PHYSICAL GEOGRAPHY
OF ASIATIC RUSSIA

OTHER BOOKS IN THE EARTH SCIENCES

A Key to Common Rock-Forming Minerals in Thin Sections
CORDELL DURRELL

Stratigraphy and Sedimentation
W. C. KRUMBEIN AND L. L. SLOSS

The Permian Reef Complex
NORMAN D. NEWELL, *et al.*

Geology of Petroleum
A. I. LEVORSEN

Petrography: An Introduction to the Study of Rocks in Thin Sections
HOWELL WILLIAMS, FRANCIS J. TURNER, AND CHARLES M. GILBERT

Rocks and Mineral Deposits
PAUL NIGGLI

Stratigraphic Geology
MAURICE GIGNOUX

Elementary Seismology
CHARLES F. RICHTER

Principles of Geology, *Second Edition*
JAMES GILLULY, A. C. WATERS, AND A. O. WOODFORD

General Crystallography: A Brief Compendium
W. F. DE JONG

Mineralogy: Concepts, Descriptions, Determinations
L. G. BERRY AND BRIAN MASON

Paleogeologic Maps
A. I. LEVORSEN

History of the Earth: An Introduction to Historical Geology
BERNHARD KUMMEL

PHYSICAL GEOGRAPHY OF ASIATIC RUSSIA

by **S. P. Suslov**

UNIVERSITY OF LENINGRAD

Translated from the Russian by

Noah D. Gershevsky, UNIVERSITY OF WASHINGTON

and Edited by

Joseph E. Williams, STANFORD UNIVERSITY

 W. H. FREEMAN AND COMPANY

San Francisco and London

EDITOR'S FOREWORD

The science of geography—particularly physical geography—was highly developed in Russia and later in the Soviet Union. One of the greatest schools of geography in Russia was directed by L. S. Berg at Leningrad University; and it was first at Moscow University and later under Berg at Leningrad that Sergei Petrovich Suslov received most of his training and experience. Berg's early work, *Natural Regions of USSR,* first published in 1937, covered the entire Soviet Union and was used by Suslov in his teaching at Leningrad. However, Suslov soon realized that a similar and more detailed work was needed for the individual parts of the Soviet Union. Since his research had been mostly in Siberia and Central Asia, he decided on that area first. His *Physical Geography of the USSR Asiatic Area* was published in 1947, with a second edition published posthumously in 1956. A sketch of Suslov's life written by A. G. Isachenko is timely:

On October 8, 1953, in Leningrad, Professor Sergei Petrovich Suslov died suddenly. He was an outstanding authority on physical geography of the Soviet Union and a talented teacher in the University of Leningrad. Professor Suslov lived through sixty difficult years, having begun a self-sustaining life of work at an early age. He was born on November 3, 1893, in Red Hill [Krasnyi Holm], a small town in the Tver province. At the age of eight he lost his parents. Because of his persistent striving for knowledge and his extraordinary ability, the future scholar obtained, after graduating from the grade school, a stipend to the Teachers Seminary in the town of Torzhok.

In 1913, S. P. Suslov became a village teacher. But after two years he entered the school of physical geography in the Moscow Pedagogical Institute, and at the same time continued his teaching as a means of subsistence.

Suslov graduated from the Moscow Institute in 1918 and left for his native town of Red Hill where, simultaneously with teaching, he conducted a large, scientifically enlightening, regional-studies work. He organized a scientific society for the study of the region and started a museum in regional studies, collecting folklore and other materials which he sent to the Geographical Society. In practice the regional studies completely defined his interests in scientific research in the field of geography. However, Suslov considered himself not yet sufficiently prepared for such activity, and in October of 1921 he entered the Geographical Institute in Leningrad. During a number of years after his graduation (in 1925) from the Institute, Suslov occupied himself with geographical research in the Baikal and other regions of

Siberia, doing basic scientific study for the fight against "road deterioration" (freezing and swelling of the roads, etc.). During 1927–30, he continued the expedition work which brought him the candidacy for the chair of physical geography at the Leningrad University. After becoming a professor at the Leningrad University, he worked in the Altai, Sayan, Taymir, and mountainous Crimea.

In 1931, Suslov was assistant to the chair of physical geography at the Leningrad University, and a year later he was promoted to the position of docent. He was entrusted with the teaching of the "Physical Geography of the USSR," and in 1933 became a candidate for the degree of doctor of geographical sciences without writing the dissertation.

As docent and, later, professor, Suslov's lectures were very popular with the students and were widely known outside the University. He won much respect as an authority among Leningrad teachers because of his lectures and work among them. During the days of the siege of Leningrad and during the evacuation of the University, he was in charge of the chair of physical geography. His wide knowledge, great experience in work on the creation of the course "Physical Geography of the USSR," and his personal acquaintance with many regions of the Soviet Union made it possible for him to create a capital work on the nation's physical geography —*Physical Geography of the USSR Asiatic Area*, for which in 1941 he was given the learned degree of doctor of geographical sciences. In 1947 this work was published as a textbook for the schools of geography.

Up to the last days of his life, Suslov worked on the second edition of this book, which was published posthumously in 1956. To his pen belonged a number of works on physical geography and geomorphology of the Sayan and Altai, and also a number of articles for the *Big Soviet Encyclopedia* and for popular scientific works.

For his many years of fruitful scientific and pedagogical activity, Suslov was awarded the order of Sign of Respect and Medals. His memory will live a long time among his co-workers, numerous students, and readers. In the science of geography, traces of his scientific activity will remain forever through his capital work, *Physical Geography of the USSR Asiatic Area*.

We hope that, by making this book available in English, other geographers will be encouraged to do similar works for their particular parts of the earth. Like Siberia and Central Asia, every other part of the earth has its peculiar biocoenoses; never before, however, has the geographer set about his work with such a determined effort to understand all the physicogeographic forces acting in a given area. The delineation of total landscape, formed by the interaction of all physical forces, was the particular goal of Suslov. The results of his work will be of value to geologists, geomorphologists, botanists, and zoologists, as well as geographers.

We have rendered a rather free translation, using the materials of both editions. Many difficulties have been experienced in translating into English the common names of rare plants and animals, some of which are peculiar to Asiatic Russia. Quite often, only the Latin names have been used to identify a plant or animal found in a given area.

We have also deleted the adjectival endings from some conventional place names. Names of less familiar places and of detailed geographic features, however, were transliterated completely. For example, for some names the case endings, such as "sky," "skoy," and "skaya," have been simplified by dropping the suffix after "sk," but for many names common usage dictates the use of the entire ending. In general, the Russian Transliteration System of the American Council of Learned Societies has been followed for the spelling of proper names. The spelling of most place names was found and verified in the *Columbia Lippincott Gazatteer of the World*. Botanical and zoological terms were checked in Bailey's *The Standard Cyclopedia of Horticulture* and *Webster's New International Dictionary*. Whenever possible, the names of plants and animals were checked against the index in Berg's *Natural Regions of the USSR*. In geologic nomenclature, Cenozoic is often used to denote both the Tertiary and Quaternary periods.

Many Russian words cannot be translated literally. For example, *"kedr"* meaning "cedar," must be changed to "pine," because cedar is a subtropical tree and does not grow in the severe winter climates of Siberia. The *Artemisia* shrub is given many common names, such as "sagebrush," "wormwood," and "polyn," in different parts of the world; rather than add to the confusion we have used only *Artemisia*. Most taxonomic names have been retained as they were in the Russian edition, unless the spelling differed greatly from that shown in the *Index Kewensis*.

The Russian volume contains not only a short general bibliography but also an extensive bibliography that follows each chapter. Since all the titles in these bibliographies are in Russian, we have included only the short general bibliography (in Russian) here. For those persons who can read Russian and want to do further research in this field, we recommend the original work, in which more than four hundred titles of research papers, on Siberia and Central Asia, are listed. Suslov did not use footnotes in his book, but prepared the extensive bibliographies.

The work of Clayton L. Dawson has been of great value in this translation. Professor Ira L. Wiggins, Director of the Natural History Museum, Stanford University, deserves much thanks and credit for reviewing the Latin names of the flora and fauna. Mr. and Mrs. Boyd Richmond and Mrs. Mary Coyle gave countless hours to the checking of botanical names and the typing and indexing of the manuscript.

Joseph E. Williams

February, 1961

PREFACE

Because this book on the physical geography of Siberia and Central Asia was intended for senior geography students in the state universities and teacher-training schools of the USSR, the manner in which the facts are presented has been determined by the systematic method of teaching geography in the Soviet schools.

Each geographic region is considered to be a basic unit and is studied in terms of its historical development and its place in the present-day landscape. Only enough Tertiary geologic history is given to provide a background for a detailed study of a region's development in the Quarternary Period. In other words, historical geology is discussed only where it has influenced the historical development of the contemporary landscape. Each region is examined as an integral part of a larger area (e.g., of Western Siberia, Eastern Siberia, or the Far East), and at the same time is treated as a single entity composed of coordinated parts—zones, subzones, districts, and landscapes.

The boundaries of major and minor geographic regions are carefully drawn. Since landscapes are considered to be a result of later developments in the life of a geographic region they are discussed after the description of each region or zone. All geographic divisions are examined genetically and are described geologically and geographically, with emphasis on their modern structure, seasonal changes, and reconstruction in relation to the economy. Animals and plants are considered, whenever possible, according to their biocoenoses. Attention is given to ecological factors, seasonal change of vegetation, and the yearly cycle of animal life.

Independent geologic, geomorphologic, climatic, geobotanic, or other explications are not provided; rather, factual data from related sciences are regarded as indissoluble components of the geographic whole. The order of presentation of the material in each chapter is not always the same, and the size of the parts, chapters, and sections varies since individual elements play different roles in different regions. For example, Chapter 4 is concerned entirely with the physical geography of Eastern Siberia, but Chapter 10 covers all the aspects of a smaller geographic area.

S. P. Suslov

CONTENTS

LIST OF MAPS

PART I

WESTERN SIBERIA

Western Siberia is the region that lies between the Ural Mountains and the mountains of Eastern Siberia and is bordered by Central Asia on the south. It is divided into two parts: the plain, or Western Siberian Lowland, and the Altai Mountain system. The latter comprises the Altai Mountains proper and the Kuznetsk Basin with its bordering mountains, the Kuznetsk Ala-Tau and the Salair ranges. Although Western Siberia is geographically diverse, it is unified by climatic influences from the Atlantic and Arctic oceans and by the hydrographic network of the Ob River system, which drains both the mountains and the lowland. Many different biotic areas occur in the region because of the varying composition and uneven distribution of the flora and fauna and their development in post-Tertiary times.

CHAPTER 1

Western Siberian Lowland

The Western Siberian Lowland, one of the most extensive lowlands in the world, forms a single physicogeographic territory. It is well defined on almost all sides by natural boundaries: on the west by the distinctly outlined terrace, 60 to 100 feet high, of the eastern slope of the Ural Mountain chain; on the east by the Yenisei River; and on the north by the Kara Sea. On the south it extends eastward from the northern Turgai Tableland along the foot of the Kazakh folded hills to the Altai Mountains near the western border of Mongolia.

The lowland, which lies between 73.5° and 50.5° north latitude, is trapezoidal in shape: narrow at its northern edge, it stretches 1,500 miles from north to south, widening to 900 miles from west to east in the south. Taken as a whole, it is a rare example of a primary flat plain, the outward appearance of which conforms very closely with its geological structure. This sea-level plain is built up almost entirely of crumbly or weakly cemented deposits. The structures are extremely simple and normal, made up of horizontally bedded unbroken Tertiary and Quaternary strata. Its flatness is shown by the fact that the Ob River at Novosibirsk, 1,800 miles from its mouth, is less than 300 feet above sea level, and that the Demyanka River, the right tributary of the Irtysh, drops only 82 feet in 175 miles of its lower course.

Morphologically, the lowland is very uniform. In the southern part it is almost a horizontal plain, where the eye detects little change in relief for vast distances; there are few hills or gullies. Low ridges and countless lakes that gradually merge with the surrounding plain somewhat relieve the monotony.

Hypsographically, the lowland is a slightly concave basin, as it is lower in the center than along its margins. On three sides the basin rises imperceptibly to the foot of the surrounding elevations. The highest parts are the western Ural section (800 to 1,000 feet in the north, 600 to 900 feet in the south), the Ob-Irtysh watershed in the south (540 feet), and in the north the Gydan Peninsula (500 to 600 feet). The general slope of the region is to the north, and is emphasized by the general north-northwest direction of flow of the chief rivers, such as the main Ob and its tributary, the Irtysh.

Climatically, the lowland is intermediate between two sharply different climatic regions—Eastern European and Eastern Siberian. The Atlantic Ocean has a marked climatic influence inasmuch as the low and narrow Ural Range is not a sharp climatic barrier. Because of the exposed character of the lowland in the north, there are strong climatic influences from the Arctic Ocean and its bordering Kara and Barents seas. Unlike the dry Eastern European Plain, the Western Siberian Lowland is wet

3

and has vast areas of swamps. The perfect flatness has given an east-west trend to the geo-

graphic zones: tundra, taiga, wooded-steppes, and steppes.

GEOLOGIC HISTORY AND MORPHOLOGY

The time at which that vast depression in which the Western Siberian Lowland was formed rose above the Paleozoic sea is not easily established, because we have no idea of the subterranean relief of the older strata on which the thick layers of Tertiary and later deposits rest. Drillings more than 1,300 feet deep do not cut through this layer; it is only along the borders that Paleozoic and Mesozoic rocks are either exposed or can be detected by shallow drilling. For example, the depth of the uneven surface of the Paleozoic series of the lowlands of the Kulunda Steppe was determined by geophysical investigation to be about 5,000 feet. Mesozoic deposits are found in small outcrops along the eastern slope of the northern Urals and in the center of the plain along the Bolshoy Yugan River. At the foot of the Ural Mountains, in the region of Novosibirsk, and on the Gydan Peninsula, there are small outcrops of igneous rock (granite, diabase). On the basis of the geological structure of the peripheral area of the Western Siberian Lowland we can assume that at the beginning of the middle Carboniferous Period it began to undergo tectonic processes and to rise above the sea. As a result of the general and unequal rise the lowlands began to fold into long, low, parallel anticlines and synclines, accompanied by faults in many localities.

The limited and discontinuous layers, the uneven depth, and the indistinct aspect of the Mesozoic deposits create great difficulties in the attempt to re-establish the geologic history of the Mesozoic Era. At that time, the Western Siberian Lowland was somewhat stabilized, but irregular displacement of the land took place and led to an alternation of marine and continental climatic regimes. The sea invaded from the north and from the Turansk Lowland on the south through the Turgai Strait. Thick layers of marine sediments were deposited. Later many areas emerged to become land, with subsequent erosion and continental deposition, and a vegetative cover developed, providing material for the formation of coal. The Mesozoic deposits, according to geophysical research, were usually laid down in synclines, where favorable conditions were created for the accumulation of numerous coal-bearing series (Triassic and Middle Jurassic) at depths to 5,000 feet. Mesozoic deposits of the Western Siberian Lowland were subjected to a very gentle folding, barely perceptible over short distances. Eight stratigraphic unconformities in the Mesozoic and Tertiary sediments indicate the beginning phases of alpine folds. Insignificant faults also have occurred.

Signs of oil-bearing strata (oil film, bitumen, natural gas, ozocerite, etc.) in many places remote from each other (Big Yugan, Ishim, etc.) are apparently related to the Upper Mesozoic. Regions with deep layers of marine sediments, especially in central and western sections of the lowland, are most favorable for oil-bearing series. Structures necessary for the accumulation of petroleum are present and the sediments often contain sandstone layers capable of collecting petroleum. The lowland evidently possesses large potential oil-bearing strata. Large industrial supplies of petroleum would permit the creation of a liquid-fuel base for industry and mechanized agriculture in Western Siberia.

The basic morphologic features of the lowland, which caused its striking levelness, were established when it was covered by the shallow Paleozoic sea. The sediments of this sea filled in all the depressions of the pre-Tertiary relief, and when the sea receded it left a plain gradually sloping northward. At this time its continental existence began: lake and alluvial sediments were deposited, and relief began to develop on the soft loamy alluvium. However, traces of water erosion between the Eocene and Oligocene and the replacement of marine facies by continental ones on the border of Oligocene and Miocene indicate that upheavals occurred in different phases of alpine folding.

That sedimentary deposits of the Tertiary are important in the geological structure of the lowland is shown by the following:

1) There is a significant change of thickness of Tertiary deposits from the west (100 to 400 feet) to the east (1,000 to 5,000 feet), the deepest layers lying below sea level. This is the re-

Central Asia by the so-called Turgai Strait. Paleocene marine deposits crop out at the present time in a narrow strip along the foot of the Urals and the Kazakh folded hills. Here, lying higher to the north and east, they are concealed under deposits of Neocene and Quaternary sediments and crop out in places as small islands.

At the end of the Paleocene, as a result of slow vertical upheaval of the country, the sea gradually abandoned the lowland, and at the beginning of the Miocene the continental regime was re-established. At this stage the widely distributed fresh-water Neocene sediments—gravels, sands, clay, argillaceous soils, and loams—emerged in the form of narrow strips of land from the Tobol to the Irtysh.

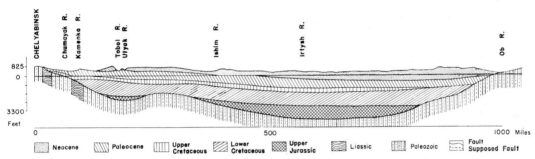

Fig. 1-1. Geologic cross section of the Western Siberian Plain from Chelyabinsk to the Ob River (near Tomsk).

sult of the epeirogenic rise of the region in the pre-Ural and its simultaneous sinking in the more easterly districts.

2) At the base of Tertiary deposits, near the foot of the Urals and the Kazakh folded hills, there is much coarse material—sand and gravel—which is replaced in the east by finer sediments.

3) In vertical cross section, thin sediments alternate with thicker ones, indicating that in the first half of the Tertiary Period the boundary of the sea changed repeatedly.

In Paleocene times, the sea once again existed here; a slow sinking of the region continued and thick marine sediments accumulated. At its greatest extension, the sea occupied almost all the area of the present-day lowland and was connected with the sea basins of the plains of

The lowland in the Neocene was well watered and studded with countless lakes.

Climatic conditions at that time were extremely favorable for plant growth and the lowland had a thick vegetative cover, judging from fossil remains of well-preserved luxuriant subtropical vegetation of bald cypress (*Taxodium distichum* var. *miocenum*), sequoia (*Sequoia langsdorffii*), broad-leaved magnolia (*Magnolia inglefieldii*), wing nut (*Pterocarya castaneifolia*), walnut (*Juglans acuminata*), and many pines. The rich woody and grassy vegetation made possible the existence of many kinds of mammals, such as giraffes, horses, camels, mastodons, and beasts of prey.

Toward the end of the Tertiary, climatic conditions were less favorable, the Ice Age set in, and the northern part of the plain was covered with a huge mass of continental ice. This glacial cover was fed by firn lying in the Northern Urals and on the uplands of the Taimyr Peninsula. It may be assumed that the Ural glaciers moved as far eastward as the mouth of the Irtysh, since there, in the boulders of the moraine, Ural rocks predominate—granite, granodiorite, and diorite. The Taimyr glacier reached the mouth of the Lyamin (the right-hand tributary of the Ob) where fragments of Siberian diabases or traps, so characteristic of the neighboring Central Siberian Plateau, are abundant.

The Western Siberian Lowland had only one epoch of continental glaciation. The southern boundary of the Siberian ice sheet crosses the Ural Ridge between 58° and 59° north latitude, extends eastward between the Konda and Tavda rivers, and crosses the Irtysh River near the mouth of the Demyanka. Farther eastward it follows the upper course of the Bolshoy Yugan and upper Maly Yugan, crosses the Ob above the mouth of the Vakh and Tym, and approaches the Yenisei above the mouth of the Stony Tunguska.

Because of the continental climate (which was then somewhat more severe and dry than now) and the high summer temperatures, the Siberian glacial covering occupied a considerably smaller area than the contemporary ice shield of the Eastern European Plain, and had a depth of only a few hundred feet instead of thousands. It moved little and thawed slowly, and consequently had little influence on its bed and left no massive boulders.

The glaciation influenced the later development of the lowland relief. The glaciers, flowing down from the Urals and the Taimyr Peninsula, encountered a weakly dissected plain, composed of loamy preglacial beds. The rocks on upper levels of these beds became mixed with the morainic material brought from the mountains. In many places the original gentle folds of the Mesozoic and Tertiary strata were planed off by the force and pressure of the ice. Slightly overthrust reverse folds and many old river valleys and lake basins were destroyed. The first glaciers made the moraine relief and

caused the uneven deposition of fluvioglacial material such as sands and clays, whose beds were broken by the successive advance and retreat of the glaciers. South of the glaciers, meltwater sediments were deposited in large lakes. Apparently parts of the Ob and Irtysh, despite being dammed by the glaciers, still flowed northward to the Kara Sea, somewhere near the converging Ural and Taimyr ice masses.

The edge of the glacier retreated gradually, with short interruptions, depositing a huge quantity of morainic material which covered the basic strata with a mantle of uneven thickness, the surface of which simultaneously was eroded by flowing water from the thawing glacier. As the glacier retreated, these morainal deposits were more deeply eroded by the slow streams which trickled over them. Traces of these meandering streams have been preserved —sandy banks and cut-off meanders that have been considerably modified by subsequent processes.

The further shrinking of the Ural and Taimyr glaciers resulted in the break-up of the solid ice cover, the creation of a channel to the ocean, and the gradual lowering of the postglacial lakes. The main rivers flowed north, clearing passages for themselves among the glacial deposits, and slowly deepening their channels by cutting through the thin Quaternary cover, and occasionally even cutting a hundred feet or more into the basic strata. At this time, vast areas of watershed and their glacial cover were destroyed by lateral erosion. Consequently, today no well-defined morainal ridges exist near the river—only the residual undamaged remains of the watersheds. The leveling processes became weak farther from the river networks; preserved moraines are hence found on raised islands of Mesozoic and Tertiary rocks. At the end of the Riss-Würm period there was a well-defined network of river valleys that cut the uneven interfluvial lands into sharply demarcated plateaus, on whose surface lakes and peat bogs continued to exist.

At the end of Würm glaciation the ice retreated, leaving no interglacial continental deposits or typical banded clays, although moraines of marine interglacial deposits were left in some northerly districts. At this time the glaciers probably withdrew to the mountain heights surrounding the lowland (northern Urals, Altai) and left the moraines that still exist near these mountains. During the Würm glaciation the volume of meltwater increased and the rivers overflowed and deposited sandy materials. The unusually wide distribution of superimposed river terraces, which are scores of miles wide and unite valleys of neighboring rivers, indicates a prolonged accumulation period, extensive meandering, and many lateral shifts of the rivers.

The central and southern parts of the lowland were covered with countless lakes and bogs. Deposits from flooding waters covered remains of tundra vegetation (polar willows) and Siberian taiga vegetation (birch, fir, pine, spruce), which indicates that the forest-tundra extended to the edge of the glacial cover. Farther south, the lowland was covered by dense coniferous forests, similar to those existing today.

The huge bones of extinct mammals found in the loess-like clay soils indicate that many animals lived in the areas not covered by ice: mammoth (*Elephas primigenius*), the woolly rhinocerous (*Rhinoceros tichorinus*), and the gigantic reindeer (*Cervus megaceros*).

The glacial period left a comparatively shallow solid covering of Quaternary deposits in the central part of the lowland (60 to 90 feet). The east-west moraine belt of the last and maximum period of glaciation formed clearly marked watersheds more than 500 feet high (at the source of the Pur River, 600 feet). These lie along the east-west sections of the right tributaries of the Ob and of the rivers flowing into the estuaries of the Ob and Taz, on which have been preserved many moraine lakes. Sharply defined moraines which extend along all the eastern slope of the northern Urals, dammed the rivers flowing from these mountains.

Quaternary deposits of the Western Siberian Lowland consist of large quantities of sand laid down by running water or on lake beaches and of moraine material that is mixed with friable and plastic debris from Mesozoic and Paleocene strata. The boundary of maximum glaciation is indicated by a belt of sand which stretches unbroken from the Irtysh across the systems of the Demyanka and Vasyugan rivers, through the Narym region, and up the river Sym to the Yenisei. In the southern wooded-steppe and the steppe sections of the lowland, loess-like clayey soils covered wide areas of the large river valleys; farther south, sand overlapped the water divides.

In the early part of the postglacial period the northern part of the Western Siberian Lowland was submerged by a marine transgression which did not penetrate far to the south except along valleys of large rivers (along the Ob to 67°), but covered a relatively large area of the northern peninsulas (Yamal, Taz, Gydan). Deposits from this marine transgression consist of fine sandy and clayey soils that contain remains of marine mollusks, *Yoldia arctica* and others, many of which still live in the Kara Sea. As a result of the subsequent upheaval, sediments from this northern transgression were raised 160 to 200 feet above sea level. The Ob and Taz estuaries may indicate a recent slight sinking of the basin.

In the postglacial period, when the weather was warmer than it is now, forests (birch groves, in particular) extended several degrees farther north. For instance, on the Gydan Peninsula, 180 miles north of the present limit of forest growth, tree trunks, horsetails, club mosses, and relic peat mosses have been found buried twelve feet deep. Today there is a shift of zones to the south, within very narrow limits, encompassing only the contact strip of present-day tundra and taiga, deciduous forests, and steppe.

The general morphologic appearance of the lowland and the basic forms of the relief were created for the most part by river erosion. This action began with the retreat and the disappearance of the Tertiary Sea, and, in somewhat weakened form, has continued to the present time. The relief has developed mainly by lateral erosion and associated alluvial accumulation; vertical erosion has been very weak.

There are several reasons why such a flat alluvial plain was formed: (1) strata that have remained horizontal since Tertiary time; (2) erosion and deposition by a large river system on a level surface; (3) the low altitude of the plain; (4) the low gradient of the entire surface; and (5) the heavy rainfall. The plain was loaded with alluvium by the rivers flowing from the surrounding mountains—Ural, Altai, and Kuznetsk Ala-Tau. The glaciers in the north dammed these rivers and created great meltwater lakes and swamps, which contrib-

by thin layers of alluvium of various ages. The landforms are quite uniform: well-defined left-bank terraces, eroded buttes of older alluvium at higher levels, remains of natural levees, and exceptionally broad and flat valleys that cover wide areas. The hydrographic network of the plain is young and poorly intrenched: the water divides are swampy and there are many landlocked, often brackish, lakes. Yet the erosion cycle seems old because the gradient of the valleys is so gradual that further dissection is limited, except possibly along the higher rim

Fig. 1-2. Typical meandering taiga stream with marshy banks.

uted to further leveling of the surface. As the glaciers retreated the rivers began meandering and lateral erosion was rapid. Meanders shifted down the gradient and channels were cut to the right in those sections of the rivers which flowed northward, thus creating wide left-bank terraces.

As a result of long erosive action the widely flooded and poorly drained plain was covered

of the lowland.

The pattern of the hydrographic network is derived basically from the major relief forms, and in the morphology of the country, the river valleys seem unimportant because they are wide and shallow with poorly developed water divides. The Ob and Irtysh, for instance, cut 200 to 300 feet into loamy Tertiary and Quaternary deposits in valleys that are seventy-five miles wide and have flood-plains as much as 25 miles wide. The lowland sections of the rivers have two terraces, one 30 and the other 120 feet above the river; in the foothills they have six terraces, the highest at 400 feet. The profiles of these valleys are usually asymmetrical, with a short steep slope on which landslides are common, and a long slope smoothed by diluvial processes. The Ob has many deep holes that have existed for a long time, and which, since they do not freeze to the bottom, provide a winter haven for large fish. In the north the valleys are so flat that their outlines are lost and the rivers appear to flow in gigantic ditches; the huge estuaries into which the rivers empty seem too large for them. Sections of the larger rivers, such as the east-west course of the Ob River or its downstream portion, exhibit youthful features and are considered postglacial streams.

Tributary streams from the hills around the lowland quickly lose their steep gradients and flow in canal-like channels with natural levees. This raises the streams higher than the land between them, and during floods the whole country is inundated: when the Vasugan River floods, for example, one can cross the divides in the area by boat. Side tributaries of the Ob and Om rivers flow in different directions during normal and flood times. In the dry southern part of the lowland the rivers flow in shallow valleys with few or no tributary streams: there, in contrast to the extreme eluvial-diluvial erosion of the north, deflation is the greatest cause of erosion.

The Western Siberian Lowland must not be considered as genetically homogeneous, with each region having an identical course of geomorphologic development. Although various regions all have a uniform distribution of definite complex forms of relief, produced by the action of common geographic phenomena during the Quaternary Period, different physicogeographic processes took place in each. It is easy to observe a certain "zonal quality" in the distribution of these geomorphologic regions.

The following five zones may be divided into many subregions, each of which can be distinguished from the other in respect to origin and age by geological peculiarities and forms of relief:

1) The zone of young coastal steppe-like plains, raised on the north coast of the lowland by epeirogenic movements during the marine transgression in the Riss-Würm period. It occupies a great part of the Yamal and Taz peninsulas and a wide coastal strip of the Gydan Peninsula.

2) The zone of glacial accumulation, which contains such glacial forms as hilly and ridge-like moraines, rocky hills, and glacial lake basins. It is located in the area of old maximum glaciation, south to 58° north latitude, and extends from the Ural Mountains to the Yenisei, north of the middle segment of the Ob River. It comprises the northern part of the forested area.

3) The near-glacial zone of alluvial plains—either flat or dissected with broad, weakly undulating or plateau-like interriver expanses. This zone stretches from the Tavda to the Yenisei, and lies within the southern part of the forested area.

4) The zone of nonglacial flat and undulating, gullied plains, which contain well-developed ravines with sloping crests, sand dunes along river valleys, and countless flat basins that were formed as a result of the erosion and suffusion of unequally accumulated loamy sediments.

5) The zone of pre-mountain dissected plains, along the bordering Urals, Altai, and Kuznetsk Ala-Tau: the pre-Ural flat plain, the pre-Salairsk elevated plain, and the hilly pre-mountain region of the Kuznetsk Ala-Tau. This zone's proximity to the mountain masses subjects it to continued erosion by streams flowing from the mountains.

The largest valleys, those of the Ob and Irtysh rivers, must be considered to be azonal subregions intersecting all the morphological zones of the lowland.

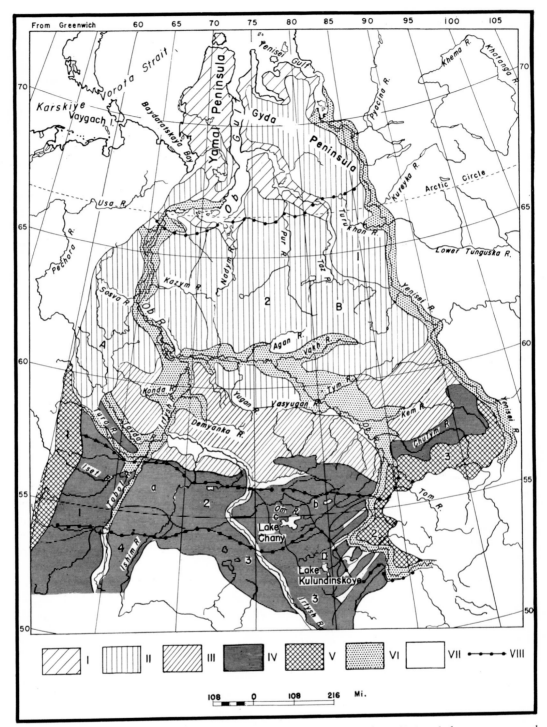

Map. 1-I. Geomorphologic divisions of Western Siberian Lowland: I—Zone of the young coastal plains created by the sea and epeirogenic movements. II—Zone of glacial accumulation, flat and hilly plains, formed at the time of maximum glaciation: 1—Gydan-Tazov rolling plain; 2—Ob-

CLIMATE

Although the low mountains bordering the Western Siberian Lowland on the west, south, and east give it little protection, it is a single climatic region. Cold winds from the north, off the Kara Sea, penetrate to its most southern part, but since it lies between two sharply differing climatic regions—Eastern Europe and Eastern Siberia—continentality, dryness, and severity of climate gradually increase from west to east. Annual and winter temperatures are low; annual and maximum daily temperature amplitudes are great, the latter occurring usually at the time of early autumn frosts. The climate changes markedly from north to south, in accord with the change in intensity of solar radiation. Toward the south, the average annual temperature and the length of the growing season and frost-free periods increase, and the thickness of the snow cover, relative humidity, and cloudiness decrease. Air masses of differing velocity—cold or warm, dry or moist—brought from the outside, may temporarily affect the climate of any part of the lowland.

In winter, two systems of pressure interact. Near Eastern Siberia is a high-pressure area where the winter high may reach 29.9 or 30.0 inches. At the same time, over the southern part of the Kara Sea, there may be a trough of low pressure—29.0 or 29.1 inches—which extends eastward from the region of the Icelandic Low to the Novosibirsk Islands and usually extends as far south as the northern parts of the lowland. Along this trough, countless depressions move from west to east, causing sharp drops in pressure. The number of deep cyclones which effect a drop in pressure of 0.8 inches and more per day averages forty-one per year.

Such a distribution of isobaric areas means that in the winter the gradient is directed from south to north; that is, the pressure decreases from the interior of the mainland to the Kara Sea. Thus, in this season, south-southwest winds prevail, blowing from the continent toward the ocean. Frequent monsoon-like winds are noted in the middle of winter. South of Tyumen, approximately along 53° north latitude, is a southern spur of high pressure from the eastern Siberian anticyclone which helps increase the south-to-north gradient.

In summer the mainland is considerably warmer than the surface of the Arctic Ocean, which has a cold and dense layer of air above it: atmospheric pressure in the higher latitudes is then higher than on the continent. The summer gradient, consequently, is directed to the south, but because temperatures increase southward, it is much weaker than the winter gradient. In summer, the prevailing winds blow from the ocean to the mainland, i.e., northerly winds which are monsoon-like with an eastern component resulting from deflection of winds to the right. The distribution of isobaric centers in Europe and Western Siberia during summer favor a transfer of air masses from west to east.

Tazov rolling plain; (A)—Western subregion; (B)—Eastern subregion. III—Zone around glaciers, fluvial flat and plateau-like plains, divided by erosion (Ob-Irtysh rolling plain). IV—Zone outside the flat-to-rolling alluvial plains: 1—Flat plain (pre-Ural); 2—Ishimsk-Barabinsk-Kulundinsk plain: a—Ishimsk region; b—Eastern Barabinsk crest region; c—Central Barabinsk flat depression; (C)—Plateau near Ob with old drainage troughs; (D)—Kulundinsk flat depression; 3—Plain near Irtysh; 4—Kustanai sloping plain. V—Zone of divided foothill plains which merge with bordering hills of Urals, Altai, and Kuznetsk Ala-Tau: 1—Eroded plain of Urals Eastern slope; 2—Pre-Salair raised plain; 3—Hilly region of Kuznetsk Ala-Tau foothills. VI—Young alluvial plains. VII—Old valleys. VIII—Border of landscape zones.

Contributing to this are a spur of high pressure extending from the Azores High to the European USSR and a sharp drop in pressure in Western Siberia. In the spring and fall, the wind varies in direction.

Thus, the most constant and regular movements of air masses are monsoon-like shifts of air northward in winter and southward in summer: westerly winds outnumber easterly winds. Local orographic peculiarities create local winds; as, for example, in the wide valleys of the Ob and Yenisei, where the wind blows along their high banks.

The highest average yearly wind velocities are found on the coast of the Kara Sea; in the forest-tundra and taiga the velocity lessens. The probability of storms is greater along the coast and at sea. In winter, storms are more frequent, being the result of the advance of deep cyclones from west to east. They are usually large snowstorms and bring about a rise in temperature. Within the seaboard zone the wind velocity is especially high in winter as a consequence of the steep barometric gradients created by the passing of the frequent and deep cyclones. In summer, the velocity of coastal winds is one-half that of winter. Inland, the wind velocity is lowest in winter. It increases in summer and reaches its greatest intensity in April, May, and October.

Because the Western Siberian Lowland extends from the temperate latitudes to beyond the Arctic Circle, the temperatures of the air in the south and in the north vary greatly. Mean annual temperatures increase southward in accord with the increase of the intensity of solar radiation. In winter, the region of lowest temperatures extends from 66° to 69° north latitude—that is, approximately along a line from Salekhard to Turukhansk—from whence temperatures increase both to the south and to the north. The northward increase is explained by the nearness of the sea and the presence of a trough of low pressure, along which, in winter, warm winds blow from west to east. The mean temperatures, in degrees Fahrenheit, of the coldest month, January or February, change from north to south in the following manner:

IN THE EAST		IN THE WEST	
Dickson I.:	−12.5	Bely I.:	−11.1
Dudinka:	−17.8	Mare-Sale:	−5.2
Igarka:	19.0	Novy Port:	13.1
Turukhansk:	−17.0	Berezovo:	−6.7
Yeniseisk:	6.1	Kurgan:	0.0

Winter temperatures fall quickly from west to east, as continentality is strengthened and the Eastern Siberian high pressure area is approached as is shown in the accompanying table.

STATIONS	DECEMBER	JANUARY
Western Stations		
Kara-Guba	1.1°F	−3.7°F
Berezovo	−2.3	−7.0
Kurgan	5.5	0.0
Eastern Stations		
Dudinka	−15.5°F	−17.3°F
Verkhne-Imbatskoye	−12.2	−10.3
Novosibirsk	3.1	−1.8

Winter has rather stable subzero temperatures. Absolute minimums vary from −48 to −64°F, depending on the duration of cold winds. There are few thaws—almost none in the east—and every day of October through April may have frost. Extremely low temperatures are usually linked with invasions of cold air from the Eastern Siberian anticyclone. Winter temperatures are also affected by the intensity of cyclonic activity in the Atlantic Ocean and northern Europe. In years when this activity is great, the cyclones raise the winter temperature; in years with less intensive cyclonic activity, winters in Western Siberia are very severe. Despite the significant coolness of the Arctic air in calm periods, the level relief discourages formation of anticyclonic temperature inversions over the Western Siberian Lowland. Therefore we observe an extremely singular phenomenon: all the year round it is warmer at high altitudes than at low ones, apparently because of a constant influx of air from the Arctic. This phenomenon must be taken into account in the choice of agricultural areas, especially for crops harmed by early frosts.

Spring in the lowland is short and cold. March, with its late subzero temperatures, is often a winter month; even through April the average temperature is either below freezing or fluctuates around 32°F. A decided rise in temperature begins only in May. The increase in temperature on the mainland comes quickly, but on the coast the rise is slow because of the north winds which blow off the cold sea. In April, the temperature decreases from south to north, as much as 3°F for each degree of latitude. The average temperature of the warmest month, July, varies from 39°F in the extreme north to 71.5°F in the extreme south, and the absolute maximum from 80.5°F in the north to 105°F in the south. July and August have stable above-freezing temperatures, and in these months early frosts occur only in the extreme north. The growing season lasts from less than 100 days in the north to 175 days in the south, and the length of the frost-free period from less than 75 days in the north to 100 days in the south.

Autumn months sharply differ in temperature: In September the average temperature may vary from 35.5° to 21.3°F in the north, 48.1° to 51.8°F in the south. In October it is either below or near freezing but the drop in temperature from October to November is remarkable—as much as 22°F. November, with its low temperatures, may be considered a winter month. The daily amplitude of temperature may reach 36° to 46°F, especially between 55° and 65° north latitude. There is a tendency for the annual and maximum amplitude to increase from the central part of the lowland to both north and south, and also from west to east.

Basic conditions influencing the distribution of precipitation on the lowland are as follows: (1) The lowland is enclosed on three sides by uplands, preventing the direct transfer of moisture from south and west, (2) it is exposed to the cold Kara Sea, (3) it is in the path of cyclones, (4) many lakes and bogs provide considerable evaporation of moisture in the summer, and (5) barometric pressures differ over various parts of the region. The zone of greatest precipitation (about 20 inches annually) stretches in a southeasterly direction from the Urals to the Altai, approximately from Samarovo to Tomsk. From this line the annual average gradually lessens both north (6.3 inches) and south (10.8 inches). In the western section, the number of days with precipitation decreases from 155 days in the north to 111 days in the south. In the eastern section, there are 145 days of precipitation in the north, 205 days in the south.

Everywhere, drizzling rains account for about 0.4 inches of precipitation monthly. In summer, heavy downpours occur everywhere—usually not more than 2 inches of rain falls in a single storm, but sometimes 3.5 inches falls at Narym, and 4.4 inches has fallen at Kamen. Throughout the lowland, distribution of the annual precipitation by seasons is uniform. The greatest amount of precipitation takes place from May to October, especially in July and August. The month of greatest precipitation is August in the tundra (less than 2 inches), July in the taiga (3 to 4 inches), and June in the steppe (1.8 to 2.5 inches). In winter, precipitation is nowhere very great, and it decreases from November to February: the average for the winter months in the tundra is about 0.1 to 0.3 inches, in the taiga about 0.4 to 0.5 inches, in the wooded-steppe and steppe about 0.3 to 0.4 inches.

The difference between summer and winter precipitation is very great everywhere; in Ust-Port, for example, it is 2 inches in August but only 0.1 inch in February. In wet years precipitation surpasses the average by 4 to 8 inches in the tundra and 4 to 10 inches in other zones. Fluctuation of monthly totals is still greater; it varies from 10 to 400 per cent of the monthly average. In winter, sometimes for months, there is little precipitation (.04 to .03 inches a month). And there have been years when half the average yearly precipitation took place in one summer month; for example, in Yeniseisk (yearly average 16.9 inches), in August, 1903, 6.9 inches of rain fell. In the taiga the annual precipitation fluctuates between 24.1 and 12.1 inches, the average per year being 18.1 inches; in the wooded-steppe (Petropavlovsk) from 23.5 to 6.9 inches, with an average per year of 13.1 inches—here during June it varies from a maximum of 7.1 inches to a minimum of 0.4 inches and during August from 5.6 inches to 0.08 inches. Thus, some years have abundant moisture and other years an extreme lack of it. Frequent and prolonged droughts in the wooded-steppe and steppe region of the lowland are unfavorable to the development of agriculture.

Approximately two weeks after the average daily temperature goes below freezing, the earth is covered with a blanket of snow that lasts all winter. The relative quantity of precipitation in the form of snow significantly lessens from north (46 per cent of the annual amount) to the center (32 per cent) and south (20 per cent). A snow cover appears in the north in the first ten days of October; by early November a cover begins to form on the more southerly sections of the lowland, and by the end of November the whole territory, except for occasional spots in the south, is covered with snow. The duration of the snow cover decreases from 270 days in the extreme north (Bely Island) to 152 days in Omsk, far to the south. It is deepest in the northern sections in April, in the taiga in March, and farther south in January or February: it is thickest in the central taiga section of the lowland—the average depth is 22.8 to 30.4 inches, and in Turukhansk, 39.3 inches—it decreases both north (11.7 inches) and south (19.5 inches). The snow cover is very compact, especially in the north, where the snow is packed by the strong and frequent winter winds.

Strong winter winds lift the fine dry snow from the earth to form snowdrifts, or to produce low snowstorms. In the forest zone, there are seventy to eighty snowstorms a year, and on the north coast there are even more; they are more frequent in the west than in the east.

Bely Island has 141 days with snow; Dickson Island has 78 days. The snow melts first in the more southerly steppe regions. At the beginning of May, more than half of the lowland is cleared of snow, and by the end of the month, almost all.

Relative humidity (83 to 87 per cent) is usually highest in November in the extreme northern section. More than half the winter days have high relative humidity. On the coast the relative humidity is high in all months. The lowest, but still rather high, relative humidity is observed in May (60 to 70 per cent). Evaporation in the north is low in the forest-tundra (15.4 inches at Salekhard); to the south it increases, reaching in the wooded-steppe 28.8 inches (Omsk), and in the steppe 42.4 inches (Semipalatinsk). The high relative humidity and frequent cyclones contribute to the development of much cloudiness. In the autumn months cloudiness reaches a maximum for the year (70 to 80 per cent), and winters are dull and cloudy, although clear sky is often observed over the northern coast along the Kara Sea. The south is least cloudy (50 per cent). The number of days with fog decreases inland from the coast of the Kara Sea—106 days at Dickson Island but only 10 days at Turukhansk. In the south fogs are very rare. The number of hours of sunshine depends on the height of the sun and the length of the day. On an average, the northern half of the district gets direct solar radiation for only about 30 per cent of the year. In winter the solar radiation is slight (in January from one hour per month in the north to 70 hours in the south); it is greatest in June–July, being from 200 to 300 hours per month in each of these two summer months.

Even though the Western Siberian Lowland has some climatic conditions common to the whole region, various sections have their own climatic peculiarities which classify them as climatic subzones and districts. The lowland can be divided into four climatic zones: tundra and forest-tundra, taiga, wooded-steppe, and steppe climates.

HYDROGRAPHY

The nearly horizontal loamy stratified deposits that are found everywhere in the Western Siberian Lowland consist of a multiple alternation of water-resistant layers (clays) with more or less water-porous gravels and sandy-clayey soils. These cross-bedded layers at various depths affect the distribution and circulation of ground water. The horizontal strata retard circulation of underground water, which is further impeded by the poor drainage of the region. A sparse network of weakly incised valleys promotes concentration of salts in the water-bearing layers and explains the intense mineralization of the water in many places. The cross-beddings, especially in the post-Tertiary layers, account for the extraordinary variation in quality and quantity of ground water obtained from shallow wells.

More constant and abundant water-bearing horizons at greater depths are linked with Tertiary deposits; they sometimes contain fresh high-quality water and at other times strong mineral water, often under weak pressure. In the younger (Tertiary) deposits, water mineralized; in the extreme north its quality and circulation is affected by permafrost. In a severe climate in which the soil freezes quickly in early winter, wells and springs that are fed by water from upper water-bearing strata become very poor by the end of winter. In deeper-lying water this is not too noticeable. The chief source of ground water is rainfall, but in the south the melting snow cover is important.

The long continental life of the Western Siberian Lowland has led to an unusual evolution of its vast river network. Nevertheless, the lowland has considerably less drainage than the neighboring eastern European plain and its rivers have a smaller flow—21 cu. ft. per second between 66° and 68° north latitude, as contrasted with 35 cu. ft. per second within the same limits in Europe. Distribution of average flow throughout the lowland has a typical zonal character. Isolines of flow usually run from east to west, but near the Ural and Altai mountains they change their direction, rounding the curves of the mountains.

Fig. 1-3. Ob River below Kondinsky during spring flood.

occurs at a shallow depth, but its quality is less uniform; it usually is not under pressure and has an unstable flow. The regime of this water is closely dependent on climatic conditions: toward the south the water becomes more

Different parts of the hydrographic network differ in age. The oldest and most important direction of flow for the rivers is northwest, corresponding to the general slope of the lowland. Not only do the largest rivers, such as the Ob, Tom, Irtysh, and Yenisei (between 56° and 61°), flow in this direction for the greater part of their courses, but the secondary rivers do also. In many places asymmetry of the river network is well marked; for example, almost all the tributaries of the rivers of the Narym region have developed on the left side, sometimes with their sources adjacent to the channel of another stream. The right slopes of the river valleys are short and steep—frequently they are high banks—whereas the left slopes are usually almost level and wide. River junctions often mark the sites of old lake beds: the characteristic accumulation of tributaries of the Lyapin River above Saran-Paul, for example. In some places, such as the Konda region, the river network was formed from united chains of lakes.

The density of the river networks is determined by the geologic history and the climate of the areas in which they are situated. The area of last glaciation has the densest river network: the Pelym River system, for example, is 200 miles long and has an area of 386 square miles. In the south, the rivers have fewer tributaries and their networks are dense because of climatic peculiarities and the existence of a lake plain along the edge of glaciation; thus, part of the Irtysh system south of Tobol is 50 miles long and 386 square miles in area. Regions never covered by continental glaciation have small river networks; however, it should be noticed that all rivers have a denser network near the source. Natural levees on some rivers raise them above the surrounding country. The rivers of the Western Siberian Lowland have insignificant gradients, which results in slow currents (Vakh: from 1.5 to 2.7 miles per hour). The sluggishness makes for extreme meandering of the channels, vast bottomlands with countless old river channels and lakes, and weak erosion of the loamy banks.

The chief river of the lowland is the Ob. Its great length (2,510 miles from the sources of the Katun), the vastness of its basin (1,821,250 square miles), and its large annual discharge (in its lower course, 8,700 cubic yards per second), make it one of the greatest rivers of the world. Its tributaries, on the contrary, are completely subject to the influence of local climatic, hydrogeologic, and hydrologic factors, and are fed by local, usually fresh, high-standing ground and surface water. In the middle of the taiga zone, vast watershed bogs feed countless tributaries of the Ob and Irtysh. In the southern wooded-steppe and steppe zones, the small tributaries that flow into the main rivers carrying the runoff that has accumulated in local basins, forming countless lakes and swamps. Because Western Siberian rivers are, for the most part, snow-fed, they have a clearly pronounced spring flooding. In the south rain water generally evaporates before it can reach the rivers.

The early and severe winter causes the rivers of the lowland to be covered with ice early and the ice remains for a long time, but there is a substantial variation from north to south in the period of breakup and freezing of rivers. Rivers in the Ob basin usually freeze at the end of October or the beginning of November, progressively later from north to south. For example, the Ob near Salekhard usually freezes by November 2 (the earliest freezing, October 3; the latest, December 1): the Irtysh, near Tobolsk, freezes in more severe winters by October 22, in warmer ones by November 27. "Shoreline," or riverside, ice that forms before the river freezes over produces an autumn ice movement on the Ob; the ice is torn away by the current and creates masses of floating ice.

The rivers of the Ob basin are frozen over 162 days in the south and 219 days downstream. The ice is thickest in April: in the steppe at the beginning of the month, in the wooded-steppe in the first half, in the taiga in the second half, in the forest-tundra and the tundra at the end. The greatest thickness of ice on the Ob, at Salekhard, is four and one-half feet. Not all of a river is covered with ice at the same time and all stretches are not covered equally. In places there are at first great unfrozen patches which, as the weather grows colder, gradually close over with level ice. In shallow sections the ice forms an uneven cover containing numerous ice-blocks. Shoal waters piled up behind such a mass of ice will freeze and block the channels of rivers to the very bottom. On the Irtysh the ice is, for the most part, smooth. Bottom-ice is encountered in almost all rivers; it usually thins on sandbanks to a layer of few inches thick.

The breakup of the ice on the rivers begins in the south and gradually advances northward. The Ob breaks up, on an average, in the wooded-steppe on April 22, in the southern taiga on May 5, in the northern taiga on May 17, and in the forest-tundra on June 4. The spring ice breakup of the Ob begins at the end of June but sometimes extends to the end of July and the beginning of August. Warm water in spring, coming from the south, overflows the ice in the north and raises the level of the Ob and other rivers in the middle of summer. In spring the ice breakup is sudden and complete and floating ice is not encountered in summer. The spring ice flow on the Ob and Irtysh continues 5 to 11 days and often is accompanied by numerous ice jams, leading to considerable destruction of the banks and of riverside structures. The flooded expanses of the Ob basin influence the temperature of the air in summer, since the temperature of the water at Salekhard may sometimes reach 64.5°F. The warm flow of the Ob decreases the amplitude of the daily fluctuations and contributes to a rise in summer temperatures even on the Yamal Peninsula.

There are many fish in the Ob and its tributaries. One of the chief commercial fish is the sturgeon (*Acipenser baeri*), (*Acipenser ruthenus*). Its spawning grounds and its winter lairs are in pits at the bottom of the river, and its "pastures" are at the mouths of the Ob and in Ob Bay. Other fish are the salmon (*Stenodus leucichtys nelma*), and the whitefish (*Coregonus muksun*), (*Coregonus peled*). They ascend to the sources of the rivers to spawn. The lower Ob and Ob Bay are of the greatest importance to the fishing industry. Blackfish, roach, pike, ide, perch, crucian, dace, and eelpout have secondary significance and are caught only in the middle Ob.

The central and lower stretches of the Ob and Irtysh are suitable only for the most primitive navigation because of their low north-south gradients, low banks, swampy and wide bottomlands, and silted beds. The downstream sections of the Ob are navigable by deep-water craft as far as Salekhard for 132 to 172 days; the Irtysh is navigable as far south as Tobolsk for as long as 189 days. Each of these rivers cuts through sparsely populated districts, poor in natural wealth. At the present time the system of the Ob is one of the links in the northern sea route because of its exit into the Kara Sea. Only the upper sections of the rivers are important for irrigation; there the water is used to irrigate large areas of the steppe, as, for example, at Kulundinsk.

The Western Siberian Lowland has many lakes. In contrast to the lakes of the neighboring Eastern European Plain, which are concentrated in the northern taiga, the lowland lakes are largely concentrated in the southern, nonglaciated wooded-steppe. In the north the lakes are scattered singly, but in the south there are numerous systems of lakes. Their shapes are extremely irregular and depend on the geography of the area in which they are situated.

On the basis of their origin, the lakes may be divided into the following categories:

1) Primary lakes, in depressions formed in the geological past under varying physicogeographical conditions.

2) Glacial lakes, which filled the sinks amid accumulations of glacial material (moraine lakes north of the mid-stretches of the Ob).

3) Lakes whose origins are linked with the activity of rivers: (*a*) cutoff meander lakes, numerous in river valleys, (*b*) lakes or lake-like widenings of river channels, (*c*) lakes that were formed as a result of breaks in natural levees because the level of the river was higher than the surrounding country.

4) Peat-bog lakes, formed in the process of the development of peat (sphagnum) swamps, numerous in the Narym region.

5) Suffusion lakes in small saucer-shaped depressions in the wooded-steppe (Baraba) and steppe zones, formed as a result of the leaching-out of salts that led to the settling and contracting of the soils.

6) Nondraining lakes, lying lower than the level of the nearest rivers (Teke, Saleta).

THE KARA SEA

The Kara Sea is a part of the Arctic Ocean. It is bordered on the west by a pair of islands called Novaya Zemlya, on the east by the Severnaya Zemlya archipelago, and on the south by the coast of northern Asia from Yugorski Shar Strait to Cape Chelyuskin. It extends northward to a line running from the northern tip of Novaya Zemlya to Graham Bell Island, thence to the northern tip of Severnaya Zemlya. The Kara Sea is connected with the Barents Sea by three straits: Matochkin Shar, Kara Strait and Yugorsky Shar. Three straits also join it to the Laptev Sea: Boris Vilkitsky, Skokalsky, and Krasnaya Armiya.

The Kara Sea lies between parallels 66°05′ and 81°09′ north latitude. At 74° north latitude, the polar "day" lasts 102 days, from May 2 to August 11, and the polar "night," with frequent and intense displays of northern lights, lasts 85 days, from November 10 to February 2. In winter the daily range of temperature is small and only with the appearance of the sun do the daily changes become noticeable. The maximum variations occur in spring; there is some warming during the day, but at night the temperature may fall to −40°F. In summer, when the sun does not set and its rays pass through the atmosphere at a very low angle, it can warm the surface of the sea and lower layers of atmosphere but weakly, and fog and cloudiness retard the heating. Most of the heat is expended in melting the huge mass of ice and snow that surrounds the sea.

The climate of the Kara Sea is intermediate between the climates of the Barents and Laptev seas: the former is determined to a great degree by the warm waters of the Atlantic Ocean and warm masses of air from cyclones, the latter by the eastern Siberian anticyclone. In winter, eastward-moving cyclones cause sharp rises in temperature, storms, and thaws in the southern districts. If the Eastern Siberian high pressure area expands and extends over the Kara Sea, weak winds, clear skies, and heavy frosts contribute to the swift development of the ice cover. The climate of the southwestern Kara Sea is relatively more moderate than the climate of the northeastern section, which extends far toward the Arctic region; for example, in the former, temperatures in winter drop to −52°F, in the latter to −63°F.

The coast of the Kara Sea must be divided geomorphologically into three tectonic and stratigraphically independent sections: western (Novaya Zemlya), southern (Ob-Yenisei), and eastern (Taimyr-Severnaya Zemlya). Each section has a different relief and seacoast.

The shoreline of the eastern part of Vaygach and the southern island of Novaya Zemlya to the parallel 73° is smooth in outline, lacks dissection, and is parallel with the geologic structure of the islands. Farther north the shore is more dissected because of the transverse movement of glaciers; Shubert Gulf, Matochkin Shar Strait, all of tectonic origin, have been modified by subsequent glaciation. The shore shows the step-like terraces characteristic of a subsiding coast.

The southern shore of the Kara Sea, part of the Western Siberian Lowland, has been formed and built up by sandy and clayey deposits of the marine transgression and is bound by permafrost. In the west it ends in low cliffs, 6 to 33 feet high; in the east low banks continue into the sea and are regularly inundated by the tide. The development of the shore zone is determined by the joint action of mechanical and thermal abrasion by the sea, intensified by the warm river water of the Ob and Yenisei. These factors cause the coast line to recede, as at Cape Leskina on the Yamal Peninsula where the shore, in the course of ten years, receded 0.9 to 1.2 miles. Unlike the southern shore of the Barents Sea, the shore line is strongly sinuous, with smooth, deeply indented embayments. Peninsulas extend far north and estuaries far south. Such a coastal outline shows the extremely simple and uniform geologic makeup of the land and the slow vertical movement of the coast in the recent geologic past, when the sea penetrated deep into the lowland along the valleys of huge rivers.

The southeastern and eastern shores of the Kara Sea, composed of crystalline rocks, have a different outline. The present configuration of the shore line was produced by: (1) lines of breaks which give the shores a rectilinear shape, as, for example, the shore of Khariton Laptev, (2) the abrasive action of glaciers, which smoothed out the shore, (3) the intensive erosion of the coastal cliffs by marine ice and frost weathering, and (4) a sinking coast, which is indicated by embayments and large sandbanks on the Taimyr Peninsula.

Three basic types of shores stand out: (1) the steep, weakly dissected shores west of the mouth of the Pyasina River, (2) the broken, dissected, cliff-like shore line of Khariton-Laptev, (3) the deep fiords east of Taimyr Peninsula. On Severnaya Zemlya the western shores of October Revolution and Komsomolets islands are low, strongly dissected, and have numerous lagoons, large littoral accumulations of sand, and gravel spits or strands. The western shore of Bolshevik Island, on the other hand, is rectilinear, steep (up to 1,200 feet high), and dissected by deep fiords. Its configuration was determined by Tertiary and Quaternary radial faults.

Although the Kara Sea lies within the limits of the continental shelf, its bottom is most uneven. Along the eastern coast of Novaya Zemlya is a narrow deepwater trough 35 miles long and more than 660 feet deep that is separated from the deep central part of the

Arctic Ocean by a submarine ridge. Within the trough, in the region of Matochkin Shar, is an enclosed basin, and south of it lies the Vaygach Basin. A broad strip of shallow water 165 to 265 feet deep parallels the coast; it is especially well marked north of the Ob and Yenisei gulfs, where a vast shoal is the product of the deposits from these rivers. The bottom of the northern part of the sea gradually drops to the level of the central part of the Arctic Ocean, and to the west and east lie basins that are 1,300 feet deep and divided by central submarine ridges whose tops are the islands of Uyedinenie, Vize, and Ushakov. The complex relief of the bottom creates considerable variation in the sedimentation: sand predominates along the littoral of the mainland and islands, silt covers the bottom of the deeper sea.

Closed circular ocean currents, turning mainly in a counterclockwise direction, are typical. The flow of fresh water from the Ob and Yenisei gulfs is spread fanwise, mingling with the surface water of the sea. The northern branch of the Ob-Yenisei current moves to the north and then to the northwest (the Sedov Current). Part of the water, driven by northeast winds, swerves to the west, moving toward Novaya Zemlya and along its shores to the Kara Strait, where considerable water is added from the Barents Sea. The merged currents flow eastward to the shores of the Yamal Peninsula, where they are joined by the Ob-Yenisei waters, closing the circle. The rate of flow is about four miles per day. The winds are important. The speed and direction of surface currents depend on the force and direction of the prevailing winds, the depth of the sea, and the relative position of shores. The Kara Sea has normal twice-a-day incoming and outgoing tides. The inflowing surge enters from the Barents Sea and the Arctic Ocean, rounding the northern tip of Novaya Zemlya; the average amplitude of the tides is 1.5 to 2.5 feet.

The Kara Sea is a separate basin containing a large amount of relatively warm and fresh water (poured in by the Ob and Yenisei) which, because of its lower density, spreads

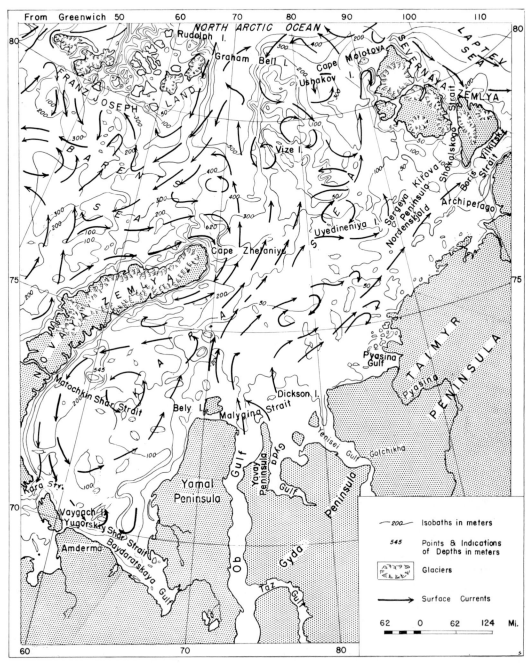

Map 1-II. Physical map of Kara Sea.

along the surface of almost the entire sea and creates a layer of water 30 to 60 feet thick that is sharply differentiated from the denser, deeper water. In summer, the presence of this fresh-water layer on the surface prevents the rise of vertical convectional currents and the penetration of heat to the depths. In winter, on the contrary, the disappearance of this layer when the rivers freeze contributes to the loss of heat to great depths.

Water of the Ob-Yenisei Shoal has a high surface temperature (41° to 46.5°F) and a low salinity. The water in the area of the shoal is muddy-brown or yellow-green and is sharply distinguished from the green waters of the Kara Sea proper. Transparency of this water is extremely slight—from 1.5 to 5 feet. The Siberian rivers carry into this water a large quantity of flotsam from their forested river-banks: the entire northeastern shore of Novaya Zemlya is covered with this flotsam, which is carried there by the current. In winter, the decrease in flow of river water causes a considerable lowering of the surface temperatures (as much as 2° to 3.5°F) and a rise in saltiness (as much as 27 to 30 parts per thousand). Near the coast there are often sharp fluctuations in temperature, caused when cold, salty water of the deep layers rises to the surface. This phenomenon often produces fogs near the coast.

In the western part of the sea, with its greater depth, the water does not warm through readily and the surface layers are more salty than those farther east. Below the 30 to 60 foot layer of fresh water there is a sharp drop in temperature and an increase in saltiness. The central part of the sea, within the circular current, has water of great density and low temperature, which fills all the basins. The Novaya Zemlya trough contains a comparatively thin layer of dense water that is highly saline and cold. A branch of the warm North Atlantic current, bringing characteristic blue water from the northwest, rounds Novaya Zemlya, enters the Kara Sea through a deep trough, and penetrates to approximately 76°36′ north latitude, where its water collides with that of the Ob-Yenisei current, mixes with it and sinks to mingle with the deep water.

The surface layer of the Atlantic water has a temperature of 34° at 30 to 50 feet; it is green, and has a transparency of more than 50 feet in the region of Zhelaniye Cape. Opposite the Kara Strait, in the depths, warm water penetrates from the Barents Sea, under the influence of west-southwest winds. Glaciers of Novaya Zemlya, descending southward, cool the littoral waters; in summer, northeast winds drive floating ice against the eastern shores of the island and hold it there, which in turn cools the water and air.

Wind and ice can change the general distribution of hydrographic elements appreciably. Ice lowers the temperature of the water; the wind, blowing across the melting ice, spreads fresh, cooled water along the surface of the sea. In broken ice, temperatures fluctuate from 33° to 34°F, while in the solid ice the temperature is never higher than 32°. Ice is the chief obstacle to navigation on the Kara Sea, which contains floating ice the year round, as the mass is too great to melt away during the short polar summer.

The ice in the Kara Sea originates there, and its spread depends on the winds. No ice enters the sea from without: the current and shoals act as a barrier, protecting the sea from the penetration of ice from the Arctic Ocean. The ice begins to form in October, at first in the shoal water near the river mouths where the water is fresher on the surface. A broad shore zone of static ice approximately 13 to 15 miles wide—somewhat wider in the east—is established quickly. It remains along the entire coast from fall to spring, having on its edge high blocks of ice frozen in as pressure ridges. The width of the land-attached floe varies from year to year, depending on the severity of the winter; sometimes it stretches so far from the shore that its edge cannot be seen from the shore heights. Along the coast of Novaya Zemlya, the shore-ice floes are narrow (2.5 to 4 miles) and are formed considerably later, not only because a lower temperature is required to freeze the more saline water there, but also because the water of the Barents Sea exerts a warming influence.

In the central part of the Kara Sea, ice 6 to 10 feet thick is formed, but the wind and rough sea do not give it a chance to solidify. It buckles, breaks up and forms floes that often rise 10 to 15 feet above the sea. These floes alternately pack together and thin out. On their borders huge heaps of ice 50 to 60 feet thick are formed. Occasionally, in the

Fig. 1-4. *Stamukha:* ice mounds in the shallow waters of the Kara Sea during August.

course of a winter, the Kara Sea, within limits of visibility, may become free of ice, only to fill up again later. Many unfrozen patches remain open during the entire winter. Icebergs sometimes run aground on Novaya Zemlya and Severnaya Zemlya, forming high (up to 60 feet) picturesque *stamukhi,* which are important in the creation of the fixed ice cover.

In the southern part of the sea, ice melts rapidly at the beginning of summer and floating ice is driven toward the northeast by southwest winds. Nevertheless, in the summer, much ice remains to hinder the navigation. Wind can shift ice with surprising speed. This has practical importance, since by waiting for a change of wind ships can often pass through straits and on open sea free of ice.

The fauna of the western part of the Kara Sea is linked to the eastern part of the Barents Sea. A great number of Arctic-Atlantic species penetrate as far east as the Ob and Yenisei gulfs. The fauna of the surface layers of the eastern part is similar to the fauna of the Laptev Sea, but comprises also some freshwater fauna, which are provided by the Ob-Yenisei current.

The resources of the Kara Sea are not yet important, although its potential is considerable. There is some commercial hunting for marine animals and fishing in the coves, straits, and mouths of rivers flowing into the Sea. Valuable whitefish, like mooksoon and broad whitefish, are significant. Several kinds of seals live in the Kara Sea. The widespread arctic ringed seal (*Phoca hispida*) lives on floating or land-attached ice, as it avoids expanses of open water. This seal can be observed lying near cracks or unfrozen patches in extensive ice fields. It makes air holes through which it may emerge onto the ice after having hunted food under it. Another large species of seal is the bearded seal (*Erignathus barbatus*); it is unable to make air holes and inhabits shoal water: its normal food consists of crustaceans.

Walruses were numerous in former times but now are rarely found. In summer, white whales (*Delphinapterus leucas*), enter the Kara Sea from the Barents in great numbers. This is a gregarious herd animal linked with the ice and effecting a regular seasonal migration. In September and October, on the eastern shores of Severnaya Zemlya, schools of thousands of white whales have been observed in the shallows. Seen from the shore, their white backs reach to the horizon, blending with the whitecaps of the sea. Near the shore, the white whales depend for food on *Boreo-gadus saida,* great masses of which converge there to spawn. White whales give a fine grade of thin oil good for precision machinery, leather of fine quality, and a coarse but edible meat. The economic exploitation of this valuable animal is important.

In and around the Kara Sea, polar bears (*Thalassarctos maritimus*) are adapted to life on the ice; they swim well, are not sensitive to cold, and travel swiftly over the ice. In summer they rove over the breaking ice, searching the crevices and open expanses for seals, which serve as their chief food; in winter they migrate to the south to find open water.

Navigation across the Kara Sea and through its straits is difficult, yet the Kara Sea is an important link in the water route, along the northern coast of the USSR. Almost two hundred years ago, M. V. Lomonosov wrote: "Having both ends and the entire shore of the Siberian Ocean in our dominion, not fearing any hindrance in quests from an enemy, and having put much effort to it with success, we let it all go to waste." Only during the Soviet regime has the northern sea route been converted into an active channel of communication with the Far East. Superpowered ice-breakers and a great number of airplanes scout the ice and accompany convoys of vessels. The construction of an official radio network, polar hydro-meteorological stations, and the organization of coal stations based on local beds, guarantee safe navigation along the northern sea route and significantly lengthen the navigation period.

With the mastering of the northern sea route, the shore line has acquired greater utility. The system of riverways that covers all of Siberia offers a convenient and cheap method of transporting its products to the shores of the polar seas. The opening of this route gives a powerful impetus to the development of natural resources of the Arctic and a new impulse toward understanding the culture of the peoples of the North.

Fig. 1-5. Ice breaker with ship convoy in thin ice along the northern sea route on the Kara Sea during the summer.

SOILS, VEGETATION, AND ANIMAL LIFE

Soil-distribution patterns of the Western Siberian Lowland are strongly influenced by a sharply expressed zonal distribution of the main soil-forming factors. There is also a sharp contrast in the central and southern parts of the lowland between the extremely variegated soils of the broad watersheds and the more uniform soils of the dissected lowlands. Northward this contrast is reduced because of the relative increase of lowland over watershed areas.

On the river plains the following zones have been identified: (1) A zone of podzolic soils in which the podzol-forming processes have been modified—soils are deeply and strongly podzolic under coniferous forests and turf; there is a transitional strip under birch forests. (2) A zone of wooded steppe soils—a typical combination of leached-out and degraded chernozems with gray, dark gray, and podzolic soils under birch forests. (3) A zone of typical chernozems and chestnut-brown soils.

On the undrained interriver areas there is a different series of zones: (1) A zone consisting predominantly of swampy soil with thick podzols under the taiga and turf-podzols under birch forests: in the south, peat bogs alternate with grassy swamps, which develop a peculiar meadow-bog soil with a high humus content; effervescence with an alkaline reaction is increased and the soils are saturated with calcium and magnesium. (2) A zone made up predominantly of meadow soil which continues into the wooded-steppe with meadow-chernozem soils that have the following genetic peculiarities: (a) a general chernozem appearance: general accumulation of humus and its proportional decline in depth; (b) saturation of the absorbing complex with alkaline-soil at lower levels; (c) the presence of elements of a hydromorphic regime—traces of gleying—and signs of solodizing. (3) A zone either of salty solonchak with typical chernozem and small spots of soloth and solodized solonetz in basins, or mixed saline chernozem and meadow-steppe and steppe soils.

The fundamental differences between the geographic spread of soils in the Western Siberian Lowland and that in the Eastern European Plain are: (1) the appearance among the podzol and chernozem strips of a special "swamp-solonchak" transitional zone with an uncommon "meadow-swamp-solonchak" complex, and (2) the important role in the southern part of the lowland, of the degree of the dissection of relief, which influences the water regime of the soil.

In the Western Siberian Lowland the influence of the relief and the petrographic character of the strata on the vegetation is weak, and the distribution of the vegetative cover has been determined largely by the general zonal changes in climate, which makes it essential to consider also the history of development of the flora. The change of geobotanic regions from north to south is so gradual that it is often impossible to draw sharp boundaries between them. The latitudinal zoning of vegetative cover is analogous to that in similar latitudes of European USSR. The tundra is replaced by forest-tundra, which is transitional to the region of coniferous forests that occupies the central part of the lowland, which has the greatest annual precipitation. Farther south, deciduous forests of birch and poplar have developed, and in the extreme southern part, where the annual precipitation is about eleven inches, steppes predominate. The general lowering of temperature eastward from the Urals has caused the boundary of the coniferous forests to swerve sharply to the south. The increase in humidity that took place in the postglacial period forced a shift of the geobotanic regions southward, but the parallel displacement of soil zones was considerably delayed. Agricultural activity of the population often strongly changes the natural process of the development of vegetation; coniferous forests disappear and areas of steppe expand.

Zoogeographically, the Western Siberian Lowland belongs to the Paleo-Arctic region. The vast territory of the lowland with its diverse fauna is not even a special zoogeographic subzone, because its animal life is generally similar to that of eastern Europe. The character of the fauna changes but slightly from west to east; many animals spread laterally through a whole landscape or geographic zone, but not one species lives on both the coast of the Kara Sea and the dry southern steppes. The character and composition of animal population is closely linked with the general landscape in which its life cycle passes; thus it is necessary to examine separately the animal life of the different geobotanic zones.

The extreme flatness of the Western Siberian Lowland gives a distinct east-west zonal distribution of the landscapes which are an eastward continuation of those of European USSR: tundra, taiga, wooded-steppe, and steppe. A large number of species of plants and animals exist on both sides of the Urals, but the zones of the Western Siberian Lowland, because of their extreme continentality and dryness, have their individual Siberian features. The subzone of mixed forests, for example, is represented only by small islands of relic linden trees in the western half of the southern taiga.

Tundra and Forest-Tundra

The subregion of tundra and forest-tundra covers three huge northern peninsulas—Yamal, Taz, and Gydan—which have two main types of relief. First, a flat or undulating alluvial plain, built up by marine clay and sand, that covers a large part of the Yamal and Taz peninsulas and a rather wide strip along the border of the Gydan Peninsula; and second, a hilly-undulating plain, built up by glacial deposits, that exists in the interior of the Gydan Penin-

sula and forms a narrow middle strip in the southern part of the Yamal Peninsula.

The Yamal Peninsula, extending north-south for six hundred miles, is an extremely young plain that emerged from the sea in the second half of the Quaternary Period. During the marine transgression it was nearly covered by the sea, and at that time layers of sandy-clayey sediments accumulated to form the peninsula. Moraine deposits were preserved only in the higher southern sections. The relief of the peninsula is young, with weak dissection and a poorly developed hydrographic network. The main ridge, with a maximum altitude of 330 feet, consists of moraine deposits and is located in the center of the southern part of the peninsula. The high sections of tundra are hills and ridges with relative heights of 490 to 660 feet above the neighboring basins. However, the northern part of the Yamal Peninsula and also Bely Island have so level a plain that even a small building may be visible from as much as thirteen miles away.

Running water and wind have created the present uneven surface. Here one sees broad, shallow, river valleys, vast swampy low places, and lake basins with expanses of raised tundra. Rivers are fed by summer rains and melting snow, but underground water flow is weak because of the permafrost. Rivers rise in lakes, flow in wide valleys with meandering courses, imperceptibly blend with the level tundra, and pass through several other lakes. Large rivers form deltas at their mouths. Lakes vary in size, depth (15 to 100 feet), and shape; on Bely Island there are vast, level, saucer-like depressions with water at the level of the tundra. Lakes are either glacial depressions or have been formed when ground ice thawed and the ground covering it settled. As a result of drifting snow and grass growth around shallow lakes, flat swamps encircle many of them.

The small amount of precipitation, frequent winds, fine soil, and sparse vegetative cover of Yamal promote the energetic erosive action of wind in the dry period of winter, leading to the formation of aeolian terrain. There are many expanses of drifted sand with deflationary depressions, tables, and hills. The plain gradually drops toward the shores, forming intermediate terraces in places. Some shores of Yamal consist of clayey precipices 60 to 80 feet high; others of flat swamps. At low tide the sea bottom on the north shores of Yamal and the island of Bely is bared for half a mile.

On the Gydan Peninsula the chief watershed, with heights to 660 feet, shifts toward the mouth of the Ob, and is a high, hilly-undulating plain, strongly dissected radially with numerous deep valleys. This plain was formed from glacial material with a rock-field on the surface and lies on an ancient Paleozoic base. The Taz Peninsula is also asymmetrical, higher in the west but low and surrounded by swamps in the east.

Basic climatic features of the tundra are: (1) severity; (2) a short cold summer; (3) frequent early autumn frosts; (4) a long harsh winter, aggravated by strong winds; (5) wide seasonal variation in insolation (in summer the sun does not set for about three months; in winter it does not rise for a like period); (6) weak evaporation on land and sea, which limits precipitation; and (7) much cloudiness and high relative humidity.

Winter in the tundra is severe and lasts from the middle of October to the beginning of May. In the extreme north the polar night extends from about November 12 to the end of January. Very short winter days mean that there is little solar radiation even in the forest-tundra; for example, in Salekhard the sun is below the horizon for all of December and in January it shines an average of two minutes per day. Temperatures in winter are extremely low, falling on occasion to −61°F. In the west the nearness of the sea modifies the extreme winter; thus in the typical tundra the average January temperature in the west is −4°F, but in the east it is −16°F. Toward the east and south the winter takes on a more stable continental character.

The climate of the forest-tundra has a continental character. Its average temperature am-

plitude is 70 degrees, its maximum temperature range 153 degrees. In the west as many as 46 days may have a temperature as low as −12°F; in the east the number may reach 61 days. In the east, there are about 12 winter days with average daily temperature lower than −40°F; occasionally the temperature reaches −81°F. Frequent cyclones, crossing the southern tundra, raise winter temperatures 27° to 36°F in 24 hours, then cause them to fall just as swiftly. Cyclones are usually followed by the invasion of masses of arctic air from the Kara Sea or from Eastern Siberia, accompanied by steady, strong frosts and clear skies.

Winter has the greatest wind velocities with the maximum of 23 to 30 feet per second in December. For many days the direction of the wind is unchanged, especially on the islands— on Dickson Island south winds have blown for 13 days without stopping; winds blow in the forest-tundra from 6 to 10 days. Particularly strong winds, which often cause snowstorms, are linked with the passing cyclones: the open terrain favors the development of powerful and frequent blizzards. Each year there are 90 to 150 days with snowstorms in the western tundra, and about 80 in the east. There is much drifting snow, because even weak winds of 13 to 16 feet per second sweep the snow from the surface: higher winds may produce a *purga,* a powerful snowstorm bearing exceedingly fine dust-like snow. The combination of low winter temperatures and strong winds create biting cold. Winter along the coast of the Kara Sea is thus harsher than the colder but calmer winter in Yakutsk. In the forest-tundra zone wind velocities are low in winter because of the predominance of high pressure: weak winds (6 to 16 feet per second) or calms are common during clear frosty weather.

The snow lies on the tundra from the middle of October to the middle of June (on Dickson Island, 265 days), but it is a thin cover, 8 to 12 inches thick, as there is little winter precipitation and strong winds drive the snow off the high spots. In the forest-tundra the thickness of the snow cover increases to 28 inches.

The snow lies in an even layer only on level terrain: winds sweep the snow from hillocks into protected spots under steep banks where it forms thick snowdrifts. These remain till autumn and serve as sources of meltwater for tundra rivers. The cold, long winters, with little snow and a thin snow cover, cause deep and prolonged freezing of soil, which leads to the preservation of permafrost, which is 300 to 1,000 feet thick along the coast. In winter, northern lights recur frequently in the extreme north but are observed in the forest-tundra only rarely. They are usually seen in the arctic tundra (Dickson Island) on 101 days, in the typical tundra (Mare-Sale) on 50 days, and in the forest-tundra (Salekhard) on 24 days.

Summer in the tundra is short and cold, accompanied by frosts and frequent snowfall: average daily temperatures range from 32° to 41°F. Almost every July and August has days with average daily temperatures of 50°F, and often temperatures reach 68°F. The average daily temperatures do not drop below 27°F in July, or below 23°F in August. Summer temperatures vary within narrow limits. The average temperature of the warmest month, July, is never higher than 46°F at littoral stations. In June there are about 20 to 23 days with frost. Some years there is no frost-free period in the north and frosts are observed during the whole summer; in others the frost-free period extends 60 to 75 days (the average annual duration is 40 days in the west and 30 in the east).

Summer is warmer in the forest-tundra. Average daily temperatures in the warmest month, July, reach 54° to 56°F, sometimes rising to 77°F in the north and to 87°F in the south, although seldom more than two or three times a year. The number of frosts is considerably lower than in the tundra; the frost-free period may last for 100 days in the west and 75 days in the east. The long northern summer day increases the insolation. In summer the midnight sun is observed at 67° north latitude, and on the 70th parallel the sun does not set at all for 73 days.

The transparency of the atmosphere is due to the absence of dust in the arctic air, and the air's insignificant water vapor content intensifies solar radiation. Even though the sun is low, there is much light, both direct and diffused. In the tundra the amount of diffused light is increased by the duration of solar radiation, a persistent layer of low, thin clouds, and a prolonged snow cover. In the forest-tundra each summer month has more than 200 hours of sunshine, but December has none.

Wind velocities decrease to a minimum in July and storms are rare in summer. High relative humidity (in the forest-tundra in July, 73 per cent), comparatively low temperature, and proximity of the cold sea cause much summer cloudiness (70 to 80 per cent). During the summer the arctic tundra has 50 days with fog, the typical tundra 11 days, and the forest-tundra 4 days. High relative humidity increases man's sensitivity to changes of temperature in the littoral regions. Precipitation is heavy in summer, with a maximum, 10 to 12.5 inches, in August. Rains are seldom more than drizzles, but sometimes are heavy downpours, accompanied by thunder and lightning. Frequent precipitation, little thawing, weak evaporation, and permafrost lead to a wide saturation of soils.

Tundra soils are similar to the swampy and podzol soils of the forest zone, but the soil-forming process in the tundra possess many specific peculiarities. Bitterly cold winter months, rapid changes in temperature, strong winds that sweep off the insignificant and irregular snow cover, all lead to an incessant breaking of the small insecure roots of the sparse vegetation. Washing-out and deflation cause the development, especially in the northern part of the zone, of a thick network of cracks that break up the surface of the soil into polygonal divisions. At the beginning of summer these cracks contribute to the saturation of soils and the forming of a sticky clay horizon; later on, however, the cracks help the draining and aeration of the soils.

Permafrost, even in the sandy soils of the tundra, hinders the percolation of surface water into the deep layers of the ground and promotes condensation of the water contained in the air that permeates the soil. This causes uniform moistening of soils of different mechanical composition and decreases drainage. The low temperatures and high humidity also hinder evaporation, and the soils of the tundra thus show, at all depths, strong swamping.

There are few drying winds in winter, so that although precipitation is light, moisture is maintained in the frozen ground, preserving the vegetation from drought. Low temperatures, the long periods in which the soils are inactive, saturation, and the lack of oxygen in the soil cause weak decomposition of mineral and organic materials. This leads to thin soils, to the weak expression of soil horizons, and to soil development on the surface of a peat layer. Very few of the micro-organisms, notably bacteria, which play such a prominent role in the transformation of nutritive elements into compounds assimilable by plants, are found here. In conditions of poor aeration and lack of oxygen, preservative processes prevail over oxidation; thus the basic soil-forming process in the tundra is swampiness. The bedrock of the tundra is extremely uniform and composed of Quarternary sand and clay deposits. Only on clean sands, with a deep layer of permafrost and good filtering capabilities, have soils of a podzol type developed.

Dissection of relief in the tundra creates some diversity in exposure of slopes and drainage, but since the sun neither sets nor rises high above the horizon in summer, it warms only the very steepest slopes more than the level terrain, and thus contributes to the relative uniformity of soil cover. The temperature of the soil in summer drops quickly with depth; in the top layer where the plant roots grow it does not exceed 50°F—and remains that high for only a short time. Thawing of the tundra soil in early summer proceeds slowly because its upper horizons contain ice layers. During thawing much heat is absorbed, but during freezing the soil holds, for a long time, the heat accumulated during summer, in spite of adjacent permafrost. Strong winds in summer contribute to swift thawing and drying of soils.

Conditions unfavorable to the existence of vegetation in the tundra are (1) the short growing season, (2) the low summer temperatures, and (3) the drying action of constant winds. This explains the poverty of flora, slow growth, remarkable ability of tundra plants to endure frosts, and predominance of low bushes and perennial—sometimes evergreen—grasses. When summer begins, plants grow rapidly. Low soil temperatures at the time of the vegetative period and strong evaporation during the frequent and powerful windstorms create such disparity between the evaporation from the above-ground parts of plants and the entrance of water into the root system (a phenomenon of physiological aridity) that woody vegetation cannot grow here.

Dwarf tundra plants, spreading along the ground or growing with many roots, are satisfied with only a thin layer of air next to the soil. This air is under the influence of the soil, which warms it in summer, and it is protected by the thick vegetation from the action of wind. The constant light in summer is favorable for plant growth. The light in the tundra is only a little less intense than in the middle latitudes, but the amount of chemical-activating rays is greater because of the transparency of the atmosphere. The winter winds carry crystals of snow which polish the exposed earth and destroy and disfigure the plants that protrude above the snow, producing bare spots on the few hills in the tundra. Perennial herbs have many large, bright flowers and grow in clumps, reminiscent of an Alpine mountain carpet. The uniform terrain and soil cover explain the uniform vegetation and small number of species.

Because of their climate, the tundra and forest-tundra are favorable for agriculture. There are short summers with 15 frost-free days in the arctic tundra, 60 to 80 in the typical tundra, and 80 to 100 in the forest-tundra. Unfavorable climate and soil are not, however, insurmountable obstacles to the development of agriculture in the tundra, since the abundance of light in the northern summers compensates for them. Physiological processes which take place in plants, such as wheat and edible root plants are directly dependent on the duration and intensity of solar light. Plants mature much faster where days are long.

Here, agriculture should be developed in order to guarantee a supply of fresh fruit and vegetables for the natives as a source of vitamins in the fight against scurvy. Raising vegetables in hothouses, the use of seed-beds to grow seedlings for transplanting, growing of herbs, and sowing of root plants and barley in the forest-tundra should be encouraged. In the tundra, it is necessary to institute measures for the improvement of drainage and aeration of soils, and fertilization is also a necessity. One month is sufficient, under favorable conditions, to develop bacterial life in the soil. The lowering of the level of permafrost is essential, and it may be brought about by the removal of the peaty horizon (which conducts heat poorly), by the action of running water, and by heating by steam with subsequent drainage. At the same time, frost-resistant strains of cultivated plants must be developed.

The fauna of the tundra, as a consequence of the severity of the climate, comprises few species and includes only those animals able to resist cold, many having thick downy white fur that acts as protective camouflage against a background of prolonged snow cover. For example, the fur of the polar fox becomes white in the winter, and the reindeer has considerably lighter-colored fur in winter than in summer. The shallow snow cover allows the reindeer to exist the whole year on green fodder. The marked increase of the length of the claws of the Ob lemming in winter is obviously connected with the need to scrape away the light snow and break the ice crust to obtain food.

In the tundra there is an especially sharp disparity between the abundance of fodder in summer and the lack of it in winter. This causes seasonal migration of many animals and also increases the propensity of such animals as the polar fox for remarkably rapid and am-

ple fattening. The tundra grouse, ptarmigan, and polar owl are more or less constant inhabitants of the tundra, but most tundra birds live there only in summer. There are a great many mosquitoes and gadflies in the tundra; in the summer they are a scourge of both reindeer and man. The Western Siberian tundra has many animals not found west of the Urals. In the east, near the Yenisei, for example, are the shrew (*Sorex vir turuchanensis*) and the field mouse (*Microtus oeconomus*). Reptiles and amphibians are few.

The northern area is divided into two broad zones: tundra and forest-tundra. The tundra in its turn is divided from north to south into arctic and typical, the latter being sometimes subdivided into moss-lichen and bushy tundra.

The arctic tundra is characterized by weak soil-forming processes, by a lack of scrub and peat swamps, and by the broad development of polygonal tundras. Typical of arctic soil formation are the predominance of physical weathering, weakness of biochemical processes, slow leaching of minerals from the soils, slight activity of microbes, slow accumulation of peat and rough humus, development of the peculiar tundra gley soil, and the lack of morphologically expressed podzol soil, even in sands. The loamy peat-gley soil cracks into polygonal blocks, and there are extensive bare spaces among the spotty arctic tundras. Along frosty cracks the hardiest varieties of arctic grasses grow: foxtail grass (*Alopecurus alpinus*), and sourgrass (*Oxyria digyna*). There are neither lichens nor hummocky tundras in this subzone. The sparse vegetation causes a paucity of fauna and only along the seacoast are there many birds. Along the coast are also found the polar bear, tundra grouse, hoofed lemming (*Dicrostonyx torquatus*), glaucous gull (*Larus hyperboreus*), and jaeger (*Stercorarius pomarinus*).

The typical tundra is characterized by the complete absence of trees, by the predominance of mossy and lichenous tundras and bogs, and by the development of peat-gley and crypto-podzolic gley soils. Podzolic soils are encountered on sands in fairly well-drained places; they have a shortened profile and are less acid than forest soils.

Mossy tundra, on clay soil with a crypto-podzolic surface of gleyed soil, has a uniform aspect resulting from the continuous shallow cover of Bryophyta, to which a few lichens are added. The comparatively rare shrubs consist almost exclusively of fine, viny dwarf birch (*Betula nana*) and some shrub willow (*Salix pulchra*). The plant cover comprises no more than two or three dozen species, of which the most common are the arctic tufted plant (*Dryas octopetala*), meadow grass (*Poa arctica*), black crowberry (*Empetrum nigrum*), cotton sedge (*Eriophorum vaginatum*), reed grass (*Carex rigida*), and cereals. In the southern part of the typical tundra, where winter precipitation increases, the role of shrubs becomes more important. In spring the deer graze on the shoots of moss and cotton grass, but in summer they

growth of herbs and grasses. At the base of hills, where in winter snowdrifts pile up on peat-gley soils, are thick overgrowths of polar willows (*Salix glauca, Salix lanata,* and *Salix pulchra*) and dwarf birch.

In flat low places between hills, monotonous *gipnovyye* bogs on peat-gley soils are found over permafrost. These tundra bogs, unlike the swamps of the forest zone, are flooded in spring and fall and have a thin turf because of the low temperature. This produces different kinds of peat, with intensive mineralization. Arctic bog moss (*Sphagnum lenense*) yields to Bryophyta, owing to the mineralization of swamp water which is accumulated in hollows with impervious bottoms. The swamping of basins is different from that in the forest zone, because the shallow basins have a mineral substratum and the vegetation creeps into them gradually.

Fig. 1-6. Low brush tundra in the basin of Euribey River, which flows into Gydansk Bay.

eat the foliage of shrubs as well. If the grazing is light, only the leaves of the shrubs are consumed, which has a beneficial influence on the lichen cover as it becomes exposed to light. Heavier grazing leads to degradation of the shrubs, lichens, and Bryophyta, and a stronger

Spotty tundra grows on slopes that are bare of snow in winter and along saddles between hills where there are patches of loam three to five feet in diameter, separated by narrow strips of vegetation along frosty cracks. There are more lichens and flowering plants than in the mossy tundras, as they are more able than bryophytes to adapt to the relative dryness of soil and the sharp fluctuations of soil temperature that result from the thin snow cover and sparse vegetation. Overgrowth of bare spots proceeds slowly, because these spots are abraded annually in winter by wind, and in spring they are enlarged by spreading mud.

On raised dry places with clayey soils and sandy hilly expanses there are lichenous tundras with a predominance of fruticose lichens: *Alectoria, Cetraria,* and reindeer moss (*Cladonia rangiferina*), grow here with a small amount of Bryophyta, but almost no grass or shrubs. This type of tundra is good winter pasture, and although excessive grazing is harmful to the slow-growing reindeer moss (in the north 1 to 4 millimeters a year, in the south 4 to 6 millimeters), it is advantageous for unpalatable lichens, particularly those which, like *Cetraria,* are able to withstand trampling.

On the well-warmed southern slopes of ravines, along the edges of snowdrifts, which often survive the summer, the vegetation is well protected in winter by snow. Here rapid and deep thawing of the soil takes place in the spring. The abundant moisture and good drainage produce tundra meadows that appear like variegated flower beds against a monotonous green-brown background of mossy tundra. Bryophytes and lichens are absent here, and grass forms a thick, short, continuous cover containing a rich and diverse blend of dicotyledons: crowfoot (*Ranunculus borealis*), globeflower (*Trollius asiaticus*), and valerian (*Valeriana capitata*). The succulent green grassy vegetation is pasture for deer in autumn, when grass and shrubs in other places have grown dry and withered. Such patches may attract many geese in summer. This grouping of plants reminds one of the Alpine meadows in mountainous regions.

In narrow strips along both sides of rivers and streams, thick clusters of willows grow to about the height of a man. Their growth is favored by the deep, rapid thawing in summer, good drainage, and the moisture provided by

snowdrifts. Deer are frequent visitors of these osier thickets. In places there are swampy meadows containing mainly sedge and grasses but also many dicotyledons.

The variety of ecologic conditions in the typical tundra may explain its relatively rich fauna. The most common mammal here is the domestic reindeer (*Rangifer tarandus*)— there are no wild deer. The reindeer is the universal animal in the tundra; without it the tundra would be almost inaccessible. Harnessed to sledges in winter and summer they serve as draft animals, and it is not necessary to carry fodder when traveling, because even in winter they get food from the tundra. Their meat is edible, their hides are used for clothes and footwear, and their sinews as thread for sewing hides. Clothing of deer hide is irreplaceable in the tundra, because even during the severest cold it is light, flexible, and retains warmth excellently, whereas sheepskin becomes stiff and brittle. All winter the deer exist on fodder, feeding on lichens or reindeer moss; in summer they eat young greens, berries, and mushrooms, and on occasion lemming and birds' eggs. Near the Yenisei, Eskimo shepherd dogs are used in herding the deer, and there are some sled dogs in the tundra. Wolves are a hazard to the reindeer herds, feeling themselves complete masters of the tundra and forest-tundra.

The polar fox (*Alopex lagopus*) plays an important role in the tundra. His chief food during the year is the abundant lemming, but with the approach of summer he becomes a bird-fancier, constantly poking about the tundra, sniffing and investigating each hillock, each small stone, until he finds a nest and does away with the eggs or the defenseless brood. The fox digs his burrow on the dry southern slopes of hills, along the high banks of rivers and lakes, always in dry sandy or loamy ground, where good drainage and warm soil have lowered the level of permafrost. So many traps are set for foxes that during a journey across the tundra they may serve as guideposts.

Lemming are widespread, especially the Ob

lemming (*Lemmus obensis*) and the hoofed lemming (*Dicrostonyx torquatus*). The lemming chooses broken turf mounds with large fissures for its burrows, since these, because of poor heat conductivity, guarantee some warmth in winter, and heat through early summer. These mounds rise above the general surface and are not covered by deep snow in winter. The lemming feeds on cotton grass and reed grass, and, since it does not hibernate, painstakingly stores them up for winter. It serves as food for such mammals as the fox and feathered carnivores like the snowy owl.

Birds prevalent in the tundra are: loon (*Colymbus arcticus*), plover (*Charadrius hiaticula*), ptarmigan grouse (*Lagopus lagopus*), snowy owl (*Nyctea nyctea*), and jaeger (*Stercorarius pomarinus*). The lakes—the most thickly populated places in the tundra in summer—serve as feeding stations for a great number of waterfowl: geese, ducks, terns, etc. Life in the tundra does not die out even in winter; the lemming wander under the snow, the fox and polar owl hunt them, and even some of the ptarmigan remain.

The forest-tundra has islands of sparse forest and many peat bogs covered with vegetation. In its transitional podzolic-gleyed soils, the bog process operates during temporary moistening. Here the podzolic process acts not only on sand, but even on clayey soil. The development of a dense mossy carpet under the sparse forest leads to much surface swampiness and a cold soil with little evaporation. Trees and shrubs are stunted on the clayey soils of the watersheds; they develop somewhat better along the well-heated slopes which are protected from wind and along river valleys. On sand, larch and spruce grow as large trees even near the northern border of their distribution. In the southern part of the forest-tundra the forest stretches in narrow strips one-half to one mile wide along both sides of the rivers, but to the north the strips break up, forested sections become few, and trees grow only in small groups or stand alone. The northern forests are so sparse and the crowns of the trees so poorly

developed that they do not modify the composition of other vegetation.

In the larch forests, on sandy soils with a thin and loose snow cover, a mossy-lichen vegetation grows. The lichens that form the base, as, for example, reindeer moss, require snow cover in winter. Under the trees the lichens are replaced by Bryophyta. The few dwarf birch and Manchurian alder (*Alnus fruticosa*) forests serve principally as winter pastures. On poorly drained soils in the southern part sparse larch forests with an admixture of spruce are found.

Valley forests provide ecologic routes along which a number of animals of the forest zone (squirrel, fox, brown bear, bald buzzard, speckled magpie, and the like) penetrate northward into the forest-tundra. The reindeer, polar fox, and tundra partridge, on the other hand, migrate southward through these sparse forests. Willow groves along the large rivers have porous soils in which burrows can easily be dug, and the presence of good forage makes them ideal homes for water rats and white hares, or snowshoe rabbits, which are eaten by the carnivores: ermine, fox, brown bear. In summer, in the thick overgrowth of willows, deer find not only their favorite fodder, but also some protection from mosquitoes. During winter, the ptarmigan migrate there and feed on willow twigs. Meadows on the drier terraces and slopes have an abundance of insects and serve as pastures for geese (*Melanonyx fabalis*) and (*Anser albifrons*) and swans. On the slopes there are many burrows of field mice, foxes, and wolves.

Among the islands of the sparse forest are sections of mossy and hilly tundra: in peat bogs supersaturated with water are mounds of different sizes whose tops are often bare of vegetation; on slopes are thick growths of "gipnovy" Bryophyta, cotton grass, cloudberry, and dwarf birch. In the postglacial xerothermic period, forests extended far into the typical tundra. There groves thrived, but the lakes turfed-over rapidly, and with the change in climate the timber line fell back and continued to retreat southward; this is demonstrated by the preservation, in the present-day tundra, of thick relic podzols and islands of forest tundra with dead trees on their edges.

Taiga

The northern, larger section of the Siberian forest zone, with individual heights of 1,200 feet, was formed from Quaternary sand, gravel, and clay. Most of it is an undulating plain with ridges and groups of moraine hills from 100 to 200 feet high, and many kames. River valleys are more than 200 feet deep along their central courses and often open into large shallow lake basins. In the west, moraine ridges run northeast-southwest. Here the moraine is composed of a gravelly-clayey soil and includes layers of crystalline Ural gravels which show that the deposits were brought from the northern Urals. West of the Ob, in the Konda region, at the level of the present-day network of the lower Lyapin and Konda rivers, are vast depressions in which there are numerous bogs. They appear to be ancient river beds and lakes, since they contain lake alluvium—bedded sand and layers of loam and gravel. Raised sections from 600 to 1,200 feet high between depressions constitute watersheds: such are the Lyulim-Vor ridge, which forces the North Sosva to make a sharp turn to the north, or the ridge west of Muzhi, where the Sinya makes a sharp turn to the south.

In the eastern part of the Siberian forest zone the undulating plain has been dissected by broad, but relatively shallow, asymmetrical river valleys into wide swampy watersheds up to 250 feet high. Moraine ridges run east-west or northwest and are formed of glacial material brought from the Taimyr Peninsula.

The southern, smaller part of the Siberian forest zone, where the maximum altitude is less than 300 feet, is also an undulating plain, formed of lacustrine sand and clay of the epoch of maximum glaciation. These are linked with huge preglacial basins of Quaternary strata,

with recent sand and clay predominating. The plain is dissected by many broad river valleys 120 to 150 feet deep. The north-south sections of rivers have asymmetrical slopes: high and steep right banks that are usually formed of strata with a gentle westward gradient and level or gently sloping left banks. Such one-sided lateral erosion is presumably a result of Quaternary tectonic movements that caused a rise in the pre-Ural district of the lowland while the pre-Salair section remained stable. Both the watersheds and river valleys are extensively swamped, with many bogs and shallow lakes. In the southern part of the Narym region, deflational basins are found.

The chief climatic characteristics of the taiga are: cold, snowy, and cloudy winters; warm and humid summers; and moderate precipitation (17 to 20 inches). The heaviest precipitation takes place in July and August (2 to 3 inches) and the lightest in February (0.50 to 0.75 inches). It is cloudy 60 to 70 per cent of the year, and there are but 30 to 50 clear days annually. The relative humidity is high (70 to 80 per cent), and winds are rather weak (10 to 12 feet per second). Clearly expressed continentality becomes stronger from west to east with an average annual temperature amplitude of 65° to 72°F and a maximum amplitude of 151°F in the west, and 72° to 81°F and 170°F in the east.

The average daily temperature in January is from −6° to −20°F. In winter 30 to 34 days have temperatures below −12°F and the absolute minimum temperature is −66°F. Steady cold with clear skies and calms is interrupted by the passage of cyclones, which raise the temperature and are accompanied by strong winds and snowstorms. Winter has approximately 12 per cent of the annual precipitation, but this is greater than in Eastern Siberia. The snow cover of 20 to 40 inches remains about 200 days, from the middle of October to the middle of May. Winter is cloudy and the hours of sunshine are few. Relative humidity is 80 to 85 per cent in December. Winter winds are weak, about 10 feet per second. There are 20 to 40 days with snow-storms in the western part of the zone; in the east, 50 to 60. Spring is relatively cold and dry, as frosts continue to mid-June and precipitation is only a little greater than in winter; cloudiness is at a minimum for the year (in March, 50 to 60 per cent); relative humidity is low (in May, 60 to 65 per cent).

The summers in the taiga are rather warm. The average temperature of the warmest month (July) is usually above 65°F, about 30 summer days have an average daily temperature higher than 68°F, and the absolute maximum reaches 95°F. The frost-free period varies from 75 days in the northern part of the taiga to 125 days in the south (from the end of May to the end of September), but there may be frosts even in July. The growing season is about 100 days long in the north, and about 150 days in the south (from the beginning of May to the first days of October). The summer months have approximately half of the annual precipitation and 10 to 12 storms or cloud-bursts. It is cloudy from 60 to 70 per cent of the time, and there are about 200 hours of sunshine a month. Relative humidity is high (65 to 80 per cent); the number of summer days with fog are few (10 or 15)—more near large rivers (at Yeniseisk about 33). In summer the velocity of winds is greater than in winter (13 to 15 feet per second). Autumn is wetter than spring (it has more than 22 per cent of the annual precipitation); relative humidity (80 per cent) and cloudiness (70 to 80 per cent) are high.

The climate of the taiga is much more suitable for the cultivation of agricultural crops than the climate at similar latitudes elsewhere. Although the short period of extreme warmth and the late spring and early autumn frosts are unfavorable for plant growth, the notable length of the summer day and lack of drought more than compensate for them. Conditions are especially favorable for the growth of grasses, vegetables, root plants, potatoes, grain, and flax. Every year great quantities of superb hay containing an abundance of grass are harvested. This is extremely important for the

development of livestock raising. In the Narym region clover grows vigorously, not only as a field crop but also as a weed, and the yield of grain per acre reaches a figure unheard of on the Russian plain. On warm exposed slopes, squash and melons grow. Flax, which is sown for fiber and oil, is of high quality. Crops of grain are dependable. On soils freshly cleared of forest, rye attains the height of a man, with heavy stands. To guarantee an annual harvest, however, it is essential to put under cultivation elevated slopes, as these are less affected by early fall frosts: if they are sheltered from cold northern winds and well drained, their soil warms quickly and deeply. In the northern half of the zone, lowering of the level of permafrost is necessary, as well as the development of early-ripening, hardy, and frost-resistant varieties of crops.

The most interesting agricultural-engineering measures are: (1) sowing grain and grass on comblike ridges, which facilitates warming and drainage of soil, and retaining the heat by mulching with peat at the end of summer; (2) allowing snow to remain on the fields in winter, but speeding-up thawing in spring by spreading mineral fertilizer on the snow, which increases the absorption of solar rays; and (3) the espalier method of growing fruit trees, which permits them to utilize the warm layer of air near the soil.

Water is always available because of the slight evaporation of precipitation and the presence of plentiful ground water, most of which lies near the surface. Soft, fresh, ground water, in the sand of Quaternary strata, forms dependable horizons 6 to 100 feet below the surface. Deeper water and good drainage are found on terraces, asymmetrical slopes, and numerous islands of firm soil.

Surface flow in the taiga zone is great because of the heavy precipitation, weak evaporation, and abundance of underground water. The rivers form fantastic meanders, which are sometimes almost complete circles on the wide flood plains. The inhabitants, for whom the rivers are almost the sole means of communication, call the meanders "tortures" and meas-

Fig. 1-7. Old and new complex meanders of the Chulym River in the heart of the Western Siberian taiga.

ure distance on the rivers by their number. Channels are dug across narrow isthmuses at the bases of large loops to straighten the course of a river. Heavy precipitation over large areas drained only by rivers of low gradient causes extensive and protracted flooding. In some years the spring floods may not drain off until late fall (for example, in the Konda region). During spring floods the bottomlands are almost completely covered with water, above which rise only isolated islands and groups of willow thickets.

Water in such large quantities spreading over extremely wide bottomland is depressing to a stranger. As the water rises in spring or in the rainy season, the current of the river becomes swift, and changes the river channels rapidly. New channels are formed, old ones are straight-ened, and meanders are lengthened by the undermining of high banks on curves. Rivers in flood easily destroy banks formed of loamy layers and deposit the silt and sand farther downstream. Log jams form, obstructing a river for miles and creating an almost insurmountable barrier to river transportation. Taiga rivers usually have floods twice a year, the strongest in spring, the weakest in fall. As a result of these floods, many rivers form braided channels.

The rivers are fed by rain, melting snow, and springs. Springs in some stretches of small rivers supply so much water that these stretches may not freeze until March, and sometimes remain open all year. The water of taiga rivers is muddy in spring, and for most of the summer it is dark, colored by organic matter, has a low salt content, a high iron content, and only a small amount of dissolved oxygen. In fall the water becomes clear and takes on a greenish tinge. The slightly mineralized water produces mossy-peaty swamps in the bottomlands, similar to those on the crests. The fast growth and development of valley peat bogs often cause clogging of shallow channels and their conversion into narrow winding bogs with steep banks.

In autumn and winter, when ice and snow stop the feeding of the large rivers at their sources, ground feeding from the widely distributed peat bogs acquires significance. When this bog water, rich in ferrous sulfate from the swampy soils, flows into a large river, it absorbs great amounts of oxygen from the river water, thus killing many fish, and polluting the water.

Lakes on the watersheds are the typical basin lakes of hilly moraine relief, partly related to the dam type. They lie at the sources of the river network and feed it. Only the deepest have survived: the shallow ones have become basins overgrown with peat, but retain their clearly defined shores. On wide bottomlands, especially in the Sosva-Konda region, there are many *tumani* or *sory* (bogs or wastes). In spring they are broad lakes, but as the water level lowers they gradually grow narrow and split into a series of channels, which, by fall, are choked with alluvium and converted into chain lakes. These lakes are strong natural regulators of rivers, retarding their fall and allowing them to be used as a means of communication during the entire navigational season.

The Western Siberian taiga, which is the central part of the forest zone of the USSR, begins approximately at the Arctic Circle in the north and extends south as far as a line from Tyumen to Tomsk. The distribution of vegetation is conditioned by the relief, the depth of ground water, and the lithologic composition of soils. The influence of the exposure of slopes is insignificant, except where steep cliffs border terraces; here it contributes to the growth of pine forests on southern slopes and spruce with fir along shaded ravines. The level relief with poor drainage, impervious clays near the surface, and 20 inches of precipitation annually make the soil swampy; a humid summer with little evaporation and high relative humidity aid in this development. Bogs are one of the three basic landscapes of the taiga. The watersheds provide optimum conditions for turf accumulation and development of strongly acid peat bogs. The same factors that create the bogs contribute to the broad distribution of podzolic soil in the coniferous forest, a thick, shady, somber, and swampy taiga of spruce and fir, to which are added larch and pine. The most favorable places for forests are raised sections along river valleys and crests and hills among swampy watersheds. The change of climate from north to south divides the taiga into three subzones: (1) sparse swampy spruce-larch forests, (2) marshy pine forests, and (3) mixed coniferous forests with swampy areas.

The sparse forests, with their low temperatures, have poor tree growth and little standing timber, resembling, in the northern part, the woods of the southern forest-tundra. Spruce-larch forests predominate, with spruce prevailing on clayey soil and larch on sand. The general swampiness leads to a broad distribution of treeless peat bogs on watersheds and to the shifting of the forest to well-drained banks of rivers. Forests on drained podzolic soils along river valleys and along the tops of watershed hills in the north are made up of spruce, larch, and European white birch; in the south pine is added, and the larch almost disappears. In these thin forests the following vegetation grows: a scrub formation, often of dwarf birch, abundant swamp underbrush, and a thick mossy cover containing a large amount of light-loving lichen, which makes these woods useful for winter pasture. Sand is overgrown with spruce-larch forest with more normally developed trees.

The Siberian larch (*Larix sibirica*) is one of the most widespread trees in western Siberia. It is undemanding as to climate, forming the northern limit of forest growth and extending southward to the dry and hot steppe. It sheds its needles in winter. Under favorable conditions larch may live for 350 years, reaching 150 feet in height and 6 feet in diameter. It grows more rapidly than other conifers in its first 30 or 40 years, and is more photophilic; it demands little moisture, and prefers soils rich in lime. It has a strong root system: a taproot and many laterals, especially where permafrost lies close to the surface. On marshes it may produce accessory roots on the lower part of its trunk—these are often overgrown with Bryophyta. The wood of Siberian larch is of high quality. It is resinous, tough, and flexible, but is not easily worked with tools. Because it resists decay, it is excellent material for crossties, piles, wooden paving blocks, and for shipbuilding. The bark of the larch is a high-grade tanning agent and a source of resin—the so-called Venetian turpentine—and wood alcohol. The heaviness of its wood makes it difficult to tow larch logs in rafts. The severe climate and low soil temperatures in the northern part of the taiga subzone act adversely on the larch; it rarely reaches great size there and trees may have dead tops or many dead branches.

Among the forests are hummocky swamps and frozen peat bogs, treeless in the north, but forested in the south with spruce and low-growing dwarf pine. In low places, on sites of former ponds are large impassable quicksand-like areas. Flooded parts of river valleys have meadows alternating with thick, tall pine-spruce forests, which are especially typical of the southern subzone.

The marshy pine forest subzone is large. Soil on drained clay along rivers and on islands among the bogs is podzolic or slightly podzolic; on sand are true podzols. Peat-bog soil forms along the borders of swamps and in the real swamp forests with thick moss cover, especially in the eastern part of the subzone. River plains with alluvial soil have trees that are better developed than those in swamp forests, no tundra plants grow under the forest canopy, and more southern species thrive in the grass cover. Because of the exceptional swampiness of the level interriver areas the forests do not occupy these great expanses, but form

strips that extend for many miles along rivers. Siberian pine forms the general background of the forest terrain, but is usually mixed with larch, spruce, fir, birch, and aspen, although there are pure stands in river valleys. In the Vakhs region, for example, forests with a prevalence of Siberian pine comprise 48 per cent of the total, larch 21 per cent, young growth on burnt-over areas 27 per cent, and peat bogs 4 per cent.

Siberian pine (*Pinus sibirica*) is a sturdy tree with a thick crown. It does not require much warmth, prefers places with rich moist clay soil, and grows well in areas with an excess of stagnant water. It is often found along the edges of peat bogs, where it is stunted, with clear signs of impoverishment. Its root system is well developed, consisting of a taproot, large strong lateral roots, and, on bogs, auxiliary roots. The Siberian pine is shade-tolerating and slow-growing, and some trees live 500 years. Fires readily destroy it, especially the young trees. Its spread is effected with the help of such birds as the nutcracker (*Nucifraga caryocatactes*). As the pine nuts ripen, these birds migrate en masse into the Siberian-pine forests, clean the nuts from the cone, eat part of them, and store the remainder for winter. The nutcracker's capacious gullet can hold eighty nuts at once. These it thrusts in little heaps under the moss, under jutting roots of trees, and near tree trunks, where the layer of snow will not be very thick, so that it can find them in winter. Not all are retrieved, however, and as a result a few succeed in germinating and producing young trees. The wood of the Siberian pine is very tough and close-grained and at the same time soft; thus it is an excellent construction material. The nuts are used as food, and pine oil is extracted from them.

Some Siberian-pine forests grow on well-drained places along the edges of watersheds and on summits of ridges and hills on strongly podzolic sandy soil and weak podzolic clay soil that has a green moss cover. The forests on clay soil contain some spruce and birch; those on sand, pine and larch; those on argillaceous soil, birch and larch. On the other hand, in the

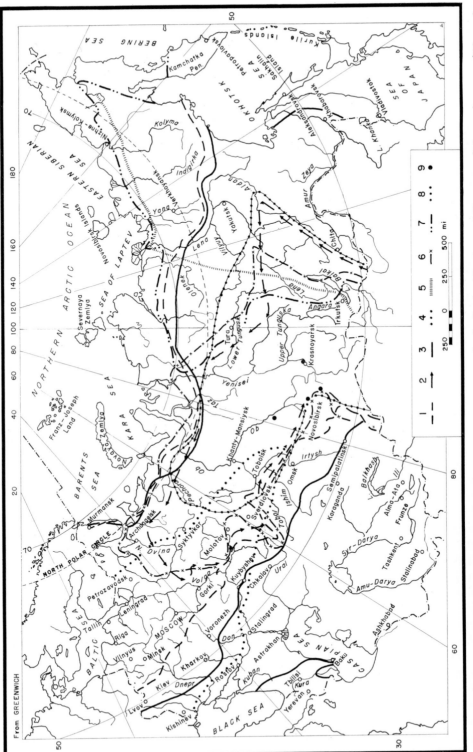

Map I-III. Distribution of principal trees (from *Flora of USSR*, V. N. Sukachev): 1—Siberian and European (Norway) spruce (*Picea obovata*, *P. excelsa*); 2—Siberian fir (*Abies sibirica*); 3—Scotch pine (*Pinus silvestris*); 4—Siberian stone-pine (*P. sibirica*); 5—Japanese stone-pine (*P. pumila*); 6—Siberian larch (*Larix sibirica*); 7—Dahurian larch (*L. daurica*); 8—Linden (*Tilia cordata*); 9—Island linden (*T. sibirica*).

southern part of the subzone, fir is admixed, having a dwarf form in some places. Siberian-pine forests with a green moss ground cover are the most productive; they grow in compact stands and support a large number of fur-bearing animals. General growth of all species is good. The trunks are solid and rapidly clear themselves of lower branches. The excellent young growth of spruce and Siberian pine guarantees renewal and steadiness of stand. Periodically recurring fires increase the dominance of pine in the forest. The undergrowth often contains single specimens of mountain ash, juniper, goat willow, dog rose, and spirea. The herb cover consists of a few species of moisture-preferring plants such as sedge and horsetail. Thick and unbroken moss covers the soil, it consists mostly of *Ptilium cristacastrensis, Hylocomium splendens,* and *Hypnum schreberi.*

On the damp clayey soil of low level places and gentle slopes, the soil-forming process is of the semibog type, because of weak surface flow and proximity of ground water. Here the Siberian pine grows poorly, the forests are sparse and contain no larch. A continuous cover of common haircap moss (*Polytrichum commune*) and moss (*Sphagnum balticum*) is characteristic. In the flooded sections of river valleys, on rich bottomland soil, Siberian pine creates almost pure thick forests, 120 to 150 years old, with rather large trees, up to 85 feet high and 14 inches in diameter; intermittent flooding by water does not injure it.

In the western part of the subzone, spruce and Siberian pine are intermixed in equal quantities. Here the moss cover of the forests is rather weakly developed—priority is taken by the underbrush and rich grass cover of typical forest plants. Siberian-pine forests on the semibog soils of depressions are the thickest. On slopes or terraces above the rivers, where water does not stand so long, are deciduous forests of birch and aspen, under which, in the herb cover, grasses such as beach grass or meadow grass are prevalent.

Areas of dry sand (river terraces, for example) produce little timber. They predominate over swamps in the western part of the subzone and are occupied by groves of stunted pine with a white-moss and lichen ground cover that contain bilberry and black crowberry (*Empetrum nigrum*). More productive pine groves with an undergrowth of red bilberry are found on moister sand and sandy loam with green mosses. These produce good timber. Burned coniferous forests are at first replaced by birch and aspen groves with a dense brushy cover of honeysuckle (*Lonicera altaica*), blackberry (*Rubus melanolasius*), and willow. A young growth of conifers (spruce or Siberian pine) quickly supersedes these groves. On sandy loam and sand, after fires, the first growth consists of pine and larch, which slowly give way to dark coniferous species.

Peat swamps, sometimes containing small Siberian pines, are distributed over large areas of watershed and along flat terraces; in many of them surface ponds alternate with spongy ground.

The Western Siberian bottomlands are numerous and diverse. Their vegetation varies greatly—from bottomland meadows to pure Siberian-pine forests. On bottomlands intermittently submerged (e.g., Poluy River) are found combinations of smooth brome (*Bromus inermis*), red fescue grass (*Festuca rubra v. barbata*), and white bent grass (*Agrostis alba*), alternating with such other grasses as reed grass (*Calamagrostis epigeios*). On long-submerged bottomlands of the lower Ob, the predominant plants are swampy sedge (*Carex gracilis*), reed grass (*Beckmannia eruciformis*), and such herbs as crowfoot, buttercup, and plantain. Downstream sections of river valleys have well-developed flooded meadows of different types, most of them with a predominance of grasses such as *Calamagrostis langsdorffii* and *Phalaris arundinacea* and sedge (*Carex aquatilis*). Less-flooded areas are occupied by bird cherry, mountain ash, dog rose, and in the east by spirea (*Spiraea salicifolia*).

The boggy coniferous forests cover an area somewhat smaller than marshy pine forests, but they are much thicker, the trees are sturdier, and there are no marsh plants in the undergrowth. In the north the thick coniferous forest consists of fir, spruce, and Siberian pine mixed in almost equal proportions; in the south there is a predominance of fir (60 per cent), with a large quantity of spruce and Siberian pine (30 per cent), and a smaller quantity of larch. This forest frames the raised and better-drained shores of rivers and edges of interriver expanses, forming so-called "walls." Under the forest are secondary strongly podzolic soils. Birch and aspen grow here and in the undergrowth there is much coarse brush— mountain ash, red elder (*Sambucus racemosa*) —and in the east, Siberian pea shrub (*Caragana arborescens*). The grassy undergrowth is variegated, with a predominance of such typical taiga plants as twin flower and oxalis. The moss cover consists principally of "shiny" mosses (*Hypnum* and *Hylocomium*). Where it is swampy, fir drops out, spruce and birch begin to predominate, but many Siberian pines remain; forest grasses are supplanted by marsh grass and in the cover are many sphagnum mosses. In valley forests there is less moss but more grass.

The boggy coniferous forest is a secondary type, having developed comparatively recently. It advances gradually, occupying a still larger and larger area and crowding out the birch forest. In the south of the subzone, on drained rich soils, there are spruce and spruce-fir forests with linden (*Tilia sibirica*) in the first tier or in the undergrowth, and with such western European herbs as liverwort (*Hepatica nobilis*) in the cover: these forests thin out on the Irtysh near the city of Tara. The soils under the forests are clayey, with different degrees of podzolization, from clearly marked podzols to transitional, to relic-forest clay soils. The latter have a deep humus horizon and a high humus content, together with extremely noticeable alkalinity, and contain more calcium than the others, as well as carbonate salts. Muddy-marsh and peat-bog soils occupy a subordinate position.

Many sections of taiga have been burned over; the growths on these areas are of different ages and represent different stages of resto-

ration; taiga not touched by fire has survived in some thinly populated places. Treetop fires, or upper-tier conflagrations, open up the surface to light and bring about the expansion of such coarse herbs as monkshood and larkspur, which form a thick tangled growth, often higher than a man. In many completely burned-over areas, willow and raspberry grow first; they are replaced by birch groves, which, in turn, give way to young growth of deciduous and coniferous trees—thus the taiga is restored rather quickly. On rich, dark-colored, weakly podzolized soil are virgin forests of full-grown birches, with linden in the second tier, thick underbrush, and a rich grass cover: on these soils the young conifers grow so slowly that they do not replace the birch. Repeated or strong ground fires, which destroy the sod and humus horizon of the soil, bring about strong growths of willow and beach grass. Turfing of the soil of a burned area and the clearing away of decaying tree trunks leads to the growth of grasses of agricultural value: meadow grass (*Poa pratensis*), brome grass (*Bromus inermis*), and meadow pea vine (*Lathyrus pratensis*). After a fire, pine groves often rise immediately on sand in dry elevated portions of the relief, but the repopulation of burned pine areas is usually slow because of the more rapid growth of other trees. Thick groves of pine suitable for lumber are situated along drained sandy terraces in narrow strips from one to three miles wide as well as in areas of fluvioglacial sand. These forests are similar to those of the pine-marsh subzone.

Many bottomland meadows in downstream sections of medium-sized rivers have been developed by farmers. Mesophyte bottomland meadows have stands of coarse grass and grain. Meadows among the northern forests contain an admixture of wooded-steppe plants: yellow lily (*Hemerocallis flava*), anemone (*Anemone dichotoma*), and aster (*Aster discoides*). Of the standing grasses, the most common and luxuriant are: meadow fescue (*Festuca pratensis*), timothy (*Phleum pratense*), and foxtail grass (*Alopecurus pratensis*). There are many legumes, such as vetch, clover, and vetchling; such coarse herbs as meadowsweet (*Filipendula ul-maria*) and burnet (*Sanguisorba officinalis*); and southern plants like *Phlomis tuberosa*.

Water divides are covered by vast peat bogs —for example, the huge Vasyuganye Marsh— formed by the swamping of large coniferous forests, a result of the abundance of precipitation and the level relief. Some parts of these bogs are former lake basins that have filled with peat, but that the greater part of them was once dry land is indicated by remnants of tree trunks found *in situ* in them and by the existence of forested areas where the process of swamping is still taking place. The various types of bogs, each of which has been given a name by the local inhabitants, are dispersed strictly according to relief and in conformity with their water regime. Near the southern border where the water on the watersheds is hard, pure hypnum bogs predominate, together with hummocky swamps and swamped birch groves.

On the southern border of the taiga there is a narrow transitional belt of forests of birch and aspen. A substantial admixture of spruce, fir, and Siberian pine, and the development of a typical taiga grass cover show that these forests are secondary, growing on the site of burned-off taiga. Toward the very southern border they change to light primary park-like groves of European birch—which withstands well the swampiness and saltiness of the soil— that have a cover of light-loving meadow-forest grasses. Approximately across the center of this belt is the border between chernozem and podzol soils. The strip of gray, wooded, clayey soils on the northern margin of the chernozem in the European USSR does not occur in Western Siberia. Patches of chernozem are found among the loess-like clayey soils at higher altitudes; in low places podzol soils prevail although there is much bog soil and solonetz. The presence of chernozem and light, dry, park-like birch groves makes this a transitional strip between the taiga and the neighboring northern wooded steppe.

In the southern half of the taiga zone almost all the population is engaged in agriculture.

Here the soil is fertile and the grain harvest is comparatively stable, since much of the territory has never suffered from drought. The basic crops of the Siberian taiga are rye, barley, and oats. In recent times, new varieties of fast-ripening wheat have been widely planted throughout Siberia, and the borders of agriculture have consequently been moved farther north. Among the nongrain crops are potatoes, flax, and hemp.

Zoogeographically, the taiga of the Western Siberian Lowland is related to the European Siberian subregion of the Paleo-Arctic, and the fauna is, in general, similar to that of the east European taiga.

The damp dark-coniferous taiga contains a typical complex of forest animals, some of them specially adapted to life in the woods. In the gloomy, purely coniferous Konda taiga, fewer animals are to be found; they prefer the secondary birch-aspen forests which grow where the dark-coniferous forest has burned off. For example, when aspen replace conifers after a fire, elk, which have avoided the old forest, appear in the new. The typical mammals are those common in the European taiga —brown bear (*Ursus arctos*), lynx (*Lynx lynx*), glutton (*Gulo gulo*), marten (*Martes martes*), otter (*Lutra lutra*), and badger (*Meles meles*). The only Siberian taiga animal not found in Europe is the sable (*Mustela zibellina*). On the lower Ob, Malaya, Sosva, and Konda rivers, where a beaver and sable game preserve has been established, and in places along the Pelym River and in the almost inaccessible Vasyuganye Marsh are polecats (*Kolonocus sibiricus*). Among the ungulates are elk (*Alces alces*) and deer (*Cervus pigargus*). Of the rodents, the most plentiful are the squirrel (*Sciurus vulgaris*), which is hunted commercially, the flying squirrel (*Pteromys volans*), and, extremely characteristic of the Siberian taiga, the chipmunk (*Eutamias asiaticus*). In places along the Malaya, Sosva, and Konda, beavers (*Castor fiber*) are still found, and water rats (*Arvicola amphibius*) are numerous. The Canadian muskrat (*Ondatra zibethicus*) was brought into the taiga and is now trapped for its fur. Field mice (*Microtus arvalis*) are numerous. Squirrel, ermine, and polecats have the greatest commercial importance.

In the Western Siberian taiga are various birds whose lives are more closely connected with the coniferous forest than are the lives of the mammals. Whereas in tundra, marine and coastal birds predominate, terrestrial birds, both settled and nomadic, prevail in the taiga. Migratory birds are not numerous. Fewer species are found in the taiga than in the Arctic: the taiga is sparsely populated by birds, and relatively few are songbirds; thus the taiga is silent as well as gloomy. Taiga species have greater geographic variability than those of the Arctic, though it is insignificant in comparison with that of the birds of southern latitudes. Taiga species of birds spread over extremely broad areas; the hazel grouse, for example, is found through the whole taiga zone of Europe and Siberia. The biotic relationships of the taiga developed in neighboring Eastern Siberia in the glacial and postglacial periods. From this center, the fauna spread gradually westward after the disappearance of the ice and the onset of the forest. This is indicated by (1) a regular decrease in the number of species of taiga birds from east to west; (2) absence in the Western Siberian taiga of endemic species of birds; (3) dominance of species found only in small numbers in Europe.

The most typical taiga birds are: of the black grouse family, the wood grouse (*Tetrao urogallus*) and hazel grouse (*Tetrastes bonasia*); of the crow family, the red jay (*Garrulus glandarius branti*), one of the most beautiful birds of the taiga, with bright-colored wings of white, black, and light blue; *Cractes infaustus;* the nutcracker (*Nucifraga caryocatactes macrorhynocha*), which during regional poor crops of Siberian pine nut moves from place to place en masse; of the mountain finches, pine grosbeak (*Pinicola enucleator*), which flies south in winter to the wooded-steppe; Siberian crossbill (*Loxia leucoptera*); of the woodpeckers, black woodpecker (*Picus martius*), and three-toed woodpecker (*Picoides tridactylus*). Some species are definitely dependent on a particular type of forest: the nutcracker is associated with the pine groves, the Siberian crossbill with larch groves, the woodpecker with spruce groves. The greatest numbers of species are found in forests that contain an admixture of deciduous trees, burned areas overgrown with birch, and groves along the shores of rivers. Here are found the waxwing (*Bombycilla garrula*), brambling (*Fringilla montifringilla*), long-tailed bullfinch (*Uragus sibiricus*), red-throated nightingale (*Luscinia calliope*), titmouse (*Parus ater*), and black-breasted thrush (*Turdus ruficollis*).

Along lakes and streams and in meadows and swamps, waterfowl and long-legged birds predominate: geese, duck, snipe. On the mossy bogs of the taiga are found the ptarmigan (*Lagopus lagopus*) which are characteristic of the tundra. Some tundra birds winter in the taiga: the polar owl and snowbird, for example.

The following reptiles are characteristic: creeping adder (*Vipera berus*), lizard (*Lacerta vivipara*), Siberian three-toed triton (*Hynobius keyserlingi*), and grass frog (*Rana temporaria*). Many mollusks of the genus *Helix,* with large and beautiful shells, are found here although they are absent in the neighboring wooded-steppe zone.

The taiga has all the conditions necessary for the life and ample reproduction of many species of insects whose lives are closely linked with the coniferous forests. The most typical are: the pine silkworm (*Dendrolimus pini*), Siberian pine silkworm (*D. segregatus*), silkworm (*Lymantria monacha*), and pine feaster (*Sphinx pinastri*), whose larvae feed on pine needles and are a dangerous blight of the forest since they reproduce rapidly. Bark beetles and long-horned beetles, or cerambycidae (*Leptura virens*) are common in the north but rarely found in the south. Near swamps, lakes, and streams there are great swarms of mosquitoes, gnats, and the like.

Wooded-Steppe

The wooded-steppe of the Western Siberian Lowland extends to more northerly latitudes than the European, has a more continental climate, and less precipitation. Small groves of trees scattered over a general steppe background constitute the wooded-steppe. Steppe chernozems, solonetz, and solonchaks combine here with soils of a podzol type. In the Western Siberian wooded-steppe, because of its level relief, light precipitation, high summer temperatures, poor drainage, and salty Tertiary clays, there are few of the ravine landscapes

Baraba Steppe. The interriver expanses, 350 to 500 feet in height, are perfect plains, although they contain an exceptional number of poorly drained depressions. In some places the wooded-steppe has a well-developed undulating ridge-and-trough relief drawn out in a northeast-southwest direction. The ridges have relative heights of 7 to 13 feet—occasionally 20 to 35 feet—thus introducing some variety into the monotonous level terrain.

Fig. 1-8. Small copses of birch trees in the southern wooded-steppe.

that are typical of the European wooded-steppe. There are, however, a great number of lakes, an abundance of ground water, and much more solonetz and solonchak soils. In place of the leached-out, fertile chernozem of the European wooded-steppe is intermediate chernozem—the northern border of the Western Siberian steppe passes through the narrow strip of southern chernozem—but no great patches of gray, forest-clay soil and degraded chernozem. Instead of vast oak forests there are a great number of separate copses of birch.

The relief of the Western Siberian wooded-steppe has all the peculiarities of primary undrained plains, expressed on much greater scale than in the European wooded-steppe. Large, shallow bodies of water—some salty, some fresh—are common on the steppe. Their outlets are rivers that flow on a level with the plain, a strikingly even surface that extends like a table for hundreds of miles. In the morphology of the plain interriver areas predominate over valleys, as is well illustrated on the

The ridge-and-trough relief developed at first as a result of accumulation and then as a consequence of the erosion of loamy, sandy-clayey layers, principally of the Quaternary. The loess-like soil which originally covered the plain was of lake-alluvial and diluvial origin. The heights are either ridges between troughs that survived the erosion, or are eroded residual mountains of a more ancient and higher level whose foundations are concealed under a thickness of recent alluvium—perhaps part of a definite system of ancient ridges and valleys. The predominant northeast-southwest orientation of the drainage conforms to the prevailing direction of the ridges. As a consequence the general slope of the surface of the Ishim wooded-steppe is to the northeast and that of the Baraba to the southwest. The troughs seem to be relics of ancient delta channels. The ridges were gradually worn away by diluvial erosion and the troughs were partly filled in. In some places the ridges were eroded to form low narrow hills, in others the surface of the ridges is wide enough to contain shallow basins. Depressions between ridges are occupied by streams, lakes, grassy marshes and wet meadows. The direction of some streams is determined by the ridge relief; others intersect ridges transverse to their course.

The present river network is poorly developed, the river valleys often being less than 35 feet deep, although the rivers in the Ishim wooded-steppe have cut to as much as 130 feet. Near the Irtysh and Ob there is still deeper dissection, often to 230 feet. In general, the relief is in the elementary stages of the erosion cycle, as is shown by a complete lack of valleys and drainage in the interriver stretches. In the wooded-steppe are many basins of various sizes, some containing water and others dry. The relief of the bottoms of the largest lake basins does not differ essentially from that of the surrounding wooded-steppe: ridges can be traced through them, sometimes under water, sometimes as islands and peninsulas that stretch northeast-southwest and divide the lake into a series of parallel coves and arms (Lake Chany).

Most of the lakes are very shallow and their shores rise imperceptibly to blend with the surface of the surrounding wooded-steppe. The lakes are virtually low flooded sections of the wooded-steppe and their origin does not differ essentially from that of the plain. Along with the lake basins are scattered countless flat, saucer-shaped basins without water. These are extremely characteristic of the micro-relief and bring about a variation of soil and vegetation. The western part of the wooded-steppe zone is better drained than the eastern, and in the eastern part of the Ishim wooded-steppe the ridges are higher (40 to 100 feet) and the river valleys are more distinctly formed.

Climatically the wooded-steppe is a transitional zone intermediate between the adjacent taiga and steppe. Summer is hot, with constant winds and frequent droughts. The average temperature in July is about 66°F but there are maximum temperatures near 100°F. The growing season lasts 150 to 160 days, from the end of April to the beginning of October, and the frost-free period 120 days, from the end of May

to the middle of September. Summer has about 50 per cent of the annual precipitation, with 2.4 to 2.6 inches in June and July. The relative humidity (65 to 70 per cent) and cloudiness (50 to 60 per cent) are a minimum in summer, and each summer has from 250 to 300 hours of sunshine. Winter is cold, especially in comparison with the European wooded-steppe; the average January temperature is —3°F but the temperature may drop to —56°F. There is little precipitation in winter—15 per cent of the annual—with the minimum of 0.2 to 0.5 inches in March and April. The relative humidity (82 per cent) and cloudiness (60 to 70 per cent) are high in winter, and there are only 50 to 100 hours of solar radiance in each winter month. A sharp shift from winter to summer temperature is typical; the average temperature may increase 18 to 21 degrees from one spring month to another so that the snow cover melts rapidly.

Abundant ground and surface water is available for most of the fertile Western Siberian wooded-steppe. The ground water in post-Tertiary deposits lies close to the surface in two water-bearing horizons, one of which, 40 to 50 feet deep, gives ample soft, fresh water with marked pressure. The water-bearing horizons in Tertiary strata yield brackish water. In the Baraba wooded-steppe the soil in low spots is so saturated with moisture that if a shallow pit or ditch is dug it fills with water immediately. Even on steppe sections of flat watersheds one can find water at a depth of 3 to 5 feet. Ground water is so diverse that if two wells are put down twenty feet apart, one may give good drinking water, and the other bitter, salty, or brackish water: the first from a layer of Quaternary alluvium, the latter from an aquifer in salty Tertiary deposits. When alluvium is cut through by streams, the circulation of ground water is revived, thus contributing to its freshness. The extent, character, and quality of ground water varies according to local conditions. In the Baraba wooded-steppe underground water of good quality lies near the surface so that it is easily possible to obtain drinking water with a strong flow. In the

Ishim wooded-steppe water obtained near the surface is not likely to be drinkable, because gypsiferous Tertiary layers often serve as aquifers; on the other hand, there are better chances of obtaining fresh artesian water from deep wells.

Surface flow on the plains of the wooded-steppe is negligible: the few shallow streams have extremely low gradients, and, in consequence, exceptionally slow currents, so that many are salty. They play a small role in the development of the relief and in the hydrography of the zone. Even the largest rivers—the Tobol, Ishim, Irtysh, and Ob—are transitory and have little effect on the hydrography of the adjacent plains.

Surface water is scattered through the wooded-steppe in numerous lakes and even more numerous shallow, saucer-shaped basins that fill with water only in spring. The Ishim wooded-steppe contains at least 1,600 lakes. In some places they are spread in disorder; in other places, where they lie in troughs, they stretch out as chain lakes. Their sizes range from insignificant to immense and they lie at different altitudes. The majority either do not have an outlet or are joined by channels to larger lakes which are without outlet. Lake water may be fresh, bitter, bitter-salty, or salty. Mineral and fresh lakes intermingle without noticeable order; often both are found in one chain. All lake basins of the wooded-steppe have poorly developed structures: even the largest lakes, like Lake Chany, do not have fully formed basins. The basins are flat and shallow, spreading over large areas in which the water stands at almost the same level as the surface of the surrounding wooded-steppe. Many large lakes are overgrown with reeds, sedges, and halophytes. Most shores and inlets trend northeast-southwest, as do numerous islands.

Lake Chany, at an altitude of 350 feet, is 1,274 square miles in area, has a maximum depth of 23 feet, and contains 70 islands. It has no outlet. The water is noticeably brackish, but in the southeast corner it is freshened by river water. Lake Ubinskoye, 332 square miles in area, is only eleven feet deep. The extreme

shallowness of these lakes makes them sensitive to meteorological changes. In dry periods they grow shallow, often even drying up, but in rainy periods they fill again with water. Wind roughens the lake water and thus contributes to better warming and faster evaporation where it is shallow. Even the largest lakes vary in level with the amount of precipitation. Traces of terraces, indicating that the lakes once had a broader spread, can be observed only on the shores of a few of the larger lakes, such as Lake Chany. The lake water contains nutritive substances and the shoal water is therefore often covered with thick vegetation which hastens the process of their overgrowth. Thus, Lake Ubinskoye has an overgrowth of reeds which stretches ten miles toward the center of the lake, and alternates with open water and patches of flotsam. Some lakes disappear because of progressive overgrowth and mossing-over, which turns them into bogs. This phenomenon appears everywhere and explains the great extent of bogs, especially in the Baraba wooded-steppe.

The fresh-water lakes of the wooded-steppe contain much plankton and many small bottom fish. There are carp in all the lakes, and in the larger and deeper ones like Ubinskoye and Tandovo there are also great quantities of fresh-water perch and pike.

The peculiarities of the soil and vegetative cover of the Western Siberian wooded-steppe are a result of: (1) the geological youth of the Western Siberian Lowland, (2) the levelness of the region and its poor drainage, and (3) the peculiar history of the development of the landscapes of the wooded-steppe zone in the postglacial period.

The pattern of soil and vegetation in open grassy spaces is extremely complex and striking. Even over short distances the soil profiles are exceedingly spotty. The vegetative cover exhibits all the transitions from feather-grass steppes to moist meadows, bogs, and open water. There is a sharp lack of conformity between soil and vegetation, although toward the forest zone such differences begin to disappear.

In the geologically young Western Siberian

Lowland, the processes of evolution of soil and vegetation are expressed so clearly that it is possible to reconstruct their three fundamental phases in the postglacial period: (1) solonchak-swamp phase, (2) solonetz-steppe phase, (3) phase of afforestation, meadow formation, and secondary swamping. The solonchak-swamp phase began in the cold moist climate of glacial times, when vast flat interriver plains were still untouched by erosion. Moisture and poor drainage brought about widespread swamping and occurrence of ground water near the surface, these leading to a universal alkalinity, not only in basins, but also on raised places. The uniform vegetation of that time grew in bogs —particularly in sphagnum bogs—and solonchack meadows. Alternation of flooding and drying led to the formation, south of the ice barrier on the area of the present wooded-steppe, of complex combinations of swamp and solonchak soils. This produced an alternation of swamp and solonchak meadows with their distinctive vegetative groupings.

The solonetz-steppe phase of the development of the soil and vegetative cover took place in the dry warm climate of xerothermic time, when the disappearance of continental ice lowered the level of erosion. The revived erosional activity converted the flat plain into a plain with undulating relief, although some places far from the rivers remained untouched by erosion. Many lakes were reduced in area or were drained, swamping was somewhat diminished, and the level of ground water dropped. Soil and vegetative cover became more sharply differentiated in high and low places: in low places they maintained their former appearance; on high places, solonchak was converted into solonetz, and solonetz into chernozem.

The phase of afforestation, meadow formation, and secondary swamping began with the return of a moist climate and was marked by the wide spread of processes that desalted the soil. The soil's development depended on the presence of calcium and magnesium: where they were present, leached-out chernozem began to form, the soil having lost almost all solonetz qualities; where they were lacking,

podzol-like soil gradually appeared. Both processes took place simultaneously and caused differentiation of the vegetation of the wooded-steppe.

Forests of birch and aspen invaded and solidly consolidated themselves in small, well-moistened low spots. The moist phytoclimate, acting on the most thoroughly desalted soil, contributed to the destruction of columnar solonetz and led to strong leaching-out and conversion of the soil into basin podzol. Feather grass and its associated plants moved to raised places, where there were solonetz and leached-out chernozem. The consequence of this process of desalting was degradation of the steppe type of vegetation to the meadow steppe. Freshening of the soil sharply reduced the xerophilous appearance of the vegetation, and grass became thicker and deeper. The reorganization of the classes of vegetation was completed when typical saline soils were invaded by a variegated family of plants from the grass, meadow, and wooded steppes. Simultaneously the forest began to advance on the steppe, and an increase in precipitation caused the formation of meadows and flooding of the low places.

The processes of desalting, forming of solonetz, leaching-out, afforestation, meadow formation, and flooding that have taken place here have had less effect on vegetation than local changes in physicogeographic conditions. The vegetative cover of a poorly drained flat plain is very closely linked with the character of the microrelief, with the water regime (especially with changes in the level of ground water), with variations in climate, and with the degree of salting and character of the soil. And all this merely provides a background for the struggle of plants for space.

A historic and geographic analysis of the present condition of soil and vegetation shows the varying ages of elements of the wooded-steppe landscape. The youngest, which are still forming, are reed bogs, grass meadows, and narrow-leafed forests. Directly beside them are ancient relic types such as sphagnum bogs, solonchak meadows, and pine groves.

The soil of the wooded-steppe develops with

little precipitation. Summer rain (about 6 inches) does not penetrate to any significant depth, since it is quickly evaporated by the high temperature and constant wind. The sharp rise of temperature in spring causes the snow to melt quickly and the high temperature and continuous wind evaporate the meltwater before it can penetrate the still-frozen and impervious soil. Consequently, soil-forming processes affect only a thin surface layer. Decomposition is retarded, so that the most common soils are thin zonal chernozems 16 to 20 inches thick, which are poorly leached and contain a high percentage of humus. Toward the northern border precipitation increases, the soil is washed deeper, and its thickness is increased. The depth of the bedrock also affects soil formation.

In large areas of wooded-steppe, Tertiary saline clay serves as a water-resistant bed for ground water, and water flowing along it is salted. Where the relief is not uniform, this water, rising to the surface in a dry period, causes the lowest and most level sections to become saline. The soil of ridges is not usually subject to this salting action. Soil in depressions, on the other hand, is strongly affected by the concentrated salts of ground water. Thus, complexes of saline soils in narrow strips that run northeast-southwest are formed on the bottoms of dry lakes, in flat depressions, and along clayey river bottoms. In the northern part of the wooded-steppe, ground water is so close to the surface that large swamps are formed and vast areas of solonetz and solonchak soil exist. Secondary solonchak is formed on pastures, in settlements, and on country roads, where the surface horizon becomes packed.

In the zone of fertile and moderate chernozem are scattered spots and strips of solonetz, solonchak, and saline soil. The morphology and chemistry of the saline soil may approximate those of solonetz, but much of the soil has a columnar structure, and resembles chernozem. In other places it has a cloddy or nutlike structure and is as productive as chernozem. Steppe basins contain podzolic soil with a light-gray podzol horizon, which gradually thins out toward the edges of the basins, and has a depth of effervescence of about 52 inches. Pure podzol soil is found only on sand under pine groves.

The flora of the wooded-steppe consists of European and Eastern Siberian plants. In the Baraba wooded-steppe more than 75 per cent of the species common to the Ufa and Saratov regions of the European wooded-steppe have been recorded. As a result of the length and severity of winter, birch, rather than oak (as in Europe), grows in small, sharply defined groves. In the European wooded-steppe the forests are confined to highly dissected riverbanks; in the Western Siberian wooded-steppe they usually avoid rivers and the riverside solonetz, and find refuge along depressions on water-divides where the soil is strongly leached out. The development of large swampy and saline expanses with vegetation adapted to them and the abundance of mosquitoes, gnats, and deerflies sharply distinguish the Western Siberian wooded-steppe from the European.

In the continental climate of the Western Siberian wooded-steppe, peculiarities of relief, the amount of moisture, and the character of the soil have more to do with plant habitats than they do in Europe. In the unstable weather and light frosts of spring, vegetation here receives sunshine on its above-ground parts while its roots are embedded in the very cold surface layers of the soil. Spring here is physiologically drier for plants than in the European wooded-steppe. If the earth is well soaked and May is warm, steppe grasses (in particular, turf grasses) develop swiftly and luxuriantly. During the warm summer, plants lose much water through evaporation, and, since rains are irregular, vegetation often suffers from severe droughts, during which the grasses become prematurely yellow and dry. May to August is the most active part of the vegetative period. The trees begin to turn green in the first part of May; toward the end of August the autumn coloration appears. Young sprouts of summer wheat and reviving deciduous vegetation are noticed during the first half of May, and by the end of August all grain has been harvested.

In the wooded-steppe the character and distribution of vegetation changes from north to south. In the north, near the southern border of the taiga, there are large areas of woods, bogs, and meadows; more and larger birch groves and fewer treeless areas than in the south. The rapid growth of meadow grass and trees indicates a good water supply, unusual for a steppe. In the southern part of the wooded-steppe, however, there is less water, and steppe species predominate, other plants growing well only in moist depressions. The grass cover thins out and the role of turf grass increases, and only near the birch groves are the grasses similar to the meadow grasses of the north. The complex associations on southern riverbottom lands do not resemble those of the plain, which consist of meadows, brush, and small poplar and willow copses. Halophytic meadows are rather similar throughout the whole territory.

The change of landscapes from north to south, although gradual, divides the wooded-steppe into three parts: (1) halophytic meadow, (2) northern wooded-steppe, and (3) southern wooded-steppe. It is also important to consider the differences in vegetation from west to east, and local changes in meso- and micro-relief, which affect the moistening and salting of soils. Copses of trees, steppes, halophytic meadows, and pine groves compose the vegetative cover of the wooded-steppe.

The alternation of plains and basins affects the distribution of vegetation. On the plains are (1) copses of birch, willow, or poplar, usually growing on podzols, (2) steppes on upper sections of watersheds, on chernozems, and (3) steppes on gentle slopes, on solonetz soil. The basins contain bogs, moist halophytic meadows, and patches of solonchak soil. Pine groves grow on river valley sand.

The halophytic meadow belt is expressed only in the eastern part of the wooded-steppe with its level relief and extremely weak dissection; in the western part, it is either lacking or appears in isolated patches. Notable are the vast thickets of tall reeds bordering fresh-water lakes or covering them solidly. These reeds, the youngest members of the vegetative cover, the conquerors of the dying lakes, represent the final stage of lake overgrowth. The basins fill with water during river flooding or after the thawing or snow; thus all settlements and roads are located on the crests. The thickets of reed (*Phragmites communis*) are in some places infringed upon by marsh vegetation: rushes (*Scirpus lacustris*), cat-tails (*Typha latifolia*), and beds of willows (*Salix sibirica*). Drainage increases the accessibility of these areas and leads to thickening of the turf and discontinuation of the swamping process, strengthens the salting of the upper horizons of the soil, and results in replacement of the reeds with sedge and reed grass. During years with little precipitation, these meadows do not suffer drought, are easily accessible, and offer excellent grazing for cattle. In wet years they are attainable with difficulty, although the majority of them can be mowed at the end of summer.

On the undrained swamped plains, there are mossy, peaty, quicksand-like bogs, overgrown with impoverished pine. The majority of them were formed by turfing-over of lakes in glacial times and are thus relic phenomena. In low spots on watersheds, on meadow–solonchak–bog soil, are meadows containing halophytic plants, such as licorice (*Glycyrrhiza uralensis*), and wetter ones with an abundance of the grass *Atropis distans*. On the crests birch copses and meadows of herbs have grown on chernozem-like soil; the vegetation consists solely of forest-meadow plants like anemone (*Anemone silvestris*) or aconite (*Aconitum volubile*). On southern slopes, where chernozem-like soil is purer, the herb meadows are enriched by steppe plants such as *Libanotis montana* or steppe alfalfa (*Medicago falcata*).

More than half of the northern wooded-steppe is covered by birch groves that grow on soils of a podzol type. Steppe-like meadows, resembling dry valley meadows of the forest zone, grow on fertile chernozem, with thick stands of many species of moisture-loving grasses completely turfed-over soil and very few steppe plants. In addition, there are swamps with swamp-solonchak soil on which grow many halophytic plants. The northern wooded-steppe is studded with birch copses which form small blocks separated by grassy expanses. These copses grow either in basins with concave bottoms or in level saucer-like depressions on elevated sections of the relief. Many of these depressions are local centers of drainage which, because of the irregularity of precipitation, are sometimes dry, sometimes flooded. At the edge of the copses, solodizing and deeply columnar solonetzes have developed, but in the central parts of the basins there are degraded solonetz, soloths, quite chernozem-like and strongly leached out, and podzolized soil with a horizon of effervescence 20 to 30 inches thick.

The groves of the wooded-steppe are the most stable ecologic formations; they complete the process of solodizing the soil, creating their own local phytoclimate. Most groves consist of rather uniform, small specimens of birch (*Betula pubescens*) with an admixture of aspen and white birch (*Betula verrucosa*) and an undergrowth of willows. The trees and shrubs do not provide a dense cover, and the soil beneath them is therefore covered by a rather thick turf, which thins out from the center of a grove to its periphery. In the lower and moister centers swamp-meadow plants, such as reed grass, predominate, and in some a sedge bog develops. Nearer the periphery the turf contains a mixture of forest-meadow plants (couch grass, vetch) with a few steppe and even halophytic species, and along the edges only steppe species are observed. On the solonetz soils of the intergrove glades the vegetation is like that of the steppe. In the Ishim wooded-steppe, on elevated places with good drainage, where the soil consists of cloddy, leached-out chernozem or soloth, the birch attains full growth—the trunks are thick and the trees are 60 to 65 feet tall—and the stands are dense. The undergrowth does not consist of willow, but of bird cherry, dog rose, hawthorn, and currant, which link the wooded-steppe birch groves with the birch groves of the forest zone; along the edges of these groves there is much steppe cherry (*Prunus fruticosa*). The grass cover is rich and diversified, and, because of the absence of swampiness, there are no bog grasses.

The chernozem expanses on the crests of ridges have almost all been cultivated, but a few small sections of steppe vegetation have been preserved, consisting mainly of steppe-like meadows. Mesophytic herbs predominate here: some are almost xerophytic, but there are no real xerophytes. Many leguminous plants are found in the meadows: pea vine (*Lathyrus pisiformis* and *L. pratensis*), clover (*Trifolium lupinaster*), and mouse vetch (*Vicia cracca*). Herbs are abundant: dropwort (*Filipendula hexapetala*), spirea (*F. ulmaria*), and yarrow (*Achillea millefolium*). Meadow rootstock grasses, such as reed grass (*Calamagrostis epigeios*) and meadow grass (*Poa pratensis*), are common. There is much turf grass, or steppe grass (*Phleum phleoides*), but turfy xerophilous grasses such as narrow-leaf feather grass and koeleria play a secondary role and are often impoverished. Spring ephemerals, such as the mosses, do not grow well here. The steppe-like meadows of Western Siberia are far more hydrophytic than, for example, those of Khahurin or northern Voronezh, and represent the transition from steppe meadows to real meadows.

Variants of the steppe-like meadows of the Baraba wooded-steppe, on rich chernozems with well-expressed grainy and clodded structure and a humus content of as much as 12 per cent, have a vegetative cover with a base of turfy grasses: fescue (*Festuca sulcata*), feather grass, steppe oats (*Avena desertorum*), koeleria (*Koeleria gracilis*), and steppe timothy. Where rich, steppe-meadow grasses grow, the most characteristic species are *Libanotis montana* and *L. sibirica,* which color the steppe white from late in June to the end of July. Near the groves are *Peucedanum officinale,* larkspur (*Delphinium elatum*), and *Lavatera thuringiaca* with its huge pale-rose flowers.

The solonetz vegetation does not stand out sharply from the background of the surrounding chernozem steppe. Solonetz soil, in this singular physicochemical regime that increases physiological dryness, creates an environment conquerable only by certain forms of plants. There is an abundance of species which thrive in saline soils such as licorice (*Glycyrrhiza uralensis*), large plantain (*Plantago maxima*), astragalus (*Astragalus sulcatus*), and *Galatella punctata*.

In strongly compressed solonetz, especially along roads in dry weather, the surface is covered with a snow-white deposit of salts and is almost bare of vegetation, but in places there may be a thick low cover of pale-green, definitely bleached grass (*Atropis distans*) and dark-red patches of succulent saltworts. The proximity of patches of solonetz plants to villages and roads forces one to suspect that their formation is connected with the compression of the upper horizon of soil and trampling of the grasses by grazing cattle—conditions under which only the hardier solonetz weeds can develop. On a surface that has been packed by trampling, wormwood, couch grass (*Agropyron repens*), and brome grass (*Bromus inermis*) replace the original grasses, but after several years these plants disappear, and feather grass and other steppe plants emerge once again.

In river valleys of the northern wooded-steppe there have developed moderately moist, coarse-grassed, slightly steppe-like bottomland meadows with an abundance of dropwort (*Filipendula hexapetala*) and clover (*Trifolium montanum*). The most common grasses are bent grass (*Agrostis tenuifolia*) and sedge (*Carex*). On preterrace sections are solonchak meadows, fundamentally made up of couch grass (*Agropyron repens*), foxtail (*Alopecurus ventricosus*), and barley (*Hordeum secalinum*), mixed with common solonchak-meadow species. In the more humid places are moist meadows containing bent grass (*Agrostis alba*) and *Digraphis arundinacea;* reed bogs; patches of hypnum; and peat bogs. Meadows are excellent, with stable productivity of standing grass.

The landscapes of the southern wooded-steppe are more complex and varied than those of the northern part. The south has many small island-like birch copses, smaller and more scattered than those of the north; steppe meadows on medium chernozem; a great number of steppe plants and many xerophilous grasses; and less turfing of the soil than in the north. Although birch copses are a noticeable part of the northern landscape, those in the south are more open and isolated. On the lighter, sandy-clay soil the groves are less dense, which permits the growth of a typical grass cover. The soils beneath the trees are clearly expressed podzols.

Steppe sections comprise meadows with varying amounts of grass; the soils are clodded or grainy chernozems with 7 to 9 per cent humus, or, in a few scattered low places, solonetz with 10 to 11 per cent humus. In these meadows, xerophilous forms predominate: fescue (*Festuca sulcata*) and koeleria (*Koeleria gracilis*); in some places, the feather grasses *Stipa capillata* and *St. joannis* are dense, but mesophilic rootstock grasses such as meadow grass (*Poa pratensis*) play a small role. The species of legumes are different from those in the steppe-like meadows: steppe alfalfa (*Medicago falcata*) and sainfoin (*Onobrychis arenaria*). Mesophytic herbs are yarrow (*Achillea millefolium*), tarragon (*Artemisia dracunculus*), pasque flower (*Pulsatilla patens*), and gypsophila (*Gypsophila altissima*), but species typical of steppe meadows, such as spirea and veronica, are absent. Spring ephemerals and mosses play no role in these meadows. The number of meadow-grass species increases in depressions and on sturdier varieties of chernozem. There is a background of turfy feather grass (*Stipa zaljeskyi*), which forms a thick leafy mass, admixed with fescue, steppe oats, koeleria, and steppe timothy. Countless flowering specimens of hog fennel (*Peucedanum officinale*) and silaus (*Silaus besseri*) also grow here.

The number and density of steppe plants depends on the character of the microrelief, salinity of soils, proximity of birch groves, and

the plain. Evidently this trough once carried water southward from the Western Siberian Lowland to the Turan Plain.

The Irtysh Plain (altitude 350 to 675 feet) slopes north and northeast, and is made up of interbedded, saline, alluvial lake clay and sand of the Neocene covered by Quaternary loess-like soil. Its extremely slight elevations, with scarcely perceptible slopes, are separated by shallow basins. It has a poorly developed network of river valleys, the larger ones 65 to 120 feet deep, the smaller ones no more than 50 feet. The plain contains many large closed lake basins, especially in its central part, and numerous suffusion depressions with gentle slopes. Some of the lake basins are below the level of the Irtysh: for example, Lake Teke is 130 feet lower than the river; Lake Ulken-Karoi, 200 feet lower; and Lake Kizyl Kak, 230 feet lower.

The Ob Plateau is a rather elevated (altitude 650 to 1,000 feet), area that slopes southwest from the Salair foothills. It is formed of post-Tertiary bedded sand and clay sediments 200 to 250 feet thick, covered with loess-like soil. It is dissected into a series of flat watershed areas, separated from each other by wide, flat-bottomed, open valleys that lie 350 to 400 feet below the plateau in the northeast and 200 to 250 feet below it in the southwest. These valleys run parallel to the northwestern foot of the Altai and to similar depressions in the Baraba wooded-steppe. To the west they widen and blend imperceptibly with the level floor of the Kulunda basin. The valleys are filled with beds of medium-grained sand, some beds being shifted by wind and others are covered by long narrow belts of pine groves. The streams that flow through the valleys, either into the Ob or into the Kulunda depression, form bead-like chains of lakes that are linked with each other by intermittent overflow channels. These valleys were formed during the last glaciation of the Altai, when the largest left-bank tributaries of the Ob, which nearly merged with the upper reaches of the corresponding tributaries of the Irtysh, were backed up by the high level (90 to 130 feet higher than at present) of the Ob and flowed in the opposite direction producing a continuous flow from the Ob to the Irtysh. These streams carried large amounts of fluvioglacial material and filled the valleys with beds of sand. Subsequent vigorous downcutting greatly lowered the Ob's level and severed its connection with the Irtysh, and today the only traces of the old channels are the residual lakes.

In the xerothermic period the smooth beds of alluvial sand were shifted and roughened by the wind and many salt lakes were formed. As the level of the Ob continued to fall some of the lakes were drained, and the young deep-cut valleys of the lower reaches of the present left-bank tributaries of the Ob were formed, as were the wide (5 to 10 miles), rolling, and slightly raised terraces of the Ob that are now covered with pine groves.

The level, saucer-shaped Kulunda basin is filled with thick beds of fluvioglacial lake and river deposits. Its central section, which is less than 330 feet in altitude—lower than the adjoining section of the Irtysh—contains several chains of lakes. This region subsided slowly during the Neocene and Quaternary periods, owing to strong faulting along a line from Novosibirsk to Bisk and simultaneous accumulation of thick beds of sediment that was washed down from the Altai by rivers draining into the central part of the Kulunda basin along a system of parallel glacial valleys. This process also resulted in the formation of a vast terraced delta plain, the water from which drained into the Irtysh. The north–northwest course of these drainage channels is marked by well-developed ravines, channels, and chains of lakes that are tributary to the right bank of the Irtysh River.

The steppes of the Western Siberian Lowland have higher average annual and average monthly temperatures than the more northerly wooded-steppe and taiga. The growing season is 160 to 175 days long, from the end of April to mid-October, and there is a frost-free period of about 140 days, from the beginning of May to the end of September. There are more than 2,000 hours of solar radiation a year in Pavlodar. The annual precipitation is less than 12 inches and there are, on an average, 111 days with snow or rain. Daily precipitation is never greater than 1.5 inches, normal relative humidity is 69 per cent, and cloudiness 50 per cent.

Summer in the steppes is hot and dry. The average temperature in July is 71°F at Semipalatinsk; the maximum is 105°F. The air is dry in summer, the relative humidity in July is 55 per cent; cloudiness is slight, 45 to 50 per cent. Summer has the greater part of the annual precipitation (both June or July have about 1.5 inches), but the high temperatures, the dryness of the air, the frequent strong winds, and the large number of clear days make summer an unproductive season because they encourage rapid evaporation, which in Semipalatinsk reaches more than 40 inches per year. The rapid evaporation of moisture from the surface of the ground and the vegetation affects the development of steppe vegetation and the yields of cultivated plants unfavorably, especially in the southern regions of the zone.

Winter in the steppes is long and cold; the average temperature in January is 1.5°F and in the course of cold spells may drop to −59°F. The air in winter is moist; the average relative humidity in January is 82 per cent. In December 62 per cent of all daylight hours are cloudy, and there are only 46 hours of sunshine at Pavlodar. In winter there is almost no precipitation—in February 0.1 inches, and March 0.4 inches—the snow cover is thus extremely thin.

Ground water of the steppes of the Western Siberian Lowland is found in the porous deposits of Tertiary and more recent times. Its depth and composition depend on the altitude, the character of the relief, and the lithological characteristics of water-bearing and water-resistant layers. It is usually saline in low places, fresh if it comes from the neighboring Kazakh hills. Its depth in low areas of the pre-Irtysh is from 6 to 26 feet; on the water divides 100

feet. In many places the depth of ground water and the lack of fresh-water lakes and springs with significant flow causes a deficiency of fresh water. However, in the Kulunda steppe, it is possible to obtain fresh water from wells even in the immediate vicinity of salt lakes. The surface flow in some steppe regions is almost nil, and near Pavlodar the Irtysh has no right-bank tributaries at all. Other regions, such as the Kulunda basin, are inland regions of interior drainage. Still other regions are watered by huge rivers in transit, such as the Tobol, the Ishim, and the Irtysh.

Salt lakes are widespread; many contain large amounts of chloride and sulphate and most are devoid of vegetation (Lake Maraldy). The few small fresh-water lakes are usually overgrown with reeds and other hydrophytic plants. Especially abundant and diverse in their mineralization are the lakes of the Kulunda steppe, which have commercial importance. Here thick pine groves approach the saline lakes, sometimes breaking off abruptly to form a solid wall. The wind carries accumulations of tumbleweed across the shores of these lakes into the water, where they are quickly covered by a white luminous crust of salt. The lakes are shallow and their basins fill only during spring flow of the rivers. Four types of lakes exist: (1) huge inland lakes without outlets, isolated from each other, with large salt accumulations, as, for example, Lake Koryakov; (2) vast lakes at the end of a chain of lakes that accumulate salt from the natural brine of inflowing rivers, for example Kulunda Lake; (3) narrow, elongated lakes along river valleys, which have varying degrees of mineralization; (4) shallow fresh-water lakes in saucer-shaped depressions. The lakes contain many salts: soda, sulphate (Glauber salt), and chlorides (mainly sodium chloride).

A dry continental climate, level relief, and many undrained basins make for a good accumulation of salts. Ground water moves toward the low spots slowly, and thus the dissolving action of the water in the saline soils in which it moves is increased. When it reaches a low place it is discharged on the surface and evaporates, which leads to the formation of solonchak and solonetz; in large, deep basins, where the water cannot all evaporate, saline lakes are formed. The saline composition and degree of mineralization of ground water depend on the relief and geologic structure of the region. In Pliocene deposits, water is usually more strongly mineralized than in Quaternary sediments.

The character of ground water is strongly reflected in the salinity of the lakes into which it flows. The strong winds of summer lift large clouds of fine salt crystals from the surface of solonchaks and deposit them on the surface of the lakes; rain water washes the saline deposits of solonchaks into the lakes; physiochemical processes and vigorous microbiological activity that take place in the lakes also influence their saline composition. Some salts are formed by old and new processes of efflorescence; some come from concentrations of old continental salts in layers; others are leached from salt-bearing Tertiary strata. Many large basins accumulated great supplies of salts in the xerothermic period, and as the climate became wetter, these basins were converted into salt lakes.

Fresh-water lakes are either recently formed or are lakes with surface or underground outlets. Lakes containing sodium chloride are landlocked and many are the last in a chain of lakes which drain from one to another. The concentration of sodium chloride increases in summer as a result of evaporation of lake water. In Burlinskoye Lake, during calm dry summer weather, a crust of salt forms on the water, gradually becoming thicker and thicker, and from this crust crystals of salt fall to the bottom; an object immersed in the water becomes thickly covered with crystals of salt in the course of four to five days. During the summer a layer of salt 2 to 2.5 inches thick may accumulate on the bottom of a lake; sometimes the salt is stained by micro-organisms to an intense rose color (Lake Vishnevoye). There are at least 350 million tons of sodium chloride of high quality in the lakes of the Kulunda steppe.

Sulphate lakes, incorrectly called saltpeter lakes by the inhabitants and on maps (for example, Kuchuk or Kulunda), contain, in solution or as sediment, decahydrate Glauber salt or mirabilite. The water of Kuchuk is such a strong brine that a person cannot sink in it. Concentration of mirabilite occurs during the advance of low temperatures in fall, but in summer the deposited mirabilite again becomes soluble, because the water at the lake shores is warmed to 86°F. On the bottom of Lake Kuchuk lies a solid blanket of Glauber salt with an average thickness of 8.25 feet. Certain lakes, e.g., Rozov, are ephemeral and soon become beds of Glauber salt. The latter is used in the chemical industry for preparation of soda and sulphuric acid, in glass manufacture, in refrigeration, in medicine, etc.

Soda lakes of the Kulunda steppe contain more soda of high quality than is found in any similar area in the world, including, besides sodium chloride, compounds of magnesium and bromine. The richest in soda is the group of Mikhailovka lakes; one of these, Lake Tanatar, has half of the bottom covered with a thirteen-foot layer of crystalline soda. The Petukhovo lakes are also rich in soda. The lakes of the Kulunda steppe contain eleven million tons. For the extraction of Glauber salt and soda, their shore deposits are used. Artificial basins are used to expedite the concentration of the salts from lake brines.

In the northern steppe zone southern chernozem soil predominates, while in the southern part there are dark-chestnut soils, distinguished from the chernozem by containing less humus, by a change from grainy structure to lumpy, and by a differentiation of the humus horizon on loamy and compact subhorizons. There is little solonetz soil or solonchak. Vegetation of the steppe zone is characterized by: (1) a flora of uniform composition; (2) numerous eastern (Siberian) plants; (3) a predomination of cereals—especially the xerophilous feather grasses and fescue grasses—over southern grasses; (4) associations of the chief species of steppe xerophytes; (5) a sharply expressed xerophilous quality of grasses

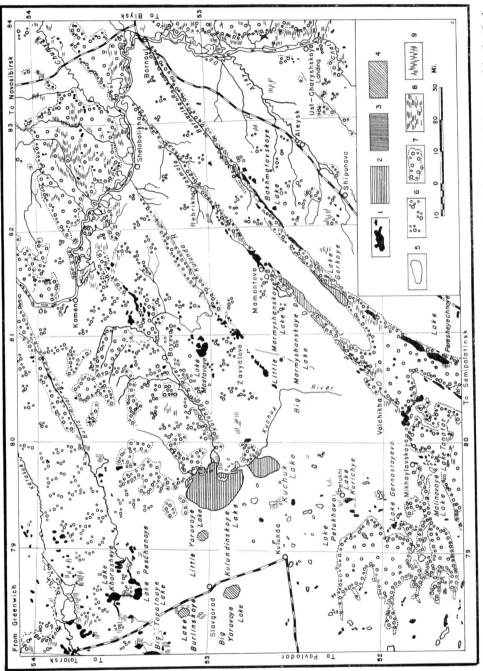

Map I-IV. Schematic map of Kulundinsk Steppe: 1—Fresh-water lakes; 2—Sulphur lakes (with Glauber salt); 3—Soda lakes; 4—Chloride lakes (with sodium chloride); 5—Lakes not in the above classification; 6—Ribbon-like pine forests of Kulunda and large areas of pine forests in Ob River area; 7—Birch forests; 8—Marshes; 9—Solonchaks.

and herbs, reflecting their persistent struggle with the insufficiency of precipitation and ground moisture; (6) less turfing of the soil than elsewhere; and (7) complex rotation of a few plant categories.

The steppes of the elevated plains of northern Kazakhstan have a vertical zonality in the distribution of vegetation. Accordingly, the southern part of the steppe zone has more northern steppe species with many additional plants appearing in rocky soil on outcrops of bedrock. A few tongues of steppe extend into the neighboring semiarid land along the Mugodzhar, Ulu Tau, and Karakaralinsk hills. On the basis of the general character of soil and vegetative cover, the steppe may be divided into two subzones: (1) the northern, or subzone of feather-grass chernozem steppes, and (2) the southern, or subzone of feather- and fescue-grass chestnut-brown steppes.

The feather-grass chernozem steppe has more steppe plants (60 to 80 per cent) and less turfiness (60 to 80 per cent) than the southern wooded-steppe. Afforestation of the steppes is slight. The monotonous vegetation of the steppes consists largely of xerophilous narrow-leafed turf grasses, especially maidenhair feather grass (*Stipa capillata*) and fescue grass (*Festuca sulcata*). Feather grass (*Stipa zalesskii*) is common and some narrow-leafed grasses (e.g., *Stipa stenophylla*) of average xerophytic quality exist, but Lessing feather grass (*Stipa lessingiana*), typical of the European steppe, is seldom encountered. There are fewer species of grasses than on meadow steppes, but the grassy cover is still quite thick and consists of numerous species; steppe vegetation contains many spring annual ephemerals.

The numerous variants of feather-grass steppes that constitute the prevailing type of vegetation are distinguished by surprising uniformity. Shallow-turf feather-grass steppe occupies large expanses on poor southern chernozem. It consists basically of small circular bunches of feather grass or maidenhair feather grass, to which are added some pinnate feather grasses, e.g., Zalesski feather grass. Steppe oats

(*Avena desertorum*) and fescue grass are always present. Brownish-gray spots of soil show through the island of grasses. The most common legumes are steppe alfalfa (*Medicago falcata*) and astragalus (*Astragalus macropus*), and the common herbs are *Jurinea linearifolia, Phlomis tuberosa,* wild thyme (*Thymus marschallianus*), cinquefoil (*Potentilla bifurca*), veronica (*Veronica incana*), and many *Artemisia,* especially the eastern species *Artemisia glauca* and *A. latifolia.* When the steppes occupy low moist places, the herbaceous cover becomes more dense: dicotyledonous plants appear in such quantity that they suppress the basic monocotyledons, and such typical representatives of meadow steppes as hog fennel (*Peucedanum ruthenicum*) and *Libanotis montana* enter the formation of grasses.

On saline soil and structural solonetz soil, which stand out because of the brighter coloring of both the vegetation and the soil, are found such halophytic plants as licorice (*Glycyrrhiza uralensis*) and a number of southern steppe species—ramose grass (*Agropyron ramosum*), kochia (*Kochia prostrata*), and sea lavender (*Statice gmelinii*). In hollows near the banks of streams and lakes, on solonized soils, one finds thickets of reeds and halophytic vegetation. In the most northern part of the subzone, in small basins, are birch-aspen groves with thickets of steppe shrubs on their edges— steppe cherry (*Prunus fruticosa*), pea tree (*Caragana frutex*), and dwarf almond (*Amygdalus nana*). On peripheral sections of the very southern steppes is a vegetation of the feather-grass type on southern chernozems, yielding many species similar to steppes on the more gravelly soil. The central part of the same region, where the altitude is 1,600 to 2,600 feet, has outcrops of Paleozoic rocks and granites and hard-crusted soil covered by pine, pine-birch, and birch forests that have a taiga-grass cover, with bog-moss turf, sundew, and cranberry. In conformity with this, taiga animals such as bear live here, whereas in the surrounding steppes there are marmots and other steppe animals.

The steppes are used as pastures, and the

meadow grass is cut for hay. The best hay meadows are on the shores of the few fresh lakes. To the south, in dry years, the steppes yield very little hay, and it is necessary to sow such fodder plants as bristly foxtail (*Setaria viridus*), sainfoin (*Onobrychis sativa*), or clover (*Trifolium lupinaster*). On places where the grazing has been heavy, and on old wastelands, are *Artemisia austriaca,* which give a dove-colored tint to the vegetative cover.

The fescue feather-grass steppe on chestnut-brown soil is connected by a series of gradual transitions with the typical feather-grass steppes in the north and the semidesert in the south. The typical feather-grass steppes contain a considerably larger number of steppe species (80 to 99 per cent) than the fescue steppe, are less turfy (40 to 60 per cent) and have more *Artemisia*. Trees and shrubs are absent. The lack of moisture and the strong evaporation on the fescue feather-grass steppe contribute to the development of such xerophilous soddy cereal grasses as maidenhair feather grass, Indian feather grass (*Stipa sareptana*), Ukrainian feather grass (*Stipa ucrainica*), and koeleria (*Koeleria gracilis*). However, pinnate feather grasses have only a limited spread. Herbs similar to grasses are represented by xerophilous, slow-growing southern species, which are scanty both in number of species and in number of plants. The less moisture, the more widely the grass roots spread in the upper layers of soil, and this decreases the turfiness and increases the area of bare soil. In the space between the clumps of grass grow moss (*Tortula ruralis*), lichen (*Parmelia vagans*), and blue-green algae (*Stratonostoc commune*), as well as mesophyllic, perennial, fast-growing grasses and annual ephemeroids such as bulb lilies and tulips which blossom beautifully in spring. The shallow root system of grasses contributes to the fast drying-out of the fescue feather-grass steppes, which toward the middle of July take on a monotonous muddy-yellow color. This is the dormant period, when the grasses bear seed and dry up.

In some places the predominant soil is rocky, dark chestnut-brown, has a humus horizon 20 inches thick, and a humus content of 3 to 4 per cent. It is weak morphologically and shows signs of salinity, has an insignificant depth of effervescence, and a large amount of gypsum at a depth of three feet. In depressions solonetz soil predominates, and on elevations there are patches of southern chernozem. Here the fescue–feather-grass steppes extend uniformly for seven or eight miles. In them, among a thick turf of the feather grasses (*Stipa capillata, S. lessingiana,* and *S. kirghisorum*) and fescue grasses, patches of chestnut-brown soils are visible, unconcealed by a poor growth of xerophytic herbs—*Allium lineare,* adonis (*Adonis wolgensis*), and sandwort (*Arenaria graminifolia*). Among these steppes are scattered growths of fescue, feather grass, and *Artemisia* or fescue and *Artemisia* in places where there are outcrops of bedrock covered with stony and gravelly soil. Here, along with the common feather and fescue grasses are scattered specimens of such shrub-like *Artemisia* as *Artemisia frigida* and *A. incana*. Eastern plants not found in the European steppes include *Iris scariosa* and *Goniolimon speciosum*.

In basins there is a vegetative cover which demands more moisture and contains many species of steppe and meadow plants that make good pastures and hay meadows. Along the shores of lakes, on deep and medium solonetz soils, have grown typical halophytic plants, such as seaside *Artemisia maritima*. Where ground waters approach the surface and along shores of particularly saline lakes are solonchaks with a halophytic vegetation of such stalky and leafy succulents as glasswort (*Salicornia herbacea*); frequently there are solonchak meadows with barley (*Hordeum secalinum*) and licorice (*Glycyrrhiza uralensis*). In valleys that face north one may encounter shrubs or small trees—willow (*Salix sibirica*) and birch (*Betula verrucosa*), for example—and many forest plants such as *Orchis latifolia*. There are also a few small pine groves containing mosses, red bilberry, and lichens.

Fescue–feather-grass steppes are used as hay meadows and pastures. They are less productive than the northern steppes, but the fodder is of good quality because of the abundance of grass. It is necessary to cut the meadows when the cereal grasses are in bloom, since later cutting yields very tough hay.

Bottomland along the large rivers (Irtysh, Ishim), with their bright green meadow grasses, thickets of reeds, and groups of shrubs along the channels, contrast strikingly in summer with the sparse dried-up steppe vegetation. On raised sections of the slightly undulating bottomlands, with their alluvial meadow soils, there are meadows of thick, medium-height couch grass: higher there are saline steppe-like and steppe meadows, lower there are solonchak meadows, and near the water, in swampy soil, are combinations of high grass with reeds and sedges. Bottomlands yield much good hay, and barley, wheat, and millet can be grown on them. Muskmelons and watermelons can also be raised there.

Outside the bottomlands, the arid and warm climate of the steppes and the saltiness of the soil discourage the formation of bogs and peat accumulation. Temporary excess moistening of the saline soil creates halophytic meadows, which contain the grass *Aeluropus litoralis* and other halophytic plants.

Unlike the wooded-steppe, with its diversity of habitat, the steppe has uniform ecologic conditions over large areas. This permits the broad spread of many animals and leads to a comparative uniformity of fauna, which is generally similar to that of the European steppes, although it comprises several species not found in Europe.

Rodents are plentiful in the steppes: ground hare (*Allactaga saliens*), small jerboa (*Allactaga elater*), and tridactylous jerboa (*Dipus sagitta*). The most common predatory animal is the tartar fox (*Vulpes korsak*). There are a number of Mediterranean, Mongolian, and European birds, but few Siberian ones: crane (*Grus virgo*), great bustard (*Otis tarda*), sheldrake (*Tadorna tadorna*), ruddy sheldrake (*T. ferruginea*), avocet *Recurvirostra avocetta*), isabellina chat (*Oenanthe isabellina*), and white-feathered lark (*Melanocorypha leucoptera*). Carnivorous birds include the imperial eagle (*Aquila heliaca*), the steppe eagle (*A. nipalensis*), and the steppe buzzard (*Buteo rufinus*).

Birch and pine groves penetrate the steppes deeply from the north, particularly in Kulunda, and give taiga animals an opportunity to live here, thus creating a merging of steppe and taiga species.

Feeding in the Kulunda pine groves, but nesting in the steppe, live the field pipit (*Anthus campestris*), bunting (*Emberiza hortulana*), and taiga wood grouse. Black grouse, oriole, and tomtit adapt themselves to life even in thin birch groves and steppe thickets. The imperial eagle, formerly a forest species, at present is more common in the steppe than in the taiga; however, it penetrates the steppe only as far as the pines or birches do. It builds its nest in trees, unlike the steppe eagle, which builds its nest on the ground.

A few species of birds are relics of the glacial period—for example, some nesting northern ducks, snipes, and speckled magpies—and there are others that are isolated from their basic habitats, such as the duck (*Oidemia fusca*), a taiga bird, the hawk (*Faleo alsolon columbarius*), which sometimes nests in the forest, sometimes in the tundra, and the ptarmigan (*Lagopus lagopus*), a tundra bird.

The deep intrusion into the steppe of wooded-steppe animals and the well-preserved remnants of an earlier, more abundant steppe fauna, show that the steppes once extended much farther to the north. The southward advance of the forests caused some animals to withdraw to the south and others to appear from the north.

CHAPTER 2

Altai

The Altai mountain system of Western Siberia has a complex history of development, which can be traced in its relief and in the distribution and nature of its organic life. It lies between 48° and 53° north latitude and 82° and 90° east longitude: the latitude is that of the steppes and semiarid lands of Soviet Europe; the Altai would stretch from Syzran to Stalingrad. This region, with its continental climate, shows both horizontal and vertical zonality in the development of its steppe, forest, and high-mountain landscapes. Among its plants and animals are species from both the Siberian taiga and steppes, from the semidesert of Mongolia, and from even more remote botanical and zoogeographic regions. The Altai is rich in mineral resources, has thick forests of sturdy trees, and a well-developed livestock industry. Since the Altai Mountains are the source of the greatest rivers of Western Siberia—the Ob and Irtysh—they provide excellent reserves of water power. Administratively, its greater part belongs to the Gorno-Altai Autonomous Oblast; a small section lies within Kazakhstan.

OROGRAPHY

The altitude of the Altai varies from 1,400 to 15,000 feet, the elevation and the area of the summits gradually increasing to the southeast. The Altai is not a sharply isolated mountain system. In the northeast it touches the Kuznetsk Ala-Tau and Western Sayan, and the Mongolian Altai branches out from it in the southeast. In the west, with noticeable traces of dislocation, the hilly steppe expanses of the Kazakh folded country form a gradual transition to the Altai. Only in the north and northwest is it sharply demarcated from the flat Western Siberian Lowland, which here lies at an altitude of 600 to 1,000 feet. The Altai is divided from the Lowland by a tectonic break in the form of a steep, weakly dissected escarpment that stretches approximately along the 52nd parallel and rises 1,000 to 1,500 feet above the plain. To the southwest the border becomes indistinct and faulted, with granite crests extending far into the steppes.

The largest mountain center of the Altai is the mountain massif Tabyn-Bogdo-Ola (Five Holy Mountains), located at the source of the Argut River on the Chinese border. Its chief peak, Kuitun, reaches 14,293 feet and is heavily glaciated. From it, the Mongolian Altai extends to the southeast beyond the borders of the USSR. The southern Altai stretches almost directly westward from the bordering Sailiugem Range—the beginning of the eastern Altai system. Within the curve formed by these two ranges lies the central Altai, which extends to the northwest.

The southern Altai, which forms a watershed between the Cherny Irtysh (which flows into Lake Zaysan) and the Bukhtarma rivers, has permanent snow and glaciers on its highest crests. It reaches 12,841 feet in the eastern part and 10,988 in the western and bears in succession westward the names Tarbagatay, Sarym-Sakty, and Narym. On the south and southwest several mountain chains descend to the Zaysan depression: for example, the Kurchum and Asyli ranges between which lies the graben lake, Marka-Kul. The ranges are only slightly dissected and the passes are difficult. Their slopes fall abruptly to the north and rather gradually to the south.

The eastern Altai consists of a group of ranges: Sailiugem (height 14,293 feet), Chikhachev, and Shapshal. Stretching tortuously southward, these ranges form the international border with the Mongolian People's Republic and provide the sources of the Ana River. From the Chikhachev chain, the Chulyshman and Kura chains extend to the west. Beyond these a fan of ranges occupies the space between the Katun River and Teletskoye Lake. At the sources of the Chulcha and Bolshoy Abakan rivers the Shapshal range becomes the Abakan Range, bending around Teletskoye Lake from the east. Characteristic of the relief of the eastern Altai are the many points at the same high elevation and the comparative smoothness of the gradual slopes and dome-like peaks of the mountain ranges. Here, at altitudes of 5,000 to 7,250 feet, are the hilly plains (the Chuya Steppe, the Kura Steppe, the Ukok and Chulyshman plateaus) that are the gates to the high steppes and semideserts of Central Asia.

The central Altai is composed of two basic mountain chains, the northern and southern, that extend almost directly east-west and drop gradually to the west. The southern chain consists of the high and massive Katun Range and includes Mount Belukha, which has two peaks, each extending from north to south; the eastern peak is 14,779 feet high, the western, 14,563 feet. Between them is a snowy saddle 13,365 feet high, which slopes gradually to the south and breaks off steeply on the north. The eastern part of the Katun Range is cut by the gorge of the Argut River, beyond which rises the southern Chuya Range, whose greatest height, attained by Mount Irbistu, is 12,982 feet. To the west, across the Katun River, is the Knolzun Range with heights up to 8,580 feet. Since many of these mountains rise well above the snow line, they are covered with permanent snow that forms some of the largest glaciers of the Altai.

Characteristic of the relief is the contrast between the heights and the broad intermountain steppe depressions with flat bottoms—e.g., the Uymonsk and Abaysk steppes, at elevations of about 3,300 feet. The northern chain of the central Altai begins in the east with the complex mountain knot of Bish-Iirdu at a height of 12,678 feet in the North Chuya Range and continues to the west under the name of Terek (up to 9,482 feet), Korgon (8,200 feet), the lower Tigiret (7,396 feet), and the Kolyvan ranges (3,926 feet at Sinyukha Mountain), which loses itself in the adjacent steppe plains.

From the Kholzun Range, the ranges of the western Altai branch out to form the Ulba, Ivanov (up to 8,670 feet altitude), and Uba mountains. From the Terek Range extends the broad fan of the northwestern mountain chains of the Altai, known as the Seminsk, Cherginsk, Anuysk, and Bashchelaksk mountains: these have been strongly eroded and nowhere reach either the snow line or the upper timber line. In the Altai, ranges with perpetual snow, or those which have patches of snow in summer, are usually called *belki,* as, for example, Katunskiye Belki (Katun Alps).

PALEOZOIC AND MESOZOIC ERAS

During the Cambrian period there was an open sea, which was part of the vast Siberian Paleozoic geosyncline, where the Altai now stand. In this early Cambrian geosyncline thick layers of limestone were formed from old oceanic reefs, but in the coastal zone an accumulation of sandy-clayey sediments were deposited which were later converted into metamorphic strata. Subaqueous volcanic activity manifested itself at times, yielding basaltic lavas, almost without exception. Orogenic processes gradually raised this geosyncline in the southwest, and in the northeast continental sediments were laid down.

At the end of the Early Silurian, the Taconian phase of Caledonian folding created the first dry land in the northeastern part of the Altai, which was washed by the Late Silurian sea. The Altai continued to rise in the southwest, where thick coral-reef limestones now alternate with layers of shale.

The end of the Late Silurian was marked by the intensive Erian phase of Caledonian folding. Huge, complex folds of northwestern trend with very steep angles of dip were created, there was shallow auxiliary folding and cleavage, and there were granite intrusions in the eastern part of the region. Deep metamorphism brought about a greenstone conversion in the Cambrian and Silurian rocks, lending a uniformity to the different kinds of rocks: chlorite caused the green coloring, which is unknown in the younger deposits. Thick layers of limestone were converted into marble. The crumpling of the folds and their penetration by different intrusions caused the rocks to become rigid and incapable of further folding. As a result of the last phase of Caledonian folding, there was a considerable increase in the amount of dry land, the sea retreated still farther to the southwest, and in the Late Devonian it finally abandoned most of the modern Altai, leaving only a small sea in the southwest.

In the Carboniferous period the Altai was an eroded land surface and towards the Permian was converted into a plain containing depressions that were temporarily swamped. At the end of the Carboniferous, the Ural phase of Variscian folding produced northwest-trending folds. Then Devonian and Carboniferous strata in the southwestern section were intruded with granodiorite, although older, intensively crumpled rocks of the Cambrian and Silurian in other parts of the Altai have no such intrusions. At the end of the Permian the ancient rocks, reinforced by intrusions of granodiorites, were broken along deep and long faults and clefts that were oriented to the northwest, in conformance with the previous folding.

Linked closely with these breaks are the principal masses of intrusives, which are the source of rich polymetallic ores. Repeated tectonic shiftings formed zones of warping several miles wide along fissures where the rocks were sharply sheared. The joints in sheared rocks were subaqueous paths along which ore-bearing solutions penetrated from the depths. Local dome-shaped anticlinal structures with impenetrable schistous strata provided extremely favorable conditions for the collection of ores from metal-bearing solutions and for the formation of huge deposits of minerals. The largest polymetallic deposits, which contain 99 per cent of the Altai's ore, are situated in a line along a comparatively narrow strip called an ore graben, which stretches several hundred miles to the northwest. It is separated from the neighboring rocks by zones of warping. Almost 98 per cent of the ore is concentrated in 14 deposits, of which those at Leninogorsk, Zyrianovsk, Belousovka, and Zmeinogorsk are best known. The metallic deposits of the Altai are among the richest in the USSR: they include much gold and silver. Among the Paleozoic rocks are many beautiful, ornamental, and commercially valuable stones—jasper, porphyry, marble, limestone.

After the Paleozoic there is a gap in the geological chronicle: neither marine nor continental Mesozoic deposits have been uncovered in the Altai. During the entire Mesozoic era the Altai was apparently a mountainous country that was being eroded away to form a peneplain.

TERTIARY PERIOD

The peneplain of the Tertiary Altai was somewhat raised above the level of the Western Siberian sea and the salty water that filled the Zaysan depression. The uniform lithologic makeup of the Tertiary deposits that are found at many places in the Altai shows that the Tertiary Altai was in many ways morphologically similar to the present low hills of the Kazakh folded country: it contained many low sloping ridges, small streams, and a great number of lakes. In the early Tertiary Period there were rather weak epeirogenic movements, which brought about the erosion of friable efflorescent rocks and the deposition of sand and clay in the fresh-water lakes. Turfing-over of these lakes followed, eventually resulting in the formation of strata of brown coal (Chuya Steppe). Because the plain was bordered by the Tertiary Sea, it had a moist and warm marine climate.

In classic profiles of Tertiary deposits (e.g., at Mount Ashutas, south of Lake Marka), thin clayey seams expose beautifully preserved impressions of leaves, boughs, flowers, and seeds, indicating the growth here of a rich Tertiary vegetation consisting of more than 70 species. This flora was similar to the Tertiary flora of East Asia, even to that of North America, but did not resemble that of Europe. Species that are now extinct or that are no longer found in the Altai grew luxuriantly: sequoia (*Sequoia langsdorffii*), swamp cypress (*Taxodium dubium*), ginkgo (*Ginkgo adiantoides*), tulip tree (*Liriodendron tulipifera*), wing nut (*Pterocarya densinervi*), walnut, beech, ash, oak, hornbeam, and many others.

In the second half of the Tertiary Period epeirogenic movements were intensified. This led to the formation of a raised section of dry land large enough to develop a hydrographic network, which carried the products of erosion beyond the borders of the Altai into the Western Siberian Lowland (where large lakes still survived) and into the vast Zaysan depression. The disappearance of the Tertiary sea and the huge lakes made the climate drier and more continental, and this, in turn, brought about sharp changes in the character of the vegetation. In the earlier moist and moderate climate the forests contained broad-leaved trees, as indicated by fossil remains in the valley of the Bukhtarma River. Certain of these species such as linden, hazelnut, alder, and spruce persist to the present; the Tertiary species of aspen (*Populus heliadum*), differed little from the modern aspen (*Populus tremula*); and the Tertiary wing nut (*Pterocarya densinervi*), resembled the modern wing nut of the Caucasus.

The Paleozoic strata of the Altai, intensively warped by several orogenic processes and made stable by repeated intrusions, were, by the end of the Tertiary Period, a rigid unyielding mass, in which further mountain-forming pressure could not be resolved by folding. Therefore, when intense Alpine folding took place at the end of the Tertiary and the beginning of the Quaternary periods, it caused deep tectonic breaks in the Altai strata and split them into a series of separate blocks that are irregularly dislocated and partly thrust upon one another. The pressure which was not accompanied by vulcanism evidently originated from the south, since these southern alpine breaks have an east-west trend—not a northwest trend, as do the Paleozoic rocks joining them. Further, in the southern parts of the Altai the masses are narrow and high, but northward they widen and sink considerably. Huge faults from the end of the Tertiary have been beautifully preserved in the modern topography of the Altai. On the borders of the Zaysan depression and the pre-Ob plain, the steep cliffs of the Altai rise hundreds of yards above the surrounding plains. Along tectonic lines there are belts of volcanic rocks and series of hot springs. The radioactive

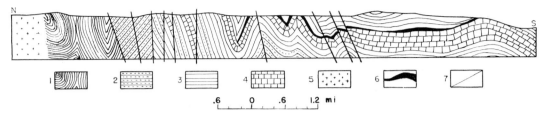

Fig. 2-1. Geologic cross section of southeastern part of the Altai; folding is complicated by small local breaks and faults. 1—Metamorphic (Cambrian-Silurian); 2—Sandstone and shale of the Middle Devonian; 3—Upper Devonian shale; 4—Upper Devonian limestone; 5—Granite; 6—Melaphyre (cover); 7—Tectonic lines.

Belokurikha hot springs are on the northern tectonic border of the Altai and the Rakhmanovskiye Klyuchi are in the central part of the region. Rich interstitial water, under pressure and carrying with it rare gases, is found along the southern tectonic border of the Altai. Cinnabar is associated with the Alpine faults in the southeastern Altai.

As a result of the displacement of large blocks, the surfaces of the Tertiary peneplain and the Tertiary deposits lying on them were raised to different levels, ranging from 1,650 to 11,550 feet in height. The Tertiary deposits were quickly eroded from elevated blocks; those on depressed blocks were preserved. For instance, in the eastern part of the southern Altai in moraine deposits lying at a height of 11,550 feet, are fragments of brown coal that are not distinguishable from Tertiary brown coal of other sections of the Altai. Almost all Tertiary deposits are faulted, and near the cliffs bordering the Zaysan depression they are highly dislocated. Tertiary grabens, somewhat modified by rivers and glaciers, now exist as large longitudinal valleys: for example, the gigantic graben just north of the southern Altai that contains the upper courses of the Bukhtarma, Sarym-Sakty, and Narym rivers. Other grabens were flooded to form two of the largest lakes of the territory—Teletskoye and Marka-Kul. On the raised, folded, fault-block mountainous country, a new cycle of erosion began and the present hydrographic network was established. The many horsts were obstacles to young river network; either the rivers went around them or succeeded in cutting through them during

their slow rise. For instance, the Katun River zigzags northward across both the Katun and Terek ranges as though it were antecedent to the uplift.

Recent studies of Altai tectonics have established the existence of many faults and show their importance in the present surface structure of the mountainous region. They have shown that the basic forces in the development of this region are those associated with large folds. According to this hypothesis, at the beginning of the Tertiary Period the Altai was a vast dome-like elevation that still retained the plasticity of the earth's inner crust. During this period its surface was fashioned into a series of large concave folds separated from each other by large depressions. The greatest rise was in the central part of the Altai, where the highest peaks are now located. In many places this process was complicated by faults. Folding of the old undulating surface and its rise to different elevations formed the flat range crests so typical of the modern Altai. The depressions are the present mountain basins.

In the mountainous country which replaces the Tertiary peneplain, the climate became more severe, and the patterns of development of vegetation and animal life began to change —a change that was sharply disrupted by approaching glaciation.

Glacial and Postglacial Periods

In the Quaternary Period the Altai was glaciated many times. There were definitely two major glaciations, but traces of three or four can be found. Evidences of glaciation are encountered everywhere in high-mountain regions: there are magnificently developed complexes of great curving moraines, drumlins, and outwash plains, numerous picturesque moraine lakes, furrowed and polished rocks, huge erratics, and deep glacial troughs with hanging side valleys. Old deep glacial cirques sometimes lie so close to one another that only sharp narrow crests remain between them. Younger cirques, evidently dating from the last epoch of glaciation, are smaller and their bottoms conform almost exactly in height to the present upper timber line. Seemingly older but poorly preserved cirques, lying 650 to 1,000 feet lower, were possibly created in an earlier period of glaciation.

The first glaciation was a solid cover, because at that time erosion had not yet dissected the mountainous country, which had been rejuvenated by the Alpine mountain building. Only huge glacial tongues, like the Bukhtarma glacier, 210 miles long, descended far onto the

Fig. 2-2. Young cirques on the slope of the Kubinsk Belok Mountains over Karakol Lake.

adjacent plains. Thick deposits of the first glaciation on the Chulyshman-Bashkaus water divide lie several hundred yards above the deposits of the last glaciation on the bottom of the Chulyshman glacial trough.

The hydrographic network of the early Quaternary noticeably differed from the modern in places; for example, until the last glaciation the Bukhtarma flowed through a wide longitudinal graben along the northern slope of the southern Altai, but today only a small part of the upper Bukhtarma flows through this graben. The Irtysh probably flowed through the wide valley of the small present-day stream Kokpektinka, passing farther on into a valley with a breadth many miles larger.

In the mid-glacial period, new tectonic movements that took place along old and new faults in the Altai were significant in the modern morphology of the region. At this time the Teletskoye Lake graben was evidently formed and there was further vertical dislocation of the northern escarpment of the Altai above the pre-Ob plain. These movements of the Altai blocks sharply strengthened erosion, thus leading to the destruction of the moraines of the first glaciation. In many places the younger deposits were covered with as much as 165 feet of alluvium, as near the northern Altai shelf. This same erosion partly rebuilt and deepened the valley network, in which glaciers of the Alpine type developed during the last Ice Age. For example, the formation of the Teletskoye Lake graben increased the gradient of a series of rivers emptying into it, e.g., the Kygy. It changed the direction of the flow of the old rivers, capturing the sources of such rivers as the Abakan. At the time of the second glaciation many rivers which had flowed northward were turned to the west.

Earthquakes in the Altai are indications of prolonged tectonic processes. More than fifty weak earthquakes have been recorded, thus adding the Altai to the seismic regions of the USSR. This must be taken into consideration as the Altai becomes industrialized.

The last glaciation on a large area of the Altai was valley glaciation, in contrast to the earlier continental type. Thick Alpine glaciers descended several hundred miles along the chief river valleys. On the lower ranges there were only short valley or hanging glaciers. New, still unturfed, marginal and end moraines from the last stages of this glaciation still exist. These moraines caused the formation of numerous mountain lakes in the upper sections of glacial valleys. Some valleys appear to have been dammed by masses of moraine alluvium brought by lateral tributary glaciers. As a consequence, the main river was forced to abandon its old glacial valley and cut a new narrow valley through the lowest gaps.

There are such eperiogenic parts of valleys in many places in the Altai. For example, the Chuya River abandoned a short section of its glacial trough (now occupied by the small Myon River), cut a deep gorge in the neighboring height, and farther downstream passed into its old glacial valley again. Thick glaciers in the main valleys or deposits left by them dammed up the tributaries, forming temporary lakes in their lower sections. Subsequently these lakes were partly filled with alluvium. After the ice in the main valley retreated or the moraine dam was broken through, the temporary lakes drained. Today these old lake bottoms form broad terraces in the downstream stretches of many rivers of the Altai, such as the Pizha and Tuloi. In many places the valleys of the main rivers are incised 500 to 600 feet deeper than their tributary valleys, from which high waterfalls plunge into the main valley, as they do in Chulyshman Valley and the Teletskoye Lake basin. The highest parts of the old Tertiary peneplain were long concealed under a fixed glacial cover and were therefore not dissected by erosion.

As the lakes of the postglacial period were drained water became abundant and erosion continued with new force. Rivers cut new gorges into the bottoms of old glacial valleys, washed out moraine dams, and released more dammed-up glacial lakes. They cut into the edges of horsts, washed out moraine and fluvioglacial materials, and created countless river terraces.

Earlier glaciation was detrimental to the local flora and fauna, and rearranged their distribution. The glaciation laid waste the territory occupied by ice. The thick broad-leaved Tertiary forests were almost completely destroyed. Only small sections survived, as, for example, in the vicinity of the Kuznetsk Alatau, which did not undergo strong glaciation and was situated far from both the thick Altai glaciers and the continental ice of the northwestern Siberian Lowland. Animals evidently perished not so much from the cold as from the absence of plant food. From the rich Tertiary forests only two linden (*Tilia cordata* and *T. sibirica*) survived, and a few Tertiary grasses the forests contained, such as asarabacca (*Asarum europaeum*), *Sanicula europaea,* sweet woodruff (*Asperula odorata*), and such other Eurasian types as the sweet cicely (*Osmorrhiza amurensis*) that are encountered today in the Far East and the Caucasus. All are widely separated from their earlier, more or less unbroken habitat. Other than the lindens and the grasses, the only remnants of the Tertiary flora are: water chestnut (*Trapa natans*) and the fern *Polypodium lineare,* which are found on the shores of Issik-Kul, in the South Ussuri region, Japan, and China.

The advance of the continental ice over the northern part of the Western Siberian Lowland pushed Arctic Circle flora southward. Arctic and subarctic plants, together with coniferous forests that lay farther south, crowded out the remnants of Tertiary flora. The advance of glaciers in the Altai led to a dying-out of alpine vegetation along their edges. This vegetation had grown before the glacial period in the arid continental climate that resulted from the drying-up of nearby regions of Asia. Arctic and alpine species were displaced from their preglacial locations and in varying degrees appeared among the flora of low mountains and plains situated in preglacial zones. Conditions in Western Siberia were more favorable than in the European part of the USSR for the preservation and open advance of arctic flora to the south. Evidently the rate at which glaciers spread was slower. Even in the period of maximum glaciation vast treeless expanses of mountainous country between the Yenisei and the Lena separated the southeastern region of the Western Siberian–Taimyr glacial cover from the glaciers of the Verkhoyansk Range.

Alpine species from the Altai spread far in the glacial epoch; both eastward into the Sayans and the mountains of Eastern Siberia and westward to the mountains of Central Asia and the Caucasus. However, there is a noticeable decrease in the number of alpine species as the distance from the Altai increases. In the period of glaciation the pre-Altai plain was thickly populated with animals, as indicated by the bones of mammoth, auroch, and hairy rhinoceros that have been washed out of loess-like soil of riverbanks.

At the close of the glacial period, arctic flora, by then mixed with many alpine species, retreated again to the north to form the modern arctic flora zone. The high-altitude flora of the Altai, enriched by arctic species, shifted to the upper zones of mountains, originating the high-altitude flora region. In addition, both floras acquired many subarctic species from the mountains of the Yenisei-Lena watershed. This explains the abundance of common arctic-alpine species (up to 40 per cent) in both the Altai and the Arctic region, despite their isolation. Arctic animals such as the tundra ptarmigan and reindeer also penetrated into the Altai and neighboring mountain systems.

Plants of the glacial period have survived even at some distance from the high-elevation zones of the Altai. Many have descended to a lower belt of mountains and to the plains. In the Charysh Valley, at 3,300 feet, arctic-alpine species are discovered amid steppe vegetation: lousewort (*Pedicularis verticillata*) or sedge (*Carex atrofusca*). In the neighboring Khakass Steppes, on dry rock slopes, such a characteristic alpine plant as partridge grass (*Dryas octopetala*) is found at a height of 2,300 feet, al-though it grows most commonly in mountain tundra at heights above 6,600 feet.

Large areas of the Altai remained dormant during the long glacial period. With the shrinkage of glacial cover the territory abandoned by the glacier began to be populated with plants and animals from the nonglaciated western and northern parts of the region and Mongolia. Alpine grass and shrubs returned first, mingling with the arctic flora. Later, as the moraines dried up, this flora advanced high into the mountains. Its place was taken by pine forests. During the last glaciation, on elevated sections that were not covered by glaciers, xerophythic steppe species began to develop. In the postglacial xerothermic period, because of the drying of alluvium, these species occupied new regions in both the surrounding plains and the Altai itself.

The poor development of glaciation in the northeastern part of the Altai developed flora and fauna with a definitely taiga character and contained species from beyond the Yenisei, such as lovage (*Ligusticum mongolicum*), which is encountered in the Altai only and may have come from the Western Sayan. Turkestanian flora and fauna have penetrated into the southwestern part of the Central Altai: such birds as the shrike (*Lanius collurio phoenicuroides*) are common. In the southeastern part of the Altai, with its sharp continental climate, poor precipitation, and snowless winters, characteristic Central Asiatic species have found themselves a second home. They blend with northern species trapped in the Altai by the glaciation: reindeer and antelope, Mongolian *Dyptychus* and typical Siberian fish live there together. In the Altai many young endemic plants have developed, especially of the general *Astragalus* and *Oxytropis,* and some animal species have been converted into special subspecies, such as the Altai mole (*Talpa altaica*) or the unique rodent *Myospalax aspalax.*

CLIMATE

The Altai, whose eastern part extends to the center of the Asiatic mainland, is a rather clearly defined climatic region. By the time warm and moist winds from the Atlantic

Ocean arrive here they are greatly modified, but cold winds from the Arctic Ocean, especially in winter, meet no obstacles or modifying influences and thus easily reach the Altai. Therefore its climate, despite its comparatively low latitudes, is much more severe than that of corresponding latitudes of the European USSR. Its complex mountain relief, with heights ranging from 1,500 feet in the foothills to 15,000 feet in the central part, sometimes influences the climate more than does its geographic position. Extensive high peneplains, where winter lasts for nine or ten months, affect the climate of the entire region much more than the presence of the highest ranges. Often the foothills of the Altai are warmer than the neighboring plains, which may be enveloped by cold air masses. Only occasional cold waves will chill the low-lying foothills.

The village of Tourakskoye, situated in a mountain valley with a good flow of air, has an average January temperature of 12°F, while Semipalatinsk, lying farther south and 1,460 feet lower, has a January temperature of 3°F. In high regions with quiet cold air in winter, average January temperatures decrease with elevation: at a height of 3,332 feet (Marka-Kul) —14°F, at 5,280 feet (Orlovsk village) —15°F, at 5,610 feet (Kosh-Agach) —22°F. Transition from winter to summer is swift, as is evident from a comparison of average temperatures of the spring months (March, April, and May), which in the village of Tourakskoye (2,154 feet) are 17°, 35°, and 50°F and in Orlovsk (5,280 feet) are 2°, 27°, and 47°F.

In summer the Altai, with its cold high plateaus, high ranges with permanent snow, and deep, moist, wooded valleys, stands out as a cool island among hot steppe plains. Again comparing Tourakskoye with Semipalatinsk, the average July temperature in the former is 61°F, in the latter 71°F. In summer, as in winter, the temperature drops as altitude increases.

On high plateaus and alpine ranges of the Altai, the winds, even at the very height of summer, are very cold, and it is necessary to be prepared at any time for snowstorms. Even in July, temperatures may drop to 23°F on

frost nights, snow may fall, and shallow lakes and swamps freeze over. Summer is relatively short. The growing period varies from 159 days in low mountains to 60 days at high altitudes. Amid the mountains there is an irregular distribution of temperatures that results from conditions favorable for the stabilization masses of cold air in enclosed valleys. At Zyrianovsk, in a locked-in valley 1,485 feet high, the average February temperature is —7°F, but in Katon-Karagai, at a height of 3,300 feet, where the cold air can circulate, it is 10°F. In Zyrianovsk spring arrives nine days later than at Katon-Karagai, but their summer temperature is similar (66° and 63°F). In the northwestern part of the Altai on a warm, clear night in July, 1910, a reversal of temperature was noted: at the bottom of the Borovlyanka Valley the temperature was 55°; on the slope 336 feet higher it was 68°.

The Altai lies in a precipitation belt with an annual rainfall of more than 12 inches which stretches from the European USSR to Lake Baikal. In winter the center of the barometric maximum, moving from Eastern Asia to the southwest, passes through the southern Altai; thus, in winter, dry southwest and south winds of continental origin prevail. In summer the warming of the neighboring regions creates a low pressure area, and moist northwest winds prevail. At altitudes of 3,300 to 6,600 feet moist westerly winds predominate throughout the year, bringing snow in winter and, in summer, rain.

The Altai, the first high mountain massif of Siberia in the path of the moist western air currents, condenses much moisture from them. Therefore precipitation is greater than might be expected for a continental region surrounded by dry areas. The westernmost mountain ranges of the Altai that rise echelon-like from the neighboring plains are the first to intercept the western winds and consequently extract the greater part of the moisture. The extreme eastern ranges, Sailiugem and Chikhachev, receive little more of it than the dry central Kobdo Valley of neighboring Mongolia. The extensive fan-like spread of the western ranges allows much of the moist wind to penetrate to the chilled ranges of the center, which swiftly condense their moisture.

Under these conditions there is much more precipitation on windward western slopes than on leeward eastern ones. This is clearly indicated by the distribution of vegetation. Valleys in the interior sections of the region, despite their high altitude, have very little precipitation; for example, the inland Ukok Plateau, at 6,600 feet altitude, has only 11.4 inches of precipitation during the year. These dry valleys are steppes which form sharply defined patches among the damp wooded landscapes. The ranges of the western Altai, however, constitute one of the most humid sections of the USSR: the annual precipitation at the sources of the Ulba River in the western Altai is 62.8 inches.

In winter low clouds drop their moisture on the lower ranges, but the high, moving clouds of summer top these ranges and leave their moisture in the region of the highest mountains, such as the Katun Range or Belukha. In the western Altai, therefore, precipitation is more seasonal than in the rest of the Altai. Besides the spring-summer maximum (May through July), an autumn maximum (October and November) is clearly observable. In autumn, cyclonic activity increases and significantly lowers the temperature of air in the mountains. Since 30 per cent of the annual precipitation consists of snow from the westerly winds, the snow cover is extremely deep (more than 10 feet at the sources of the Maly Ulba River).

The heavy precipitation in the western Altai is clearly indicated by the wide spread of green fir taiga, the tall and luxuriant hydrophilic grasses in the meadows, and the swampy soil. The foothills receive much less precipitation (16 inches) and are also subjected to the drying influence of the adjacent flat steppes; therefore steppe vegetation penetrates along them far into the mountain region.

A second humid area is the northeastern section of the Altai, which is reached by westerly winds that deposit moisture on the ranges jut-ting farthest to the north. The annual precipitation here is 36 inches, with a single sharp maximum in summer and a minimum in winter. The deep snow on the slopes, especially on the southern ones, slides down them in spring, destroying the woody vegetation. The abundance of moisture is clearly manifested by the solid growth of a dark-conifer taiga of spruce, fir, and Siberian pine.

The central Altai, despite the high elevation of its ranges, has 20 to 24 inches of precipitation annually, and thus is covered largely by larch, which is more tolerant of semiarid conditions than are most conifers. The southern Altai is subject to the strong drying influence of the surrounding steppes and semidesert. Along the lower sections of the Bukhtarma River there is less than 12 inches of precipitation a year. The closed grabens in the central and especially in the southeastern Altai are located in the rain shadow of the high western ranges and constitute an area of transition to the continental Mongolian climate. These grabens have a small annual precipitation—a single summer maximum in July and August and almost none in winter—as it is only in summer that high moving clouds can top the tall mountain ranges to the west. On Ukok Plateau, out of 11.4 inches of annual precipitation, the winter has only 0.7 inch. The snow cover is so thin that there is no snow route, travel by wheel or pack is possible the year round. Cattle graze on green fodder for the whole winter. Young crops, because there is so little meltwater in the spring, need irrigation. The grabens have approximately the climate that would prevail if the Altai was a plain. This is indicated by the steppe and semiarid character of their vegetation and the development of chernozem, chestnut, and brown soils.

The Altai is enclosed between isolines of 75 per cent annual relative humidity in the north and 65 per cent in the south. As in all continental regions, the relative humidity is highest in December and January (75 to 80 per cent) and lowest in May (55 to 60 per cent). The air of the southern Altai and the foothills of the western Altai is especially dry. In the mountains, evaporation is considerably less than in the foothills. Autumn is cloudiest, spring clearest. The number of cloudy days in a year increases from south to north and is higher in the mountains. High mountain peaks are so often enveloped in clouds that they are seldom visible. The local mountain-valley winds affect the distribution of temperature and humidity. Many of them are foehn winds that raise the temperature and lower the relative humidity. The accompanying table shows the relationship between wind, temperature, and humidity for two autumn days in Katon-Karagay.

Foehns cause the growth of steppe patches, as at Katon-Karagay and in the Chuya and Chulyshman river valleys. Under their influence night chilling is moderated, autumn's first frosts appear later, and those of spring disappear sooner. Their dryness and warmth melt the snow cover quickly. Because of them, the lower course and the delta of the Chulyshman River serve as a wintering place for birds, which gather in this deep narrow valley lost amid high mountains continuously covered with snow. Foehns and foehn-formed currents of air are observed also near glaciers (i.e., the Katun Glacier) and evidently hasten their thawing.

DATE	OBSERVED TEMPERATURE (°F)			RELATIVE HUMIDITY (%)			WIND DIRECTION AND STRENGTH (FEET PER SECOND)		
	7 hrs.	13 hrs.	21 hrs.	7 hrs.	13 hrs.	21 hrs.	7 hrs.	13 hrs.	21 hrs.
October 8	43	63	59	48	39	32	NE 19.8	0	0
October 9	59	66	61	25	28	29	E 39.6	S 26.4	S 33

MORPHOLOGY OF THE ALTAI

The modern morphology of the Altai results from its complex geologic history; both old and new landforms can be clearly seen in the present landscape. It is a folded-fault block mountain region altered by subsequent glaciation and erosion. The repeated folding of the past affects the modern relief of the northwestern part of the Altai, giving a north-south trend to its valleys—the trend of the modern hydrographic network. Valleys and ridges conform in broad outline to the prevailing trend of rock structures but are greatly complicated by selective erosion, especially in the volcanic-rock areas. Epeirogenic upheavals and the consequent strengthening of erosion in the Tertiary and perhaps in the Mesozoic, when the Altai was completely raised above the Western Siberian Lowland, have been important. Peneplanation, quite strongly reflected in the modern relief of the Altai, was completed during the long continental period.

The disjunctive dislocation of fault blocks in the Altai at the end of the Tertiary has been the dominant factor in creating the present relief. Basically, the Altai is a high plateau, dissected by tectonic breaks into uneven sections of different height that often consist of two or more benches and are divided by deep and broad dislocated valleys. In much later times large-scale movements along these breaks greatly altered local levels of erosion. This caused new cycles of erosion to be superimposed on the foregoing ones, and thus further complicated the relief. The many high plateaus gave space for large ice fields during early glaciation and has had a far greater influence on the present landscape of the Altai than the narrow snow-covered mountain ranges. The total glaciation affected the present relief of the Altai, especially in the central and southern parts. It helped preserve the weakly dissected relief that existed at the beginning of glaciation and created (1) meso- and micro-relief on the plateaus; (2) typical glacial landscapes with alpine forms; (3) glacial valleys containing a whole complex of glacial deposits; and (4) countless lakes.

The present cycle of erosion, retarded by glaciation, has not yet reached the stage of maturity. Erosion has cut deeply the margins of the highest benches, where it has cut narrow lateral gorges, but the central parts of the plateau are still very weakly dissected. Remnants of the former plateaus exist as massive table-like blocks that drop off sharply toward elongated valleys. It seems as though a level might almost be laid across the tops of the mountains—from which it is possible to infer the existence of an ancient peneplain. In the present climate, vigorously active frost weathering is important in the creation of relief forms at high altitudes.

Karst phenomena are less important, although in some sections of the Altai where there are widespread limestones there are karst landscapes with numerous caves (along the Charysh River), deep sink holes, streams that

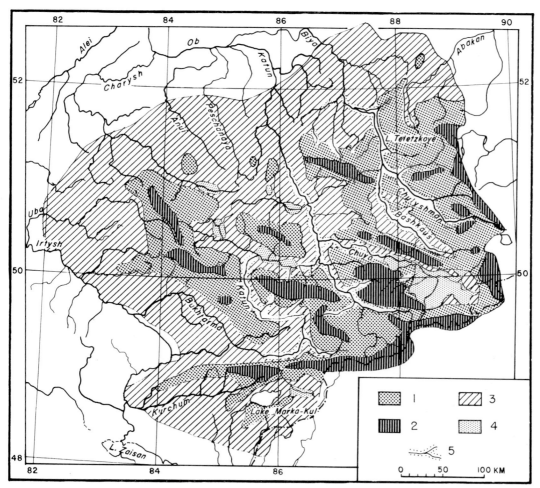

Map 2-I. Basic types of relief in the Altai: 1—Landscape of ancient peneplain; 2—Alpine landscape; 3—Central mountain area; 4—Flat-bottom valleys; 5—Glacial valleys.

Fig. 2-3. Well-preserved parts of the ancient Tertiary peneplain at 6,000 feet—the surface of Terektinsk ridge near its abrupt slope to the Uymon steppe.

disappear and reappear (source of the Elikmanar River), and deep springs. Different stages of the geologic history of the Altai are expressed in the relief of various sections.

The most outstanding feature of the Altai relief consists of remnants of the ancient peneplain—well-preserved horsts whose surfaces are broad plateaus. Even on plateaus half-destroyed by erosion it is possible to trace the former level surface. The crests of most of the mountain ranges of the Altai, from the highest eastern ranges to the lowest northwestern ones, are relics of the peneplain.

The peneplain rose above the timber line in the east, to heights of 6,600 to 8,250 feet; in the northwest it was approximately 3,500 feet high. The very broad (about 12 miles wide) and flat water divides of the present ranges are slightly rolling plains from which a few isolated peaks emerge. Some of these peaks are flat domes, others have narrow crests, and others are cone-shaped. The plateaus have sheer cliffs that border longitudinal valleys with even rectilinear edges; some are cut by only a few deep gorges. After a long and difficult ascent along thickly wooded, deeply cut, narrow gorges, the traveler finds himself on the broad flat or rolling terrain of a mountain summit. Here he is given a sense of spaciousness and may travel for

dozens of miles without ever thinking of the elevation. On these broad plateaus are many large swamps, rocky deposits, and snow fields from which rills of meltwater run through thickets of polar birch. Mature river valleys with slightly intrenched meandering streams of low gradient are common. The channels of many of these streams are braided, some connect a series of lakes, and others pass through large swamps. Near the edges of the plateau, the gradient steepens, and rivers either cut impenetrable gorges or form hanging valleys from which high waterfalls descend. At the base of the waterfall, the water often disappears into large talus slopes.

Many plateaus (for example, Chulyshman Plateau) have a glacial landscape with moraines, huge erratic boulders, glacial lakes, and tundra streams, although there are no glaciers here now. In the severe climate—spring, summer, and autumn together lasting but two or three months, and winter ruling nine or ten, as in the polar tundra—it would be surprising if no relics of the glacial period had survived to the present day.

The high, flat plateaus in some parts of the Altai—e.g., the Katun, Chuya, Sailiugem, and Chikhachev ranges—have alpine landscapes with strongly dissected relief and great contrasts in elevations. Here are sharply defined groups and chains of craggy peaks and ridges, isolated peaks with extremely steep slopes, and a mass of glacial cirques and glaciated valleys. Despite the deep dissection, the relief was formerly different, as indicated by the ring of plateaus. There is a certain crudeness of rectilinear outline, many summits have broad flat surfaces which may be remnants of the peneplain, and many of the ridges and peaks have the same elevation. The alpine landscape lies in the highest sections of the former peneplain, which because of their maximum upheaval and narrowness were subjected to intense erosion. Subsequently, strong glacial abrasion and extremely vigorous frost weathering destroyed their primary features. Thus, Katun Range, which has typical alpine relief, exemplifies a large tapering horst separated from the adjacent ranges by deep tectonic breaks. Some of its peaks appear to be monadnocks and others to be highly raised horsts. Some parts are almost undissected: in one stretch of 36 miles there is not even a single narrow pass.

Typical of the alpine landscape are the cirques; the tortuous sharp peaks owe their configuration to the destruction of the rear walls of the cirques by glaciers which grooved both slopes of the range. The sources of the rivers that begin in the cirques glaciers are in places so close that the dividing range is little more than a comb. The difference in snow depth and glacial cover in various parts of the Altai also has an effect on the alpine relief. The Katun Range is higher than the Chuya, but in the Chuya the alpine relief is expressed more sharply. Probably this is because the Katun Range has a thicker and longer-lasting snow cover, which protects it from continuous frost weathering. On the Chuya Range, where the snow cover is thinner, frost weathering is active for a longer period. The exposure of a slope also affects weathering. Since a north-facing slope has a snow cover longer it is less subject to destruction because the greater moisture causes soil to form, and this in turn is secured by vegetation. Therefore north-facing slopes are gradual and south-facing slopes are steep and craggy. The alpine landscapes that lie far above the snow line have a thick snow cover and constitute a region of present-day glaciation.

Fig. 2-4. Northern slope of Katunsk ridge at the source of the Kulcherla River broken up by glacial cirques.

The intermediate mountain landscape, at an altitude of 1,600 to 3,300 feet, occupies approximately half the Altai, and predominates in the more inhabited northern and western sections. Its lower elevations have a smoother relief, and less contrast in heights than those of higher areas. The intermediate mountain landscape nowhere extends above the timber line. Along the periphery it is dissected and mature, owing to the strong action of the complex hydrographic network: mountain ridges are narrow, the summits are sharp, the valleys are deep and narrow, but the relief still preserves its mildness. The higher sections of the intermediate mountain landscape, in the vicinity of the old peneplain, have not attained maturity. The existence on isolated peaks of remnants of the Altai peneplain, and the general leveling-off of surrounding mountain ridges, indicate that the intermediate mountain landscape is a secondary one. It was probably formed when dissected parts of the peneplain were reduced through erosion. Evidently, in these areas the peneplain resembled a weakly rolling mountain plateau, was about 3,300 feet high, and sloped gradually to the west and somewhat more abruptly to the north. It was deeply dissected by the complex river system into wide ranges, whose flat peaks survived as remnants of the peneplain. The marginal sections were more vigorously eroded and now form the intermediate mountain landscape; that selective erosion was important is indicated by the fact that most higher points of irregularity are formed of the most resistant rocks.

The intermediate mountain landscape, with its good dissection and drainage, lies almost entirely within the forest zone, which in the foothills gives way to steppe.

The river network of the Altai is fairly young, since conditions on the Tertiary peneplain made such a river network impossible. At present, the Altai drains from southeast to northwest and from east to west: since the general slope of the region is to the northwest, most water runs off in this direction. Selective erosion has developed in conformity with the direction of old folding, although young faults from the end of the Tertiary period have had an influence on the river network. The rivers that begin in the Southern Altai at first flow northward, but soon turn west along the Tertiary fault lines. Where the general slope of a locality intersects these faults, the rivers make a sharp turn (for example, the Katun at the mouth of the Argut). Separate sections of river valleys differ greatly from one another.

In the Altai, longitudinal valleys are called steppe valleys. They are enclosed grabens with wide flat bottoms, and are sharply demarcated from the surrounding horsts by distinct faults. For instance, Uymonsk steppe, at an altitude of about 3,300 feet, is locked in by the high, almost perpendicular walls of the Terek Range on the north and by those of the Katun horst on the south. The flat bottoms of these grabens are Tertiary surfaces that were preserved by alluvial cover brought down by glaciers that descended from thick neve fields on neighboring ranges. Thus in the Chuya steppe the glaciers moved so slowly that they left no signs of abrasion, but did leave a thick ground moraine. Shallow glaciers of the last glaciation deposited end moraines at the mouths of tributary streams. After the disappearance of the glaciers from the grabens, strong glacial streams that flowed down the slopes of the surrounding ranges carried great quantities of fluvioglacial material to the grabens. They rewashed and sorted the moraine deposits and covered the bottoms of the grabens with a thick layer of rolled and angular gravel, thereby raising their level.

Some flat-bottomed valleys are former lake basins that were formed when streams flowing into a valley were dammed by moraines or by the mass of the glacier in the main valley (Ursulsk steppe). In many valleys there is an intricate complex of interstratified lake, moraine, and fluvioglacial deposits that crop out in terraces, some of which (Chuya steppe) have loess-like clay soil containing shells of land mollusks that resemble those of the present. On the flat bottoms of the grabens, the rivers flow slowly, and lateral erosion is vigorous, forming

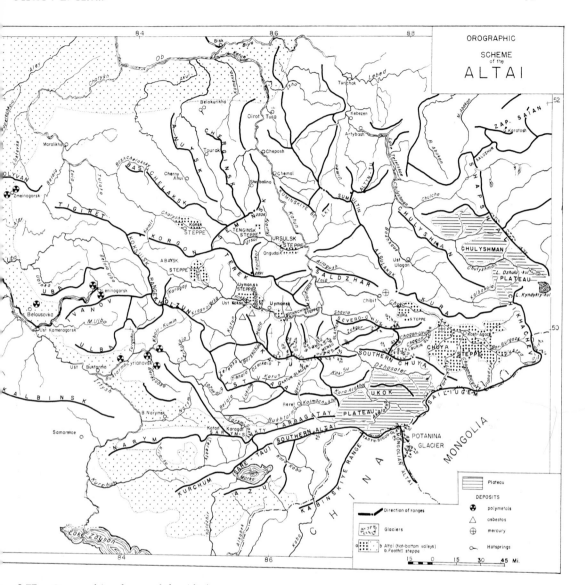

Map 2-II. Orographic scheme of the Altai.

braided channels, cut-off meanders, and lakes (Chuya steppe). They sometimes form broad swamped expanses, as on the Kansk steppe.

Valleys with flat bottoms, well warmed and protected from moist winds by the ranges, are warm and arid oases, which present a sharp contrast to the cold and moist narrow valleys deepened by erosion. Their landscapes depend on elevation and climatic peculiarities, varying from meadow steppes with productive chernozems (Uymonsk steppe) to semideserts with light-chestnut or brown soils (Chuya steppe) that are useful only as pasturage.

Where deep valleys already existed at the beginning of glaciation, ice and snow eroded them more deeply. The existing relief was not preserved, as it was on the peneplain, but new landforms were created by valley glaciation. The best example of this type of valley is that of the Chulyshman River, which is 90 miles long and has a typical **U**-shaped transverse profile. It is no more than 1,650 feet wide, and long

Fig. 2-5. Glacial valley of the Pyzha River: in the distance, the upper border of the forest is seen
at the lake—fir trees on the slopes.

stretches of its perpendicular and craggy sides are devoid of vegetation. Tributaries of the Chulyshman enter from hanging valleys that cut but slightly into the steep edge of this glacial valley. The Katuyark River falls more than 60 feet into the Chulyshman, and many other tributaries fall dozens or even hundreds of feet, creating clouds of spray and then disappearing in the thick talus. Only the channels of the larger tributaries (Bashkaus, Chulcha) have been eroded to the level of the Chulyshman, but even they have steep gradients in their lower valleys and dark, narrow, impassable gorges, although their middle and upper sections flow through typical broad glacial valleys.

Deep glacial troughs were filled by vast terminal moraines and fluvioglacial deposits from each stage of glaciation that finally raised their bottoms more than 600 feet above the level of the present rivers (Chuya, Katun, Chulyshman). The best-preserved moraines are in the upper glacial valleys, but there are terminal moraines in the lower courses of some, as in the Katun Valley at the mouth of the Mayma River. Here the moraine is a high embankment on which gigantic boulders of granite from far up the valley are scattered in chaotic disorder. The moraine in the valley of the Chulyshman is composed of a gray clay soil containing boulders that it has cemented into a tight conglomerate; this has eroded into badlands of pyramids of soil capped by huge boulders. Repeated erosion of the moraine material and the fluvioglacial deposits has formed from three to ten terraces. The piling-up of packed glacial deposits at the mouths of tributaries sometimes dammed the main Katun and Chuya rivers. Above these dams the rivers formed sandy islands and below them cut deeply eroded canyons. The solid ground of the fluvioglacial terraces provides a good base for roads because of its mixed composition and porosity. These terraces are covered with stony chestnut soil on which steppe vegetation grows. Present rivers flow in deeply eroded terraced channels up to 500 feet wide.

Erosional transverse valleys with V-shaped profiles are widespread in the Altai. Their steep slopes are covered with trees and huge patches of talus. They have comparatively narrow bottoms and two or three alluvial terraces. There are also fault valleys that intersect the east-west horsts, as, for example, the famous gorge of the Argut River that separates the Katun Range from the Chuya.

The present glaciation of the Altai is remark-ably simple and uniform. The landscape of the old peneplain, most of which lies below the line of perpetual snow, is not modeled to any appreciable degree by the modern glaciers. Only a few of the mountain massifs of the Northern Altai rise above the snow line. Notwithstanding the heavy precipitation and the severe climate, which lower the snow line to between 7,600 and 7,900 feet, large snow fields are found only on northern slopes. They usually last far into the summer and if conditions are favorable may survive for several years.

The snow line in the Altai (1) rises from west to east, (2) is higher on south-facing than on north-facing slopes, and (3) is higher on the central ranges than on the outer. In the western and northeastern Altai it lies between 7,600 and 7,900 feet. In the higher central Altai it is 7,900 to 8,500 feet on north-facing slopes and 10,200 feet on south-facing ones. In the southern Altai, owing to the proximity of the hot dry steppe, it lies, in the east, at a height of 9,240 feet, and in the Sailiugem and Chikhachev ranges it is 10,230 to 11,500 feet high.

Fig. 2-6. Mensu, largest valley glacier of the Belukha River.

The 754 glaciers of the Altai cover an area of 230 square miles. Hanging and valley glaciers are the most common. Hanging glaciers are small but are the most numerous (385), cover an area of 53 square miles, and lie at heights of 8,500 to 10,000 feet. Valley glaciers (155 of them, with an area of 150 square miles) are less common, but nevertheless are significant in the general picture of glaciation, particularly since their snouts descend considerably lower (6,500 to 8,000 feet). The majority of these glaciers are not fed by large firn fields but often receive snow and ice from avalanches, which break away from suspended snow and small glaciers attached to steep slopes of surrounding ranges. The remainder of the glaciers are tributary to the large valley glaciers.

The rate of movement of the lower courses of many Altai glaciers has been measured: for example, the daily advance of Mensu is 5.6 inches; Katun, 4 to 10 inches; and Akkem, 10 inches. The rate at which their fronts are retreating can be determined by the discharge of meltwater at the autumn flow (September), which varies from 1.5 to 6.1 cubic yards per second, depending on the location of the glacier. Altai glaciers recede and shrink rapidly as they become separated from their ice fields. The western section of Katun glacier is now completely isolated and its connection with Berelsk glacier has disappeared. During the past twenty or thirty years Mensu glacier has retreated 62.7 feet annually; Katun 36 to 55 feet; Akkem, 33 feet; and Bolshoy Maashey, 30 feet.

There are four large glacial centers in the Altai: Katun Range, South Chuya Range, North Chuya Range, and the southern Altai. These four glacial centers contain 93 per cent of all Altai glaciers and 97 per cent of the Altai glaciated area. There are more glaciers on the north-facing than on the south-facing slopes: the north slope of the main Katun Range has 133 glaciers with a total area of 45.5 square miles, the south slope has only 69 glaciers with an area of 21.2 square miles.

Low ranges whose peaks rise no more than 600 to 1,300 feet above the snow line have glaciers only on their north-facing slopes. If they rise 1,600 to 2,600 feet above the snow line, then glaciers also appear on the south-facing slopes, although the northern slopes will have more glaciers and wider areas of glaciation. High mountain masses that rise 3,300 feet or more above the line of permanent snow are equally glaciated on both slopes (Belukha) or have a more heavily glaciated windward slope (Tabyn-Bogdo-Ola).

Details of each of the Altai's quartet of glacial centers follow:

1) The Katun Range has more glaciers than any other range in the Altai: 40 per cent of the area of all Altai glaciation (89 square miles) and about 45 per cent (342) of all the glaciers are concentrated here. The focal point of glaciation is Mount Belukha with its 31 glaciers that cover an area of 27 square miles. But there are numerous hanging glaciers both in the higher eastern and in the lower western sections of the range and in its many spurs. The slopes of Belukha are completely covered with snow; only sharp ridges and isolated declivities exposed to the sun remain bare. The Belukha glacial center has thick deposits of snow and firn fields from which there are frequent firn glacial falls; the snow line is at a height of about 8,900 feet. The steeply falling Belukha glaciers have few side tributaries. Lateral glaciers are seldom connected with the main glacier, which is fed mainly by ice avalanches from the hanging glaciers. The snouts of the main glaciers descend 6,600 feet lower than any other Altai glaciers. Belukha is the junction point of the range; high spurs fan out on all sides. The glaciers descend into deep valleys between these spurs and are thus arranged radially. The five largest valley glaciers are: Mensu (length 6.8 miles, area 4.63 square miles); Katun (length 4.86 miles, area 3.4 square miles); Berelsk (length 4.86 miles, area 3 square miles); Myushtuayry, or Kochurlin; and Akkem.

2) The South Chuya Range, the second glacial center, has (a) a comparatively large number of small valley glaciers; (b) a concentration of glaciers in the central, higher part of

the range where heights reach about 13,200 feet; (*c*) especially irregular distribution of glaciers along slopes; (*d*) glacier snouts at higher altitudes than on the Katun Range. Slight dissection of the southern slope and the presence, parallel to it, of the large valley of the Dzhasater River, explain the small area of glaciation there (15 glaciers covering 3 square miles). The northern slope, on the other hand, is heavily glaciated (191 glaciers with an area of 49 square miles) and has many rather large valley glaciers. The biggest of these is Big Taldurin at the source of the Chagan-Uzun (Chuya River system), 4.9 miles long, with an area of 7.6 square miles. It lies in a wide slanting cirque and descends only to a height of 7,722 feet, conforming to the upward rise of the snow line.

3) The third glacial center of the Altai is the North Chuya Range. It contains 118 glaciers in an area of 50 square miles. The glaciation is concentrated in the Biish-Irdu massif. The largest glacier, Bolshoy Maashey, is about 6 miles long and has an area of 5 square miles. It lies on the northern slope and descends to an elevation of 7,775 feet, which is 330 feet lower than the timber line.

4) In the southern Altai, insolation is strong, dry steppes and semidesert are near by, and precipitation is light because the moist winds are intercepted by mountain chains lying farther south. On the weakly dissected northern slope numerous small cirque glaciers descend to 8,500 or 9,000 feet. Only the deeply dissected relief at the sources of the Ak-Alakha (Argut system) provides conditions favorable for the accumulation of snow. Here peaks 11,800 feet high that alternate with lower saddles at 10,500 feet have complex cirques occupied by firn fields. Alakhin Glacier, 4.8 miles long and 7.7 square miles in area is, evidently, the largest glacier of the Altai within the USSR.

The high ranges of southeast Altai—Sailiugem and Chikhachev—are regions of smaller glaciation. They have a small amount of precipitation but a high snow line. Few of the eastern ranges, however, rise above the snow line: Kura, Korgon, and Sumultin. These ranges have very small glaciers and semipermanent snow fields.

The majority of Altai glaciers do not have large firn fields connected with them. Most are fed by snow and ice avalanches that break away from the snow and ice that cling to the steep slopes surrounding the glacier. The Altai glaciers move approximately 5.5 inches to 18 inches in 24 hours, and they continually recede, contract, divide, and separate. The western half of Katun Glacier has completely separated from the eastern, the junction between the parts of Berelsk Glacier has disappeared, and the thickness and width of the glacial tongues has decreased. The rate of recession in the past few years, according to direct measurements, is from 16.5 feet to 82.5 feet.

HYDROGRAPHY

There are many lakes in the Altai. They vary greatly in size, origin, regime, and connections with the river systems. There are lakes in tectonic depressions—(Teletskoye and Marka-Kul, for example) a great number of shallow mountain lakes, and many glacial lakes.

Teletskoye Lake lies at an altitude of 1,550 feet, far in the mountains of the northeastern part of the Altai. Its area is 89 square miles, it is 48 miles long, its average width is 2 miles, and it consists of two parts. The longer, south-ern part trends approximately north-south; the shorter, northern section extends east-west. The southern part resembles a Norwegian fiord, but its shoreline, instead of being dissected and tortuous, is straight and almost devoid of peninsulas and bays. In many places cliffs as high as 6,600 feet rise perpendicularly out of the water, and there is practically no low shoreline. Because of the steep banks, the area of the lake is the same at both high and low levels. The sides of the lake consist principally of epidote-chlorite schists, although in the southern part of the western shore there is a thick outcrop of granite (Altyn-Tau Range). The large rivers flowing into this part of the lake have cut deep gorges (Koksha River) and formed deltas extending far into the lake: the Chulyshman River delta is growing, that of the Koksha River is disintegrating. Many shallow streams empty into the lake over waterfalls. The shores of the northern (east-west) section are considerably lower (less than 2,600 feet) and descend gradually to the level of the lake. The shoreline is winding and is made up of loamy deposits.

Teletskoye Lake, which is a typical mountain lake, is the fourth deepest lake in the USSR. The depth of the southern part exceeds 660 feet for its entire length, except in the southern end, which is being filled with alluvium by the Chulyshman River. The shores drop abruptly to the lake bottom, the central part of which has a level surface: the depth, a few yards offshore, may reach 132 feet. The east-west section is much shallower, especially in the west, where it is not more than 66 feet deep. The deepest parts of the lake bottom are covered with dense layers of gray silt.

The high cliffs of the lake basin form a narrow, deep trough, into which air masses burst from the surrounding mountains. These air currents come from two directions: one flows from the southern tip of the lake to the source of the Biya River at the western end of the east-west section and is known as the *verkhovka,* the other, the *nizovka,* flows in the opposite direction—one may give way to the other within a single day. The more constant *verkhovka* rushes out of the narrow gorge of the Chulyshman River with much force and sweeps onto the lake, setting up waves as much as four feet high along its whole length. On clear summer days it blows from midnight to noon, and in winter, almost without interruption day and night, often not subsiding for several weeks. This wind, like a foehn, is accompanied by clear warm weather, low relative humidity (20 to 30 per cent), and a small but constant amount of precipitation. Thus,

along the southern part of the lake, on steppe soil that receives little precipitation (16 inches annually), the population gets good harvests. The *nizovka* is changeable and acts as an indicator of harsh weather and heavy rainfall.

Teletskoye Lake's chief tributary is the Chulyshman River, which contributes 72.5 per cent of the total flow into the lake. The only natural discharge of the lake is the Biya River, which carries out 98 per cent of the incoming water; the remaining 2 per cent is evaporated. The average annual variation in the lake level is about 13.2 feet. It is lowest at the end of March or the beginning of April. The level begins to rise with the first spring thaws, which come slowly until the average daily temperature increases nine degrees, at which time the snow in the mountains thaws rapidly and precipitation increases. The lake then rises very swiftly and reaches its highest level in June, only to begin to drop in July, which it continues to do for eight and a half months. Teletskoye regulates the water discharge of the Biya River and thus plays an important part in the economy of the province.

Teletskoye is a temperate lake although the low temperature of its water brings it close to the polar type. Temperatures of 57° to 61°F are never maintained for more than ten days, and then only near the surface of the water. On occasional days in August surface temperatures in the deep part of the lake may rise to 64°F. The top 30 feet of water are often warmed to above 50°F in summer but at a depth of 330 feet the constant temperature is 39°F, and at 890 feet is between 38° and 39°F. The low temperature of the lake water is a result of its depth, the lack of well-warmed shoals, and the mixing of the water by prolonged strong wind. The ice cover comes too late to insulate the lake against loss of warmth to the winter air. The extent of the ice cover varies from year to year; in three out of five years (1928–1932) the lake froze over completely. Breaking-up begins with the separation of ice from the shores about the end of April. Early in May the *verkhovka* breaks up the ice and by the middle of the

Map 2-III. Bathymetric map of Teletskoye Lake.

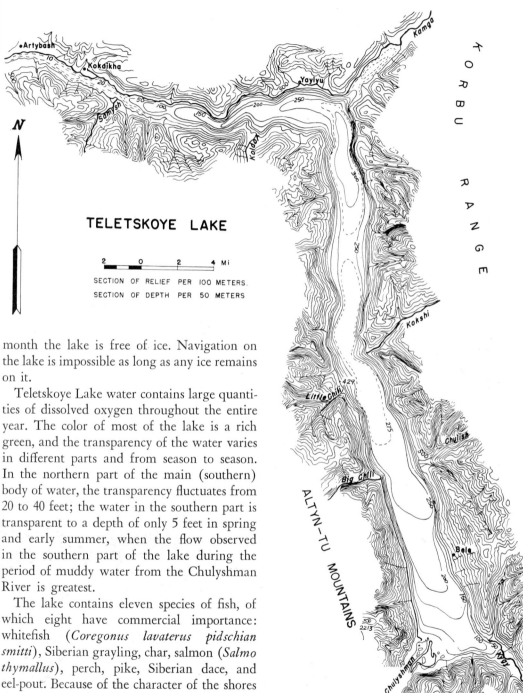

TELETSKOYE LAKE

SECTION OF RELIEF PER 100 METERS.
SECTION OF DEPTH PER 50 METERS

month the lake is free of ice. Navigation on the lake is impossible as long as any ice remains on it.

Teletskoye Lake water contains large quantities of dissolved oxygen throughout the entire year. The color of most of the lake is a rich green, and the transparency of the water varies in different parts and from season to season. In the northern part of the main (southern) body of water, the transparency fluctuates from 20 to 40 feet; the water in the southern part is transparent to a depth of only 5 feet in spring and early summer, when the flow observed in the southern part of the lake during the period of muddy water from the Chulyshman River is greatest.

The lake contains eleven species of fish, of which eight have commercial importance: whitefish (*Coregonus lavaterus pidschian smitti*), Siberian grayling, char, salmon (*Salmo thymallus*), perch, pike, Siberian dace, and eel-pout. Because of the character of the shores there are very few birds, and the lake seems deserted, yet the fascination of the unspoiled severe landscape of the lake attracts tourists.

Geologists differ as to the origin of Telet-

Fig. 2-7. The source of the Biya River in the northwest end of Teletskoye Lake. (*Drawing by S. P. Suslov.*)

skoye Lake. Some consider its basin a graben that originated in comparatively recent time, basing their opinion on its well-preserved exterior form and the fresh traces of tectonic processes which they believe created it—processes which certainly had a great influence on the morphology of the surrounding regions. Others consider Teletskoye Lake to be a tongue-like depression formed by a large Chulyshman glacier which expanded and deepened an elongated valley which was already here, leaving moraine deposits in the depression.

Marka-Kul is the largest alpine lake in the Altai; it has an area of 175 square miles and lies in the deepest part of a graben between the Kurchum and Asyu ranges at an altitude of 4,900 feet. The southern shore of the lake is steep, consisting of the edge of a horst that drops directly to the water. This cliff is cut by only a few streams; along its underwater base is a high pile of coarse products of erosion. On the lake's northern shore, where the face of the horst is four to six miles inland, there is space for the accumulation of alluvium from five large tributaries. The Topolevka River, the chief tributary, has built a wide delta into the lake and is gradually filling the eastern edge with alluvium.

The outlet of Marka-Kul is the Kaldzhir River, which flows into the Cherny Irtysh. The lake is of rather uniform depth with a maximum of 78 feet. Its gradually sloping bottom becomes flat near the center, and is covered with ice almost the entire year. The mountain streams fed by melting snow and springs; their water is only slightly mineralized, and this helps to keep it a fresh-water lake. The temperature regime of Marka-Kul is that of a temperate lake. The temperature of the surface layer in July is 61° to 62.5°F, the bottom temperature about 45°F. The lake freezes over at the end of November and the ice breaks up in the middle of May: the average duration of ice cover is 173 days. The water is deep green—lighter in the north—its transparency is 20 to 23 feet. Many fish breed here: grayling is the most common. Because of the wealth of fish there are numerous birds on the shores.

Many shallow lakes of the Altai were created by glacial activity—there are three different types, each with a different origin: (1) tarns, (2) ground-moraine lakes, and (3) moraine-dam lakes. The first are most common in high-mountain relief, the second as usually found on surviving sections of the ancient peneplain, and the third in the upper parts of glacial valleys.

1) Tarns, which lie on the bottoms of cirques and are often found at the very edge of the permanent snow, are always small, 20 to 35 feet deep. Their bottoms slope abruptly away from the precipitous wall of the cirque, along whose base are high cones of talus. On the opposite side, the tarn is dammed by bare, coarse moraine rocks, across which water usually flows. Some large tarns are dammed by material from mountain landslides. The tarns' sources of water are snow and rainfall; thus mineralization is extremely slight. When the snow thaws the level of the tarns is raised. In summer the upper six-foot layer of water in most tarns is well warmed, yet some are covered with ice almost the entire year. The water is dark green; transparency is slight. Few contain fish.

2) Ground-moraine lakes are scattered by the hundreds in the landscape of the ancient peneplain, especially in the eastern Altai with its gradually sloping water divides and poor drainage. They have sloping shores, formed of shallow deposits of moraine material. Their water is dark, since it contains an abundance of organic matter carried from nearby peat bogs. They vary greatly in size and shape. The largest is Dzhulu-Kul, on the Chulyshman plateau at an altitude of 7,210 feet; it is 6 miles long and its greatest depth is 23 feet.

3) Numerous picturesque moraine-dam lakes are located in glacial valleys at heights of 3,300 to 8,580 feet. Their number is explained by the gradual gradients of many rivers of the Altai. Their basins reflect the shape of the bottom of the glacial valley containing them, hence most are elongated and have precipitous shores. The longitudinal gradient of the lake bottoms is slight. The thick terminal moraines that dam these lakes may rise dozens or even hundreds of yards above the level of a lake. The depth of the lakes averages about

Fig. 2-8. Balyktykol, a cirque lake which is the source of the Uymen River.

Fig. 2-9. Kochurlinsk Lake, a morainal lake at the foot of the northern slope of the Katun Ridge.

30 feet but increases with the size. The largest of them (Taymenye) has the greatest depth— 224 feet. Glaciers feed these lakes, and retreating glaciers are slowly filling them with silt: their water may contain so much glacial silt that its color is a cloudy white. Those situated near glaciers gradually silt up and form broad shallows or swamps (Shavlinskoye), and some (Nizhne Kochurlinskoye) are being converted into river beds with marshy banks. Outlets may cut through the moraine embankment and deepen to such an extent that the lake is drained.

Not only elevation and depth but also glacial feeding influence the thermal condition of moraine-dam lakes. In summer shallow lakes in the immediate vicinity of glaciers (Nizhne Akkem) have the lowest surface temperatures; the highest are those of shallow lakes far from glaciers (Nizhne Multin). Deep lakes have comparatively low temperatures, a thin snow cover that can be blown off by strong winds,

and the formation of ice on some tributary rivers.

The color and transparency of lake water depend entirely on the presence and magnitude of glacial feeding. The farther the lake is from a glacier, the greater the transparency. This is noticeable in the little Multin lake chain: transparency in the upper lake is 72 inches, in the middle 145 inches, and in the lower 148 inches. Transparency increases during the winter, reaching a maximum in spring, when much clarifying snow water from the neighboring slopes enters the lakes. In the hottest part of summer, when the glaciers thaw vigorously, transparency is at a minimum. The color of the water depends on the amount of glacial silt it contains. In the lakes with the least transparency, the color of the water is milk-gray (Lake Akkem), as the transparency increases the color becomes milky-green (Kycherlinskoye) and finally changes to rich, dark turquoise (Taymenye). The lakes contain only a few cold-water fish: arctic grayling (*Thymallus arcticus*) or Siberian miller's thumb (*Cottus sibiricus*).

The Altai has a complex hydrographic network. The water divides of river basins do not conform strictly with its ranges. Some rivers (Argut, Katun) cut gorges through the highest mountain ranges, and the sources of some rivers that flow through different basins begin on the same marshy plateau or even in the same valley, without a visible watershed: for example, the sources of the Bashkaus and upper Chuya rivers. The longitudinal profile of most rivers is concave: that is, their gradients are very steep in the upper stretches (150 to 250 feet per mile), swiftly decrease in the middle course (5 to 25 feet per mile), and in the lower course become almost a level, dropping no more than 2.5 feet per mile. The sections of rivers on the old peneplain or in valleys with flat bottoms, regardless of altitude, have low gradients. The rapids in the rivers of the Altai make navigation impossible and flotage difficult. There are few waterfalls on the large rivers because of the relatively uniform thickness and structure of the rocks composing the Altai. The Katun River, which flows from south to north across the Altai, joins the Biya, which flows out of Lake Teletskoye, to make up the Ob River. The Irtysh also collects water from the western and southern Altai.

The hydroelectric importance of the Altai rivers is great because of their steady supply of water. Thawing snow yields most of the water; second in importance is the runoff of the abundant precipitation, which is great because of the imperviousness of the rocks and the steepness of the slopes. Ground water con-

Fig. 2-10. The Uymen River, typical of the Altai Mountains.

tributes a small amount. Thus, the water of the Uba River consists of 50 to 55 per cent meltwater, 25 to 35 per cent rainwater, and about 15 per cent ground water.

The majority of the rivers (Biya, Kaldzhir) flow out of lakes—natural settlement tanks and regulators of discharge—and thus have a steady supply of pure, transparent water. Rivers fed by glaciers even though they are short and have small basins, may have a heavy discharge; for example, the Iyedygem River, whose total length is 15 miles, has a summer discharge of 33 cubic yards a second. The Katun River, in whose basin is concentrated 80 per cent of the glaciation of the Altai, receives 30 per cent of its water from glaciers. The water of rivers fed directly by large glaciers is saturated with glacial silt which makes it muddy or milky-green; such glacier-fed rivers are usually avoided by those birds that feed on fish.

The varying elevations and trends of ranges cause climatic conditions to differ and this in turn causes variations in the discharge patterns of the rivers. The snow begins to thaw first in the valleys, then on the upper parts of the slopes, and finally in the high mountains; this provides natural regulation of the summer discharge. The long period of maximum flow during which there are sharp fluctuations of level, is followed by a rather long period of steady flow in late summer. The combination of meltwater from rapidly thawing snow and runoff from the warm spring cloudbursts cause large floods in the spring. The floods of autumn, when precipitation increases, are smaller than those of spring, because at this time there is little meltwater discharge and part of the precipitation in the mountains consists of snow. The rivers discharge the least water at the end of February and the beginning of March.

In winter most sections of the rivers are covered by ice more than 3 feet thick, but the rapids do not freeze over until the middle of winter and this causes the formation of bottom ice, a typical phenomenon in the Altai, and also leads to the formation of ice layers on the rivers. In some sections the water can neither pass under the ice because the channel is clogged with sludge and bottom ice, nor raise the thick layer of ice frozen to the shores. Below the unfrozen rapids it overflows the surface of the ice, then freezes to form thick layers. In spring the movement of ice is hindered by ice jams in narrow parts of river valleys, where thick ice layers have not yet broken. The spring ice movement takes place with comparatively small discharges of water, and the rivers are usually clear of ice before the main flood from thawing snow in the upper basin begins.

In the Altai conditions are favorable for the construction of hydroelectric stations. Rivers are deep with steep gradients and there is an alternation of narrow sections of valleys for dams and wide sections for reservoirs. The main disadvantages are the rapid silting and the small winter flow, which will necessitate the construction of huge catch basins and artificial reservoirs.

A mighty flow of cheap electric energy is now being transmitted across a high-voltage line from the new Ust-Kamenogorsk hydroelectric station on the Irtysh. In the narrow pass of the Irtysh that lies just below the mouth of the tributary Bukhtarma, the construction of the Bukhtarma hydroelectric station will be started soon. Above the dam will be a vast artificial lake that will be joined with Lake Zaysan. This will allow a uniform flow of water independent of the annual fluctuation in precipitation. It has been estimated that the rivers of the Altai can produce more than ten million kilowatt hours of electricity annually.

The existence of salmon (*Salmo thymallus*), char, and grayling in the rivers of the Altai associates them with Siberian lakes. The presence, in the southeastern part of the Altai, of three species of *Oreoleuciscus* suggests the influence of Central Asia.

SOILS, PLANTS, AND ANIMALS

To accord with its geographic position, the northern and central Altai should be covered by steppe vegetation, the southern part with semiarid vegetation. These features of east-west zonality are clear in the foothills of the Altai and show up against a background of vertical zonality in other landscapes of the region, as in the deep and broad grabens and glacial troughs. In this mountainous region, where the altitude ranges from 1,500 to 15,000 feet, and the relief is complex, the basic pattern of the distribution of vegetation, soils, and animals is vertical zonality, in some places (e.g., western Altai) so well expressed that it is possible to visualize the relief from a map that shows only the soil cover.

Steppe, forest, and high-mountain vertical zones are distributed in conformity with local conditions, often they jut into each other and interweave closely. The borders between these zones are gradual transitions; on northern slopes they are lower than on southern ones. The upper borders of the forest zone rise sharply from north to south and from west to east. Similarly, the lower timber line lies at an altitude of 1,200 feet in the west, at about 3,300 feet in the south, and at 4,620 to 6,000 feet on the Mongolian side. Only in the extreme northeast does the forest zone of the Altai blend with the lowland taiga. Thus, to the east and south, the forest zone rises upward along the mountain slopes, gradually plays out, and finally disappears in the extreme southeastern region, where the steppe zone abuts directly against the high-elevation zone. For example, in the Sailiugem Range, areas sparsely overgrown with fescue and wormwood not only lie alongside damp, green, alpine meadows and thickets of small polar birch, but also alternate with them in the most complex manner, depending on such local conditions as insolation, drainage, and moisture in the soil. This attracts the most surprising faunal combinations, so that, for example, the steppe eagle and the tundra ptarmigan dwell here side by side.

The distribution of vertical zones is complicated by the forms of relief and the exposure of the slopes. Forests do not grow on high, level plateaus, even though these plateaus are below the timber line. The Ukok Plateau, with an average height of 7,260 feet, is treeless, whereas in the neighboring valley of the Kara-Alakha River the forest rises to an altitude of 7,850 feet. The southern slopes of the mountains, especially in the east-west ranges of the southern part of the region, are subject to desiccation by insolation and southwestern winds. Northern slopes, where a large amount of snow accumulates, are shaded and thaw slowly. Thus, in a valley, the dark strip of forest on the slope with northern exposure may contrast sharply with the bright treeless slope with southern exposure—a typical feature of the landscape of Central Altai. In many places dry steppe with typical xerophytic vegetation, many locusts, and such steppe birds as the horned lark lies near typical spruce-fir-pine taiga where wood grouse find shelter. Larch grows on the southern slopes of some ranges because it demands less humidity than the dark coniferous taiga on the northern slopes.

Here it is possible to observe the well-known struggle between vertical zones at their points of contact. The forest, whose upper border is the high-elevation zone and whose lower is steppe zone, subsists at the limits of its possible existence; therefore, the slightest alteration in external conditions may cause a shift of the forest boundary in one direction or the other. Young, sturdy, and healthy larches on moraine terraces near Mensu (Belukha) glacier suggest an encroachment of the forest upon the steppe zone. On the other hand, the gradual downward withdrawal of the forest is graphically marked by the multitude of dry, dead trees and the lack of undergrowth near its upper border: a thick mossy cover and thickets of small polar birch have without doubt supplanted the taiga. The moss cover and the closely entangled boughs of the birch do not permit the seeds of the conifers to fall directly onto the surface of the ground. The shade and excess moisture destroy the young shoots of the few seeds that succeed in reaching the earth. Further, one severe winter can destroy trees of many years' standing, and seedlings replace these trees only with great difficulty.

Man's strong influence on the natural vegetation is especially noticeable in the inhabited districts. Logged or burned-over sections of the dark coniferous forests are replaced by temporary forests of birch and aspen. Prolonged grazing of cattle leads to a changed composition of forest, alpine meadows, and steppe pastures.

Human activity in subalpine regions and in the upper part of the forest belt (brush burning, logging, cattle grazing, haying) have aided grass in the struggle between it and the forest. Widely separated meadows among spotty deciduous forests have been slowly transformed into vast regions capable of sustaining hundreds of thousands of cattle. With the aid of sedge (*Carex pediformis*) a very dense turf was formed, which interfered so much with the further growth of forests that trees and brush surrendered the region to meadows. A major part was played in the creation of the meadow landscape of Altai by Siberian stag-breeding, which began here a hundred years ago. The building of fences to enclose the Siberian stag required thousands of large stakes which were procured from the neighboring forests. The enclosures were built on the south-facing slopes because of the better pastures there, but the north-facing slopes were used to grow grasses since the Siberian stag required great supplies of hay in winter. Because of this, the land was cleared of forests. The enclosures were often moved to new pastures, causing further clearing of forested areas. Thus, the peculiar mountain-meadow landscape so characteristic of the southern Altai is in part a creation of man.

In the northeastern part of the Altai, agriculture is possible only to about 1,500 feet, but in the southern and eastern parts, in deep steppe valleys, cultivation takes place up to 4,125 feet (Chulyshman River). The development of grain crops in elevated regions is affected by early autumn frosts and frosts caused by local inversions of temperature during the growing period. Consequently, it is necessary to plant the warm southern slopes with wheat, tomatoes, and cucumbers, and barley and oats only in the colder bottoms of valleys. The continental climate of the Altai, with its rather high temperatures during the growing period, should make it possible to raise the altitude at which crops are grown to approximately 6,000 feet in some parts of the region. For example, in the Chuya Steppe, at an elevation of 5,775 feet, experiments in sowing Abyssinian barley and peas, lettuce, turnip, rape, and alfalfa were successful. The chief problem is the selection of early-ripening and frost-resistant crops. It is also possible to utilize valuable wild plants such as raspberries, currants, and gooseberries, which are encountered at a height of 5,900 feet, have an excellent flavor and aroma, and are quite large. Plants such as giant onion are also found as high as 5,280 feet; here, too, are such first-class fodder grasses as yellow lucerne and sainfoin.

The Altai fauna is rich and diversified: 328 species of birds alone have been counted. The main reasons for this are: (1) convergence in the Altai of European-Ob fauna such as wolverine and trydactylous woodpecker, eastern Siberian fauna such as Siberian stag and stony wood grouse, and Central Asian fauna such as antelope and mountain turkey; (2) a complex history of landscapes with recent destructive glaciation and penetration into the Altai of arctic fauna such as reindeer and tundra ptarmigan; and (3) a diversity of modern faunal environments. Thus, the Altai is not a single faunal unit that has received its animal population comparatively recently from surrounding zoogeographical regions. The Altai fauna contains many fur-bearing animals (squirrel, otter) and birds of commercial value (wood grouse, hazel grouse). For the protection of sable and stag, which are being rapidly exterminated, a large game reserve has been set up south of Lake Teletskoye. The steppe pasturage, forests, subalpine and alpine meadows of the Altai offer broad prospects for the development of grazing land for cattle, sheep, and horses. In the southeast, camels, domesticated yaks, and hybrids of yaks and cows can also be raised.

Steppe Zone

The steppe zone in the northern, western, and southern foothills of the Altai is a rather broad strip of mixed grass, feather-grass, and chernozem steppe. Narrow strips of steppe penetrate deep into the mountain region along broad river valleys which are open to the premountain plains. In the central Altai, at a height of about 3,300 feet, the strips break up into islands that are called mountain steppes. In the southeast, the steppe zone rises above 5,000 feet and becomes more arid; here highmountain steppes blend into semideserts. In the foothills of the Altai, with their gentle intermediate-mountain landscape, the meadowsteppe vegetation forms a wide belt that surrounds the mountain-taiga center of the Altai. Nearer the mountains, the amount of moisture in the soil increases and in many places loamy chernozem develops into fertile soil with deep effervescence—frequently 56 inches deep, as compared with a norm of 20 inches elsewhere.

The narrow and in some places discontinuous fringe bordering the flat steppes consists of a brushy steppe containing thickets of honeysuckle (*Lonicera tatarica*), dog rose (*Rosa acicularis*), spirea (*Spiraea hypericifolia*), and pea shrub (*Caragana arborescens*). In the south, the dwarf almond (*Amygdalus nana*) is predominant. Amid thickets are separate patches of richly colored vari-grass steppe with yellow blossoms of the lily (*Hemerocallis flava*), fragrant white caps of dropwort (*Filipendula hexapetala*), and rose blossoms of sainfoin (*Onobrychis sativa*). Grasses spread abundantly in the higher mountains, where

feather grasses attain a luxuriant growth, but they do not drive out the dicotyledons.

On the rocky soil of steep slopes and craggy ridges there are large areas of stony steppe which penetrate far into the Altai along river valleys, at first along both slopes, then along the south-facing slope only. In the rocky steppe, on an equal footing with the plentiful dicotyledons, especially species of *Astragalus* and *Oxytropis,* are much desert oat (*Avena desertorum*) and eastern feather grass (*Stipa orientalis*). Deep in the mountains near outcrops of granite, solitary pine groves and clusters of aspen and birch begin to appear. Clusters of bird cherry and mountain ash find shelter in places along the northern slopes of ridges, and the grass beneath them, which contains many steppe species, gives the landscape the character of a wooded-mountain meadow.

Steppe vegetation resembling that of Central Asia penetrates deep into the central Altai from the Zaysan depression and the Irtysh River valley, where there are semideserts with *Artemisia* on brown and light-chestnut soil. This vegetation climbs, in places, to a height of 5,000 feet. A belt of feather- and fescue-grass steppe at an altitude of 2,000 to 2,800 feet consists largely of feather grass (*Stipa capillata*) and fescue grass (*Festuca sulcata*) and large areas of shrubs: spirea (*Spiraea hypericifolia*), pea shrub (*Caragana frutex*). The steppes are used as pasturage during the growing period, and crops of millet, wheat, muskmelons, and watermelons are also grown where water is available for irrigation.

The belt of feather-grass and mixed-grass steppes occupies the high foothills and lower sections of mountain slopes from 2,800 to 5,000 feet and is noted for the height and thickness of its grass cover, the abundance of such grasses as steppe alfalfa (*Medicago falcata*), of *Artemisia sericea,* and of the pinnate feather grasses (*Stipa joannis* and *S. rubens*). One finds sections of brush steppe with almond (*Amygdalus nana*) and barberry (*Berberis heteropoda*). In these steppes, the cultivation of rye, barley, wheat, oats, and flax, which do not require irrigation, is widespread. Rivers and streams that flow through the steppe are fringed by walls of huge black poplars, silver poplars, and willows, under which tall grass grows. In the narrow valleys of the north-facing slopes are thickets of bird cherry, dog rose, spirea, and hawthorn.

Mountain steppes in discontinuous strips and separate patches—such as Uymonsk, Abaysk, Kansk, Tenginsk, and Ursulsk steppes —extend deep into the forest zone. Their vegetation is similar to that of the steppes of the western foothills. Locked-in valleys have a definite continental climate with less precipitation than the adjoining mountains. In summer they warm up considerably, but in winter they are very cold because of the stability of the cold air that flows into them from the neighboring mountains: the amplitude of their temperature is thus rather high. The well-weathered fluvioglacial lake deposits in these valleys are porous, and water quickly percolates into the soil. This good drainage, in conjunction with the small amount of precipitation and the high summer temperatures of the air and soil, contributes to the development of xerophytic vegetation. The soil of the mountain steppes is principally southern chernozem and dark-chestnut with a humus content as high as 8 per cent. Solonchak soil is also found.

In early spring, when the moisture content of the soil is high, the mountain steppes are covered for a short time with a variegated cover of such blooming perennials as crowfoot, aconite, adonis, and anemone. On the rapidly drying soil, under the hot sun, this spring vegetation quickly burns out and is replaced by steppe grasses among which are many found in the rocky-steppe and some semiarid species. In these steppes the grass covers 80 to 90 per cent of the soil and grows to a height of 20 to 30 inches. The cover comprises the following grasses and herbs: feather grass (*Stipa joannis*), Siberian feather grass (*S. sibirica*), capillary feather grass (*S. capillata*), fescue grass (*Festuca sulcata*), koeleria (*Koeleria gracilis*), steppe alfalfa (*Medicago falcata*), and sainfoin (*Onobrychis sibirica*). Among the grasses of the rocky steppe there are many species of

Astragalus and *Oxytropis,* of which one hundred kinds have been counted in the Altai, and edelweiss (*Leontopodium sibiricum*). The vegetation of the rockiest mountain steppes (Ursulsk) has a semiarid character; scarcely 50 per cent of the soil is covered and the grass is one to two inches high. Typical is the pres-

Fig. 2-11. Siberian edelweiss (*Leontopodium sibiricum*) on the steppes within the Altai Mountains.

ence of such semiarid species as summer cypress (*Kochia prostrata*), winter fat (*Eurotia ceratoides*), and lichen (*Parmelia vagans*).

The mountain steppes of the Altai constitute the main pastures of the region. Their vegetation has much value as fodder because of the abundance of salts that it contains; this makes it more nutritious than the fresh forage of subalpine meadows in the forests. In winter these steppes have almost no snow cover, and cattle can pasture the year round on green fodder. Large areas of the steppe are cultivated, as at Uymonsk, but in some at higher elevations, such as Abaysk at 4,290 feet, grain does not always ripen and plowed fields are rare. In especially arid years, it is necessary to resort to artificial irrigation. In the stony soil wheat ripens quickly, but the early autumn frosts have compelled the inhabitants to develop early-ripening varieties of grain. *Uymonka* wheat is early-ripening (its vegetative period is 73 days) and hardy, like barley; both are grown rather high in the mountains. The mountain steppes are rich in fragrant plants from which valuable volatile oils can be extracted, e.g., *Panzeria lanata:* if these plants were cultivated it would be unnecessary to import the volatile oils that are the raw material for the perfume industry.

In the mountain steppes are countless susliks, red duck (*Casarca ferruginea*), crane (*Grus virgo*), and chat (*Oenanthe isabellina*). Grasshoppers chirp and cicadas crackle at the height of summer.

The steppe is indigenous to the broad glacial troughs of the large rivers, such as the Katun, Chuya, and Chulyshman. Especially in their lower courses, where the valleys are widest, the steppe is broadly developed. Higher in the valleys the character of the steppes changes from Siberian to Mongolian. In the lower part of the Katun River valley, on loamy chernozem of second and third terraces, such typical vegetation of foothill steppes as steppe alfalfa grows. On rocks and large accumulations of talus are stone-loving plants: *Rhododendron dauricum,* covered in spring, and sometimes in fall, with beautiful lilac-rose flowers; Siberian barberry (*Berberis sibirica*), gooseberry (*Ribes aciculare*), and other drought-resistant shrubs. Farther south, on high terraces with chestnut soil, the proportion of steppe plants increases to 90 per cent. The cover becomes more sparse and stunted, and mixed with feather grass (*Stipa consanguinea*) are steppe wheat grass (*Agropyron cristatum*), thistles (*Echinops ritro*), and aster (*Aster altaicus*). At higher altitudes the vegetation has a semiarid Mongolian appearance; growing on crags are *Panzeria lanata* and gigantic (three feet high) ephedra (*Ephedra nebrodensis*).

The lower part of the Chulyshman Valley is an *Artemisia* and grass steppe with soil of a chestnut type. Yet at a height of 4,250 feet, on south-facing slopes, meadow-steppe plants grow on dark-colored chernozem-like soil. On north-facing slopes, semiswampy soil that freezes to a depth of 35 to 40 inches is found under dark-coniferous forests. In a narrow strip along the northern rivers are isolated pine trees; farther south these are replaced by laurel poplars (*Populus laurifolia*) and thickets of shrubs, e.g., *Hippophae rhamnoides*. On terraces along the river valleys are many small fields where wheat and barley are grown by artificial irrigation.

The vegetation of the high-mountain steppes in the higher southeastern Altai, strongly resembles that of the stony steppes of northern Mongolia, but has nothing in common with that of the steppes of the western Altai. A valley, 5,722 to 6,270 feet in altitude, with a level bottom, constituted of thick layers of conglomerate, and surrounded by high mountains, forms the Chuya steppe. It has a very harsh climate and only 4.4 inches of precipitation in summer. Winter is severe, with temperatures as low as −44.4°F. The snow cover is very thin (2.8 inches) and is often blown off by strong winds; permafrost exists at a depth of three feet. Rivers often freeze to the bottom. Summer has sharp daily amplitudes of temperature. On the passes (e.g., Tashanty) in the Sailiugem Range, caravans often are surprised by snowstorms in the middle of summer. Chuya steppe has many features of the Mongolian semidesert. An extremely scanty, dwarfed, and thin vegetation, withered and gray, covers no more than one-tenth of the soil and is barely noticeable on gravelly areas. The vegetation is uniform and contains purely Mongolian or endemic species: a mixture of feather grass (*Stipa glareosa*) *Dontostemon perennis, Astragalus dilutus,* pea tree (*Caragana bungei*), and chee grass (*Lasiagrostis splendens*). Under this vegetation brown carbonaceous soil has developed, sometimes with efflorescences of salts. The bottomlands contain carbonaceous solonchaks with unusual solonchak vegetation. Along riverbanks are solitary larches.

Another and similar steppe is the Kura steppe, which lies along the Chuya River at an altitude of 4,950 feet. Here most plants creep along the ground; various species of astragalus bury themselves in the earth and display only flowers and leaves above it. The plants appear to be dwarfs, but the underground parts have almost normal growth.

The Ukok Plateau, lying among the mountains at a height of 7,260 feet, resembles in many ways the Chuya and Kura steppes. Its climate is severe, it has only 10 inches of precipitation, sharp changes in temperature, and a snow cover 2 to 5 inches thick. Surrounded by high mountains, the surface of Ukok Plateau is made hilly by numerous old moraines, among which are many lake basins. Because of the plateau's high elevation and the peculiarities of its relief, the vegetation of the Ukok Plateau differs from that along the Chuya River: (1) there are no trees or shrubs; (2) it does not comprise the plants peculiar to the Chuya Steppe; (3) rocky-steppe plants are widespread. On the Ukok Plateau chestnut soil has developed, and large areas are covered with efflorescent salts, to which a few saliferous species such as *Elymus dasystachys* are linked.

The fauna of the high-mountain steppes has Mongolian characteristics. Many species establish the connection of the Altai with Central Asia: of the mammals, the black tailed Persian gazelle (*Gazella subgutturosa*); of the birds, the goose (*Eulabeia indica*) buzzard (*Buteo hemilasius*), *Syrrhaptes paradoxus,* and Mongolian ground sparrow (*Pyrgilauda davidiana*), which in summer dwells at altitudes as high as 10,000 feet but in winter descends to about 4,000 feet. The high-mountain steppes provide good fodder for numerous flocks of sheep, and for the yaks (*Poephagus grunniens*) and *sarlyki* kept by the natives.

Forest Zone

The forests of the Altai, unlike the lowland taiga, do not contain vast bogs; grass grows vigorously beneath the trees. The dark-colored soil is of a podzolic type, some is swampy, and near the steppes the soil is clayey. The five basic coniferous species are larch, Siberian pine, fir, spruce, and pine. The relief, climate, and types of soil affect the distribution of each. There are few deciduous trees in the mountain forests. Only birch and aspen are found there and they occupy cut-over land, burned areas, and narrow strips along the riverbanks. To the south and southeast, the decrease in precipitation and humidity causes the thick forest to die out gradually. It is replaced by a thin forest of larch with an undergrowth of meadow-steppe and subalpine grasses. In the humid northeast Altai, forests of spruce, fir, and Siberian pine, similar to the Siberian Lowland taiga, are common. In the western Altai, where precipitation is heavy, fir forests predominate. In the central Altai, the forest zone becomes discontinuous, being broken by strips and patches of steppe. In the southern and southeastern sections, which are extremely dry, the forests are unimportant.

The distribution of the species of trees varies with altitude. Pine is not found above 2,300 feet, birch climbs to 4,950 feet, and aspen goes somewhat higher; spruce and fir are stunted within a hundred yards of the timber line. Siberian pine and larch form the timber line, Siberian pine being dominant where the slopes are always moist. Near the timber line the continuous taiga cover begins to thin out, and the trees grow in compact groups with glades between them. Here are scrub birch (*Betula humilis*) thickets, and stunted fir and spruce with deformed trunks, flag-shaped crowns, and branches that spread along the ground. If the weight of the snow presses young fir saplings to the ground they may send out auxiliary roots from which young shoots with thick needles spring up. The result is a group of closely growing young trees, joined by a horizontal trunk that is concealed beneath Bryophyta. Siberian pines near the timber line have gnarled crowns, somewhat blunt at the top, and one-sided, inclined in accord with the direction of the prevailing wind.

Fig. 2-12. The character of the pine forest near its upper borders among the sources of the Kara-Kokshi River. (*Drawing by S. P. Suslov.*)

Larch trees, the sturdiest of the conifers, are not one-sided; however, they lose their tops. In severe winters the young needles of Siberian pines may be killed by the sharp fluctuations of temperature and desiccation. This leads to the starvation and death of entire branches. Isolated Siberian pines may grow far above the timber line; in the central Altai they are found at a height of 8,500 feet.

In the dense, mixed forests of spruce, fir, and Siberian pine in the cold and moist northeastern Altai, Siberian pine is the dominant species. In many places it may yield to spruce—e.g., above 3,000 feet on soil saturated with cold water—although higher up almost pure stands may grow. In the drier central Altai it forms only a narrow strip in the upper part of the forest zone, girdling the high-mountain zone and separating it from the deciduous forests below. In the arid southeastern and southern parts of the Altai, Siberian pine forests resemble the sparse subalpine forest, with an undergrowth of small polar birch.

There are many well-defined types of Si-

berian pine forests. In the lower part of the forest zone the forests are of two kinds: those with a ground cover of thick grass and those in which the cover consists mainly of green moss. The first, the most productive forests, grow on the well-moistened fine podzolic or weakly podzolic soil of mountain slopes. They have an undergrowth of spirea (*Spiraea chamaedrifolia*), honeysuckle (*Lonicera coerulea*), and dog rose (*Rosa acicularis*), and the first tier of the tall grass cover consists of beach grass and monkshood, the second of white geranium and forget-me-not. The forests in which the green moss grows are found on terraces where there is much moisture and considerable podzolizing of soil; they are less productive. Their undergrowth is sparse and contains many such northern plants as red bilberry, whortleberry, oxalis, and honeysuckle. The green-moss cover is almost solid. The dead branches of trees are hung with countless lichens; white ones of the genus *Usnea*, black ones of the *Bryopogon*.

The Siberian-pine forests of the higher part

Fig. 2-13. The pine forest on the mountain slopes near Teletskoye Lake.

of the forest zone are considerably less productive and have thin stands. The Siberian pine forests on rocky watershed crests and upper slopes, where there is very little fine soil, grow above a cover of bergenia. The individual trees are covered with branches and needles to the very bottoms of their trunks. Under the forest canopy are the broad, shiny leaves of *Bergenia crassifolia,* the roots of which contain much tannin and are used for tanning hides. Forests on the wider watersheds and the bottoms of the upper stream valleys have a crowberry ground cover. On slopes of low gradient, fine soil containing much moisture has accumulated, leading to the development of sandy–peaty–podzolic soil. Here, under the sparse stand of trees, many with dead tops, there is a solid moss-lichen cover and thick growths of small polar birch. Among subalpine meadows are islands of Siberian-pine forest whose trees are densely covered with needles.

These grow on rich, turfy, and latent podzolic soil that is well moistened by mountain streams. The undergrowth consists of honeysuckle, willow, and mountain ash, with stands of dense grass three or four feet tall and a moss cover growing on isolated loamy patches. The Siberian pine forests contain many squirrels, offer excellent wood for the manufacture of paper, and supply abundant harvests of pine nuts.

On the ranges of the western Altai, which have much more moisture than the other, there is a typical mountain-taiga region. Siberian fir and Siberian pine grow both in deep valleys and on slopes of all exposures and climb to high altitudes to form the timber line. In the central Altai there is less fir. It is confined mainly to the shady northern slopes of narrow, moist valleys, where it forms isolated islands at an altitude of about 3,000 feet and loses many of its grassy companions. None grows in the southeastern Altai. The typical shady fir forest of the western Altai is not the mossy taiga of the northern slopes, but is a forest with an admixture of aspen, a thick undergrowth, and ungovernable tall grasses. Here, such typical taiga plants as whortleberry or pyrola are not present, although oxalis is found. A great many species typical of European deciduous forests, such as *Paris quadrifolia,* grow here, as do many plants associated with linden forests—sweet woodruff (*Asperula odorata*), for example. There are many large forest ferns, but the moss cover is sparse. The soil, too, is different from that of the taiga, it is not podzolic but is a type of gray forest soil. In the fir forests on gentle slopes, the moisture content of the soil is greater, and the soil is more podzolic: many plants of the moist meadows grow here.

In the northeastern Altai pure stands of spruce grow on the bottoms of deep, narrow valleys, where the cold air that rolls off the mountains stagnates, leading to the formation of permafrost. Many of these spruce groves grow on wet peaty areas that fill old stream channels. Because the soil is cold and wet the spruce have many dead branches, which are

Fig. 2-14.   The pine forest near the upper forest border west of Teletskoye Lake. In the foreground, polar birch (*Betula rotundifolia*).

covered with white lichens. In the undergrowth are scrub birch (*Betula humilis*), most of it near the borders of the groves; scrub cinquefoil (*Potentilla fruticosa*), and a polar species of *Polygonum viviparum*. There is also a luxuriant mossy cover of green bryophytes (*Hylocomium* and *Aulacomnium*): groves on shaded portions of northern slopes have a sphagnum ground cover.

Pine is a tree of the foothills and low mountains. The greater humidity in the high mountains gives larch an advantage in the struggle for space, and pine does not grow above 2,300 feet. Along the warm dry valleys of large rivers, larch penetrates rather deeply into the mountains: to Leninogorsk, to Korgon village on the Charysh, to the village Cherny Anuy, to the mouth of the Bolshoya Sumulta River (tributary of the Katun), and above the mouth of the Shavla River on the Chulyshman. In the southern part of the Altai, it is encoun-

tered in the Narym Range. Pine keeps to stony, dry, open slopes, either on limestone outcrops or on rocky fluvioglacial terraces, forming narrow gallery-like forests along rivers. In the foothills it is mixed with birch and aspen, but somewhat higher it is mixed with larches. The undergrowth of the pine forests near the foothills contains no red bilberries or pyrola and few bryophytes: it consists mainly of meadow-steppe grasses—for example, steppe alfalfa (*Medicago falcata*)—and in spring, anemone (*Anemone altaica*), pasque flower (*Pulsatilla patens*), and lady's-slipper (*Cypripedium guttatum*).

Even below the limit of the spread of pine, Siberian larch appears, at first as single trees, then small groves. Gradually it takes preponderance over pine, and, above 2,300 feet, forms solid stands. In the northeastern Altai, and in some parts of the dry southeast, the mountain forests consist exclusively of larch. It occupies more space and occurs in more vertical zones than any other tree. It rises to a height of 6,600 feet, often forming the timber line, either alone or together with Siberian pine. Since it endures dryness and a rocky substrata well, it grows at lower altitudes than other conifers, descending into the open dry mountain steppes along the channels of mountain streams. Larch prefers the moderately moist gentle slopes of open valleys, but will grow almost anywhere, either in pure stands or mixed with other species.

Most mountain larch forests are light and park-like and contain many glades. The trees do not grow close together; centuries-old trees stand alone above a ground cover of thick grass. They have long branches with thin needles, which let the sun through; hence the earth is warmed more under larch forests than in the dark coniferous taiga, and underbrush and grasses grow directly under the trees as well as on open patches. Everywhere there are thick, almost impenetrable thickets of spirea (*Spiraea trilobata*), dog rose (*Rosa acicularis*), honeysuckle (*Lonicera coerulea*), currant (*Ribes rubrum*), barberry (*Berberis sibirica*), and the like. No flowers or grasses are exclusive to the larch forests; the ground cover is composed of common meadow-forest plants: e.g., iris (*Iris ruthenica*), globe flower (*Trollius asiaticus*), and pea vine (*Orobus luteus*). Atragene (*Atragene alpina*) climbs through the trees and masses of white blossoms hang from the branches. Countless larch seeds fall off the trees, but the thick, tall grasses choke the young shoots and larch is therefore not restored easily.

The two types of larch forests that are most productive are (1) the dense forests with scrub undergrowth of spirea and open grass cover that grow on weakly podzolic clayey soil, and (2) those with thick tall grass cover containing such brightly blooming plants as peony (*Paeonia anomala*) and anemone (*Anemone caerulea*). Some larch forests have a solid lichen cover that crackles underfoot, reminding one of the pine groves. Alpine plants, such as

violets, grow beneath the trees in the forests at high altitudes. In narrow valleys, above 3,300 feet, on moist soil, larch is mixed with dark conifers. The narrower and more moist the valley, the more Siberian pine, spruce, and fir appear, larch being displaced to the upper, more open slopes. Where the mixed forest is thick, typical taiga plants appear in the undergrowth, and the cover consists largely of moss. The larch suffers some oppression—the crowns become meager, many dead trees appear, and young trees develop slowly.

Forest fires have destroyed large areas of valuable forest, leaving vast burns. The spread and intensity of a forest fire depend on the kind of trees in the forest. Siberian-pine forests are easily destroyed by fire because the dense taiga vegetation allows the fire to jump swiftly from tree to tree. Other aids to fire are the thick needle cover, the lowness of the crowns, and the resinous quality of Siberian-pine needles. Pure larch forests suffer less from forest fires, since they are park-like and the trees stand far from one another. Larch has thick bark and a juicy needle with little resin; its dead lower branches drop off soon after dying. A rapid fire only chars the bark on the lower trunk, destroys the undergrowth, and interrupts fertility for a few years. In mixed forests a conflagration is selective; Siberian pine, spruce, and fir are completely burned out, but larch is preserved. The burns have an especially dismal appearance because a fire usually leaves the charred tree trunks standing; only the needles and the lower branches are destroyed. Rising high above the moist ground and thoroughly dried by the sun, the scorched trunks and branches of Siberian pine gradually shed their charred bark and, like gigantic white brushes, they stand for years, until their root system decays. They decay slowly; it takes thirty or forty years for the trunks to fall to the ground. Then, with the trunks pressed to the damp earth, decomposition is more rapid; bryophytes and lichen tighten about them, maintaining constant moisture, and the trunks gradually crumble into rot.

Fig. 2-15. Old pine burn with beach grass in the upper Biya River basin in the Altai Mountains. (*Drawing by S. P. Suslov.*)

The restoration of the forest takes place slowly, since it passes through a series of intermediate stages. In the first years after a fire, a burn is populated by beach grass, willow-herb (*Epilobium angustifolium*), and raspberry, which crowd out the remnants of taiga vegetation and choke the young growth of conifers. Then, birch and aspen form independent secondary stands that may survive for many years. Finally, under a canopy of birch and aspen, fir, spruce, and Siberian pine revive and slowly replace the birch and aspen. Above 4,600 feet, the restoration of Siberian pine and larch takes place without the intermediate stages because of the absence of raspberry, birch, and aspen. Soon after a fire, a brisk young generation of Siberian pine and larch is propagated without dangerous competitors.

Forest meadows attain exceptional growth in the Altai, and glades and open valleys adjoining forests are occupied by rich meadows that yield good harvests of hay. The majority of species are either those common to European wooded-taiga meadows or others that are similar: for example, European anemone (*Anemone ranunculoides*) and the globeflower (*Trollius europaeus*), may grow beside their Siberian counterparts, blue anemone (*Anemone caerulea*), and the globeflower (*Trollius asiaticus*). The species in the wooded meadows vary with the amount of moisture. The drier glades are covered with orchard grass (*Dactylis glomerata*), brome grass (*Bromus inermis*), meadow grass (*Poa pratensis*), and various dicotyledons—geranium (*Geranium pratense*), vetch, clover, and European pea vine (*Lathyrus pratensis*). Many southern slopes that are bare of forest because of the action of snow slides or

Fig. 2-16. Umbrella-like large herb, *Heracleum dissectum,* in the foreground, found in the damp glades of the mixed forest along the Ulalinka River.

the heat there, are moistened by meltwater from slowly melting patches of snow on their crests. On such slopes a thick and rich grass cover containing cow parsnip (*Heraclum dissectum*), *Bupleurum aureum,* and *Aconitum septentrionale* may grow to a height of three feet.

The taiga has unusual meadows of tall rich grasses that do not form a sod; between the thick stalks of the plants are patches of bare soil. These meadows grow near creeks that flow through the forest, in narrow and moist valleys, and in places where there are many springs. The grassy plants are gigantic, sometimes as much as twelve feet tall. A caravan can get lost in these seas of weeds, since a rider can orient himself only with the greatest difficulty. When resting or camping one must take precautions against losing one's horses in the weeds. Larkspur (*Delphinium elatum*) and aconite (*Aconitum septentrionale*) vie in growth with angelica (*Archangelica decurrens*); there are also such plants as violet (*Viola tricolor*) and starwort (*Stellaria holostea*).

The fauna of the forest zone of the Altai is rather similar to the fauna of the Western Siberian Lowland taiga. It consists of bear, wolverine, polecat, ermine, squirrel, flying squirrel, hare, elk, wild goat, musk deer, and roe deer. On the border of the zone are red deer (*Cervus elaphus canadensis n. sibiricus*), which have nonossifying horns. These are cut off annually, treated with boiling water, and exported to China, where for more than two thousand years they have been used in Chinese and Tibetan medicine. Other animals extremely common in the northeastern Altai taiga—e.g., susliks—are encountered only sporadically.

Characteristic birds of the thick spruce, fir, and Siberian-pine taiga are: wood grouse (*Tetrao urogallus*), hazel grouse (*Tetrastes bonasia*), the deaf-cuckoo (*Cuculus obtatus*), three-toed woodpecker (*Picoides tridactylus*), and nutcracker (*Nucifraga caryocatactes*). Other birds, such as forest pipit (*Anthus trivialis sibiricus*) or thrush (*Turdus viscivorus bonapartei*), populate the light larch forests.

High-Mountain Zone

The high-mountain zone of the Altai has no forest, but there are mountain meadows and thickets of small polar birch with a moss and lichen ground cover. The lower border of the zone varies considerably in height, from 6,300 feet in the northwest to about 8,000 feet in the southeast. The zone has a short growing period, strong insolation, sharp fluctuations of daily summer temperatures, and much wind. Snow remains on the high mountains until the end of May and in August the first snow falls. In the course of three months plants must blossom and bear fruit, otherwise early snowstorms and drifts will bury them before they can reach maturity.

In the high-mountain zone of the central Altai it is still early spring at the beginning of June. Everywhere thin patches of snow alternate with bare strips of ground; only the grasses have begun to break through; polar birch is just starting to blossom. Migratory birds appear, but only small flocks of them. The nesting period of birds begins early and the young hatch while the ground is still covered with snow; the parent birds search for food in the thawed patches of earth. Vegetation awakens quickly; spring is short and summer soon arrives. Night frosts and snowfalls are frequent throughout the summer. An alpine meadow in full flower, glittering with frost at sunrise, is a common picture in the Altai. Snow may fall toward evening or at night during the first half of summer, sometimes covering the ground to a depth of ten inches. Usually the snow begins to melt with the first rays of the rising sun, and by the end of day or on the day following, there is no trace of it. Such temporary changes bring harm neither to vegetation nor to animals—the blossoming of plants continues and birds sing and remain on their nests.

Plants of the high-elevation zone have made many diverse adaptations that safeguard them against the sharp lowering of summer temperatures and the increased evaporation at these heights. These plants are stocky or stretch out along the ground, which does not chill as quickly on cold nights as do the overlying layers of air. They have large roots, a small number of leaves, and an abundance of bright, large flowers; for example, the gentian (*Gentiana altaica*) has a small rosette of leaves, directly above which is a large deep-blue flower that is wider than the rosette. Even a woody plant, the willow (*Salix reticulata*) has a trunk no more than two or three inches long, only two leaflets, and an amentum at the top. Many plants, such as aconite (*Aconitum anthora*), that are large in wooded valleys are dwarfed here, but even though the stalk and leaves of these plants are much smaller the flowers maintain their size. Thus they appear relatively large and form a thick ground cover.

Flowers are more brightly colored in the high mountains than on lowlands, and this gives alpine meadows a striking brilliance. For protection from winds and cold, many dwarf plants conceal themselves in crevices, hiding their long runners under a layer of rocks and exposing only their leaves and flowers above the rock waste. Many plants decrease evaporation and cooling not only by stockiness, but by developing a thick fur whose thickness increases with elevation—e.g., edelweiss (*Leontopodium sibiricum*). Others secure protection by drawing their leaves and flowers together: as, for example, the saussurea (*Saussurea sorocephala*), which resemble grayish clumps of dirt. Plants such as swertia (*Swertia obtusa*), with smooth stalks and leaves, grow in the moist soils of northern slopes and along the banks of cold streams that run out of snow fields, where together with primrose (*Primula nivalis*) they stand above the neighboring grasses. These plants have large intercellular cavities containing air; during the day the bareness of the stalks allows this air to be highly warmed; at night the warm air in their tissues keeps the plants warm from within.

By the end of July autumn has begun and grasses wither. The plants which were first out of the snow have ripe fruit and seeds. Yet on meadows which thawed late, spring flowers, which had finished blossoming a month and a half earlier in the valleys, are now in bloom. About the twentieth of August the small polar birch begins to redden, adding bright new tints to the variegated carpet of dying high-mountain vegetation. Birds abandon high-altitude lakes. By the fifth of September it is late autumn in the high-mountain zone of the central Altai; ponds are covered with ice all day long, despite the fine weather and the radiance of the sun. In mid-September the snow cover is solid. In winter the drying winds attack the scrub vegetation and are especially destructive because the plants are dormant. Thickets of small polar birch later appear to have been trimmed at a single level—the level of the surface of the winter snow. On exposed places, where the snow is blown off or there is little of it, the small polar birch is a low, small brush creeping along the ground. In more protected places, where the snow is deeper and the action of the winds is less injurious, it grows three to five feet high.

Of the 297 species of high-mountain vegetation, 39 per cent are common to the Arctic zone and 61 per cent are mountain species. Most of the mountain species also grow in other mountain regions of the USSR. In some places steppe species are admixed, especially in the arid eastern Altai.

The high-mountain zone is divided into two subzones, the mountain meadow and mountain tundra. The mountain-tundra subzone is so much larger than the mountain-meadow subzone that it dominates the high-mountain zone of the Altai and gives it a flora similar to that of the polar tundra. It is quite different from the corresponding zone of the Alps, where the small polar birch is very rare. This is explained by the relatively northern position of the Altai and by the broad remnants of the peneplain with their gravelly soil. Further correlation with the polar tundra is indicated by the poor drainage and consequent swampiness and the unique history of the Altai in glacial and postglacial times. Thus, the mountain-tundra subzone contains a great number of pure mountain and arctic-alpine species, as is shown in the following table.

BASIC TYPES OF LANDSCAPES OF THE HIGH-MOUNTAIN ZONE	SPECIES OF PLANTS			
	NUMBER	FOREST AND STEPPE (%)	MOUNTAINOUS (%)	ARCTIC–ALPINE (%)
Mountain Meadows				
Subalpine Meadows	93	63	24	13
Alpine Meadows	137	38	38	24
Mossy-Lichenous Tundra	151	9	47	44
Rubbly-Lichenous Tundra	119	6	56	38
Stony Tundra	157	8	53	39

The mountain-meadow zone is divided into three belts: (1) alpine shrubs; (2) subalpine meadows; (3) alpine meadows.

The belt of alpine shrubs begins a short distance below the upper timber line. In it groups of stunted trees alternate with vast thickets and subalpine meadows on rubbly, poorly developed podzolic soil. The most characteristic shrubs are: small polar birch (*Betula rotundifolia*), dwarf willows (*Salix glauca, S. arctica*), honeysuckle (*Lonicera hispida*), and mountain currant (*Ribes fragrans*) with extremely fragrant leaves. Small polar birch, which propagates by runners or implanting branches, forms impenetrable thickets in which creeping, bent trunks and branches covered with fine, serrated leaflets rise and intertwine among themselves. These thickets, consisting of birch about three feet high, cover many square miles and hinder the movement of men and animals.

Subalpine meadows cover the slopes of mountains within the zone of sparse forest and somewhat above it. In appearance they are similar to forest meadows, and at lower levels they form a transition to them. Their soil is moist, and on them the grass may grow as much as five feet tall. A group of riders passing through these meadows, breaking and pressing down the stalks, lays down a marked trail like a narrow corridor. The subalpine meadows contain a large percentage of forest-meadow grasses that grow only half as tall as at lower altitudes: larkspur (*Delphinium elatum*), aconite (*Aconitum septentrionale*), and cow parsnip (*Heracleum dissectum*). Of the high-mountain plants the most important are: *Leuzea carthamoides* with large dark-lilac flowers and found only in subalpine meadows, swertia (*Swertia obtusa*), lousewort (*Pedicularis verticillata*), and alpine timothy. At high altitudes the predominating plant is the broad-leafed saussurea (*Saussurea latifolia*) with grayish-lilac racemes. The soil under the meadows contains little humus and has latent or turfed-podzolic characteristics, indistinct morphologic structure, and a deep profile. Higher yet, the meadow cover begins to change; forest plants become fewer and alpine grasses more common. The plants are smaller and flowery, but they still grow densely and form a solid turf.

Alpine meadows occupy a narrow expanse of dry mountain-meadow soil along the mountain slopes. The grass stands 8 to 24 inches high, and as many as 30 or 40 different species, many brightly colored, may grow in a section 100 yards square. The meadows are intensely variegated and made especially attractive by countless columbines (*Aquilegia glandulosa*) with big, blue, five-petaled flowers that have a yellowish-white center. Among them, standing out in contrast, are the bright orange flowers of the globeflower (*Trollius asiaticus*), the crimson satiny-glossy heads of chive (*Allium schoenoprasum*), and the white umbrellas of mountain anemone (*Anemone narcissiflora*). Attracting attention with their dark-blue color are the bilabiate blossoms of dragon's head (*Dracocephalum altaiense*) that grow close to one another in large racemes. There are large patches of violet (*Viola altaica*) with large, blue-violet flowers, and many gentians (*Gentiana altaica*) with tight clusters of ten or more deep-blue, beaker-shaped flowers.

The brilliance of the alpine meadows is somewhat dulled by more modestly colored flowers such as yellow or speckled saxifrage (*Saxifraga hirculus, S. melaleuca*) and light-colored lousewort (*Pedicularis alpina*), and by the black spikes of sedge (*Carex atrata*). Here, too, are grasses in great number: hair grass (*Deschampsia caespitosa*), sweet-scented vernal grass (*Anthoxantum odoratum*), and grass (*Phelum alpinum*). Together with several sedges they make the meadow cover thicker and more turfy. Intense grazing of the meadows gives such plants as lady's mantle (*Alchemilla vulgaris*) and geranium (*Geranium pratense*) primary importance. At higher altitudes the mountain meadow thins out and the grass becomes shorter, plants disappear one after the other, the soil becomes exposed and swampy, and we enter the mountain-tundra subzone.

The mountain-tundra subzone occupies an area many times larger than the mountain-meadow subzone and is especially typical of the landscape of the peneplain. Disruption of the soil cover, abundant rocky outcrops, and talus suggest the skeletal quality and primitiveness of the soil. Weak genetic horizons and in the more eroded valleys, weakly marked podzolic horizons, are characteristic of mountain-tundra soil. The ground cover contains little grass, consisting mainly of some fifty species of bryophytes; there are many thickets of small polar birch. The three basic types of landscape are (1) mossy-lichenous mountain tundra, (2) rubbly-lichenous mountain tundra, and (3) rocky mountain tundra. These replace one another from bottom to top, but their interrelations are so camouflaged by relief and the na-

Fig. 2-17. Chief representatives of vegetation in alpine meadows and mountain tundra. 1—Svertzia (*Swertia obtusa*); 2—Onion (*Allium schoenophrasum*); 3—Ptarmigan grass (*Dryas octopetala*); 4—Globe flower (*Trollius asiaticus*); 5—Golden crepis (*Crepis chrysantha*); 6—Yellow gentian (*Gentiana algida*); 7—Saxifrage (black-white) (*Saxifraga melanoleuca*); 8—Swamp saxifrage (*Saxifraga hirculus*); 9—*Pedicularis amoena*; 10—Altai violet (*Viola altaica*); 11—Forget-me-not (*Eritrichium villosum*); 12—Sedge (dark-colored) (*Carex melanantha*); 13—Sedge (mountain) (*Carex perfusca*); 14—Cotton grass (*Eriophorum vaginatum*); 15—Cinquefoil (snow) (*Potentilla nivea*); 16—Poppy (alpine) (*Papaver nudicaule*); 17—Buttercup (snow) (*Ranunculus altaicus*); 18—Gentian (Altai) (*Gentiana altaica*); 19—Columbine (*Aquilegia glandulosa*). (*Mounting by S. P. Suslov.*)

ture of the substrata that to demarcate these belts of the subzone is extremely difficult.

Despite the seeming poverty of the stunted cover, cattle graze in the tundra in good weather, even preferring it to the alpine meadows, to which the herds usually descend when the weather is bad.

The mossy-lichenous mountain tundra is found in moist places not affected by desiccating winds, on the bottoms and gradual slopes of broad valleys, and at the sources of rivers. In many places it penetrates deep into the forest zone, creating forests with a mossy ground cover that are very similar to those of the polar wooded-tundra. This type of tundra, in its pure form, has a continuous mossy cover of *Hypnum schreberi* and *Hypnum splendens*. It also has, in places, a lichenous cover and many dense thickets of stunted polar birch and willow on peaty-podzolic soils. In dry areas these thickets gradually thin out, leaving open expanses into which the lichenous cover penetrates.

Through the mossy-lichenous cover are scattered many typical alpine plants, which may form magnificent flower beds, some comprising only a single species. Forest-meadow species and many alpine meadow plants do not penetrate this subzone, which contains numerous species not found at lower altitudes: claytonia (*Claytonia joanneana*), with delicate pale-rose blossoms; chickweed (*Alsine verna*), which forms small thick clusters of fine white flowerets; and similar species. Higher are found blue corydalis (*Corydalis pauciflora*), golden crepis (*Crepis chrysantha*), sedge (*Carex atrata*), and the pale and pallid *Lloydia serotina*. There are also many grasses not found below: alpine sweet grass (*Hierochloe alpina*) and dark-spiked koeleria (*Koeleria atriviolacea*), for example.

Amid the mossy-lichenous tundra are swampy, boggy expanses covered with grass and bryophytes. They lie in undrained depressions, on level sections of watersheds, near creeks, and in areas where meltwater stagnates. The surface of such a swamp is somewhat hillocky and in the depressions are heaps of dark,

chocolate-colored soil. When one walks over the solid, thick, mossy cover, one hears underfoot the sucking sound of water impregnating the subsoil. There are no lichens in these swamps; the rather dense grassy cover consists of bog-alpine plants: several species of sedge (*Carex limosa, C. rigida*), cotton grass (*Eriophorum altaicum*), and saxifrage (*Saxifraga hirculus*).

Near snow patches the vegetation is extremely variegated. A few feet from the snow there may be clusters of large, bright-colored flowers which look very attractive against the background of a snow field—blue flowers of the columbine (*Aquilegia glandulosa*), orange-colored poppies (*Papaver croceum*), and masses of little stars of saxifrage (*Saxifraga sibirica*). Nearer the snow, plants will be only beginning to break through the recently thawed soil—traces of vegetation can be found at the very edge of a snow patch. Here crowfoot (*Ranunculus altaicus*), which blossomed long ago in the mountain tundra, is just casting off its calyx, which is thickly covered with long blackish-brown hairs. Sometimes the bud of the crowfoot breaks through the thin snow crust and is displayed above it, but not until the thawing snow retreats a few inches do its golden-yellow blossoms open up.

The rubbly-lichenous mountain tundra occupies the higher, windy slopes which are amply warmed by the sun, and well drained. The comparatively high temperature of soil and the intense evaporation, aggravated by the rubbliness of the mountain-tundra soil, explain this tundra's solid lichenous cover, which, in its turn, aids in the warming of the soil. Because mosses (*Cladonia alpestris* and *Cetraria islandica*) predominate here, covering the thin soil, the landscape resembles the mottled lichenous polar tundra. The reindeer that dwell in the rubbly-lichenous tundra of the east Altai strengthen this resemblance. Amid the lichenous cover, are unusual alpine plants that tend to grow in big grassy clumps. A plant of this type is partridge grass (*Dryas octopetala*); its whitish-green, leathery, serrated leaves, large milky-white flowers, or the white crests of its fruit are visible over large areas in summer, as are patches of chickweed (*Alsine arctica*), *Sibbaladia tetrandra, Thermopsis alpina,* campanula (*Campanula pilosa*), and blue forget-me-not (*Eritrichium villosum*).

Rocky mountain tundra occupies the highest part of the mountain-tundra subzone; it lies just below the snow line. This type of tundra represents the earliest stage in the development of a vegetative cover. On soil that has just emerged from the snow are a few stocky plants with a sharply expressed alpine character. It is here that the most uncommon and interesting plants of the Altai are found: *Braya rosea* (near the glaciers and snowfields of Chuya), *Dryandanthe bungeana,* and *Saussurea sorocephala* are not common in the Altai, but the few specimens that grow in the rocky tundra connect its flora with that of the mountain ranges farther south.

Only the hardier plants of the lower-lying tundras have settled in the rocky tundra. Those which are able to survive the severe conditions on the exposed summits, ravaged by cold winds and often closed-in by clouds, include several species of claytonia, lousewort, and saxifrage. To these plants are added others that are still hardier: plain white-blossomed whitlow grass (*Draba wahlenbergii*), small four-petaled sedum (*Sedum quadrifidum*), stocky saussurea (*Saussurea pygmaea*), and gentian (*Gentiana tenella*). Here and there is groundsel (*Senecio frigidus*), wrapped from top to bottom in a fur coat of soft, tufty, web-like, white fuzz that covers its stalk, leaves, and the envelope of its floral calathide. All these blossoming plants rise higher and higher, among the isolated patches of snow, until they reach the snow fields. Even here on exposed cliffs, especially on south-facing slopes, are small oases amid the snow waste, where, in cracks, rose saxifrage (*Saxifraga oppositifolia*) and small veronica (*Veronica densiflora*) have caught hold. Still higher, in small pits protected on all sides by rocks, are miniature stalks of poppy, whose flowers never rise above their shelter. Lichens are found up to 11,000 feet. The only vegetation within the zone of perpetual snow is the *Sphaerella nivalis,* which tints the snow red, and a few lichens that cling to exposed rocks.

The landscapes of the high-mountain zone are more uniform than those of the other vertical zones, and the different mountain regions do not differ from one another as much as, for example, the steppes of the northern and southern Altai. Yet the high-mountain zone in one part of the Altai may lack a landscape found in all the others, in another a landscape may be more prominent than it is elsewhere. In the western Altai, luxuriant alpine meadows that cover large expanses near the timber line mark the beginning of the high-mountain zone, and the mountain tundra contains a large number of flowering plants. In the central and southern Altai the mountain-meadow subzone reaches an intense development, and the high-mountain tundra has a poorly developed moss and lichen cover. The northern slopes of the southern Altai are the last refuge of the small polar birch; thus the mossy-lichenous tundra is missing here. In the northeastern Altai the belt of small polar birch reaches exceptional development, but the mountain-meadow subzone is very poorly represented. In the southeastern Altai, the belts of alpine shrubs and subalpine meadows are lacking, and the alpine meadows contain only a few bright-colored alpine plants. The high-mountain tundra covers vast areas, but is more uniform and does not have the great variety of species that it has elsewhere. High elevations, the proximity of Mongolia with its dry continental climate, the presence of locked-in elevated plateaus edged by ranges contribute to the wide spread of mountain-steppe plants which occupy the higher open and arid sites in the southeast. In the central and western Altai the high-mountain and steppe zones are separated by a wide strip of forest, but in the southeastern Altai the zones are in direct contact—side by side one may encounter alpine tundra, alpine meadows, thickets of small polar birch, and high-mountain steppes with many features of a semidesert.

Many different animals live in the high-mountain zone. Where the upper timber line adjoins the belt of alpine meadows, conditions

are extremely favorable for the existence of ruminant animals: roe deer, Siberian and Caucasian stag, elk, and musk deer. Along cliffs of the southern Altai are cautious mountain goats (*Capra sibirica*), as well as mountain sheep (*Ovis ammon*); in winter both feed on dry grass and lichens on mountain summits where the wind blows away the snow. There are reindeer on the Chulyshman Plateau. In the region are such rodents as the pika (*Ochotona alpina*) and the Mongolian pika (*O. pricei*); the marmot (*Arctomys baibacina*), which yields a valuable pelt and supplies breeding stock for acclimatization to other regions of the USSR (Bashkiria, Dagestan), lives near the snow line. From the lower-lying forest zone come bear, wolf, and fox; in the southern Altai are the cat (*Octocolobus manul*), red wolf (*Canis alpinus*), and snow panther (*Uncia uncia*). Many species of birds live in the belt of small polar birch: white ptarmigan (*Lagopus lagopus brevirostris*) and alpine blue-throated warbler (*Cyanecula suecica altaica*). In the subalpine and alpine meadows are mountain water pipit (*Anthus spinoletta blakistoni*), mountain finch (*Fringillauda nemoricola altaica*), and dotterel (*Eudromias morinellus*).

In the rocky tundra are many other birds, of which one of the most interesting is the snow pheasant (*Tetraurogallus altaicus*), a pedestrian and poor-flying bird. It avoids the forests and lives on steep mountain slopes, to which little snow adheres in winter, and on which, after the occasional storms of summer, the snow melts quickly. In particularly severe winters this bird may descend a little lower. There is also the red-beaked jackdaw or chough (*Pyrrhocorax pyrrhocorax*), easily distinguished by the bright red of its beak and legs; it flies swiftly, and generally lives on stony ledges above precipices, up to altitudes of 8,250 feet. Higher up lives the yellow-beaked alpine clough (*Pyrrhocorax graculus*), which in winter descends to the lower reaches of the Chulyshman River. The stony-white ptarmigan (*Lagopus mutus nadesdae*) avoids the thickets of small polar birch but ascends to 10,000 feet. The snow-mountain finch (*Montifringilla*) and mottle-breasted hedge sparrow are also found here. The insects on the alpine meadows include many bumblebees and many diptera, especially flies; they obtain food from many different alpine plants.

Fig. 2-18. Characteristic fauna in vertical belts of Altai. I—On the edge of forest-steppe: left—crane (*Anthropoidus virgo*), right—duck; II—Representatives of taiga belt: left—nutcracker, right—chipmunk (*Tamias sibiricus*); III—Among sparse mountain forests: right—stag (*Cervus elaphus sibiricus*) and muskdeer (*Moschus sibiricus*), left—mountain goat (*Capra sibirica*) and snow leopard (*Felis pardus*); IV—Left—representative of fauna from Chuisk steppe-sadzha, Next right—representatives high mountain (alpine) belt: altai pischukha (*Okhotona alpina*), mountain turkey (*Tetragallus altaicus*); redbeak jackdaw. (*Mounting by S. P. Suslov; drawing by V. V. Trofimov.*)

CHAPTER 3

Salair-Kuznetsk Mountain Region and Kuznetsk Basin

The Kuznetsk Basin and the mountains surrounding it—the Kuznetsk Ala-Tau, Salair, and Mount Shoriya—have the same geologic history and constitute the northern extremity of the Altai mountain system. The Kuznetsk Ala-Tau and Salair ridges extend northwest-southeast almost parallel to each other, for a considerable distance, and converge south of Stalinsk in Mount Shoriya to form the slightly hilly Kuznetsk Basin, which is open to the northwest toward the Western Siberian Lowland.

KUZNETSK ALA-TAU RANGE

The Kuznetsk Ala-Tau, which is a continuation to the north of the Abakan Range, extends almost directly north-south until it reaches the source of the Tom River from which it trends northwest to the main line of the Trans-Siberian Railway. It appears to be a group of massifs of an ancient folded-mountain system, irregularly shaped and surrounded on all sides by tectonic breaks. The Kuznetsk Ala-Tau is sharply bounded by two large areas of hilly foreland, the Kuznetsk Basin on the west and Minusinsk Basin on the east; on the south it abuts against the Altai and the Western Sayan.

The Kuznetsk Ala-Tau is strongly dissected by numerous tributaries of the Tom, Kiya, and Chulym rivers into separate mountain massifs. The greatest heights are concentrated in its southern section, at the sources of the Tom and Bely Iyus rivers. At the source of the Bely Iyus is a narrow craggy range with a row of peaks called Tegir-Tyz (sky teeth) with a height of 6,640 feet. The highest point of the Kuznetsk Ala-Tau is Mount Amzas Taskyl, with an altitude of 7,100 feet. Northward the altitude gradually decreases, reaching 4,750 feet at the source of the lower Ters River. Near the northern extremity of the mountainous country at Mount Chernishnay, the ridge is only 1,020 feet high. Still farther to the north the Kuznetsk Ala-Tau ends just south of the mainline of the Trans-Siberian Railway.

The main watershed is closer to the western border of the range than to the eastern; thus the southwestern slope is shorter and steeper and has very simple outlines, dropping with an escarpment from 1,000 to 2,000 feet high into Kuznetsk Basin. In some places, the northeastern slope also descends steeply, with an escarpment as high as 1,300 feet, into Minusinsk Basin; in other places, where eastern spurs of the ridge jut out varying distances into the Minusinsk Basin, it is scarcely separated from its bordering hill country. The valleys of the southwestern and northeastern slopes are

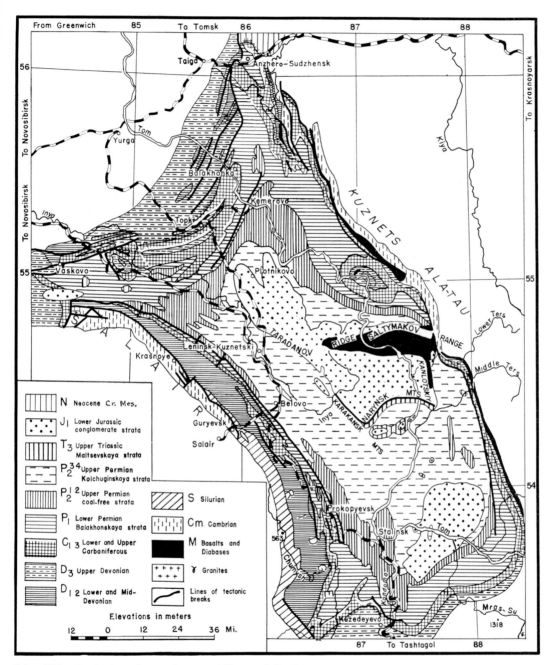

Map 3-I.   Geologic and tectonic map of Kuznetsk Basin.

quite different. The valleys of the northeastern slope are well developed, with broad bottoms that in places are completely flat and are covered with alluvial deposits. Present-day rivers meander over the alluvium, not reaching the bedrock. On the southwestern slope there are extraordinarily clear traces of comparatively recent rejuvenation of the erosion cycle. Narrow V-shaped valleys contain swift and turbulent mountain torrents which rush over the bedrock in small rapids and waterfalls. In places the bottoms of the valleys are clogged with such a large quantity of coarse rocks that it is impossible either to navigate or to ride along the river.

The altitude of the foot of the Kuznetsk Ala-Tau varies from 1,650 to 2,140 feet in the northeastern and from 1,050 to 1,250 feet in the southwestern foothills; in other words, the border of the Kuznetsk Basin lies lower than the border of the Minusinsk Basin. This suggests that a change of the level of erosion, effecting a rejuvenation of the erosion cycle, was a result not only of the upheaval of the Kuznetsk Ala-Tau, but also of the lowering of both basins, and that the Kuznetsk Basin settled more than the Minusinsk Basin. The main rivers diverge from their watershed sources, creating radial valleys. This indicates that, since the beginning, the pattern of the river network in the Kuznetsk Ala-Tau has remained the same.

The Kuznetsk Ala-Tau is formed of Lower Paleozoic deposits. The oldest sedimentary rocks, which have undergone the most intense folding, are crystallized banded limestones of varying color and structure: a subordinate role is played by quartzite and clay shales of the Cambrian. Where faults have taken place, there are many large intrusions of plutonic rocks. Limestones have been subjected to very strong contact metamorphism, which recrystallized and transformed them into marble of different colors and coarseness of grain; connected with the marble are the majority of small ore deposits—copper, iron, molybdenum, lead, and zinc. On the Cambrian limestones is a stratum

of flaky tuff (Silurian), that has an over-all greenish color and is composed of alternate layers of sand, clay shale, breccia, tuff, and tuffite. Both of these beds underwent intense Caledonian folding. They form systems of more or less complex folds with two main directions of dislocation—northwest and northeast. After the Caledonian folding, masses of volcanic rocks flowed onto the surface.

On the whole, the outline of the Kuznetsk Ala-Tau does not conform to the direction of folding. The present range is a complex system of massifs which were raised and subsequently broken into separate sections by faults, the lines of which are distinct, not only along the borders but also within the mountain mass. There are many horsts of different heights. The entire Kuznetsk Ala-Tau was further raised as a result of repeated epeirogenic movements, which took place even after the formation of the hydrographic network, as is shown by certain epeirogenic sections of river valleys (Cherny Iyus River).

The morphology of the bald mountain zones of the ridge shows the influence of glaciation. At the sources of all rivers are huge glacial cirques—some solitary, others arranged in staggered rows—with well-expressed moraines, damming up countless lakes. At the mouths of the valleys that open into the Minusinsk Basin there are no glacial remnants, either moraines or fluvioglacial deposits. In the glacial period the area evidently contained many small isolated hanging glaciers that had very small accumulative areas, short but comparatively

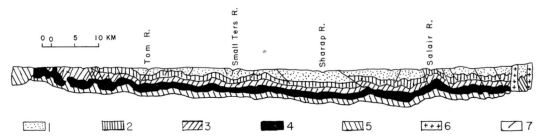

Fig. 3-1. Geologic cross section of Kuznetsk basin. 1—Kolchuginsk; 2—Upper Permian; 3—Balakhonsk; 4—Carboniferous; 5—Devonian; 6—Diabases and basalt; 7—Faults.

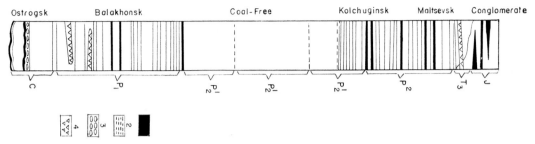

Fig. 3-2. Stratigraphic diagram of coal deposits in Kuznetsk Basin. 1—Coal; 2—Coal-shale; 3—Conglomerate; 4—Basalt.

broad tongues, and moved very slowly. At the present time there are no glaciers in the Kuznetsk Ala-Tau, but the mountains are covered with snow for the greater part of the year, although on southern slopes it may survive only in the depths of gorges. The northern and northeastern slopes of the highest mountains are covered with huge patches of permanent snow that forms sheet-like firn fields, the lower limit of which lie at 4,300 feet.

Geomorphologically, the Kuznetsk Ala-Tau consists of the remains of an old high-altitude peneplain that has undergone extraordinarily prolonged erosion. On water-divides are remnants of the old peneplain: isolated high points with flat or basin-shaped crests, among the rolling hills. The highly broken relief, the number of chaotically heaped mountains, makes it impossible to demarcate the separate mountain ranges exactly. The general appearance of the country is characterized by the contrast between the predominant mountain massifs and the smooth outlines of the watersheds. The alternation of metamorphosed limestones and shales, the countless outcrops of igneous rocks, and a well-developed hydrographic network caused the irregular dissection of relief. Sharply defined alpine forms of relief are rare; they are closely connected with the numerous cirques, which introduce some variety into the general monotonous picture, especially in the lower northern section of the range, where heights do not exceed 3,300 feet. They were formed during the Pleistocene and their continued growth is explained by the intense frost

weathering, which has covered the peaks and slopes of the higher mountains with talus and alluvial deposits that often support a thick vegetative cover.

The climate of the high-mountain section of the Kuznetsk Ala-Tau is similar to the climate of the northeastern part of the Altai. The distribution of subterranean water varies greatly. In regions of massive crystalline rocks, ground water lies comparatively near the surface. These rocks, being compact and impervious, contribute to the accumulation of moisture in the porous detritus covering them. The circulation of water in the rocks themselves takes place along crevices and depends on their character and frequency. In limestone, the distribution of underground water is that which is typical of karst regions, and the water level is only slightly above that of the surface water in the nearby valleys. Everywhere the water is fresh and good to drink. The sources of some rivers are on vast, swampy, flat or saddle-shaped watersheds; other rivers originate in narrow gorges or in tarns. During melting of snow or after rains, the rivers rise swiftly and recede just as quickly. There are lakes in the highest parts of the region, at the bottom of *kar* formations or old cirques; they are small, and circular or oval in shape.

The vegetation of these mountains does not offer great diversity. Much of the surface is covered by forests. In the lower foothills these are light larch or larch-birch forests containing many broad glades. Higher, there are three basic belts of vegetation: (1) mountain fir, spruce, and Siberian pine forests, (2) mixed fir and aspen forests, and (3) the alpine region of bald mountains.

The most common trees of the mountain taiga are Siberian pine, fir, and spruce. These trees are very tall, but have thin trunks, narrow crowns, and lower branches that are withered and completely covered with hanging lichens. Young undergrowth is inconspicuous among the deciduous woody species such as birch, aspen, and mountain ash. The forests have a thick mossy cover above which a few typical taiga plants raise their heads: pyrola, oxalis, red bilberry, whortleberry, and club moss. On the more rocky portions of the southern part of the region *Bergenia crassifolia* and *Rhododendron dauricum* are found. On swampy or somewhat bare ground are species common in the tall-grass forest meadows. The soil under these forests is extremely moist; water will appear even in a shallow pit.

Mixed forests of fir and aspen are characterized by: (1) a general moderately humid regime, (2) a mixture of coniferous and deciduous species, (3) a poor mossy ground cover or none at all, and (4) a large number of relic species. Even where there is no linden, relic species associated with it are found: asarabacea (*Asarum europaeum*), enchanter's nightshade (*Circaea lutetiana*), sweet cicely (*Osmorrhiza amurensis*), campanula (*Campanula trachelium*), and fescue grass (*Festuca gigantea*). Amid the forests are scattered large burned-over areas and there or on places too wet for trees are tall-grass meadows that contain swiftly growing plants six to nine feet high: cow parsnip (*Heracleum dissectum*), *Angelica silvestris,* alfredia (*Alfredia cernua*), aconite (*Aconitum septentrionale*), and *Bupleurum aureum*. Meadows of most river valleys also consist of tall taiga grass. Only in the widest valleys are there large dry meadows that are useful for agriculture. The upper timber line lies at approximately 4,300 feet, its height is determined here not so much by climatic conditions as by the spread of rocky deposits which in places slide off slowly to hinder the growth of trees. On the more stable deposits trees grow directly on large rocks where a real soil cover has not yet formed; here the forest appears as though it had just recently begun to grow.

Alpine vegetation grows on the high mountains far above the timber line. In general, it

Fig. 3-3.   The uniform ridge tops and domes of "white mountains" of the Central Kuznetsk Ala-Tau.

Fig. 3-4. Park-type forest of Siberian larch on the piedmont of the Kuznetsk Ala-Tau.

resembles that of the northeastern part of the Altai, but fewer species grow here. In the subalpine meadows, immediately beyond the timber line, is tall grass and such high-elevation plants as swertia (*Swertia obtusa*) and saxifrage (*Saxifraga punctata*). Above them are alpine meadows containing columbine (*Aquilegia glandulosa*), lousewort (*Pedicularis versicolor*), Altai violet (*Viola altaica*), and Altai dragon's head (*Dracocephalum altaiense*). Higher yet are stony or spotty tundra and continuous rock waste.

SALAIR RIDGE

The Salair Ridge is a separate elevation rising from the lower course of the Biya River. It extends northwestward, in the same direction as the Chumysh River, and ends before reaching the Inya River, a tributary of the Ob. The ridge is basically an arc of large radius with the bulge facing eastward. Its altitude varies from 1,300 to 1,550 feet; only in the north do separate peaks reach a greater height: Kopna Mountain is 1,980 feet high and Mount Pikhtovka 1,850 feet. The Salair ends with a small hill—Mokhnataya—and beyond to the north-west lies the isolated picturesque group of small conical peaks, 1,280 feet high, called Bugotakski: these are formed of igneous rocks.

The Salair Ridge, morphologically considered, has lost the typical features of a mountain range—the sharp variance between the forms of relief and the geologic structure. The complexity of its geologic structure is expressed in the juxtaposition of sandstones and shales with crystalline limestones of the Cambrian period and greenstone tuffs of the Silurian. The intense folding and large tectonic dislocations with faults and overthrusts closely connect the morphology of the ridge with that of the Kuznetsk Ala-Tau. It is rich in polymetallic ores that contain zinc, lead, silver, and copper; reserves of zinc alone are estimated at 600,000 tons.

The Salair is asymmetrical in shape with the water divide nearer its eastern border. The western side slopes gradually to the Ob River and blends imperceptibly with the Western Siberian Lowland. Many parts of the northeastern slope have an extremely steep escarpment, bearing the name *tyrgan,* that in the south rises more than 300 feet above the adjoining plain. Because the strip of rigid limestones that constitute the tyrgan is broken by meridional faults and dissected by longitudinal valleys, the region contains a series of somewhat parallel cuestas, some of which form mesas or buttes. The precipitation on the gradually sloping western side is greater than on the eastern slope. Hence wide river valleys penetrate deeply into the west, whereas the east has a weakly developed river network with short steep gradients.

Many features of the Salair indicate that it was at one time part of an ancient peneplain that was later subject to complex faulting. At the beginning of the modern period a thick accumulation of continental alluvium covered this highly denuded fold-fault region, which created the base of the present relief. Today horizontal forms of relief predominate: wide undulating watersheds, few outstanding peaks, and broad valleys. As a result of complex prolonged erosion by running water the fault scarp is highly dissected by the hydrographic network and the flat watersheds are covered with friable alluvium and argillaceous soil.

The climate of the Salair Ridge is similar to that of the northeastern Altai. The average July temperature is 59° to 64°F, that of January 3° to −3°F, the absolute maximum is 93°F, and the absolute minimum −52°F. The growing season is 137 to 145 days, 82 of them frost-free. Despite its slight elevation above the surrounding plain, the Salair Ridge acts as a condenser of moisture from air cur-

rents coming from the west, thereby bringing about natural climatic asymmetry; in the western Salair the annual precipitation is 19 inches, whereas in the extreme eastern part it is only 17 inches.

On the eastern foothills of Salair Ridge the vegetative cover is a combination of steppe and forest species. Scattered patches of birch and aspen grow on northern slopes. On the southern slopes, where the soil consists of thin, rubbly, saliferous chernozems, are such steppe plants as cinquefoil (*Potentilla subacaulis*), *Artemisia frigida,* and similar xerophytic species found in the mountain steppes of the Altai. These plants, in a habitat isolated from their main center of propagation, may be considered remnants of a landscape of the xerothermic period.

In a narrow strip in the extreme eastern part of the Salair Ridge, there are park-like forests of birch, larch, and pine, with pine and larch in the first tier and birch in the second. Pine formerly predominated sharply over birch, but the cutting of pine allowed birch to spread. The underbrush contains much spirea (*Spiraea media*) and dog rose (*Rosa acicularis*). Under the trees dark-colored carbonaceous soils have developed. Westward, more and more aspen appear in the forests, solitary spruce are seen, fir at last mixes in, and finally taiga trees become preponderant.

In the Salair, an increase in aridity during some postglacial period led to the expansion of larch and pine forests. Then, in a subsequent moist period, the forests were invaded by broad-leaved trees; these trees migrated from the western spurs of the Kuznetsk Ala-Tau. A peculiar gray and light-gray forest soil developed beneath these forests because their mossy cover was thin and a thick growth of tall grasses provided large amounts of humus and ash. Forests of aspen and fir with a tall grass ground cover are widespread on the moist western slope. The aspen provides raw material for match production, and the fir may be useful for the production of pine oil, which is used in the cellulose and camphor industries.

In the west the contact of the Salair with

the Ob and Chumysh valleys is a slightly hilly wooded-steppe zone, parallel to the ridge and trending northwest. In it there is a gradual transition from the light-gray, strongly pod-zolic soil of the taiga to the leached-out cher-nozem of the wooded-steppe. Large park-like birch groves alternate with wide strips of grassy meadows. On the sandy or loamy-sandy soil of old river terraces are pine groves and occasional sphagnum bogs. Farther west and lower, on leached-out, slightly sandy cher-nozem soil are meadows that contain grasses and herbs characteristic of the mountain steppes of the Altai. There, small groves of birch and aspen are found only on the northern slopes.

KUZNETSK BASIN

The Kuznetsk Basin forms an irregular quad-rangle. It is bounded on the east and northeast by the Kuznetsk Ala-Tau, on the southwest by the Salair Ridge, on the south by the foot-hills of Mount Shoriya, and on the northwest by a low ground swell with no special name that gradually and imperceptibly merges with the Western Siberian Lowland.

The Kuznetsk Basin, in places, is sharply divided from the Kuznetsk Ala-Tau and the Salair by high and steep escarpments that are visible for dozens of miles. In some places the scarps, which may consist of a series of steps, run along both sides of the foothills— i.e., separating the foothills from both the basin and the mountain. In others, the basin con-tains gradually rising foothills that pass imper-ceptibly into the mountain ridges: here it is diffi-cult to trace the orographic border. The geologic boundary is easier to trace because it corre-sponds approximately to the contact between the Cambrian and younger formations. The term "basin" is rightly applied to the area, since from the periphery to the center there is an uninterrupted and significant downslope: in some places it is gradual, in others there are scarps. The lowest points are in the central part of the basin, where it is cut by the broad valley of the Tom River, which descends from an altitude of 630 feet at Stalinsk to 350 feet at Kemerovo. Because the basin contains many coal-bearing deposits, it is also called the Kuz-netsk coal basin.

The Kuznetsk Basin and its peripheral hills contain rocks extremely diverse in composition, origin, age, and structure. Coal-bearing strata of the Upper Paleozoic and Mesozoic form most of the deposits. Middle Paleozoic deposits adjoin them along the periphery, and in places tectonic breaks have brought them close to the Lower Paleozoic rocks that form the mountain ridges bordering the basin. The younger rocks of the center are surrounded by concentric belts of older rocks that extend to the periph-ery. The structural geology of the coal-bearing deposits is also unusual. Folding along the edges of the basin occurred as a result of tan-gential pressure from the mountain ridges circumscribing it, especially the Salair. This pressure also produced many large faults.

Both types of dislocations—abrupt faults and overthrust folds—are distinctly visible in the marginal zone of the basin. They are trace-able for dozens of miles, but toward the center both types gradually begin to disappear. Among the folds of the central part there are no large anticlines containing deposits older than Upper Permian.

The two most important events in the geo-logic history of the basin were (1) the forma-tion of the basin itself, which occurred when the surrounding mountain ridges were raised in the early Paleozoic, and (2) the formation of the coal-bearing strata, when vast layers of coal deposits accumulated in the sinking geo-syncline. There was a general tendency toward subsidence in the late Paleozoic, although the height of the basin's shore line fluctuated. Intense dislocations in the bordering ranges, a result of Caledonian folding, were accom-panied by the subsidence of the basin. To-ward the beginning of the Devonian, the crests of the Salair and Kuznetsk Ala-Tau were small islands or peninsulas in the vast Ural-Siberian Sea, but toward the end of the Devonian the shallow sea began to recede toward the Kuznetsk Ala-Tau side. At the beginning of the Carboniferous, a deeper sea, that covered a large area, invaded the region. Orogenic processes in the Carboniferous led to the upheaval of the bordering ranges. After this time there was no folding: in the whole vast uniform layer of sediment of the Upper Carboniferous and the Lower and Upper Permian, there is no trace of it, although there are traces of epeirogenic movements. Physicogeographic conditions changed sharply at the time these sediments began to accumulate. The sea broke up, along the shores, into a series of somewhat isolated small bays. The shore line of the Kuznetsk Basin became very irregular and its connection with the open sea gradually disappeared, until the basin was converted into a landlocked, shrinking lake.

Conditions were favorable for the development of a luxuriant vegetation and the consequent accumulations of organic matter on the shores of the shrinking lake. Along them were vast swamps and swamped forests of tall tree-like ferns, mammoth sigillarias, lepidodendrons, calamities, and other species of terrestrial plants that do not exist today, which served as raw material for the formation of coal beds. There were several different periods in which much organic matter accumulated, and productive coal-bearing strata were created. Because deposition alternated with long periods during which conditions for such accumulations were unfavorable, a geologic cross section of the Kuznetsk Basin shows interstratification of coal and carbon-free deposits. The absence of coal in the latter is apparently a result of a shrinkage of the basin's area, caused either by subsidence of its bottom under the weight of the accumulated deposits or by the partial upheaval of its borders. Frequent fluctuations in the level of the basin, as a result of which the shores of the landlocked lake were at times covered by water and at other times left dry brought about the formation of a num-

ber of coal seams, most of them thin, along the borders of the basin.

The Kuznetsk coal basin contains more high-grade coal than any other coal basin in the USSR. Coal reserves, to a depth of 5,900 feet, amount to many billions of tons, half of which lie above the 1,650-foot level. Counting the fine seams, there are more than 150 coal beds, with a total thickness of over 600 feet; the 83 that are of working thickness have an over-all thickness of 535 feet.

The most significant for industry are the Balakhonsk and the Kolchugino formations, which contain the richest beds of coal, some with single seams as much as 50 feet thick. This coal was formed from accumulations of organic matter on the site of bogs and forests in the late Paleozoic. This is confirmed by the consistent trend of the separate beds, by the purity of the coal, by the unsorted character of the organic matter, and by the presence of undisturbed small roots of plants and mineralized trunks of trees in a vertical position. In places the coal beds are highly dislocated (Prokopyevsk), in other places slightly so (Kemerovo), and in still others the beds are complex in structure and contain seams of barren rock (Leninsk-Kuznetsk).

Coal of the Kuznetsk Basin varies greatly in quality: it ranges from poor anthracites to rich and gaseous long-flames; there are both bituminous and sapropelite coal. This makes possible its varied utilization for power production, transport, coking, and the production of fuel oil and many industrial chemicals. The coal is very pure, containing about 90 per cent carbon and insignificant amounts of ash (4.3 to 5.1 per cent) and sulphur (0.36 to 0.52 per cent); the phosphorus content may vary from 0.008 to 0.08 per cent in a single seam.

The coal of the Balakhonsk formation is deposited in numerous thick strata that stretch for long distances; much of the coal is very clean, containing 90 per cent carbon and only 4 to 5 per cent ash. The length of the strata indicates that it was formed in a vast peat bog. The thickness of the strata indicates the luxuriant growth and richness of the plants creating it, and also suggests a long period in which physical and geographic conditions remained the same. The coal of the Balakhonsk deposit contains little moisture (3 to 4 per cent) and is therefore a very valuable fuel; some types of it can be used for coking.

The coal of the Kolchugino deposit was formed under very swampy conditions by an accumulation of vegetative residues, and the numerous and well-expressed coal strata are not very thick. The coal is bright and shiny and is not striped. The prevailing gaseous coal contains 14 to 16 per cent primary coal tar. From it may be obtained liquid fuel, gas, and various other chemical products. North of Kemerovo are found Devonian sapropels with a high content of pitch that chemically resembles petroleum. These sapropels are a valuable raw material from which artificial liquid fuel and lubricating oils can be produced.

At the present time coal is mined in ten large centers: Prokopyevsk, Kemerovo, Anzhero-Sudzhensk, Kolchugino, and six others. These comprise 48 mines of different sizes—the largest has an annual output of more than three million tons. Through integration of Kuznetsk coal and Ural iron ore, the Ural-Kuznetsk coal-metallurgical combine was organized. The Kuznetsk metallurgical plant in the city of Stalinsk, the largest in the USSR, is based on local coal and iron ores from both the neighboring Shoriya Mountains and Magnitnaya Mountain in the Urals.

The Mesozoic in the Kuznetsk Basin was marked by the appearance of stratified intrusive veins of close-grained blue-black basalt, which, together with the rocks holding them, were subsequently dislocated. Exposed later by processes of denudation, these stratified intrusions of basalts formed ridges that extend northwest or almost latitudinally and at the present time serve as water divides of tributaries of the Tom and Ob rivers. Such are the Karakansk Mountains—which have an extremely narrow (15 to 35 feet) and sharp crest, a northwest trend, and a height of about 1,700 feet—and the Taradanov and Saltymakov

ridges. In the Early Jurassic Period there was an accumulation of organic matter which now constitutes seams of inferior brown coal. In the Late Jurassic a continuous cycle of erosion began, as a result of which a peneplain was formed from the highly folded country. At the present time it is dissected by numerous river valleys. The uniform height of the flat watersheds of Salair and the residual mountains in the middle of the Kuznetsk Basin indicates the ancient leveling of the surface of the complex geologic structure.

The Quaternary deposit that plays the greatest role in the modern relief is the loess-like soil that covers almost all elements of relief, from the highest ridges to the low bottomlands. It lies either directly on the basic rocks or on clay, and in the larger valleys it is underlain by sand. This soil is yellowish- or reddish-brown; it may be coarse or fine grained, bedded or not bedded, more or less sandy. It is fluvioglacial alluvium that was deposited in dammed basins. This is shown by the alternation of layers of sand with stratified soil, which has assumed a modern character only where the steppe soil-forming process could act on the fluvioglacial alluvium. In this soil calciferous concretions and parts of bones of large mammals are often found: mammoth (*Elephas primigenius*) or ox (*Bos priscus*).

The Kuznetsk Basin is an erosion landscape with a well-incised, dense system of valleys, which gives it an undulating-hilly character that conceals the complex geologic structure of the basin. The mantle of loess-like soil softens all forms of relief, despite considerable dissection and variation in relative heights. The relief of most of the basin looks as though it had been smoothed out; only along the borders, where the depth of the soil decreases rapidly, do the forms of relief acquire a distinct sharpness. The tops of the water divides, which rarely rise more than 300 feet above the level of the river valleys, are flat and narrow—seldom more than a mile wide. Their area is insignificant when compared with that of slopes of valleys and ravines. The size of valleys does not correspond to the present-day runoff; they are 3 to 6 miles wide, and some are over 650 feet deep. They have wide bottoms across which the rivers form countless meanders. Rivers form graduated slopes, with a strongly dendritic pattern of lateral tributaries, and their sources lie in deep cirques with steeply turfed slopes. Intensive epeirogenic elevation of the mountain regions adjacent to the basin has rejuvenated the river network. This is shown by the depth to which the modern rivers have cut into the floors of the old Quaternary valleys. It is also demonstrated by the gorges that rivers have cut through hardrock ridge crests, such as the one the Inya has cut through the basalts of the Karakansk Mountains. It is further indicated by the redistribution of the hydrographic network; for example, the Tom River was rejuvenated at its source by the elevation of the Kuznetsk Ala-Tau near an old valley in the lower region of the Kondoma River. This explains the extremely sharp bend to the north of the modern Tom River near Stalinsk.

In the northern part of the basin the relief is level and broad slopes alternate with shallow valleys. The south-central part is more sharply dissected, and has deep valleys and narrow-crested slopes. In the extreme southern part of the basin, the relief is still more sharply dissected, because of its greater altitude and the close convergence of such large rivers as the Tom and Kondoma. However, the profile of the landforms is softened because the slopes are covered with a mantle of soil.

The Kuznetsk Basin lies in a region in which atmospheric pressure is high in winter and low in summer. Therefore, most of the precipitation takes place in summer and the winter is dry, with little snow and low temperatures. Like the adjacent parts of the Western Siberian Lowland, the basin has great annual temperature amplitudes (Stalinsk: 97° to −62.3°F), cold winters (January average 1.5°F), and sharp transitions from winter to spring (February 3°F, March 15.3°F, April 33°F, May 49°F). The humidity is low, strong winds blow throughout the year, and summer precipitation is much heavier than

that of winter (August 2.9 inches, February 0.6 inch).

The southern part of the basin is warmer than the northern: January and July average temperatures at Stalinsk are 1.2°F and 66°F; in the north, at Leninsk-Kuznetsk, the average temperature in January is 1.0°F and in July 64.2°F. The growing season is somewhat longer in the south—Stalinsk, 159 days; Leninsk-Kuznetsk, 152 days—and summer precipitation is greater—at Stalinsk, June has 2.8 inches, July 2.88 inches, August 2.9 inches; at Leninsk-Kuznetsk, June has, respectively, 2.28, 2.56, and 2.6 inches. The thickness of snow cover at Stalinsk is 19.4 inches and at Leninsk-Kuznetsk 7.6 inches. In the northern part, the low winter temperatures and the thin snow cover lead to the deep freezing of the soil. Hence, when the snow melts in spring, the water is not absorbed by the soil, but either runs off on the surface or evaporates, which clearly affects the river regime.

The Tom River and the majority of its tributaries have two pronounced maximums of discharge: in spring, after the snow melts, and in fall or at the end of summer, when the rainy period begins. The rise of the river, as well as its fall, is usually very abrupt: in the Kemerovo region the Tom rises more than 20 feet above its level. It may rise 6 to 10 feet in the course of a single day, and fall almost as swiftly. In spring and occasionally in fall the Tom River is navigable below Stalinsk.

Complex faults and folds, alternation of permeable and impermeable rocks, undulating relief, and a highly developed hydrographic network have produced an extremely complex occurrence of ground water. The structure of the basin itself, a closed syncline, offers favorable conditions for the accumulation of artesian water; contributing to this is the composition of the coal-bearing strata, in which water-permeable and water-tight rocks lie side by side. Clay soil is a rather poor aquifer, so the water seeks the lower, more sandy horizons. Further, clay yields more or less brackish water, and where it predominates, as in the northwestern part of the basin, there is a shortage of good drinking water. Both old and new alluvial deposits, on the contrary, provide good supplies of fresh water because of the sand and gravel they contain, and in some places they serve as the main source of water.

The wooded-steppe that occupies the center of the Kuznetsk Basin comprises, for the most part, chernozem soil that, unlike the loesses of the Ukraine and Central Asia, has a uniform, heavy physical composition: it is a clayey soil, with 67 per cent of its particles less than 0.01 millimeter in diameter. It has a high content of silicon (ranging to 70 per cent) and contains 5 to 13 per cent of calcium carbonate, the percentage decreasing with depth. It is highly productive.

The most widespread soil in the Basin is leached-out and slightly degraded argillaceous chernozem that has humus only in the very upper part of its profile and an excellent grainy structure. Distinct signs of degradation are observed in this chernozem: thin streaks and patches of siliceous material occur in the lower part of the humus horizon; grainy structure changes into a dusty-clotted one; it acquires signs of saliferousness and becomes solonetz-like. Light-gray podzolic soil is common in the forests. It has a thick podzolic horizon, coarse physical composition, flaky structure, and a compressed-clay lower horizon. Various kinds of bog soil have been formed, principally under the influence of ground water. They have developed on lower river terraces and along the bottoms of ravines: for example, carbonaceous meadow-bog soil in the central section and a solonchak in the western part of the basin. When subjected to systematic cultivation with periodic fallowing, the acidity of the soil drops, the humus is distributed evenly throughout the whole humus horizon, the amount of absorbed calcium decreases, and the structure changes from grainy to lumpy.

The distribution of vegetation and soil in the basin accords with the basic elements of relief, depending on the exposure and angle of slopes and the character of river valleys. Forests of fir and aspen have developed at the higher elevations on extremely podzolic soil,

e.g., on the steep slopes of the Taradanov Ridge. On the other hand, steppe-like areas on chernozem are found in the lower parts of the basin. The gradual eastern slopes have chernozem under the grassy vegetation, but on the steep western slopes weakly podzolic soil lies beneath the birch groves. Broad river valleys with terraces covered with clayey soil have steppe meadows on chernozem, and the sides of narrow valleys are covered by taiga on highly podzolic soil. The most complex combinations of vegetation and soil can be observed in the transitional strip between the wooded-steppe and the forests.

Local geomorphologic and climatic peculiarities divide the Basin into five clearly-defined physicogeographic regions: (1) northwest arid region with grassy steppes, (2) central wooded-steppe region with patches of grassy steppe and birch groves, (3) pre-Salair meadow-forest strip, (4) transitional subtaiga strip, and (5) region of real forest.

1.) The northwest part of the Kuznetsk Basin, between the Salair escarpment and the right bank of the Inya River, is the driest. It lies at an altitude of 625 to 850 feet, is almost flat, and has poor drainage. The soil cover is uniform; there are deposits of calcium carbonate and sodium sulphate in hollows. Patches of mixed and feather-grass steppe are common. Here separate tufts of feather grass (*Stipa joannis*) are found against a grassy background of steppe grass (*Phleum phleoides*), meadow grass (*Poa pratensis*), couch grass (*Agropyron repens*), koeleria (*Koeleria gracilis*), fescue grass (*Festuca ovina*), steppe alfalfa (*Medicago falcata*), clover (*Trifolium lupinaster*), valerian (*Valeriana officinalis*), and pasque flower (*Pulsatilla patens*). In other places fescue grass, koeleria, and meadow grass predominate and among these there are scattered such herbs as cinquefoil (*Potentialla bifurca*), campanula (*Campanula sibirica*), and dropwort (*Filipendula hexapetala*). As a result of grazing, the amount of fescue grass and koeleria is increased, but the herbs and other grasses begin to be replaced by annual weeds. Of the greatest importance as fodder in steppe areas are alfalfa (*Medicago falcata*) and sainfoin (*Onobrychis viciaefolia*), which can be successfully used for pastures and hay.

Trees and shrubs play an insignificant role in the region, being confined to solitary, rare copses of birch and aspen on the north slopes of valleys, in closed depressions on water divides, and on slopes of river valleys. Under the canopy of the birch copses, on degraded chernozem, grow such plants as reed grass (*Calamagrostis arundinacea*), and spirea (*Filipendula ulmaria*). The valleys have solonetz and solonchak soil with impoverished solonetz vegetation, such as *Artemisia frigida,* and solonchak vegetation, such as glasswort (*Salicornia herbacea*). In shallow depressions, meadow grass is common, but wet depressions on bottomlands contain much sedge grass.

2.) In the wooded-steppe region of the central part of the basin, the dissection of the relief is greater than in the north, because of the forking of the hydrographic network. Instead of the xerophytic fescue and feather grasses of the northwest, mesophytic plants begin to predominate: burnet (*Sanguisorba officinalis*), violet (*Viola canina*), and vetch (*Vicia sepium*). Birch does not form open copses, but dense thickets with a thick undergrowth of shrubs: spirea (*Spiraea media*), wild rose (*Rosa cinnamomea*), pea tree (*Caragana arborescens*), and cranberry tree (*Virburnum opulus*). Although pine and larch are not found here, there are many plants usually associated with them—e.g., peony (*Paeonia anomala*)—as well as others that grow in the fir and aspen forests, e.g., cow parsnip (*Heracleum dissectum*). Despite the low altitude, Taradanov Ridge is covered with a solid mantle of aspen and fir.

3.) The weakly dissected meadow-forest strip at the foot of Salair Ridge, at an altitude of about 1,000 feet, has a predominance of dusty and grainy slightly degraded chernozem that passes over into chernozem-like meadow soil. The grassy cover is meadow-like, and there are many hummocky reed-grass marshes; only in a few places, on southern slopes or on second terraces of rivers, do xero-phytic steppe plants grow. Birch groves are rarer than in the wooded-steppe, and are open and park-like. In places pine and larch are found.

4.) In the transitional subtaiga strip, deep dissection prevents the stagnation of ground water. However, the sharpness of the relief causes so much soil erosion that the soil has become shallow and rubbly, a condition further aggravated by intensive agricultural activity. Numerous remnants of forest vegetation, such as pyrola, find shelter in the birch copses amid open steppe expanses. Larch stumps and young fir trees are scattered on patches of peculiar soil which shows podzol characteristics and contains about the same amount of humus as chernozem. All these things indicate that this area was once part of the fir forest lying above, and has been cleared by man, a change that introduced some features of the steppe landscape. In the subtaiga strip there is little tillage; the main crops are winter rye, oats, and barley. Wheat does not grow well on this soil that has recently emerged from the forest, although a few miles away in the wooded-steppe wheat yields excellent harvests.

5.) Forests of fir and aspen occupy the southern and eastern part of the basin, where the altitude ranges from 1,150 to 1,300 feet. The basic soil cover consists of light-gray, highly podzolic, thick soil on a loess-like alluvium; however, there are shallow rubbly soils along the slopes. The vegetation is similar to that of the fir and aspen forests of the Kuznetsk Ala-Tau.

Agriculture thrives in the Kuznetsk Basin. For many years the basin has produced large quantities of grain and livestock. The level relief, which is extremely adaptable to mechanical cultivation, the chernozem soil, and the basin's homogeneity make it an ideal place in which to develop large-scale grain raising. The increasing population of the fast-growing cities and workers' settlements in the basin, the most highly industrialized region of Siberia, has created a demand for vegetables and dairy products that becomes greater each year. Thus, large dairies and truck gardens have been developed near all the large cities. Natural conditions have made it possible to create an agricultural industry that can supply the entire region with all the food its rapidly growing population needs—vegetables, grain, fruit, meat, and dairy products. The development of electro-energy in the Kuznetsk Basin has made possible a complete electrification of rural economy.

MOUNT SHORIYA IRON-ORE DISTRICT

The Shoriya iron-ore district lies south of the Kuznetsk Basin in the basin of the Kondoma River. The district's intermediate-mountain relief reaches its highest altitude, 5,200 feet, in the mountain group Mus-Tag. The principal mineral resource is magnetite ore, which is used by the Kuznetsk metallurgical combine. The iron ores are contact-metamorphics that are found, for example, in Telbes, at the contact of granodiorite with porphyrites and metamorphic rocks of the Middle Devonian. The biggest beds are: Telbes, Temir-Tau, and the Kondoma group. The Telbes bed contains 1,500,000 tons with average iron content of 45 per cent; these ores are mined in open pits, and although they are variable in composition, contain very little sulphur. Deposits at Temir-Tau include large supplies of sulphide ore with an average iron content of 46.7 per cent. The most important reserves (approximately fifty million tons) are those of the Kondoma group: they include the ores of the Tashtagol deposit on the right bank of the Kondoma, which are of high purity, contain a very small percentage of sulphur and zinc, and have an average iron content of 50 to 55 per cent.

PART II

EASTERN SIBERIA

Eastern Siberia is a vast mountainous region extending from the Arctic Ocean on the north to the Mongolian People's Republic and the Soviet Far East on the south and from the Yenisei River on the west to the Bering Sea on the east. The islands in the seas which border Eastern Siberia are closely associated with the mainland. The Yenisei River is a distinct geographic boundary separating two different worlds. Although the Western Siberian Lowland differs little from the Eastern European Plain, from the Yenisei eastward the relief, climate, and organic life vary sharply. Eastern Siberia is morphologically diverse; its altitude ranges from more than 10,000 feet to slightly above sea level. In contrast with Western Siberia, mountains and plateaus predominate and there is only a small area of lowland.

CHAPTER 4

Eastern Siberia

The geologic composition and structure of the region are extremely complex: rocks from pre-Cambrian to Quaternary exist—rigid massive blocks instead of the recent alluvium of Western Siberia. Many areas contain Paleozoic and Triassic rocks that include outcrops of granites and trap rocks (diabases). Associated with these rocks are rich metallic and nonmetallic mineral deposits. Geologic history begins with the formation of the rigid Paleozoic block of the Siberian platform, which rests on a folded Pre-Cambrian foundation. This platform is bordered by younger folded ranges, such as the Sayan and western Trans-Baikal mountains, and the intensively folded northeastern part of Siberia, which is of Mesozoic age.

Unlike the northern parts of Western Siberia and the Eastern European Plain, Eastern Siberia did not have a complete glacial cover. Glaciation was local, on only the highest mountains. Since the lowlands were free of ice, much of the flora and the fauna was able to survive this period by adapting itself to the severe climatic conditions. As the ice retreated, the flora and fauna swiftly populated the more westerly territory. This explains the survival of Tertiary relics and the presence of indigenous flora and fauna in Eastern Siberia. The xerothermic period that followed the Ice Age made possible the introduction of certain plants from the steppe into the eastern taiga and tundra.

Eastern Siberia is far from the warm seas; therefore it has a sharply continental, so-called "Eastern Siberian" climate. The temperature has wide annual and daily ranges. During the severe winters there is little snow; lengthy periods of calm allow frequent inversion of temperatures. The summer is rather dry with hot days and cool nights. This climate is appreciably different from both the climate of Western Siberia, which is transitional to that of Europe, and the monsoon climate of the Far East. The even colder climate of the glacial period caused the formation of the large areas of permafrost that have such a strong influence on the present-day landscapes of Eastern Siberia.

The complex hydrographic network of Eastern Siberia belongs principally to the basin of the Arctic Ocean. The huge rivers begin in the high-mountain regions of the south and flow northward into the ocean. These rivers, unlike those of the Western Siberian Lowland, are characteristic mountain streams, with swift currents, stony beds, and sandbanks. The peculiar Eastern Siberian climate and permafrost give the rivers an abundance of water, an exceptionally irregular flow, and many special features of their winter regime.

Eastern Siberia has vertical as well as latitu-

123

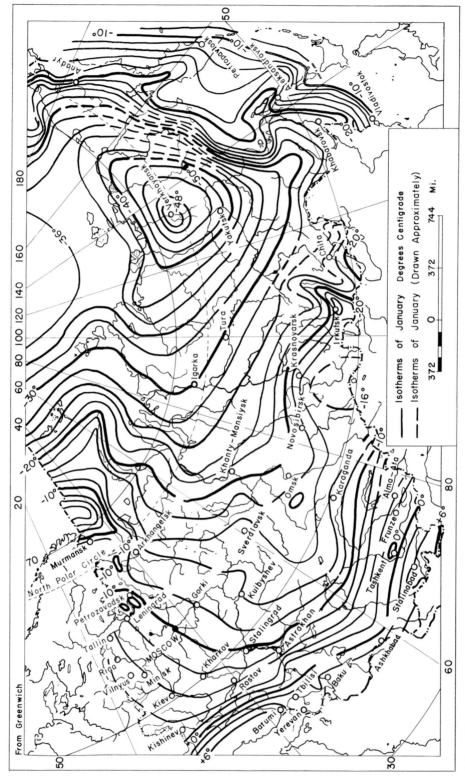

Map 4-I. January isotherms.

dinal zonality, with tundra, forest-tundra, taiga, wooded-steppe, and steppe in both types of zones. In the high ranges there are winding strips and patches of high-mountain vegetation. The continental climate of Eastern Siberia allows the forest landscape to advance far to the north, and, at the same time, the mountainous character of the region promotes the spread of these forests southward to Mongolia. Therefore, the taiga zone extends farther from north to south than that of the Western Siberian Lowland. On the other hand, the wooded-steppe and steppe is broken here, consisting of strips of steppe that jut northward from adjacent Mongolia into the taiga.

In the forest landscape the Dahurian larch predominates, being well adapted to the severe climate and permafrost. Although the pine plays a smaller role, dark-coniferous species are prevalent in places. This indicates a notably wider spread of coniferous species than in the Western Siberian Lowland. The forests of Eastern Siberia have few swamps, most of which are shallow because permafrost lies near the surface. In the diverse landscapes of Eastern Siberia, all types of soil are encountered— from swampy and podzolic in the north to chernozem, chestnut soil, and solonchak in the southern wooded-steppe and steppe areas. In the taiga zone, amid mature podzolic soils,

are islands of solonetz steppe soil. There are also patches of rocky soil found on the bald mountains.

The fauna of Eastern Siberia differs from that of Western Siberia. Many European and Western Siberian species are replaced in the Eastern Siberian tundra, taiga, and steppe by indigenous species and subspecies and by endemic species closely related to Eastern Asiatic and American ones; high in the mountains an unusual biocoenosis of Central Asiatic origin is found. Many common Siberian mammals and birds as well as some southern species have migrated northward. Because of the predominance of taiga in Eastern Siberia, taiga birds spread from the tundra to the steppes of Mongolia, whereas in the territories farther west, these birds are found only in the north.

Eastern Siberia is divided into five geographic regions: (1) Arctic, (2) Central Siberia, (3) mountains of northeastern Siberia, (4) Sayans, and (5) Trans-Baikal and Pre-Baikal.

Although Eastern Siberia has diverse geographic conditions, it is nevertheless a physicogeographic unit sharply distinguished from other parts of the USSR. The basic contributors to this unity are: (1) the climate, (2) the permafrost, and (3) the hydrographic network.

THE CLIMATE

The climate of Eastern Siberia is more severe than might be expected in a region near the 60th parallel. This results from the vigorous winter anticyclone—a high-pressure area in which barometric pressure is higher than anywhere in the world—that in winter (approximately from October through March) lies above Central Asia. The center of the anticyclone is south and southwest of Lake Baikal, over Mongolia and North China. In winter, to the east and west of the Siberian anticyclone are two deep barometric lows: the Aleutian low in the North Pacific Ocean and the Icelandic low in the North Atlantic Ocean. Near

the Chukchi Peninsula, a high pressure spur branches out, almost fully covering the central and northeastern parts of Eastern Siberia. The region north of this spur of high pressure is subject to Atlantic-Arctic influences; the region south of it is subject to the influence of the Pacific Ocean.

Cyclones penetrate into the first region from the Icelandic low-pressure area during early winter. Their centers usually move along the northern margin of the continent or along a trough of low pressure usually found over the adjoining seas. The cyclones carry a great amount of warmth. In the winter these lows draw the cold continental air from the region of the anticyclone and warm it. In the extreme north this creates strong southwesterly and westerly winds with accompanying snowstorms. If there is much cyclonic activity on the polar outskirts of Siberia, the winter in the central part of Eastern Siberia will be warm, but if there is only mild cyclonic activity, the winters are very cold.

South of the spur of high pressure—for example, at Ust-Maya—the influence of the Pacific Ocean predominates in summer, but in winter, cold continental air rushes in and produces northwestern and severely cold northern winds. In the northern half of Eastern Siberia—for example, in Kazachye—the north wind, blowing from the unfrozen expanses of the sea, is warmer. The continental winds are colder, particularly southeasterly winds, which make winter near the Yakut coast extremely cold.

In September the Siberian anticyclone begins to form. The Arctic air masses along the northern regions of maximum pressure promote its growth and cooling. Through October and November, air temperatures drop sharply, especially in depressions. In Verkhoyansk the temperature may drop as much as 39 degrees in one month. Both south and north of Verkhoyansk, the monthly drop is less (in Kazachye 26.9°F, in Nerchinsk 27.3°F). The Siberian anticyclone reaches its maximum development in the period from December to February, which determines the extremely stable character of air circulation.

The typical anticyclonic winter of Eastern Siberia has many calms. The probability of calms is very great in the central part: in January at Olekminsk, 69 per cent; at Verkhoyansk, 63 per cent; and at Yakutsk, 40 per cent. Along the coast the probability of calms drops strongly—at Kazachye to 21 per cent, at Russkoe Uste to 23 per cent. Winds with a velocity of 3 to 6 feet per second are common: at Yakutsk they average 5.5 feet per second, and at Olekminsk 5.3 feet per second. Although these winter winds are so light that they cannot even be used to winnow grain, only the lower layers of air are calm. Toward the periphery of the anticyclone region, wind velocities increase: on the seashores from 6 to 10 feet per second (Kazachye, 8.6 feet per second). Along the lower Yenisei River the yearly wind velocity is 22.4 feet per second, and in winter it averages 24.4 feet per second. The velocity of wind in the course of a day in the winter does not change appreciably. Away from the area of the anticyclone, the air is exchanged for masses of colder air. Since these contain little water vapor, there is little cloudiness and consequently the lower layers of air are cooled swiftly by radiation.

The breakthrough of warm air from the oceans in April and the gradual warming of air and soil cause the anticyclone to collapse, and in summer a low-pressure system is established over Eastern Siberia. There is high pressure at this time of year in the subtropical part of the Pacific Ocean and in the Arctic Ocean, and from May through August the cyclonic type of air circulation predominates. Air masses flow in from the seas to mix with the substrata of air of the central parts of the continent. Summer weather, although it is typically continental, changes frequently. The instability of the lower atmosphere in summer is due, on the one hand, to the warming of the earth's surface and, on the other hand, to the mass of incoming cold air from the Arctic. This modification sometimes takes place violently. Streams of cold air advancing rapidly through the lower layers of atmosphere between the Polar Seas and Verkhoyansk average 33 feet per second.

The influence of the Pacific Ocean is not great in summer because the thermal gradient between the central part of the region and the Pacific is less than between the center and the Arctic. Cyclones from the Atlantic often break in from the west. In summer the prevailing movement of lower air is from sea to continent to sea; consequently, the direction of wind has a monsoon character. Winds usually blow from the north in summer, and their velocity in the lower atmosphere is greater than in winter. At Verkhoyansk the average wind velocity in January is 1.9 feet per second and in June

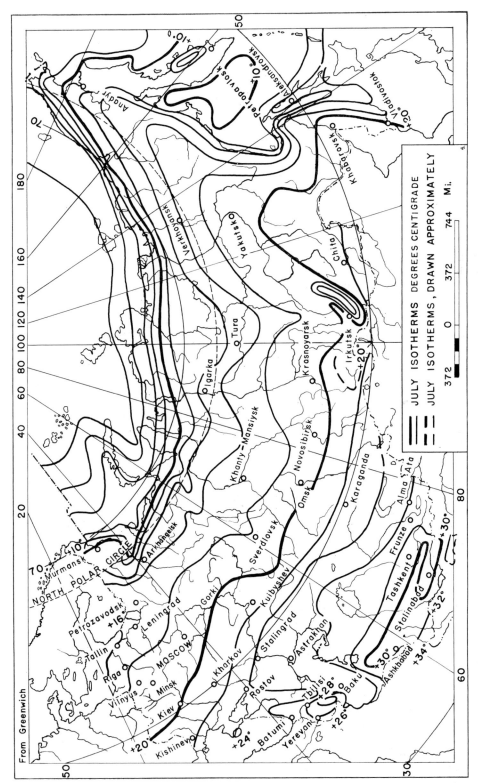

Map 4-II. July isotherms.

9.5 feet per second; in Kazachye it is 8.5 feet per second in January and 17.2 feet per second in July; at Ust-Maya 2.6 in January and 10.2 in June. Maximum wind velocities are recorded in the central part in June, in the south in May, in the north in July. During the summer the velocity is somewhat greater in the middle of the day than in the morning and evening; on the coast it varies less.

The climate of Eastern Siberia is determined by its northern geographic position; by the direction, speed, and nature of air currents; and by the character of relief. The climate is sharply continental: in winter, temperatures are uncommonly low; in summer, comparatively high. The distribution of isotherms is normal in the western part but not in the eastern part, in which there are two cold areas, one at Verkhoyansk, the other, and colder, at Oimyakon.

Verkhoyansk lies in a vast basin, surrounded by an almost solid ring of mountains. The presence of these mountains and the prevalence of winter calms, or extremely weak winds not exceeding 3 feet per second, lead to the "supercooling" of the lower layers of air and the accumulation of this air in the basin. Owing to this supercooling, exceptionally low temperatures are observed. Isotherms encircle Verkhoyansk more or less concentrically. Conditions even more favorable for the stagnation of air exist in Oimyakon Basin, which, isolated and locked-in by mountain ranges, is approximately half as large as Verkhoyansk Basin. In winter, Oimyakon is covered by a "lake" of cold air that results in temperatures even lower than those at Verkhoyansk, although summer temperatures are higher. At Verkhoyansk, the January average is −57°F, the July average 59°F, and the annual amplitude 116°F. At Oimyakon: January −67°F, July 65°F, annual amplitude 132°F. In Verkhoyansk the absolute minimum is −88.9°F and the absolute maximum 93°F; this gives an amplitude of 181.9°F.

At elevated points the summer is somewhat cooler and winter is warmer than in the lower places. For example, in Mangazeya, a silver-lead mining town at 3,345 feet on the southern slope of Verkhoyansk Range, the January average is −20°F, whereas in Yakutsk, at an altitude of 336 feet, it is −45°F. On the average, the winter temperature increases 3°F for each 330 feet of rise.

The −92.3°F registered at Yakutsk was the lowest temperature ever recorded on the globe until 1958 when −132° was recorded in Antarctica. Near Verkhoyansk and Oimyakon frosts are possible in any months except July and August. In October and May temperatures may be lower than −21°F; in November and April, −57°F; from December to March, −76°F. The rivers are under ice for almost eight months. Daily amplitudes are very great: in summer the temperature in the Yakutsk district may reach 95°F and after sunset drop to 41°F. At Yeniseisk during February the temperature has risen from −39° to 1.5°F and, at the end of January, it has been known to drop from 10.5° to −43.2°F in a single day. Even when the temperature is as low as −12°F, low humidity and clear skies permit the sun's rays to melt snow on roofs. There may be times between October and May when the temperature rises above 32°F. Farther inland, summer is warmer and winter is colder. The warming influence of the sea in winter, when there are very large areas of ice on the sea, is less than the cooling influence of sea ice in summer. Whereas in Kazachye the annual amplitude is 90°F, the absolute maximum 53.1°F, and the absolute minimum −62°F, in Verkhoyansk they are correspondingly 116°F, 93.5°F, −89.6°F, and in the more southerly lying Ust-Maya 108.4°F, 99°F, and −76.1°F, respectively.

Many wild and cultivated plants that are well suited to this dry climate, when transferred to milder but more humid climates suffer from spring or autumn frosts. For example, wild currants brought into the Leningrad region were destroyed by the early morning frost in March. Most animals easily survive the low winter temperatures but do not have the same habits that similar species have elsewhere. Rabbits run but little and spend

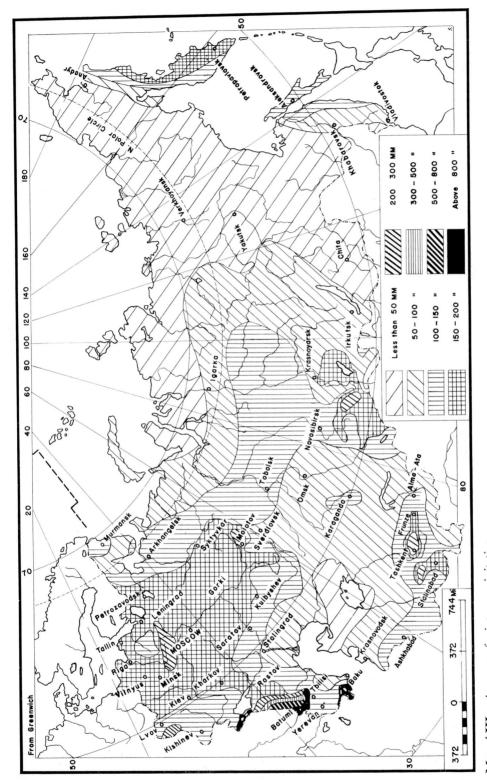

Map 4-III. Amount of winter precipitation.

most of their time buried in the snow. Partridges, grouse, and guinea hens spend most of their time huddled in the loose, porous snow, with only their heads protruding above the surface; when they do make their infrequent flights into trees, they stay only long enough to eat a few birch and willow buds, then hasten to plunge again into the snow. In times of bitter cold birds are sluggish and fly slowly, only *Cractes infaustus* flies easily from one tree to another in its quest for seeds. But by February one can hear the rapping of the black and varicolored woodpeckers.

At higher altitudes the daily weather fluctuates less and the wind is stronger. For example, the probability of calm at Mangazeya mine is 30 per cent, in contrast to 70 per cent at Yakutsk. The magnitude of temperature inversion may be extremely great. In the Yenisei ridge, the temperature at the Eldorado mine (2,300 feet altitude) has been known to be 18 degrees higher than at the Novo-Mariinsk mine (528 feet altitude) for four consecutive days. Although there has been a difference of 44.1 degrees in January, the annual temperature at Eldorado averages only 3.6 to 5.4 degrees above that at Novo-Mariinsk. The lowest temperatures have been recorded during calms: strong winter winds, from wherever they may blow, generally cause a rise in temperature— even though the wind is not warm, any vertical mixing of air disrupts inversion and warms the air near the ground. In winter there is a close correlation between air temperature and wind velocity. Thus, in Yakutsk, January temperatures rise as the wind becomes stronger— an increase of 30 feet per second may raise the temperature 40 degrees.

In the central part of Eastern Siberia, cold fogs are common—in Yakutsk, approximately every other day in the middle of winter is foggy. Exceedingly low temperatures and the slight snow cover lead to the freezing of the soil to a considerable depth. In the dense frigid air, sounds acquire an unusual force. The slightest rustling is heard at a great distance, the creak of a sled can be distinguished for

almost two miles, and the rumble of the ground and crackling of ice, from cold, sounds like gunfire. Because of the stillness of the air, the severe winters are endured comparatively easily by man. Heat loss during a calm with temperatures down to −50°F is little different from loss at −3°F with a moderate wind or at 32°F in a gale.

Although the winter is long and cold, thawing is rapid and continuous when spring comes. The average daily temperature at the end of March and the beginning of April rises faster in Verkhoyansk than anywhere else in the world—1.08° per day. The temperature rises .54°F daily in Kazachye. In spite of this, only May is a real spring month; the wind regime of March is purely that of winter, in April it is transitional, and temperatures are still rather low: in Verkhoyansk in March −21°F, April −11.5°F, and May 29°F; in Kazachye, correspondingly, −17.2°F, 0°F, and 25°F; and in Olekminsk 0°F, 22.7°F, and 22°F. Late spring frosts are common.

Summer, with hot days and cool nights, has comparatively little cloudiness and is often dry, but the prolonged dry periods are interrupted by torrential rains. The average temperature of July is quite high. For example, it is 66.2°F in Yakutsk, the highest July temperature at that latitude anywhere on the globe. The temperature sometimes rises to 100°F. In summer, stones and sand are often so hot that it is impossible to walk on them barefooted. To escape the heat, people work at night, despite the multitude of mosquitoes. In July the temperature seldom falls below 32°F; only at Verkhoyansk does it ever fall as low as 28.5°F. During the summer, cold winds that blow inland from the north coast of Siberia at a rate of 26 to 33 feet per second may lower the temperature as much as 18 degrees. The temperatures of the central part are also affected by the amount of ice in the adjoining seas.

In summer, fogs are rare along a narrow strip of coast. The growing season and frost-free period increases from north to south: (Kazachye, 81 days; Verkhoyansk, 105 days;

Ust-Maya, 126 days; and Nerchinsk, 150 days) and from east to west (Russkoe Uste, 63 days; Vilyuisk, 118 days; Olekminsk, 129 days; and Yeniseisk, 140 days). The frost-free period lasts 73 days in Verkhoyansk, 98 days in Yakutsk, 102 days in Olekminsk, and 107 days in Yeniseisk.

Grain and vegetables planted in May ripen during the short, warm summer and barley is harvested in the middle of July, although some crops do not ripen fully or are destroyed by late spring and early fall frosts. Intense freezing of the soil hinders the sowing of winter grain. Rye and wheat are sown during the hot, dry summers when the permafrost is at least 3 feet below the surface of the soil and it is necessary to irrigate. However, at Yakutsk ground water collects above permafrost and is available to plants so that they do not suffer from drought. Farming is limited not so much by climatic conditions as by the lack of knowledge of vast areas of the Siberian north. Because of the hot summer of Eastern Siberia many animals are found much farther to the north than they are in Western Siberia. Along the middle Lena at a latitude of 62° or 63°, birds such as field lark and horned grebe make their nests, whereas along the Yenisei they go no farther north than 58°.

In the central part, September is the only autumn month: it usually has many clear days and intense morning frosts. During the day the temperature usually reaches 68°F, but at night it may fall as low as 10.5°F. There is a rather sharp decrease in temperature from September to October, which, according to its wind regime and temperature, is a winter month. For example, at Verkhoyansk the temperature from September to October drops from 36° to 6°F, at Kazachye from 34.6° to 10.5°F.

The autumn precipitation is of agricultural importance. If, in autumn, rain falls now and then and soaks the ground down to the permafrost, next spring the soil will warm easily and rapidly. Thus grain sown in spring will grow for a long time without rain, being fed by moisture released by the gradual thawing of the active layer of the soil. But after a dry year it is possible to find dry soil, which the snow cover could not soak, at a depth of 4 to 6 inches.

The precipitation in Eastern Siberia is not great, the annual amount fluctuating between wide limits. Winter is dry because of the anticyclone, and in summer moist winds off the Pacific Ocean deposit their moisture on surrounding mountain ranges. Precipitation is lightest on the coast of the Laptev Sea—3.4 inches at the delta of the Lena—and near Verkhoyansk—5 inches. (On the periphery the amount of precipitation increases to 10 inches at Olekminsk and 18 inches at Yeniseisk.) Although Verkhoyansk's annual average is 5 inches, during some years there has been as much as 9.1 inches, during others as little as 2.0 inches. The precipitation in south Trans-Baikal (Olovyannaya), where the annual average is 10.6 inches, has been as much as 18.7 inches, and as little as 7.2 inches. Although the total amount of precipitation may be small, the number of rainy days is rather large—at Yakutsk, 104 days; at Olekminsk, 110.

Although Eastern Siberia sometimes receives no more precipitation than do deserts, the seasonal distribution of it is entirely different. August has the most and March the least. At Verkhoyansk all months except June and December may be completely devoid of precipitation. Winter has 4 to 14 per cent of the precipitation, spring 7 to 19 per cent, autumn 19 to 38 per cent, and summer 30 to 63 per cent. For instance, in Yakutsk, 1.6 inches during August and only 1.2 inches during March. Although most of the rain usually falls in July and August, a hot summer may be almost completely dry, especially the first half. Along the middle Lena the small amount of precipitation is indicated by the character of the wooded-steppe, which contains steppe plants and animals and has carbonaceous solonchak soil.

Since there is little precipitation in winter, the snow cover is thin. At Yakutsk in November the snow cover is only 4 inches thick and

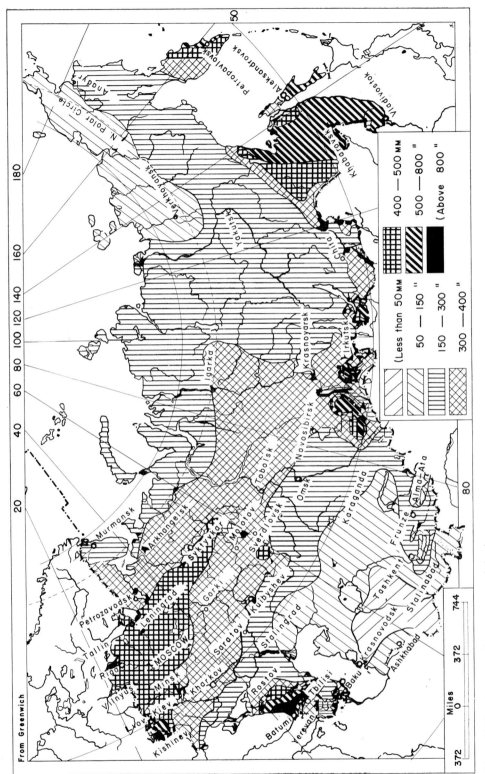

Map 4-IV. Amount of summer precipitation.

the temperature of the air drops to —17.2°F and lower, as a consequence of which the ground freezes deep. Toward the periphery of the region the amount of winter precipitation, and thus the thickness of snow cover, increases: the snow cover at Kazachye reaches 4.8 inches; at Verkhoyansk, 10.8 inches; at Olekminsk, 14.4 inches; and at Yeniseisk, 30.4 inches. The start and the duration of the snow cover differ yearly and from place to place. For example, the first snow may fall at Kazachye on September 12, but at Amga on October 8. Snow lies on the ground for 230 days at Verkhoyansk and 185 days at Yeniseisk. The snow, falling at very low temperatures, is extremely fine and dry, and thus easily transported by the wind.

The number of cloudy and overcast days is greatest on the coast. The annual cloudiness in Kazachye is 61 per cent, in Verkhoyansk 51 per cent, in Ust-Maya 36 per cent. The number of overcast days in Kazachye is 126 and in Verkhoyansk 84. The sky is clearest during winter and spring. Thus the number of clear days in January at Verkhoyansk is 12 and at Russkoe Uste 16; the number of clear days in July at Verkhoyansk is 3 and at Kazachye 2. On the coast there is a predominance of summer fog, and in the central part there are many winter fogs. Relative humidity is highest in the central part (Yakutsk) in November (83 per cent), lowest in May (60 per cent), with an annual average of 75 per cent. In winter, the daily march of relative humidity is even; in summer, it varies more, except on the coast, where there is little variation. Absolute humidity is lowest in the central part from December to February because of the low temperatures, and is highest in July; that is, it increases as the temperature rises. Local climatic peculiarities within Eastern Siberia are a result of geographic position, character of relief, and the influence of large bodies of water.

The fact that there are few cloudy days in winter—a result of the anticyclone—contributes to radiation of heat from the earth and intense lowering of the temperature; a 10 per cent increase in cloudiness raises the temperature, on the aevarge, 1.8 degrees. February, March, and April have more clear days than cloudy ones. October and September are cloudiest; May is next. For example, the monthly cloudiness at Yakutsk (in percentages) is:

January	52	July	56
February	45	August	60
March	37	September	63
April	49	October	73
May	59	November	61
June	56	December	56

For the year: 56 per cent

PERMAFROST

Permafrost is ground that has been frozen for many years. It occupies approximately 20 per cent of the earth's surface, and in the USSR about 3,860,000 square miles, or nearly 45 per cent of its area. The undulating layers of permafrost are of different thicknesses (the term thickness is used here to mean the vertical distance between the upper and lower surfaces of the layer at any one point), and lie from a few inches to several yards below the surface of the ground. Climate; relief; the physical composition, moisture, content, heat conductivity and capacity of the soil; peculiarities of the soil-forming processes; and kind and degree of vegetative cover are factors which help to determine the upper limit of permafrost. Its lower limit is the point at which warmth from the earth's interior or circulating ground water raise the temperature above 32°F.

Permafrost is covered by a layer of soil of varying thickness, called the active layer, which usually contains much moisture and varies in temperature with the seasons. This layer freezes every winter; a warm summer may thaw it down to the upper surface of the permafrost,

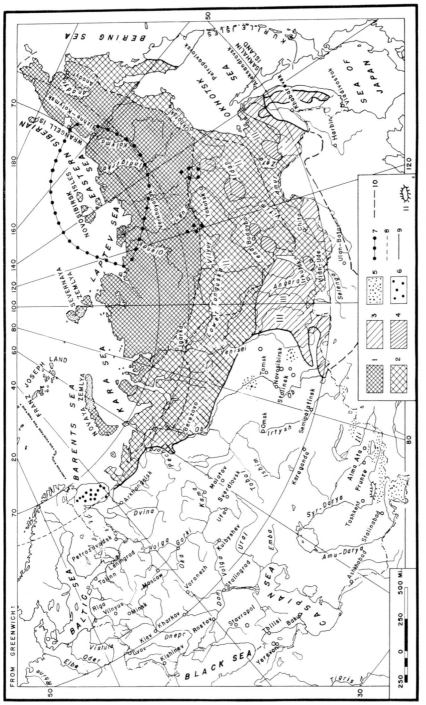

Map 4-V. Permafrost distribution: 1—Continuous permafrost; 2—Permafrost with islands of thawing ground, rare in north, increasing southward in number and size; 3—Islands of permafrost in thawing ground; 4—Permafrost with islands of thawing ground; 5—Islands of permafrost separated from general mass; 6—Permafrost in mounds of peat bog; 7—Border of regions with large chunks of ice in frozen ground; 8—Borders of subregions with different ground temperatures, at 10 to 15 meters deep (I, usually lower than −5.0°C; II, −5.0° to −15°C; III, usually higher than −15°C); 9—Southern border of permafrost within USSR; 10—Assumed southern border of permafrost (outside limits of USSR); 11—Present-day glaciers in northern USSR.

and a cool one may not. The root systems of plants and the soil-forming process are confined to this active layer. Islands of unfrozen soil with water circulating in it that are surrounded by permafrost are called *taliki;* islands of unfrozen soil, no matter how deep, that do not extend downward beyond the lower limit of the permafrost, are called pseudo *taliki.*

There are two types of permafrost. Some is solid: the soil is frozen to great depth without a break. Some, commonly found on the periphery of a solid layer, has alternating frozen and unfrozen layers, the latter being kept from freezing by the ground water that constantly or periodically circulates through it.

The border of a permafrost area is very similar to the shoreline of a highly dissected continent, edged by numerous islands. The southern boundary of permafrost in the USSR cuts through the northern part of the Kola Peninsula, crosses the narrowest part of the White Sea to a point 12 miles north of Kamenka, crosses the Pechora River near Rosvinskoe (65.5° north latitude). It begins to move to the south in the Urals, crosses the Ob near Kondinskoe, passes slightly north of Surgut, crosses the Yenisei near Nizhne Shadrino, below 60° north latitude, and then drops sharply southward. Below Krasnoyarsk, it turns west and then continues southward through the Western Sayan, the Tannu-Ola, and the southeastern Altai mountains, and enters Mongolia and China. From here it again enters the USSR along the eastern slope of the Bureya Range, runs along the lower course of the Amur, curves around the northern end of the Sikhote-Alin Range, follows the coast of the Sea of Okhotsk, and then cuts through the north-central part of Kamchatka.

This area contains sections solidly occupied by permafrost (e.g., along the northern coasts), other sections with many *taliki* (e.g., along the upper course of the Aldan River and in the mountains between the Olekma River and Lake Baikal), and still others with more or less thickly scattered islands of permafrost amid vast unfrozen expanses (e.g., along the southern boundary).

Islands of permafrost are also to be found outside the area, either in such soil as peat or in mountainous regions. There are many in the central part of the Kola Peninsula; along the Ob just north of Novosibirsk; in the Kuznetsk Ala-Tau, at the source of the Tom River; on Sakhalin; in the Saur Range; and in the

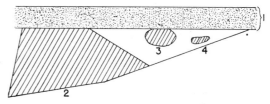

Fig. 4-1. Cross section of an area of permafrost near its southern border. 1—Active layer; 2—Area of permafrost; 3—Island of permafrost; 4—Lens of permafrost.

Dzungarian Ala-Tau. Others exist in the high ranges of the southern Tien Shan and the Pamir mountains, in both the northern and southern Urals (e.g., Mount Iremel), in the northern Caucasus (e.g., Razvolka), and on Mount Ararat in Armenia.

The permafrost generally decreases in thickness from the central parts of the frozen zone to the periphery, where it cracks in fantastic patterns and thins out. The permafrost in the USSR is thicker than that in North America—and knowledge of its thickness is necessary if the minerals and ground water beneath it are to be exploited. Its thickness generally varies from three feet to several hundred yards. The maximum thickness (approximately 2,000 feet) was discovered by drilling near Kozhevnikov Bay. At Amderma the permafrost was penetrated by a drill to a depth of more than 915 feet, but the full thickness, judging by temperature (at a depth of 700 feet, 23.2°F), evidently reaches about 1,300 feet. At Ust-Port it is 1,070 feet thick.

Farther south the permafrost is less thick: at the Norilsk plateau about 700 feet; in the mountains near the Utina River, a tributary of the Kolyma, 590 feet; at Yakutsk 450 feet; at Ugolnaya Bay 300 feet. Nearer the edge of the permafrost area the thickness seldom exceeds 250 feet: Vorkuta 230 feet; Taldan 265 feet; Bushuley 220 feet; Zilovo 170 feet; Skorovodino 165 feet. And farther yet it thins to less than 100 feet: Ulan-Bator 80 feet; the estuary of the Vorkuta River 80 feet; Naryan-Mar 55 feet; near Lake Khubsugul in Mongolia 45.2 feet. Near its southern limit, its thickness drops to a few yards: Berezovo 23 feet; Yanov, on the Turukhan River, 18 feet; the shore of Lake Kizi 3 to 6 feet.

The temperature of the permafrost provides a clue to its origin and can be used to calculate its thickness. In summer, the thawed active layer of soil extends to the depth at which the temperature is 32°F. The upper surface of permafrost may, during the summer, reach

found in the north and on high mountains, especially in permafrost containing many thick layers of solid ice. Temperatures lower than 23°F at depths of 30 to 50 feet are common in solidly frozen areas. Thus, in Ust-Port the permafrost temperatures (Fahrenheit) during the second half of September are: at a depth of 3.3 feet, 29°; 6.6 feet, 27.5°; 13.2 feet, 22.2°; 19.8 feet, 21°; 26.4 feet, 17°; 33 feet, 19.1°; 39.6 feet, 20°; 52.8 feet, 20.5°; 59.4 feet, 20.8°. On Mount Botugolski in the Eastern Sayan, at an altitude of 7,650 feet, just below 52° north latitude, the temperature of permafrost is 22°F at a depth of 50 feet. In the central part of the permafrost region at depths of 30 to 50 feet, temperatures fluctuate from 23° to 29.2°F, and nearer the periphery from 29.2° to 31.0°F.

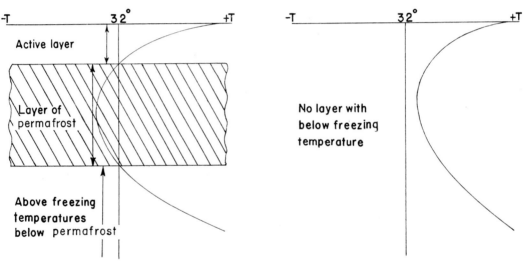

Fig. 4-2. Summer type of distribution of soil temperatures in depth: left, in regions of distribution of permafrost; right, in regions where permafrost is absent.

32°F but the temperature within the permafrost is always below freezing. Its lower surface lies where the temperature of the earth is 32°F. Below the permafrost the temperature is above freezing. In permafrost many bodies of animals of past epochs, such as mammoths or woolly rhinoceroses, are preserved. Many persons believe that either spores, eggs, or even animals themselves in an anabiotic state, may someday be found in permafrost.

The lowest permafrost temperatures are

In order to raise the temperature of a column of permafrost 69.3 feet high and one centimeter square a little above 32°F, it would be necessary to expend, for example, in Petrovsk-Zabaikalski 30,000 gram-calories, and in the basin of the Usa River 68,000 gram-calories. And for purposes of agriculture it would be necessary to lower the upper surface of permafrost 6.6 feet. It would require more than 6,000 tons of burning coal to thaw approximately .4 square mile of permafrost.

Permafrost as a Geographic Factor

In Eastern Siberia the formation and preservation of permafrost are promoted by: (1) the long duration of low temperatures, which vary from 29°F along the periphery to below −70°F in the district of solid permafrost; (2) the light, almost negligible, precipitation in winter; (3) the thinness of the snow cover; (4) lack of clouds in winter, which contributes to extensive heat radiation and intense cooling of the earth; (5) the many calms which result in temperature inversions and supercooling of the air in depressions and river valleys; (6) short, dry, and comparatively cool summer, during which high mid-day temperatures are followed by cold nights.

Permafrost affects the character of relief, and where it is present the normal processes of erosion and soil formation are altered. The shell of permafrost moderates the processes of erosion by protecting the subsoil from extreme dissection. Summer precipitation and floods lead to the development of wide valleys on permafrost because it is impervious to water: lateral erosion replaces downcutting along small, shallow rivers. This explains their wide channels, whose depth does not correspond to the magnitude of the flow of the streams, which are braided on vast bottomlands and have slow currents and many islands. Large rivers may form deep channels in permafrost and lower its upper surface for some distance from their banks, and thus cause extensive erosion of alluvial sand; for example, near the Tynda River (Zeya system) there are many gullies 40 to 50 feet wide and 10 feet deep.

Permafrost explains the asymmetry of valleys that trend east-west. On the southern slopes where the permafrost is less than a foot from the surface the active layer thaws slowly in summer and there is little erosion by water from the melting snow cover, which causes the slope to have a low gradient. The more highly warmed northern slopes, which have a southern exposure, either have no permafrost or else it lies 10 to 15 feet below the ground. The direct rays of the sun quickly melt the snow and

ice of winter. Because the melting of snow and the thawing of soil takes place swiftly, the meltwater and spring cloudbursts crumble these slopes, forming deep gullies and washing off the topsoil, so that the slopes become steep.

In valleys that run north-south, the depth of the permafrost is the same on both slopes, which gives symmetry to the valleys' lateral profiles. In the broad, well-warmed valleys of Trans-Baikal, the upper surface of the permafrost lies far below the ground even on the slopes that face the north, whereas in deep, narrow, and highly shaded valleys it is near the surface on both slopes.

Rapid thawing of the active layer has its affect on the relief of steep slopes. The soil becomes highly saturated with water and great masses of it creep slowly along the unfrozen upper surface of the permafrost. The creeping layer forms wrinkles along the lower slope— bulges and hillocks from 4 to 6 feet high. Because of this solifluction, which takes place each summer, there is a slow but constant lowering of hills and a general leveling of the relief.

In limestone regions of Eastern Siberia, permafrost and the prolonged winter freezing retard the development of karst topography, the ice acting as a cement in the walls of karst craters, sinks, and caverns. Here, as elsewhere, the expansion of the active layer in the course of freezing leads to the creation of mounds several yards high (*bulgunnyakhi*) or hilly bogs (*maryi*). Systems of polygons bounded by deep cracks develop in the loose alluvial strata, and the thawing of layers of ice in the permafrost leads to the broad development of "congealed karst"—craters, saucers, and sinkhole lakes.

Altitude has a strong influence on the distribution and thickness of permafrost. Many watersheds have no permafrost or only a very thin deep-lying layer, because the heavy rains that fall on them penetrate the soil to the upper surface of permafrost and slowly melt it. A thick snow cover, falling early and thawing late, does not favor the development of permafrost, nor does the inversion of temperature. At Turgutu station (Yablonovoi Range) at an elevation of 3,360 feet, the permafrost is from 10 to 25 feet thick and in the valley of the Ingoda River at Chita (2,250 feet) it is 100 feet thick; at the pass across Borshchovochny Range (3,070 feet) there is no permafrost, but at Buryatski station (2,860 feet) 5.5 miles away, shale is frozen to a depth of 110 feet.

The below-freezing temperature of permafrost makes it impervious to air and water. The depth to which the active layer freezes and thaws annually is important in soil formation and depends on many natural temperature-regulating factors: (1) climate—the farther south, the thicker the active layer, other conditions being equal; (2) relief—the active layer is thicker on northern slopes (that is, slopes of southern exposure); (4) water—running surface water drives the upper surface of permafrost downward and standing water raises it; (4) soil—in sandy soil the active layer is deepest, in peat it is shallowest; (5) vegetation—beneath a mossy cover permafrost is near the surface of the soil.

The depth of summer thawing depends on the thermic properties of the soil—its heat capacity and conductivity—which, in turn, depend on the mechanical composition of the soil, its density, and its humidity. Both capacity and conductivity increase as the amount of water in the soil increases. Heat balance depends on the character of the movement of moisture in the soil, the amount of organic matter it contains, and the thickness and density of its vegetative cover. In general, well-drained stony soils absorb and conduct heat most easily. Dry and moderately moist soil, poor in humus and covered with sparse vegetation and sand, thaws out rather thoroughly and rapidly. Clay soil thaws less deeply, and peaty soil thaws least of all. On the coast of the Arctic Ocean, the thickness of the active layer in sandy soil is 4 to 5 feet, in clay 2 to 3 feet, in peat 8 to 16 inches; west of Irkutsk, it is 7 to 17 feet thick in sand, 5 to 6.5 feet thick in clay, and 20 to 30 inches thick in peat.

Shallow-lying permafrost lowers the temperature of soil. This inhibits soil formation, as is shown by the absence of genetic soil horizons.

It also shortens the active period, or interval between the beginning of thawing and the beginning of freezing. With the onset of freezing, soil formation in the upper horizons of the active layer ceases, and the soil solutions formed during the short active period move deeper and soon freeze. Hence the soil layer is thin. On Dickson Island, under a moss cover 3 to 4.5 inches thick, half an inch of clay soil had thawed by June 17, 12 inches by July 15, and 16.5 inches by August 15, but on September 20 it began to freeze from above. The upper layers of soil were thawed for about 100 days.

Vertical movement of water in the soil is limited by the thickness of the active layer: since water cannot penetrate frozen ground, it will be stopped at the upper surface of permafrost. Soil horizons immediately above the permafrost are always in a state of supersaturation; for example, at Ust-Port the relative humidity of the lowest horizon of the active layer sometimes reaches 80 per cent. Capillary action raises water through the upper horizons and moistens the surface. In the soil below the permafrost and in the thawing active layer, vapor tension is greater than in the permafrost itself. Thus permafrost is a strong condenser of the water vapor in the thawing active layer, and of that always present in the soil below the permafrost throughout the year. This has tremendous practical significance in regions with little precipitation—for example, along the middle Lena and in Trans-Baikal—because auxiliary stores of water exist in the soil. The supersaturation causes swamping and the coloring of podzols.

Directly above the upper surface of permafrost is an accumulation of clayey particles less than 0.01 millimeter in diameter, washed down from above or forced down by the pressure generated when the active layer freezes. The resulting abrasion of particles causes pulverization. Washing down of humus leads to the formation of secondary humus horizons: for example, in the Pikan River Valley (Zeya River system) there is a secondary humus horizon in boggy soil at a depth of 10.5 feet. The movement of soil solutions of different concentrations and the enrichment or impoverishment of the separate horizons by salts take place only in the active layer. Under conditions like those on the Yakut meadow-steppe, easily soluble salts are washed down to the frozen soil by autumn rains and remain there because of the negligible circulation of ground water, which freezes rapidly. The water released in spring and summer by the gradually thawing soil, and the small amounts supplied by precipitation are completely absorbed by the roots of plants before enough accumulates to flow laterally. Thus, soil solutions at any given point are always the same, and no salts are washed out of the soil: the salts that are carried downward in solution collect in big rusty patches and streaks just above the permafrost.

Permafrost retards microbiological processes in the active layer, and none whatever take place in the permafrost itself. Consequently vegetative residues decompose slowly, which leads to the accumulation of organic matter and to the formation of peat.

Permafrost is a physical barrier to the downward growth of roots and its low temperature retards plant growth. Only in the upper part of the active layer can plant roots survive, although such physical processes as capillary rise of moisture take place in the lower horizons. The cold shield of permafrost compels the roots to spread horizontally in the thin upper strata of the active layer. Because of this, strong winds may blow down trees that grow above permafrost: in some places, as on the shores of Lake Doroninskoye in Trans-Baikal, whole forests consist of trees that have been tipped and tilted in different directions—these are called "drunken" or "dancing" forests.

Because Dahurian larch, which is extremely cold-resistant and has a superficial root system that it supplements with auxiliary roots, is by far the most common tree in Eastern Siberia, the forests have an extremely monotonous appearance. Larch will develop new needles when the ground is solidly covered with snow or even when its trunk is covered with a layer of ice. When the level of permafrost is raised by the development of peat, it kills pine, but larch

forms new roots to replace those destroyed, but the lower the permafrost drops and the higher the temperature of the soil, the better the quality of a larch forest. Where permafrost lies near the surface the trees are dwarfed and impoverished, with short, gnarled, and twisted trunks: the stands are thin and as many as 86 per cent of the trees may be defective. In many forests the trees are inclined in many different directions because of the periodic "heaving" of thawing soil. On slopes where solifluction takes place their trunks may be asymmetrically elliptical in cross section—shaped somewhat like the blade of a saber. The best grade of larch grows on clay soil that is more than three feet thick. Linden, poplar, and cork (*Phellodendron amurense*) grow only on large *taliki*.

The presence of permafrost, which is impenetrable by water, just below the surface of the ground, causes surface swampiness, not only in valleys and on gentle slopes but also on water divides. These swamps have a flourishing boggy vegetation, especially peat mosses. Bog vegetation, in turn, owing to its exceptionally low heat conductivity, leads to an increase of moisture and contributes to the rise of permafrost—in places it almost reaches the surface of the soil. Because peat is a good heat insulator, the bogs freeze deeply in winter and thaw out to a depth of only 8 to 16 inches in summer. Therefore these bogs are shallow and knobby —in contrast to those in the southern half of the taiga zone, which are 30 to 40 feet deep.

The depth to which soil thaws in summer is in large part determined by the kind of vegetation that grows on it. In forests, the thawing depends on the density of the forest canopy, the thickness and spread of the mossy ground cover, the character of the dead litter, and the thickness and depth of the humus horizon. Moss, litter, and humus, being poor conductors of heat, greatly retard the thawing of the soil. The deepest thawing (6 to 10 feet) is in sparse forests of larch and pine on dry sandy crests. Where the ground cover is not continuous, there is little litter and the soil contains little humus. Beneath dense shady forests and dense thickets, on soil with thick peaty horizons, the soil seldom thaws to a depth of more than 30 inches; moist meadows and bottomlands thaw to a depth of from 3 to 5 feet; dry meadows from 5 to 7 feet. On bogs containing reed grass there is deeper thawing (2 to 4 feet) than on mossy bogs, which thaw least of all—for example, on August 15 on Dickson Island soil with a mossy cover 1.5 inches thick had thawed only to a depth of 2 feet, and only 16 inches of soil with a similar cover 3 to 4 inches thick had thawed.

Open treeless land thaws deep enough to permit cultivation. In the southern part of the permafrost region, spring plowing often proceeds when the ground has thawed only to the depth of a plowed furrow. The plow skids along the frozen subsoil as along a stone, and the ice crystals in the furrow glisten in the sun like newly minted kopecks. By the time the grain is harvested, the soil has thawed to a depth of from 6 to 10 feet.

A series of actions that minimize the loss of soil heat in winter and accelerate thawing in spring make it possible to drive permafrost to such a depth that the temperature and humidity of the active layer will be favorable for agriculture. As a first step, it is absolutely essential to create conditions that favor the accumulation and preservation of a snow cover in winter and its quick melting in spring. One way of doing this is to leave tall stubble on the fields. This precludes autumn burning of grass and autumn plowing, but the melting of the snow cover is accelerated by spring burning, and by scattering dark cinders, which absorb the sun's heat, over the fields. It is possible to raise the temperature of the soil several degrees by spreading dung evenly over the soil. On such artificially warmed soil, as far to the north as Igarka and the Lower Tunguska, not only truck-garden vegetables but also certain varieties of early ripening barley can grow to maturity.

Permafrost in arid districts is agriculturally beneficial. The water from the melting snow and the part of the water from the periodical rains that are stored on the permafrost supply the vegetation with moisture during the first half of summer. Throughout the summer the thawing of frozen ground releases ever-new supplies of moisture that give vegetation a chance to complete its growth, even though there is little rain and the water from melting snow is spent. Deeply thawed and dried out by the end of summer, the soil absorbs almost all of the water received from autumn rains; this water freezes quickly and is safely stored until spring. The cold water derived from recently thawed ice preserves the ice, with which the roots of plants are in contact, for a long time. Strangely enough, ice and ice-cold water accelerate life processes and produce natural vernalization of plants. Experiments at Irkutsk have shown that young plants, a month or more old, that have been grown in soil irrigated with ice-cold water, still, if placed in a warm environment, develop quickly and mature in one or two months.

Earthworms cannot live in permafrost, although they descend to its upper surface. Some animals conceal themselves in burrows in the permafrost. The Kamchatka suslik, or black-headed marmot, hibernates in burrows where the temperature may be as low as −21°F.

There is less ground water where there is permafrost than in regions without permafrost. Classified by location, it is of three types: above-frost, below-frost, and inter-frost.

Above-frost ground water—which lies on the permafrost, a waterproof base—is sometimes liquid, sometimes solid, depending on the time of year, the depth to which freezing temperatures penetrate the active layer, and the depth of summer thawing. Above-frost water is cold —close to 32°F—contains a wealth of organic substances and much oxygen, but few minerals, except in the arid districts of Eastern Siberia. The above-frost water consists principally of water from precipitation, surface water, and water from vapor that condenses on the cold upper surface of the permafrost. The supply is small and inconstant; above-frost water has no pressure and flows only if local relief permits. It cannot be used as drinking water because for the greater part of the year it is frozen solid, and in summer, when it is not, the thinness of the water-bearing horizon, which is near the surface, makes it impure. In farming it is necessary to consider the consequences of disturbing the natural regime of above-frost water: for instance, a raised embankment will raise the level of permafrost; this forces the water to the surface and leads to swamping.

Below-frost ground water lies beneath the permafrost. It never freezes and is kept under constant pressure by its watertight roof. This water contains less oxygen and organic matter than the above-frost water, but much carbon dioxide. Although its temperature is generally above 32°F, the range is wide. It emerges to form springs at the foot of slopes with southern exposure, which are comparatively warm in winter and actually hot in summer. Where there are large outlets for this water, the ground around them may thaw completely through, thus creating large "windows" in the permafrost.

The inter-frost water lies within the permafrost, filling cracks either with flowing water or solid ice. It connects the above-frost and below-frost water, and is therefore known as transit water. The permafrost and the water are in constant conflict: permafrost, absorbing the heat of water, tends to convert it into ice; and water, giving off its heat to permafrost, tends to thaw it. The water that flows through permafrost carries with it, into the depths, the heat energy released as the frozen ground thaws.

In summer, warm rain water sinks far into the permafrost before it freezes. It gradually widens the cracks through which it flows, and may create islands of thawed ground (pseudo *taliki*). With the cessation of rains much of the water flows off into the below-frost zone. With the return of winter the water remaining in narrow cracks freezes solid, but only the walls of wide fissures ice over, especially if the water in them is in motion. Most thawed spots, however, are preserved from the grip of permafrost by water that flows into them from outside sources: these spots are of many shapes—lenticular, sheet, veiny, pipe-like, and stock-shaped. The temperature of the inter-frost water does not depend on the meteorological conditions at the surface but is determined by the length of paths along which it circulates through the permafrost: its temperature is always close to 32°F. The chemical content of the water may vary greatly—descending, it may be rich in oxygen; ascending, laden with carbon dioxide. Although the source of inter-frost water lies outside the layer of permafrost, the permafrost may yield much water with a steady pressure. Prospecting for water under such conditions is extremely intricate.

Much ice is enclosed in permafrost—filling cavities, cementing loose rocks of very diverse composition, and making the permafrost watertight—and the forms of its stratification vary greatly. Extremely fine crystals barely noticeable to the naked eye form veins only a fraction thick, and layers of so-called fossil ice. Seams or lenses of ice less than three feet thick are rather infrequent: along the banks of the Indigirka River, most outcrops of ice are 13 to 16 feet thick, and in some shoreline banks ice outcrops are as much as 165 feet thick (Sypnoy Yar). On the Novosibirsk Islands and the coast of the Arctic Ocean, on both sides of the mouth of the Lena River, there are especially thick seams of fossil ice covered by a thin layer of loose deposits. Thick blocks of ice form shear cliffs at the seashore, on the tops of which masses of semiliquid quicksand collect and drip off to form alluvial fans. Quicksand has completely filled many of the cracks in the ice and exists today as veins of soil inside the fossil ice. The bodies of such animals as mammoths and rhinoceroses that were caught in this quicksand and perished are, in many places, found fully preserved by the permafrost.

Buried ice has many origins: (1) small buried glaciers; (2) snowdrifts covered with rocks and soil and turned to firn; (3) lakes frozen through to the bottom and subsequently covered with alluvium; (4) underground ice-layers; (5) water which has frozen in crevices; (6) river ice thrown onto banks by high water or jammed in estuaries of lateral tributaries, where it was covered with alluvium or by landslides and cave-ins from undercut banks.

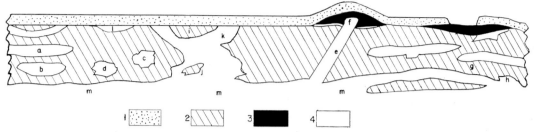

Fig. 4-3. Forms of water and ice in permafrost. 1—Active layer; 2—Permafrost; 3—Ice; 4—Thawed areas: a—layers and strips, b—lenses, c—pipes, d—nests, e—stocks, f—veins, g—hydrolaccolith, h—foliated permafrost, i—spring lake, j—permafrost island, k—nest-like lens of permafrost, l—*talik* window, m—pseudo-*talik*, n—subfreezing water.

The thawing of ice buried in permafrost leads to the formation of "frozen karst," such as sinkhole lakes. Forest fires, clearcutting of forests for plowland, and overturning of trees by storms may all expose soil to the sun's rays and bring about the thawing of seams of ice and the formation of basins which gradually fill with water. At first the affected area starts to settle and then forms a swampy hollow that is gradually converted into a shallow lake, from which protrude tree trunks devoid of bark and branches. The expansion of sinkhole lakes proceeds energetically: ice underlying the banks thaws, and then sections of the banks settle to the bottom, leaving crevices in the ground, cave-ins, slides, unsubmerged chunks of earth, and twisted and inclined trees in their wake.

Because the heat capacity of water is greater than that of soil, lakes increase the thawing of the permafrost beneath them during the summer: its upper surface is lowered, lenses and veins of ice melt, the bottom settles, and the depth of the lake is increased. For instance, beneath the bottom of one of the lakes near the lower course of the Anadyr River, permafrost was discovered (by drilling) only at a depth of 66 feet, but on the shores of the same lake it is found at a depth of 2 to 3 feet. The bottom of the lake usually does not freeze in winter because it is protected by the layer of water covering it, but when it does freeze, an ice bottom may survive a long time. Cave-ins of banks caused by erosion and thawing enlarge lakes, and this expansion leads to rela-

tively swift union with neighboring ones. Those from which the water drains may become sinks whose bottoms gradually turn into meadow surrounding one or more shallow ponds.

Lake formation proceeds rapidly. On one section of farmland that had been cleared 15 years earlier a small lake began to form as the permafrost beneath it melted: a winter cabin that stood 60 feet from the shoreline of a lake 13 years ago is today on the very shore, and cracks have already appeared under one corner of the house. Sometimes a much-used dirt road will suddenly be cut off by a lake that develops on the site of a burned-over forest.

Seacoasts that consist of frozen strata of loose material containing lenses and streaks of ice are rapidly eroded by waves. As soon as the glacial cement of the soil is converted to water, the rocks warmed and loosened by the sun and sea water succumb to the movement of the waves and the forces of gravity. Constant wave-cutting intensifies the process, and the sliding debris rapidly washes off and is distributed along the bottom of the coastal zone. Very sharp and swift changes occur in the configuration of shores built of permafrost.

Freezing of the active layer begins in October, and in February and March the frozen active layer and permafrost gradually converge. Intense dynamic pressure is created in the active layer at this time, causing horizontal movement of water or diluted soil. Ebonite tubes of soil thermometers have been bent or broken by this movement, which is due to the volume expansion that occurs when the temperature of the water drops to 32°F. Water expands 10 per cent when it freezes, when the compact molecules of water change into the larger molecules of ice. This increase in volume creates pressure within the ground and forces the still unfrozen water, and sometimes even quicksand, to move in the direction of least resistance. Below it is a waterproof layer of permafrost, which can be compressed but slightly; above it the frozen active layer, which may not only be compressed, but also raised, buckled, and broken. In summer, when the active layer thaws out, it returns to the original volume, but this process takes place more gradually. This annual expansion and contraction of the active layer, accompanied by a rise (from 2 to 6 inches) and fall of the soil surface, bears the name "yearly pulsation" and is responsible for the destruction of buildings built on frozen soil.

In winter the above-frost water, squeezed between two impervious frozen layers, acquires all the characteristics of artesian water, and during its freezing in the enclosed space causes extremely powerful pressure in the soil. The pressure of the water seeking to escape from the enclosed space plus the pressure produced by the increased volume of the ice in the frozen active layer may cause mounds to form on the surface. Trees raised with the mounds acquire a fan-like shape. The growth of a mound ceases when the resistance of the active layer equals the pressure of water. The water remaining inside the mound is converted into an ice core with numerous cracks that extend to the surface. Often trees fall into these cracks and split. In spring the bulging mounds settle as the ice melts.

If the pressure of water is great, it may raise the frozen active layer and break through it, and flow out on the surface before it has time to freeze, sometimes forming a fountain as high as a man. As the escaping water spreads along the snow and soil, it freezes immediately.

The ice formed by the complex processes that begin with the freezing of the active layer and conclude with the discharge of ground water onto the surface in winter bears the name *naledi*. When sharp differences between the temperature of *naled* water (32° to 34°F) and that of the air (−40°F) cause clouds of vapor to form it is said that "the *naledi* boil." As new compression forces more water to the surface, it either contributes to the gradual building-up of a layered ice mound with a vent at the top or pours across level land to form ice-layer fields. These fields vary from a hundred to a million square yards in area, may be 15 feet thick and may be the result of a water outflow of more than 300 gallons per second (along the Oyegordakh River in the Tas-Khayakhtakh Mountains). The ice produced when ground water freezes on the surface differs from lake or river ice: it is whitish, from the countless air bubbles contained in it, and sometimes contains chunks of clay soil. The source of the water feeding a mound extends far beyond the mound itself.

Conditions necessary for the annual formation of *naled* ice fields are: a large quantity of water in the active layer, low temperatures with little snow at the beginning of winter, and permafrost at a shallow depth. Ice layers may be formed not only as a result of tensions produced by the convergence of the freezing active layer and permafrost, but also by the outflow of weak springs active the year round, fed by below-frost water. These form hanging ice sheets on rocky slopes—beautiful and shapely ice cascades that are often cloaked in diaphanous negligees of vapor, as, for example, along the high banks of the Gilyuy River (Zeya River system). *Naledi* may also form as a result of the complete or partial freezing of those paths along which ground water circulates between the active layer and the permafrost.

As spring approaches, the mounds begin to collapse, and by the second half of summer, only disordered tracts of fallen trees and torn-up turf remain in their place. Or their sites may be marked by thick accumulations of large stones, since the water pulsating through the opening in the ground throws out and washes away all the fine soil and small pebbles. Where fields of ice form each winter, vegetation is scanty and develops slowly because of the curtailed growing period and the low temperature and poor aeration of the soil that result from the prolonged covering by ice. In June, bushes on the sites of such fields have not yet turned green and willows are only beginning to bloom, although a few steps away lily of the valley and peony have already finished flowering (Trans-Baikal). Bog bilberry, willow, and dwarf birch, which are prevalent on ice-layer sites, lend a tundra-like appearance to the parts of northern Trans-Baikal that are covered by ice fields in winter.

Besides the mounds of ice that form each winter and disappear each spring, there are many with a longer lifespan: these are called *bulgunnyakhi,* or hydrolaccoliths. Because they develop in the course of several dozen years, these mounds are large, reaching 120 feet in height and 660 feet in diameter at the base, and are resistant to melting. Most are circular or oval with flattened tops and steep slopes, and have an outer covering of peat that is as much as a yard thick and is cemented together with ice. Under this peat is a layer of earth—for example, lake sand—from one to several yards thick that is underlain by a thick (as much as 23 feet) layer of ice with a dome-like surface; inside this is water.

That such a fragile stratum as bedded sand would remain unbroken in its rise to a height of more than 100 feet, shows the extreme evenness of upheaval of *bulgunnyakhi* and the absence of any sort of catastrophic phenomenon accompanying their formation. Yet *bulgunnyakhi* grow rapidly: some have grown, according to the natives, 5 to 7 feet in twenty years. No *bulgunnyakhi* are built in a day, nor in such a short period can one melt. As they grow, they are riven by cracks from within, for interior growth exceeds that of their skin. Frozen soil and ice are then thawed by the sun; the tops shrink, and the day of their doom has begun. A series of concentric cracks appears on the surface; these cracks widen and deepen until a crater is formed, on the bottom of which

there is a small pool or bog. Mature trees 30 to 40 years old with unbent trunks that have been found in craters indicate the duration of their development. Annual mounds lie wholly within the active layer, with its poor supply of above-frost water, which explains their small dimensions and short life. But the roots of the *bulgunnyakhi* lie within permafrost, and the growth of the mounds is linked to the hydrodynamic pressure of the inter-frost and below-frost water.

Most mounds are formed on the bottom of basins of drained or turfed-over lakes in the middle of swamped sections of river deltas. For example, in the delta of the Indigirka River, 56 large *bulgunnyakhi* have been counted. The *bulgunnyakhi* in the northern tundra are all dead. On the shores of certain lakes in Trans-Baikal, such as Doroninskoye, unusual variants of the *naled* process are observed: for example, small frozen mud volcanoes and mounds from which there is an outpouring of mud in winter, and in which, even in July, it is possible to detect 10-foot-thick blocks of ice on the bottom.

Construction in the area of permafrost is plagued by problems created by the *naled* process. Hanging ice sheets shoot out from the banks of railroad cuts, covering the rails and clogging the drainage ditches, or they penetrate tunnels, forming large icicles on the arches and covering the walls. In the search for an outlet, *naled* water breaks through the frozen active layer in the places where it is the thinnest. Under warm buildings *naled* water often bursts forth and floods the subcellar and living rooms. One February, for example, water suddenly appeared in the subcellar of a building in Trans-Baikal, burst into the house, poured out of cracks and windows, and froze so swiftly that finally the whole house was filled with ice clear to the ceiling. A spring that emerges in a river channel in summer has been known to break through the ground into the warmed subcellar of a house on the second terrace when its natural outlet was blocked by the freezing of the river. *Naled* water may even escape under unwarmed structures, which provide some protection and heat and thus cause less freezing of the ground. For example, water has flowed upward into an empty icehouse, and even into a keg turned upside down in the yard, filling it half full and running out the bunghole.

In the first winter after the construction of an automobile road along the side of a hill, it was noted that *naled* mounds were strung out along the side of the road that was against the slope—the cleared level surface of the road had permitted the soil beneath it to freeze completely through, transforming the active layer into a frozen plug that arrested the movement of ground water down the slope and caused it to burst through to the surface. *Naledi* may form along even a small path beaten through the snow that packs it and provides deeper freezing of the active layer. The above-mentioned keg, which functioned as a vacuum vessel, drawing the *naled* water to it, and also the formation of ice mounds along the side of the automobile road have suggested ways of protecting buildings in permafrost areas—particularly hilly ones—by artificially freezing the active layer some 150 or 200 feet higher on the slope and parallel to the building. Here the vegetative cover and the top 1 or 2 feet of soil are removed from a strip 15 or 20 feet wide, and this strip is regularly cleared after every heavy snowfall. The downhill flow of water that might break through the thin frozen layer beneath the building is checked by the artificially formed frozen plug, and *naled* water can be drawn off into an auxiliary ditch. In summer it is necessary to cover the bottom of the strip with insulating material such as peat, which must be removed at the beginning of the first autumn frosts.

In many places *naledi* provide the only water available in winter, and the ice is used for preservation of food. When bogs, rock wastes, and ground covered by windfallen trees and other obstacles are covered with *naled* ice, they become passable for sled travel.

There are two diametrically opposed theories on the time of origin of permafrost. Some believe that permafrost is a relic of the glacial period and that it is slowly but constantly growing thinner and less widespread. Others believe that it is a product of the recent climate. This question has practical significance, since the correct answer may indicate: (1) whether —or how deep—to melt the permafrost before constructing buildings; (2) whether the thickness of the active layer will decrease or increase —a question of great importance to agriculture. It seems likely that neither theory gives a full explanation, but that neither is entirely wrong. It has been determined that the age of permafrost differs from region to region, and at different depths in a single region. For example, in the north much of the permafrost was certainly formed in the glacial period, but it is also true that it is still developing.

There is indisputable evidence of the antiquity of permafrost. (1) The bodies of dead mammoths, woolly rhinoceroses, and musk oxen that are found in the permafrost confirm that it was formed in the Pleistocene. From the moment of death, these animals have remained frozen. (2) Thick seams of fossil ice 30 to 40 feet below the layers of glacial debris indicate that permafrost has existed continuously since the glacial period: in the modern climate, too little snow falls for the formation of fossil ice. (3) Permafrost is slowly disappearing in many places, such as Skovorodino, Amderma, along the Selemdzha River in Khabarovsk, and along the Usa in Komi.

The following facts indicate that the permafrost is retreating downward and that its area is decreasing. (1) The upper limit of permafrost in some places lies 60 to 100 feet from the surface: that is, since the soil freezes from the surface downward, and present-day freezing does not reach that depth, the upper surface must be lower than it once was. (2) The retreat to the north of permafrost—in 1837 there was permafrost in Mezen, but in 1933 it was no closer than 25 miles north: that is, it is retreating northward about one-fourth of a mile per year. (3) Sunken lakes have formed where there were once thick layers of ice. (4) The upper surface of permafrost has dropped near inhabited places: for example, at Bomnak it dropped 132 feet between 1911 and 1933, and soil temperatures at Skovorodino indicate that it has dropped there.

The distribution of permafrost in Eastern Siberia is due to the fact that the lowlands and plateaus were not under a solid cover of ice during the glacial period. Glaciation was local. The climate was similar to that of modern Eastern Siberia, only colder. Severe winters and the absence of solid glacial cover were favorable for permafrost formation. During the glacial period there was intense freezing of the soil, formation of thick layers of *naled* ice, transformation of lakes into solid lenses of ice, great accumulation of snow, and the conversion of large snow patches into firn. Ice in depressions could easily be buried by deposits from areas not covered by ice.

Once more widespread than it is now, permafrost has retreated northward. However, present-day climatic conditions there contribute not only to its preservation but also to its active formation, as the following facts testify. (1) Permafrost is found in postglacial deposits of Eastern Siberia or in young alluvial islands of the Pechora River delta. (2) Dumps in the Kolyma gold fields have, in the course of several years, frozen through to a depth exceeding the thickness of the active layer. (3) When wells were sunk near the village of Tunka in the Irkut Valley, pieces of Neolithic pottery and human bones were found at a depth of 45 feet in frozen muddy sand, which confirms the formation of permafrost after man was living here.

Permafrost and Construction

The vast permafrost region contains a wealth of natural resources. These include the latent power in the large Siberian rivers, rich stores of minerals, immense areas of forest, tundra pasturage capable of feeding millions of reindeer, and large regions in which agriculture is rapidly advancing northward. The development and use of the former land of penal servitude and exile depends on the construction of factories and mills, mines, ports, dams, rail-roads, highways, airports, schools, hospitals, laboratories, and so on.

Permafrost is an obstacle to the economic development of any territory. Experiment has shown that a structure built on permafrost according to conventional engineering specifications quickly buckles and is ruined. Where permafrost lies near the surface one need only remove sod, cut brush, dig ditches, build terraces, set up a fence, or build a house to upset the thermal and water balance of the soil. The warmth and protection of a building usually cause the permafrost level beneath the building to drop, which may cause the following: sagging foundation, cracking walls, jamming doors and windows, eruption of *naled* water into the subcellar, bursting water mains, slipping slopes along ditches and terraces, and the like. Strengthening buildings for the battle against collapse is not always possible, because the stresses brought about by the geophysical processes associated with permafrost are estimated to be many thousands of pounds per square inch. Thus construction requires a knowledge of the physicomechanical, aqueous, and technical properties of both the active layer and the permafrost. In order to forecast the ways in which permafrost will affect construction and ways in which construction will affect permafrost—their dialytic interaction—it is necessary to acquire a thorough knowledge of both. Only by such study may we control the subtle processes operating in frozen soils and develop the technique of antifrost construction.

Permafrost is sturdy and resistant to mechanical influences; for example, gold-bearing sands that are solidified by permafrost are a solid monolith. The resistance of frozen soil to compression has a wide range and exceeds many times the resistance of the same soil in a thawed state, which depends on the mechanical composition of the frozen soil, its humidity, and its temperature. As the humidity of frozen sandy soil is raised, its resistance to compression increases, but the resistance of clay soil decreases with rising humidity. Frozen soil is extremely hard to work: even friable soil becomes so hard that the simplest digging requires heavy tools, such as crowbar or pick, and goes very slowly. Consequently a fire is usually built above ground that is to be worked and the thawed soil is then cleared away. Often several fires must be built on the same spot before the soil is thawed to the required depth. A small amount of ground water makes the work easier, but if thawed spots containing too much water are struck when digging in frozen ground, work must be stopped until the exposed surface has frozen and sealed off the inflow.

Blasting is not effective in frozen clay soil: clay will not crack, breaks up but slightly, and does not disintegrate. Drilling is difficult in any frozen soil. The drill heats during the work, transfers its warmth to the ground, and thaws the soil: the soil then loses its abrasiveness and binds the drill. If, during a pause in the drilling, water runs back into the hole, it freezes quickly, making it necesary to rebore. A ten- to fifteen-minute pause is enough to allow water to freeze in the hole and jam the drill. The hole must be filled with warm water and a 10 per cent solution of salt to prevent this—and salt soon corrodes the metal of the tools and pumps.

Underground ice must be avoided during construction. Buildings constructed over strata or lenses of ice many feet deep may collapse soon after they are finished—if ice is near the surface even while they are under construction. Many railroad carloads of gravel were thrown into a section of sagging road which passed over a lens of ice 13 feet thick, but the road continued to sag. In order to facilitate earthwork, steam, hot water, and electricity must be used to thaw frozen ground and to warm the soil. For example, steam or hot water is forced through an open pipe under pressure, warming the pipe and the ground surrounding it; when it reaches the open end, steam and water flow out of the pipe and shoot upwards between the pipe and the earth. The use of hydraulic equipment has expedited the washing of frozen gold-bearing sand.

The natives store perishable food in permafrost. For instance, in the Indigirka River valley, geese killed in the fall are kept in the permafrost until late the next summer. Occasionally cellars are built in frozen ground, providing temperatures as low as 23°F. These cellars are insulated with peat, may consist of a system of compartments with two or three insulated doors, and the ground above them should be well drained. At one of the fish-canning factories, a 60-foot-deep tunnel with lateral passages was dug in the permafrost; the lateral passages served as storehouses for the complete output of the factory. The stability of such structures is guaranteed by the known stability of the frozen soil: in mining pits columns of frozen earth replace timbers.

Frozen sandy loam or clay are converted into quicksand when thawed, become viscous and tacky, and have high water content. If railway roadbeds are constructed on such frozen soil, engines, railroad cars, rails, crossties, and ballast may all disappear without a trace when it thaws. If it is necessary to dig out and remove thin patches of thawed clay or loam (thick ones must be bypassed), brush roads or wooden stagings must be built to serve as bases from which to scoop out the half-liquid earth. Otherwise the workers have to stand knee-deep in cold mud. Under some conditions dry sand and slag must be mixed with the quicksand to thicken it before it can be worked. Occasionally artificial freezing is necessary to strengthen quicksand and make it workable.

Under the first rays of the spring sun the edges of depressions and the walls of ditches begin to thaw, and the half-liquid ground slides downward along a slip surface of frozen ground that glistens in the sun. Meltwater from ice formed in cracks in which the rains of autumn collected, and early spring rains further liquefy the soil and increase the speed of solifluction. If a rainy autumn is followed by a warm spring huge earth slides take place, some leaving large scars 100 feet long and 16 to 20 feet deep. To reinforce recesses, drainage ditches are built on top of and below them, and stone supporting walls or posts are used.

Water supply in the permafrost area is extremely uncertain in winter because small rivers freeze to the bottom and there is little ground water. The nearness of permafrost to the surface does not permit the digging and use of wells or the laying of water supply lines without complicated warming devices. Therefore, many of the people living along small rivers are forced to melt river ice to obtain their water; in other places fossil ice is melted or *naled* water is used. Water is also impounded in reservoirs that are made deep enough so that they do not freeze through, but the broad valleys with meandering streams that are common in the permafrost area are poor places in which to try to build reservoirs. Since water-supply pipes are surrounded by below-freezing temperature at least part of the year, it is necessary to protect them from freezing and breaking. Pipes are placed in trenches at a depth where the temperature fluctuation is slight and the minimum does not drop below 29°F; the trenches are then filled with some sort of insulating material, such as peat, and sometimes a second pipe, through which warm water is circulated, is placed in the trench. If water is warmed to above 50°F before it enters the pipes it will generally remain in a liquid state for a full 24 hours.

The main causes of the destruction of buildings constructed on frozen ground are: (1) irregular settling of the foundation as the permafrost beneath it thaws; (2) the buckling of the foundation as the active layer expands and contracts.

The layer of permafrost is stable only during long periods of below-freezing temperature. Warmth conducted downward by the walls and foundation of a building thaws the permafrost and liquefies the soil at the foundation. If the composition and particle size of soil are right, quicksand will form. Then the building begins to settle. The upper surface of permafrost lowers under the building, particularly under its warmest part. A deep thawed spot with frozen walls impenetrable to water—a sort of pseudo-*taliki*—in which ground water is held and into which surface runoff from rain may flow is formed: it is not symmetrical because of the irregular heating of walls of dif-

ferent exposure. The water in this thawed patch may rise and actually enter the subcellar of the house.

Because of prolonged exposure to sunshine during the many clear days in Eastern Siberia, south-facing walls receive a great amount of warmth, which passes down through the heat-conducting (particularly stone) foundations. Intense thawing and considerable dropping of the permafrost occur. Under the southern walls of one building, whose foundation extended 13 feet below the surface, liquefied ground could have been scooped out by buckets to a depth of two feet. Because north-facing walls are more shaded the permafrost below them thaws less rapidly, if at all.

The thawing of the permafrost and the formation of quicksand under the foundations cause buildings to settle unequally; cracks usually appear first, and a building may collapse because of this unequal settling. Because ice will melt with an increase of pressure, even at below-freezing temperatures, it is possible that unstable quicksand-like masses are formed under a heavy building even before the soil reaches a temperature above 32°F. Even unheated buildings, such as sheds and warehouses, disturb the thermal regime of the soil beneath them: in summer the soil is not warmed as much as uncovered soil; in winter it loses less heat by radiation and does not freeze through.

In order to use the best features of frozen soil—for instance, its great resistance to stresses, its sturdiness as a foundation—for construction, it is essential to preserve the permafrost under the building by decreasing the influence of the building on the permafrost as much as possible. To keep the upper surface of the permafrost constant (or to raise it) from year to year, the thermal flow from the building to the permafrost must be eliminated, and the amount of heat received and lost must be balanced.

The principal methods of preserving permafrost under a building are: (1) construction of double or triple floors separated by heat-insulating layers of dry peat or cinders with a covering of felt and lining of asphalt; (2) use of a material with a low heat conductivity (e.g., hollow bricks) for foundations and walls; (3) installation of subcellars that can be ventilated in winter and shut up in summer; (4) lessening of building weight; (5) installation of a system of pipes to cool walls and foundations, opened in winter and closed in summer; (6) use of arches or pillars to decrease the foundation surface in contact with the ground; (7) installation, under ovens or chimneys, of wooden rather than stone foundations; (8) use of drains to remove water from under the building and to prevent ground and surface water from flowing under it; (9) equalization of the temperatures under the southern and northern walls. This equalization may be accomplished by so orienting the building that the least possible wall area is exposed to the direct rays of the sun; shading the southern walls with fences, arbors, or trees; and painting the southern walls white. If a building houses a forge, a bakery, a public bath, or anything else that gives off a great amount of heat and if the permafrost has a temperature just below 32°F, the maintenance of the permafrost is, of course, difficult. For these buildings it is necessary to plan for the gradual elimination of permafrost and construct them as on thawed earth, replacing the liquefying soil under the foundation with thick gravelly pads.

The other basic cause of the destruction of buildings on permafrost is the buckling of foundations that results from the yearly pulsation of the active layer. During winter freezing this layer expands and the ground and any building on it are raised; in summer building and ground drop the same amount. Because the strata within the active layer are heterogeneous, particularly in physical composition, expansion caused by freezing is irregular, and as a consequence deformation of only part of a building may occur. Posts or piling supporting simple structures—fences, gates, garden benches, bridge piers—may be raised as much as 8 or 10 inches a year, and after two or three years may be 20 inches higher than when it was first placed in position. One of the piles of a bridge, for example, may be raised more than the others, so that after a few winters it may be

completely extruded and rest on the river bottom, or even hang from the bridge, and the bridge may curve and sag. Stone or brick foundations crack and lose their facing and may finally crumble entirely. Railroad rails may be bent six inches or more.

The reasons why a column or post is bent or raised are many and complex. As the moist upper horizons of soil—the active layer—freeze, a post embedded in them freezes to the soil around it, and the lateral expansion of the freezing soil compresses it strongly against the post. When freezing has reached a depth of 12 inches the active layer begins to expand upward. If the post is firmly embedded it will not rise with the soil, and the buckling earth will slide along its surface, but as the depth of freezing increases and the buckling ground exerts greater force the post is plucked out of the lower strata of unfrozen soil and moved upward, leaving an empty space below its base. Water and quicksand flow into this space and are solidified when the freezing reaches them. The ground continues to buckle and the post continues to move upward with it, but the formation of an open space under it ceases. When the freezing of the active layer reaches the permafrost, a state of rest sets in, during which the ground does not swell and the post does not change its position.

With the onset of warm days in spring, the thawing ground begins to settle. The post, whose base rests in the frozen ground or ice beneath the surface, does not settle, thus registering the height of its winter movement. As the earth warms, cracks open in the ground around the post and water flows in, thawing the frozen soil around it and causing both post and ground to settle. However, since the post can only settle to the sand that flowed in beneath it, it is left higher out of the ground than it was the year before.

The movement of a post is determined by the intensity with which soil and post freeze together, and this in turn depends on the depth of freezing and thawing, and the mechanical composition, moisture content, compactness, temperature, and heat conductivity of the soil, the weight of the post, the roughness of its surface, and the shape of its base also affect its movement.

The thicker the active layer and the deeper the post is embedded in it, the greater the area of contact between post and soil and the more intense the pressure of the swelling ground. The finer the particles of soil, the greater the swelling (for example, the pressure exerted when fine grains of sand freeze together is 331 pounds per square inch; gravel, about 37 pounds per square inch; and pebbles, 13 pounds per square inch): the moister the ground the more cementing water, and hence the greater the swelling; the greater the density of the earth the less the amount of water required for its saturation, and the greater the swelling—thus posts in tightly packed soil are raised more than those in loose dirt. Light-weight posts with sharpened, tapering bases in soil that is a poor conductor of heat are likely to be moved most.

Foundations are raised in the same way as posts and to approximately the same height. To prevent this it is necessary to take many measures to decrease the intensity with which foundations and soils freeze together. Such measures are: (1) Removing fine-grained soil from around the foundation and replacing it with material that freezes less solidly, such as coarse gravel or conglomerate. (2) Decreasing the area of the foundation by using a system of arches rather than solid walls. (3) Draining away rain water and ground water from near the foundation. (4) Giving the foundation a smooth and slippery surface so that the frozen ground will slide along it easily: e.g., coating the foundation with heavy grease and soaking the soil with oil. (5) Constructing the foundation in such a way and of such material that it is able to absorb distorting stresses: e.g., if heavy rocks are fastened with cramp irons the foundation becomes a unit that responds to the pulsation of the soil as a ship does to a wave. (6) Sinking the foundation (posts or bridge piles) to twice the depth of summer thawing. A porch, which is usually much lighter than the building to which it is attached, is thus raised higher by expanding soil: if its connection with the main building is not broken, its roof will dip, its floor will tip, its steps will slip.

The geographer, climatologist, hydrologist, soil scientist, geomorphologist, botanist, entomologist, zoologist, agriculturist, geologist, biochemist, engineer, architect, geophysicist, paleontologist, archaeologist—all may find much to study and ponder in the regions where permafrost is found. Perhaps the time is not far off when the obstacle that permafrost places in the way of utilization of territories will, dialectically, turn into its opposite and become a powerful productive force that man can control and regulate.

THE HYDROGRAPHIC NETWORK

The rivers of Eastern Siberia empty either directly or indirectly into the marginal seas of the Arctic Ocean. The two largest rivers, the Yenisei and the Lena, are each more than 2,400 miles long, have basins that comprise more than three-quarters of a million square miles, and have average discharges greater than 20,000 cubic yards per second, which places them among the greatest in the world. The chief sources of the rivers lie in the high mountains of the south, where the hydrographic network is densest and the runoff is greatest.

Since the rivers flow from lower to higher latitudes, they transport much warmth northward and play a conspicuous role in the hydrologic regime of the polar seas. The influence of this fresh warm river water is indicated by the relatively high temperature of the surface water of the Kara and Laptev seas, and its low salinity. The river valleys are mountainous in their upper courses and the streams have swift currents, many rapids and cataracts, rocky beds, and pure transparent water.

All the rivers have an abundance of water,

an exceptionally irregular discharge that is smallest in winter, and comparatively brief but intense spring floods—none is free of ice for more than a short period. Because the winters are long and cold, the ice is unusually thick; some rivers freeze to their bottoms, and others become clogged and overflow to create large ice fields.

The Eastern Siberian climate and its permafrost control the flow and water regime of the rivers. Summer precipitation uniformly decreases from the southwest, where as much as 16 inches of rain falls, to the northeast, where, in the basin of the Yana and the lower courses of the Indigirka and Kolyma, less than 6 inches falls each summer. The thickness of the snow cover decreases from 36 inches in the northwest to 8 inches in the southwest (Trans-Baikal): in the north central part, between the Yana and the lower Lena, is an area where the snow cover is seldom more than 16 inches thick. Snow cover has an important effect on the volume of discharge of the rivers. The runoff on the northwestern slope of the Khamar-Daban Range in Trans-Baikal, owing to the climatic influence of Lake Baikal, may reach 9 gallons per second, but on the northern slopes of the Stanovoi Range and in the mountains of northern Chita, the mean runoff is only 3 gallons per second, and in the steppes of Trans-Baikal near the Mongolian border and in the Verkhoyansk depression, it drops to half a gallon per second.

The water of the rivers is largely derived from the runoff of spring and summer rains and the melting of snow, ice, and permafrost. Because of the widespread occurrence of permafrost, the rivers do not receive much ground water, but even though the total annual precipitation, except in the high ranges, is not great, the rivers of Eastern Siberia have plenty of water. This is because of the extremely slight evaporation (a result of low temperatures), the long duration of ice cover, and the brevity of summer. In the mountainous regions, with their steep slopes and permafrost layer impervious to water, as much as 90 per cent of the heavy summer rain is quickly swept into the rivers. Thus there are high and rapid floods on many rivers, whose enormously increased water volume and accelerated current often create a destructive force of colossal proportions.

Summer temperatures and precipitation determine the amount of water derived from melting permafrost and ground ice. This ground water imperceptibly fills shallow streams which flow into and raise the level of large rivers. If autumn precipitation is heavy, following a summer in which the soil has thawed deeply, and if the snow cover is so thin that the active layer freezes completely through in winter—then there will be floods in spring. The flow of many rivers, after the snow mantle of their basins is gone, is sustained by the thawing of *naled* ice in the mountains. This ice is thick and thaws slowly, so that a rather uniform flow of meltwater maintains the rivers through the summer. Some rivers, despite the intense cold, do not freeze in winter (Yukhtochka of the Aldan system, Yasachnaya of the Kolyma system); others (Omolon, Anyul) are only partly frozen in winter. These rivers are fed by warm water from sub-permafrost springs that emerge along tectonic breaks on the river bottoms. The yearly amount of ground water in the total water balance of the rivers, however, is not more than a few per cent (Kolyma, 5.8 per cent; Yana, 1.8 per cent).

Even the large rivers have an exceptionally irregular annual flow: 90 to 95 per cent of the annual discharge takes place in the warm spring and summer months. All rivers are lowest in winter and highest in summer: some rivers flood at one time, some at another, depending on the geographic position of their basins, the temperature, and the depth of snow cover. In regions where the snow cover is thick, spring brings an intense and rapid thaw. The runoff of the resulting meltwater often causes a spring flood, although spring precipitation may be light.

The Yana and Indigirka rivers whose basins have only a light snow cover (6 inches along the Yana in February) and few spring rains, do not have spring floods. The water rises almost imperceptibly; the rivers, which have lost much water during the winter, slowly fill with meltwater from the thin snow cover and late-thawing ice. Wind and sun cause part of the snow to evaporate before it can melt— thus the rivers raise their level only slightly in spring.

Most of the summer rains along the upper stretches of these rivers are prolonged and steady. Slightly thawed soil is quickly saturated with water, and the water that cannot be absorbed begins to run into the rivers: some water is supplied by ice melted by the warm rain. The Yana has several periods during which its level rises, including one in June, when the snow finally melts, and another at the beginning of August, which follows heavy rains in the mountains, and is higher than that of June, especially in rainy years. The annual fluctuation of the river's level may be as much as 16 feet. The Yana's discharge is lowest in February, highest in July: its spring rise is sharper than its autumn fall. The level of the Indigirka rises at five different times in the course of a year, and the difference between its highest and lowest level may exceed 26 feet. The Indigirka has no discharge at all from November through April, its maximum discharge is in August 3,447 cubic yards per second, unlike other Siberian rivers it does not have high water in June, and the increase from July to August is gradual. In autumn its discharge decreases more rapidly than that of other rivers.

Rivers that have their sources in the high mountains have more or less uniform distributions of flow. The snow at different altitudes melts at different times so that the rivers are fed by meltwater from early spring until July, when the summer rains begin. If there are early rains or the snow in the mountains does not melt until late, the runoff may be so heavy as to cause floods. In June the discharge of the Lena is 80,420 cubic yards per second, that of the Yenisei 95,700 cubic yards per second, and that of the Kolyma 15,600 cubic yards per second. The increase in river flow from May to June is very sharp: that of the Kolyma is

90 times as great, that of the Lena 10 times, and that of the Yenisei 5 times. The discharge of each is smallest in the winter and in early spring (March and April): the Lena discharges 1,540 cubic yards per second, the Kolyma only 60 cubic yards per second. The maximum monthly discharge of the Kolyma is 260 times the minimum, the Lena's maximum is 52 times its minimum, and the Yenisei's maximum 20 times its minimum. The Lena also rises sharply in September following the onset of autumn rains. The discharge of the Angara is regulated by Lake Baikal, a natural reservoir, of which it is the only outlet. It has an exceptionally uniform flow throughout the year, even in winter.

The average temperature of the water in Eastern Siberian rivers from January through April is about 32°F. In spring the temperature begins to rise rather rapidly, reaching the maximum in July and August: the drop in autumn is slower than the rise in spring. Daily fluctuations of water temperature are especially great in May and August.

The temperature regime of the Angara River is unlike that of any other Siberian rivers. It receives very cold water from Lake Baikal the year round. Near the lake its temperature in August is only 47°F, but in its lower course the water is warmer, not only because the sun and air have warmed it but also because warmer water has entered it from tributaries. In winter, the water it receives from the lake, though colder than in summer, is comparatively warm (December, 38°F; January, slightly over 32°F) and the river never freezes over near its source.

The breakup of the ice on the large rivers is an exceedingly complex process. In spring direct and diffused radiation, water running off the banks, and melting snow that lies on the ice, cause the river ice to become pitted and fissured. Water from melting snow and spring rains in the mountains swell the rivers—pressure from beneath makes small cracks into large crevices, the water forces the blocks of ice apart and the breakup has begun. Although the rising water causes mechanical destruction

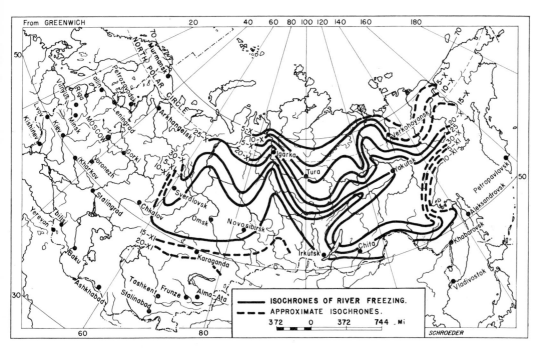

Map 4-VI. Isochrones for freezing of Siberian rivers.

of the ice, it melts it but slightly since its temperature is very close to 32°F. The ice cover on rivers flowing from south to north breaks up first in their upper courses, later in the lower channels. Water from the south reaches the lower sections almost before spring has begun in the north; the rivers begin to rise before they are uncovered—spring floods overtake spring itself.

On an isochronal map, on which lines connect points with identical dates of breakup in a given year, it is possible to trace the gradual progression of the breakup of the ice cover from south to north. The Lena and the Vitim begin to break up in mid-May; the Bulun in mid-June. The Yana and Indigirka, whose sources are farther north, break up later: the upper courses at the end of May, the lower in the middle of June. The bend of the isochrones on the Yenisei indicates an earlier breakup than would ordinarily have occurred because of an April flood at the sources. The mechanical action of the rising water is greatest along the lower courses of the rivers. Thus, the ice may break up while it is still very thick; for

example, ice on the lower stretches of the Kolyma is from 3 to 6 feet thick when it breaks up.

Floating ice may accumulate and pile up in a section of a river that is still solidly frozen, forming vast obstructions and damming up the already high water (at Turukhansk on the Yenisei, 50 to 60 feet). The spring ice movement, lasting on an average from 7 to 11 days, is accompanied by a considerable rise of water in the narrow sections of rivers; for example, at the rapids on the Lower Tunguska in June, the water has risen 76 feet above its average level. While being moved, large chunks of ice, which do not melt quickly, abrade and destroy the river banks. Thick blocks of ice, in the bottom of which rocks of different sizes have frozen act like junior glacial rasps, abrading the beds of the rivers, and undercutting high bluffs along the rivers so that they collapse. Agglomerations of boulders cemented with ice may so abrade the surface of rocky banks to whose level the flooding water has raised them that these banks have the appearance of natural roadways; the best roadmakers could not pave

Fig. 4-4.   Lena River in the Bulunsk region during breakup of ice in June.

roads that would be so smooth, so firm, so tightly packed.

The level surface of sandy river banks may be gashed deeply by ice carried by the overflowing water, the gashes resembling furrows made by a gigantic plow. The ice tears out and carries away trees, which increases the amount of flotsam along the Siberian shores of the polar seas. Elsewhere, the ice may push boulders and rubble that strew the banks to the side, forming embankments as much as 30 feet high that parallel the banks. These embankments are particularly well developed on the Lower Tunguska River, where sandbars up to 330 feet long with flat tops in which much rocky waste and gravel are embedded rise 10 feet or more above the normal level of the river. In spring tributaries carry out, together with the ice, many large stones, which, caught up by the water of the main river, are deposited a short distance below the mouth of the tributary, forming bars. In summer the warm river water energetically destroys the banks that have frozen solid during the winter. Beginning in June, all Eastern Siberian rivers gradually drop, with occasional small rises, and reach their lowest level in February to

April. Rivers are free of ice in the northern and central sections for from 134 to 162 days. In small rivers that freeze through to the bottom, there may be no ice flow; the ice is thawed from the top by the sun's rays and the water slowly melts the ice beneath.

The winter regime of Eastern Siberian rivers is extremely peculiar, and their freezing-over is a very complex phenomenon. In autumn, the water in the lower reaches of rivers flowing from south to north has a temperature higher than that of the surrounding air. The farther north, the greater the temperature difference between water and air; for example, at Sredne-Kolymsk, the water in the Kolyma in August and September is five degrees warmer than the air. As winter sets in the water loses heat to the colder air and is further cooled by the cold water that enters from tributaries which flow east-west—the heat gained from the water of the upper regions and from solar radiation is dissipated. When the loss of heat exceeds the gain, it is said that the river has reached the phase of cooling in the hydrologic regime.

Large rivers in the more southern latitudes are warmer in the summer than are small rivers in more northern latitudes, and require greater cooling in the winter to reach freezing temperature. Because of this, the isochromes joining points with the same dates of freezing display a sharp curve to the north, where they intersect such large rivers as the Lena or the Yenisei and the space between them narrows toward the south. This phenomenon is less evident in the northeast, where the rivers are smaller, and their water is colder. The freezing spreads gradually from north to south. The lower Lena freezes over in the first ten days of October, the upper part at the end of October or the beginning of November. The upper Angara freezes much later. The Yana, the Indigirka, and Kolyma freeze over more rapidly but separate patches near sandbars often do not freeze over until December. Ground discharge, which is small but is usually the primary source of water in early winter, stops completely when the active layer is frozen all the way to the permafrost. Consequently, there is a sharp drop in water discharge, the levels of the rivers drop, and the rivers seem to hibernate for the winter.

There are four reasons for the formation of the thick ice cover on the large rivers and the freezing-through of many smaller ones: (1) severity of climate and the thin snow cover; (2) the small amount of ground water; (3) slow current of the rivers; and (4) low temperature, close to 32°F, of the river water. Shallow rivers freeze through to the bottom: water moves only inside the alluvium deposited on its bed, and sometimes that freezes too. Only the shallow sections of the larger rivers freeze through, and rivers with a great quantity of water do not freeze to the bottom, their flow continuing beneath the ice although the discharge is greatly reduced. Rivers with steep gradients that receive no replenishment from ground water may drain in the very first days of winter, leaving no water to form an ice cover. At the beginning of winter, intense cold sometimes freezes the surface of such rivers before they can drain, covering them with a layer of ice up to eight inches thick, which, after the water level drops, hangs suspended from bank to bank. Under this first layer of

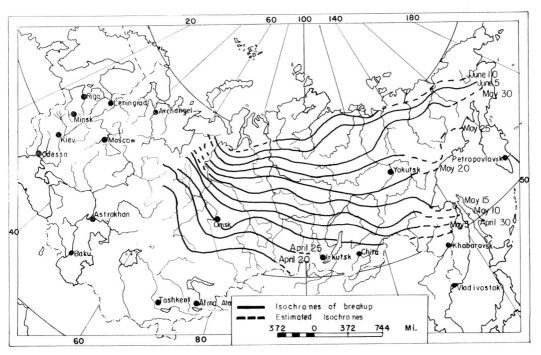

Map 4-VII. Isochrones for breakup of Siberian river ice.

ice a second layer may be formed at the lowered level of water, and sometimes a third one. Such a frozen river in which several layers of ice are separated by air cavities is called a *sushnik,* and if a horse is ridden across it the sound of his hooves striking the ice echoes hollowly through the chilling air. Deep pools in some small rivers may not freeze solid, and if no ground water flows into them they stagnate, acquiring a repellent odor and taste. When a pool is fed by active subsurface springs, it may not freeze at all, and fish will gather there in great numbers to spend the winter. These spots are live fish tanks from which the natives supplement their food stores. In severe winters shallows on even such large rivers as the Indigirka freeze through to the bottom, and the discharge drops to zero for many months.

The duration and thickness of the ice cover increase from south to north. Freeze-over lasts in the south less than 200 days and in the north more than 250 days. The ice on the Lena at Olekminsk is 53 inches thick, at Yakutsk 85 inches, and at its mouth 90 inches. The thinnest ice has been observed on the Aldan (18 inches) and the thickest on the Lena (112 inches). The thickness of river ice depends on the duration of the winter, the temperature of the air, and the thickness of snow cover on the ice—a thick cover acts as an insulator and slows freezing from above, leading to the formation of bottom ice. The upper stretches of many rivers with rapid currents and rocky beds do not freeze over for a long time, and the water becomes supercooled. These streams may form bottom ice, especially in years of strong winds and low temperatures in October. On the Yenisei bottom ice has been as thick as 10 feet at the end of October. Part of the bottom ice is washed away as sludge ice and driven under and frozen to the ice cover lower down the river, increasing the thickness of the cover, clogging narrow sections of the river and bringing about unexpected floods, or causing the development of vast ice-layer mounds.

After the formation of the ice cover, the water in the large rivers subsides rather rapidly, so that where the rivers are wide the unsupported ice sinks to the level of the water, forming an enormous trough with the raised edges of ice lying out of the water on the dry banks. On the lower course of the Lena, water has often risen as a result of autumn precipitation in the south, causing the ice in the middle of the river to bulge upward and allowing water to flow out of the cracks and inundate low places along its banks. At sites where springs with water as warm as 48°F flow from the bottom of the river, the ice is either thin, or missing: unfrozen spots are called *polynias.*

When the flow of water beneath the ice is obstructed or the inflow is too great to be carried by the constricted channel, the water may burst through a thin patch of ice and freeze on the surface, forming ice mounds resembling *naledi* from which water will pour, flooding entire valleys and creating ice fields that cover several dozen square miles. Such fields may also be created when an unfrozen spot overflows: they appear from year to year on the same sites; they arise, grow, and disappear annually.

In winter an active ice field presents a unique spectacle—as water is forced out over the already frozen river valley during periods of intense cold, mists resembling vapors from hot springs rise above the field. This mist results from the temperature difference of water and air: the temperature of the water overflowing onto the ice is slightly above 32°F, whereas the air temperature may be −40°F. Ice mounds begin to form in December or January and attain their greatest height in March, by which time they may be 13 feet high. On the mirror-like surface of such a mound, on a clear and quiet frosty evening, a network of fine cracks appears as the lower and upper surfaces of the mound cool unequally. Later, more and larger cracks form, and if the ice is thick and the amount of incoming water small, the water emerges through the cracks more or less quietly; but if the pressure of the water is great and the freezing intense, the mounds may explode, as they have been seen to do on the Onon River in the Urkan-Zeya system. Here, water from springs on the slopes above the river flowed through unfrozen ground into the river, producing colossal hydrostatic pressure beneath the ice. This caused the explosion of mounds 10 to 13 feet high and 50 to more than 200 feet in diameter, whose ice was 6 feet thick. These mounds, after cracking and shuddering in the evening, burst the next morning with a great noise like gunfire. The gushing water carried enormous ice blocks—fragments of the mound—along with a sound resembling that of a railway train. A small bridge was destroyed in a few seconds, leaving in its place a few pilings. In an hour or two everything had calmed down: the water subsided, blocks of ice were strewn on the valley bottom 300 feet from the mound, and adjacent mounds that had not exploded ceased cracking.

When sleds are being pulled over ice fields water may gush out of nearby mounds and, upon freezing, stick to the feet of horses and fasten the sleds to the ice. The horses are unharnessed and the drivers ride out on horseback, abandoning the sleds. In spite of this, sleigh routes are established on the smooth ice fields along rivers. River water forced through the ice floods roads, destroys bridges, and deforms buildings. Scraping the ice from a road near an active ice mound is hardly worthwhile, for a road cleared one day is again impassable the next. Trunks of trees and rocks are often frozen into the ice.

With the first spring thaws, the growth of the mounds and ice fields stops. On the surface of the ice, depressions are formed around sticks and stones, where thawing is faster, and rills flowing from them cut narrow, deep channels, gradually cutting entirely through the ice to the ground beneath. Ice mounds settle, leaving craters in the ice. Rain gradually disintegrates the ice field into loose gray pieces of ice, which may be carried off by a flood. Since the ice reflects the sun's rays, it thaws slowly and may survive until July or August, presenting a singular sight amid the summer landscape. Old larch trees turn green in the ice field, even though the lower parts of their trunks may still be surrounded by ice. Near

the ice fields and on islands of open ground amid the ice, plants do not blossom until the same plants are elsewhere already in full bloom; birds fly above the ice; insects buzz; reindeer may enter the fields to protect themselves from the heat and the gadflies.

Huge ice mounds may survive for many years. They may sink beneath the surface of the soil, be covered by alluvium and converted to ground ice, which is distinguished from ordinary river ice by its foliation, whitish-yellowish color, and opaqueness. Some rivers must change their direction of flow to pass around them, and the water of the melting ice contributes to the river flow during the summer.

The hydrostatic pressure that forces the river water upward and forms ice mounds is generated when, with the onset of extremely cold weather, the river ice expands greatly and alluvial deposits freeze through. This reduces the channel capacity and thus the amount of water then can pass through the channel. As the amount of ice increases, the amount of channel area that is open decreases until the water must break through the alluvium or lift the ice to form an unbroken mound. As the ice continues to thicken and the deposits that line the banks and the bed of the river freeze more deeply the channel becomes so constricted and the pressure so great that the water breaks through the ice at the point where the formation of the mound has weakened it. (Here in nature are the conditions which Pascal duplicated in his "barrel experiment"—the pressure of a small amount of water pumped into a closed barrel after it has been filled will burst the barrel.) If a watertight dam is created by the clogging of the channel with floating ground ice or with the ice cover, which may collapse from the weight of snow on it, the water impounded behind it may overflow and form an ice field.

Large rivers with highly developed alluvial deposits have wide channels (and thus large channel capacities) and deeper active layers beneath their channels. In winter the reduction of channel capacity by ice formation is slight and does not hinder the water flow, the amount

Fig. 4-5. Cracked ice mound in the river near Anuysk.

of which is decreased. Thus there are fewer ice mounds on large rivers than on small ones.

Ice fields are often found in those places where the river has cut many braided channels through gravel. In these places, with their vast cooling surface, shallow channels freeze solid during the first intense cold spell and stop the movement of water. But only the shallow channels freeze through; deep stretches of water remain mantled with the normal ice cover, and the streams are converted into a chain of lakes separated by ice dams and locked in on all sides. Here nature performs on a large scale the experiment of freezing water in a hermetically sealed vessel: swift and intense freezing causes so great an increase in volume in such a short time that ice mounds burst almost as soon as they form. The larger ice fields—such as the gigantic Ulakhan-Taryn on the Moma River—which contain several hundred million cubic yards of ice, are formed where large quantities of below-frost water break through thawed openings in the permafrost into river beds and prevent their freezing-through.

Almost the entire course of the Yenisei River is navigable. It is a natural highway uniting the sparsely inhabited far north, which is rich in forest, fur, and fish, with the economically stronger, more densely populated south—rich in agriculture and cattle raising—through which runs the great Trans-Siberian Railway. All the land in the Yenisei Basin is combined in one administrative and economic unit, Krasnoyarsk Territory.

The Yenisei River has no less importance for central Siberia than the Volga has for the region it traverses. The largest rivers of Eastern Siberia serve as approaches to the Northeast Passage, which links northern Europe and Siberia, thus allowing export of Siberia's raw materials to all parts of the world. The connection of the Yenisei with the Ob system by the five-mile-long Ob-Yenisei Canal, which unites the Kas with the tributaries of the Ket, creates a continuous waterway 625 miles long. The importance of Eastern Siberian rivers has greatly increased with the development of industrial centers, the transformation of the Northeast Passage into a normally functioning waterway along the northern shores of the

USSR, and the general growth of the economy.

The length of the rivers from north to south and the wide diversity of the geographic regions through which the rivers flow affect their navigability. The upper stretches of the rivers are shallow, rocky, full of rapids and rushing currents, and are little used for navigation, although on some of the larger rivers vessels with powerful engines but of very small draughts are used (in the upper course of the Yenisei, as little as 4.5 feet draught) to overcome the strong currents. On the rapid-filled tributaries of the Yenisei—the Angara, Stony (or Middle) Tunguska, and Lower Tunguska rivers—large, flat-bottomed, high-prowed, roofed boats are used. These boats are often pulled by manpower or use sails, because the coarse-rock towing patch is not suitable for horses.

The lower courses of the rivers are broad, deep, and generally suitable for navigation. The Lena below the mouth of the Vilyui is 52 to 66 feet deep, and the Yenisei below Turukhansk is 46 to 75 feet deep so that large sea-going ships can ascend them. They are aided on both by a slow current of 1.8 to 2.5 miles an hour. The Indigirka, however, is navigable only for the four months (June through September) that it is free of ice. Strong winds which raise waves on wide stretches, compel tugs towing strings of barges to stop over in protected places. Narrows, and rapids only 6.6 feet deep in the upper Lena and 2 feet deep on the Indigirka above Khonu, and shallow bars in the mouths of the Yana and Indigirka limit their navigability.

The following characteristics of Eastern Siberian rivers are favorable for the utilization of waterpower: abundance of water, steep gradients, hardrock bottoms and banks which can provide firm foundations for dams, and the alternation of narrow sections containing rapids and waterfalls with broad stretches—a circumstance favoring the construction of large reservoirs. The extremely irregular discharge of the rivers, however, would severely curb the winter output of power stations, unless reservoirs large enough to regulate the rivers' flow could be built. Conditions on the Angara River are especially favorable for the utilization of waterpower: it has abundant water; it has the most uniform discharge of all the Eastern Siberian rivers (because it drains Lake Baikal, a large natural reservoir); it flows across beds of igneous rocks; and it drops 1,240 feet in 1,110 miles—the steepest gradient of any of the large rivers of Eastern Siberia—for example, Padunski rapids on a

Fig. 4-6. Blocks of ice on a river in Northeastern Siberia.

stretch 4,150 feet long have a total drop of 20.6 feet and Shamanski rapids drop 42.5 feet in 18,000 feet.

The work has already begun toward controlling the Angara for the utilization of cheap electrical energy, which will facilitate the development of local deposits of aluminum and other mineral resources from the Angara-Ilinsk region, the development of the chemical industry, including the production of liquid fuel from Cheremkhovo and Tungussk coal, and the manufacture of cellulose, wood, and viscose by the chemical treatment of wood pulp. These and other branches of industry are guaranteed the availability of cheap electrical energy.

Despite the extensive hydrographic network in Eastern Siberia, there is not enough water the year round. The development of industrial centers, the expansion of gold mining, and the extension of railroads await the solution of the problem of supplying water during the eight-month-long winter to areas far from the large rivers. Shallow streams freeze through to the bottom, the larger ones are covered by thick layers of ice, ground water freezes, and permafrost lies so near the surface in many areas that it is difficult to lay pipes, let alone maintain the flow of water through them. On some small rivers, high dams have been built in the hope that the depth of the water they impound will be great enough so that it will not freeze through entirely and thus may provide a source of water in winter.

Eastern Siberian rivers contain many fish. Although salmon constitute 97 per cent of the catch, there are several species of whitefish (*Coregonus muksun, C. sardinella, C. autumnalis, C. nasus, C. tugun,* and *Stenodus leucichthys nelma*). In the east there are Siberian salmon (*Oncorhynchus keta*) and suckers (*Catostomus catostomus*), and in the Yenisei Gulf, many flounders. There is some commercial fishing on the lower Lena and Yenisei, but the fishing industry still remains in its infancy.

CHAPTER 5

Eastern Siberia Arctic Region

The arctic region of Eastern Siberia is the narrow strip of continental tundra within the Northern Siberia Lowland and the Laptev, Eastern Siberia, and Chukchi seas, and including the Severnaya Zemlya and Novosibirsk archipelagoes. This region, the most northerly in Siberia, has an extremely severe arctic climate under the strong influence of the Eastern Siberian climate. The strip of tundra adjacent to the sea and the islands have certain unique features of marine climate, which is clearly distinguished from the climate of the forest zone of the neighboring mainland. The region has a landscape of glacial and tundra zones. It lies within the limits of the Taimyr National Okrug of the Krasnoyarsk Territory and in the northern part of the Yakut ASSR.

SIBERIAN POLAR SEA

The Severnaya Zemlya Archipelago is a natural extension of the Taimyr Peninsula. Jutting far out into the seas, it is an important barrier separating the Kara Sea from the eastern seas of the Soviet Arctic. These seas, which have many common geographic features and a pronounced polar character, bear the general name of Siberian Polar Sea. This northern border is the continental shelf (with an isobath of 660 feet), beyond which it joins the central part of the Arctic Ocean. The Siberian Polar Sea comprises three rather clearly defined seas that maintain their own individual characteristics against a background of common geographic features. The Laptev Sea has the Taimyr Peninsula and Severnaya Zemlya on the west and Novosibirsk Archipelago on the east. The East Siberian Sea lies between the Novosibirsk Islands and Wrangel Island, and the Chukchi Sea is farther east along the Bering Strait and the coast of Alaska. The waters of these seas are linked by straits to each other and to the Kara and Bering seas.

Along the coasts the Laptev Sea is only 66 to 132 feet deep. These shallow waters extend from 270 to 330 miles, and in the region of the Novosibirsk Islands as far as 600 miles, northward from the coast. At the outskirts of the continental shelf, maximum depth ranges from 198 to 264 feet; only at the northeastern end of the Taimyr Peninsula are there depths of 660 to 1,320 feet. Vast expanses of the East Siberian Sea average between 60 and 80 feet deep; maximum depths run from 148 to 181 feet. The average depth of the Chukchi Sea in its southern and middle sections is only 148 feet, but east of Herald Island there is a northward jutting submarine trough whose depths have a strong influence on the sea regime. Beyond this submarine trough is Herald Bank, which retains ice for a long time. Along the north-south trough, however, the water from the northern limits of the Chukchi Sea flows southward.

Soil on the bottom of the seas is diverse. The Lena and Yana rivers deposit suspended material close to the shore in the Laptev Sea. West of the Lena River delta, sandy soil predominates; only near the Taimyr Peninsula are there stones and pebbles. As the depth increases 120 miles from the shore, the sand is replaced by silt. East of the Lena River delta, most of the sea floor is covered with a gray silt. Sand and pebbles are usually found on the sea floor close to islands.

These seas, and particularly the Laptev Sea, which is equidistant and most removed from the influence of the Atlantic and Pacific oceans, have a climate more severe than that of the Kara Sea. This is because much heat is expended in the thawing of large masses of ice and because the seas are subject to the severe continental climate of Eastern Siberia. Cyclonic activity from the Atlantic Ocean passes over the Laptev Sea. In winter, when there is a high-pressure system on the mainland, on which weakened cyclones have very little influence, the sea becomes warmer, cloudiness increases, and snowstorms occur as late as April or May. During winter, which is long, there are clear skies, weak southern winds or no wind at all, and temperatures higher than those on the adjacent mainland. The eastern part of the East Siberian Sea has milder winters, and thaws may occur even in mid-winter. In the short, cool, and cloudy summer, the temperatures are lower than those on the continent; there are many early morning frosts and fogs and frequent drizzles. In the Laptev Sea there is a counterclockwise current. The flow of river water, especially that of the Lena, forces the sea water from the shore and forms a steady weak current moving toward the Novosibirsk Islands and northward along their western shores. There is another current flowing southward along the eastern shore of Severnaya Zemlya that carries great masses of ice.

During summer the Kamchatka Current of the East Siberian and Chukchi seas penetrates through the Bering Strait. It moves, in its main current, to the middle of De Long Strait between Wrangel Island and the mainland. Here a strip of open sea forms a deep channel in the ice, which is pressed to the mainland shore. Along the shore of the Chukchi Peninsula a weaker current flows from west to east, joining the Kamchatka Current to move in a counterclockwise direction. In winter the entire current has a reverse direction.

Steady and periodic currents are changed and stopped altogether by strong winds which can alter both the force and direction of moving water. Along the entire coast, these winds create waves with an amplitude of 3.5 feet or more, a factor which is important in navigation between the mouths of large rivers. A wave entering the Laptev Sea from the north increases in amplitude in the southwestern part of the sea. In the East Siberian Sea, the incoming current from the north of the Novosibirsk Islands passes to the southeast in the upper layer of water with a speed of from 0.8 to 2 inches per second. In the Chukchi Sea, the influence of the Pacific Ocean is evident in the general tidal conditions. The distribution of land and sea, the contours of the shores, the depths, winds, and constant currents all sharply influence the sea level, which varies from 1 to 80 inches and more. Near Bear Islands the fluctuation is 1 inch; at the mouth of the Lena River, 10 inches; at Bennett Island, 42 inches; at Wrangel Island, 52 inches; and in Khatanga Bay, 85 inches; as a consequence of which the movement of ice does not stop all winter. Ebb and flow in the Laptev Sea have a regular semi-diurnal character.

The temperature, salinity, and transparency or clarity of sea water are affected by the enormous amount of river water entering these seas. This river water causes direct stratification of the sea water. A layer of warm water of insignificant salinity and low density lies on the surface, above denser, colder, saltier, and clearer water. The water of Siberian rivers can be traced far beyond the estuaries. For example, the fresh, muddy water and flotsam of the Lena can be found as far as three hundred miles from shore. In summer the water entering the Chukchi Sea from the Bering Strait is warm and supplies much heat.

The warmest, clearest, and least salty water is found near the mouths of rivers. In the Bykov channel of the Lena River the salinity is 8 to 10 per cent, but it increases farther out in the sea: at 75°30′, 14.9 per cent; at 76°30′, 18 per cent; at 77°, 23.7 per cent; and at 77°30′, 27.4 per cent. Temperature of 59°F and salinity of 17 per cent are found in the freshened southeastern part of the Laptev Sea, and there is higher salinity (28 per cent on the surface in summer) in the deeper northwestern part, where there are below-freezing temperatures even on the surface. In summer, surface temperatures and salinity depend on the extent of the ice cover, which yields during thawing an immense quantity of fresh water, especially on the shoals and near the shores. In winter, the water of the Laptev Sea has a freezing temperature (for water of its salinity) or close to it; bottom temperatures are below freezing the year round except near river mouths. Salinity generally increases with depth. In water strongly subjected to the influence of rivers, however, there are little salinity and above-freezing temperatures even in deep water. This is apparent from the following tables.

In the Laptev Sea below 74° north latitude and 120° east longitude from Greenwich:

DEPTH (FT.)	TEMP. (F)	SALINITY (%)
0	37	17.4
33	33	22.5
66	30	28.6

Seventy-five miles northeast of the mouth of the Lena:

DEPTH (FT.)	TEMP. (F)	SALINITY (%)
0	40	4.9
33	40	4.9
66	39	6.2

Temperatures of the East Siberian and Chukchi seas are not known, although surface temperatures from 32° to 41°F have been recorded. The proximity of the continent, with its rapid cooling in autumn and severe cold in winter, contributes to the formation of ice in these seas.

Convectional circulation, owing to the lowering of air temperature, takes place in only the comparatively thin, least dense, surface layer of water, causing ice to form easily. Ice forms faster in the Laptev Sea and the East Siberian Sea than in the more western seas of the Arctic. Because of the rapidity of ice formation in these seas, ships may be stopped by the freshly formed ice. Even in summer, ice may form with a snow cover, and the difference between the ice formation in winter and in summer is small: in winter 36 inches freeze, and in summer 32 inches. In coastal water with its shallows and small ebb and flow, low temperature and low salinity in autumn lead to the development of shore ice. In the eastern part of the Laptev Sea and the western part of the East Siberian Sea, this ice reaches a width of from 180 to 300 miles. In the Chukchi Sea it is less developed—for example, in the region of the Kolyuchin Bay its width is 21 miles.

In autumn, the ice becomes solid over vast expanses. In the region of Tiksi Bay during early October, a land-attached floe forms; between the middle and end of October, the ice cover develops on the more open expanses of the sea. On the northern edge of the coastal land-floe lying a little north of the Novosibirsk Islands, huge pieces of ice often break loose and drift away from the land-floe, leaving large areas of open water behind. These areas are important in the life of ice in the polar seas.

Expanses of open water on the margin of the coastal land-floe opposite the mouth of large rivers are sites of origin of polar ice. Ice is formed here in winter because of (1) the low temperatures, (2) the river water being carried to these places, and (3) the winds. When the temperature becomes sufficiently cold, the river water arriving here freezes, forming thick ice.

This ice is then broken loose by the winds and drifts from the edge of the land-floe. In the open water left by the drifting ice, new ice begins to form. This process of ice formation and break up is repeated many times during the winter.

The ice that breaks loose drifts away and collects in large ice hummocks, some of which are more than 30 feet high. Ice hummocks are especially well developed in the eastern part of the East Siberian Sea. In the Wrangel Island region, for example, the ice formed a hummock 50 to 66 feet high, approximately 3.5 miles wide, and stretching for dozens of miles—a real barrier to vessels. In summer, the coastal land-floe breaks up into separate floating fields and finely broken ice of varying density. Thick polar ice usually does not drift to the shallow coastal regions; only in the deep western part of the Laptev Sea do large ice fields or icebergs from the glaciers of Severnaya Zemlya sometimes run aground, forming large, picturesque, immovable *stamukhi*.

Ice thaws faster near the mouths of rivers than it does in the open sea because of the direct contact of coastal waters with the warmed shores of the mainland, the rapid warming of shallow water by the sun, and the low salinity of the surface water. Boris Vilkitski Strait is ice free only in the most favorable years, but more often, usually in August and September, the only free channel is very near to Cape Chelyuskin. The amount of ice does not remain constant from year to year, and the ice present during the summers is determined by the force and direction of the winds.

A fundamental factor of ice formation is the intensity of cyclonic activity at high latitudes. In years of little ice, cyclones in the area of the Barents Sea move east by the high-arctic route. As a consequence, there is a flow of masses of warm air into the Laptev Sea and the Novosibirsk Archipelago zone; thus the amount of ice in the Laptev Sea in such years is small. With a decrease in atmospheric circulation, the cap of cold air in the polar regions enlarges, displacing the polar front southward and, in turn, causing more freezing of the sea. The

amount and disposition of ice in the Chukchi Sea are determined by hydrologic factors, such as a warm current from the Bering Sea entering from the south and a weak cold one from the East Siberian Sea, as well as by atmospheric influences. The magnitude of the warm currents which thaw and force the ice northward does not remain constant. This is reflected in the condition of the ice and the position of its southern border. If a high-pressure area is stabilized above the Chukchi Sea and cyclonic activity is within the limits of the Barents Sea, a northern current is created that introduces masses of cold air which retard the thawing of ice, cold arctic water, and thick polar ice. With the reverse distribution of pressure, south and east winds predominate, bringing warm air from the coast which promotes the active thawing of ice. This warm air increases the flow of warmer water from the southeast and impedes the entry of cold water from the East Siberian Sea.

The route along the Siberian Polar Sea is one of the links of the Northern Sea Route. The coasts are icy, both by reason of the amount and extensiveness of the ice on the coasts between the mouths of the rivers Pyasina and Khatanga on the west, and between the capes Shelagski and Shmidt on the east. These parts of the coast receive no discharge from large rivers. But opposite the outlet of the powerful Lena current, the southern border of ice in August withdraws to Severnaya Zemlya.

The abundance of organic and inorganic substances discharged by the rivers plays a substantial role in the biology of the seas. However, the broad, shore-attached ice floes hinder the development of littoral life and freshen surface waters durng thawing. The waters beyond the limits of the Arctic Circle and on the north are not separated physically from the central part of the Arctic Ocean. In composition of fauna, however, they are, because of their hydrologic peculiarities, highly distinct. The animals of the northern Laptev Sea, where freshening is the least, are high-arctic genera. Arctic-Atlantic animals enter from the west by

Fig. 5-1. Glacial tongues on October Revolution Lake.

the northern route. In the fresher southern part of the sea, several species of many genera are found. Brackish-water species and a few marine ones survive the intense freshening; but near the Lena delta purely fresh-water species live. The Chukchi Sea contains boreal species which enter with the warm current through the Bering Strait.

The richest and most diverse fauna is found in the Laptev Sea, especially in the waters closer to the Taimyr Peninsula. Here mollusks are found in abundance: for example, sea lilies (*Yoldia arctica*), starfish, sea cucumbers, vermes, crustacea, and especially marine cockroaches (*Mesidothea entomon*). Sponges and Bryozoa are also plentiful. The most common species of fish, near the coastal islands, is the four-horned sculpin (*Myoxocephalus quadricornis*). Although Baikal hair seals, sea hares, and white whales live in these waters, there are fewer here than in the Kara Sea. Walrus (*Odobenus rosmarus*) cling to the shoals and usually feed on bottom mollusks and crustacea. The skin of walrus is used for making high-quality belts and for polishing optical glass. When the Bering Strait is clear of ice, Greenland whale, narwhale, and pteropods (sea butterflies) penetrate to the north into the Chukchi Sea and remain there until October. They then return south, as do certain fish.

ISLANDS OF THE SIBERIAN ARCTIC

The islands of the Siberian Arctic are linked in their origin and history of development with the adjacent mainland. They are on the broad continental shelf bordering the northern shore, and are separated from the mainland as the result of tectonic or epeirogenic movements of the earth's crust. Severnaya Zemlya, a highly denuded and reduced ancient folded massif, is similar to the Byrranga Plateau on the Taimyr Peninsula. The Novosibirsk Archipelago was until recently joined to the spurs of the Verkhoyansk Range; Wrangel Island is allied geologically with the mountan massifs of the Chukchi Peninsula. All the islands experienced more energetic movements in the Quaternary Period than did the adjacent mainland.

Most of the island groups have some recent glaciation, such as the glacial caps of Severnaya Zemlya and Henrietta Island and the glaciers on Bennett Island. Where glaciers have retreated, thick layers of fossil ice play a large role in the development of landscape, as, for example, on Bolshoy Lyakhov Island. The islands exhibit a definite unity of landscape, which is a result of their position in the high latitudes, similarity of climatic conditions, and common geographic features of the seas around them.

Severnaya Zemlya Archipelago

Severnaya Zemlya (Northern Land) comprises four large islands—October Revolution, Bolshevik, Komsomolets, Pioneer—and many nearby small ones, situated in groups and singly. In the central part of the archipalego lies the largest one, October Revolution Island. The rectilinear, high, and weakly dissected eastern bank of the island runs along a fault line and is formed of intensely folded, green chloritic and talc schists set mainly on end. These schists of the Cambrian Period have seams of quartzite and form rocky cliffs from 650 to 1,000 feet high. A terrace 165 feet high and several miles wide runs farther seaward and ends in a steep ledge. The slopes of the east coast are notched by many valleys through which glaciers flow from island snow fields. Most of these glaciers end at their emergence on the terrace, or even in the valley itself. The lower parts of many ancient glacial valleys are

sometimes inundated by the sea; one has formed Matusevich Fiord, which cuts into the island 36 miles. The western shore of the island, formed of easily eroded red marl of the Silurian Period, is low, containing a multitude of bays and gulfs of very diverse sizes and abounding in lagoons, sandbars, and spits. Here glaciers do not form tongues but massive terminals in the form of glacial barriers 16 to 18 feet high.

The interior of the island has smooth, rounded relief. A former single glacial cap has broken down into four individual caps at the corners of the island; the northern one has an elevation of 2,227 feet, which is the highest point of the entire archipelago. The hydrographic network is well developed, with separate streams reaching lengths of 30 miles. They either flow from the central part of the island, fed by snow and glacial water, or begin immediately at the foot of the glacial caps. Because of the elevation of the island, streams everywhere flow through deep canyons with perpendicular banks several dozen yards high. Southeast of the island lies Shokalski Strait with a meridional trend and a depth of from 600 to 1,000 feet, which is a clearly expressed graben. It is fully accessible for navigation, because of the strong currents, absence of islands, and rather frequent freedom from ice. The eastern and western shores of the more southerly Bolshevik Island are similar to the eastern shore of October Revolution Island, and the northern and southern shores are similar to the western shore. The island interior has a smooth, undulating relief. Two comparatively small glacial caps do not influence the relief; the hydrographic network is weakly developed. The island is separated from the mainland by the deep Boris Vilkitski Strait.

Farthest north and third in size, Komsomolets Island has Cambrian rocks only in the southeastern part, where the outcrops form nunataks amid glaciers. The remaining area of the island, with low (33 to 66 feet) hills, slight slopes, and low shores, is formed of exceptionally loose Quaternary alluvium. Shoals which extend several miles are broadly devel-

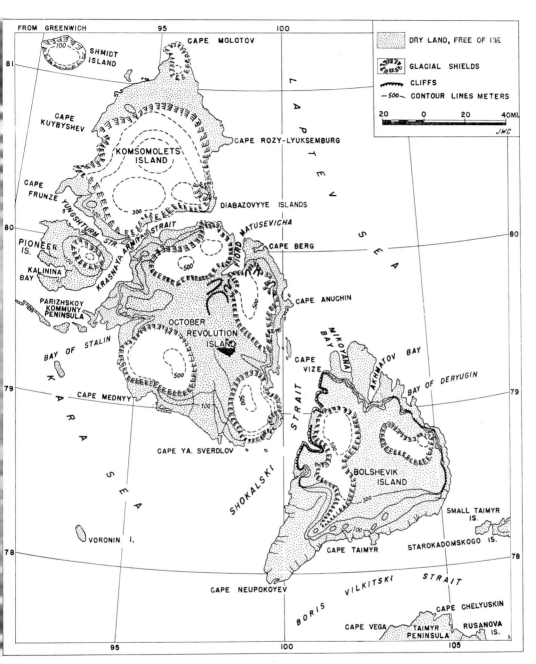

Map 5-I. Severnaya Zemlya.

oped, so that the configuration of the shore changes with the tides. The great central glacial shield, with a height of 1,650 feet, has a regular dome character. The smaller glacier in the northern part of the island completely overlaps the shallow seashore, masking its true con-

tours. Here lies the northern tip of the island and of the whole archipelago—Cape Molotov (81°16′ north latitude). Only Cape Morris Jessup on Peary Land in Greenland and Cape Fligely on Rudolf Island in Franz Josef Archipelago are farther north (166 and 40 miles, respectively) than Cape Molotov. South of the island is the narrow (1.8 to 9 miles) Krasnaya Armiya Strait (Red Army Strait), an ancient glacial valley half submerged by the sea. The narrowness of the strait, the many rocky islands of limestone and diabase, the many floating icebergs, and a breakup of ice only in exceptionally favorable years make it unsuitable for navigation.

The geologic history of Severnaya Zemlya is inseparable from that of the Taimyr Peninsula, from which Severnaya Zemlya was split in recent geologic time. Paleozoic deposits thousands of feet thick formed the archipelago and were deposited in a deep sea basin of the geosyncline type, which grew shallow gradually with the accumulation of sediments. The deepwater uniform series of clay and lime shales of the Cambrian alternated with limestones and later with Upper Silurian marls, clays, and sandstones containing seams of gypsum. These were precipitated in lagoons and bays of the coastal sections, from which the sea was retreating. Subsequently, they were covered with gray sandstones of the Permian Period, often containing fine carbonaceous seams and charred fragments of tree trunks of local origin.

The tectonics of the archipelago are extremely complex. Rocks were dislocated intensively and steep folds were compressed, faulted, and overturned, accompanied by many overthrusts and foliated reverse faults, sometimes for dozen of miles. The strike of folds changes from northeast to northwest. Outcrops of igneous rocks accompanied by veins of tin and lead ores are observed. The mountainous region formed toward the end of the Paleozoic Era extended considerably farther south and north of the modern archipelago. It was subsequently eroded to the base and converted into uneven country with low elevations.

In Quaternary times, all of Severnaya Zemlya was subjected to solid glaciation which extended many miles into the sea. The glacial cover was as thick as 2,300 feet. There are indications of two phases of glaciation, separated by a period of marine transgression, sediments

of which are found from 220 to 330 feet above the present sea level. There are also indications of a weaker postglacial transgression: deposits 50 to 75 feet in height; half-inundated valley fiords at the bottom of the modern sea, close to shore; and rubbly soil with shells of the first transgression. At the end of the glacial epoch, the earth's crust in the region of Severnaya Zemlya and Taimyr was broken by a series of tectonic cracks which separated the archipelago from the mainland. Certain lower portions were inundated and formed Boris Vilkitski and Shokalski straits. These radial dislocations determined the recent contours of the shores. At the present time an uplifting of Severnaya Zemlya is taking place, more rapidly on the eastern side than on the western side.

Recent glaciation of Severnaya Zemlya is fairly great, the ice covering an area of 6,021 square miles. There are ten large ice shields which occupy 42 per cent of surface of the archipelago. The distribution of ice varies from 100 per cent on Shmidt Island to 18 to 20 per cent on Pioneer and Bolshevik islands. On the island of Komsomolets there is a large glacial cover with an area of 2,200 square miles. The glacial shields rise to a height of 2,805 feet and reach a thickness of from 660 to 825 feet. In the north, long stretches of the shields are washed by the sea. The large, floating, fan-like tongues penetrate into Krasnaya Armiya Strait and Matusevich Fiord, fully bridging the latter. The Severnaya Zemlya district produces many icebergs of "table form." These icebergs, several hundred yards long and 60 to 80 feet high, drift toward the Central Polar Basin. In the south most of the glaciers are of the alpine type and terminate on land. On a part of October Revolution Island having alpine relief and a height of 2,790 feet, there are independent hanging and cirque glaciers. The glaciers of Severnaya Zemlya are underlined by a layer of permafrost. Since their nourishment is meager, the glacial activity is slight. Often there is no sign of movement. Nevertheless, traces of retreat and disappearance of the ice cover can be found everywhere in the form of old mo-

Fig. 5-2. Hanging cirque glacier on October Revolution Lake.

raines, hanging valleys, boulders, and dead ice, all separated from the caps feeding them. As the arctic climate became milder, the glaciers on Bolshevik Island retreated sharply. In the northern parts of the archipelago, the retreat was slower.

The high latitude of the archipelago, the abundance of ice on land and in the adjacent sea, and the cooling of the lower layers of air (from the expenditure of heat in thawing ice) establish a severe polar climate for Severnaya Zemlya. A feature of this climate is the change from the period (of many days' duration) of continuous insolation during the polar summer to the period of absence of solar heat during the long polar winter. Although the climate is severer than on other polar islands, the winters are not as cold and the summers not as hot as the more southerly parts of the mainland.

Rather low average annual pressure indicates that the archipelago is under the influence of cyclones from the Barents Sea. Intense influence is observed only in winter (from November to February). Moderate northeast winds, of from 16 to 26 feet per second, predominate; only in summer are there western and northern winds.

The temperature regime, according to observations on the small western islands of the archipelago, is very severe and greatly enhances frost weathering.

The normal daily change of air temperatures stops during the prolonged polar night. With the appearance of the sun, the daily temperature variation begins to be defined more clearly, revealing the greatest amplitude in April. During four years of observations on the islands of the western part of the archipelago, the longest continuous period without early morning frost was eight days in July. Severnaya Zemlya is warmer than the adjacent mainland during the winters. The average temperature of the coldest month (March) is —16.8°F. In Dudinka, more to the south, the January temperature is —22°F. There is a warm spell in the middle of winter (February —10°F), and an abrupt lowering of temperature from October (13°F) to November (—3°F). In winter there are about 96 days of snowstorms, the maximum occurring in January. Because of the finely crystallized dust-like structure of the snow, a snowstorm of drifting snow can be started by weak winds of only 13 to 16 feet per second. A severe snowstorm develops with winds of 26 feet per second, making travel by dogs very difficult or even impossible. The snow cover is established at the end of September and lasts until the beginning of July. There is a sharp rise in temperature from April (−7°F) to May (15°F). Summer, in comparison with the mainland, is colder, with frequent early morning frost. The average temperature of July is 33.5°F (in Dudinka, 55°).

The annual precipitation averages 3.6 inches. There are as many overcast days as there are clear days, with the cloudiest month being August, the clearest March. There are 91 days of fog per year, the greatest number occurring during July and August. There is no fog during December and January. The aurora borealis has been observed for 113 nights, from the end of September to the end of March.

The ice condition near Severnaya Zemlya varies greatly from year to year. Years with heavy ice, when even icebreakers cannot approach Severnaya Zemlya, alternate with extremely favorable years, when movement by ships is very easy.

Severnaya Zemlya, in comparison with other polar islands, has an extremely meager vegetative cover of green mosses, bushy lichens, and a few flowering plants. Vegetation is to be found on terraces and coastal plains of porous clay and sand formations, on which have developed small patches of primitive rocky soils with insignificant accumulation of peat. In the southern sections of the archipelago, the vegetation is richer. Here wild reindeer pasture on large mossy expanses. The short growing period (two to three months) ends in the middle of October during favorable years, but at the end of August in cold, cloudy summers. In the colder summers the buds of arctic poppy remain unopened and other flowering plants exist in a clearly impoverished state. Snow cover affects the development and distribution of vegetation. It controls the freezing and moistening of soils and protects the plants from mechanical injury during winter snowstorms.

The small western islands of the archipelago have patches rich in fine-grained, sufficiently moistened soil on which grow grassy-mossy cover containing dense, scattered stands of hair grass (*Deschampsia arctica*) and meadow grass (*Poa glauca*). Because of the permafrost, the thick, fiber-like root system of this grass can penetrate to a depth of only six inches. These grasses grow luxuriantly near the burrows of lemmings. Amid the grasses are strewn small sod clumps of mosses (*Torula ruralis, Ditrichum flexicaule*). Encountered individually are such flowering plants as arctic poppy (*Papaver radicatum*), saxifrage (*Saxifraga oppositifolia*), sour grass (*Oxyria digyna*), whitlow grass (*Draba alpina*), and scurvy grass (*Cochlearia arctica*). Near patches of snow, crowfoots (*Ranunculus glacialis*) are found. The sole representative of the shrubs, the willow (*Salix polaris*), has a delicate herbaceous, pale-green stalk buried in the moss cover, above which only one or two inches of leaves and stalk project during flowering. Moss and lichen plants grow on the highly moistened, clayey soil. On drained sections, the mosses are replaced by lichens: at first cetraria (*Cetraria islandica, C. cucullata*) and later alectoria (*Alectoria nigricans*). Much saxifrage grows at nesting places of white terns; on old nestings of birds, much starwort (*Stellaria*) is found.

The animal life of Severnaya Zemlya is poor. On the littoral plain of Bolshevik Island there are small groups of three to five animals of wild reindeer. The polar fox and lemming (*Lemmus obensis*) are widespread, preferring the gentle southern slopes with a certain amount of vegetation. Lemming have young twice during a warm summer and extended autumn, but only once during a cold summer. Severnaya Zemlya has fewer species of birds than other Arctic Islands: Novaya Zemlya, 77; Franz Josef Land, 28; Severnaya Zemlya, 20 species. However, there are bird-gathering places on the eastern coast of the archipelago where guillemot (*Cepphus grylle mandtii*), white tern (*Pagophila eburnea*), polar seagull or glaucous gull (*Larus hyperboreus*), and others live in colonies of thousands. Sparrows (*Plectrophenax nivalis*) arrive during the first days of May to breed, and are found everywhere. Black geese (*Branta bernicla*) are also evident. During two years of observation, no insects were found on Domashny Island.

Novosibirsk Archipelago

The Novosibirsk Archipelago, a broad group of islands of different sizes, forms, and structures, are north of the coast between the mouths of the Yana and Indigirka rivers. The archipelago is broken into three separate groups of islands: (1) the De Long Islands (Bennett, Jeannette, Henrietta); (2) the Novosibirsk Islands proper (Kotelny, Faddeyev, Novaya Sibir, Belkovsky), and associated with these is the so-called Zemlya Bunge, a vast, sandy lowland, frequently inundated by the sea in its marginal sections; (3) the Lyakhov Islands (Bolshoy and Maly Lyakhov, and Stolbovoy).

The small De Long Islands (for example, Henrietta Island is 2.5 by 2.1 miles), are high plateaus ending in the sea as steep, inaccessible slopes or separate large cliffs of rather sharp outline, reaching heights of from 1,039.5 feet (Henrietta Island) to 1,650 feet (Bennett Island). The islands are formed of horizontal Cambrian schists (Bennett Island), sandstones, cherts, and porphyrites (Henrietta Island) or young basalts.

Recent glaciation has developed on the three northern islands. This glaciation occupies 25.9 square miles, or 52 per cent, of the islands' surface. At the top of Jeannette Island lies a small remnant of glacial cover 264 feet thick. Hoarfrost plays the principal role in feeding the glaciers. A marshy tundra with polygonal formations predominates on the De Long Islands. There is no small stream on the islands.

Fig. 5-3. Tufa rocks along the southern shore of Henrietta Lake in the De Long Archipelago.

The Novosibirsk and Lyakhov islands differ in geologic structure and relief. Kotelny Island is formed of Paleozoic limestones. On Bolshoy Lyakhov Island, Mesozoic shales and sandstones plus varied igneous rocks (granites, grandiorites) are exposed in low places. Scattered on the islands are small isolated patches of Tertiary rocks rich in fossil flora (sequoia, swamp cypress). Considerable areas are covered by early Quaternary deposits with thick layers of fossil ice containing fossil fauna (mammoth, rhinoceros); there are also deposits of northern marine transgression. The large forms of relief are either small, separate elevations or massive horsts bounded by the complex network of fault scarps of northeast and northwest directions. These peaks are not as high as those on the De Long Islands: Emiy Mountain on Bolshoy Lyakhov Island, 890 feet; Malakatyn-Tas Mountain or Kotelny Island, 1,150 feet.

There is no trace of recent glaciation on the Novosibirsk and Lyakhov islands. The small amount of precipitation does not allow glaciation and greatly lessens erosion. Most important in the formation of relief is frost erosion, which is furthered by the almost uninterrupted condensation of mosture during frequent shifts of temperature above and below freezing.

The mountain peaks are windy. In areas of igneous rocks, the wind has shaped blocks or eroded columns of basalt into fantastic "castles" and transformed narrow cracks in jointings into wide corridors. Enormous cup-shaped depressions are also evidence of the intensive corrosive work of the wind. Mountain peaks are strewn with angular rock waste of original rocks, broken up by the action of frost weathering.

The higher parts of the islands determine the character of the hydrographic network. The river system is rather weakly developed because of the almost complete absence of ground water and slight amount of precipitation. The rivers either flow along tectonic depressions, forming narrow and deep canyons (as on Kotelny Island), or flow through well-developed valleys (as on Bolshoy Lyakhov Island). They enter the sea directly or, as on Bolshoy

Lyakhov Island, empty into the graben of the central part of the island to form a flat low plain containing many lakes and rivers with watersheds which are often of fossil ice.

The Novosibirsk Archipelago is closely associated in its geologic composition and structure to the northern Verkhoyansk Range, although the Paleozoic System is less intensively dislocated. Mesozoic folding manifested itself to a lesser degree and weak, late Tertiary folding brought about deep cracks, accompanied in the northern part of the archipelago by outpourings of basalts and a slight warping of Tertiary sediments. The oldest Quaternary deposits (on Bolshoy Lyakhov Island) are fossil ice.

Quaternary deposits are widespread on the Novosibirsk Islands and along a 930-mile coastal stretch (from the delta of the Lena River to the mouth of the Kolyma River) of the adjacent mainland. Only the mountains and wide stretches along the large rivers remain free of fossil ice. The fossil ice extends below sea level and forms an icy bottom in the eastern part of the Laptev Sea and the western part of the East Siberian Sea. The thickness of the recent strongly degraded fossil ice can be measured in hundreds of feet, which means that it was even thicker in the past. Because of the absence of large orographic glacial centers, the unfavorable conditions of glacial feeding, and the comparatively thin glaciers, the very slow glacial movement from the center to the periphery stopped, and a zone of stationary firns developed around the perimeter. The exceptional purity of the fossil ice indicates that the adjacent heights did not contribute a surface cover of debris during the period of ice accumulation. The fact that these heights were also covered by the ice reveals the extent of this glaciation.

The whole stratum of well-developed Quaternary deposits is a younger formation. Its countless accumulations of animal bones and forest residue extend north to Faddeyev Island. These remains from the last warm period were deposited either on the surface of the fossil ice or in deep crevices (formed in the Quaternary Period) which did not cut through the entire

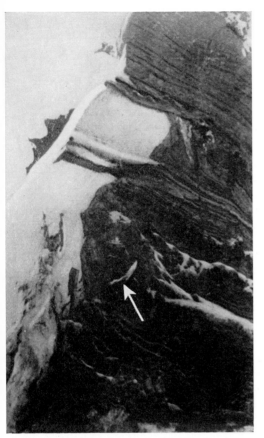

Fig. 5-4. Mammoth tusk in the frozen silt of Lake Lyakhov.

thickness of ice. From these early Quaternary deposits, especially in earthen veins cutting through the ice, specimens of mammoth tusks were washed out from sea cliffs by marine and wind erosion. There is much evidence showing beyond all doubt the recent upheaval of the shore. For example, near Bolshoy Lyakhov Island there is a vast lowland terrace extending northward which is not shown on earlier maps. Along the southeastern shore of the same island a beach with a narrow strip of drift material brought in formerly by the sea, was found under a layer of moss and modern vegetation. In the lower course of the Etirikan River, two systems of meanders, one 10 to 12 feet above the other, are visible.

The recent epoch may be described as one of melting and degradation of fossil ice. This melting and degradation of ice produces many unusual forms of relief, contributes to the feeding of rivers, and affects the retreat of the coast line, despite the rising of the shores. When fossil ice melts, it leaves deep pits as well as caverns and other thermokarst features. Frozen earthen veins, exposed during the melting of the ice, melt and crumble, forming conical mounds up to 50 feet high. Similar formations are mounds created by frost warping, as a result of dynamic tensions between the layer of winter freezing and the permafrost.

The unusual regime of rivers and lakes is determined by the water from the melting fossil ice, by the weak development of ground water, and by the small amount of winter and summer precipitation. With the thawing of snowdrifts, blown by the wind into depressions, the energetic activity of the rivers begins; but since rivers must force their way across packed snowdrifts, they are impeded and checked, which limits stream erosion. In summer, the rivers are fed by the thawing fossil ice on the bottom and banks. That is why rivers not receiving tributaries abound in water toward their mouths. As a result of a river alternately crossing seams of frozen Quaternary deposits and accumulations of fossil ice, a chain of deep pits occurs within the ice. These pits are separated by shallow sandbanks that crop through the ice in places along the river bottom. The feeding of lakes by the melting ice on their bottom and edges shows that despite the increase of water in the lakes, a lowering of their level occurs. This is because the volume of the ice is greater than its volume when it becomes water. With the thawing through of the frozen ground or ice partition separating one lake from another, the lakes unite and often form an outlet to the sea, which results in flat, swamped expanses.

Coast lines are modified by fossil ice banks. At the top of an ice bank is a perpendicular cornice 5 to 6 feet high, back from which runs a recess 50 to 60 feet in width, descending to a broad terrace of fossil ice covered with earth, which protects it from thawing. At the water line, the sea undercuts the shore, leaving concave walls and caves. Under solar heating and above-freezing temperatures of sea water, the fossil ice melts. Then, with a loud noise, various-sized pieces of ice and frozen ground cave in, flowing into depressions and, finally, into the sea. Because the erosion of fossil ice by sea water ceases at a depth of 33 to 50 feet, the ice bottom of the sea may be traced within a hundred yards from shore. Temperatures remain below freezing at these depths, even during the entire summer. Thus this ice survives for a very long time.

The basic factors acting on the typical polar climate of the Novosibirsk Archipelago are: (1) its location close to the southern border of the polar front, which may shift either northward or southward; (2) the proximity of the East Siberian winter anticyclone, influencing the climate with the migration of the polar winter front to the north; (3) the cyclones moving eastward from the Barents Sea and bringing masses of warm air; (4) the warm Siberian winds which raise the air temperature (18 to 27 degrees) and the relative humidity, thus contributing to the appearance of fogs.

Characteristic of the archipelago are the uniform low temperatures of January, February, March, July, and August ($-22.5°$, $-23.2°$, $-20°$, $37.5°$, and $36.5°F$, respectively) and the early morning frost during the entire summer. The annual precipitation is only 3 inches, the greatest amount being in August (0.72 inch), the least in April (0.04 inch). Relative humidity is higher than on the adjacent mainland (August 92 per cent, February 80 per cent). Overcast skies predominate during the whole year, and there are many days with snowstorms.

Winter is stable, cold, and windy. From November to April there are no thaws. The many foggy days in winter are a result of the Siberian warm air. The snow remains on the ground for nine months, even though there is a small amount of winter precipitation (from December to February a total of 0.28 inch), and strong winds blow the thin snow cover from elevated places into depressions. The snow is in patches; it is extremely compact and often exhibits a granular structure. Although the temperature may be as low as $-4°F$, the direct rays of the sun can, and especially on sharply dipping slopes, melt the snow.

Summer is cool (July average is $37.5°F$), but temperature fluctuations are not great because of the proximity of the sea, which has a temperature of $32°F$. During a 22-day frostless period in July and August, the temperature of the air varied from $32°$ to $39.3°F$. However, early morning frost and light snows at the peak of summer are possible. Although intense fogs prevail in summer, especially in August, they seldom last for more than 12 hours.

The short, cool summer limits the soil-forming process and also the amount of vegetative and animal life. The soil cover is poorly developed, and in many places is replaced by a gravelly and rubbly eluvial layer without continuous sod cover. Polygonal soil is little developed because there is insufficient rough material on the islands for its formation. There is no tree and shrub vegetation. Separate species of grass grown in clusters and turfs, separated by areas of bare soil, a few of which are covered with mosses and lichens. Conspicuous on the drier tundra are: saxifrage (*Saxifraga caespitosa, S. hirculus*) in very dense clumps cinquefoil (*Potentilla fragiformis*); arctic poppy (*Papaver radicatum*); *Luzula hyperborea;* and glacial avens (*Sieversia glacialis*) with a big golden-yellow blossom. Some grasses are also found. Clumps of grasses, among which are most of the mosses and lichens, are more abundant on moister places along the slopes. Oxalidaceae (*Oxyria digyna*) are found on sandy-rubbly hills, and crowfoots (*Ranunculus nivalis*) near snowy patches. On ground fertilized by bird droppings, there is a dense green of grasses, with a predominance of scurvy grass (*Cochlearia arctica*). On Bennett Island, alpine poppy and partridge grasses grow heavily on rocky tundra patches that are free of snow.

The New Siberian Archipelago and the adjacent mainland, which were not separated until recent geologic times, have the same impoverished fauna. Some of the animals, such as reindeer, wolf, polar fox, and white ptarmigan, owever, migrate across the ice from the islands o the mainland and return to the islands oward summer. Widespread throughout the slands is the lemming (*Lemmus obensis no- rosibiricus*). Despite the nearness of the archi- pelago to the mainland, northern birds do not requently live on even the closest islands, hough they are very common on the opposite oast of the mainland. Although birds do not ind the steep, craggy shores of the islands uitable for nesting, guillemots and gulls gather n these places temporarily (as, for example, on Bennett and Belkovsky islands). Birds that usu- lly nest on the islands include the red-throated oon (*Colymbus stellatus*), polar duck (*Clan- gula hyemalis*), and white ptarmigan (*Lagopus agopus birulai*). Certain birds, such as the king ider duck (*Somateria spectabilis*), appear on he islands in the first days of May.

Wrangel Island, 75 miles long, lies in the northern part of the Chukchi Sea and is sep- arated from the mainland by De Long Strait, 72 miles wide. In the central and southern parts of the island are two mountain chains. The mountains, which extend from east to west and reach 3,300 feet (Sovetsky Peak, 3,300 feet), are devoid of glaciers. The northern part of the is- land is a gradually sloping lowland, called "Akademiy Tundra," which descends toward the sea. The climate of the island is marine, with winter temperatures that are compara- tively high (February, −13°F) and summer temperatures that are comparatively low (July, 36°F) for those latitudes. On about half the days of the year there are early morning frosts. The annual precipitation is approximately 6 inches, the greater part of which is snow. There are many foggy days, as the relative humidity is high the year round. North winds prevail throughout the year. Mountain foothills and low places are covered by rocky tundra with mosses, lichens, grasses, and creeping bushes. Willow beds are encountered in the river val- leys of the southern mountain slopes. Countless gulls, noddies, geese, and ducks and many foxes and polar bears inhabit the island. The many walruses, nerpa seals, and sea hares living in ad- jacent waters are the objects of commercial interests. East of Wrangel Island lies Herald Island, 1,200 feet high.

CONTINENTAL TUNDRA AND WOODED-TUNDRA

The subregion of continental tundra and wooded-tundra occupies the North Siberian Lowland and Byrranga Plateau. In comparison with the corresponding subregion of Western Siberia, it has a more rigorous climate, less an- nual and winter precipitation, less swampiness, and a predominance of lichenous alectoria with hummocky tundra. Dahurian larch grows there in place of Siberian larch, and dwarf birch (*Betula exilis*) in place of *Betula nana*. This region has the greatest northward advance of woody plants.

The North Siberian Lowland joins the West- ern Siberian Lowland in the lower Yenisei and extends eastward, as a comparatively narrow coastal strip, along the Kara, Laptev, and East Siberian seas to the lower Kolyma River. Most of the North Siberian Lowland maintains the uniform character of a low hill country with many lakes. It is formed of Quaternary depos- its which are partly glacial and partly of a boreal marine transgression type. The Meso- zoic continental deposits are only between the Khatanga and Lena rivers. Farther eastward, beyond the Yana River, shallow outcrops of granite are found.

The lowland on the Taimyr Peninsula from the Yenisei to the lower Khatanga, between the Byrranga Plateau and the Central Siberian Plateau, is called the Pyasina-Khatanga depres- sion. Separated from the Central Siberian Pla- teau by fault lines, this depression is formed of sand, silt, and gravel of the Quaternary marine transgression. It is partly washed-up moraine material, partly the usual littoral deposits with fossils of animals similar to those now living in the adjacent seas. At the highest points among these marine deposits are belts of moraine deposits, which were raised above the sea as islands at the time of the marine transgression and have survived to the present. From beneath uniform layers of Quaternary sediments, small strips and patches of rocks of the Permian-Carboniferous and the Cretaceous periods crop out. Broad valleys of large rivers are filled with alluvium.

The depression is an undulating plain. The typical moraine landscape is made up of low hills, with lakes in the depressions between them. There are many ridges extending in an east-west direction with elevations of from 495 to 825 feet. The latter are formed of moraine material and studded with many various-sized boulders. There is very little dissection of relief in the depresson by postglacial erosion valleys, which frequently made their way along ancient glacial valleys. The upheaval of dry land, which followed the period of marine transgression and continues to the present time, rejuvenated the erosional activity of the rivers. But the small amount of precipitation, lack of ground water, and short summer explain the limited role of erosion in the formation of the modern relief.

Between the lower Khatanga and Lena rivers is a flat synclinal basin filled with Mesozoic deposits. These deposits are almost horizontal or form gently sloping dome-shaped folds. Within this basin rise low Mesozoic ridges: Pronchishchev Range (500 feet) rises between the mouths of the Anabar and Olenek rivers; the Chekanovskiy Range (1,650 feet) rises west of the Lena River delta. Because of the porous Mesozoic rocks, most of the rivers are in wide, flat-bottomed valleys, many of which abound in meander lakes. Of the Mesozoic salt domes, Solyanaya Sopka, near the western shore of Nordvik Gulf, is the most important. Its salt stock is worked in shafts 1,320 feet deep. The salt, reserves of which measure millions of tons, is of high quality and contains an insignificant amount of impurities. The known deposits of oil in this region are not, as yet, of industrial importance.

The morphology of the North Siberian Lowland is directly linked with the rising and sinking of the coast. Its western section at the mouth of the Olenek River has the character of a coastal plain, imperceptibly but gradually descending from the south toward the sea. Since large rivers like the Yenisei, Khatanga, and Anabar form estuaries, this indicates the comparatively recent advance of the sea into the land. An appreciable upheaval of the coast followed this advance, and continues even now. This is manifested by the following: (1) young terrace deposits overcrowded with rich fauna similar to that now living in the adjacent seas, (2) the abundance of drift material on the surface of young low terraces, and (3) the formation of coastal lakes, lagoons, and shoals. The character of the coast varies sharply beyond the Olenek River, where the shore is either stable or rising. At the mouths of the large rivers are deltas rather than estuaries. The large delta of the Lena River is an example. The shore line becomes much more winding and dissected, and large bays extend inland. Some, such as Tiksi Bay in the Gulf of Buor-Khaya, have protected coves favorable for harbors. On the continent and the adjacent islands, there is a general upheaval of dry land and a retreat of the sea. Recent shores which are formed of loose Quaternary alluvium with masses of fossil ice quickly recede as a result of the mechanical activity and the above-freezing temperatures of the sea. Thus the subsidence of the shores of Vasilyevsky and Semenovsky islands in the Lyakhov group reached 132 feet a year. The first of these islands has now vanished. Because of the subsiding process, there are many hanging valleys.

The North Siberian Lowland, even on level water divides, is covered with lakes of different sizes and shapes. The lakes are sometimes joined by grass-filled streams and sometimes separated by swamps. Looking at the area from an elevated vantage point, an observer would be hard pressed to decide whether the greater part of the surface is water or dry land. Almost all of the lakes are small (one-half mile long) and shallow (five feet deep). All the lakes are either the result of glaciation or permafrost. The glacial lakes are in depressions between morainic hills which have survived erosion during the subsequent marine transgression. An example of this type is Lake Pyasina, dammed from the north by a terminal moraine, which has been cut by the Pyasina River to form an outlet. Although the lake is 42 miles long, its depth is slight: in the north 3.3 to 6.6 feet, in the south 19.8 to 33 feet. The lake receives water through the Norilsk River which drains large deep mountainous lakes (Lama, Keta, and Glubokoye) lying at the edge of the northwestern shelf of the Central Siberian Plateau.

Many of the shallow, lowland lakes may be the result of the thawing, during the warm continental summer, of ground ice in the permafrost. The bottom of most of these lakes is pure ice covered with a peaty layer. A decrease in the number of these lakes is now indicated by their drainage into rivers, into lower-lying lake depressions, and into the sea. The drained lakes leave behind flat, swamped expanses. Because of strong winds and the small amount of snow, thick ice forms in the lakes in winter, and the shallower ones freeze solid.

The rivers of the North Siberian Lowland do not have many tributaries. The large transit rivers such as the Yenisei, Lena, Yana, and others which carry warmer water from the south begin as shallow streams that start from lakes and flow directly into the sea. Comparatively low summer temperatures limit evaporation, so that stream discharge is relatively great. The shallow depth of permafrost promotes the accumulation of above-frost ground water. Even with the small amount of precipitation, streams continue to flow throughout the summer. Permafrost limits the flow in winter, however. The sources of river water are meltwater and summer rains. Fluvial discharge continues high during the short warm period. In winter, however, because of the absence of ground feeding, the flow of the rivers stops.

The Lena delta is the largest in the USSR and the third largest in area (12,352 square miles) in the world. It contains many islands, islets, and sandbars which are cut through by many channels. Although there are more than 800 channels in the delta, the hydrographic skeleton is formed by ten large channels, the more important of which are Bykov, Trofimov, Olenek, and Bolshoy Tumat. Channel direction and depth not only change from year to year but also change abruptly during the navigational period. With the gradual fall of the water level from spring through late summer, many sandbars appear and the general pattern of the channels becomes unrecognizable. Tides and moderate winds sharply alter the channels near the river mouth. There are more than a thousand islands in the delta, most of which are small. More than ten of the large islands are located in the southern and western parts of the delta. Erge-Muora-Sisse (solid and uncut by channels, with an area of 2,702 square miles), Khardanga-Sisse (almost 386 square miles in area are included in this group. These islands are covered by a damp mossy tundra and tundra swamps of sedge grass. On elevated and well-drained parts of the islands, the growth of lichens increases, and some dwarf birch and willow grow.

The greater part of the delta is very young geologically, exhibiting the exceptional dynamism of the process of land creation, development, and destruction. The factors governing this process are: (1) the colossal quantities of sand and silt carried and deposited by the Lena, deposits which pile up during the period of spring flood and, after being fastened by vegetation, create new islands and unite them to form larger ones; (2) the river water itself, which is active in undermining the banks; and (3) the wind, which dries the sand and carries great masses of it from place to place. Continuous permafrost, with an abundance of fossil ice, explains the origin and development of underground lakes, bulging ridges, and ice mounds. The permafrost also helps to destroy the banks, creating cliffs very characteristic of permafrost regions. Innumerable frozen lakes are scattered over the surface of

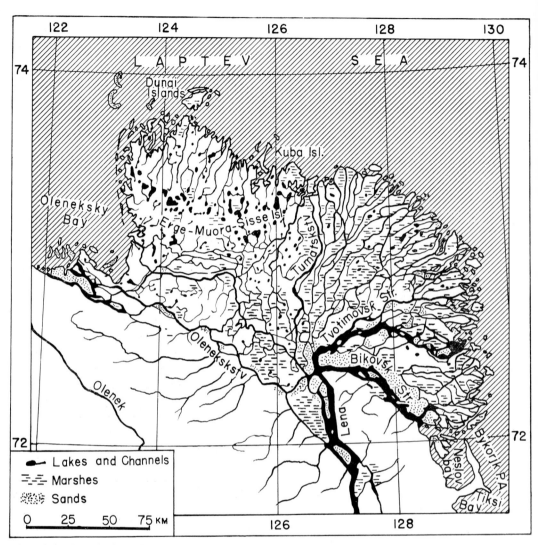

Map 5-II. Lena delta.

the tundra. The thawing activity of the water causes the small, separate lakes to grow slowly in depth and washes out the bars between them. Thus, these small lakes join one another and form larger lakes which cut into the surface of the tundra. As a result, the erosion basis for the streams which empty into the lake is lower, and the general drainage of the locality is improved. This causes the tundra to become dry. The small streams change into rivers with clearly defined beds and valleys. The 120 ice mounds rise to heights of from 33 to 130 feet and rest on bases ranging from 30 to 500 feet across. There are eight permanently inhabited places in the delta. The visitors who come during the hunting and fishing season are quite mobile. Dogs are the only means of transportation in winter, and the channels provide the sole means of transportation in summer.

Byrranga Plateau, on the northern part of the Taimyr Peninsula, starts with two low elevations east of the Yenisei Gulf. Farther on, it gradually rises, forming a continuous plateau between 3,300 and 4,950 feet in height. In the basin of the lower Taimyr River, and to the east, the plateau breaks up into separate ridges which extend to the shores of the Laptev Sea. Byrranga Plateau is a one-sided horst, bordered on the south by a steep, and often almost perpendicular, dissected escarpment. It has an east-northeast trend sloping down gradually to the north into a series of low (up to 330 feet) elevations directly approaching the shores of the Kara Sea. In the south, the plateau is formed of coal-bearing strata of the Tungusk series (Permian-Carboniferous) with intrusions of basalts and diabases. The coastal section of the plateau is formed of highly dislocated gneisses and metamorphic schists of the Pre-Cambrian with large outcrops of granite. The latter compose many sections of the coast and the Nordenskiöld Archipelago, which has typical cliff-like character. In the central part of the plateau are large overthrusts: Silurian limestones are thrust up on rocks of the Tungusk

series, and metamorphic schists are on Silurian deposits. The strike of these overthrusts coincides with the east-northeast direction of folding and the lines of fractures along both the southern scarp of the plateau and along the northern brim of the Central Siberian Tableland. Within the limits of the plateau, along lower stretches of the Pyasina River, are coal deposits of commercial importance. There are known to be six working seams of coal, 1.5 to 10 feet thick, of high calorific value and little ash. This coal may serve as excellent fuel for marine and river vessels of the Northern Sea Route.

The Taimyr Peninsula evidently stood considerably higher during preglacial time than it does today, and the islands of Severnaya Zemlya and the Nordenskiöld Archipelago made up a single unit with the Byrranga Plateau. In the Quaternary Period, they were

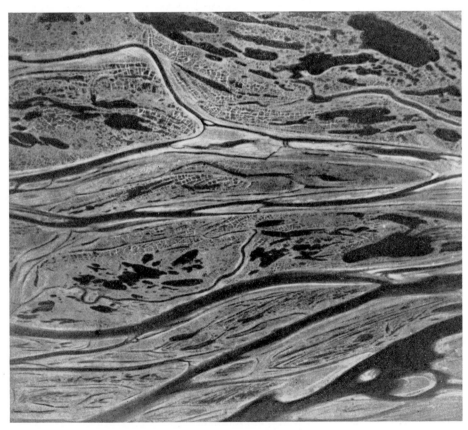

Fig. 5-5. Lena delta with distributaries, lakes, and islands.

covered by glaciers which superimposed prominent features on the region. Everywhere on the plateau there are glacial depressions (now filled by lakes), polished rocks, erratic boulders, and moraines. The plateau is bordered by deposits of the arctic marine transgression which rise along its slopes to a height of 330 feet. There are no glaciers on the plateau today. Dissection of the plateau is negligible. The largest rivers of the Taimyr Peninsula, the Pyasina and Taimyr cut across the plateau and offer a clear picture of its youth in the form of weakly developed valley-gorges and a large number of rapids and waterfalls. The shallow streams have scarcely begun their destructive work of dissecting the plateau.

Near the southern edge of the plateau, with embayments jutting into it, lies the largest lake of the Arctic, Lake Taimyr (1,795 square miles). Its northern banks are steep and high (165 to 330 feet) and its southern banks, which are composed of Quaternary marine and glacial deposits, are low. The lake basin was flooded by the waters of marine Quaternary transgression, evident from the organisms of marine origin preserved in the lake. The water level of the lake, which is only several yards deep, is gradually lowering. The spring floods fill the lake basin with water, which empties through the Taimyr River during the year. Before the lake freezes solid in winter it has lost 75 per cent of the water accumulated in spring. The period of open water lasts about three months. The lake is exceptionally poor in flora and fauna: whitefish "muksun," and "chir" are the most numerous fish; less frequently found are "goletz," "kharius," "ryapushka," and "omul."

The climate of the subregion of lowland tundra and wooden-tundra of Eastern Siberia, in comparison with that of the Western Siberian tundras, is very severe. Since the moderating influence of the Atlantic and Pacific oceans does not quite reach this region, it is wholly subject to the continental climate of northern Asia. Typical are the great contrast in winter and summer temperatures from west to east. Absolute amplitudes are very large but

rather uniform through the whole subregion: 152.3 degrees (−69.5° to 82.8°F) in the western part (Dudinka) and 148 degrees (−63° to 85°F) in the eastern part (Russkoe Uste). The average January and July temperatures reach −22° and 55°F in the western part of the subregion (Dudinka), and −36.5°F in the eastern part (Russkoe Uste). Indicative of the severity of the climate are: (1) the average below-freezing temperatures eight months a year, from October to May; (2) the number of days with frost, 264 at Khatanga and as many as 298 days a year at the Lena River delta (Sagastyr); and (3) the short vegetative period, which ranges from 78 days in the western part (Dudinka) to 63 days in the eastern (Russkoe Uste). There is an extremely rapid shift from winter to summer: March, April, and May in the western part (Khatanga) are −18°, −1°, and 29.7°F, respectively, and in the eastern part (Kazachye) −18°, −3°, and 24.8°F, respectively. Soil temperatures are extremely low: on Taimyr below 76° north latitude, in the period of the greatest thawing of the soil (July and August), the temperature of the earth did not exceed 33°F at a depth of 8 inches.

The annual precipitation is less than in the Western Siberian tundras, varying from 6 inches (Russkoe Uste) to 9.1 inches (Khatanga). However, in the Lena River delta (Sagastyr) it is only 3.4 inches. Most of the precipitation is in summer: 50 per cent of the annual amount from July to September; 10 per cent from January to March. Although from 33 to 50 per cent of the annual precipitation is snow, there is so little of it that the snow cover is slight (in the Taimyr tundra, 2 to 6 inches; in the eastern part of Kazachye, 6 to 8 inches). Winds easily carry off the thin snow cover into depressions, where the accumulation may reach a depth of from 13 to 16 feet. There is little cloudiness, especially in the eastern section. The annual average in the Taimyr tundras is 72 per cent (the greatest in September is 85 per cent; the least in January, at Dudinka, is 65 per cent). In the eastern part (Kazachye) the average is 61 per cent (the greatest in August is 79 per cent; the least in January 41 per cent). The winds are strong only in the tundras of the western part: the annual average in Dudinka is 22.4 feet per second; in Kazachye only 12.34 feet per second.

The continental climate of the subregion of tundra and wooded-tundra of Eastern Siberia, the small amount of precipitation, and the thin snow cover severely affect the soil-forming process and the character and distribution of vegetation. Despite the continental climate in the tundras of Eastern Siberia, swamping is more prevalent than in the western part of the tundra zone, which has a more oceanic, moist climate. This swamping is caused by the intensive inter-soil condensation of vapor, owing to the difference between the very cold perma-

underlies the soil and contains abundant seams of ground ice.

Because of the severe climate in the subregion, lichenous and polygonal tundras predominate. But east of the Lena River are hummocky tundras where there are fewer scrub thickets, which contain another form of dwarf birch (*Betula exilis*), than there are in the Western Siberian tundras, and tundra meadows become more scarce. Under these dry and hot summer conditions, woody vegetation reaches to within 39 miles of the seashore at Buor-Khaya Gulf in only a few places.

As in Western Siberia, the subregion is divided into three east-west belts: arctic tundra, typical tundra, and forest-tundra.

Fig. 5-6. Arctic tundra of the Lower Lena River area.

frost and the rather warm (during the summer) surface soil. There is enough condensation to maintain the soil in a supermoistened state, which is why the gleying process gains predominance and suppresses the process of podzol formation even on sandy soil. Under warm summer conditions, strong capillary actions may cause solutions to rise in clay soil. As a consequence, unique arctic carbonaceous solonchaks develop. They exist, if only temporarily, under the influence of excess moistening by carbonaceous water. Strongly affecting the soil-forming process is the permafrost, which

Arctic tundra has almost no lichenous tundra and only a small amount of mossy tundra. Dryadaceae tundra is broadly developed in dry, elevated places where there is a light snow cover in winter and deep frost thawing in summer. The development of a squat but rather dense cover of partridge grass (*Dryas punctata*) depends on a certain calcareousness of the soil, good drainage, and aeration by a dense network of shallow frost cracks. The diverse flowering plants vary with the soil and the geographic position. Polygonal boggy tundra with porous surfaces is typical, especially in river valleys and on the sites of former lakes. Vegetation nestles along the cracks of polygonal structures and consists of mosses, lichens, some flowering plants such as saxifrage (*Saxifraga caespitosa*), and small creeping polar willow. Low bogs saturated with moisture are often underlain by ground ice and show a predominance of sedges and cotton grasses. Cereal grasses such as sweet grass (*Hierochloe pauciflora*) or foxtail grass (*Alopecurus alpinus*) and dicotyledons such as lousewort (*Pedicularis hirsuta*) are rare. On steep, well-protected slopes of mellow and richer soil are found small tundra grass plots with discontinuous cover of mixed grass and herbs.

Typical tundra, owing to the variation of climatic features from west to east, is divided into western or Taimyr-Anabar tundra and eastern or Trans-Lena tundra. These are rather sharply marked by different vegetation patterns.

In the western part of the subregion, large areas are occupied by lichenous alectoria tundra which yield poor and monotonous species. An extremely hardy lichen, *Alectoria ochroleuca*, which suffers little from frost and strong wind, and much cetraria lichen (*Cetraria cucullata*) predominate. Reindeer moss (*Cladonia*) and certain bryophytes are also admixed. Grassy cover is meager. Polar birch and willows do not form a special pattern. Besides the dryness of summer, the grazing of reindeer contributes to the development of alectoria. They eat out the reindeer moss but leave the alectoria. Since it is eaten only if there is a lack of other fodder, the alectoria tundra is of little economic importance. One can observe traces of the podzol-forming process under these tundras on sand and sandy loam. In little-drained depressions with clay soil are cetraria tundras on peat-gley soil. On slopes and the summits of ridges and hills, turfy tundra with thick, turfy vari-grass of partridge grass is widespread on well-drained, dry, sandy-loamy soil. To these are admixed in varying quantities cassiope (*Cassiope tetragona*) and isolated specimens of herbs. Mosses are scarce, but a rich lichen cover is developed in some areas. In others, the

moss cover is developed, but lichens are absent. Mossy tundra with cotton grass (*Eriphorum vaginatum*) and with polar birch (*Betula exilis*) in the vegetative cover do not occur as widely as turf tundra. Under it is developed peat-gley soil, with permafrost at a depth of from 16 to 20 inches.

Bogs of varying types are widespread. Low, hillocky, cotton-sedge-grass bogs are found in low places, on broad plateaus, and on low sections of slopes. In some places, cotton grass (*Eriophorum vaginatum*) predominates; in other places, sedge grass (*Carex rotundata*) is dominant. To the latter is added moisture-loving, marsh marigold (*Caltha palustris*) or marsh-cinquefoil (*Comarum palustre*), plus a dense mossy cover of *Drepanocladus*. There are also flat-knobbed bogs, where elongated flat mounds with permafrost at a depth of from 8 to 12 inches alternate with moist spots with permafrost at a depth of 5 feet. Vegetation of the mounds is mainly moss-lichen with borders of dwarf birch or willow beds at the base. The vegetation of the moist spots consists of water sedge (*Carex aquatilis*) and a dense moss cover.

More thickets of tundra scrub grow in the southern part of the typical tundra. In the northern part they grow only as a component of other tundra plant groups. The density and height of the scrub formations are determined by the shelter from desiccating winds and by the thickness of snow cover. The shrubs themselves contribute to the uniformity of the snow cover by preventing the snow from being completely blown off. Patches of tundra meadow, adapted to steep, well-drained slopes where much snow collects during winter, are sparsely scattered. In them are found meadow grass (*Poa arctica*), foxtail grass (*Alopecurus alpinus*), arctic poppy (*Papaver radicatum*), astragalus (*Astragalus arcticus*), and other species.

In the estern part of the subregion, despite the small amount of precipitation, there is so much swampiness of clay soil that mossy tundra cannot exist, and *Hypnum sphagnum* hillocky tundra prevails. Because the surface layers of soil are well warmed during a warm

Fig. 5-7. Larch grove with ivy along the Novaya River near the Khatanga River.

summer, mosses have a chance to develop satis-factorily and to survive in those inter-hum-mock expanses which are sufficiently protected by the snow cover in winter. Little peat ac-cumulates because, at a certain depth (16–20 inches), the temperature drops and water con-ditions deteriorate, the permafrost is reached, the growth of mosses is suspended, and lichens get the upper hand over mosses. From 30 to 50 per cent of the surface of the hummocky tundras is covered by mounds of cotton grass. Cetraria instead of reindeer moss makes up the lichen cover. Hillocky tundra provides good winter grazing for deer herds because the tops of the hillocks, covered with cotton grass or fodder lichen, rise above the snow. In spring, the rapidly growing green of the cotton grass and sedge of this tundra attracts deer.

The sharply continental climate of the low-land forest-tundra of Eastern Siberia contrib-utes to the advance northward of wooded plants. Dahurian larch (*Larix dahurica*) is well adapted to the conditions of wooded-tundra. It changes, east of the source of the Pyasina River, to Siberia larch. This tree grows northward to latitude 72°25′ in sparse forests along the rivers. In the western part of the forest-tundra there are many stunted trees. To the east, beginning at the Khatanga River, the forests become better in all respects. Beyond the Yana River the sparse forest dwindles to nothing. This is evidently linked with the de-crease of wind velocity to the east and with the higher temperatures of the vegetative period. In the postglacial xerothermic period the for-ests extended farther north. Trunks of larch and birch have been found buried in the tundra 120 miles north of the present-day timber line. Tundra plant groups of the forest-tundra are more often scrub thickets and hillocks of cotton grass. Through these are scattered 20 to 40 specimens of larch in 2.5 acres. Four types of vegetation are found in the larch forest: (1) woody, of collected groups of larches; (2)

Fig. 5-8. Wooded-tundra in the Norilsk region.

scrub formation of alders (*Alnus fruticosa*), willow (*Salix pulchra*), and dwarf birch (*Betula exilis*); (3) grass and scrub formation with tundra and forest flora; (4) moss-lichen. On slopes with slightly podzolic-gleyey soils, lichen predominate; in swampy sections, *sphagnum* mosses are found.

Along with the geographic and geologic study of the Soviet north, much work has been done on the organization of agricultural economy in the tundra. Soil specialists have completely altered polar agriculture. In 1913 agricultural areas did not extend north of 68° north latitude, but they now reach the 72nd parallel.

Norilsk collective farm, located 198 miles north of the Arctic Circle, is a large agricultural enterprise. Before this development of polar agriculture, the reindeer herders, fishermen, and hunters did not know the taste of potatoes and cabbages. Now, however, vegetables are grown on even the most remote collective farms of the Taimyr National Okrug. Cabbages, radishes, and potatoes are grown on open ground. Thus, the inhabitants provide themselves with vegetables for the entire winter.

The dairy and vegetable farms were organized during the five-year plans. Large collective farms gather rich harvests and provide the industrial centers with vegetables, including cabbages, radishes, carrots, beets, turnips, tomatoes, and cucumbers. With the availability of these vegetables, scurvy has now been eradicated. Compensating for the short vegetative period, the late spring's early frost, and the lack of soil-nourishing substances is an abundance of light during the long polar days. Scientists have developed selective plants, such as fast-ripening and frost-resistant vegetables, suitable for polar agriculture. The strictest adherence to the rules of northern agronomy explains the excellent vegetable harvests on open ground. Included in these rules are: autumn plowing, use of large quantities of organic and mineral fertilizer, placing of young plants in the ground in pots containing peat and manure, carefully timed irrigation, and meticulous care of plants. In January, during the long polar night when the outside temperature is −58°F, cucumbers and tomatoes are grown under artificial lighting in greenhouses. Fresh vegetables are available to the inhabitants of Dickson Island in April.

Wild reindeer, still to be found in the tundra of Eastern Siberia, migrate to the forest-tundra in winter. The feed available in reindeer-moss grazing areas of the northern Taimyr will allow the present-day reindeer herd to be increased at least seven times. Efforts to acclimatize the Kolym marmot (*Marmota kamtschatica bungei*) and musk ox (*Ovibos moschatus*) on rocky tundra of steep mountain slopes—for example, on the Byrranga Plateau —seem to be successful. The musk ox may be kept as a domesticated animal, because it is easy to tame and successfully protects itself from wolves and bears. It yields valuable wool, savory meat, and a good hide, since its skin is not attacked by the larva of the gadfly. The eastern part of the subregion contains fauna similar to that of the Chukchi Peninsula and the adjacent sections of North America: for example, the wealth of shrews (*Sorex*). Ob lemming is replaced by Kolym lemming (*Lemming paulus*).

Birds stay in the tundra only two to two and one-half months for nesting, and spend the rest of the year wintering in the southern latitudes. Only the tundra ptarmigan (*Lagopus mutus*) and polar owl (*Nyctea nyctea*) remain in the tundra during the winter. Plant-eating birds, of which there are very few in the tundra, arrive earlier than other birds and remain longer. The sparrow (*Plectrophenax nivalis*) spends 142 days in its home latitudes. The first herald of spring, the sparrow arrives while the tundra is still covered with snow and the temperature even at noon does not rise above 3°F. It remains in the tundra until the water is frozen by the winter cold. At the beginning of June the mating cry of the ptarmigan commences. This bird feeds on saxifrage leaves or willow buds.

The polar summer, which comes on rapidly, begins with the intense thawing of snow. The number and size of dark thawed patches is noticeably increased by the warm rays of the sun. Insects, such as flies, mosquitoes, beetles, and butterflies, appear. Flock after flock of

Fig. 5-9.   Reindeer pasturing on the tundra near the Lena River.

new birds arrive and at once set about nesting. The arrival of snipes, because of their great number and because of their mobility, immediately brings great animation to the monotonous brown tundra. Many of them attain their food from the soil, so temporarily thawed out. Most of the snipes limit their stay in the tundra to the period between the thawing and freezing of the soil, or from 55 to 80 days. Because they require open water, waterfowl, such as the duck, loon, and goose, appear relatively late in spring, but remain longer than other birds. With the ice breakup on the sea, many birds migrate to the coast.

In summer the tundra is a picture of great regeneration. In the July sun the vapor-filled air vibrates above white patches of snow against a background of water-saturated soil. The sandworts (*Arenaria interpres*) are jostled by the wind and fill the air with an alarming crackling. The melodic sighs of the Icelandic sandpiper (*Erolia canutus*) and the lengthy, melancholy whistles of the plover (*Squatorola squatorola*) are heard. Everywhere pairs of sparrows and Lapland longspur (*Calcarius lapponicus*) are seen. Near the shores of lakes, still full of thawing ice and snow, are groups of black geese (*Branta bernicla*). Polar duck (*Clangula hyemalis*) appear in separate dark spots. The intermittent cry of the laughing-gull (*Larus cachinnans*) or the cry of a goose (*Anser fabalis*) is heard, the latter fowl being the object of mass plunder in the time of moulting. The great bird of prey, the polar owl, hunts ptarmigan and lemming.

Day and night do not differ during the polar summer. The sun drops slightly closer to the horizon toward midnight. The temperature at night hardly differs from that of day. The voices of birds do not become silent on those rare days when a damp, thick mist hangs over the tundra for twenty-four hours or when unexpected snow falls, covering the birds' nests.

Toward the end of nesting, when the fledglings begin to take flight, the snipes become silent, and the tundra appears dead. Toward autumn, the tundra is enlivened by mature birds and by the young flocking together for the migration. In July and August, the bird migrations begin, and the tundra becomes empty. Before long it is completely covered with snow.

Although the same birds are found east of the Lena River, many species found there are not native to the western tundra. These include the rare white goose (*Chen hyperboreus*), the rose-colored sea gull (*Rhodostethia rosea*), which flies to China, Japan, and even to Australia in winter, and the American black-billed loon (*Colymbus arcticus pacificus*). There are few birds from nearby Chukchi. About 45 species do not extend west to the Kolyma River.

Much attention is being given to the further development of fishing, hunting, and the reindeer industry. The reindeer is the basis of life for the inhabitants of Taimyr. At present, dairy cattle are being used as far north as the settlement of Khatanga. The dairies of large Soviet state farms have cows which give record yields. Since the government has mechanized the fish-catching industry, river fishing has become important in the region. Fisheries have appeared on the banks of the Yenisei and its tributaries, and large fish canneries have been built. The following valuable fish are caught: sturgeon, white salmon, "muksun," "sig," "chir," "ryapushka," and "pelyad." The fishing industry of the extreme north is supplied with salt from the large reserves from Solyanaya Sopka, near Nordvik. There is organized sea fishing in the Yenisei Gulf and the eastern part of the Kara Sea. Dolphins, seals, sea hare, Baikal hair seal, and even polar bears are caught. The natives of the region hunt fox, polar fox, ermine, wild northern deer, geese, ducks, and ptarmigan.

CHAPTER 6

Central Siberia

Central Siberia is the vast territory lying mainly between the Yenisei and Lena rivers and between 52° and 72° north latitude. This territory is a single geologic unit (the Central Siberian Plateau) which differs sharply from the adjacent regions in geologic history and morphologic appearance. On the west, it borders the Western Siberian Lowland along the Yenisei River; on the east it extends beyond the Lena River into the basin of the Aldan River; on the north it borders the North Siberian Lowland approximately along a line from Dudinka to the lower stretches of the Olenek River; on the southeast it is bordered by Trans-Baikal, and on the southwest by the Sayan Mountains. The territory is chiefly drained by many large rivers: by the eastern tributaries of the Yenisei—the Angara, the Stony Tunguska, and the Lower Tunguska—and by the tributaries of the Lena—the Vilyuy, the Aldan. The highest elevations of the Central Siberian Plateau are at the sources of the Kureika, Lower Khatanga, Kheta, and Kotui rivers: 6,560 feet in the Putorana Mountains. Along the Lower Tunguska the highest points do not exceed 2,500 feet, and the low slopes along the Yenisei rarely reach more than 500 feet.

In its geologic structure the Central Siberian Plateau resembles the Eastern European Plain in many respects. The folded foundation of the plateau is also formed of Pre-Cambrian rocks,

in places raised to the surface to form a crystalline shield (Anabar massif). In other places it drops below the mantle of horizontal or slightly dislocated Paleozoic and Mesozoic rocks. This accounts for the vast depressions such as the Vilyuy Valley. Unlike the Eastern European Plain, the plateau has many faults, extremely prolonged epeirogenic upheavals, and a broad development of Upper Paleozoic basic igneous rocks (trap). Athough it has the general appearance of a horizontal tableland, the character of relief differs.

The river network cuts the plateau into many parts of different size, some parts in the form of isolated mesas, other as elongated range-like elevations. Both types of formations are similar in height since, genetically, they composed a single common peneplain surface. An observer at the bottom of one of the large river valleys would have the impression of being in a mountainous country, especially if the rim of the water divide is sufficiently dissected by transverse valleys. But having climbed out of the valley, the observer would see before him a slightly undulating surface, solidly covered by dense forest, which becomes more monotonous the farther he moves from the river toward the center of the water divide.

Central Siberia belongs to the taiga zone; only in separate patches to the south are there islands of wooded-steppe. Because of the elevated relief, more continental and dry climate, and wide occurrence of permafrost, this territory, in comparison with the corresponding taiga of the neighboring Western Siberian Lowland, is characterized by (1) less swampiness, (2) the predominance of Dahurian larch and fewer dark coniferous species, (3) the presence in many places of steppe plants and animals in taiga areas, (4) indigenous fauna, and (5) the far northward spread of Siberian species generally.

Administratively, the western part of the region belongs to the Krasnoyarsk Krai, the eastern part to the Yakutsk ASSR, and the southeastern part to the Irkutsk Oblast.

GEOLOGIC HISTORY

The Central Siberian Plateau is a geotectonic unit formed mainly of Paleozoic deposits lying on a Pre-Cambrian foundation. From the beginning of the Cambrian Period, it experienced little folding and remained a massif, which yielded noticeably to pressure only along its periphery. The region underwent slow, rhythmic, epeirogenic movements, causing the transgression and regression of the seas and the formation and eventual drying of huge lake basins. The number of terraces in the valleys of the large rivers (10 to 12) is considerably greater than in those of the Eastern European Plain. This indicates many stages of retardation and cessation in epeirogenic upheavals. During these stages, depth erosion gave way to lateral erosion.

In the Cambrian Period the region was inundated at first by a shallow and later by a somewhat deeper sea, in which thick layers of limestone accumulated. Toward the end of the period, this sea became shallower and in places was even converted into lagoons, in which beds of gypsum and rock salt were deposited. In the Silurian Period fluctuating movements were resumed. The Erian phase of Caledonian folding drew the sea back to the periphery and created folds of the marginal type. At the beginning of the Devonian Period the region became dry land. In the middle of the Carboniferous Period, there developed a vast network of lakes and bogs which resulted in the accumulation of coal-bearing strata. At the beginning of the Permian Period and even to some extent in the Upper Pennsylvanian, there were powerful Variscan mountain-forming movements. The rigid block of the Central Siberian Plateau, unable to resist this pressure of intense folding, buckled along the edges where Caledonian folds were intensified, and was broken along the rim and in the central part by a network of large tectonic fractures. Along these, as along channels, trap intruded into strata of the Paleozoic deposits and extruded on their surface. In and around the lakes life disappeared, and masses of tuff rocks, broken through by trap dikes, were deposited. There was a long period of tectonic quiet after this eruption. In the Mesozoic Era the main part of the Central Siberian Plateau remained dry land. It was subjected to erosion, which gradually carried off the products of vulcanism and revealed, in places, the older strata under younger extrusive rocks (trap).

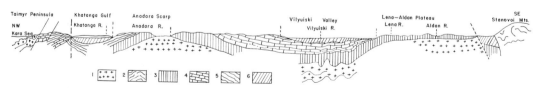

Fig. 6-1. Geologic cross section of Central Siberian Plateau, from Nordensheld Archipelago to Stanovoi Range. 1—Pre-Cambrian; 2—Paleozoic; 3—Cambrian; 4—Silurian; 5—Permo-Carboniferous (Tungus formation); 6—Mesozoic.

Fig. 6-2. Trap rock imbedded in Silurian formations, Moyer River basin.

A series of weak vertical movements caused Mesozoic transgressions. The Jurassic sea penetrated deeply along the river course of the modern Lena, Vilyuy, and Aldan valleys, creating an interior basin which was converted, toward the beginning of the Upper Jurassic Period, into a series of lagoons and lakes. In the lakes which existed at this time in the south, in the Kansk and Irkutsk regions, coal-bearing strata were deposited. The weaker transgression of the Lower Cretaceous sea covered only the northernmost Lena River valley. Tectonic movements of the Upper Cretaceous Period drove the sea back to the north and caused the weak folding of Mesozoic deposits. Subsequently the entire territory became dry land and underwent erosion. Traces of ancient glaciers, discovered in only a few places on the plateau, indicate that glaciation was local and was limited to high mountain regions such as the upper reaches of the Kureika and Kheta rivers or the Yenisei Ridge. The modern relief is being developed by intensive frost weathering under conditions of dry continental climate and by the erosive forces of the complex and powerful hydrographic network.

GEOMORPHOLOGIC DISTRICTS

Within the Central Siberian Plateau the following geomorphologic districts are rather well-defined: (1) the Tunguska Basin (coal) and the Putorana Mountains; (2) the district with near-surface Pre-Cambrian outcrops including the Anabar massif, Lena–Aldan Plateau, and Yenisei Ridge; (3) the district of Mesozoic marine transgression, including the Vilyuy and Lena basins; (4) the southern district outside the trap area, comprising the upper Lena flat elevation and the Cheremkhovo and Kansk coal basins.

Tunguska Basin–Putorana Mountains

The Tunguska Basin occupies the western and central part of the plateau, within the area of trap occurrence. Its margins are marked by Lower Paleozoic rocks, crumpled in slanting folds of a northeastern strike, and the central part is formed of continental lagoon deposits of the Upper Paleozoic. These deposits are composed of sandstones and shales, with subordinate seams of coal and tuff masses, with intermittent tuffs and tuffites and inter-stratifications of sandstones and shales. The horizontal continental lagoon deposits of the Permian-Carboniferous Period contain all types of commercially important coal beds—from anthracites to rich sapropelite and brown coal. The width of the mixed coal seams sometimes reaches several yards. Most of the coal is concentrated in the central and lower course of the Lower Tunguska River, where there is a syn-

Fig. 6-3. Trap rock exposed in the rapids of the Khatanga.

clinial trough of carboniferous deposits that reaches 5,000 feet in thickness (Bugarikhta, Noginsk, and other beds).

Igneous rocks are found throughout the basin. Siberian trap is mainly diabases, the main mass of which was extruded in pre-Jurassic times. The area occupied by them is so great (up to 385,000 square miles) that it may be compared only with the greatest basalt deposits on the globe, such as the Deccan Plateau in India. The conditions of occurrence of the trap are extremely diverse. It appears as blanket deposits of varying width, as sills, as thick dikes, and as extrusive surface flows. Columnar structures of five- and six-sided prisms are typical. Intrusive trap is the source of a series of ore deposits, such as the Angara iron deposits along both sides of the rapids of the meridional segment of the Angara River. Linked with the extrusive trap is a commercially important deposit of Iceland spar, formed by the filling in of cavities in the volcanic rock. Beneath the culture base in Tura (Turinskaya Kultbaza), along the Lower Tunguska, are large, rich deposits of spar suitable for the manufacture of optical instruments.

As a result of the thermic influence of the trap intrusions, part of the coal deposits were converted from noncoking to coking coal and part into graphites of high quality, with a carbon content of from 80 to 95 per cent. The graphite deposits are large enough to satisfy the

Fig. 6-4. Trap rock on the Lower Tunguska.

world demand for many years. In the largest graphite deposit on the Kureika River, where there is a complex seam approximately 50 feet in width, the graphite resources amount to more than ten million tons. Post-Tertiary formations are glacial deposits.

Modern relief of the district was formed as a result of (1) intricate epeirogenic movements; (2) many large faults—for example, along the northern border of the basin; (3) dissection of the ancient peneplain by erosional processes, which is indicated by the many terraces at considerable heights above the present level of the rivers; and (4) glaciation in the higher areas. From the ancient peneplain have survived vast structural mesas with monoto-

agents, the trap has contributed to the preservation of large (up to 20 square miles) areas of ancient peneplain. Frequently these large areas of peneplain are formed by denudation of layers of sedimentary rock and occupy dominating positions above the surrounding locality. Often the tops of the mesas and the slopes of valleys are set with countless picturesque trap columns having prismatic structures. The trap, because of its exceptional tendency toward disintegration by intensive frost weathering, yields thick rock fields on the summits. Along the slopes there are vast talus slopes which descend into the valleys. As a result of the alternation of horizontal layers of hard trap, which yield easily to disintegration, the slopes

Fig. 6-5. First rapids of the Kureika River.

nous, flat, swampy summits, cut through by erosional trenches or, infrequently, deep river valleys.

The trap, having intruded in sedimentary rocks, placed a particular stamp on the morphology of the distict. Owing to its durability against the destructive activity of external

of the mesas and the rims of the river valleys acquire an unusual step-like profile.

No less distinct is the role of trap in the development of negative forms of relief. Valleys in sedimentary rocks are broad, with flat bottoms and very little lengthwise gradients, which results in a slow current. But rivers intersecting areas formed by trap are full of rapids and form steep-walled gorges, on the slopes of which are typical columns and fragments of trap with striking outlines. Accompanying the alternation of trap and sedimentary rocks is the alternation of wide and narrow sections of the valleys. In the slow-moving rivers of the wide valleys are many islands and channels. In the trap, the fast-moving streams make narrow, vertical gorges. In the valleys of shallow streams are series of step-like breaks of longitudinal profile, accompanied by many high waterfalls. Layered intrusions of trap may form rapids, and trap dikes jutting far out into the river impede ice movement and cause gravel and boulders to pile up. Where the trap intrusion is small, the river by-passes it, forming loops characteristic of many rivers cutting through trap areas. In the higher regions subjected to glaciation—for example, in the Norilsk region—glacial forms of relief have evolved. There are ancient glacial valleys, many cirque formations, accumulations of moraine material, deep long valleys ploughed out by glaciers in which are moraine-dammed lakes (Lake Melkoye).

The Putorana Mountains make up a unique geomorphologic region which stands out sharply from the Central Siberian Plateau. The mountains occupy the higher, northwestern part of the plateau, which stretches from Lake Pyasino to a deep, eroded depression forming Lake Yessei. This lake was formed by the activity of the Kotui and Moyero rivers

Fig. 6-6. Lake Lama.

and their tributaries. The average elevation of these mountains is approximately 2,300 feet, although in the northwestern part they reach 4,620 to 5,280 feet. These greater elevations are at the water divide of the Kotui and Kheta rivers. Mount Kamen is 6,681 feet high. The elevation of the Putorana Mountains, which is unusual for the general character of the Central Siberian Plateau, is due to the great thickness of the traps developed here and the presence of a highly lifted massif. This massif is limited by the erosion lines which can be seen in the steep escarpments rising several hundred feet above the Central Siberian Lowland. The presence of igneous-rock cover accounts for the wide appearance of table mountains. In the Putorana region, which was subjected to ancient glaciation, mountain glacial forms give the relief a very dismembered appearance. A dense network of ancient glacial valleys plays an important role in the contours of the relief. These valleys divide the Putorana massif into individual mountain groups. They are long, relatively narrow and deeply cut (2,300 to 2,600 feet), and spread out radially from the central part of the region. Their bottoms are filled with deep lakes, which give the impression of widely flooded rivers. The general features of these glacial valleys are: (1) an oval basin profile; (2) steep, in places precipitous, slopes; (3) lengthy basins and lakes—Khatanga 68 miles, Kita 56 miles, Lama 53 miles; (4) noticeable widening of basins and lakes toward the lowlands—from 0.6 to 10 miles; (5) low elevations—Lama 175 feet, Bolshaya Khatanga 241 feet, Kita 307 feet; (6) presence of moraine material in the lower parts of most of the lakes; and (7) well-developed deltas at the mouths of the tributaries emptying into the lakes. Wind erosion acts longer and more strongly on the more heated slopes that face south. Permafrost also thaws deeper, leading to a much faster destruction of these slopes.

Glacial accumulation, of which there are traces, played a small part in the morphology of the region. These traces are found at the base of the mountains as moraine material and

Fig. 6-7. Glacial cirques on the north slope of the Putorana Mountains; stunted alder in the foreground.

bogs. On bald mountains with very steep slopes and a continuous outcrop of solid rock, frost erosion caused by the severe polar climate proceeds on a grand scale.

Anabar Massif, Lena-Aldan Plateau, Yenisei Ridge

In the Anabar massif in the basin of the upper Anabar River, the Pre-Cambrian foundation outcrops on the surface in complex steep folds with a northwest strike, and is surrounded by ancient Paleozoic rock deposits that lie horizontally or undulate with slight folds and faults. Since volcanic processes have been very little developed, trap is absent here. Structurally, the block resembles a dome-shaped anticline, with the Pre-Cambrian rocks at the core. The Pre-Cambrian foundation drops steeply away from this core on all sides. Morphologically, the block is a highly eroded plateau, sloping to the north and northeast, which explains the direction of flow of the Anabar and Olenek rivers. The elevated southern rim of the plateau, the so-called Vilyuy Mountains, is on the watershed between the Olenek and Vilyuy and reaches 3,445 feet in the Lyucha-Ongokton massif. In the east, however, the elevation of the southern rim drops to 1,980 feet. Within the limits of the Pre-Cambrian shield are flat smooth slopes, now and then broken by isolated peaks which extend into the mountain tundra zone. Rivers meander in stony beds amid broad valleys whose slopes are heaped with talus. A monotonous relief of low hills characterizes the area of the Cambrian outcrops. Placer gold is a known mineral deposit.

The Lena-Aldan Plateau extends to the south from the Vilyuy Valley, approximately to the wide central part of the Aldan River. It is formed, as is the Anabar block, of a Pre-Cambrian foundation covered with Cambrian limestones and dolomites. However, the Lena-Aldan Plateau is not so well proportioned as the dome-shaped Anabar massif. Highly dissected by the river network, it reaches an elevation of 1,650 feet in the western section and drops toward the east. Since the watersheds are from 330 to 1,000 feet above the level of the large rivers, there is intense dissection of the margins of the plateau. Thus an intricate valley relief has evolved principally in the vicinity of the large rivers. In the Lena River Valley above Yakutsk, there are high, sheer, craggy bluffs formed of Paleozoic limestones. These are dissected by narrow erosional trenches and modified by processes of the karst type, with the formation of picturesque columns and towers.

On the flat, higher parts of the plateau lies a thick layer of Quaternary deposits—sands, gravels, and clayey carbonaceous soil. These deposits contain seams and lenses of fossil ice that vary from 6 to 100 feet thick. Since the plateau was never covered by glaciers, evidently this fossil ice was formed in the glacial period by accumulations of stationary masses of firn in depressions.

On the divides, a lake and gentle-slope landscape prevail, containing low-gradient slopes, vast bogs, and many lake depressions in different stages of extinction and conversion into bog areas. The lakes were formed from fossil ice, the size and shape of the lake depressions being determined by the size, shape, and character of thawing ice blocks. Some of the lakes are evidently of a karst character. The river network is weakly developed and frequently connects the lakes; the current is slow and streams are often overgrown. Since there is only a slight thawing of the soil, the supply of ground water is negligible, and the rivers often dry up in summer.

The Yenisei Ridge begins somewhat north of the main line of the Trans-Siberian railway between the cities of Krasnoyarsk and Kansk and extends approximately 540 miles in a northwesterly direction, corresponding to the direction of folding. Somewhat above the mouth of the Stony Tunguska River, the ridge is intersected by the Yenisei Valley, which runs in a narrow gorge amid crystalline schists, forming the Osinovskiy rapids. These can be passed only with difficulty during low water. Farther down, having received the Middle Tunguska, the Yenisei at once widens its valley to 60 miles. Beyond the Yenisei, the ridge is gradually submerged under the Quaternary deposits of the Western Siberian Lowland, then extends toward the upper stretches of the Taz River. On the northeast it does not have a pronounced boundary and forms a weakly inclined surface, which gradually blends with the Central Siberian Plateau. On the southwest, where it rises above the Yenisei, the ridge breaks off in a steep tectonic shelf which is clearly evident in the relief. In places its rocks extend also to the other side of the river, forming rapids—for example, the Kazachinsk rapids above the mouth of the Angara. The ridge is separated from the Eastern Sayan by a comparatively wide valley composed of Paleozoic and Mesozoic formations. Vertical dissection of the ridge is marked; elevations range from 2,640 to 2,970 feet; its highest point is Enashimskiy Polkan, which is 3,680 feet; and the valley of the largest river, the Bolshoy Pit, is cut into the ridge 660 feet.

The Yenisei Ridge is formed of Pre-Cambrian crystalline schists and gneisses, which are disrupted by large intrusions of granite. Within its limits, there are no outcrops of trap. In the northern part, Lower Paleozoic sandstones and limestones lie on Pre-Cambrian strata. The fundamental tectonic process must have been an upthrust or overthrust, which sharply elevated the ridge above the adjacent areas to the west. The ridge is one of the richest gold-bearing areas in Siberia.

The Yenisei Ridge is an intermediate-mountain landscape. It is deeply dissected by prolonged erosion, with smooth relief forms and is isolated in the middle of the lower regions surrounding it. As a result of intensive erosional activity, the Bolshoy Pit River has cut across the ridge. The fact that almost all the Pit river's upper tributaries are now directed toward the course of the main river indicates their comparatively recent capture. The smoothness of the relief, the swampiness of the divides, and the thick, loose deposits (more than 132 feet) in certain deep valleys are the result of glaciation, traces of which are found in various parts of the ridge. Permanent snow survives only on the highest points today. In the region of gneisses and crystalline schists on the flat, gradually sloping watersheds are vast bogs, from which rivers begin in formless channels whose direction of current is scarcely detectable. The rivers cut into the slopes of the ridge and flow along a canyon amid bare rocks. Farther on, the valleys are wider, and contain sand-gravel deposits along the riverbanks. Valleys in the middle of granite regions are narrow, their slopes are covered with talus, and their channels are littered with large boulders. Rivers in limestone and sandstone regions flow through wide valleys and amid low gravel islands in a series of shallow branches.

Vilyuy-Lena Basins

The Vilyuy Valley, between the Anabar massif and the Lena-Aldan Plateau, is a large, flat-floored, synclinal depression with a northeast-southwest trend. It is filled with Jurassic deposits and possesses clearly visible borders. Lower Jurassic continental deposits, cropping out along the edges of the valley, occur transgressively on Cambrian and Silurian limestones. The central part of the valley is made up of a thick series of these deposits, which lie horizontally or form gradually sloping folds. This series shows an uneven alternation of sands, porous sandstones, clay shales, and, in places, seams of brown coal.

Morphologically, the region is a large, dissected, low plateau with gently sloping divides and broad river valleys. The elevation of the plateau varies from 429 to 660 feet in the large valleys, and from 1,000 to 1,320 feet on the higher watersheds. In the glacial period, there was a mantle of stationary firn lying on lake-river deposits and on the ice of lakes frozen to the bottom. Part of the firn and lake ice survived to the present time as large lenses of fossil ice under recent unconsolidated deposits. After the glacial period the plateau received much more precipitation than it receives at present. This is indicated by the highly developed river terraces, which do not correspond at all to the modern activity of the river systems. In this same period the deposit of alluvium took place. Today it has the character of fine, sometimes loess-like clay soil and usually contains a certain amount of carbonate. Centuries of activity by atmospheric agents have smoothed off sharp rises and steep slopes, filled valleys with thick masses of unconsolidated deposits, and in general left soft, only slightly undulating contours.

The slight dissection and low slopes, the insignificant precipitation and negligible ground water, and the solid vegetative cover are the causes of the scant runoff that occurs only during the period of spring thaw, when the soil is still frozen. From an airplane an observer sees countless large and small lakes against an ocean of dark-green, dense taiga. In places the lakes are so close together that, from above, they look like a continuous light ground-fog. The network of shallow riverlets and streams, meandering fantastically among the lakes but usually not joining them, resembles a fine silvery web.

There are so many lakes in some places that the line of travel is from one lake to another. Most of the lakes are in the interfluvial areas farthest from the rivers—that is, in areas that favor the collecting of water and excavation of channels but do not nourish stream runoff. Even in sandy areas many lakes exist because permafrost makes the sand impervious to subsoil drainage. There are also many sinkhole lakes, formed by the thawing of lenses of ice in unconsolidated deposits. In the middle of some of these lakes are groups of larch or willow, standing in 3 to 6 feet of water.

The levels of sinkhole lakes, even those lying close to one another, sometimes differ considerably. When a stream gradually cuts back upstream, there is a discharge of water from a higher lake into a neighboring lower one. Consequently, the first lake may dry up. A lake is often drained in order to use its bottom for the development of hay meadowlands. Both the bottom of drained lakes and the narrow border around the lake shore are called *alasy* and provide the best meadows and pasturage. There is a seasonal variation in the amount of water flowing into the lakes. The greatest amount is observed in spring from meltwater; in summer the inflow is greatly diminished. Many water-divide lakes are in a stage of extinction. The leveling work of denudation proceeds gradually and leads to the lakes being filled by sand and silt. As a result, shoaling has taken place. Vegetation growing in ponds and producing a great amount of peat finishes the process of converting the lakes into bogs.

The Lena Basin, which is part of the Vilyuy Valley on the north, is a narrow, deep depression along the lower course of the Lena River from the North Siberian Lowland almost to the mouth of the Aldan. It is formed of Cretaceous and Jurassic sediments which are almost horizontal. In the valley of the Lena River there are pronounced terraces: the flood plain itself and two above the flood plain. The valley abounds in both dry and swampy beds of old rivers. These extend along the courses of the rivers, separated by flat crests and sandy hillocks. Alluvial deposits are sandy through their entire thickness; sometimes in the upper part they are more clayey or covered by loess-like, carbonaceous clay-loams.

Southern District

The southern district of the Central Siberian Plateau lies outside the trap region and to the south of the Tunguska Basin. It extends south of a line approximately from Tulun to Kirensk, and is the southern shelf of the plateau between the Baikal region and the Sayans. It is formed of Lower Paleozoic rocks, adjoined by a strip of coal-bearing deposits on the south which stretch along the foothills of the Sayan. The district is a horizontal, elevated plateau, which is dissected by the deeply notched valleys of the tributaries of the Angara, Lena, and Kirenga rivers, on a broad, swampy divide. The relief takes on sharper features in the northeastern part, where there are close-grained limestones and sandstones of the Cambrian and Silurian periods, on which karst topography is widespread. In the southwestern part, where the summits of the divides are formed of easily disintegrated, weakly cemented Jurassic sandstones, the relief generally bears a soft, horizontally sloping character.

The Cheremkhovo Coal Basin, in a strip 45 miles wide along the Trans-Siberian railroad between Krasnoyarsk and Irkutsk, and the Kansk Coal Basin, to the east of the southern part of the Yenisei Ridge toward the Biryusa River and south to the foothills of Eastern Sayan, closely resemble each other in origin and development of carboniferous strata. In the Jurassic Period this area was a slowly sinking lowland occupied by lakes and bogs.

Coal seams originated from lake and bog peat mosses not connected with the seashore and were interrupted in their development, not by the advance of the sea but by the drying of the basins or by their complete overgrowth. The area and thickness of the carboniferous deposits were determined by the shape of the bottom of the basin. Thus, the coal seams at times are not continuous. The varying and noncontemporaneous occurrence of a Jurassic carboniferous stratum on the eroded Paleozoic surface explains the following features: the comparatively slight depth of the coal-bearing series (660 to 1,320 feet), the small number of seams, their variable thickness (5 to 15 feet) over great distances, and the fracturing of coal basins into separate islands owing to the erosion of many coal beds. Reserves reach 75 billion tons in the Cheremkhovo Coal Basin and 40 billion tons in the Kansk Basin. Bituminous and sapropelite coal predominate in the Cheremkhovo and lignites in the Kansk. Ash content of the coal is 7 to 14 per cent, and the sulphur content reaches 1.5 per cent. The heat capacity of the coal in Cheremkhovo is 6,000 to 7,000 calories, and in Kansk 3,200 to 5,500 calories per kilogram.

The Chulym-Yenisei basin closely resembles the Kansk-Cheremkhovo basin in geologic structure and development. This basin lies outside Central Siberia. It stretches in a wide strip (37 to 56 miles) along both sides of the Trans-Siberian railway from Bogotol to Krasnoyarsk. It continues along the left side of the Yenisei River to the mouth of the Angara River. In the south the basin is bounded by Kurbatov and Solgon ridges. In the north the lignite coal-bearing strata are hidden under shallow deposits along the line from Bogotol to Predivinsk. The coal of this basin has a rather high heat capacity and a variable ash content. The strata of coal vary greatly in thickness. Combustible shale is present in large quantities. The brown coal is used for locomotives, and the combustible shale is a source of liquid fuel. The location of these basins along the Trans-Siberian railway and near large waterways greatly increases their economic significance.

SOIL AND VEGETATION

The vast taiga of Central Siberia differs considerably from the corresponding taiga of the Western Siberian Lowland in types of soil and vegetative cover. The higher, partly mountainous relief and the wide expanses of rocky surfaces contribute to good drainage. The extreme continentality and dryness of climate result in less swampiness and podzolizing of the soil and in the infiltration far into the taiga of a steppe-soil complex with solonetz and solonchak. These factors have led to: (1) the predominance of a uniform, light-colored coniferous taiga, especially containing Dahurian larch, many pines, and a few dark-colored conifers; (2) the growth of scrub alder as a forest undergrowth; (3) the presence in the drier larch forests of many steppe species, and even small islands of steppe with feather grass and fescue; and (4) fewer and smaller bogs. In the highest parts, vertical zonality is noted. In Western Siberia most of the conifers have the same northern limit, but in Central Siberia their northern limits vary widely. The borders of hydrophytic fir and Siberian pine drop sharply to the south.

The Pacific slope variety of Dahurian larch (*Larix dahurica*) plays the greatest role in the composition of the forests of Central Siberia. This species, which closely resembles the American larch (*Larix laricina*), is distinctly different from the neighboring Siberian larch. The Dahurian larch, tolerant of extreme cold, is the most northerly tree on the globe. It grows from the northern timber line to the steppes of Trans-Baikal, and also extends to the timber line high in the mountains. As a light-loving tree, the larch prefers the most exposed summits, slopes, and ridges. The Dahurian larch is not finicky about its soil, growing well on the rubbly soil of dry slopes and on sphagnum bogs. With its thick network of lateral roots in the upper part of the active layer, it is also adapted to the use of shallow soil above permafrost. Although its root system allows it to grow over permafrost, the tree is defenseless against blizzards. Because the larch can form auxiliary roots on any part of the trunk above the root neck, it can grow on sphagnum bogs without being choked by the rapid growth of moss cover. In these bogs the larch may reach an age of 300 years, whereas under similar conditions the pine usually dies before it is 50 years old. Because it likes light, has a thin crown, and grows in comparatively sparse stand, larch does not create such a sharply pronounced phytoclimate as the shade-enduring spruce. Hence, a diverse vegetation may develop under its canopy. However, there may be little moss cover in very dry places. Its rapid growth as a young tree and its resistance to cold favor the growth of larch in new territories. But the fact that it loves light retards its spread in those places where the climate and soil conditions permit other trees to exist. Larch is easily replaced not only by spruce and fir but even by pine.

The wood of Dahurian larch has excellent industrial qualities: it is strong and resinous, and has negligible shrinkage and swelling. Larch is difficult to finish, and owing to its high specific gravity, sinks after prolonged immersion. The wood has a very high heat value. It serves as an excellent building material, because it is extremely resistant to moisture; it becomes very hard during constant exposure to water because of surface sliming, which prevents both external and internal decay. Larch is irreplaceable in the manufacture of crossties (serving up to 15 years), telegraph and telephone poles, mine braces, bridge piles, ends for street pavements, and in the construction of ships.

The distribution of vegetative cover in Central Siberia differs from that in other parts of Eurasia. First, there is little of the latitudinal zoning that is found in the vast plains of European USSR and Western Siberia. The east-west zone of dark coniferous taiga does not have latitudinal spread even in the low, southern parts of Central Siberia. It stretches along the belt of higher elevations which run along the Yenisei River. Maximum precipitation in the zone occurs along a meridional strip which gradually narrows and wedges into the polar circle. Central Siberia lies within the bounds of the forest zone, but the entire plateau and the table mountains exhibit a "bald-mountain" vegetation at 2,900 feet in the south and at 1,150 to 1,320 feet in the north. The absence of Siberian pine is characteristic. More fully expressed is the vertical belt in the western region. Here the dark coniferous taiga and the larch taiga meet, and an alder belt is present. Here (in the Putorana Mountains) the vertical vegetation belts have the following schematic form: from 132 to 1,320 feet, dark coniferous taiga with larch; from 825 to 1,810 feet, larch forests; from 1,320 to 2,480 feet, dense, mixed forest; from 2,310 to 2,640 feet, alder (*Alnus fruticosa*) belt; from 2,480 to 2,970 feet, mountain tundra with dwarf birch; from 2,640 to 3,960 feet, mountain, lichen tundra: and above 3,960 feet, rocky, mountain, polar deserts. Eastward these belts diminish and finally disappear. The role of the dwarf birch belt is lessened.

It is possible to divide Central Siberia according to vegetative and soil cover into three parts: (1) northern subzone of sparse swampy forests; (2) central, or Tunguska-Yakutsk, subzone with predominance of drier larch forests; and (3) southern, or Angara-Lena, subzone with pure stands of pine forests. South of the taiga zone lie four forest-steppe "islands": Achinsk, Kansk, Krasnoyarsk, and Balagansk–Irkutsk.

Northern Subzone

The northern subzone of sparse, larch forests is between the southern boundary of the wooded-tundra and the polar circle, and has a clayey, podzolic, and swampy soil, with many rocks in mountainous areas. It has a prevalence of Dahurian larch, with some pine and spruce but no fir. Here many tundra fauna, such as polar fox and white ptarmigan, are found. However, such typical taiga forms as the Siberian polecat are absent. In the northern half, sparse, swamped forests, which are transitional to the forest-tundra, predominate; in the southern half, they become drier and denser. Larch forests are found at higher altitudes, and there is also a subalpine strip of brushwoods and bald-mountain vegetation.

The northern boundary of the forest is an irregular, broken line. It juts deeply northward along the valleys of large rivers and retreats southward hundreds of miles from the seacoasts along water divides. Wedged into the forest zone are large areas of tundra. Individual islands of forest grow on coarse-grained soil and advance far to the north of the border of the dense forest. The most northern groves of Dahurian larch are in the Khatanga River valley below 72°23', and in the Lena River valley below 72° north latitude. These groves are surrounded by moss and brushwood tundra. They contain trees 10 to 16 feet high, which have irregularly situated branches hung with strands of lichen. The undergrowth is made up of polar willow and dwarf birch.

der for reindeer. Grasses grow only on bottom-land. Even farther south there are very few healthy, thick forests. On low, gentle slopes and at their bases, there are thin larch forests with a few healthy dwarfed trees and an undergrowth of willow and dwarf birch. The denser and best-formed larch forests which contain trees 40 to 50 feet in height and an undergrowth of scrub alder (*Alnus fruticosa*), are along the warm, wind-protected slopes of river valleys and riverbanks. The trees are used only for firewood; it is necessary to bring timber into the lower sections of the Lena from the upper course of the river. Burned-over patches are little developed. The regrowth of trees after a fire does not take place as quickly as in the more southerly subzones. The restoration of a larch forest is a slow process. Sometimes the destruction of a forest by fire leads ultimately to the formation of tundra patches. At higher altitudes a subalpine strip of scrub alder 100 to 130 feet wide is found. The alpine belt occupies the highest parts of the mountainous regions. On horizontal summits of high plateaus, and

Fig. 6-8. Dahurian larch on the northern margin of the taiga.

The northern strip of the taiga is a monotonous sparse forest of Dahurian larch. The crowns of the trees are narrow and thin. Instead of green grasses there is a monotonous, gray, lichenous cover, providing excellent fod-

along crevices and depressions with fine soil accumulated amid rocky patches, there are often beds of Alectoria lichen (*Alectoria ochroleuca*). Lower, on shallow, rocky, peat-bog and peat-gley soil, there is a strip of turf and moss tundras with willow (*Salix reticulata*), partridge grass (*Dryas octopetala*), and cassiope (*Cassiope tetragona*).

Central Subzone

The central subzone extends from the Arctic Circle to approximately the 60th parallel on the west (the northern border of the continuous pine groves), and to the east-west section of the Aldan River valley on the east. In the Aldan Valley are found Far Eastern flora, such as Yeddo spruce (*Picea jezoensis*), Okhotsk clematis (*Atragene ochotensis*), and *Listera brevidens*. The *Listera* is found in the Okhotsk region, in Japan, and in North Korea. Because of the increase to the east of a dry continental climate, the decrease in winter precipitation, and the slight snow cover (which contributes to the occurrence of permafrost close to the surface), the makeup of vegetation varies from west to east within the boundaries of the subzone. In the moister western part, forests of Siberian larch prevail, and a large role is played by the dark coniferous forests of Siberian pine, fir, and spruce. Here more strongly podzolic soils of a different mechanical composition are found. In the drier eastern part, the Dahurian larch is more prevalent because it is best adapted to the conditions of permafrost. The light-loving pines join it in more or less significant numbers. Steppe forms grow under the forest mantle, and there are even patches of meadow steppe. Less podzolic and swamped soils are to be found here, and under the meadow steppe there are even solonetz and solonchak soils. Because of these differences it is possible to divide the subzone into two districts: the Tunguska on the west, approximately up to the Yenisei and Lena divides; and the Yakutsk, which is east of these boundaries.

The Tunguska district, which includes the basins of the Lower and Stony Tunguska rivers, has mostly Siberian larch. Spruce is a definite element of this forest; Siberian pine is common; and pure stands of fir stretch for dozens of miles along the rivers. The grassy

Fig. 6-9. Larch forest of Central Siberia on the Chun River.

cover of the taiga is poor in range of species and is devoid of tall grasses. The upper slopes of divides are covered with dense Siberian pine (20 per cent), spruce (40 per cent), and larch taiga. Individual trees grow to a height of 66 feet. There is a well-developed undergrowth of scrub alder, willow, juniper, mountain ash, and dog rose, and a rich grass cover of Jacob's ladder (*Polemonium coeruleum*), cow parsnip (*Heracleum dissectum*), and reed grass (*Calamagrostis villosa*).

The dark coniferous taiga may be classified as follows: (1) spruce, Siberian pine, larch taiga, with larch in the first place and spruce and Siberian pine in the second; (2) spruce, Siberian pine, mossy taiga, with the predominance of Siberian pine and spruce, a small admixture of larch, with a poor grass cover; (3) spruce-fir mossy taiga, with a prevalence of spruce and fir, infrequent admixture of Siberian pine and larch, typical grassy taiga species, such as honeysuckle or pyrola, and with a complete mossy cover eight inches deep. On burned-over areas, the first plant to appear is usually willow herb (*Epilobium angustifolium*). Later birch-aspen forests develop along with fast-growing grassy cover. And still later, spruce and Siberian pine are added. On coarse-grained and gravelly soil, especially on the slopes facing south, burns are gradually covered by larch-pine and pine groves, at first with grass, and then moss. Ultimately the burns are replaced, by dark coniferous taiga. Along the riverbanks thick, grassy vegetation is often found. There are many mossy bogs. In the valley of the Lower Tunguska, the forest does not extend more than 1,650 feet above the level of the river, although a strip of scrub alder grows beyond the forest. On the bare rocky peaks, and packed on soil which preserves the red-brown color of the original rocks, mosses and lichens have developed. On fine soil, dwarf birch grows in patches along with partridge grass, cinquefoil (*Potentilla nivea*), and other mountain-tundra plants. The best forests provide a large quantity of wood pulp for the sawmills of Dudinka, and Siberian pines give good yields of nuts.

The Yakutsk district, occupying the basins of the Lena, Vilyuy, and Aldan Rivers, has forests predominantly of Dahurian larch, plus pine (especially on sand), birch, and aspen. Spruce is extremely rare. In the western part of the district, larch forests with admixtures of pine, birch, and aspen are common. The undergrowth is mountain ash, pyrola willow (*Salix pyrolifolia*), scrub alder, and dog rose. The grassy vegetation is columbine (*Aquilegia parviflora*), raspberry (*Rubus saxatilis*), lady's-slipper (*Cypripedium guttatum*), and a single liana, Siberian clematis (*Atragene sibirica*). In moist places in the undergrowth, dwarf birch (*Betula exilis*) is found.

Fig. 6-10. Fir–moss taiga in the Tunguska Valley.

In the eastern part of the Vilyuy basin, there are many clearly defined types of forest. The most widespread type, occupying large stands for hundreds of miles, is the green taiga. It grows on level areas and in depressions where ground water and permafrost occur close to the surface. The green taiga also grows on podzolic soil of different mechanical composition, but mostly on medium podzolic soil and soil with a thin podzolic horizon. The Dahurian larch, with trees 60 to 70 feet high, prevails in the forests. There is little undergrowth except for a monotonous cover of wild rosemary, columbine, red bilberry, and sedge. In the dense moss cover grow good stands of larch.

Large areas of red-bilberry taiga are found where there is clay soil with moderate moisture and the permafrost lies at a depth of three feet. Below the bilberry taiga are found brown-gray podzolic soil that resembles the gray, forest clay soil. The stands of Dahurian larch are thicker and better here than in the preceding areas and restoration is faster. In the undergrowth are willow, spirea, and dog rose, enmeshed by Siberian clematis. The monotonous grass cover is pyrola; the moss cover is thinner than in the green taiga.

On the sandy, well-drained, podzolic soil of gentle slopes throughout the whole district pine-grove taiga is encountered. The pine with larch and the larch alone which make up these forests are sparse, low (50 to 53 feet) trees of slow growth, which produces compact and close-grained wood. The displacement of larch by pine has proceeded intensely. Secondary birch forests grow on burned-out forest sites and cut-over land. Scrub birch (*Betula viluica*) and dwarf birch (*B. exilis*), the common undergrowth of the landscape, are found in those places where the taiga has undergone systematic burning. The very dry vegetation burns furiously. If a pine forest burns, leaving the larch, then islets of meadow steppe may grow. Amid the solid dark mass of forest, meadows form narrow light-green fringes along rivers and around lakes. The most widespread type of meadow in valleys has a dense undergrowth of reed grass (*Calamgrostis langsdorffii*), five

feet high, with a small admixture of sedge and other grasses. Meadow expanses near lakes have less luxurious vegetation than the valley meadows.

In the middle of pure taiga expanses in the Vilyuy Valley, in the Lena River valley, and on the Lena-Amga water divide grow the most northerly patches of wooded-steppe. Here dense taiga comes in contact with feather grass and fescue grass, and swampy soil is found near solonetz soil. The preservation and development of meadow steppes may be attributed to the features of the continental climate, namely: (1) the small amount of precipitation and high summer temperatures (higher than in the southern steppes of Kazakhstan); (2) permafrost, preventing significant leaching of soil and the surface deposition of salt through capillary action; and (3) a wealth of matrices of carbonates and other salts.

Beneath the meadow steppes on terraces of the Lena River and on the Lena-Amginskiy water divide, the soil is a boulder-free, unstratified, brown-gray, carbonaceous loam which lies in layers from 30 inches to 16 feet thick—all of which contributes to its fertility. The loam was deposited in the glacial and ensuing xerothermic periods and acquired a loess-like appearance. It has survived because of the hot, dry summer. The composition of the local soil, especially the chemical composition of separate horizons, varies with the season: In summer, when the permafrost thaws and there is little rain, soil solutions rise upward; in autumn, when rain falls, there is a washing in of the salts to the upper limits of the permafrost.

The meadow steppes on the terraces of the central Lena are most unusual. On the first of them, which rise 20 to 30 feet above the river level and are more than 6 miles wide, there extend parallel rows of ridges from 6 to 10 feet above the elongated swampy troughs dividing them. These ridges have iris (*Iris sibirica*) scattered along them. The tops of the ridges and the upper parts of the slopes remind one, by their outer appearance, of typical feather-grass steppes of more southern latitudes. Maidenhair feather grass (*Stipa capillata*) predominates. To this species are added fescue grass (*Festuca lenensis*), koeleria (*Koeleria gracilis*) and xerophytic mixed grasses, such as Siberian edelweiss (*Leontopodium sibiricum*) and veronica (*Veronica incana*). Beneath these meadow steppes is an interesting, dark-colored, extremely fertile clay soil. This soil is very similar to chernozem in content of humus (12 to 17 per cent), nitrogen, phosphoric acid, and potassium. There is a gradual decrease of humus with depth. But along with that, soda is encountered (the soil is saliferous) in all horizons, and a great impoverishment of colloidal-clayey particles is noted in the upper horizons. Besides, at a depth of from 40 to 60 inches, permafrost appears.

Along the lower slopes there extend narrow strips or patches of crusty, columnar or typically columnar solonetz soil. This soil effervesces from the surface and is sometimes covered with efflorescences of salts. On this soil, almost pure thickets of *Atropis tenuiflora* grow. The middle, and widest, parts of the slopes are covered by black solonchak soil. The amount of harmful salts in this solonchak is greater than that in the worst solonetz soil of the southern steppes. In dry weather the surface is covered by efflorescence of salts and, during the rain, acquires almost a black tint owing to the solution of salts. The sparse vegetation on black solonchak is halophytes such as *Suaeda corniculata,* glasswort (*Salicornia herbacea*), and *Artemisia jacutica.*

On the second terrace, which has the broadest development of forest according to relief, the tops of the narrower ridges are covered by meadow steppes. The covering does not consist of pure feather grasses, but mainly of fescue grass and koeleria, to which are admixed fine steppe sedge (*Carex stenophylla*), lychnis (*Lychnis sibirica*), sea pink (*Statice sibirica*), and *Artemisia pubescens*. Beneath this vegetation is a dark-colored clay soil. On the terraces, in podzolic soil, are larch and pine copses, and in depressions in the middle of meadow steppes are small individual islets of birch groves. The grass cover of the adjacent meadow steppe is on solodized soil.

Some islands of meadow steppe are the result of the warmer and drier xerothermic period; the taiga has subsequently moved onto them. The solonchak soil is a relic of former drier conditions, and the formation of solonetz soil is linked with the modern moister climate and the approach of taiga. Many meadow-steppe islands exist because man destroyed the red-bilberry taiga, which grew on carbonaceous clay soil. The large accumulation of snow beneath the trees and its slow melting and evaporation lead to leaching of the soil. Because of this, chloride salts and sulphates are washed down to the level of the permafrost. Because of the destruction of forest, small amount of precipitation, and high temperatures during summer, the frost layer descends, the soil dries, and the soil process is adjusted to the chernozem-steppe type. The greatly increased evaporation of water from the surface of the soil after the destruction of the forest plus the rise (by capillary action) of saline ground water lead to the accumulation of soluble salts in the upper layer of soil. This explains the solonchak quality. As a result of the decrease in the amount of rising ground water and the processes of leaching, solonetz soil is formed.

The fertility of soil and the intensity of solar radiation favor the development of agriculture on meadow steppes. Grains have been successfully adapted to the comparatively short vegetative period. Local breeds of barley have been developed that will ripen in 71 days. Farmers sow mainly spring rye and barley and some wheat and oats. The vegetables cultivated are cabbages, potatoes, and cucumbers. Watermelons are grown on the warm ridges. Unfavorable features for agriculture are the small amount of precipitation, the spring droughts (necessitating irrigation), the early frosts, and the abundance of pests, such as Locustidae and marmots.

Southern Subzone

The southern subzone of taiga, stretching approximately from the 60th parallel to the southern islands of forest-steppes, has a predominance of pine in the west, larch in the east, and dark coniferous taiga along the high watersheds. This distribution is explained by the diversity of soil and climate within the area.

The western part of the subzone has a warmer climate and slightly more precipitation. Permafrost lies deep or is absent, and the sandy and clayey podzolic soil is better warmed. Pine prefers this warmer but poor sandy soil.

The eastern part of the subzone has a colder climate and less precipitation. Permafrost is close to the surface, and the slightly podzolic soil is richer. Larch tolerates the cold clayey soil and the permafrost.

On the high watersheds, which have a cool summer and ample precipitation, there is a rich clayey soil which is moist and cold. Dark coniferous taiga of fir, Siberian pine, and spruce is to be found.

The subzone was formerly covered by dark coniferous taiga. Only sand on second terraces and warmer southern slopes is now covered with pine forests. As a result of fires on the watersheds, the continuous stand of Siberian pine, fir, and spruce taiga, on moist and cold soil, was replaced by secondary birch. Along the slopes, the lowering of permafrost beneath the burns, the strengthening of the podzol-forming process, and the presence of limestones contributed to replacement of the dark coniferous taiga by pine. The southern subzone of taiga may be divided into two districts: the Angara on the west and the Lena on the east.

Of the forests in the Angara district, pine forests have the greatest economic importance. On clayey soil two types of pine groves are found: the red bilberry, mixed grass pine grove, which has excellent wood and good restoration on burns and fellings, with mixed grasses of Siberian iris (*Iris ruthenica*), *Pulsatilla patens,* beach grass, and red bilberry; and the mossy pine grove, which is found on the boundary between the preceding pines and the Siberian pine-fir taiga, with solid mossy cover. On sand of the second terrace of the Angara and other large rivers, the rhododendron-pine grove, with

undergrowth of Dahurian rhododendron (*Rhododendron dahuricum*) or the lichenous red-bilberry pine grove, has developed. Depending on its composition, character, and age, the vegetation of burned areas is replaced with birch and aspen, or pine is restored on them. Sometimes, also, an undergrowth of spruce, fir, and Siberian pine develops. There are narrow strips of meadow in a few places. On bottomland meadows, meadow grass (*Poa pratensis*), bent grass (*Agrostis alba*), and hellebore (*Veratrum album*) predominate. Far more diverse and rich are the meadows on unswamped or seldom-flooded places.

In the Lena district, the grass cover of the larch forests consist mainly of shade-loving plants and a rare underbrush made up of dog rose, spirea, honeysuckle, and alder. Light larch groves, some with an admixture of pine, occupy the drier and more open places, and have an underbrush of Dahurian rhododendron, honeysuckle, and dog rose. Included in the grass cover are crepis (*Crepis sibirica*), and iris (*Iris ruthenica*). Many steppe plants grow on the warmed northern slopes (facing south). Burned-over areas are widespread in the district.

The southern wooded-steppe zone in Central Siberia comprises four isolated islands: the Achinsk, Kansk, Krasnoyarsk, and Balagansk–Irkutsk wooded-steppes.

The Achinsk wooded-steppe has a well-defined relief and a complex distribution of vegetative cover. On the slopes facing north, steppe vegetation composes 30 to 40 per cent of the growth and is often found even in birch groves. On the slopes facing south the amount of steppe vegetation increases to 70 to 80 per cent. The vegetation on the north-facing slope of the northern area of northern steppe is: oats (*Avena pubescens*), *Onobrychis sativa, Libanotis sibiricus, Aster alpinus,* valerian (*Valeriana dubia*). Other forest species can be found near birch groves. In the southern part, cereals are present, and on the slopes facing south, steppe species comprise 65 per cent of the vegetation. Predominant are: koeleria (*Koeleria gracilis*), feather grass (*Stipa rubens*), oats

(*Avenastrum desertorum*), *Artemisia sericea,* iris (*Iris ruthenica*). In depressions near lakes, where solonchak is encountered, are uniform, poor solonchak meadows with *Atropis distans,* foxtail (*Alopecucus ventricosus*), and barley (*Hordeum seculinum*).

The Kansk wooded-steppe has smooth forms of relief and clay soil. The soil cover is made up of a combination of chernozem and podzolic soils. In the south, on large level watersheds is a fertile and leached-out chernozem that has a well-expressed grainy structure which is stable during plowing. To the north, because of the lower elevations, it is replaced by a moderate chernozem. A unique type of podzolic soil is very widespread. It has a brown tint when fresh and exhibits a marked, substantial, grainy structure. Along the bottom of wide ravines there is a meadow saline soil. On both gentle slopes and watersheds the alternation of shallow depressions and elevated areas strongly affects the distribution of vegetation.

The higher places bear a more xerophytic vegetation which is composed of koeleria, steppe timothy, steppe sedge, and sometimes much pinnate feather grass. There is a more luxuriant cover in depressions, with a predominance of meadow and meadow-steppe species, such as iris, anemone, and mint (*Phlomis tuberosa*). Thin birch saplings grow in some of these depressions. On the divides, birch groves separate plowed fields. In these groves is the grassy cover indigenous to them, containing globeflower (*Trollius asiaticus*), iris (*Iris ruthenica*), and anemone (*Anemone narcissiflora*). Along the outskirts of the groves, larch is added to birch, and the grassy cover becomes enriched with forest species, such as *Maianthenum bifolium* and lady's-slipper (*Cypripedium guttatum*). *Suaeda maritima* and barley (*Hordeum secalinum*) are adapted to low riverbanks. Much of the district is covered by fields, meadows, and pastures.

In the Krasnoyarsk wooded-steppe, a region north of Krasnoyarsk on the left bank of the Yenisei River, mild, soft relief forms are predominant. Basically, the soil is of the chernozem type; it is replaced by leached-out chernozem at greater heights and by gray forest soil of high productivity on the edges. In the northern part of the forest-steppe island there is a regular alternation of birch groves on the

Fig. 6-11. Steppe on the southern slopes of ridges in the wooded-steppe near Kansk.

slopes facing north. On the slopes facing south, steppe groups are present. The region has characteristic steppe flora, ranging from feather-grass steppes to meadow and rocky steppes. The general vegetative background of the steppes is made up of grasses such as fescue, koeleria, maidenhair feather grass, and several species of wormwood. On the steep slopes facing south is found unique xerophytic vegetation peculiar to rock steppes. These species are *Umbilicus spinosus,* rock cress (*Arabis incarnata*), and *Patrina sibirica.*

The Balagansk–Irkutsk wooded-steppe has a unique character. It is a complex of narrow steppe strips (two to three miles in width) along the valleys of large rivers such as the Angara, Oka, and Iya. The upper part of the slopes and also part of the level ground on higher places are forested. Steppe, however, occupies the slopes facing south and the first terraces of river valleys. There are mild forms of relief. Clayey and, sometimes, loess-like soil exists in layers several (6 to 20) feet thick and contains the shells of terrestrial mollusks. The soil cover, similar to that of the Kansk wooded-steppe, is mainly a combination of the leached-out, moderate, and rich chernozem and the unusual podzolic soil which guarantees high productivity.

The most typical are the steppes on the first river terraces which bear fescue grass (*Festuca pseudovina*), crested wheat grass (*Agropyron cristatum*), maidenhair feather grass (*Stipa capillata*), and cinquefoil (*Potentilla subacaulis*). On slopes facing south there is a more drought-loving vegetation: *Artemisia frigida* and kochia (*Kochia prostrata*). Solonchaks of littoral sections of valleys are not rich in vegetation, although plantain (*Plantago maritima*) or glasswort (*Salicornia herbacea*) are common. The few boggy meadows and mounds supply very little fodder. On watershed plateaus, dry-valley birch forests have developed, with the usual species—geranium (*Geranium pratense*), day lily (*Hemerocallis flava*), anemone (*Anemone narcissiflora*)—in the grass cover.

ANIMAL LIFE

The fauna of Central Siberia, in comparison with that of the more westerly regions, has a different appearance and seems older. This antiquity is indicated, for example, by the many species of shrew. Owing to the pronounced continental climate, and especially to the summer heat, the significant advance of many mammals and birds to the north is well marked. In regions to the west, these mammals and birds are usually found farther south. The local species of suslik (*Citellus jacutensis*) dwells along the middle Lena and along the Vilyuy; and another rodent, the *Mus major,* inhabiting the mountains of the Altai and Sayan penetrates to the Yakutsk region. Certain birds, such as the dark-blue dove (*Columbia livia*) and bittern (*Botaurus stellaris*), which nest along the Yenisei between 54° and 55° north latitude, reach 62° to 63° in the Lena Valley. The Yenisei serves as the eastern bound-ary for such species as the double snipe (*Capella media*) and gray crow (*Corvus corone charpii*). Certain Western Siberia species—for example, the Altai mole (*Talpa altaica*)—are found inside the borders of Central Siberia, but do not cross the Urals. Western species are supplemented by species of eastern origin, such as white Yakutsk wagtail (*Motacilla alba ocularis*) or reddish thrush (*Turdus naumanni*). To the east, the Verkhoyansk Range serves as the distinct zoogeographic boundary for many species of the west. Mountain elements are absent in the faunal makeup.

The diversity of fauna from north to south is clearly manifested. The polar fox is encountered in the bordering southern wooded-tundra, and such taiga species as squirrel and chipmunk are absent. Squirrel appears in the northern zone of sparse forests. The polar fox migrates in for the winter; the polecat as well as the sable and musk deer live in the southern section. All of these do not appear farther north.

Carnivorous animals in Central Siberia are: brown bear, wolverine, wolf, fox, polecat (*Kolonocus sibiricus*), and sable (*Martes zibellina*). There are many of these animals in rocky patches of mountainous regions in the dense taiga and in regions of Siberian pine and other trees. The hoofed animals in Central Siberia include elk and musk deer. The following rodents are numerous: squirrel, which is the basis of the local fur industry and which prefers dense, dark coniferous taiga; chipmunk (*Eutamias asiaticus*), which lives along the borders where there are tall hollow trees for shelter and which feeds on pine nuts, the fruit of the currant, and dog rose; flying squirrel (*Pteromys volans*), which is found in the dense forest thickets at the banks of rivers; pika; *Ochotona hyperborea turuchanensis,* which is widespread along rocky patches and which stores tufts of dried grass but does not make small stacks as it does in the Altai; *Sorex aroncus jacutensis; Microtus oeconomus;* and *Evotomys rutilus vinogradovi,* a common small rodent serving as food for the fox, polecat, and ermine. The "harvest" of valuable fur animals varies, according to supply, in different years. The acclimatization of American mink (*Lutreola visou*) and the re-establishment of beaver and sable, which were abundant here in the past, are desirable.

The birds closely linked with the forest are: common wood grouse (*Tetrao urogallus*), which reaches its eastern limit here; hazel grouse; ordinary cuckoo; and large variegated wood-pecker. Nesting everywhere near water are the loon (*Colymbus stellatus*) and *Capella gallinago.* Certain birds, such as the field lark (*Alauda arvensis*) and warbler (*Sylvia curruca*), avoid dense forests and frequent the more southerly wooded-steppe.

CHAPTER 7

Northeastern Siberia

The region extending from the Lena River to the Bering Strait differs substantially from the other regions of Eastern Siberia in its geologic history and development of relief. It is a combination of (1) mountain ranges arranged either in the form of arcs or separate mountain groups; (2) rolling plateaus more or less dissected by erosion, and (3) vast swampy lowlands, slightly raised above sea level and broken by the intricate network of the Yana, Indigirka, Kolyma, and Anadyr river systems.

The geologic systems of Northeastern Siberia can be traced from the Cambrian to the Quaternary periods. Especially notable is the Upper Paleozoic and Mesozoic developments, with many Mesozoic and Tertiary igneous rocks. Tectonically, this is the youngest part of Eastern Siberia, since mountain building here is much more recent than in the other regions. Because the recent structure is linked to the Mesozoic phase of alpine folding, it became a part of the continental mass only at the end of the Lower Cretaceous period. This is in contrast with adjacent Central Siberia where active mountain-forming movements had already occurred in the middle of the Paleozoic Era— after the Caledonia folding, which played an essential role in uniting its different parts.

Although the climate of the region, like the climate of Eastern Siberia, is continental, the climatic peculiarities of the high mountains have not been fully reported. In summer the cold currents and dense, prolonged fogs of the Bering and Okhotsk seas cool the coastal lowland regions.

The region belongs to the taiga landscape, containing weakly developed, swampy, and podzolic soil. Because of the high mountains and the cooling influence of the adjacent seas, however, a bare-mountain vegetation belt of subalpine bushes is widespread, and the lowlands exhibit a forest-tundra landscape. In contrast with the Yakut taiga, the dark coniferous forests are absent and Dahurian larches with rather low timber lines predominate. Only in large river valleys with their specific physico-geographic conditions are bottomland forests of poplar and Korean willow found.

The fauna of the region is different from that of Western Siberia, but is similar to the fauna of adjacent parts of North America, and includes an unusual biocoenosis in the mountain-tundra landscape.

Administratively, the region belongs to the Yakut ASSR in its western half (approximately to the line from Okhotsk to Nizhne-Kolyma) and to the Khabarovsk territory in the eastern half.

GEOLOGIC HISTORY

The various features of relief of the mountainous region of northeastern Siberia have a single geologic background. In Paleozoic and Mesozoic times the region contained a geosynclinal basin—extendng from the present-day mouth of the Lena River to the shores of the Bering Sea—in which thick layers of sediments accumulated: Paleozoic-Mesozoic, 33,000 to 49,-500 feet, including Triasic-Jurassic, 16,500 to 19,800 feet. These sediments were formed by the alternation of marine advances (in the Devonian, Permian, Triasic, and Jurassic) with periods of retreat related to the Caledonian orogeny and to subsequent Mesozoic and Tertiary phases of alpine folding, and by younger epeirogenic upheavals. Indicative of a prolonged sagging of the geosyncline and the instability of the extent of the sea basins is the variation in lithological composition of the shale series, sandstones, and limestones, which are interbedded with extrusives and their tuffs, formed as a result of active submarine volcanic activity. Apparently, only the Kolyma—Yukagirsk platform was stable during the entire geologic history of Northeastern Siberia. Geosynclinal development was disrupted by periods of violent interrelated folding. These periods overlapped one another and masked, to a great degree, earlier folding. Maximum folding gradually moved to the periphery and to the Pacific Ocean side.

The basic structure of the region was formed by the initial stages of Alpine folding, of which the most intense was in the Lower Cretaceous Period. Owing to the considerable width of the folded zone and the comparatively small area of the Kolyma-Yukagirsk rigid massif, the formation of folds took place freely, quietly, and regularly. The Lower Cretaceous folding seized and worked over the weak folding of the earlier cycles. In places it was weakened by the rigidity of earlier dislocated sections and, in the end, adapted itself to the contour of the old rigid massif, which was squeezed into the belt of young folding. At this time Verkho-yansk and Cherski ranges were formed, and the region entered the prolonged continental period. During Lower Cretaceous folding, many faults occurred at the border of the sagging geosyncline. These faults, which are associated with the rigid Paleozoic deposits, generally pass in the direction of folding. Because they were filled by diabases or granites, the faults are easily detected for a distance of several dozen miles. At this same time, intense volcanic activity yielded thick masses of igneous rocks, rich and diverse in metals.

After Lower Cretaceous folding, a great part of the region did not undergo further folding but was converted into a rigid mass. It responded to the subsequent Alpine folding with exclusively epeirogenic movements and irregular upheavals along large fracture lines. These lines correspond to the strike of Mesozoic folding or travel in a direction perpendicular to it. Examples are the large transverse fractures running from Okhotsk to the Chaun Bay. By these young fractures, which originated as recently as the beginning of the Quaternary Period (for instance, in the Kharaulakhsk Mountains), a series of large ranges was finally shaped, and the borders of horsts and grabens were determined. Toward the end of the Tertiary Period, the great part of the dry land, and its young mountains, underwent energetic erosion. In the Tertiary Period, the orogeny was concentrated in the extreme east, which was flooded along the coast by the Pacific Ocean. The last phase of alpine folding took place here in Cretaceous and Tertiary deposits, folding ranges in a meridional direction. An example is Koryak Range or the heights of the Taygonos Peninsula, in which the coal-bearing Neogene is crumpled into slanting folds. Only in the Quaternary Period was the subregion of the Koryak Range finally consolidated with the remaining continental mass of the region when folding was replaced by faulting.

Repeated folding, especially of Upper Mesozoic deposits with intrusions of various igneous rocks, accompanied by a series of volcanic cycles, entailed mineralization which is exceptional in wealth and diversity. The erosion of the comparatively youthful mountain ranges was deep enough to uncover mineral zones; in many places the development of cherty formations indicates the presence of intrusions not yet uncovered by erosion. Traces of tin, copper, antimony, arsenic, silver, lead, zinc, and gold ores have been found. Particularly noteworthy are: (1) the extremely rich gold-bearing district of Kolyma, where mineralization is connected with granites which have broken through Triassic strata; (2) the Endybalsk group of lead-zinc deposits containing silver; (3) the Imtandzha tin deposit in the basin of the upper

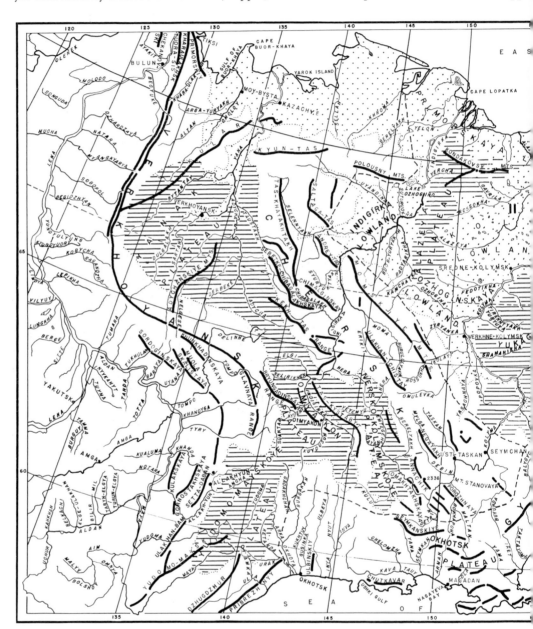

Map 7-I.   Orographic scheme of Northeastern Siberia.

stretches of the Yana River; and (4) the Mangazeya lead deposit on the southern slope of the Verkhoyansk Range. In contrast with the Central Siberian Plateau, the region is poor in nonmetallic minerals. Conditions were not favorable for coal formation until the Upper Cretaceous Period, when lagoons and swamps were left along the shores of the drying sea. A coal-bearing basin is located along the tributaries of the left bank of the Kolyma and the right bank of the Indigirka rivers. Here the Zyryanovsk deposit has 56 seams of coal, ranging from 2.5 to 30.5 feet thick. Twenty-three of these seams are being mined. The coal is of high quality, contains little ash and little sulphur, and has an average heat capacity

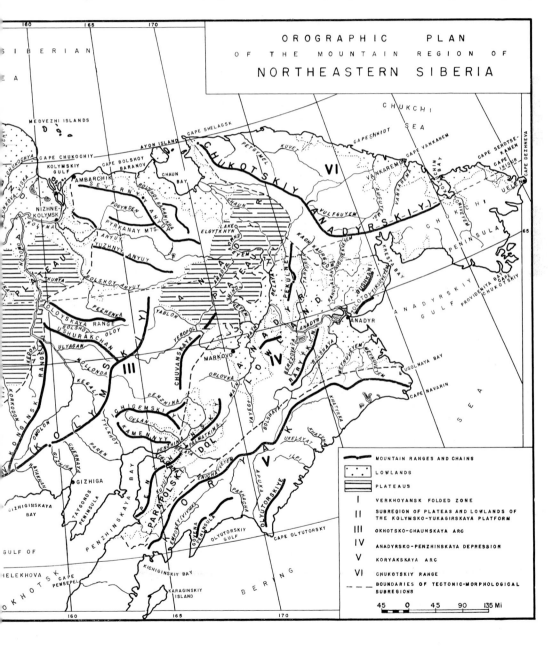

OROGRAPHIC PLAN
OF THE MOUNTAIN REGION OF
NORTHEASTERN SIBERIA

		MOUNTAIN RANGES AND CHAINS
		LOWLANDS
		PLATEAUS
I		VERKHOYANSK FOLDED ZONE
II		SUBREGION OF PLATEAS AND LOWLANDS OF THE KOLYMSKO-YUKAGIRSKAYA PLATFORM
III		OKHOTSKO-CHAUNSKAYA ARC
IV		ANADYRSKO-PENZHINSKAYA DEPRESSION
V		KORYAKSKAYA ARC
VI		CHUKOTSKIY RANGE
		BOUNDARIES OF TECTONIC-MORPHOLOGICAL SUBREGIONS

45   0   45   90   135 Mi

of about 7,500 calories per kilogram. There is also a substantial deposit of coal near Olyutorsky Gulf on the coast of the Bering Sea, where more than six seams of brown coal have been discovered, one of which reaches 17.5 feet in thickness. The territory is rather rich in structural rock materials, although it lacks lime.

Glaciation and faulting are the important recent (Quaternary) events that strongly affect the molding of modern relief. They have continued intermittently, even to the present time.

Periodic large-scale upheavals of land above the sea level with conditions of cold climate, with great fluctuation in the amount of precipitation, brought about repeated and extensive glaciation. Evidence of it is observed in individual mountain ranges (Chersky, Verkhoyansk, Kolyma, Suntar-Khayata, and Koryak) and in the mountains of the Chukchi Peninsula. The glacial traces are the many cirque formations, glacial troughs and hanging valleys, terminal and lateral moraines, crags worked by ice, glacial lakes, and vestiges of surviving small glaciers (as in the Kharaulakhsk Mountains).

From the slopes of the Verkhoyansk and Chersky ranges, the glaciers advanced onto the outskirts of adjacent plateaus and lowlands. The glaciers came down almost to the present level of the sea on the Chukchi Peninsula and the northern shores of the Okhotsk Sea. In some parts of the Koryak Range, they formed an ice barrier that projected far into the sea. Valley glaciers were predominant. They ranged from 60 to 215 miles in length and from 1,320 to 1,485 feet in thickness.

On the low through passes of the Yansk Plateau, where the snow was driven from the adjacent watersheds, there are areas of ice accumulation. Several valley glaciers of different basins branched off from these firn fields. On the Oimyakon and Nera plateaus extensive glaciation developed because of the transfer and accumulation of ice from contiguous ranges.

Moraine deposits are unknown within the lowland regions. Although the glaciers did not penetrate deeply into the lowlands, they did deposit moraines along the outskirts. During the glacial period snow accumulated and turned into stationary firn, lakes froze completely through, and ice layers were buried. The landscape during the glacial period exhibited glacier-covered mountain tops, low-mountain regions covered with coniferous and larch forests, and meadows in the wider river valleys. In this landscape there existed a mixture of southern (tiger, antelope, bison, wild horse), polar (polar fox, lemming, northern deer), and older (elephant and rhinoceros) fauna. The glacial period climate was slowly replaced by the present sharply continental, colder, drier climate. This caused the retreat of glaciers, the appearance of large areas of permafrost, the formation of fossil ice, the destruction of the fauna, and the wide spread of polar and present-day species of taiga.

Vertical movements during the early Quaternary Period unevenly and intermittently raised separate blocks of the mountain ranges. The border zone on the south and east was more strongly elevated, but the coasts at times were dropped below the level of the ocean. The modern relief was sometimes conditioned by this differential upheaval. The Chukchi Peninsula has experienced, and is now experiencing, a more rapid upheaval than the adjoining section of Kolyma Range and the Yukagirsk Plateau. Koryak Range had a tendency toward upheaval, but the Anadyr depression has lagged in raising or even subsided. The series of marine transgressions is of the Quaternary Period. The last of them completely flooded the flat country of the Penzhina and Anadyr rivers, but in the lowlands of the Kolyma and Indigirka the sea covered only the coastal regions. Owing to the submersion of individual sections bounded by tectonic breaks—partly formed earlier and partly a result of the upheaval before the last glaciation—the Chukchi Peninsula was separated from Alaska by the Bering Strait. Far to the west the Novosibirsk Islands were kept isolated from the mainland.

The deep Quaternary breaks were sometimes accompanied by volcanic phenomena. Recently, in the upper reaches of the Moma River, amid the lava cover, a young well-preserved, extinguished slag volcano (Balagan-Tass) was discovered. It is a regular truncated cone, rising 595 feet above the surrounding area. Its crater, 395 feet wide, has become a lake, on the surface of which pumice frequently floats. In the northern part of the Anadyr Plateau, a round pond (Elgytkhyn) with a diameter of 40 feet lies in the eruption caldera of a Quaternary volcanic tube.

The fact that the erosional cycles linked with

There are many signs of streams being captured by different rivers. Permafrost shows its influence on the development of the modern microrelief and on the formation of the lake landscape in the lowlands. In the most recent alluviums, there are buried frozen lakes, firn ices, and ice seams. Mechanical weathering also plays an important role in molding the landscape.

Fig. 7-1. Relief of the main southern Verkhoyansk Range.

the repeated vertical movements changed is indicated by the number of terraces in the river valleys. There are ten terraces at heights of from 6.5 to 1,320 feet. The terraces of 115 and 130 feet were formed after the last glaciation, and the remaining ones in the glacial epochs—the very highest perhaps in the Tertiary Period. Valleys were deeply notched and became extremely diverse in their configuration. Narrow valley gorges of the Indigirka and Kolyma are older than the last stages of upheaval of the ranges intersected by them.

Until recently it was supposed that, in spite of severe climate and high mountain ranges, extensive modern glaciation could not exist in Northeastern Siberia because of the meager precipitation, especially in winter. However, substantial glacial zones have recently been discovered and given preliminary study. This general area of glaciation covers more than 115 square miles, and contains more than 200 glaciers and large firn basins. The principal area of glaciation, with a prevalence of big valley glaciers, is in two glacial zones—in the Suntar-

Khayata Range (more than 100 glaciers in a general area of about 77 square miles) and in Buordakhskiy massif of the Cherski Range (area of glaciation more than 38 square miles). Considerably less glaciation has been discovered in Koryak Range, with several valley glaciers from 1.8 to 2.5 miles long. Still less glaciation—mainly cirque glaciers and large firn basins—has been recorded on the high-mountain sections of Yanski-Indigirka and Okhotsk-Indigirka watersheds, on Mount Chen, in Tas-Khayakhtakh Range, and in the Kharaulakhsk Mountains. The average elevation of the snow line in the Indigirka basin is between 775 and 792 feet. The glaciers terminate at an average altitude of approximately 6,640 feet in the first zone and 2,640 feet in the second. The thickness of glaciers is between 660 and 825 feet. Types, forms, and dimensions of glaciers vary. Valley glaciers in high parts of the valleys make up 30 per cent of the over-all number of glaciers and occupy more than 68 per cent of the area of present glaciation. The length of valley glaciers varies from 1.2 to 6.8 miles, and the area from 0.8 to 8.1 square miles. Cirque glaciers—the largest group in number—occupy the bottom of cirques. The average cirque glacier covers approximately one square mile in areas. There are a number of small hanging glaciers, which adhere to steep mountain slopes, and firn basins, which remain in small depressions the year round. The exposure of slopes affects the distribution of glaciers: On the north-facing slopes of Suntar-Khayata Range are concentrated 114 glaciers which cover 57 per cent of the general area, and on the south-facing slopes are 6 glaciers which occupy 3 per cent of the general area of glaciation. Very slowly the glaciers melt away and retreat more and more. And sometimes a single glacier breaks into two glaciers, and a gap forms between them; also large ice blocks break off from the glaciers and become small hanging glaciers. The presence of glaciers in the central part of the region is explained by the unique geographic and climatic conditions. The principle glaciation is in high-mountain zones, considerably south of the

Arctic Circle. These mountains have more moisture than lower places. Above 8,000 feet an appreciable part of the yearly precipitation is snow, which accumulates throughout the year. The maximum thawing, which occurs during the long, sunny summer days, is limited by nightly frosts and, besides, lasts for little more than a month. The continuing rise of the region apparently favors the preservation of glaciation.

Although the separate sections of Northeastern Siberia are linked geologically, they still differ from one another in genesis, local history of development, and morphology. Six subregions are noted: (1) the Verkhoyansk folded subregion, (2) the plateaus and lowlands of the Kolyma-Yukagirsk platform, (3) the Okhotsk-Chaun arc, (4) the Anadyr Plateau and Anadyr-Penzhina depression, (5) the Koryak Range, and (6) the Chukchi massif.

Verkhoyansk Folded Zone

The Verkhoyansk folded zone has a symmetrical structure and consists of two parallel ranges—the Verkhoyansk and the Chersky—and the plateaus between them. It is a complex of sedimentary rocks which have been deposited in a marine basin isolated in the Upper Paleozoic and which have been highly dislocated by Lower Cretaceous folding. The central, less elevated part of the subregion received its outlines and dimensions in the Upper Triassic Period and was formed of thick, dislocated Triassic deposits. The marginal mountain ranges—Verkhoyansk and Chersky—are formed by a series of Paleozoic deposits.

The curving Verkhoyansk Range comprises the western marginal section of the region. It begins somewhat west of the Dzhugdzhur Range, dropping echelon-like beyond its northern tip, extends far to the north, curving in an S-shape similar to the curves of the lower courses of the Aldan and Lena rivers, and ends near the Lena River delta. The range is the divide between the system of the Lena and the systems of the Yana and Indigirka. In its separate sections, it bears different names. It is highest in the southern part, where average altitudes are approximately 6,600 feet and individual peaks rise to 8,250 feet. Peaks of the central meridional section, or Orulgan Range, rise from south to north from 3,630 to 6,600 feet. In the northern part of the range—the Kharaulakhsk Mountains—only individual peaks reach more than 3,300 feet. As a single tectonic formation, the Verkhoyansk Range has the following characteristic peculiarities: (1) asymmetry, (2) preservation on the summits of parts of the ancient peneplain, and (3) laterally distributed hydrographic network.

The Verkhoyansk Range slopes steeply toward the Lena and Aldan valleys, sometimes as a perpendicular wall that rises as much as 1,650 feet above the neighboring Central Siberian Plateau. There are pronounced alpine forms of relief and deep-cut valleys, bearing traces of recent glaciation of an alpine type. The eastern slope, facing laterally the Yana and Oimyakon plateaus, has a gentle gradient, with mild, smooth mountain shapes and runs into broad flat valleys with signs of ancient glaciation of a continental character. The summit of the range has a slightly undulating surface with a great number of elevations of the mesa type, accentuated by a series of tooth-like peaks of approximately uniform height, as though cut off at a certain level. There are relic peneplain surfaces of both small and large areas on the summits of many mountains; they survived under caps of ice, when erosion was especially intense.

The hydrographic network is principally lateral and, more rarely, **V**-shaped valleys. The Lena slope has true turbulent mountain streams which cause extremely energetic erosion: the formation of narrow, canyon-shaped valleys and alpine forms of relief, and the capture of the sources of the rivers of the Yana system. For example, the Tompo River (Lena system) intercepted the upper tributaries of the Adycha River (Yana system). The rivers of the Yana slope of the range begin on swamped, almost plain-like areas. Often the current moves slowly

in broad glacial valleys but becomes swift when it reaches the many sandbanks. At their emergence from the mountains, the streams once again become calm. The causes of the differences in gradients of the rivers are: (1) the asymmetrical rise of the range; (2) the difference in height of local erosion levels since the rivers of the Lena Basin have almost twice as great a gradient as the rivers of the Yana Basin; (3) the heavy precipitation on the western and southern slopes (covered with deep snow) and light precipitation in the Yana basin (almost no snow). Branching out from the northern end of Orulgan in a northeastern direction and rising sharply above the adjacent country is the Kular Range, with heights of 1,980 feet and steep northwest slopes and gentle southeast slopes. It is a pronounced anticline with a series of granitic masses along its axis. As a continuation of the Kular Range, the Polousny Range reaches altitudes of from 2,475 to 4,290 feet. It bears a mesa character with smooth mild forms of relief showing signs of glaciation.

The Chersky Range forms the eastern marginal section of the Verkhoyansk folded region. It is a broad area, distinctly elevated above the plateau adjoining from the southwest, which extends 600 miles from the lower part of the Yana River to the Okhotsk-Kolyma divide. It parallels the Verkhoyansk Range and also curves in an **S**-shape. Chersky Range is extremely complex in structure, composition, and strike of strata. It has a very diversified picture, like that of a series of parallel mountain ranges. These ranges are often highly dissected and divided into separate groups, individual peaks of which reach 9,900 feet. The outer northern mountains of the Chersky Range are composed of Paleozoic rocks. The inner and western sections are formed of sandy schistous strata of the Lower Mesozoic, which are crumpled into folds and broken by many intrusions of granites. These strata make up the highest parts of the ranges. The central part of the Chersky Range, in the basin of the Indigirka River, is composed of nine ranges with average elevations of 6,600 to 8,250 feet. It reaches its highest point in Pobeda Mountain —10,322 feet. The parallel mountain chains, stretching in a west-northwest direction, are clearly expressed and have alpine forms of relief. Traces of glaciation are revealed in the morphology, and there are small glaciers. The northern ranges contain very flat, weakly dissected, plateau-shaped mountains. They reach 6,600 feet and exhibit parts of the ancient peneplain.

In conformity with the Triassic strata, the tributaries of the Indigirka and Kolyma, as well as the sources of these rivers, lie in longitudinal valleys between the separate ranges of the Chersky Range. The main channels of the Indigirka and Kolyma cut through the ranges along transverse valley gorges. The majestic, narrow valley of the Indigirka cuts across a very narrow section of the Chersky Range below the mouth of the Inyala tributary, where the difference between the valley bottom and adjacent peaks is 4,950 to 6,660 feet.

The southern Triassic ranges are cut on the west by a fault, but the northern Paleozoic ranges continue western as the Tas-Khayakhtakh Range, which is composed of two principal mountain chains with elevations to 8,250 feet. From the northeast the rocky wall of Tas-Khayakhtakh is easily seen. Capped by a crest of bald peaks, it is covered in many places by patches of snow even in summer. Clear traces of glaciation have survived in the range, and small hanging glaciers are exposed. The Buordakhskiy mountain massif in the upper course of the Moma River rises to 9,570 feet and has an alpine form of relief. It is the largest glacial region of the range. The gently sloping western side of Tas-Khayakhtakh gradually and imperceptibly blends with the Yana Plateau. The ranges of the central part of the Chersky Range which are notched by the Indigirka continue to the east into the basin of the Kolyma. Here the short, northwest-trending mountain chains give the Chersky Range the character of a plateau. These chains rise to 6,600 feet.

Between the Verkhoyansk and Chersky ranges is the central belt of the Verkhoyansk folded region. It is considerably lower and is composed principally of a group of plateaus.

The Yana Plateau is an elevated, broad, flat-bottomed bowl. It becomes lower from south to north, and its borders gradually rise toward the surrounding ranges. This bowl is called a plateau because of its elevation—to 2,970 feet in the south. Its monotonous relief is a combination of broad slopes extended in a meridional direction, flat hills, and separate mountain groups with the deeply cut valleys of the Yana River and its chief tributaries. The divides and depressions owe their origin to anticlinal upheavals and synclinal saggings of a meridional trend. The plateau is formed of Triassic and Jurassic rocks. These are broken by igneous rocks and are covered by a fine mantle of Quaternary clayey, sometimes carbonaceous, soil. On the right bank of the upper Yana, standing out sharply because of its height (more than 5,570 feet) and northeastern strike, is a mountain chain with separate mountain groups (the so-called Adchanskiye Mountains). This chain exhibits gentle slopes and smooth summits, connected with outcrops of granodiorites.

The Oimyakon Plateau, in the upper stretches of the Indigirka River, extends to the northwest, where it passes imperceptibly into the Yana Plateau. In many places it is highly dissected by the river network and converted into sections with intermediate mountain relief. To the south and northwest it gradually rises (to almost 5,000 feet) and develops into a water-divide plateau. Along the upper stretches of the Indigirka extends the Oimyakon Depression, the bottom of which lies at 2,310 feet. It is the cold pole of the earth.

The Nersko-Kolymsk Plateau is a conspicuous depression of scarcely expressed, flat relief between the high Chersky and Tas-Khayakhtakh ranges, and gradually descends to the valley of the Indigirka. It is higher in the south (up to 4,290 feet), and in the north becomes a low-mountain group dissected by rivers. Individual peaks rise only about 330 feet above the average ridge level; only isolated mountains reach 5,280 feet. In the upper stretches of the Nera River lies the Nera Valley at an elevation of about 2,640 feet. It abuts the Tas-Kystabyt Range on the east. The Nersko-Kolymsk Plateau, like the Oimyakon, is formed of Triassic black schists and sandstones, gathered in gentle folds.

The independent Tas-Kystabyt Range extends in a northwestern direction (in the south in a meridional direction) along the right bank of the upper Indigirka, parallel to the southern sections of the Chersky and Verkhoyansk ranges. It rises sharply above the Oimyakon and Nera depressions, being separated from them by huge tectonic breaks. These breaks are marked by flows of andesite and tuffs along the outskirts of the range. In the north the range is a rather complex picture of peaks and summits (to 7,260 feet) of the alpine type that show traces of glaciation. Toward the south the range drops (to 4,950 feet), taking on the appearance of a sharply dissected plateau. The range is formed of highly dislocated Triassic formations, broken by outcrops of granites and sometimes overlapped by extrusives.

The Suntar-Khayata Range is in the upper reaches of the rivers Okhota and Yudoma and the left-bank tributaries of the Indigirka (Suntar, Agayakan, Kuydusun). This northwest-trending range is 93 miles long and 31 miles wide. This isolated mountain center, the largest independent orographic unit, is separated from the neighboring Verkhoyansk Range and Indigirka-Okhotsk watershed by sharply lowered and clearly expressed depressions. This high range numbers twenty peaks with heights near 9,400 feet. The sharp peak in the central part rises 10,000 feet and is one of the highest points in Northeastern Siberia. The range has apline relief with considerable development of glacial forms. Here are found narrow, tooth-like crests, pyramid-shaped peaks, steep slopes, young glacial troughs, open valleys with many glacial lakes and moraine hills, and glacial cirques, all so close to one another that the regional soft contour of the surface of the range has almost dissappeared. In the central part of the range a continuous ice cover occupies

the divide and is nourished from the general firn region. In the northern and southern parts the glaciers are of the alpine type, separated from each other and fed from isolated regions. The glacial valleys are of recent formation. Recent erosion works over the glacial forms, but its influence on the development of a modern relief is still insignificant. Young erosion valleys have a **V**-shaped latitudinal profile and an undeveloped, step-like longitudinal profile.

Kolyma-Yukagirsk Platform

The subregion of plateaus and lowlands of the Kolymsk-Yukagirsk platform is the most rigid stable block in the entire Eastern Siberia. Evidences of this are: (1) the encircling platform, in the south, of Paleozoic folds form the Chersky Range; (2) the difference in the character of Permain and Mesozoic deposits—thick masses of limestones within the borders of the Verkhoyansk folded zone and the thin, shaly sandstone series on the platform; (3) the horizontal Mesozoic deposits. The irregular upheaval of separate sections of the platform in conjunction with river erosion led to the formation of two plateaus and two lowlands.

The Yukagirsk Plateau, the highest part of the subregion, occupies the eastern section between the Kolyma and Omolon rivers and extends farther to the south. In the north it has a flat, weakly dissected surface with broad, shallow valleys. The plateau merges with the high Quaternary terrace of the valleys of the Kolyma and Omolon rivers. Rising above the general level of the plateau are small isolated mountain groups (1,650 to 4,950 feet) composed of intrusive rock. The southern part of the plateau varies from 1,320 to 2,640 feet in height, but there are few outstanding mountain peaks. With the exception of two Lower Paleozoic ridges in the west and Upper Paleozoic folds passing around them, the plateau is formed of Mesozoic deposits: In the southern part are horizontal Triassic formations; in the east are Triassic formations that are intensively crumpled into folds of a northwest strike. To this is added the dislocated Jurassic. Small masses of granites and syenites are scattered in the middle of the Mesozoic sedimentary rocks.

The Alazeya Plateau occupies the middle part of the platform, along the right bank of the Indigirka, and is surrounded on all sides by lowlands. Its western slope is steep, dropping off in scarps to the Indigirka lowland, but the eastern slope is more gentle. The undulating surface of the plateau's broad valleys is disrupted by rounded, low summits and a few larger mountain groups, formed of crystalline rocks. In the northern part of the plateau rise the mountain range Ulakhan-Sisse and Kondakovsk Mountains, with elevations to 2,970 feet. These are formed of Mesozoic and Paleozoic sedimentary rocks with intrusions of granites and patches of extrusives. The raised southern part of the plateau has heights to 3,168 feet. Extremely complex fractures as well as horst elevations are developed on the Alazeya Plateau. These originated on the individual sections with different amplitudes and, probably, at different times.

The Kolyma and the Indigirka lowlands, with elevations up to 165 feet, are formed of loose Quaternary deposits. These ideal plains are highly swamped and, in low sections, occupied by a countless number of lakes. In certain regions the total area of lakes approximately equals the area of dry land. Owing to the lowness and slight incline of the lowlands, the flow of water is so hampered that thousands of lakes have formed, and the large rivers with their numerous tributaries flow northward in broad valleys of very slight gradients and weakly cut meanders. For example, the Kolyma at Sredne-Kolymsk (360 miles above the mouth) has a maximum elevation of 60 feet. Since most of the lakes are connected with each other and with the rivers by channels, river water enters the lake basins during floods. On the other hand, during low water, the lakes feed the rivers. There are also sinkhole lakes (created by the thawing of fossil ice in the permafrost), lakes in old river beds, and glacial lakes amid elevations of moraine ma-

terial. Most of the lakes are circular or oval shaped, are not more than 2.2 miles long, are shallow (6.6 to 13.2 feet), and have gentle, sloping banks. The shallowness of the lakes and their prolonged (from October to the end of June) and deep freezing, starve most of the fish toward the end of winter. By draining lakes, which is easily accomplished, good bottomland for meadows is reclaimed. On the elevated dry areas, which are remnants of the higher Quaternary terraces, the inhabitants have settled and developed the good meadows.

Okhotsk-Chaun Arc

The Okhotsk-Chaun arc, extending northeast in a narrow strip from Okhotsk to Chaun Gulf, is a young (Cretaceous and Lower Tertiary) tectonic subregion. In the Paleozoic and Mesozoic eras, its separate parts belonged to different tectonic regions, as sections of the ancient platform and Verkhoyansk folded zone, but subsequently its development took another course. As a result of the Tertiary phase of alpine folding, when large-scale arc-shaped tectonic breaks occurred, these sections of different origins were reorganized in conformity with the tectonic arc and were united in a single unit.

The Okhotsk Plateau is the southern part of the arc, and forms the watershed between the Okhotsk and East Siberian seas. Its shape and location are determined by the erosional activity of the rivers of the Okhotsk and Kolyma slopes. It differs from the neighboring Nersko-Kolymsk Plateau by extensive development of highly dislocated volcanic rocks of the Upper Cretaceous and Tertiary periods. Another difference is the predominating latitudinal direction of folds and mountains. The plateau is formed of dislocated sedimentary Mesozoic rocks intruded by granite. Patches of young igneous rocks are also to be found.

The plateau drops off in escarpments toward the coast. This produces deep dissection by rivers, cutting canyons between which are some irregularly disposed mountain groups and chains. Among them are: (1) the Chutkavar or the Primorskiy Range, with heights to 3,960 feet in the central part, and with alpine forms of relief; (2) the Seimchan Range, to 5,775 feet; and (3) the Olsk basalt plateau, to 5,610 feet. From the upper sections of the Buyunda River, right tributary of the Kolyma, Okhotsk-Kolyma watershed runs along the Kolyma Range.

The Kolyma (or Gydan) Range is a broad, extremely complex formation along the Okhotsk-Chaun arc. It is composed of many finely dissected mountainous ridges and clusters of ranges (to 6,600 feet), between which lie broad glacial valleys. On the coastal side, the southern part of the range drops abruptly. The valleys of this slope are deeply notched and have a glacial character. Branching off to the north from the main axis of the range is the long Konginsk chain with heights to 6,000 feet. In the northern half, the Kolyma has a rather broad and high central axis with a series of parallel ridges to 6,600 feet high. It separates the Ushurakchan chain to the northwest, having heights of 6,080 feet, and it is characterized by alpine forms of relief with traces of glaciation. The main axis of the Kolyma ends very abruptly in the north before reaching the Bolshoy Anyuy River. In the northeast it abuts the Anadyr Plateau. The Kolyma Range is formed of marine sedimentary rocks (Permian, Triassic, and Jurassic) and extrusives and their tuffs, in folds of a northeast or meridional strike.

The Anadyr Plateau and Anadyr-Penzhina Depression

The Anadyr Plateau, with heights of 2,640 to 3,300 feet (but with peaks to 3,960 feet), lies between the higher elevations of the northern end of Kolyma and the western part of the Chukchi ranges. It has uniform relief and massive forms, often in the shape of completely flat mesas and gently rounded hills. This is explained by the horizontal blanket deposits of extrusives. The circular pond Elgytkhyn, with a diameter of 7.2 miles, lies in a Quaternary volcanic crater in the northern part of the plateau.

The Northern and Southern Anyuy ranges, divided by the valley of the Anyuy River, branch off from the northwestern part of the Anadyr Plateau. The Northern Anyuy Range, with heights of 4,290 to 4,950 feet (but peaks to 5,940 feet), is a recent fold-fault formation. The steep and inaccessible slopes indicate that the range is bounded by breaks. The range has typical alpine relief and fresh traces of widespread glaciation—with countless intricate cirque formations, moraines bare of vegetation, and river valleys still not incised to the bottom of glacial troughs. The Southern Anyuy Range has steep southern and more gentle northern slopes.

The Anadyr-Penzhina depression is a region of subsidence between the Okhotsk-Chaun arc, the Koryak Range, and the Chukchi block. In the past it was an area of volcanism. Intermittent outpourings of extrusives filled in great areas of the depression. It was also recently inundated by the sea. Many elevations were subjected to glaciation; for example, distinct traces were left near Zolotoy Range. Three lowlands in the depression are the Anadyr Lowland, the Penzhina Lowland, and Parapolskiy Valley, plus isolated mountain groups.

The Anadyr Lowland, the largest of the three lowlands, has a comparatively flat relief and is only a few dozen yards above sea level. Only toward the mountains does it exhibit undulation. The lowland is dotted with many small circular lakes, most of which are remnants of cutoff meanders left in the flood-plain by the rivers. Some of them have formed from the thawing of fossil ice buried in the permafrost. A few of the lakes in the coastal sections have the appearance of lagoons cut off from the sea.

The Penzhina Lowland and the Parapolskiy Valley are of the same character, with maximum heights to 660 feet.

Scattered amid the depression are small ranges. They extend from an east-northeast to a meridional direction and are either completely isolated or linked with the Chukchi and Koryak ranges. The most recent fold-fault ranges are: (1) Pekulney Range, a long narrow mountain chain with an average height between 4,950 and 5,280 feet, alpine forms of relief, and distinct traces of recent glaciation (many glacial lakes and the presence of a small hanging glacier on the western slope at 4,290 feet); (2) Rarytkin Range, with elevations to 2,970 feet; and (3) Penzhina Range, with elevations to 1,980 feet.

Koryak Range

Koryak Range, which is a part of the Koryak-Kamchatka arc, is a typical marginal Tertiary-Quaternary folded zone of the Pacific coast and is convex to the west. It is distinctly different in its structure and history from the interior regions of Northeastern Siberia. Koryak Range is a young alpine fault and volcanic zone but, in contrast with the eastern volcanic region of Kamchatka, does not have Quaternary volcanoes. The volcanoes are related to an earlier epoch. Koryak Range extends along the shore of the Bering Sea from Kamchatka to Anadyr Bay and descends to the Anadyr plain in a steep cliff, demarcated by an east-west tectonic line. The range consists of many parallel mountain chains, separated by longitudinal valleys. Toward the southwestern end, the range widens (from 60 to 150 miles) as the chains diverge radially to the south and are cut off by the coast line of the Olyutorsky Gulf. Only the very northern range joins with the central Kamchatka Range. It is separated from it by a small gap six miles wide, across which Parapolskiy Valley unites with the low eastern coast of Kamchatka. The average height of the range varies from 3,300 to 4,950 feet. Even at the shore, there are 3,300 and 4,290 foot peaks. Separate peaks of the range rise to 6,600 feet.

The clay shale composing Koryak Range was crumpled into folds parallel to the axis of the arc and the coast line; subsequent arc-shaped upthrusts generally conformed to the direction of folding and determined the borders of the range. Regions of sandy-schistous strata have a very smooth relief. In many places, especially those formed by extrusive tuff rocks, the range has an alpine character and is heavily dissected by glaciation (glacial troughs) glacial cirques, moraines). Separate mountain groups are divided by deep glacial valleys. In the central part of the Bering slope the range has increased precipitation, and at the snow line (3,300 feet) there are glaciers up to 2.4 miles long and 82.5 feet thick. The ends of these glaciers descend to 2,640 feet, and are receding.

Chukchi Massif

The Chukchi massif is between the Anadyr basin and the Chukchi Sea coast. It is a Paleozoic and Mesozoic folded zone. After Mesozoic folding it was converted into a rigid region which subsequently reacted as a solid mass to epeirogenic fluctuations. The present-day boundaries of the mountain range are marked by tectonic breaks.

The Chukchi block consists of two parts. They are divided by a line from Kresta Gulf to Kolyuchin Bay and differ in basic forms of relief. From Cape Shelagsk to the southeast extends Chukchi Range (Anadyr Range), which reaches to 7,590 feet in the central section. It drops rather steeply to the Anadyr Plateau and is sharply distinguished from it by highly dissected alpine forms of relief with deep glacial valleys. To the east the range drops to 4,620 feet and then rises again near Kresta Gulf, where Iskaten Range (in which there is a small hanging glacier) reaches 4,950 feet. Farther on, it turns to the east toward Kolyuchin Bay.

The eastern part of the mountain range, Chukchi Peninsula proper, contains many mountain groups and short ranges trending in different directions. These exhibit smooth rounded contours, average between 2,640 and 3,300 feet in height, and contain a few peaks in the central sections to 4,950 feet. The mountains are separated by broad valleys which cross the country in a northwest direction and do not conform to the present-day trend of the rivers—for example, the large valley from Mechigmenskaya Bay to Kolyuchin Bay, which is very shallow. Where there are larger coastal mountain groups (in the southeastern section of the Peninsula, with its extremely dissected shore line), the deep and narrow bays—Lavrentiya (Lawrence), Provindeniya (Providence), and Tkachen—are typical glacial fiords with characteristic depth distribution and origin linked with the very youthful glaciation of the peninsula.

HYDROGRAPHY

The Bering Sea, the triangle-shaped, northernmost marginal sea of the Pacific Ocean, is bounded on the west by the northeast coast of Asia, on the east by the northwest coast of North America, on the north by the Bering Strait, and on the south by the peninsula of Alaska and the Aleutian and Komandorski (Commander) Islands. The broad (to 205 miles) and deep (to 9,900 feet) western straits of the Aleutian archipelago allow the water from the depths of the Pacific Ocean to flow into the basin. The single, narrow (21 miles) and shallow (to 194.7 feet) Bering Strait seals off water from the cold, deep, northern seas, reducing to a minimum the influence of the Chukchi Sea. The bottom of the Bering Sea may be divided into two sharply differing basins by a line passing approximately from Cape Navarin to Unimak Pass. The shallow north-northeastern basin (with depths less than 660 feet) occupies 44 per cent of the whole area of the sea, and the south-southwestern, broad, deepwater basin (with depths to 13,200 feet) covers 43 per cent. The natural boundary between them is a very sharply pronounced ridge (with depths from 660 to 6,600 feet) that occupies, altogether, 13 per cent of the sea floor. The average depth of the sea is 4,731 feet, and the greatest depth in the southern part is 13,422 feet.

The diverse relief of the bottom, in particular the steep ridge running across the entire sea, with irregularities, pockets, and shelves, hinders the movement of water from south to north and through the Bering Strait. The difference in climatic conditions and degree of freshening of separate basins, the cold temperatures, and the dissected coast line, all create the complex and, in places, tortuous scheme of over-all circulation of the Bering Sea. During summer there is a strong, steady flow of surface water from the Komandorski Channel northeastward. This current approaches the continental slope only in the center to provide the two large circular motions of the central part of the sea. The western current moves in a counterclockwise direction, and the eastern one in a clockwise direction. The left current runs along the western shore of the Bering Sea to the south, incorporates the waters of the Olyutorsky cold basin, and passes between Kamchatka and the Komandorski Islands. It then merges with the current from the Sea of Okhotsk to form the cold Oyashio Current. The very strong current of the saltier and heavier water warmed during summer passes north in a second current from the southeast along the coast of North America. In the northern part of the sea, the extremely stable main current flows north through the Bering Strait into the Chukchi Sea, and the return current plays a negligible role. Winds strengthen or weaken the main current, but do not change its direction. Important for the dynamics of the sea water is the inflowing 24 or 12 hour tidal surge from the Pacific Ocean.

The water temperature depends, in the first place, on the over-all climatic and geographic conditions of this sea. The sea is at rather high latitudes (between 52° and 65°30′ north latitude) and is between highly chilled lands, including the region of the severe Siberian winter. Consequently, the sea has an extremely cold, moist climate with abundant, prolonged,

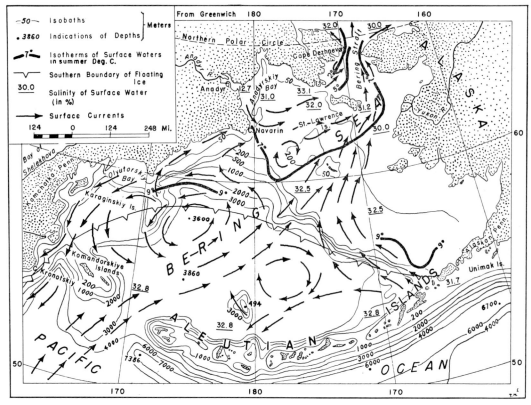

Map 7-II. Physicogeographic map of the Bering Sea.

and thick fogs. The average temperatures in the Bering Strait are −2°F for January and 41°F for July; near the Aleutian Islands 32°F for January and 50°F for July. The coldness of the water links the Bering Sea with the circumpolar seas. In the central part of the Bering Sea the water has these temperature stratifications in summer: surface water warms to 50°F in summer; at a depth of from 100 to 130 feet, which is usually the layer of temperature discontinuity, it is 39 to 43°F; lower down, to a depth of 330 to 500 feet, there is a cold intermediate layer with temperatures of 33° to 34°F. The water warms to a stable temperature of 38.5°F at the depth of from 660 to 1,650 feet. Below this, at the depth of 6,600 to 9,900 feet, the temperature falls again to 34° and 35.5°F. There are two pronounced cold spots—in the Olyutorsky Bay and in the Anadyr region—where freezing temperatures (to 29°F) have been registered even at depths

of 1,650 feet. The spots are the result of the hydrologic regime associated with the intense cooling of the mainland in winter. The spots contribute to the formation of fog, prolong the duration of ice cover, and affect the distribution of commercial fauna. Annual vertical circulation does not spread farther than the cold intermediate layer.

Vertical distribution of salinity in the Bering Sea is rather uniform: 32 per cent on the surface, to 34.5 per cent at a depth of 9,900 feet. In the layer from the surface to 1,650 feet, salinity increases from 32 to 34 per cent; and from 1,650 to 9,900 feet, it varies only 0.5 per cent. The rather high salinity is explained by the enormous interchange of water with the Pacific Ocean. Only in regions receiving discharged water from large rivers (Anadyr and Yukon) is the surface layer less saline. Water transparency varies from 8.25 feet near Anadyr Bay to 50 feet in the open sea. In winter the northeastern part of the Bering Sea is covered for several months with floating ice, and only its southern part remains ice-free. Ice from the Chukchi Sea does not enter the Bering Sea through the Bering Strait. At the beginning of May the ice begins to thaw; by the middle of May it is found in quantity only along the western shores; in June it remains only in Anadyr Bay. The ice border moves northward beyond the Bering Strait in summer, leaving the Bering Sea free of ice.

Fauna of the northern part of the sea is related to the arctic region, whereas fauna of the southern part belongs to the subarctic, indicating a transition to the temperate sea. Conditions along the Asiatic coast are favorable for most species of plankton which emigrate from the cold, very salty depths. On the rocky bottom at a depth of 100 to 330 feet, biocoenoses of fixed species predominate—sponges and Bryozoa. Of the echinoderms there are many brittle stars and starfish, whose numbers increase with depth. Various polychaeta and ribbon worms creep amid the water vegetation, and diverse crayfish-decapods poke about displaying their unusual coloring of red-brown stripes. As sand and slimy mud are added to rocky ground, mollusk and many crabs appear. The Kamchatka crab, with its large meaty claws, is of commercial importance. At a depth of 9,900 feet on clayey ground live countless polychaeta in fine white tubers, sea cucumbers, mollusks, deepwater fish (*Lampanyctus beringensis*) with phosphorescent organs. These fish indicate the close connection of the great depths of the sea with the Pacific Ocean. The most characteristic features of fauna of the Bering Sea are (1) the great number of species—280; (2) the originality; (3) the arctic character of species which live here in large numbers and are native to cold waters—gobyrock fish (22 per cent of the fish fauna), cod, and Siberian humpback, blue-backed, and silver salmon.

The following are commercially important: (in the northern part) Greenland whale (*Balaena mysticetus*), (in the southern part) Japanese whale (*B. japonica*), white whale (*Delphinapterus leucas*), and killer whale (*Orca gladiator*); walrus (*Odobaenus rosmarus*) near the western shore of the sea, seals—especially long-eared seal (*Eumetopias jubatus*) and marine fur seal (*Callorhinus ursinus*). The marine fur seal is nearly exterminated now and, together with sea otter (*Enhydra lutris*), is encountered in very small numbers only near Pribilov Islands, Island of Mednyy, and, rarely, Kamchatka coast.

VEGETATION AND SOIL

Despite the extreme cold and minimum precipitation, a forest landscape prevails over a considerable area of the mountain region of Northeastern Siberia. In the east the vegetation of bald peaks is more predominant than forest vegetation.

Severe climatic conditions limit the assortment of woody plants. The sole conifer and predominating tree is the Dahurian larch (*Larix dahurica*). It reaches 70°15′ north latitude in the Indigirka Valley and within 18 miles of the beginning of the Yana delta. Typical Yakut taiga, with the predominance of pine and spruce, does not grow beyond the Verkho-yansk Range. The severe climate is also responsible for the sparse forest stands which are typical for a subpolar region. Only on narrow riparian sections and on islands does a dense forest develop. At a short distance from the river, in a direction toward the mountain slopes, terraces show unfavorable forest growth. The severe climatic conditions also impose a low vertical limit on the spread of woody vegetation. In the Verkhoyansk Range the forest rises to 3,135 feet, and separate trees to 3,465 feet. On Chersky Range, near the mouth of the Moma River, the timber line is 2,145 feet; and on Kolyma Range, at the sources of the

Omolon River, the timber line is 2,970 feet. Although larch grows almost everywhere, it prefers dry, elevated places and avoids low swamped sections, yearly inundated bottomlands, and rocky alluvial deposits. East of the Kolyma River basin, the mountains are treeless, except along the upper Anadyr, its tributary the Mayn, and the middle course of the Penzhina, where there are islands of larch forest. The character of a larch forest varies with geographic position, slope exposure, and altitude. The denseness of larch forests decreases toward the north. On south-facing slopes, the growth is more successful; on north-facing slopes, vegetation bears a wooded-tundra character. Mountain larch forests are replaced on the lowlands by sparse, swamp stands. In the river valleys, separate specimens, 10 to 22 feet high and 4 to 6 inches in diameter, grow 6 to 10 feet from one another.

Most of the trees are crooked, dead-topped, and of little use even for the building of primitive Yakut huts. Construction timber is usually obtained from stands growing on large islands of thawed ground. The poor undergrowth is composed of scrub alder, wild rosemary, blue currant, red bilberry, bog bilberry, and rare patches of grass cover or thickets of birch and reindeer moss, which is fodder for reindeer. Close to the timber line, the forest takes on a wooded-tundra character, of dwarf larch with curved and misshapen trunks, and is replaced by a narrow strip of dense thickets of dwarf stone pine (*Pinus pumila.*) All crests and tops, plus a large part of the slopes of high mountains, are free of woody vegetation and are covered by a solid mantle of rocky alluvial deposits and taluses. For example, on Orulgan Range, in a 9- to 18-mile strip along both sides of the main watershed range, woody vegetation is absent even along river valleys. Therefore, when crossing the range, it is necessary to stock up with enough wood for two to three days. On gentle slopes of bald mountains grows lichenous high-elevation tundra, rather rich in flowers.

In many river valleys there are widespread forests of balsam poplar (*Populus suaveolens*),

used in the building of large hollowed-out boats. There are also forests of full-grown relic Korean willow (*Chosenia macrolepis*), the straight trunks of which are used for the construction of bridges and telegraph poles. In the southern part of the region the following deciduous trees grow; aspen, mountain ash, bird cherry, and birch. The terraces of the broad river valleys often have solonetz soil and abound in excellent meadows favorable for cattle raising. Despite the occasional early frosts and snowfall in summer, climatic and also soil conditions are not an insuperable obstacle to agriculture within the limits of the riparian terraces. Conditions in the south permit the sowing of barley and rye, but for the raising of many vegetables, warmed beds are necessary.

Summer is cool in the east, beyond the Kolyma basin. Because of the cold and moist sea winds, the many fogs, and the cold currents of the Bering and Okhotsk seas, the permafrost cannot thaw rapidly or deeply and the growing period is shortened. Consequently, considerable areas of water divide are covered with the vegetation of bald peaks and subalpine underbrush, and in the lowlands of the Anadyr-Penzhina depression a wooded-tundra landscape prevails. The severe weather has imposed the mountain conditions of a subalpine belt on a sea-level area. Only within the favorable physicogeographic conditions along bottomlands are there islands of good poplar, Korean willow, and larch forest.

The yearly flooding of light alluvial soil and well-drained gravel subsoil permits some thawing of the permafrost, and a rather thick snow cover creates favorable conditions for the wintering of plants. In the bottomlands this contributes to the development of forest vegetation whose grassy cover resembles that of forests more to the south. The development of bottomland vegetation changes from groves of Korean willow to poplar groves or larch forests, which have many common features in their structure. But this development is affected by the constant shift of the river channel.

The first wooded vegetation on young

Fig. 7-2. Aspen forest on the Anadyr River.

gravels is Korean willow. On high spots of bottomland with circulating ground water and sandy-gravelly soil are found tall (up to 60 feet) straight Korean willows with narrow, compact crowns. Balsam poplar is encountered singly. The sparse undergrowth consists of bushes of currant (*Ribes dikuscha*), red currant (*Ribes triste*), and wild rose (*Rosa acicularis*). The grass cover is dense, displaying principally cacalia (*Cacalia hastata*) and reed grass (*Calamagrostis langsdorffii*). Moss cover is absent.

On fine sand and somewhat muddy soil, poplar is predominant. In the poplar groves, straight trunks of balsam poplar 60 feet high and 18 inches in diameter are found. Korean willow grows solitarily. The undergrowth consists of red currant and wild rose, under which

a thick tall cover of reed grass and a rare moss cover is developed. On weakly podzolized, muddy-sandy bottomland soil, underlain by gravel with admixture of sand at a depth of more than 18 inches, grow Dahurian larch forests. The high, well-proportioned, straight trunks of these larch trees are used for construction. In the undergrowth are: willow beds, wild rose bushes, currants, and Sakhalin raspberry. A luxurious cover of reed grass reaches the same level as the undergrowth; low moss carpets on logs have given shelter to typical taiga species of pyrola and honeysuckle.

Higher along the slopes on weakly podzolic, clayey soil are mountain larch forests with a thick undergrowth of scrub alder 6 to 10 feet high. Farther up the slope, the stand of trees thins out, the trunks become highly twisted and crooked, and the crowns grow in widely spread knots. Encountered here are dead-topped trees and deadwood and, in the undergrowth, dwarf creeping pine, Middendorf birch, and dwarf birch (*Betula exilus*). Above the larch limits, dwarf creeping pine predominates completely. (On low parts of the slopes and along streams, there are good, dense growths of this dwarf pine that reach 6 feet in height. These thickets are exploited for the pine nuts, which are very rich in oil.) Higher up, the slopes are covered with rubbly rock waste, amid which grow occasional beds of dwarf creeping pine no more than 2 to 4 inches above the ground. Above the zone of dwarf creeping pine, lichenous-rubbly mountain-tundra prevails. At first the tundra exhibits a solid vegetation cover, but higher up it has a thin scattered cover because of the energetic activity of snow corrasion. Detritus projects through the thin cover everywhere, and there are outcrops of large stones.

There are spots of flowering vegetation amid the white areas of lichen where reindeer moss and cetraria are found. Partridge grass (*Dryas punctata*), *Alsine arctica,* lousewort (*Pedicularis lanata*), cinquefoil (*Potentilla nivea*), anemone (*Anemone narcissiflora*), and other high-altitude species grow here. There is also a mountain tundra of sedge and cotton grasses. From a height of about 2,640 feet upward, there are large rock patches almost devoid of vegetation.

Soil conditions of the region are rather diverse. The soil is shallow and rocky and contains considerable moisture and peat but little humus. Soil in the valleys is from washed-over moraine deposits, and on slopes is the rocky soil of taluses. The upper slopes of mountains are devoid of soil cover, but the lower slopes have a soil cover from one to five inches thick. Only along the valleys are there thicker podzolic, slightly podzolic, podzolic-gleyey, muddy-boggy, and peat-bog soils.

The patches of steppe which extend north of the Arctic Circle (as far as 67.5° north latitude) are of great geographic and economic interest. There are known steppe areas in the broad val-

leys of the Yana (between the mouths of the tributaries Dulgalakh and Adycha), Indigirka (at the mouth of the valleys of the tributaries Kuydusun, Elga, Inyala, and Moma and of the adjoining segments of the main valley), and Kolyma. The steppes coincide with steep slopes on the main banks of rivers which have a southern exposure. There are also steppes on the open, higher, and well-drained ridges of terraces located over bottomlands. The temperatures on the steep south-facing slopes are favorable for the growth of xerophytic steppe vegetation. Exposed to the warming rays of the sun and protected from the cold north winds, these south-facing slopes thaw quickly and thus allow the development of vegetation. The shallow rubbly soils are close to the dark-chestnut type. Found on the slopes are various kinds of steppe vegetation with a predominance of sedge (*Carex duriuscula*), meadow grass (*Poa botryoides*), fescue grass (*Festuca lenensis*), crested wheat grass (*Agropyron cristatum*), and oats (*Avenastrum krylovii*). Included in the mixed grasses of the steppe are veronica (*Veronica incana*), cinquefoil (*Potentilla tollii*), a Verkhoyansk endemic species, *Dracocephalum palmatum,* and saxifrage (*Saxifraga bronchialis*). Beneath the steppe vegetation, on the crests of the terraces located above bottomlands, a soil is developed which has little humus and which does not effervesce, is sometimes weakly gleyed, and is of the cryptopodzolic type.

The lack of moisture in the soil during a hot summer does not restrict the growth of steppe xerophytes, but it hinders the normal development of forest, meadow, and cultivated plants. Permafrost restrains the development of vegetation in the spring. In summer, however, the permafrost, if it does not lie at a great depth, actually fosters the growth of vegetation by contributing moisture to the very dry soil. The following are the basic types of steppes of the terraces: (1) the fescue–cereal–mixed grass steppes on the higher, well-drained crests, with the predominance of fescue and sedge, with *Artemisia tanacetifolia,* rock jasmine (*Androsace septentrionale*), anemone (*Pulsatilla flavescens*), and crazyweed (*Oxytropis deflexa*); and (2) the sedge–cereal–mixed grass steppes, which lie somewhat lower and have as their background plant the narrow-leafed sedge (*Carex obtusata*). Linked with the steppe crests is an abundance of steppe fauna, including marmots and locusts.

In composition, character, and in the seasonal cycle of their development, the steppes of northeastern Siberia are very similar to those of the steppe zone. They are a direct continuation of the steppes of central Yakut, but contain fewer species. Common in the vegetative composition are the typical Mongolian-Dahurian species—for example, sedge. The mountain and northern plants, such as astragalus (*Astragalus arcticus*) or cinquefoil (*Potentilla nivea*), indicate the close relationship of the Yana-Indigirka steppes to the mountainous steppes of Central Asia. Even above the Arctic Circle the steppes keep their biological characteristics. They have a very abbreviated period of quiet in the middle of July; when the air temperature is high and there is almost no growth, the steppe turns yellow and "burns out." The isolated islands of steppe in the midst of the swampy taiga of Northeastern Siberia are relics of the post-glacial period, when the climate was warm and dry and the steppes had a wide distribution and adjoined the steppes of central Yakut.

When the climate became colder and wetter, forest landscapes appeared and the steppes were pushed to the south. Only on the steep south-facing slopes have patches of steppe survived as small islands separated from the large steppes by thousands of miles of taiga. Recently the steppe has been descending from the slopes to the level of the terraces. Evidence that the steppe is occupying the open drained crests which have been freed of taiga and swampy meadow is old stumps of larch found in the steppes, the buried layers of peat, and the traces of gley soil. The continental climate of severe winters and warm summers, the insignificant precipitation, and the dryness of the air and soil foster the growth of xerophilous vegetation. After a rigorous winter, the wasted

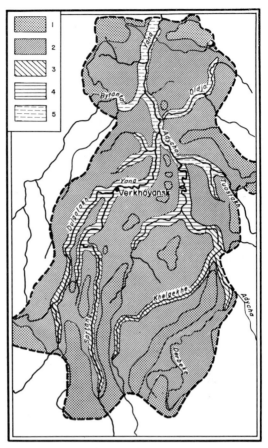

Map 7-III. Distribution of vegetation in the Verkhoyansk region: 1—Tundra, rocky, lichenous, dwarf pines; 2—Deciduous forests, watershed; 3—Valleys, 50 to 80 per cent forested, marshy meadows, poplar groves on banks and islands of rivers; 4—River valleys of Verkhoyansk depression, with forests (50 to 60 per cent), naturally irrigated meadows and irrigated pastures (20 to 30 per cent), open steppe spaces of terraces and steppe on south-facing slopes (to 10 per cent of area); 5—River valleys with marshes most prominent.

livestock quickly recover on the green pasturage of the steppes, and particularly the early spring vegetation on the south-facing slopes. In fall, after the rain, the steppes are again covered with vegetation and mantled by snow while they are still green. In order to get concentrated fodder for domestic animals, forage grain crops, such as oats, are introduced into cultivation. The steppe sections which have permafrost lying deeply are the most suitable for agriculture. Fast-ripening varieties of grain and vegetables can be grown by using irrigation and fertilizers, although summer frosts endanger the growth of potatoes.

ANIMAL LIFE

The fauna of the mountain regions of Northeastern Siberia differs from that of the western regions of Eurasia at the same latitude. The fauna of these two regions are separated by the high arch of the Verkhoyansk Range. Certain widely ranging species of the forest zone of the Subarctic either do not enter from the west (polecat) or are represented by other species (Kolyma hare). On the other hand, many of the mammals, birds, and fish are similar to those in adjacent North America, including: local species of elk; the white-necked goose (*Anser canagicus*) that nests on the Chukchi Peninsula, on the lower Anadyr, and in Alaska and winters in North America as far south as California; the white goose (*Chen hyperborius*); the white-necked loon (*Colymbus pacificus*); and the original Dallia fish (*Dallia pectoralis*). The Dallia fish is an ancient species that dwells in shallow streams, lakes, and sphagnum bogs of the Chukchi Peninsula, islands of the Bering Sea, and in Alaska; during the winter it conceals itself amid the sphagnum, where for weeks it may remain as though frozen, but when brought into a warm room it thaws out and returns to life.

The fact that the Bering Strait is a sharp geographic boundary is indicated by the many species of birds which do not cross the strait in either direction. For example, the dotterel (*Eudromias morinellus*) and the Mongolian plover (*Charadrius mongolus*) do not cross the straits toward the east, and the Alaskan-swan (*Cygnus columbianus*) and the Canadian brant do not cross to the west.

The mountain-tundra landscape contains biocoenoses not duplicated anywhere on Eurasian territory. Here lemmings form a deep-seated southern projection of their arctic habitat. Elements clearly of southern Central Asiatic origin (for example, mountain sheep, black-headed marmot, mountain finch) extend far to the north in places. They can live here because of the warm, continental summer. These animals are relics of a bygone landscape.

Fossil remains indicate inhabitants of arctic latitudes (fox, musk ox), typical northern forest species (elk, wolverine), southern mountain animals of open expanses (marmot, sheep). These lived in a continental climate similar to that prevailing in Central Asia—a cold, snowless winter, lingering cold and windy spring, and short hot summer. As a result of this, animals of that country were able to make their way northward along watershed ranges of Arctic and Pacific Ocean basins.

Since the Bering Strait was evidently formed at the end of the glacial period, territorial links with North America have also influenced faunal composition. The onset of the forest in postglacial time isolated the animals, of the open expanses, in the extreme north. Such animals as Kolyma suslik are representatives of a relic fauna of a warmer and drier xerothermic period.

The many species of small rodents, which provide a rich feeding base for commercially valuable carnivora, include: the red field mouse (*Evotomys rufocanus kolymensis*), the rust-colored field mouse (*E. rutilus jochelsoni*), the north-Siberian field mouse (*Microtus hyperboreus*), the field mouse (*M. oeconomus koreni*), and the forest lemming (*Myopus schisticolor thayeri*). Along stony alluvial deposits and along the craggy banks of rivers, the pika (*Ochotona hyperborea kolymensis*) is widespread, and along valleys in thickets of

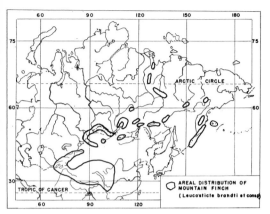

Map 7-IV. Geographic distribution of mountain finch (*Leucosticte brandti et consp.*). This map shows the spread of this Central Asian (Tibetan) species through the high open ranges and deep into the taiga zone of Eastern Siberia.

willow dwell white hare (*Lepus timidus kolymensis*). Squirrel is the most important game animal commercially but, owing to the scantiness of food, the squirrel population in one-third less than that in the forests of Belorussia. The most characteristic rodents, the Kolyma suslik and black-headed marmot, are active for only three to three and a half months a year. During the winter which lasts eight and a half to nine months, they hibernate in burrows in the permanently frozen ground, at temperatures of 4° to 21.7°F. Although the Kolyma suslik (*Citellus eversmanni buxtoni*) lives mainly in the forest zone, it may be found in pure tundra to the shores of the East Siberian Sea and in the mountains to the forest boundary. Typical is the insular rather than the continuous propagation of the suslik. It chooses for its burrows dry open places on posi-

tive forms of medium relief, where fine-textured soil is present along the edges of forests, but does not inhabit moist meadows. The black-headed marmot (*Marmota kamtschatica bungei*) lives above the timber line in the rocky tundra on bald peaks. The grass it stores in its burrow serves as a bed in winter and as fodder in spring.

The common carnivora in the taiga include the bear, fox, weasel, and ermine. Lynx and wolverine are rare. Of the hoofed animals, wild reindeer is widespread and especially abundant west of the Indigirka. It passes the winter in full-grown forests and the summer in the bald-mountain zone. Elk (*Alces americanus pfizenmayeri*), on the other hand, lives only in the forest zone. It prefers thickets of willow and feeds on the shoots. The endemic subspecies of musk deer (*Moschus moschiferus arcticus*) is encountered singly on wooded and rocky slopes of mountains. Snow sheep (*Ovis nivicola lydekkeri*) are found on bald-peak and nearby zones; the farther north, the lower it descends from the mountains (in the Verkhoyansk Range up to 4,980 feet, and in the Anyuy Range to 1,980 feet).

Among the birds encountered in the forests are: rocky-wood grouse (*Tetrao parvirostris*), hazel grouse (*Tetrastes bonasia kolymensia*), Siberian jay (*Perisoreus infaustus*), and teal (*Nettion crecca*). In the lake-forest district of the lowlands are found waterfowl, including duck (*Oidemia fusca steinegeri*) and goose (*Anser fabalis*). The nutcracker (*Nucifraga caryocatactes macrorhynca*) is found in thickets of stone pine. Nesting in the mountains are: *Hystrionicus pacificus,* mountain-tundra partridge (*Lagopus mutus transbaicalicus*), and Polynesian ash-colored tattler (*Heteractitis incana brevipes*).

CHAPTER 8

Sayan Mountains, Tannu-Ola Range, and Tuva Basin

The Sayan Mountains lie south of Central Siberia and southeast of the Western Siberian Lowland. On the western periphery the mountains are in contact with the Altai; on the east they are separated by the narrow Tunkin graben from the Khamar-Daban Mountains, one of the ranges of Trans-Baikal. The Sayans consist of two ranges: the western Sayan and the Eastern Sayan, which unite in the shape of an inverted **Y** at a point near 96° east longitude where the Kazyr River (Yenisei system) and the Uda River (Angara system) originate. In this mountain center, some elevations reach 9,900 feet. Although both mountain ranges have fundamental geographic features in common, each has its individual peculiarities.

The Western and Eastern Sayans are strongly dissected uplands—ancient peneplains raised above the timber line. They consist principally of Paleozoic rocks (in the Eastern Sayan Pre-Cambrian rocks are also present) and were formed by intense Caledonian folding followed by repeated epeirogenic upheaval and glaciation. In the Eastern Sayan there are small glaciers. The basic trend of the mountain strata and the direction of tectonic lines of the chief ranges differ. In the Western Sayan a northeast and east-northeast trend predominates; in the Eastern Sayan the trend is north-

west. In both Sayans the basic development and relief forms are uniform, but in the Eastern Sayan the eruption of basalts has contributed more to the leveling off of the country and to the preservation of the ancient peneplain. The hydrographic network belonging to the Yenisei system unites the Sayans. Although a continental climate prevails in the Sayans, it is more pronounced in the Eastern Sayan, where precipitation is not so great.

The vegetation in the Sayans, which lie between 56° and 52° north latitude, corresponds to that found in the subzone of mixed forest and wooded-steppe between Moscow and Kursk, or the Western Siberian wooded-steppe and feather and mixed grass chernozem steppes between Ishim and Atbasar. Steppes of latitudinal zonality are also encountered in the Sayans. The more arid climate in the forest, wooded-steppe, taiga, and higher places of Eastern Sayan allows pine and larch to attain major growth. In the Western Sayan dark-coniferous forests predominate.

Administratively, the western part of the Sayans and Pre-Sayans belongs to the Krasnoyarsk territory, the central section to the Irkutsk Oblast, and the eastern part to the Buryat-Mongolian ASSR. The Khakass autonomous region penetrates the western part.

THE WESTERN SAYAN

The Western Sayan is a highly dissected mountain block beginning at the source of the Abakan River and extending in a broad belt 390 miles northeast to the upper reaches of the Kazyr River, where it joins with the Eastern Sayan. In the west it is joined to the Shapshal Range of the Eastern Altai system at Shebin-Daba pass, and in the upper stretches of the Abakan it is separated from the Kuznetsk Ala-Tau by a tectonic break which is poorly ex-

Sayan is interrupted by an escarpment dropping 330 to 660 feet to the plain of the Koybal steppe.

The Western Sayan is divided into narrow individual mountain chains by many energetic rivers. They flow on a massive, gradually undulating upland. The strike of the ranges varies from an east-west to an almost north-south direction. The chief axial Sayan range begins at the source of the Greater Abakan River and

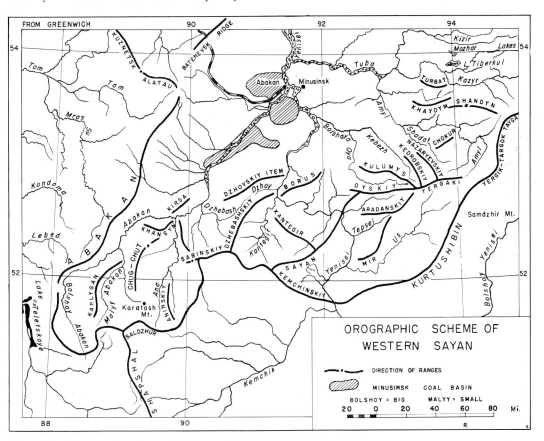

Map 8-I. Orographic scheme of Western Sayan.

pressed in the relief. The Western Sayan is separated from the Minusinsk Basin on the north and the Tuva Basin on the south by different tectonic boundaries. In the north this fault line is quite prominent; it is clearly evidenced east of the village of Beya, where the

extends to the northeast. It forms the watershed of the Kemchik River on the one side, and the Smaller Abakan and Kantigir rivers on the other, and intercepts the Yenisei at Greater Porog. Over this expanse it rises far above the timber line. At the junction with the Altai, individual summits reach higher than 9,900 feet, but toward the Yenisei they gradually drop to 8,250 and 6,600 feet.

The axial range is formed of granites or contact cherts. As a result of extensive glacial quarrying on both sides of the range, the crest is sharp, and the slopes are steep, bare, and rocky. To the north and south of the axial range elevations drop to 1,650 feet at the boundary with the Minusinsk Basin. West of the Yenisei, the axial range is known as the Oyskiy Range; from the Yenisei it stretches east to the source of the Us River as the Yergaki range; from the Us the range extends northeast to the summit of Kazyr, under the name of Tazarama Range, or Yergik-Targok-Tayga (toothed-wooded-ridge). In the section beyond the Yenisei, the range is not so straight and is formed of metamorphic schists, which are susceptible to erosion.

Between the Western Sayan, the Kuznetsk Ala-Tau, and the Eastern Minusinsk mountains lies a depressed region, which in terms of its altitude, its geologic structure, and its relief, differs sharply from the mountains surrounding it. The depression is divided by Batenevsky Ridge into two basins: the Yenisei-Chulymsk on the north and the Minusinsk on the south. The first extends 136 miles to the west of the Yenisei as far as the Black Iyus River. Its highest points (nearly 2,970 feet) lie along the periphery near the adjoining mountains; the elevations of the central part descend to 1,120 feet. Toward the north, the basin gradually turns into the weakly hilly plain of the Western Siberia Lowland. The Minusinsk Basin is elliptical in shape. Its axis extends more than 124 miles from southwest to northeast. The Yenisei cuts across the basin from south to north for nearly 60 miles. The central part of the basin is nearly 790 feet in elevation, increasing to approximately 2,300 feet near the periphery. The section of the basin which lies between the Yenisei and Abakan rivers is named the Koybal steppe; that located to the west of the Abakan is the Uybat steppe; north of the city of Abakan is the Abakan steppe;

the Minusinsk steppe occupies the right side of the basin.

Geologic History

The Western Sayans, formed primarily from Lower Paleozoic strata, contain rocks of the Lower Cambrian through the Upper Silurian. Middle and Upper Paleozoic rocks play but a slight part in the formation of the Western Sayan, occurring chiefly in Minusinsk Basin. The oldest Cambrian rocks compose the marginal section of Sayan, appearing in long, narrow strips. In the interior of the region, they are revealed only in the deeply eroded part of axial sections of anticlines. The fact that a great part of Western Sayan is made up of metamorphic rocks gives a monotonous appearance to the lithological composition and distinguishes the region from the neighboring Kuznetsk Ala-Tau and Eastern Sayan. The nature of the Silurian strata indicates a period of instability. A geosyncline, stretching in a northeast direction, was formed on a section of Western Sayan and existed through the Upper Silurian Period. The accumulation of Silurian deposits took place under quiet conditions: the basin gradually sank and was filled by an extremely thick mass (up to six miles) of clay shales and sandstones—fine clastic rocks. At the end of the Upper Silurian Period, owing to the Erian stage of Caledonian folding, the Cambrian and Silurian rocks were collected into folds which extend parallel to the over-all strike of the Sayan. Massive rocks of the Cambrian (extrusives, conglomerates, sandstones, and limestones) still secured to the basement rock by intrusions, resisted pressure and were consequently broken up by faulting: the northern tectonic boundary of the Sayans is linked with these faults. However, the fine clastic rocks of the Silurian behaved in quite another manner. When mountain-forming pressure concentrated in these masses, strata were gathered into isoclines and folds tilted to the northwest. In the process of folding the

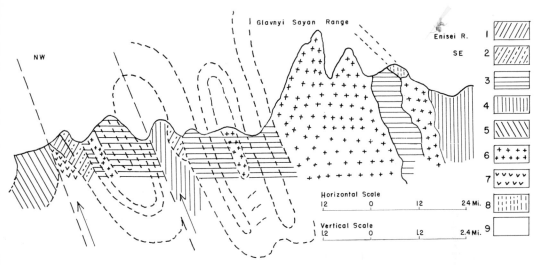

Fig. 8-1. Geologic cross section of the central part of Western Sayan. 1—Cambrian effusions; 2—Cambrian limestone and sandstone; 3—Lower Silurian chlorite schists, amphibolites, and marble; 4—Upper Silurian limestone and sandstone; 5—Normal Middle and Upper Paleozoic of Minusinsk depression (Upper Devonian, Lower Carboniferous); 6—Dzhoysk granite; 7—Mainsk granite; 8—Peridites; 9—Planes of distortion.

pliable, easily crumpled shales and sandstones of the Lower Silurian Period slipped along the surface of fixed Cambrian strata. Under strong lateral pressure, the rocks experienced intense metamorphism, with recrystallization and shearing in the deeper horizons and zones of the greatest crumpling, and the formation of green chloritic schists characteristic of Western Sayan. Folding was accompanied by the intrusion of acidic and basic intrusive rocks such as pyroxenites and peridotites. In contact zones minerals such as copper (Main deposit), molybdenum, and iron (Abakan deposit) were deposited. During the last phase of Variscan folding, a powerful movement took place. The Lower Paleozic rocks of the Sayans were lifted on top of the Upper Paleozoic deposits of the adjacent Minusinsk Basin.

The mountain region which had emerged as a result of folding was rapidly denuded, and the reddish stratum of the Lower Devonian was deposited on the eroded surface. After the Middle Devonian Period, the sea abandoned the mountain region of the Western Sayan. Devonian and more recent deposits were con-

centrated in the Minusinsk Valley. Its bottom was covered by marine deposits of the Lower and Middle Devonian, by thick continental masses of the Upper Devonian and Carboniferous, and by coal-bearing Permian deposits of varicolored conglomerates, sandstones, and limestones. These deposits are relatively undisturbed: strata are almost horizontal, sometimes gentle dipping, but in some places they curve in smooth wide folds. Only close to the mountains are dislocations of a fault type noticeable. The folds have been well eroded and appear as craggy ridges traceable for many miles. They are asymmetrical in profile. Slightly dislocated, thick, coal-bearing, sandy-clayey Permian deposits form flat synclines separated by dome-shaped elevations which appear as isolated patches scattered in the center of Minusinsk Basin. Often they are covered by a mantle of rather thick alluvial deposits of the Yenisei and Abakan. In the northern part of this Minusinsk coal basin, which has total stores of coal amounting to fourteen billion tons, there are 38 seams of coal with thicknesses of from 0.6 to 14.8 feet and a total over-all thickness of

Fig. 8-2. Alpine forms of relief on the granite ridge of Yergak.

133.6 feet. This coal is excellent fuel (heat capacity is 7,800 calories per kilogram) and may be used to make gas.

In the second half of the Tertiary Period, in connection with alpine folding, a powerful epeirogenic upheaval of Western Sayan caused a buckling of the axial section of the range and a gradual subsidence of the northern and southern regions. The upheaval did not take place at once, but in stages. This is indicated by the development of three to five old river terraces in the valleys of the large rivers. Corresponding to this upheaval, movement occurred along the northern tectonic border of Western Sayan. In addition to the rejuvenation of its streams, the ancient peneplain surface of Tertiary Sayan, was subjected to glaciation which left its traces in the highest sections in the form of erratic boulders, eroded cirques, and remnants of moraine deposits. Glaciers descending from the

Fig. 8-3. Bald mountain type of relief in the Kulumyss Range of the Western Sayan.
(*Drawing by S. P. Suslov.*)

mountains terminated at a height of about 990 feet. This glaciation was not connected with the existing hydrographic network, and separate glacial tongues intersected the present river valleys. After the disappearance or abridgment of the glaciers, the deepest incision of the river network took place, and, corresponding with the new dissection, glaciers invaded the ready-made valleys. The snow line of this (the second) glaciation, according to the altitude of the bottom of cirques, lay at about 6,270 to 6,600 feet—that is, somewhat above the present timber line. Glacial tongues, having a length to 9.6 (and even to 12) miles, ended not far from the area of feeding, and terminal moraines of these glaciers are found today at about 5,280 feet.

Traces of the last glacial epoch in centers of glaciation have survived in exceptionally fresh form. The excellent preservation of glacial forms, in places almost untouched by river erosion, indicates that the retreat of glaciers took place quite recently. Even at the present time, in southwestern Sayan, within the borders of Tuva Autonomous Oblast (region), there are cirque glaciers. Following the glacial epoch, extensive development of lakes and the meandering of river channels took place in the adjacent valleys, and in the xerothermic period energetic weathering of sandstones and the shifting of sand occurred. Subsequently the climate became moist, the hydrographic network achieved its present appearance, loose sand in the depressions was covered with pine groves, and the timber line in the mountains began to rise and cover the talus partly. The physicogeographic conditions which influence the present climate were established.

Geomorphologic Character

In the morphology of Western Sayan four stages of the development of relief may be noted: (1) the oldest, prolonged stage of denudation, belonging evidently to the Tertiary, which brought the region to peneplain; (2) the recent epeirogenic upheaval, which rejuvenated old eroded regions; (3) the glacial period, with its dissection of the highest peaks and the formation of areas of rock waste; (4) the postglacial phase, characterized by the erosional dissection of uplands and by the abrasion of irregularities in the relief.

The Western Sayan is characteristically a dissected region with a predominance of rounded, smooth mountain forms amid vast rolling expanses. Separate groups of higher and more sharply outlined summits are scattered throughout, and are formed, for the most part, of massive rocks. The tops of individual mountains are almost level. To the north and south of the main Sayan range, the mountains gradually become lower.

In the recent past the Western Sayans were a peneplain from which isolated monadnocks of resistant granites and contact cherts rose to heights of 660 to 1,980 feet. Along this plain quiet rivers twisted in intricate meanders over their broad, mature valleys. Remnants of the old denuded surface, in the form of flat plateau-shaped expanses, are found at a height of about 6,600 feet. This level is fairly well maintained throughout the range, and is only difficult to establish in places where the peneplain is dissected by many energetic rivers into sharp-crested ridges. At the junction of the Western Sayans and the Altai, the peneplain is distinctly expressed, owing to the fact that there are no deeply notched glacial troughs, but poorly developed valleys. Great heaps of moraine material are strewn everywhere; shallow lakes lie on the surface, with rocky bogs overgrown by polar willow and birch. Erosion of the peneplain continues at present. The snow is important in this process of leveling: it fills the lower areas of the high rolling plains and protects them from destruction by atmospheric agents; at the same time, the ridges of bedrock rising above the level of snow cover undergo intense decomposition. Fine eluvial products thus developed are removed by the wind, and coarse ones are rolled off into low places where they accumulate, eventually filling in the depressions and leveling the relief.

The main types of relief are: (1) the highest,

much-dissected mountain ranges of the alpine type, (2) the vast, flat-topped bare-mountain masses, and (3) lower surrounding bald-mountains of the intermediate mountain landscape.

Ranges of the Alpine type are generally higher than 6,600 feet, with individual summits to 7,920 feet. They have jagged shapes, with high finger-like peaks—such as the granite range Yergaki—or with saw-like outlines—such as the Aradanskiy Range. Alpine forms

quarry so close together that the almost perpendicular mass dividing them is like a sharp comb with a width at the upper part of not more than 6 feet. The highest point in Western Sayan, Karatosh Mountain, lies in the upper stretches of the Ana River at 9,652 feet. It is a peak that has been carved by the drawing together of three enormous cirques. At the present time cirques serve as places of snow accumulation. Even though a large amount of

Fig. 8-4. A greatly dissected mid-mountain landscape near the small Kebezh River. (*Drawing by S. P. Suslov.*)

of relief have been brought about in the glacial period and at the present time by the joint activity of intense glacial weathering and energetic frost erosion caused by the severe high-mountain climate.

Mountain ranges more than 6,600 feet high are often dissected by large and deep cirques cutting in from the north and south sides. These generally occur above the level of the present-day timber line. Narrow ridges, sharp peaks, and steep rocky slopes are all evidence of abundant *kar* glaciation. In places cirques

the snow melts toward the end of August, new snow begins to fall early in September.

The river valleys of the high-elevation zone exhibit the characteristic effects of glaciation. In their upper reaches, the valleys are typical glacial troughs, terminating in the steep walls of cirques, at the base of which lie small lakes with transparent, greenish water. Small streams meander along the broad, flat bottoms of the **U**-shaped valleys amid accumulations of moraine material and many ponds and bogs. The shallow streams of lateral hanging valleys drop

Fig. 8-5. Yenisei River in the Sayan Canyon.

into the main valley in steep cascades and waterfalls up to 160 feet in height (at the source of the Ana River).

The bald mountains average 5,775 to 6,105 feet in elevation. Rising 330 to 660 feet above the timber line, the characteristic dome-shaped tops lend a massive appearance to the mountains. In this area may be seen flat-topped bald-

Fig. 8-6. The moraine dam of Lake Oysk.

Fig. 8-7. Thick coniferous taiga on the north slope of the Western Sayan.

mediate-mountain landscape. Watersheds exhibit typical features of an old, eroded relief. They contain mesas which are formed by outcrops of more stable mountain rocks. Closer to the deep river valleys in the area of shales, which are susceptible to erosion, the flat mesas are replaced by more dissected but smoothly outlined crests—often broken up into separate cone-shaped summits.

In contrast to the relatively mature upland forms, most of the valleys are distinguished by features of energetic erosion, indicating relative youth and recent epeirogenic upheavals. Signs of the rejuvenation are observable along most of the rivers. Narrow gorges drop hundreds of feet from their well-expressed valley edges to the turbulent, rapid-filled rivers that rush along their notched bottoms. The Yenisei has cut across the entire Western Sayan mass and flows in a deep gorge with almost vertical walls rising hundreds of yards. It forms countless

mountains, each capped with a horizontal peneplain. Quiet streams flow off the bare plateaus into narrow, dark, taiga-covered gorges.

Alluvial deposits and taluses play a prominent part in the morphology of the bare mountains. These deposits of the angular fragments of rock differ in size and are heaped in disorder. They cover the surface of high mountains and descend in long tongues into the upper parts of mountain valleys. The movement of these taluses is extremely slow and irregular because of the pressure of the upper talus material on the lower, plus the flow of water draining along the bedrock. The water carries the finely grained material out of the talus and brings about the settling and sliding of individual rocks. It also causes mechanical pressure between the boulders when it freezes. In the glacial period the conditions for rapid disintegration of mountain strata were especially favorable.

Relief of the taiga zone is that of an inter-

Fig. 8-8. Mountain stream in the coniferous forest of the Sayan.

and dangerous rapids. The character of the rocks cut through by the river also influences the width of the valley. For example, the Ana River valley (Abakan system) narrows in granites and widens in regions of chloritic schists.

In conformity with the general structure of Sayan, a combination of typical lengthwise valleys (Us River) and typical lateral valleys

river, flowing along the ancient peneplain, but swift and considerable upheaval of Sayan and subsequent rejuvenation caused the river to entrench its old meanders.

The Minusinsk and Yenisei-Chulymsk basins have a dissected relief; from slightly hilly to intermediate-mountain type. Three stages in the development of the relief may be distinguished: (1) a preglacial period; (2) a phase

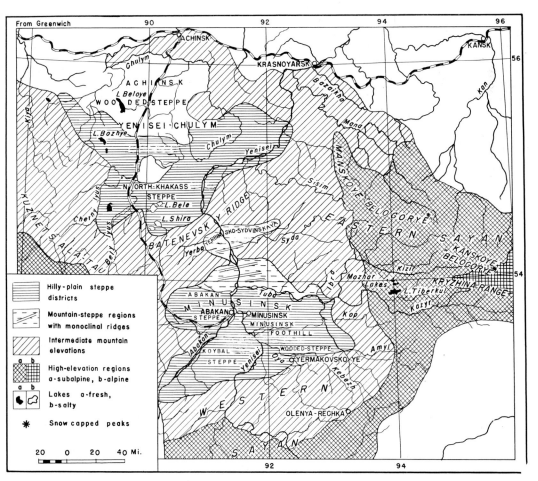

Map 8-II. Geomorphologic districts of the southern Krasnoyarsk region.

(Smaller Kebezh River) is seen. There are indications that tributaries of the Yenisei belong to the older hydrographic network. The Kantigir and Greater Oya rivers form long, narrow loops in the bedrock, analogous to the meanders of lowland rivers. Originally the loops might have been formed by a mature, calm

(corresponding to the glacial period in time) of widespread development of lakes and meandering river channels, during which old-lake and old-river sands were deposited in the valleys and loess was deposited on the interriver expanses; (3) the phase preceding the present one and having a somewhat drier climate, so that water was less abundant and sand deposits were exposed to wind action.

The relief of the depression has developed and is developing on a more or less folded, sedimentary, Paleozoic foundation. The morphology of the region closely reflects the underlying geologic structure. Most of the rivers are antecedent, having made their way along strata which yield easily to erosion; lengthwise valleys are monoclines, because they are laid out along the strike of strata of shales and marls, which are inclosed between the more solid sandstones. One slope of the water divide drops off to the bottom of the valleys in steep, rocky cornices, but the opposite descends very smoothly. Therefore the landscape sometimes takes on a typical cuesta character. In the formation of the relief, the slope exposure is important, influencing the extent of moistening and insolation and disintegration of the bedrock. The north-facing slopes covered by woody vegetation prove to be more abrupt and more rocky; the south-facing slopes are more gentle and are covered by steppe vegetation. The many, dry dead valleys are conspicuous. They are either completely devoid of water (even in springtime) or are drained by negligible streams—small in proportion to the valleys they occupy. These dry valleys owe their origins to the intensive erosional work of abundant water in the past. Indicative of this are the dry former channels of the Yenisei in Minusinsk Valley.

The smoothness of the valley relief is explained by the solid mantle of carbonaceous, loess-like soil. This soil cover has a depth of from a few inches to several yards, and covers the upper parts of the slopes of valleys and the surface of water divides up to an elevation of 330 feet. The soil bears many characteristics of typical loess: whitish-yellow color, porosity, an abundance of calcium, and a tendency to stand in vertical walls.

The loess was formed in the favorable climate of the drier and warmer period preceding the recent one. Paleolithic tools found in the soil indicate its age. Loess is the subsoil for rich chernozem, adding to its productivity.

The distribution of thick layers of limestone in the valley favors the development of a karst relief. Many caves of variable size are located on the right bank of the White Iyus. Other karst forms such as karst lake depressions, funnel-craters, wells, and inclined fissures may be found in the valley.

The relief forms change sharply in regions of igneous rock, as on Batenevsky Ridge. The relief here is an intermediate-mountain landscape with very soft features. The higher places frequently have the appearance of irregularly conical or cupola-form hills and jagged ridges; the depressions are like wide ravines or locked-in basins.

Under conditions of continental dry climate, energetic weathering of weak sandstones once yielded a mass of sandy material which was carried off into river valleys by surface water, or blown about and subsequently fixed in place by pine groves. With the destruction of the pine groves, the sand began to undergo intense shifting. In the southwestern part of the valley the soil cover is thin or completely absent. In snowless winters and in late autumn, when the sparse grass cover drys up, the fine sand is carried by the wind beyond the limits of this area.

The hydrographic network of the Western Sayan is unified because most of the streams drain into the Yenisei. It is a highly-branched, dendritic network, of which the trunk stream is the Yenisei. Its large branches (Abakan and Tuba rivers) separate into many secondary tributaries. The sources of the large tributaries are far back in the timbered mountains and the high-mountain zone.

Western Sayan has a high relative humidity and an abundance of running water. Almost every broad gulley or narrow valley contains a stream, brook, or spring. Snow accumulation in winter, with the gradual melting in spring and the summer runoff regulated by the densely wooded slopes replenish the taiga rivers and provide an abundance of water during the entire first half of summer. Because of good filtration of rain water on the slopes, the water in mountain streams is clear. At the end of

May and the beginning of June, the sun's warmth accelerates the melting process and the water level in the rivers rises, sometimes causing great floods. During this time the most energetic erosion and the transportation of alluvial material take place. Rain falling in the upper stretches of the rivers results in marked fluctuations of the water level. Occasionally, the water rises 6 to 12 feet during the night, flooding the shores, causing much destruction, and forming extensive log jams. Owing to the deepness of the Yenisei valley, floods take place only when there is an extreme rise of the river (15 to 20 feet). Sometimes all the islands in the valley bottom and the lowest points of the terraces are inundated. The Yenisei freezes over at Minusinsk by the middle of November, and breaks up late in April. It is free of ice for approximately 205 days. Shallow streams originate from snow drifts or lakes and swamps. Many lakes have been formed by cirques, moraine dams (Lake Osykoye), and landslides (lakes of the Ana upper stretches). The distribution of ground water is irregular and depends on the character of the rocks: for example, compact and hard-to-penetrate rocks contribute to the accumulation of moisture in the loose deposits covering them, but in loose and broken rocks the circulation of water takes place along the cracks.

The steppes of the adjacent valley (Minusinsk) are poorly drained. Steppe streams, not having their sources in the mountains, are generally poor in water, have a slow current, and become very shallow in summer—in places almost drying up. The water of these streams never reaches the main river, and is often taken up in the irrigation of fields and meadows. The shallow valleys usually contain intermittent streams.

In Devonian and Carboniferous and some saliferous rocks, there are many aquiferous seams which produce springs. Some of these springs have brackish water. In places where ground water flows unobstructed in one direction, wells yield fresh drinking water. However, in places where the subterranean relief prevents good ground water circulation, the well water is salty. Likewise, the lakes in undrained valleys that are fed by terminating steppe streams or by brackish springs contain salty water (Lake Tagarskoye).

The chemical composition of the water of lakes differs: there are chloride-sulphate lakes with salt content up to 18 to 23 grams per liter (Lake Tagarskoye), lakes with considerable supplies of Glauber salts (Lake Shunet), and others with sodium chloride deposits (Lake Solenoye). On the shores of Lake Tagarskoye and Lake Shira, health resorts offer treatment that includes bathing in and drinking of lake water and application of the oily mud obtained from the bottom.

Once every five or six years droughts necessitate irrigation of meadows and young crops. Remnants of ancient irrigation ditches may still be seen in the steppes. Enormous, waterless expanses (Koybal steppe), containing thousands of acres of the most fertile soil, require a substantial irrigation network, although the flatness of the region could result in the stagnation of irrigation water, saliferousness, and subsequent deterioration of the fertile soil.

The geographic landscapes of the Western Sayan owe their over-all arrangement and diversity to many factors. Longitudinal zonality is rather clear, although it is greatly disrupted by the orography. According to its geographic position, the Western Sayan should be a latitudinal steppe zone analogous to the steppes of northern Kazakhstan. A certain similarity to Kazakhstan is observable in the Minusinsk Valley. In the north at low elevations it has mild forms of relief and a maximum annual precipitation of 12 inches. In the south the mountain ranges of the Sayan border on the steppe and wooded-steppe of the vast Tuva Basin and its northern extension—the small Usinsk Basin. Because the height of the Western Sayans reaches more than 6,600 feet, vertical zones exhibit a sharp diversity of climates, soils, and plant and animal life. Landscapes belong to steppe, wooded-steppe, subtaiga, taiga, and high-mountain zones. The almost west-east trend of the main ranges strongly affects the disposition, character, and level of vertical zones. In general, the zones extend from west to east; symmetrical zones—as on the lower slopes—are similar in structure. The exposure determines the nature of the landscape; on the north, zones are influenced by the Siberian steppes, and southward they are influenced by the Mongolian steppes. The dryness of the south-facing slope allows the wooded-steppe to reach 3,300 feet, whereas on the colder north-facing slope it rises only 1,200 feet. On the southern slope, light larch forests predominate, along with steppe brushwood and grassy forms of the Mongolian type; dark-coniferous taiga covers the northern slope.

Felling and burning of forests on the lower slopes, plowing of new areas, and intensified pasturage of cattle lead to modification of the landscape by promoting the following phenomena: (1) rapid melting of snow, (2) intense erosion of slopes, (3) development of taluses and large slides, (4) replacement of wooded hydrophytic meadows by xerophytic types, (5) an advance into the mountains (especially along rocky open slopes warmed by a southern exposure) of plants from the neighboring wooded-steppe, and (6) replacement of dark-coniferous forests by secondary birch groves or larch forests.

Climate

The location of the Western Sayan near the center of the vast Asiatic continent, which in winter is the region of the anticyclone, gives the sharply continental, severe climate to the region. Winter in the foothills is warmer than in the neighboring valleys, where orographic conditions depress the temperatures under conditions of the anticyclone. Annual and average January temperatures increase with the elevation of a place, and July averages regularly decrease.

At higher places the climate is very severe. This is shown by the low average annual temperature of 11.2°F, by the annual fluctuations in temperature, and by the abundance of frost, of which only July is free.

Spring in the mountains is late; March is definitely a winter month with minimum temperatures of 22°F. By the end of May the average temperature over a 24-hour period is more than 83°F. The snow disappears completely in June.

Summer in the mountains is short and cool: the change of temperature with elevation is close to the mean figure of 1.18 degrees for each 330-foot rise. Over a distance of 50 miles, between Yermakovskoye and Olenya Rechka, which differ 4,260 feet in elevation, the summer is shortened by 40 days; or, stated another way, summer is lengthened one day for each vertical descent of 132 feet.

The amount of precipitation varies with altitude, as shown in the following table:

	ALTITUDE (FEET)	ANNUAL PRECIPITATION (INCHES)
Bottom of Minusinsk Basin (Minusinsk)	813	11.1
Sayan foothills, northern slope (Yermakov)	984	23.6
High-elevation zone of Sayan (Buybin Lake)	4,838	46.5
Central part of southern slope (Buyba)	2,853	17.4
Bottom of Usinsk Basin (Usinsk)	2,200	15.6

It may be seen that the amount of precipitation in the high Sayans is four times as great as that in the adjacent steppe and wooded-steppe valleys, and therefore the depth of snow cover in the mountains is also great.

The climate of Minusinsk Valley is sharply continental. This is evident from the average annual temperature and temperature range of 71.6 and 155.1 degrees, respectively, in Minusinsk, and daily fluctuations over 54 degrees in May (77°F in the daytime, down to 23.1°F in the morning). As a result of this temperature change, there is active physical weathering of mountain rocks and the accumulation of talus on the slopes. The average temperature of the coldest month, January (−3°F), is lower than in Krasnoyarsk, much farther north; and the July average reaches 68°F.

The amount of precipitation in general is slight: 12.2 inches in Minusinsk, 10.8 inches at Koybal steppe. Toward the mountains precipitation increases. The greatest precipitation occurs in summer (56 per cent), and the least in winter (9 per cent); spring and fall receive intermediate amounts of 15 per cent and 20 per cent respectively. At Minusinsk an average of 2.5 inches of rain falls in August, with 2 inches in February and May. Rains in summer are often accompanied by intense thunderstorms, and sometimes by hail. Rain water rapidly runs off the slopes and does not percolate deep into the soil. The scantiness of precipitation in winter is remarkable. Snow begins to fall at the end of October in Minusinsk and accumulates slowly, with 2.8 inches during November, 5.3 inches in December, 7.4 inches in January, and 2.6 inches in March. In April the snow is gone. The snow mantle is very thin and is quickly blown off into low spots. Thus it is possible to travel all winter and cattle find fodder the year round. The thin snow cover allows intense freezing of the ground, which preserves ice in wells at a depth of 10 to 13 feet during the entire summer, and forms frost with ground ice in the turf-mound bogs—as, for example, on the shore of Lake Itkul in the more northerly Yenisei-Chulymsk Valley. The absence of a snow cover promotes deflation, sometimes leading to a condition like that in the Uybat steppe, where all the fine soil is blown beyond the steppe borders and the surface soil strewn with gravel and fine rubble.

Southwest and northwest winds prevail, having their greatest velocities in spring and autumn. These contribute to evaporation and drying of the soil. Dryness of the air is explained by the continentality of climate and very late freezing of the reservoirs. Relative humidity is greatest in January (81 per cent), and least in May (55 per cent), when it may drop as low as 39 per cent. The greatest cloudiness is in October (69 per cent); the least in March (49 per cent).

Although the vegetative period lasts 160 days and is frost-free for 113 days, climatic conditions, during the spring months especially, are not favorable for agriculture. High summer temperatures foster the ripening of muskmelons and watermelons, but harsh winters are destructive to fruit trees. Early-morning frost in May, little precipitation, little cloudiness, and the great disparity between daytime and nighttime temperatures exert harmful effects on plants. Violent storms in spring may last all day without letup, removing the scanty snow cover. Winds dry out the soil, carry off the loose, upper arable layer, and expose the roots of plants, thus constituting a menace to local grain cultivation. Dew is neither frequent nor abundant and evaporates rapidly. Early hoarfrost at the beginning of autumn, and many downpours—sometimes accompanied by hail—injure young crops.

Lying between the Mir and Kurtushibin ranges at an altitude of 2,310 feet, the small Usinsk depression has extremely cold winters. The January average of Usinsk village (−20.1°F) is 18 degrees lower than that of Minusinsk and 1.4 degrees lower than that of Turukhansk lying at 66° north latitude. Temperatures in January reach an absolute minimum of −60°F. The unusually cold winters are explained by the accumulation, in an enclosed valley, of chilled masses of air descending from the neighboring mountains.

The average July temperature is 60.8°F, but temperatures may rise to 80°F. Frosts are absent at this time. The growing period (160 days) at Usinsk village is 19 days shorter than at Minusinsk; nevertheless, the average temperature of the period is above 64°F, sufficient for ripening cultivated plants. As a result, the greater part of the valley is covered by fields under cultivation. The total amount of precipitation (15.4 inches) is less than at Minusinsk, but the snow cover reaches a somewhat greater depth (10 inches) and melts in late April—early May. Winter has the least precipitation (9 per cent of the annual). The existence of permafrost, as suggested by the thin snow cover, has been confirmed by the discovery of ice layers

4 to 8 inches thick found in the summer at a depth of 9 to 20 inches.

In the higher, mountain taiga zone, the seasonal and annual fluctuations of temperatures are not as sharp but are nonetheless considerable. The amount of precipitation in the lower part of the zone reaches 27.8 inches (Abaza), but nearer the higher zone it increases to 32 inches (Buyba). The depth of snow cover is substantial and snowslides are frequent, as evidenced by the scarred slopes.

The climate of the higher zone is sharply continental, but the amplitude of temperature, 119.3 degrees (from 79.3° to −40°F), is nevertheless smaller than in the neighboring Minusinsk Valley. Early-morning frosts occur frequently; only July is free of them. Daily amplitudes are great; for example, in Buyba at the end of September at 7:00 A.M it was 32°F, at 1 P.M. it was 58.8°, and at 9 P.M. it was 38.5°. Summer is short and cool; the average temperature of the warmest month is 54°F. Winter is long and harsh, with the January average −4.5°F (Olenya Rechka). Spring is late, for March, with minimum temperatures near −21.8°F, is a winter month. Only at the end of May does the average daily temperature rise above 41°F. The snow finally melts in June. In mid-September sharp chilling accompanies the falling of new snow. From October to March the average daily temperature is below freezing. The severe climate explains the extremely widespread development of talus slopes.

The Western Sayans have a large amount of precipitation (Olenya Rechka—47.8 inches), owing to the fact that the ranges of Western Sayan are a barrier to the prevailing northwest and west winds. In summer, when dense rain clouds enshroud the mountain peaks, blue sky is visible above Minusinsk Valley. Most precipitation falls in summer (48 per cent); the least in winter (10 per cent). Summer brings considerable cloudiness and abundant daily rains (daily amount of precipitation is often up to 2.1 inches). As a result, there are many mountain springs and swampy expanses.

Snow covers the ground from the beginning

of October to the middle of June (255 days). Its depth reaches record figures: 99.2 inches at Lake Buybinskoye, 84.4 inches at Olenya Rechka. In winter, the snow falls during intense storms and is blown in great quantities off exposed places into depressions, where it accumulates to depths of 14 feet. At the bottom of deep cirques and in deep shaded ravines, highly packed drifts, similar to firms in consistency, lie throughout 10 to 11 months of the year. In a cold summer, they do not thaw out and can survive for many years. The snow slowly melts in spring, when a hard glaze forms on it. Throughout the summer deep reservoirs form, which regulate the water balance of most of the large rivers. In spring and at the beginning of summer, movement along roads is hindered by large drifts and deep snows which remain in the depressions be tween the mountains.

Steppe and Wooded-Steppe Zones

In the three depressions lying north of the Western Sayan range there is found a complete transition series from the wooded-steppe of the Western Siberian type (Achinsk wooded-steppe) to feather–mixed grass chernozem steppe (North-Khakass steppe) and to dry feather–fescue grass steppe on chestnut soil (Koybal steppe). The landscape, influenced by the proximity of the mountains, the dissected undulating relief, the wide development of rocky and rubby soil on the slopes, and the outcrops of bedrock on the tops of hills and slopes is distinguished from the lowland Western-Siberian steppe and wooded-steppe in species composition and in species distribution. Many new eastern and mountain-steppe species such as Siberian edelweiss (*Leontopodium sibiricum*) grow here; but, on the other hand, species such as dropwort (*Filipendula hexapetala*)—common to the lowland Western Siberian steppes—are absent. Dissection of the relief disrupts the unity of the vegetative cover, favoring the growth of woody vegetation on south-facing slopes of rises and hills, and the development of dry rocky steppes on north-facing slopes. On low sections where solonetz and solonchak are present, vegetation indigenous to them is found.

steppes). Chestnut (sometimes saliferous) soil, columnar solonetz soil, solonchak, and salty bog soil attain wide distribution. Many steppe species may be noted with the steadily

Fig. 8-9. Minusinsk wooded-steppe with grass on the southern and birch trees on the northern slopes.

In the central section of the North-Khakass steppes, north of Batenevsky Ridge, feather–mixed grass steppes predominate with a base of maidenhair feather grass, koeleria, and *Diplachne squarrosa,* to which are added *Artemisia glaua, A. sacrorum* and various steppe grasses: aster (*Aster altaicus*), cinquefoil (*Potentilla bifurca*), gentian (*Gentiana decumbens*), and edelweiss (*Leontopodium sibiricum*). Underlying this type of steppe are local variants of fertile chernozem. Along the shores of vast acrid lakes there are places with uniform and poor solonchak-meadow and bog vegetation, including *Atropis distans,* Siberian barley (*Hordeum sibiricum*), foxtail grass (*Alopecurus ventricosus*), and the like. These solonchak meadows contain many valuable fodder grasses, and may be used as meadows and pastures for sheep. In broad ravines and on the south-facing slopes at the borders of steppes grow small islets of larch forests and birch copses.

There is an island of feather–fescue grass steppe along each side of the lower course of the Greater Abakan (Koybal and Abakan

decreasing moisture. Chief of these is the feather–fescue grass steppe, with 100 per cent steppe species. Of these, the following predominate: Maidenhair feather grass, fescue grass, *Diplachne squarrosa,* and koeleria. There are also many xerophytic grasses. The large areas that are almost completely without water present a desolate view of burned-up steppe at the end of summer; but in places where the steppes have been successfully irrigated, the soil bears rich harvests. Near the forest zone the proportion of steppe species drops from 60 per cent to 40 per cent, the grass stand becomes thicker, and is formed of mixed grasses such as pasque flower (*Pulsatilla patens*) and astragalus (*Astragalus absurgens*).

Higher up and still closer to the timber line is the turf-meadow steppe; 20 to 30 per cent of the species here are steppe forms, including thick stands of grasses and luxuriant weeds, such as steppe grass (*Phleum boehmeri*), brome grass (*Bromus inermis*), *Libanotis montana,* and iris (*Iris ruthenica*). Amid this steppe are scattered larch-bird groves. On many

Fig. 8-10. Northern Khakass artemisia and grass steppe with feather grass, gray artemisia, and veronica.

solonetz soils purely halophytic species are found: *Artemisia maritima* and *Kochia prostrata*. On the shores of dried-up lakes, on solonchak soils, grow glasswort (*Salicornia herbacea*) and chee grass (*Lasiagrostis splendens*). Bottomland meadows of the Greater Abakan River, remaining green all summer, yield hay of good quality.

In over-all character and distribution of soil, vegetation and animal life, the eastern Minusinsk Valley belongs to the wooded-steppe of the foothills. Pure steppe expanses on chernozem, inhabited by such typical steppe animals as the long-tailed marmot, alternate with pine groves on littoral sand. Birch groves grow on water divides, often on soil of a podzolic type, where such forest animals as the chipmunk live. Near salty lakes, carbonaceous solonchak with indigenous halophytic vegetation may be found.

The vegetation on the north-facing and south-facing slopes is so different that one can immediately determine which direction is north without the aid of a compass. On the north-facing slopes, which are more moist because the snow thaws more slowly, small birch trees grow with an admixture of aspen and hawthorn. Beneath their canopy, meadow-forest grassy vegetation thrives even though some steppe species infiltrate. Under the copses, podzolic soil and degraded chernozem are found. Groves are on the tops of hills and ridges, and extend downward along deep wide ravines in ribbon-like patterns.

The south-facing slopes and summits of watersheds, because of the stronger insolation, are drier, burn out more easily, and are occupied by turf-meadow steppe. Beneath these steppes is a gravelly loose-structured ordinary chernozem, which changes in the drier sections to varieties of southern chernozem and, where the water-divide is very high, to varieties of thick chernozem. Near the mountains, because of the greater annual precipitation, ordinary chernozem becomes degraded. At present, steppe areas are intensely cultivated. Pine groves stretch in narrow strips along sandy areas in river valleys. In their shade thrive typical forest plants such as pinks (*Dianthus superbus*) and representatives of the turf-meadow steppe such as aconite. On periodically moistened areas in river valleys and along the shores of salty lakes solonetz and solonchak soil is developed on which solid patches of iris (*Iris ensata*) may be found. By the end of May, the saline steppe areas have a dismal appearance. The sparse grassy vegetation turns yellow, becomes dusty and partly withers.

Birds, such as the field lark (*Alauda arvensis*), Siberian steppe pipit (*Anthus richardi*), and partridge (*Perdix dahurica*), and mammals, such as the long-tailed marmot (*Spermophylus eversmanni*), Dzungarian hamster (*Phodopus songarus*), and steppe lemming (*Lagurus lagurus*), exhibit protective coloration which blends perfectly with their surroundings.

Bog-meadow and meadow soil is found on bottomland and on islands in the Yenisei and its large tributaries. On these soils grow meadows of the southern type with some steppe plants included.

South of the main Sayan range along the lower course of the Us River is the Usinsk birch-larch mountain wooded-steppe. Here, the boundaries between forest and steppe areas are very sharp. On the more shaded, north-facing slopes grow thick spruce-larch forests with the taiga plant cover peculiar to them and with taiga birds such as wood grouse. On open gentle slopes of northern and western exposure, park-like larch forests grow with rich, flowery plant cover made up of columbine (*Aquilegia glandulosa*), lady's-slipper (*Cypripedium calceolus*), and lily (*Lilium martagon*). On slopes with a southern exposure and mountain, rubbly, southern chernozem grows an extensive steppe grass cover of koeleria, steppe timothy, and pinnate feather grass (*Stipa joannis*), as well as steppe shrubs such pea (*Caragana pigmaea*) and spirea (*Spiraea hypericifolia*). Marmots are abundant, and swarms of grasshoppers (*Locustidae*) are everywhere.

Fig. 8-11. Abakan steppe with artemisia and bushes.

Taiga Zone

The taiga zone occupies almost the entire mountain region of the Western Sayan, with the exception of separate strips and islands of high-mountain zone distributed throughout. Between the wooded-steppe zone and taiga, there is a transitional zone—the subtaiga—on the north-facing slopes at a height of 1,320 to 2,310 feet. It is characterized by deciduous and mixed forests and owes its existence to the activity of man. In the subtaiga there are two types of forests: (1) temporary birch-aspen forests which replace the dark coniferous taiga species when they are destroyed by fire and cutting, and (2) remnants of unchanged taiga. Swampy, solid, secondary birch-aspen forests predominate with an admixture of bird cherry, mountain ash, and alder. Beneath their canopy, on soil covered with rotting leaves, a hydrophytic grassy vegetation grows. On the edges of the forests are moist, luxuriant meadows with tall forest grasses, such as reed grass (*Calamagrostis langsdorffii*), aconite (*Aconitum volubile*), *Allium victorialis,* and globeflower (*Trollius asiaticus*). On higher places, peony (*Paeonia anomala*), bushes of wild rose (*Rosa cinnamomea*), and spirea (*Spiraea chamaedryfolia*) grow. Beneath the forests, clayey soil is formed because of the proximity of the steppes and the retreat of the taiga under man's onslaught. Along riverbanks are impassable thickets of willow, bird cherry, mountain ash, currant, and alder. In river valleys, on bottomland meadows with muddy-boggy soil, grassy vegetation is luxuriant and stands as high as a man. Amid vast birch-aspen forests and fields are scattered islands of taiga surviving as spruce groves or pure pine plantings, under which slightly podzolic soils are developed.

The animal world of the subtaiga is made up of species which have reconciled themselves to man's intrusion. A few steppe species and some taiga inhabitants have adapted themselves to the changed conditions. The boar, river beaver, Siberian Caucasian stag, and sable, all of which were still living near Minusinsk in the middle of the nineteenth century, have disappeared. Of the mammals in the birch-aspen forests these have survived: the roe deer, flying squirrel, white hare, wolf, fox, polecat, ermine, and weasel. Facilities for nesting in the many forest islands, the nearness of man with his vast grain sowings, and the abundance of rivers, streams, and lakes have attracted more than a hundred species of birds into the subtaiga. Most common of them are: the black grouse *Lyrurus tetrix*), the Dahurian partridge (*Perdix dahurica*), oriole (*Oriolus oriolus*), and gray-headed woodpecker (*Picus canus*). In islands of taiga, it is sometimes possible to find animals that were formerly more widespread: bear, elk, grouse (*Tetrao urogallus*), black woodpecker (*Dryocopus martius*), and large tomtit (*Parus major*).

The taiga, or mountain strip of coniferous forests, occupies the principal area of the mountain region, on the north-facing slopes at a height of from 2,310 to 5,610 feet. The taiga on steep slopes of mountains is developed on coarse soil; on gentler slopes it is on clayey soil of a podzolic type; and in depressions and valleys it is on peat-bog soil. Most prevalent on the lower north-facing slopes is the moist fir–pine–spruce taiga with the addition of aspen, birch, and balsam poplar (*Populus suaveolens*), with a subgrowth of fir, spruce, and pine in rare patches of forest cover. The underbrush consists of typical shade-loving taiga species—bird cherry, mountain ash, honeysuckle, and alder. On the solid moss cover of green Bryophyta, club mosses, and ferns grow much red bilberry, whortleberry, and bog bilberry. In this ordinary taiga complex thrive shade-loving flowering plants such as pyrola. Many century-old trees have intertwined crowns which filter the sunlight to such an extent that dampness and darkness prevail. Monotonous crypto-podzolic soil is widespread beneath these forests.

On gentle slopes irrigated by the many springs are areas of tall-grass hydrophytic forest meadow. The springs which feed the meadows all summer receive their water from fields of melting snow, preserved under the forest canopy. Ground water lies at a depth of 8 to 30 inches. The floral makeup of the meadow is rather monotonous. Plants such as aconite (*Aconitum septentrionale*), larkspur (*Delphinium elatum*), globeflower (*Trollius asiaticus*), cow parsnip (*Heracleum dissectum*), and European hellebore (*Veratrum album*) ordinarily reach 16 to 24 inches in height, but some species are more than 6 feet high. Under the meadow, crypto- and weakly podzolic soil have developed with a thick humus layer. In broad valleys, swamps extend for distances of several miles beneath which peat-bog and peat-podzolic soils are developed.

At about 3,300 feet, deciduous trees disappear and mixed taiga is replaced by purely coniferous forests. Fir predominates, and pine grows in great quantity. Spruce prefers the narrow valleys of mountain brooks and the areas of coarse-rock talus where ground water is abundant. Under the canopy of the spruce forest, honeysuckle and currant grow above a solid ground cover of green mosses. There is some sphagnum moss, much whortleberry, and red bilberry. Farther up in the mountains meadows increase in number and acquire a conspicuous alpine character. At 4,125 feet and higher, plants such as the Altai violet are found. In the upper taiga zone—under the forest— typical podzolic soil prevails, linked with good irrigation of the disintegrated schists. Beneath the meadows, shallow, undeveloped, rocky soil of the podzolic variety is found. In the western taiga zone of the north-facing slope there are stands of light larch (along the Ana River) and park-type forests of pine-larch (along the Greater Abakan River) with a scanty undergrowth of honeysuckle, spirea, and grass.

In the upper section of the south-facing slope of the main Sayan range, spruce-fir taiga with an admixture of pine predominates on a podzolic soil. On rocky patches in the middle of the forest there are groupings of such lithophytes as Dahurian rhododendron, spirea (*Spiraea media*), and valerian (*Valeriana dubia*). In the lower section of the slope, mountain larch forests are developed. Pine forests may sometimes be found to contain wooded-steppe species, such as lady's-slipper. On chernozem-like soil of the rocky south-facing slopes

there are plants indigenous to the steppes, such as artemesia, phlomis, and other species.

In the taiga zone, burned areas are widespread. The growing-over of burns in the region of dark-coniferous taiga follows the same sequence as that of the Western Siberian taiga: it begins with a stage of overgrowth by beach grass, willow herb, and raspberry; and is followed by invasions of birch and aspen, spruce and fir, and finally pine. On the south-facing slope burned areas are covered rapidly by a thick undergrowth of larch and are soon repopulated by such taiga animals as the squirrel and the nutcracker.

The silence of the Sayan taiga, if there is no wind, is broken only by the roar of mountain creeks descending along their steep stony channels. The animal population of the taiga conducts its daily struggle for subsistence quietly and efficiently. In summer, wolverine and lynx —almost impossible to catch—and bear roam through the taiga. The sable, a bold and vigorous carnivore, is one of the common inhabitants of the Sayan taiga; its chief prey are hazel grouse, nutcracker, grouse, chipmunk, and squirrel. The range of a sable is about 7.6 to 9.6 square miles. In the strip of taiga adjoining the shores of lakes and streams live otter, ermine, weasel, polecat, and white hare. Squirrels and chipmunks occupy every niche. The cony dwells in rock waste. Stag and musk deer prefer the rocky banks of the upper sections of mountain rivers.

The bird life of the taiga is diversified. Grouse and their broods forage among the berry bushes, nightly seeking protection in the bushy spruce and firs. Hazel grouse, calling to one another, wander in flocks among the willow thickets. Double-snipes and snipes peck at the shore mud in search of food. River ducks feed and sleep in the sedge and horsetail near the shore. The predatory osprey, the goldeneye, and the merganser obtain fish from the rivers and lakes. The ousel (*Cinclus cinclus lencogaster*) dives into the water for insects. The falcon (*Falco peregrinus*) and other carnivora hunt waterfowl.

In the rivers are found grayling and salmon

(*Salmo thymallus*), burbot, and miller's thumb (*Cottus sibiricus*). As soon as the ice clears, many of the fish go upstream along small creeks where they pass the entire summer in deep holes. Lakes contain a larger number of fish species, including whitefish, dace, perch and pike.

When summer passes, the inhabitants of the taiga begin to prepare themselves for winter. Toward the end of August many have already moulted, matured, and gathered their strength. Some get ready to hibernate, others secure stores for the coming winter. Birds which migrate gradually set off for warmer regions. Flocks of bullfinches fly through the taiga, feeding on the berries of mountain ash. Flocks of finches hover about burned-over areas in search of birch seeds. Nuthatches with their broods look for insects. Long-tailed tomtits roam through recent mowings. Jays, nutcrackers, and cuckoos frantically rob pine groves, gathering stores for winter. At the end of August the first snow falls in the lowlands. Rabbits and weasels begin to bleach out, ermine and polecats start to mature. The thin summer fur of the sable changes from an unassuming light ocher-brown to a luxuriant winter coat with a brown-black hue. In September ice masses float along the rivers, streams and shallow lakes are covered by ice, and the exodus of geese, ducks, and other waterfowl commences. Fish return from the shallow rivers and spend the winter in deep holes along the large rivers.

By October, winter has begun in the Sayan taiga. Reindeer descend from the high-mountain zone, abandoning the safety of the snow-covered peaks for the comparative warmth and abundant fodder of the taiga, where they are preyed upon by lynxes, wolverines, and large packs of red wolves. Stags gather in herds of up to twenty head, eating grass which they dig out from under the snow with their hooves. They remain all winter on a single area of 10 to 15 acres. Carnivora such as sable and wolverine are active throughout the winter. Birds remaining in the taiga have adapted themselves to the winter conditions. Nuthatches, during warm, calm days, hunt insects

and their larvae, and at night seek protection in the hollows of trees. Hazel grouse, which subsist on birch and willow shoots, gather in small flocks and fly out to forage with the first rays of the morning sun, nestling in the snow at dusk to spend the night. Wood grouse also sleep in the snow but feed in the pines, eating the needles. Jays, nutcrackers, and cuckoos, in winter, live on stores gathered in autumn.

In April, moulting begins and the antlers of the stag grow. In spring all the winter wool of the sable gradually drops out, being replaced by that of summer. At the end of April the sable young are born and by mid-July they are big enough to fend for themselves. National game preserves have been established for the protection of the valuable sable and stag.

High-Mountain Zone

The high-mountain zone begins at an altitude of 4,950 feet and extends upward to a maximum of 8,250 feet. At a height of approximately 4,620 feet the pine–spruce–fir taiga is replaced by high-mountain sparse forests of pine and fir, among which are scattered subalpine meadows. Solitary crooked pines 8 feet tall, and impoverished firs converted into compact green bushes cling to slopes of small valleys most protected from the cold mountain winds. In the sparse forest, the grassy vegetation is typically taiga, and has many representatives of the meadow vegetation such as globeflower; but on rocky soils, *Rhododenron chrysanthum* and the herb *Bergenia crassifolia* grow in great quantity. In depressions, bushes of fragrant rhododenron (*Rhododendron fragrans*) with redolent delicate-rose blossoms are found in great numbers. Peaty-podzolic soil with a thick peat layer is developed under the sparse forest. The sparse forest ends in a belt of scrub alder (*Alnus fruticosa*), the knotty trunks of which together form a barrier about five feet tall, edged by thickets of dwarf birch.

Subalpine and alpine meadows are less prominent here than in the neighboring Altai, and the proportion of alpine species common to the arctic region is 55 per cent, as compared to that of the Altai (39 per cent). The composition of the subalpine meadows is rather diverse—both the lower meadows and the high-mountain tundras are represented by such species as: *Parnassia palustria, Allium victorialis,* globeflower (*Trollius asiaticus*), columbine (*Aquilegia glandulosa*), and swertia (*Swertia obtusa*).

The alpine meadows are scattered on slopes that are sheltered from the wind and well irrigated by springs and melting patches of snow. Meadow flowers include the primrose (*Primula elatior*), violet (*Viola altaica*), gentian (*Gentiana altaica*), and dragon's head (*Dracocephalum altaiense*). Certain forest plants, such as globeflower, grow, but their growth is dwarfed. In the moister depressions grow marsh marigold (*Caltha palustris*) and cotton grass (*Eriophorum alpinum*). Under meadows with good drainage, mountain meadow soil is developed; but in spots with surplus moisture the

soil is boggy. The high-mountain tundras are not conspicuous.

The large amount of precipitation, the abundance of fog enveloping the tops of mountains, long-lying patches of melting snow, negligible drainage, and slight evaporation all create favorable conditions for the moss-lichen mountain tundra which gives a dismal coloring to the bald-mountain landscape. Scattered on the basic moss-lichen cover are specimens of flowering alpine plants, such as lousewort (*Pedicularis oederi*), lloydia (*Lloydia serotina*), gentians, and violets. In depressions, patches of fine-leafed dwarf birch and miniature willow bushes (*Salix myrsinites*) grow, with brown, projecting catkins equal in height to the rest of the plant. Under this moss-lichen cover, shallow tundra soil of a swamp type has developed. On the more open slopes, there is a rocky mountain tundra. The stones are covered with lichens which lend a gray tone to the tundra. In great numbers, *Rhododenron chrys-*

Fig. 8-12. Kashkara (*Rhododendron chrysanthum*) from the high mountain belt of the Western Sayan.

anthum with profuse white-yellow flowers, characteristic of these areas, are found pressed to the earth. A few flowering plants adorn the bare mountain tops. They are scattered amid fragments of rock along cracks and do not even form beds. Beneath the rocky tundras is found shallow, slightly moist soil with a thin upper layer of peat.

The fauna of the high-mountain zone varies sharply in composition and population density according to seasons. In summer the high-mountain zone is covered with meadow and tundra vegetation and is fanned by cool winds which mitigate the sultriness and carry off mosquitoes and gnats. Thus it attracts many animals and provides good pasture for wild ungulates of the Sayan. On the exposed, rocky bald-peaks covered with mosses and lichens, herds of reindeer pasture. Musk deer graze everywhere incessantly during the short summer, fattening up for the winter, when food is scant. The Siberian stag often comes here from the sparse high-mountain forests. In wild, craggy places, mountain goats may be seen

clinging to sheer cliffs and rocky patches (e.g., near the Yenisei gap through Western Sayan). Along with the deer resides their most malicious enemy, the red wolf (*Canis alpinus*). Bears often feed in the zone. In rocky patches there are found countless conies, or pikas, and mice.

The more common birds of the high-mountain zone are mountain water pipit (*Anthus spinoletta blackistoni*), and snow pheasant (*Tetraogallus altaicus*). Ptarmigan (*Lagopus mutus nadezdae*) may often be seen near patches of snow, ordinarily nesting in the tundra of the north.

Snowless areas in the bald-peaks offer shelter and food to ungulates during the spring and summer, but in winter icy winds force them to descend to the taiga, which is warmer and rich in food. Only musk deer remain near the timber line during the winter. Conies and mice live off their summer stores underneath the snow. The red wolf and the sable are the only animals which range the high-mountain zone in winter.

THE EASTERN SAYAN

The Eastern Sayan is a mountainous region located south of Central Siberia and extending in a northwest direction for more than 600 miles. The Eastern Sayan forms the watershed between the systems of the Angara and upper Yenisei rivers. Morphologically, it is a high upland, deeply disected by river valleys, gently inclined to the northeast from the main water divide towards the Central Siberian Plateau and steeply dropping to the southwest—toward Lake Khubsugual (Kosogol) and the upper Yenisei. Geologically and orographically, the Eastern Sayan is sharply demarcated from the Central Siberian Plateau in the northeast by a scarp 1,320 feet high. The Eastern Sayan is divided from the neighboring mountain system Khangay and Tannu-Ola in the southwest by the Selenga graben, the basin of Lake Khubsugal-Dalay, and the vast Tuva Basin. At the Tunkin graben, the Eastern Sayan joins the

Pre-Baikal mountain region. The latter, with a northeast trend in its many ranges, is set at a right angle to the predominating tectonic elements of the Eastern Sayan. Its axial range, Pogranichnyy or Greater Sayan, drops down and ends at Obo-Sarym Pass. On the west, the Minusinsk Valley borders the mountain region, and separates it from the Kuznetsk Ala-Tau and the Western Sayan.

The Eastern Sayan is superficially uniform in relief and altitude, but its origin and disposition of its structural elements divide it into two sharply diverse parts: the western and the eastern. The western part (up to the Iya River) is bounded on the north by a zone from Krasnoyarsk to Nizhneudinsk and on the south by the Tuva Basin, which has fault lines of a northwest and north-northwest strike. Four plateau levels extend in these directions with varying relief forms. The first, and marginal

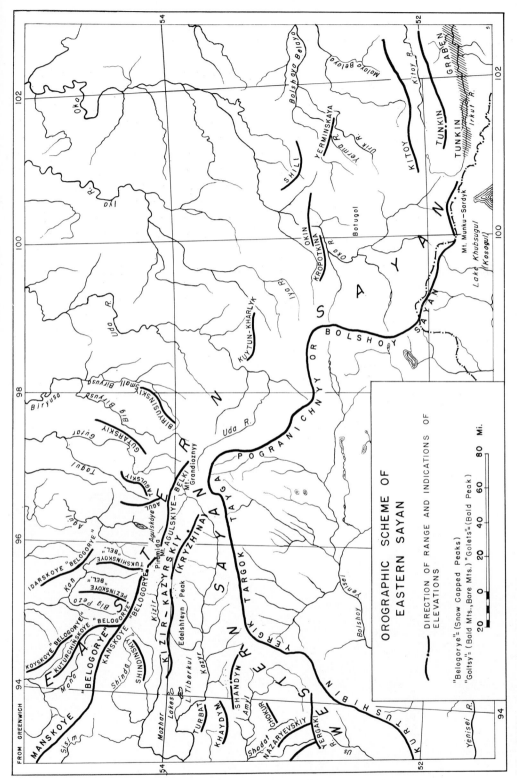

Map 8-III. Orographic scheme of Eastern Sayan.

level is a plateau 40 to 50 miles wide consisting of erosional mountains 3,300 to 4,125 feet high. Rivers have cut the plateau into a complex system of mountain ridges of varying orientation and form. The depth of dissection is not more than 1,650 feet, but the maturity of the landscape indicates extensive lateral erosion. The second level of the plateau has average heights of 4,950 to 5,950 feet, and individual summits reaching to 7,250 feet, which rise above the timber line. The third level contains the most representative type of relief in the Eastern Sayan—extensive flat watersheds called "white mountains." In the west these white mountains are found even inside the limits of the second level. The white mountains receive their name from the abundant patches of snow which lie on them for prolonged periods of the year and from the large areas that are covered by white lichens. The watershed areas are an ancient peneplain which has undergone dissection. Above the over-all surface rise low individual summits and ridges which are covered with alluvia; they are composed of the more stable rocks. In places the plateau is cut up by

deep erosional river valleys with steep slopes. The third level breaks off at the second with a distinct cliff. The individual white mountains have their own names: beginning at Pyramid Mountain (7,445 feet) in the Agul white-capped mountains is the Kanskoye white mountain (5,725 feet), a continuation of which is the lengthy Manskoye white mountain (4,950 feet). The Eastern Sayan reaches the Yenisei and ends in the Kuysumy Mountains, at the northern end of which, near Krasnoyarsk, is a national preserve. In this preserve are 35 magnificent tall rocks with fantastic forms called *stolby*, pillars. They are weathered intrusions of seamed granite and syenite rocks. The preserve is famous for its beauty, and is visited yearly by tens of thousands of tourists. The fourth level, 6 to 12 miles in width, rises sharply above the Sayan upland to a height of more than 6,600 feet. Here and there are small suspended glaciers and traces of ancient glaciation are everywhere. The range has alpine relief forms; vertical dissection exceeds 3,300 feet. Toward Uda Range in the sources of the Kazyr it adjoins the intensely dissected Kizyr-

Fig. 8-13. "Pillars," a state-owned forest.

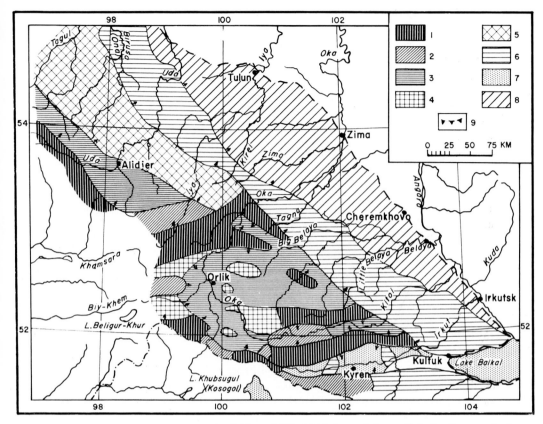

Map 8-IV. Relief of Eastern Sayan: 1—Ridges 8,250–9,900 feet, alpine relief; 2—Steppe of plateau 7,260–9,240 feet (heights affected by last glaciation); 3—Steppe of plateau 5,940 to 7,260 feet; 4—High parts of this steppe, to 8,250 feet, were affected by last glaciation; 5—Steppe of plateau 4,950–5,940 feet; 6—Border steppe of plateau, from 3,300 to 4,125 feet in west, from 4,620 to 4,950 feet in center, from 3,300 feet and lower in east; 7—Axial depressions of Baikal-Kosogol heights; 8—Cheremkhovo-Kansk depression; 9—Main fault lines.

Kazyr (Kryzhina) Range. It is highest in its eastern part, in the so-called Figuristye Belki, where Grandioznyy Peak is located.

The eastern part of the Eastern Sayan has relief based on wide tectonic zones. The northeastern border zone has flat crests surrounded by peaks, some of which reach 5,280 feet. The surface descends gently to the north and then falls as a steep cliff for several hundred feet. The central plateau of the Eastern Sayan rises 7,260 feet from the basin of the upper Oka. Its highest point reaches 8,580 feet, and its flat valleys dip to approximately 6,270 feet. In the southwestern part of the plateau the surface of

the ancient peneplain is well preserved, as are the many areas of Tertiary basalt cover. The plateau lies almost wholly above the timber line. The uniform landscape is unusual for elevations of more than 7,260 feet. The streams flow slowly in very broad gentle valleys and meander intricately within marshy swampy banks; the rock talus alternates with swampy depressions. The central plateau is surrounded by alpine mountains: to the north it is guarded by the long Oka and Erminsk alpine mountains (to 9,900 feet), which lie adjacent to the eroded surface of the narrow Shili ridge. To the west, it is bounded by the Uda and Great

Sayan. The plateau consists of three sections, each with a different origin. One has elevations of 10,560 feet, with sharp alpine relief and small glaciers; the other two are high borderland levels with datum marks at 7,260 to 9,240 and 9,240 to 9,900 feet. To the south lie the broad, intensely dissected and picturesque ranges of the Kitoy and Tunka Belki bald-mountains which rise to a height of 10,890 feet. They rise high above the bottom of the river valleys; for example, the summits of the Tunka bald-mountains are 4,950 to 8,250 feet above the Irkut Valley. Between the Tunka bald-mountains and the massif of Munku-Sardyk is the extensive and relatively depressed plateau Nukhu-Daban. The ranges have alpine relief forms: sharp pyramidal peaks, razorback ridges, dissected cirques and gorges. The mountain group Munku-Sardyk is a tectonic continuation of the Tunka bald mountains, although it is separated from them by the erosional valley of the Irkut. The mountains terminate in the east in a system of tectonic depressions extending from Baikal to the upper reaches of the Irkut.

The Eastern Sayan reaches its greatest height (11,453 feet) at Munku-Sardyk peak lying north of Lake Khubsugul. The high Tunkin and Kitoy Mountains extend in an approximate east-west direction and northwest of them lies Botugol, an isolated bald peak 7,672 feet in height. Farther to the north, in the system of the Oka and Greater Belaya rivers, are alpine-type mountain ranges (Okin, Yermin, and Shili). At the sources of the Uda, Biryusa, and Kazyr rivers, at the junction with the Western Sayan, is the recently raised Mount Ary-Dag (9,900 feet) area. From it, the Eastern Sayan spreads out to the northwest, where it may be distinguished by the nature of its more or less isolated orographic units: (1) the high and greatly dissected Kizyr-Kazyr or Kryzhina Range, extending in an east-west direction between the Kizyr and Kazyr rivers (Yenisei system) and reaching an 8,830 feet altitude on Edelshtein Peak; (2) Agul Belki mountains with sharp alpine relief; (3) Kanskoye Mountains (6,600 to 8,250 feet), Manskoye Moun-

tains (4,950 to 5,280 feet), and Idarskoye white mountains.

Geologic History

The oldest sedimentary and igneous rocks of the Eastern Sayan are Pre-Cambrian slates and limestones, which extend in a northwest direction as separate wedges, bounded by sharp tectonic breaks. The entire Pre-Cambrian mass is gathered in steep, sometimes reversed folds of a west-northwest strike, often crumpled and twisted, complicated by shallow second-order folding, and by slight upthrusts and overthrusts. Large sections in the central part and at the periphery are formed of Cambrian shales, limestones, conglomerates, and different extrusives. Two stages of intense Caledonian folding in the Silurian Period gathered the Cambrian deposits into folds. Marine sediments of the Devonian Period are found in separate islands. Intense volcanic activity occurred in the beginning of the Devonian Period, with the eruption of molten syenitic rock. The foundation of Eastern Sayan was established as a rigid block; it reacted to further orographic movement only by shearing of rocks and by fractures, with which the intrusion of igneous rocks is linked. Mesozoic folding did not take place in Eastern Sayan. Jurassic continental deposits were not widespread, but are found in separate spots in valley-grabens and on the tops of bare peaks, occurring horizontally on eroded ancient sedimentary series set on end (for example, in the basin of the Oka River on Ospin bald mountain). Tertiary deposits are found in a few places: in the upper stretches of the Oka and Urik, on the Tissa River, clay shales contain the fossil remains of 30 species of Miocene plants, and outcrops of brown coal have been found.

During the prolonged continental period the mountain region was converted into a peneplain. Associated with the alpine orogeny was an upheaval of the eastern part of Eastern Sayan which faulted and partly thrust the rocks onto the Central Siberian Plateau. Lines of overthrust folding are detectable over considerable distances and have a northwest strike, apparently conforming to primary Pre-Cambrian folding. Through fissures formed during the uplift there have issued great quantities of basalt. Extrusions have continued to occur up to the glacial period, and possibly even later as well; for example, on Ospin bald peak, basalts overlap Tertiary deposits. In certain places, as in the Tunkin Mountains, recent upheaval has had large scope. Basalt deposits have been disrupted by faults, sharply disconnected, and set on two completely different levels; some parts have remained on the bottom of the graben, and others have been uplifted, to be found as fragments on some bald-mountain summits.

Many mineral deposits are linked with igneous and sedimentary rocks. Along the lower tributaries of the Kizyr River are rich gold ores associated with contact zones of granites and limestones. The gold deposits are noted for their richness and for their large nuggets. The Irbin deposit of magnetite and hematite (north of the mouth of the Kizyr), distinguished by high content and great purity of metal (up to 60.6 per cent) and with total reserves not below 20 million tons, is related to contact zones of syenite and extrusive rocks. The upper valley of the Biryusa River is the richest mica-bearing region of the USSR, with mica content of from 1 to 2 per cent, with the highest grade rock yielding flakes 8 by 12 inches in size. The mica (Muscovite) is linked with pegmatite veins, intersecting gneisses, and crystalline schists. The Eastern Sayans contain the sole deposits in the USSR of valuable nephrite (jade) stone. Distinguished for high quality and beautiful tints, these are scattered as rock waste along the river valleys, and crop out amid crystalline schists in the Tunkin and Kitoy bald mountains. The deposits were formed by the recrystallization of ancient basic extrusives and their tuffs. The Aliberov graphite deposit on Botugol bald peak is famous for

Fig. 8-14. Large cirque with snow field on Kizir-Kazirsk ridge.

its high quality. It was formed by contact metamorphism when syenitic magma intruded into Pre-Cambrian clay shales and limestones rich in carbon. Good construction stone, especially marble, is found everywhere.

Traces of extensive and intense ancient glaciation are encountered literally at every step. It is said that Eastern Sayan experienced at least two glacial epochs in the Quaternary Period. Indications of more ancient glaciation are large glacial troughs, sometimes lying transverse to the modern river network, and elevated more than 500 feet above the level of the bottoms of the glacial troughs of the last glaciation. In the first glacial epoch the glaciers descended far into the depths of taiga valleys (in Kizyr Valley a typical glacial landscape prevails from an altitude of 1,320 feet, containing moraine-dammed Mozhar lakes studded with the rocky islands that represent typical *roches moutonees*). In Irkut Valley, glaciers of the first glaciation descended to an altitude of 2,689 feet. Traces of glacial activity, because of their freshness and direct connection with the sources of past glaciers, are undoubtedly related to the recent period of glaciation. The remains of these have survived as small modern glaciers and firm fields. Moraine deposits have only just recently begun to be worked over by the modern hydrographic network, as, for example, at the sources of the Iya River. The snow line at the time of the last glaciation, just as at the present time, had a slight gradient to the west; that is, the western part was subjected to more intense glaciation than the eastern, despite the lower altitudes in the west.

The recent glaciation bore an alpine character. Valley glaciers reached lengths of several dozen miles and, creeping along narrow and deep valleys notched during the preceding interglacial epoch, developed them into deep and comparatively narrow glacial troughs. The glacier in the Irkut Valley descended to an altitude of 3,355 feet and had a length of over 36 miles and a depth of about 1,000 feet. In the valleys of the Kitoy, Belaya, and Oka, the foot of the glaciers descended to altitudes of 4,031 feet. Glaciers from Munku-Sardyk extended to

Lake Khubsugul. In the Manskoye-Kanskoye district great glaciers filled almost all the large valleys, reaching 96 miles in length along the Uda, and forming typical glacial troughs with walls 990 to 1,320 feet high. The trough bottoms are covered with moraine deposits which form chaotic heaps of hills 100 to 130 feet high, amid which lie moraine lakes (e.g. Greater Agul with a length of 6.6 miles), many of which have since been drained. The peaceful shallow streams flowing here do not correspond in size to the old glacial valley containing them. The lateral tributaries for the most part have hanging valleys and open onto the main valley at heights of 660 to 825 feet above its bottom. Glacial valleys originate in deep cirques, sometimes set on three and four levels and forming natural cirque stairways.

Traces of erosional rejuvenation are noticeable on rivers (for example, the deep dissection of valleys in the period previous to the last glaciation) and indicate a recent upheaval of the mountain region. The upheaval of Sayan undoubtedly continues even today, as manifested by: (1) fresh and deep intrenchment of valleys since the last glaciation; (2) increasing number of earthquakes, and (3) the presence of mineral springs linked with recent fractures, such as the hot carbonate springs (104°F) and chalybeate springs in the Arshan Tunkinsk, and the springs in the system of the Biryusa and Kitoy rivers. Owing to recent rejuvenation, the upper course of the Kazyr River has almost cut off the eastern part of the Kizyr-Kazyrskiy Range from the Yergik-Targok-Tayga Range and approaches close to the sources of the Uda, which it will probably capture in the near geologic future. The newest erosional cycle has not even spared young basalts, which at present survive only on water divides, protecting the ancient peneplain from erosion.

Although it is not extensive, one of the factors in the formation of relief in the Eastern Sayan is modern glaciation. Affected by glaciation are the higher mountain groups of the watershed of the upper Yenisei and Angara from Munku-Sardyk to the sources of the Iya River and the eastern part of the Kizyr-

Kazyrskiy Range. On the highest peak of Munku-Sardyk, there are two glaciers—the northern and the southern, partly united by their firn fields. The larger, northern glacier occupies 0.25 square mile and has a maximum thickness of about 280 feet, and descends in two tongues to 9,160 feet. The glacier drops steeply, forming a regular terminal moraine. The lower part is tinted a bright purple color by colonies of algae (*Sphaerella nivalis*). The smaller southern glacier has a firn field completely devoid of a tongue and lies in a valley that opens to the southeast. The snow line on the north-facing slope is 9,240 feet and on the south-facing slope 10,461 feet. The proximity of Lake Khubsugul whose water surface occupies about 1,158 square miles influences the feeding of the glaciers of Munku-Sardyk. In summer the diurnal lake breeze carries moist air from the lake to the mountain range, thus sustaining these glaciers.

In the eastern part of Kizyr-Kazyrskiy Range, in a broad step-like cirque, is the largest glacier in Eastern Sayan, Stalnova Glacier—1.8 miles long and 1.2 miles wide—which descends in three tongues to a lake below it. In this same range, below the sources of the Kazyr, is a hanging glacier, Solovyeva, with a maximum depth of 330 feet. Small glaciers and large snow fields are also found in other parts of Eastern Sayan. Noteworthy is the exceptionally low snow line in the Kizyr-Kazyr Range (6,600 to 7,590 feet in height, or 1,650 feet lower than on Munku-Sardyk), indicating heavy precipitation.

Geomorphologic Character

The stages in the development of Eastern Sayan's relief are almost analogous to those of Western Sayan, but early glaciation was more

Fig. 8-15. Cirque Lake, source of the White River in the Kizir-Kazirsk Lake.

intensive. Modern glaciers continue to mold relief in the higher parts of the Eastern Sayan. The surfaces of an ancient Tertiary peneplain have survived and are covered by young extrusive basalts.

The mountain region of Eastern Sayan, despite its deep dissection by erosion and glacial activity, is an ancient peneplain raised to great heights, with rocky outcrops above the timber line. The general northerly trend of the hydrographic network responds to the weak, but nonetheless perceptible, northerly slope of the peneplain. It is obvious that the original peneplain has been raised in the region of the axial part of the Sayan. The broad, flat tract along the Kanskoye River stands in the north at maximum heights of 3,960 to 4,290 feet; farther south the land rises and reaches a height of 5,610 to 5,940 feet; at the sources of the Kanskoye and Agul rivers the peneplain surfaces lie at 6,600 to 6,930 feet, and the surfaces of mesas on them stand at 7,920 feet.

The Sayan, has almost level water divides with random mountain-mesas projecting to heights of 990 and 1,320 feet above their surfaces. Sometimes these are rounded or flat-topped hills separated by eroded valleys from the general mass of snow-capped mountains. They represent residual sections of the original peneplain. It is impossible to distinguish any clearly expressed directions of the watershed ranges. Individual high mountains appear as upland plains, elevated above the timber line; they are unusually level, smooth and swampy. Only individual high bald peaks such as Botugol have the regular shape of a flat dome.

Contributing to the preservation of the ancient peneplain was its flooding by basaltic lavas, which formed a uniform cover with a thickness not exceeding a few dozen yards. Basalts form residual mountains hundreds of square yards in area on most of the water divides, and are visible over long distances because of their conspicuous black color. The basalts lying on horizontal surfaces and forming upright dark scarps striated by vertical cracks contribute to: (1) the table-shaped character of the hills and (2) the step-like appearance of the valley edges, owing to the uneven stability of the basalts and the horizons of tuffs and breccias alternating with them. There are several dozen such steps with a width of 16 to 33 feet, indicating the variable intensity of volcanic activity, and its prolonged character.

In places one encounters sharp alpine relief forms with saw-like crests; high, pointed peaks; steep slopes; and an abundance of crags. For example, Kitoy and Tunkin bald mountains, and also Munku-Sardyk, Kizyr-Kazyr, Agul Belki, and Oka chain, and Uda and Great Sayan ranges are sharply contrasted with the smooth relief of the neighboring range in Trans-Baikal, the Khamar-Daban Range. In its eastern more uplifted section, the Kryzhina Range contains alpine forms. The Agul Mountains are similar in character, and are no less bold in their contours nor less picturesque in their relief than any region of the Altai or Alps.

The alpine character of the highest ranges is not in contradiction, however, with the over-all massive character of the Eastern Sayan. From a high point one may see that all these pyramidal peaks reach approximately one level. Even here some sections of the ancient peneplain have survived. Sharp alpine forms have been carved as a result of the destructive work of ice and snow during the period of more intensive glaciation. Today, it is possible to trace all the stages in the process of glacial quarrying, from the occasional deep cirques cut in at the periphery of horizontal masses, to the complete glacial erosion of an area. Often separate cirques gradually cut into the mass of snow-capped mountains and their receding walls converge. Sharp crests are created near the points of convergence, and sometimes triangular peaks are formed between the cirques. The water divide between adjacent cirques in the upper stretches of the Uda and Kazyr rivers is a sharp saddle about 0.6 of a mile in width. Such a relief is formed by the disintegration of the walls separating cirques and the subsequent formation of a deep saddle-shaped mountain pass between neighboring river systems. A typical divide of this sort is the deep and long pass which intersects the bordering Sayan mass and connects the system of the Usa River to the upper Yenisei system.

Some parts of the ancient peneplain have been subjected to greater dissection than others, because they were uplifted to a greater height. The narrowness of the upraised sections also contribute to their rapid erosion. Tunkin Mountains, elevated by fault dislocations to a great height, did not exceed 18 to 21 miles in width. Subsequently, the surface of their peneplain was almost completely destroyed, owing to the thickness of glaciation and the rapidity and intensity of erosion. Only the small level sections on the tops of mountain peaks withstand as remnants of the peneplain. The northern part of Eastern Sayan bears features typical of an intermediate-mountain landscape. It has uniform watershed levels rising in general from the periphery to the center of the mountain region. In some places the mountain landscape acquires the more gentle character of a high-mountain plain. Here it resembles an old relief, containing occasional scattered buttes—outcrops of the harder rocks (quartzites, or granites) which have withstood erosion. Near the deep valleys the uplands are extensively dissected. The depth of dissection, however, does not exceed 1,650 feet.

Morphologically, the rocks of the river valleys have greater significance in directing the stream than the primary stratum of the mountain region. In contrast with the Western Sayan, lengthwise and transverse valleys are not predominant. Some rivers have cut through and others coincide with the strike of the folds. Beginning on the slopes of the high mountain massifs, the river arteries fan outwards, creating a radical grouping of the valleys.

In every large river valley of the Eastern Sayan, one may note three basic divisions: (1) The upper section of the valley is carved into a broad glacial trough, containing a quiet flowing river, with traces of glacial work so fresh that they would seem to have been left by a recently retreated glacier. (2) The glacial trough is succeeded by a narrow canal-shaped section, to 3,300 feet deep, where the river,

taking on the character of a turbulent mountain torrent, cuts intensively into the mountain mass, forming rapids and waterfalls. Lateral tributaries have not succeeded in cutting their gradients to the main channel, so their valleys hang at a height of 577 to 660 feet. (3) Farther on, the valley widens and becomes accessible to pack travel. Emerging from the narrow gateways of its valley to the spaciousness of the plain-hill expanses abutting the mountains, the river loses velocity and deposits part of its suspended clastic material in islands divided by a series of channels. The greatest role in molding the morphologic character of the valleys is played by selective erosion.

Climate

Little is known about the climate of Eastern Sayan. Only the extreme eastern part has been studied. It has an Eastern Siberian continental climate: severe winters (January average from $-1.8°F$ at Arshan to $-14°F$ at Tunka) with many hours of sunshine, warm cloudy summers (July average from 57°F at Okin village to 62.7°F at Tunka village), and a temperature range of 146.4 degrees (93.2°F to $-53.2°F$). In this part of the mountain region temperature inversion is clearly expressed: Arshan (2,946 feet), lying 12 miles from an only 557 feet higher than Tunka (2,389 feet), is warmer in winter but colder in summer. The January average increases and the July average decreases according to rises in elevation. At Mondy (4,290 feet), lying 1,900 feet above Tunka, the January average is 9.12 degrees higher, but on the other hand, July is 3.8 degrees colder, owing to the high elevation. As would be expected, the location of the villages also influences the temperature average: For example, Okin (4,210 feet), at the bottom of a mountain depression enclosed on all sides, is colder than Mondy, lying at almost the same height (4,290 feet) on a slope with a southern exposure.

Continentality is shown in the daily temperature fluctuations: For instance, in Mondy during half of June the temperature during the day reached 90.5°F and at night fell to 61°F. On Botugol bald mountain (7,672 feet) summer lasts two and a half months: from the middle of June to the first of September. Nights in summer are very cold: in the first half of August the temperature drops to 14°F. Snow may fall even in the middle of June. Only at the end of summer does the snow melt completely, and in 15 or 20 days new snow falls. The snow cover is established by the end of September. On the bare mountain, permafrost is prevalent. Rivers freeze through to the bottom.

The small amount of precipitation, especially in the winter months, is characteristic of the Eastern Siberian climate. The annual precipitation varies from 10.8 inches (Okin) to 19.0 inches (Arshan), and even on Botugol bald mountain is only 12 to 16 inches. Toward the southeast, which is influenced by the climate of Mongolia, the annual amount of precipitation decreases and the percentage of summer precipitation increases. Thus, at Mondy: summer 8.5 inches (71 per cent), winter 0.16 inch (1 per cent), spring 1.5 inches (13 per cent), fall 1.8 inches (15 per cent). In places lying farther from Mongolia the percentage of winter precipitation increases; for example, 3 per cent in Okin. Even high in the mountains summer precipitation is frequent but light. The greatest number of days is in summer and the least in winter: at Mondy during the three summer months there were 40 days of rain (11, 16, and 13 days, respectively); during the three winter months there were 5 days of precipitation (2, 2, and 1, respectively). From 9 to 10 per cent of the annual precipitation is snow. The depth of the snow cover is negligible (in Mondy up to 0.4 inch). However, in the ranges of the western part of Eastern Sayan, heavy snows fall which do not melt off till June or July, and in places remain almost the year round.

Southward toward the borders of Mongolia cloudiness decreases from 60 to 45 per cent. The greatest cloudiness is in summer, the least in winter. Thus, in Mondy, with an average annual cloudiness of 40 per cent, the maximum cloudiness in July reaches 62 per cent, and the minimum in February drops to 20 per cent. The vegetative period in the eastern part of Sayan fluctuates from 147 days (Tunka) to 125 days (Mondy).

As in Western Sayan, there are three basic types of vegetation: steppe, taiga, and high-mountain vegetation.

The outstanding characteristics of the soil cover of the Eastern Sayan are its swampiness, which is unusual for mountain regions, and the extreme slowness of its formation. The latter is explained by: (1) the northerly location of the Sayan among mountain regions of southern Siberia; (2) the wide distribution of subsoil which is impermeable to water owing to the presence of permafrost; and (3) the weak decomposition of vegetation resulting from the brevity of the summer.

Predominant over most of the Sayan is an undeveloped rubbly soil. At heights of 3,300 to 5,900 feet is found a distinctive humus-eluvial soil having a thick, partly decomposed peat layer with little podzolization. The deep layers of the soil profile are developed from rocks rich in basic oxides. Weakly podzolic soil poor in humus content has a wide distribution on crystalline rocks in the forest belt. Peat-bog soil is developed primarily on the bald-mountain tundras, at the upper reaches of rivers, and on gentle north-facing slopes under a moist moss taiga. Meadow-bog soil with a thick layer of humus is found under meadows in the river valleys, and is replaced on dry meadows by turf-meadow soil. On limestones, particularly on south-facing slopes, the warmer and more fertile humus-carbonate soil, used for tillage and gardening, has a wide distribution. A chestnut soil which is not fully formed and is poor in humus may be found on the low terraces of open, broad valleys (for example, the Oka, below the mouth of the tributaries Sentsa or Irkut in the Mondy region. It is developed in sand and gravel under good drainage conditions and with the absence or deep position of permafrost.

The Eastern Sayan mountain region (approximately as far as the Iya River) is divided into two parts: The southwestern is moist, having a thick snow cover and no permafrost; the northeastern is drier, since it has severe winters with little snow and contains permafrost lying close to the surface. The eastern half of the mountain region differs from the preceding in having very little precipitation and an extremely irregular distribution of it according to season. This results in a corresponding variation in vegetation: in the lower half of the forest belt is forest vegetation of an xerophilous nature, and in the high-mountain valleys are small islands of steppe. In the lower forest belt of the western half of the region there is a predominance of dark-coniferous taiga of pine, spruce, and fir, but higher up in the mountains the difference between vegetation of the northeastern and southwestern parts is pronounced. Only in the northeastern part is the swampy pine-larch taiga found. The subalpine pine groves have a forest-tundra character, and instead of subalpine or alpine meadows in the high-mountain zone, there is mountain tundra. In the eastern half of the Eastern Sayan there are pine groves on the lower south-facing slopes, mountain larch forests on the higher slopes, and above these—up to the high-mountain belt—a continuous strip of pine forest. Moreover, under conditions of a continental and dry climate of the Mongolian type, the vegetation belts extend higher up, and the timber line of the pine or larch forest rises from 5,115 feet in the west to 6,600 feet in the extreme southeast, with some trees found at a height of 6,960 feet.

Steppe Zone

Steppes in the lower part of the taiga zone may be found in the valley of the Oka River. These steppes are situated on rubbly slopes of southern, southwestern, and southeastern exposures and are influenced by the more northerly-lying Irkutsk-Balagansk wooded-steppe. Another variety of steppe is encountered at the sources of the rivers flowing from the main Sayan range; for example, steppes lie on terraces and slopes of moraine hills of the Mondy village district, and are influenced by the nearby Mongolian steppes. Typical steppe flora of a Mongolian appearance and makeup is found here, including *Smelowskia alba* and willow (*Salix caspica*). High in the mountains, steppe, forest, alpine, and bog-meadow species are mingled in confined areas. Mongolian feather grass grows alongside bog plants and mountain edelweiss. Steppes in the midst of a solid forest zone at 4,950 feet are sustained by local conditions: the southern location of the region, the openness of wide valleys, and the sandy terraces where ground waters lie deep. The south-facing slopes are especially favorable for steppe vegetation, because of their intense insolation and calcareous soil. The sandy soil, weak in humus, has a humus horizon of a cinnamon-chestnut color. It is covered by steppe mixed-grasses and herbs which are ordinarily indigenous to the more arid sections of the Trans-Baikal steppe zone. On steppe sections of the Oka River valley grow as many as 50 species of steppe plants; the more completely covered surfaces contain 40 to 60 per cent of steppe species, and the height of the grass stand is 8 to 10 inches. At the source of the Oka two basic types of steppe plants are found: (1) a meadow-mixed grass group and (2) a feather-grass group. In the first group are: meadow grass (*Poa botryoides*), koeleria (*Koeleria gracilis*), and crested wheat grass (*Agropyron cristatum*); among the mixed grasses are iris (*Iris flavissima*), gentian (*Gentiana macrophylla*), and Siberian edelweiss (*Leontopodium sibiricum*). The second group includes: feather grass (*Stipa decipiens*), cinquefoil (*Potentilla subacaulis*), *Artemisia frigida,* and steppe sedge (*Carex stenophylla*).

The fauna also has a steppe character: marmots and Locustidae may be found. The steppes are used as pasturage, because the rockiness of the slopes prevents mowing of the grasses. In winter the steppes are snowless; thus cattle may pasture on them the year round. Local varieties of livestock—Mongolian sheep, Mongolian oxen, and *sarlyki* (a hybrid of Tibetan yak with Mongolian cow)—adapted to the intricately dissected relief, clamber with ease along the steep slopes. They are well protected from the winter cold by thick fur.

Taiga Zone

To the Uda River, the vegetation of the western part of Eastern Sayan is analogous to the vegetation of Western Sayan. There is an unbroken distribution of dark-coniferous taiga, including pine, fir, and spruce; with pure pine forests growing along steep rocky slopes. Close to places inhabited by man the taiga is replaced by subtaiga with a predominance of deciduous plants; this in turn is succeeded by thin wooded-steppe forests of birch. The eastern part of the mountain region, which receives comparatively little precipitation, is occupied, in its lower zones, by woody vegetation of a more arid character. On the lower north-facing slopes are many stands of pine; higher up are mountain larch forests; and still farther up are solid forests of Siberian pine. The timber line, formed of larch-Siberian pine, is 6,270 feet (Mondy) to 6,600 feet (Botugol bald mountain), but individual trees are found at 6,930 feet in the Tunkin bald mountains.

In the southwestern part of the Eastern Sayan below 3,300 feet, the fir-spruce-pine taiga predominates with high grass on typical podzol or humus-eluvial soil. The trees grow to two levels: The first, 32 feet high, is comprised of spruce and pine; the second, thicker, and up to 100 feet high, is made up of fir, with frequently dead trees. The undergrowth is mountain ash, elder, meadowsweet, currant, raspberry, and occasionally spruce. Under the forest canopy is a dense and high (to 4 feet) grass stand. In the valleys is spruce-fir taiga on swamp-podzol and peat-gley soil. On humus-eluvial soil at 3,300 to 3,960 feet is the mixed fir-pine, moss shrub taiga. This taiga has an undergrowth of bird cherry, mountain ash, and currant, and an abundance of green mosses, but little grass cover. In the lowlands are peat bogs with sphagnum, cloudberry, and sundew. The forest belt terminates in a sparse subalpine forest of

fir or pine alternating with patches of subalpine meadows and undergrowths of rhododendron. The timber line is made up of pine and fir.

In the foothills of the northeastern part of the western half of the mountain region, sparse birch forests with mixed grass lie on the border of the mountain taiga with a forest-steppe plain. Many steppe species are found in the vegetation of the open places. Most of the forests have now been cut down and turned into fields to be used for grazing lands or hay fields. Higher up (2,640 to 3,300 feet), along the edges of the mountain region, is the pine–spruce–fir taiga on weakly podzolized, clayey soil with a moss-grass cover. On river terraces are thin larch forests with extensive sections of swampy meadows. Along the old rivers is a taiga consisting of spruce, pine, larch, and birch, and also there are sphagnum bogs with pine. On huge areas are extensive burns, now grown over with birch. At 3,300 to 3,960 feet there is a scrub taiga of sphagnum moss and pine and larch, with a thick moss cover and permafrost lying at a shallow depth; this taiga is developed on swampy and peat-humus soil. The south-facing slopes, which are rocky and insolated, are devoid of swamps and covered with drier larch forests and thick grassy vegetation. On the south-facing slopes made up of limestones is a shallow humus-carbonate soil that supports the growth of park-like larch forests, abundant grass cover, and geranium, *Allium victorialis,* and peony (*Paeonia anomala*). Characteristic of the valleys are thickets of scrub birch (*Betula fruticosa*), pea tree (*Caragan jubata*), and cinquefoil (*Potentilla fruticosa*). Between the swampy forests and flat tundras of the watersheds is a transitional strip grading in series from lichen-moss to subalpine to pine groves. The timber line is made up of larch and pine.

In the northern part, adjoining the Irkutsk-Balagansk wooded-steppe and birch forests, especially in river valleys (with the exception of the Oka Valley), are many dry pine groves on sand, sometimes with an admixture of Siberian larch. The groves are in the lower mountains, from 2,145 to 3,300 feet high. Pine groves with mixed grass cover are widespread. In this type of forest are found weakly developed underbrush, with solitary specimens of mountain ash, spirea, alder, willow, and rhododendron, with a grass cover of reed grass (*Calamagrostis arundinacea*), meadow grass (*Poa sibirica*), anemone (*Anemone narcissiflora*), and hawkweed (*Hieracium umbellatum*), and a rare moss ground cover. Under these forests are crypto-podzolic clayey soils, often lying on limestones. Less widespread are mossy pine groves and pine forests with highly developed undergrowth of scrub alder (*Alnus fruticosa*). Pine restoration takes place satisfactorily in all types of forest. A subgrowth of Siberian pine indicates that the pine has occupied these sites temporarily as a result of fires.

Above the pine forests, larch forests are predominant. On the slopes of northern, northwestern, and northeastern exposure a moist larch taiga is found, with solid lichen cover of reindeer moss and cetraria. Subgrowth in this type of forest includes pea tree (*Caragana jubata*), willows (*Salix arbuscula*), and much dwarf birch; and in the grass cover are saxifrage (*Saxifraga hirculus*), lloydia (*Lloydia serotina*), and primrose (*Primula farinosa*). These forests are capable of sustaining not only hundreds (as today), but thousands of reindeer. On the slopes of southern, eastern, and southeastern exposure larch forests grow with grassy undercover: the undergrowth on the drier slopes contains rhododendron and—in addition to the usual forest species such as pyrola—steppe plants (aconite and koeleria); on the moister slopes are sphagnums and hypnum covers, sometimes associated with thickets of wild rosemary and dwarf birch.

Playing a prominent role in the landscape are birch thickets located above the midline of deep gullies. Amid the basic plant, scrub birch (Betula fruticosa), there is a luxuriant grassy cover consisting of a mixture of forest species (cornflower), meadow-bog species (cotton grass), and subalpine species (gentian). Systematic felling and burning of the thickets lead to the development of moist sedge and cobresia meadows. Uniformity of the grass stand and an increase in its thickness and succulence may be achieved by cultivation.

Farther up in the mountains dark-coniferous species begin to be mixed in. At river sources on rocky slopes, spruce predominates, having occupied small areas in the bottomlands. Rising above the larch forests are pine-larch forests with thick lichen and moss cover. Among the grasses are forest species such as *Allium victorialis,* steppe species such as Mongolian feather grass (*Stipa mongolica*), and high-elevation species such as cobresia (*Cobresia filifolia*). Forests of this type are the best deer pasturages.

A zone of Siberian pine forests, several dozen miles wide and at a 5,610-foot maximum altitude, forms an unbroken ring around the high-mountain region. These pine grow on weakly-podzolized, rubbly soil, underlain by crystalline rocks. In the lower part of the zone is a group of mossy Siberian pine forests in which a few fir, spruce, larch, and pine trees may be found. Underbrush is almost absent. The grass cover is composed of the common taiga species. There is much whortleberry and red bilberry. The solid moss cover is composed of the ordinary forest types (most often *Pleurozium schreberi*). These forests are rich in timber and nuts.

Closer to the high-mountain zone lies a group of Siberian pine forests with a thin tree stand, a thick undergrowth of rhododendron, an abundance of whortleberry, red bilberry, and sedge, and a well-developed moss cover. Siberian pine woods with a subgrowth of dwarf birch, alder groves, and impoverished rhododendron. Restoration under the canopy of the pine woods proceeds poorly. The pine has abundant seed years recurring every five to seven years.

The lower zone contains vast burned-over areas. In the recent past the Siberian pine forests were devastated by the pine silkworm (*Dendrolimus sibiricus*), and the taiga was completely bared for hundreds of miles. In a few years time the silkworm had managed to dry up immense areas of pine forest. The number of caterpillars increased from year to year, persisting even with the falling of snow in August and September. There were so many caterpillars that their chewing of the pine needles produced a noise in the forest. All the shallow streams were continuously strewn with dead caterpillars, the decay of which made a stench in the forest. Wild animals, including squirrel and sable, escaped from infected areas of Siberian pine taiga. The pine and trapping industries, the chief sources of income of the local population, ceased. Large areas of dried-up forests created favorable circumstances for fires. Fire completed the work of the pine silkworm and even destroyed those small islands of pine which had been spared from it. Only subalpine pine woods survived. The restoration of pine on the vast burned-over areas is just beginning. Where there are groups of old pines nearby the restoration is more successful because of the scattering of the seeds by chipmunks, squirrels, and nutcrackers. The restoration has proceeded very slowly because of repeated fires, which have burned out the mossy bedding, and laid bare the rocky soil. The fir forests suffer greatly from the larva of the taiga beetle (*Monachanus urisori*).

Pine reaches the high-mountain zone only in those places where there is fine-grained soil, and retreats when talus begins to accumulate. Thus the timber line depends on the character of the soil, as well as the climate. Amid pines with flag-shaped crowns, fir is encountered in small quantity.

The animal life of the taiga is analogous to that of the Western Sayan, but here elk is often found, reindeer is abundant, and the flying squirrel is widespread. The climatic conditions, however, are unfavorable for wood grouse and hazel grouse. It would be desirable to introduce a hardier species, such as the grouse (*Falcipennis falcipennis*), which lives in the forests along the coast of the Okhotsk Sea.

High-Mountain Zone

The high-mountain zone has the same appearance as that of the Western Sayan. The belt of subalpine shrubs is poor and often mixed with alder groves, alpine willows, and birch (*Betula fruticosa* and *Betula gmelini*). Dwarf stone pine (*Pinus pumila*), which in the neighboring Trans-Baikal embraces the summits of bald mountains in a solid narrow strip, is conspicuously absent. Many animals are absent in the high-mountain zone of Eastern Sayan, because they are usually associated with this creeping pine. For example, sable, which is habitual to the bald mountains near Lake Baikal, is rare in the Sayan. Subalpine meadows at a height of 5,280 to 7,260 feet have tall grass stands (28 to 40 inches) which are rich in composition and dense in growth. These meadows are valuable for their luxuriant reed grass (*Calamagrostis macilenta*) and grass (*Agropyron mutabile*), which make excellent fodder for cattle. Amid the grasses there are also many colorful blossoming herbs.

The alpine belt is occupied primarily by mountain tundra. Alpine meadows are encountered only in small patches between the forest belt and the high-mountain tundra. On alpine meadows as many as 120 species of plants are found, including: alpine sweet grass (*Hierochloe alpina*), koeleria (*Koeleria altaica*), chive (*Allium schoenoprasum*), astragalus (*Astragalus alpinus*), and poppy (*Papaver alpinum*). Moist meadows with cobresia (*Cobresia bellardii, C. schoenoides*), sedges, and rushes, may be found.

As in the Altai, the mountain tundra consists of three types: moss-lichen, rubbly-lichen, and rocky tundra. These have a mosaic pattern of distribution on small areas. Moss-lichen tundra grows on flat plateau-shaped summits, gentle slopes, and depressions, in which mosses may predominate over lichens, and there is much sedge and rush. Rubbly-lichen tundra, like polar tundra, is mantled by mounds of bulging grassy sod with many cracks. Here patches of bare substrata, strips of lichens, alpine willow, partridge grass, and groups of individual alpine species are found. In the rocky tundra single plant specimens are scattered; only near patches of snow are there groups of bright alpine plants such as violets, gentians, and primroses.

Fig. 8-16. Subalpine meadows in the Kizir-Kazirsk Range; glacial cirque in the distance.

The domestic reindeer in Eastern Sayan is exclusively a saddle and pack animal and is never used as a draft animal. Vast forests of the subalpine zone with abundant thickets of reindeer moss, together with high-mountain tundras and meadows, fully guarantee deer fodder the year round. Mongolian sheep are raised here. Thus local livestock breeding combines two such extremes as polar reindeer husbandry and steppe sheep breeding.

TANNU-OLA RANGE

United under the name Tannu-Ola are a series of ranges stretching in a general east-west direction, each with a different geologic structure, strike, and morphologic appearance. They form a single orographic unit as the main boundary between Siberia and the region of northwestern Mongolia. The western section of Tannu-Ola—the Tsagan-Shibetu Range—is narrow, craggy, and very steep on both sides, especially on the south. Narrow river valleys are deeply notched in the slopes of the range. Its serrated crest is capped by cone- and pyramid-shaped peaks rising above the snow line. Between them lie deep cols with almost inaccessible passes more than 9,900 feet high. Firn fields sometimes survive for several years. The hardness of the mountain rocks contributes to the preservation of the range elevations and the alpine relief forms. The rocks are metamorphic and crystalline schists, serpentines, quartzites, and solid conglomerates with siliceous cement.

The central part of the mountain system—Tannu-Ola proper—appears as a uniform, high-mountain bulwark, broad at the base and with flat summits. Above them rise craggy, bare peaks devoid of snow, with a maximum altitude of more than 8,250 feet and a relative height of more than 500 feet, with broad, flat passes at an altitude of 6,600 feet, sometimes accessible to wheeled transportation. The range has terraced slopes (of which the southern is steeper) with rather gently sloping river bottomland. The Tannu-Ola Range is made up of friable limestones, sandstones, marls, and shales, and has been greatly reduced and broken into separate mountain groups, with more resistant material forming the high individual bald peaks. Cambrian rocks compose the chief massif of Tannu-Ola, but the superficial strata are Silurian rocks and rocks of the Biy-Kem complex. In the range are many tectonic breaks and overthrusts: Cambrian deposits are thrust on the Silurian and the Biy-Kem complex from the south.

The eastern section of Tannu-Ola—the Sangilen Range—is similar to the Tsagan-Shibetu and has been uplifted quite high. It has sharply defined alpine relief forms, high passes, deep gorges, and small glaciers. The sedimentary rocks of Tannu-Ola proper are abruptly replaced here by massive crystalline rocks such as granites, syenites, granodiorites, and gneisses, on which rest shales and crystalline limestones with a northwest (Eastern Sayan) strike.

TUVA BASIN

The Tuva (Uryankhay) Valley lies in the upper part of the Yenisei River basin, between the Western and Eastern Sayan on the north and the Tannu-Ola Range on the south. On the west it is bounded by the Shapshal and Chikhachev ranges, belonging to the East-Altai system, and on the east by Bain-Ola Range, separating it from the basin of Lake Khubsugul and linking Tannu-Ola with the Eastern Sayan. The valley is in the central part of Asia between 50° and 54° north latitude, which is approximately the latitudinal distance from Tula to Kharkov, and between 89° and 99° east longitude. It is a pear-shaped valley with its narrow end pointing westward. The valley is more than 420 miles long and from 54 to 270 miles wide. It is approximately 63,690 square miles in area and has a population of 150,000. The lower central section of the valley lies between 1,650 to 2,640 feet in altitude, and the ranges surrounding it rise to a height of 8,250 feet. The valley is intersected by many spurs from the bordering mountain ranges and is broken into several isolated depressions, extending along the largest rivers.

The geologic history of the Tuva Valley from the Miocene is closely linked with the history of the neighboring Altai. In the development of the region's relief, as in the Altai, the following episodes were important: (1) the Tertiary upheaval of horsts (of a somewhat smaller scope than that in the Altai); (2) repeated glaciation, traces of which may be seen in several localities; (3) a post-Tertiary upheaval, indicated by hot springs, earthquakes, and the deep notching of rivers into the bottoms of old valleys. As in the Altai, the continental climate causes energetic frost weathering. The valley contains a transitional landscape grading from the low-lying Siberian taiga to the semiarid lands and steppes of the high-mountain region of northwest Mongolia.

Geology and Morphology

Of the sedimentary rocks which took part in the building of the Tuva Basin are marine layers of the Lower Paleozoic, marine and continental deposits of the Middle Paleozoic, and continental deposits of the Jurassic Period. Igneous rocks play a significant role in the geologic structure of Tuva, especially in its eastern part, which has extensive fields of granites and quartzite porphyries. The basic intrusions (pyroxenites and peridotites) are in the western and central part of the region. Of the effusive rocks, basalts are predominant; they are distributed in the eastern part. The age of the igneous rocks varies from Pre-Cambrian (micaceous granites) to Quaternary (basalts). The geologic structure of Tuva is characterized by the following: (1) a two-layered structure of comparatively thin, weakly dislocated Middle Paleozoic and younger strata, lying unevenly on a tough foundation of Cambrian and older layers; (2) the absence of geosynclinal formations of the Lower Silurian, highly characteristic of the neighboring Western Sayan; (3) the accumulation and preservation of Carbonaceous and Jurassic deposits, which are absent in the Western Sayan; (4) the frequency of periods having weak tectonic-denudation activity.

The Tuva has a platform structure, in contrast with the Western Sayan and the Eastern Altai (to which the northwestern and south-western parts of Tuva belong) with their typical lineal Caledonian folds. Following the early Paleozoic, Tuva began to rise (although some of the stages of its history were signified by large-scale subsidences, but with lesser vertical displacements). At the beginning of the Lower Silurian Period, Tuva was separated from the Sayan. Intensive upheavals in the Tertiary and Quaternary periods, led to the emergence of large orographic units, the Tannu-Ola and Kurtushinbin ranges, which isolated the Tuva Basin.

The Tuva has great diversity of relief. It is

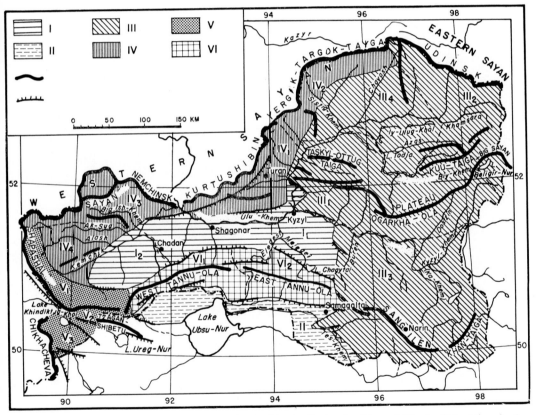

Map 8-V. Geomorphologic regions of Tuvin; I—Tuvin Basin: 1—Central Tuvin (Ulu-Khem); 2—Western Tuvin (Kemchik). II—Ubsunursk Basin. III—Eastern Tuvin Mountains: 1—Central Mountains; 2—Sayan Mountains; 3—Khangaisk Mountains; 4—Todzhin Basin. IV—Western Sayan subregion: 1—Kurtushibinsk Ridge; 2—Ergak-Targak-Taiga Ridge; 3—Kemchik Ridge; 4—Alash plateau. V—Southwestern high-mountain region: 1—Shapshalsk Ridge; 2—Tsagan-Shibetu Ridge; 3—Mongun Taiga. VI—Tannu-Ola Ridge: 1—Western Tannu-Ola Ridge; 2—Eastern Tannu-Ola Ridge.

a combination of bald mountain ranges, high flat uplands, more depressed and intensely dissected mountainous sections (giving the entire region the character of a mountain country), broad valleys, and large basins covered with the low relief or undulating hilly plains. Morphologically, Tuva is divided into two parts: the narrow western and central basin of the Ulu-Khem and Kemchik, and the wide eastern basin of the Biy-Khem and Kha-Khem. The first is the extensive Tuva Basin 220 miles in length and from 25 to 75 miles in width; the second is the high Eastern Tuva upland. The boundary between them may be drawn ap-

north it is bounded by the steep straight ledge of the Kurtushibin Range, and on the east by the tectonic precipice of the Eastern Tuva upland. The Ulu-Khem depression lies at a higher altitude than the Minusink Basin. The altitude of its lowest parts vary from 1,729 feet in the downstream area to 2,093 feet near the point at which the Biy-Khem (Great Yenisei) and Kha-Khem (Little Yenisei) merge. A characteristic feature of the Ulu-Khem depression is the abundance of isolated mesas, high crests, and mounds. Their relative elevations vary from several dozen to hundreds of feet. Some of them are connected with the Western

Fig. 8-17. General view of the Ulu-Khem depression.

proximately along the meridian of Kyzyl. The Tuva Basin is in turn divided into two isolated depressions—the Central Tuva, or Ulu-Khem, and the Western Tuva, or Kemchik. The mountains on the edge of the Tuva Basin may be subdivided into three well-delineated morphologic units: the Alashy Plateau, the southwestern high-mountain region, and the Tannu-Ola Range.

The Central Tuva depression lies along the Ulu-Khem River (the upper Yenisei). On the

Sayan or Tannu-Ola, but many belong to the basin itself. The Tannu-Ola, more or less isolated groups of hills (Argalykta, Utuk-Kay, Karatag), have a unique geologic structure and morphology and form a narrow chain extending for more than 120 miles along the northern edge of the depression. The picturesque mountain Khayrkhan which figures in Tuva legends stands solitary in the middle of the plain made up of white marbleized limestones. Tectonically, the Ulu-Khem depression is a region of subsidence bounded by fractures along the ranges and uplands surrounding it. In general, it has a folded structure.

The most important structural element in the Tuva Basin is the anticline, which subsides to the east and extends in an east-northeast direction. Its axis coincides with the valley of the Ulu-Khem, and its slopes with the southern chains of the Western Sayan and the Tannu-Ola Range. Superimposed on this large structure are anticlinal and synclinal folds. The main anticline is composed of deposits ranging in age from the Cambrian to the Jurassic. In the axial part of the anticline lies a Middle Cambrian sedimentary layer with shallow intrusions of igneous rock. It is laid out in large folds complicated by small fractures. Parallel displacements of this and an overthrust of the rocks formed the monoclinal ranges at the northern edge of the basin. The Cambrian layer is covered with a later series of younger sedimentary rocks. Belonging to them are the gentle folds of Upper Silurian and Lower Carboniferous rock: sandstones, shales, and clays. Steeply erect, compressed folds lie along the edges of the depression near the ranges. In the eastern part of the depression a uniform, fresh-water, Jurassic, coal-bearing layer is widely developed; it consists of conglomerates, sandstones, and clays with thin layers of bituminous marls and coal. The rocks have a number of very gentle bends, and in some places they lie almost horizontally. The folded depression is separated from the Western Sayan by a complex deep fracture, which extends for a distance of 120 miles. Besides this fracture, there are smaller faults which run at various angles toward the major fractures of the depression; these lines limit small depressions such as that of Elegest-Mezhegey. More fault tectonics are indicated by a system of irregular fissures, the local shaling of the rocks, breccias, and slickensides.

The western part of the Ulu-Khem depression, containing hard siliceous and igneous rocks, was folded in the Paleozoic. The present relief is highly dissected with the wide development of small mounds and an abundance of buttes and crags cropping out of the softer sedimentary rocks. This relief, the variety and brightness of color in the outcrops, the steppe or semidesert vegetation, the salt lakes, and the scattered barchans—all give to the depression the character of a Gobi landscape of the Central Asiatic basins. The eastern part of the depression is weakly hilly and in places flat; more elevated sections have a tableland character.

The lowest place in the Ulu-Khem depression is occupied by a valley of the Ulu-Khem River and is a broad alluvial plain made up of gravel covered with a loess-type loam. This plain is bounded by terrace-like ledges of bedrock, on which remnants of ancient gravel and sand deposits lie 260 feet above the river. Owing to an uplift of the southern part of the main anticline, the river was gradually displaced to the north as far as the foothills of the Kurtushibin Range, transforming the primary relief of the depression. The valley of the Ulu-Khem is in some places very wide and terraced, with vast steppes along both sides of the river. In places where the river cuts into mountain ridges, the valley is very narrow. The Ulu-Khem, where it passes through broad flat valley sections, becomes a braided stream. One such place, toward the western part of Khayrkhan Mountain, has the characteristic name "Forty Yeniseis."

The immediate western structural and morphologic continuation of the Ulu-Khem depression is the Western Tuva, or Kemchik, depression. Bounded on all sides by mountains, it extends in an east-northeast direction along the Kemchik River for a distance of nearly 60 miles, with a width of from 12 to 15 miles. In the east, the highest bench marks reach 2,900 feet, in the west 3,100 feet, and along the edges 3,630 to 3,960 feet; the local relative elevations do not exceed 500 to 650 feet.

The Kemchik tectonic depression was formed on an anticline. Its arch is made up of Cambrian deposits and its edge is Lower Silurian. The depression is bounded by faults formed during the end of the Tertiary and the beginning of the Quaternary periods. In relief, it is a slightly concave plain filled with low

Fig. 8-18. Upper Kemchik Valley at 4,500 feet elevation.

mountains which slope gradually down to the river and separate into the smaller ridges and hills of a small-mound relief. Near the foothills of the surrounding mountains are located huge alluvial fans; along the large rivers are thick alluvial deposits and in the center of the depression, sandy soil is blown around by dry westerly winds. The Kemchik depression became a place for accumulation of friable Quaternary materials. In the most depressed part, the accumulation was so intensive that the ancient mound relief was buried under alluvia; buttes and isolated peaks crop out above the alluvial plain. The periphery, being at a higher level, was not buried, and remains exposed to the continuous action of weathering. The depression was filled with alluvia at an especially high rate during the glacial epoch. The valley glaciers of two glacial periods, descending from the Shapshal Range, deposited large terminal moraines in the Kemchik valley near Baytal. Deposits were left by lakes temporarily formed at the head of glaciers. The accumulation of friable material, as well as the intensive wash-

ing away of ancient alluvial fans, is taking place at the present time, indicating that the surrounding ranges are continuing to rise. The upper sections of the right tributaries and the lower sections of the left are typical mountain rivers flowing in narrow **V**-shaped valleys are characteristic of the right tributaries of the Kemchik.

The Ubsu Nur Basin, only the northern part of which belongs to the USSR lies to the south of the Tannu-Ola Range in the huge depression of the Great Lakes in northwestern Mongolia. It is egg-shaped, with the pointed end on the east. To the west, the basin is bounded by spurs of the Tsagan-Shibetu Range, and to the east by the low Agardag-Tayga Mountains. The northern part of the basin is a plain which rises gently toward Tannu-Ola. The boundary between them is rather sharp, since the foothills are cut off by a steep slope. Near the base of the mountains there is a long strip of large alluvial fans formed by temporary mountain streams. The basin lies at an altitude of 2,300 to 3,000 feet. Its foundation is made up of Archean and Paleozoic rocks which crop out on the surface forming small mounds. Upheaval in the Tannu-Ola was accompanied by relative subsidence in the Ubsu Nur Basin, which was a region of intensive accumulation of friable Tertiary and Quaternary deposits. Its bottom was gradually filled by lake deposits and alluvium from the surrounding heights. The basin has no drainage. Neither the locked-in lake Ubsu Nur, nor the river Tes-Khem which drains into it has terraces. The eastern extreme of the basin (also an area of accumulation) is separated from the Ubsu Nur Basin. The river cuts into the ancient alluvial sediments, forming terraces of up to 30 feet in height, and carving deep into the bedrock. At the present time the individual mountain-buttes and the range of Agardag-Tayga appear to be buried in friable alluvia.

The eastern half of Tuva, which includes the basins of the Biy-Khem and the Kha-Khem, is occupied by the complexly dissected Eastern Tuva upland, containing plateaus, mountain chains, and depressions. This large orographic unit is a part of the extensive Khangi upland of northern Mongolia. The Eastern Tuva upland narrows gradually to the west. On the side toward the neighboring Ulu-Khem and Todzhin depressions, this narrow part of the range is bounded by a sharply indicated tectonic edge. The average altitude of the upland is 4,950 to 5,280 feet. Rising from its surface are narrow, low ranges, separated by shallow troughs. The over-all orientation of the ranges is east-west, but in the eastern end they begin to extend in a west-northwest direction. The geologic composition which distinguishes the upland from other parts of Tuva are: (1) the presence of Pre-Cambrian layers which, though abundant in the Eastern Sayan, are absent in the west; (2) the extremely insignificant deposits of the Middle and Upper Paleozoic, which are widely represented in the neighboring Tuva Basin; (3) huge areas of granites, granodiorites, and quartzite porphyries; and (4) the abundance of Tertiary and Quaternary basalts linked with young fractures.

The Eastern Tuva upland is the most ancient structure in the Tuva oblast. It is formed of Pre-Cambrian gneisses compressed into complex steep folds, crystalline schists, amphibolites, marbles, dolomites, and acid intrusions. Between the folds of the Pre-Cambrian are folds containing volcanic tuffs and porphyries. To the north of Biy-Khem, at an altitude of 5,270 to 6,600 feet, large areas are covered by Tertiary basalts 3,300 feet thick. Blanketing the basalt is a layer of tuffs having a thickness of 660 to 1,150 feet. At the same place the remains of a Tertiary volcano have been discovered. Along some of the wide fractures there are extrusions of Quaternary basalts, most of which date from the Pleistocene. The present-day relief of the upland reflects the underlying geologic structure, which is characterized by large intersecting fractures. The fractures determined the boundaries of the mountain chains, of horsts, and of plateaus, the distinct edges of the depressions, and the directions of the river valleys. The hot springs located along the fractures indicate recent tectonic activity. The upheavals at the end of the Tertiary and the beginning of

the Quaternary periods led to a rejuvenation of the relief and the emergence of a system of young river valleys. The mass of the upland is dissected by the Biy-Khem and Kha-Khem into three mountain regions: the Cis-Sayan with the Todzhin Basin to the north of the Biy-Khem, the Cis-Khangai to the south of the Kha-Khem, and the central mountain region located between the two.

The central mountain region, framed by the lower and middle courses of the Biy-Khem and Kha-Khem rivers, is a complex watershed consisting of two parallel chains of narrow (from 1.5 to 3 miles in width) bald mountain ranges extending in approximately an east-west direction for a distance of nearly 80 miles. They lie on the basic massif of the upland. The average altitude of the upland is 4,950 to 5,610 feet, and the average height of the mountain chains above the level of the upland is 990 to 1,650 feet. The northern chain consists of Ottug-Tayga and Taskyl. The southern chain extends westward from the Ottug-Tayga to Tumat-Tayga (7,075 feet) and Atcholdug-Tayga; and branches into the Khertesh-Tayga and Dongul-Tayga ranges. The ranges can be classified into two types: the alpine and the flat-top. The higher ranges, such as Ottug-Tayga or Khertesh-Tayga, have narrow dissected crests, and the lower ranges, such as Dongul-Tayga or Tumat-Tayga, level plateau-shaped surfaces. Fault-block depressions divide the ranges. Farther east, the mountain chains turn into a broad strip of flat bald mountains; they are known by the name Ogarkha-Ola or Orangyula-Tayga and contain evidence of ancient glaciation, such as cirques, trough-shaped valleys, erratic boulders, and moraines.

The Cis-Sayan mountain region has a similar structure, with a dissected plateau-shaped base from which rise bald mountain ranges. However, in the Cis-Sayans the upland itself is developed: isolated ranges, such as Kuu-Tayga and Oyva-Tayga stand out on the over-all massif of the upland with mean altitudes of nearly 6,600 feet.

The Todzhin Basin is occupied by the middle Biy-Khem and its tributaries, the

Khamsara, Iya, Azas, and Sistig-Khem. The western part is a complexly dissected locality with the deeply cut wide valley of the Biy-Khem. The eastern part of the basin has an altitude of nearly 3,300 feet, and individual peaks rise to 6,600 feet; it bears the name Khamsara-Azas plain. Twofold large-scale glaciation is indicated by the wide distribution of hilly-moraine landscape, glacial lakes in chains along the rivers. After the last glaciation, intensive erosion conditioned by the lower base-level of erosion on the southern rivers led to a shift in the watershed; these rivers captured the tributaries of the Biy-Khem and cut into the northern glacial valleys.

The Cis-Khangai mountain region is somewhat more dissected and depressed. The upland is a complex system of low mountains which are covered by a dense swampy taiga. On the surface of the upland are set narrow mountain massifs of the alpine type with heights up to 10,500 feet. The ranges coincide with the southern and southeastern edges of the upland. The Sangilen high-mountain chain has steep, high inaccessible passes, and strongly dissected alpine forms of relief with traces of ancient glaciation. On the southeast rises the Khan-Tayga Range (9,240 feet); viewed from Lake Tere-Khol, it is a high, steep-walled range with serrated crests, and from the east it ap-

pears to be a high plateau above which the watershed section rises as flat denuded mountains. The river valleys in the ranges reach depths of 3,300 feet; inaccessible gorges alternate with broad sections filled with alluvium and lake deposits.

The Alash Plateau is in the northwest corner of Tuva in the basin of the left tributaries of the Kemchik: the Alash, the Ak-Sug, and the Big Ish-Khem. Above the general level of the plateau there rise isolated cupola-shaped bald mountains covered by extensive fields of talus. One of these is the granite massif Bay-Tayga (9,240 feet). The south edge of the plateau has, in places, the flat appearance of a sharply expressed ledge; elsewhere it is dissected by gorges. Eventually, the terrain modulates into the small-mound relief of the Kemchik depression. Ancient glaciers have left many traces of their activity on the plateau—cirques, troughs, moraines, boulders, and moraine-dammed lakes.

The southwestern high-mountain region is the highest and most strongly dissected orographic knot at the junction of the Altai and Tannu-Ola ranges. This region is linked with the southeastern Altai and with it underwent all the basic stages of relief development. The layers which compose the ranges have a west-northwest to east-southeast strike. The moun-

Fig. 8-19. Continuous loose rock fields on the taiga of the Alashkoy Plateau.

Fig. 8-20.   Peneplain surface of the Tannu-Ola Range at 6,000 feet.

tains were subjected to large Tertiary upheavals and the tectonic relief is comparatively youthful. Nearby are the Tsagan-Shibetu and Mongun-Tayga ranges, and parts of the Shapshal and Chikhachëv ranges, which belong to the Altai.

The Tsagan-Shibetu Range is a direct southeastern continuation of the Shapshal Range and extends eastward into Mongolia. It is south of the western Tannu-Ola, and is connected with it. The range is composed of green-rock effusions and schists of the Cambrian and Lower Silurian; thrust onto these on the north and south are strongly dislocated conglomerates, sandstones, and shales of the Upper Silurian. In the area of permanent snows, the range contains well-expressed alpine relief forms. Part of the north-facing slope is a plateau that is cut through by deep gorges and has steps which descend toward the north. This is the highest part of the range (11,550 feet). The south-facing slope drops in a sharp ledge 1,650 to 1,980 feet high toward a narrow, open tectonic valley, on the bottom of which lie the Khindik-tig-Khol Lake and the Khargin-Gol River. Glacial traces are not significant on this range.

South of Tsagan-Shibetu on a high plateau is the large isolated mountain massif of Mongun-Tayga. The highest peak, Munku-Khayrkhan-Ula (12,982 feet), is covered with snow the year round and contains small gla-ciers. Taking part in the geologic structure of the range are crystalline schists—possibly of Pre-Cambrian origin—and quartzites and clayey schists of the cambrian, these are cut through by large-scale intrusions of granites. The direction of the folds, like the lines of fault disturbances, is northwest, which is characteristic of the adjoining regions of the Altai. From the northeast, the massif is bounded by a sharply expressed tectonic ledge. On the southwest the terrain of Mongun-Tayga is smoother, lowering gradually into a small-mound relief. Everywhere the mountain massif contains evidence of ancient glaciation—solid fields of moraines in the upper reaches of rivers, many boulders, and chains of glacier-fed lakes. Mongun-Tayga has typical alpine relief forms with deeply-cut cirques and troughs.

Mineral Resources

The Tuva Valley is one of the richest regions of the USSR in quantity and variety of mineral resources. The thickness of the rich ore-bearing veins and their proximity to the surface contribute to easy and profitable mining. The wealth of gold-bearing placers of Tuva is exceptional. Districts in the northeastern part contain thick series of gold-bearing sand. Original deposits of gold, linked with intrusions of granitic magma, have also been discovered. In enormous outcrops of pyroxenites, serpentine deposits of platinum have been found, as well as huge deposits of high-quality asbestos. Native silver is often encountered, sometimes in large masses. Various copper ores may be found in the western part of Tuva in contact zones between limestones and greenstone igneous rocks. There are also indications of the occurrence of hematite and magnetite.

Carboniferous and Jurassic coal of economic importance is found in the central part of the valley. The seams are of a working thickness and occur close to the surface. The coal is of good quality and is transitional between bituminous and brown coal. Graphite and oil may be associated with these deposits. Tertiary deposits in the southern slope of Tannu-Ola contain a thick mass of rock salt of high quality. There are many cold carbonate and hot sulphuric mineral springs. Marble, kaolin, sandstones, and gems are of economic significance in the Tuva Valley.

Salt with an admixture of Glauber salt and bromide is extracted from several highly mineralized lakes of the Ulu-Khem depression, such as Chedar-Khol' and Tus-Khol'. The bottom of the former lake is covered with a thick layer of mineral mud, and for this reason a local resort has grown up near it. There are many mineral springs, of varying temperature and chemistry, in Tuva. A group of some 150 highly mineralized springs—sour and bitter, cold and hot—has been discovered in the system of the upper Khamsara. There are warm springs in the downstream area of the Kha-Khem, hot sulphur (with a temperature of 132°F and carbonaceous springs in the valley of the river Tayrisin-Gol, and sulphur springs on the left bank of the Alasha River.

Climate

The Tuva Valley, almost in the middle of the Asiatic mainland, possesses a sharply continental climate. This is expressed in the comparatively low average annual temperature

(22.2°F at Tolbuk) and in the great daily and annual amplitudes (in the Tuva steppes in summer the temperature reaches 104°F; in winter it may drop to −57.5°F). The small annual precipitation is also characteristic of the sharp continentality. Factors which determine the climate are: (1) the location of the valley along the northern rim of the highest mountain zone of Asia; (2) the isolation effected by the barrier of the surrounding mountains; (3) the local relief; (4) the exposure of the slopes. Tuva is an intermediate region which combines climatic features of the inner-Asiatic steppes and semidesert with those of Siberian Taiga and high-mountain zones. Tuva has a harsher climate than the European part of the USSR lying at the same latitudes (for example, the strip from Saratov to Chernigov) because of its distance from the ocean. Despite its relatively small size, the region contains a series of transitions from west to east, from north to south, and from lower to higher elevations.

The change of wind regime, according to seasons of the year, occurs with the change of pressure. The isobar pattern indicates that westerly winds prevail in the Tuva Valley during winter, and easterly winds prevail in summer. These general courses are altered by local conditions, inasmuch as the direction of river valleys strongly influences the wind direction. At Tolbuk during the entire year northwest and north winds prevail (in January the frequency of these winds is 76 per cent, in July 58 per cent). The average wind velocity alters sharply according to seasons. Characteristic for the anticyclonic winter regime is a very large number (to 90 per cent) of calms. In spring the wind velocity increases, and reaches its greatest magnitude in May (9.2 feet per second at Kyzyl). In summer the wind velocity decreases (4.6 feet per second in August). Strong winds also blow in autumn. Although the wind may blow strongly during the day, it dies down during the night and early morning. Between the bordering mountains and lower steppe plains and valleys a daily exchange of air takes place.

The temperature regime of the Tuva Valley

is marked by the abruptness of change from winter to summer and from day to night, as well as extreme temperature diversity of individual districts. The warmest month of the year is July (the monthly average at Kyzyl is 67°F and the maximum temperature is 89.8°F), the coldest is January (at Kyzyl the average is —27°F, and the minimum is —62°F). At Tolbuk, from February to June, temperatures ranged from —27°F to 34°F. With specific conditions of relief (for example, valley bottoms) bringing about winter temperature inversions and intensive summer heat, the over-all continentality of climate is increased. On the slopes the annual course of temperature is smoother and the annual amplitude smaller. Since the difference in elevation between Kyzl (1,980 feet) and Tolbuk (3,036 feet) is 1,056 feet, Tolbuk should have a winter temperature 3.2 degrees below that of Kyzyl. Actually, however, the January temperature at Tolbuk is 11.5 degrees higher than that at Kyzyl. A characteristic of depressions is stable periods: from December to March at Kyzyl, thaws were not observed; on the other hand, from June to August the air temperature did not drop below 32°F. At Tolbuk, which is at a greater height, early frosts were observed in all the summer months. In the mountains sharp drops of temperature, even in the middle of summer, are possible. The western part of Tuva Valley is warmer in summer and colder in winter than the eastern part. Slope exposures clearly influence the distribution of temperatures.

The Tuva Valley has little precipitation. North and northwest winds predominate over drying winds from the south and carry a sufficient amount of moisture for precipitation, but the high transverse ranges of Eastern Altai and Western Sayan intercept them, creating a "rain-shadow" on the eastern side. Summer winds pass above the scorching dry steppes of the low central part of the valley, but when they meet the chilled mountain tops in the east of the region, they precipitate part of their moisture. Thus in eastern Tuva heavy downpours are frequent and peat bogs are common in the midst of the moist taiga, but in the "rain-shadow" in the west lies the driest part of Tuva, where under dry steppe conditions artificial irrigation is necessary for agriculture.

Of the mountains surrounding the valley, Tannu-Ola has the least precipitation. The annual average at Kyzyl is 7.2 inches, at Tolbuk 12.6 inches. Most rain falls in summer and (excluding mountain zones) least in winter. The rainiest month is August (4.1 inches at Tolbuk during 18 days with precipitation, 2.6 inches at Kyzyl during 13 days with precipitation). The driest period is from February to April (about 0.16 inch to 0.20 inch a month at Tolbuk during 6 to 9 days with precipitation, about 0.08 to 0.36 inch at Kyzyl during 3 to 5 days with precipitation). The daily maximum precipitation is small: 0.81 inch at Tolbuk, 0.80 inch at Kyzyl. In summer many thunderstorms occur (at Tolbuk there are 24 thunderstorms during the year; 7 to 8 occur in July and August). There is only a thin snow cover during winter in low-lying parts of the region, and livestock can obtain fodder the year round. At Tolbuk, a yearly average of 69 days of snowfall has been recorded; at Kyzyl there are 41 days of snowfall. The forest zone of the mountainous eastern part of Tuva has so much snow that it is almost impossible to travel there. During calm weather snow sometimes falls two days in succession. On Tannu-Ola Pass, snow more than 20 inches deep hampers passage for three to four months.

The relative humidity of the air is not high: the annual humidity at Kyzl is 70 per cent; the greatest is observed in November (89 per cent), and the least in May (48 per cent). January and October have the most cloudy days (about 15 per month); the clearest period is March to July (about four to six cloudy days). Owing to the diversity of relief, the frequency of fogs is not the same everywhere. At Tolbuk, during an average year, there are 54 days with fog; from November to March two to three days with fog occur monthly. During April, May, and October of some years fog was not observed; July is foggiest (18 days).

Because of the pronounced anticyclonic type

of weather, winter is long (up to 170 days) and severe in the valleys. Here strong inversions occur, with weak winds or calm, a steady cold period without thaws, slight precipitation, and thin snow cover. March is also a winter month. Although spring, commencing with April, has drier air and powdery snowstorms, it is warmer, rainier, cloudier, windier, and foggier. Summer is warm—often hot—with more and heavier precipitation, few cloudy days, and fogs. Autumn is short. A rapid drop of temperatures in September is accompanied by early-morning frosts, weak winds, slight precipitation, and little cloudiness. The growing period in the central part of the valley lasts 139 days.

The shortening of the growing season from west to east explains the difference in the altitudes at which plowed fields may be found: in the west plots are cultivated at heights up to 4,712 feet, in the central part to 4,068 feet, and in the east to 3,366 feet. In Eastern Tuva spring is dry, summer rainy, winter snowy, and temperatures may fall below 32°F even during the

period in which cereals flower. Nevertheless, there are luxuriant meadows necessary for animal husbandry. Grains do not ripen every year, although in favorable years they yield exceptional harvests. In Western Tuva, owing to the moist spring and warm and less rainy summer, agriculture is dependable but requires artificial irrigation.

Hydrography

The Tuva Valley, surrounded by mountain ranges, contains the sources of the upper Yenisei and forms a single enclosed hydrographic region. Only the mountain streams of the Tannu-Ola southern slope belong to the undrained interior basin of Mongolia, where the rivers (for example, Tesiin-Gol) end in large water reservoirs (Lake Ubsu Nur).

Tuva has a centripetal hydrographic system. Water from all the rivers of the valley are collected by the two main sources of the Yenisei, the Kemchik and Ulu-Khem (the latter is

Fig. 8-21. Kha-Khem River in its lower course.

Fig. 8-22. Kemchik River with wide meanders and sandbanks.

formed by the junction of the Biy-Khem and the Kha-Khem). Subsequently, under the name Yenisei, they flow across the single narrow opening in Western Sayan to the boundaries of the Siberian plains. All the upper forks of the Yenisei are mountain rivers, flowing in narrow gorges, and have a swift current, rocky bed, many small falls, and occasional rapids. In depressions and steppe valleys the river currents slow down, and beds become braided and form many small lakes and islands (the rivers of the Khamsara-Azasskaya plain or the section of the Ulu-Khem bearing the name "Forty Yeniseis"). In its downstream section the largest river of the valley, the Ulu-Khem, has a main channel 742 feet wide, a maximum depth of 14.8 feet, and a 6-mile-per-hour current. The discharge of the Ulu-Khem River in its upper course is 1,193 cubic yards per second, and that of the Kemchik is 286 cubic yards per second. The upper Yenisei receives the greatest volume of its water near the sources of the Biy-Khem and Kha-Khem, which lie in the zone of the

Sayans with prolonged rain and abundant snow, and where countless lakes drain into the rivers, regulating their flow during summer. Consequently, most of the rivers have plenty of water.

Low water is observable in early spring and fall. The Kemchik River, irrigating a large district with negligible amount of precipitation, has a low supply of water. Its many tributaries are not amply watered and as they emerge from the mountains they disappear in their own alluvia. The large rivers freeze over in October. By mid-April the Ulu-Khem is free of ice, and at the beginning of May the Biy-Khem breaks up.

The rivers of Tuva oblast serve as the fundamental paths of communication for the more remote corners of the basin; thus the population is usually concentrated along their shores. The Yenisei is the most important connecting link between Tuva and Siberia, although rocks must be cleared from its channel and rapids. The Ulu-Khem River is navigable throughout its extent. The rivers flowing among the steppes of the central part of the valley guarantee irrigation during summer drought. Irrigation canals or "mochagi," flow on the surface of the steppes in all directions, irrigating young crops and enriching pasturages. The great rivers and mountain streams possess colossal reserves of water power. The fish in the rivers are as follows: grayling (*Salmo thymallus*), char, pike, whitefish, dace, perch, and burbot.

Many of the lakes of Tuva are found in the mountains, especially in the eastern half. The Khamsara-Azassakaya plain, because of the abundance of lakes covering it, may be called "lake country." Lakes both large (Noyon-Kul) and small stretch in a long chain, through which flow the rivers Iy-Suk, Azas, and Khamsara. These lakes lie amid a hilly moraine landscape on the paths of retreat of ancient glaciers. On the southern slope of Sayan and in the mountain region of the upper stretches of the Kemchik are found cirque lakes (Chapsa) and moraine-dam lakes (Kara-Kul). There are many salt lakes in the central steppe section of the valley, such as Lake Tuz-Kul (only 10 feet deep, from which salt is extracted). At the foothills of the southern slope of the Tannu-Ola Range at a maximum altitude of 2,673 feet, lies large, salty Ubsu Nur Lake, 77 square miles in area.

Vegetation, Soil, and Animal Life

The Tuva Valley, at 51° to 54° latitude and at altitudes from 1,650 in its lowest part to 8,250 feet in the adjacent mountains, contains sharp contrasts in relief, climate, plant and soil cover, and animal life. Since it is small, it contains an intricate distribution of geographic landscapes. The landscapes of the Tuva deservedly merit the name "natural landscapes," because cultivated landscapes still occupy a negligible area. The valley is completely isolated from the neighboring regions by mountain ranges with vast taiga expanses. The valley is a transitional region from the Siberian swamp forests to the arid steppe expanses of

Mongolia; thus the natural character of Siberian Taiga is intricately combined with that of Mongolian Steppe. In Tuva, which is a mountainous region with heights of more than 6,600 feet, three vertical zones are clearly expressed: steppe, taiga, and high-mountain. Eastern Tuva is a mountain district with larch-pine forest and broad meadow valleys, but in the "rain-shadow" of Western and Central Tuva, steppes predominate. In the mountains, islands of high-altitude landscape are found. Along the warmer, south-facing slopes of the southwestern part of Sayan, there is no intermediate forest belt between the steppe landscapes and high-mountain landscapes. Soil, flora, and fauna of the south-facing slopes differ sharply from those of the north-facing slopes: steppes are developed on the south-facing; taiga is common to the north-facing slope.

The soil cover of Tuva is diversified. Arid-steppe soil; chernozem; gray, clayey, forest soil; and podzolic, bog, and rocky tundra soil may be found. The biotic world of Tuva belongs to the northern subzone of the paleoarctic region. It does not have an indigenous flora and fauna because it lies on the intersection of East-Siberian (Dahurian), European (West-Siberian), North-Asiatic, and Central-Asiatic borders. The organic world of Tuva tends to be European, although the sharp continentality of climate results in the absence of broad-leaved forests. Most of the flora and fauna of Tuva are Altai types, although there are fewer species—especially those of the high altitudes; there are almost no endemic plants and animals.

Steppes, which occupy about one-third of the region, are widespread along the large river valleys and high mountains. The complex relief and the broad lowlands, which are divided by wooded ridges, break up the steppe into individual islands. The lowland steppes are sometimes completely flat, sometimes hilly. In depressions, there are saline and fresh-water lakes. Steppes are widespread in the central, western, and southern parts of the valley, especially along the rivers Ulu-Khem and Kemchik. In comparison with the Minusinsk Val-

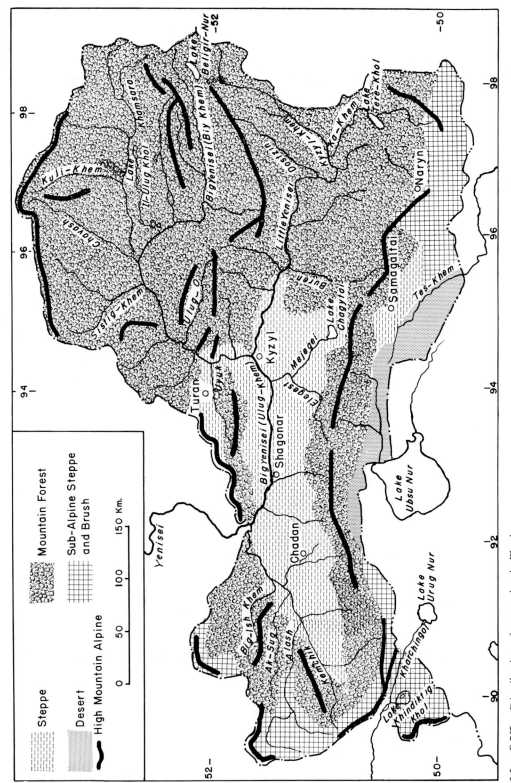

Map 8-VI. Distribution of vegetation in Tuvin.

ley, the steppe and desert character of vegetation in Tuva is expressed more sharply and more typically: the area of arid soil is greater; there is no chernozem zone, as this soil is found only in patches. Sand is not secured by pine groves but by grassy vegetation. Steppes cover not only lowland but rocky hills and mountains. Riverside forests are well developed.

Soil of the Tuva steppes is developed on fine-grained products of weathering of shales, on alluvial sandy-clayey earth with pebbles, and on the loess-like loam of slopes. Clayey desert-steppe soil, and more rarely chernozem, contains a sufficient amount of lime, phosphoric acid, and potassium salt, but is poor in nitrous compounds. With artificial irrigation the soil provides good harvests. Solonchak soil is scattered in small patches and islands.

The steppe's character varies with altitude, relief, level of ground water, and soil–ground cover. On the lower terrace of the Ulu-Khem, in places inundated by water during spring flood, are the dense, bright green feather grasses (both pinnate and maidenhair types) and mixed grass, which sometimes is replaced by low bush steppes. On the upper terrace of the Ulu-Khem the steppes bear a more arid character and contain many Mongolian species suggestive of the Chuy steppe in East Altai and the steppes of Mongolia. Grasses and small bushes reaching six inches high are scattered widely. In this type of steppe, *Artemisia frigida* predominates, and *Nanophyton erinaceum,* pea tree (*Caragana bungei*), winter fat (*Eurotia ceratoides*), *Ceratocarpus arenarius,* kochia (*Kochia prostrata*), and chee grass (*Lasiagrostis splendens*) grow in places.

Solonchak meadows are abundant in depressions near rivers, where ground water is sufficiently near. Plants growing luxuriously here are licorice (*Glycirrhiza uralensis*), desert barley (*Hordeum secalinum*), and foxtail grass (*Alopecurus ventricosus*). Growing on the 400,000 acres of lowland suitable for agriculture are: various cereals, buckwheat, hemp, and flax; such truck-garden crops as cucumbers, cabbage, and watermelons. Although there are

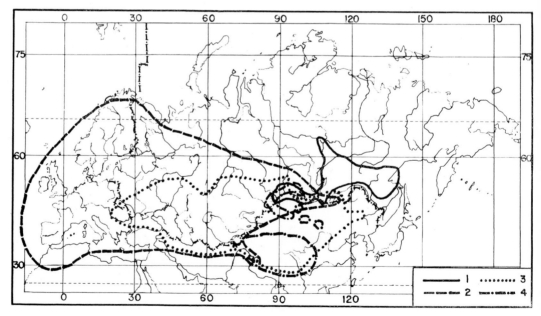

Map 8-VII. Fauna composition of Tuvin: 1—Eastern Siberian, 2—European, 3—Mongolian, 4—Tibetan. 1—Area of Siberian lentil (*Erythrina rosea*); 2—Area of gray flycatcher (*Muscicapa striata*); 3—Area of baloban (*Falco Cherrug*) from the falcon family; 4—Area of Tibetan and Altaic Urals fauna (*Tetraogallus tibetanus, T. altaicus*).

Fig. 8-23. General view of the northeastern part of the Ulu-Khem depression with small copses of larch.

rich harvests of grains, sometimes the young plants are ruined by early-morning frosts.

In the mountain steppes against a background of sheep's fescue grass (*Festuca ovina*) and other grasses (*Poa alpina*), one encounters astragalus (*Astragalus dahuricus*) and edelweiss (*Leontopodium sibiricum*), to which are added high-altitude species such as poppy (*Papaver alpinum*). At lower altitudes, where the steppe loses its alpine character, grow artemisia, feather grass, and many mixed grasses, such as steppe lucerne (*Medicago falcata*), not encountered above.

Mammals dwelling in the Tuva steppes include suslik, marmot, jeroba, wolf, and steppe fox. The birds include the great bustard (*Otis tarda dybowskii*), quail (*Corturnix coturnix*), and demoiselle crane (*Grus virgo*). Adapted to rocky hills are lapwing (*Vanellus vanellus*), hoope (*Upupa epops*), and stone-dancers (*Saxicola izabellina*). Associated with brackish lakes are ruddy sheldrake (*Casarca casarca*), gray heron (*Ardea cinerea*), noddy, goldeneye, and pintail duck. In the mountain steppes are large mountain sheep (*Ovis ammon*), and such birds

as red-beaked chough (*Pyrrhocorax pyrrhocorax*).

The chief occupation of Tuva inhabitants is livestock raising. Along the valleys are luxuriant meadows, on which graze herds of large and small-horned cattle. The horses which are bred in Tuva are celebrated for their endurance. Along the Ulu-Khem one may encounter camels and yaks.

The rivers meandering along the steppe are visible from a distance by their narrow dark-green fringe of bottomland forest. Trees predominating in it are laurel-leafed poplar (*Populus laurifolia*), birch, alder, bird cherry, barberry, and, as undergrowth, dogwood (*Cornus alba*), pea tree (*Caragana spinosa*), and dog rose (*Rosa acicularis*). Rocky terraces are covered with impenetrable thickets of buckthorn (*Hippophae rhamnoides*). The grassy vegetation comprises a mixture of plant types: water plants such as pond weed, bottomland bog plants, steppe plants such as Siberian aster, and forest species as well. In the upper section of streams, larch is found. Because of the contact of river, forest, and steppe, this riverside forest is thickly populated by a mixture of bird species such as the titmouse, forest species such as the woodpecker, steppe birds such as the crane, and various waterfowl.

The plain adjacent to the southern slope of the Tannu-Ola Range bears a pronounced semiarid character. On its surface, covered by fine rubble or gravel, there is a sparse, exhausted, and monotonous cover. Prominent are individual specimens of chee grass, gray strips of artemisia, impoverished pea tree, solid groves of saltwort (*Halogeton glomeratus*), and little clusters of small feather grass. In these places representatives of Central Asiatic fauna are found, such as Persian gazelle (*Gazella subgutturosa*), grouse (*Syrrhaptes paradoxus*), and rock partridge (*Caccabis chukar pubescens*). The valley of the Tesiin-Gol is noted for a strip of tall forest in which there are boar and countless waterfowl.

Forests occupy approximately one-half the area of Tuva, and grow above 3,300 feet, and extend to an altitude of 6,600 feet in the mountains. The timber line is higher on the south-facing slopes and, in general, in the southwest. The forests, for the most part, have the characteristics of Siberian taiga; that is, they consist of larch, fir, spruce, and Siberian pine (*Pinus sibirica*), with *Pinus silvestris* only rarely encountered. In distribution of tree species through the mountains, a certain regularity is observed, depending on the altitude of the place, but the upper limits of individual species vary in different sections of the ranges. Larch is predominant throughout the mountains, forming the timber line and in places extending downward into the steppe along wide ravines and shaded slopes. On Tannu-Ola the first spruces and Siberian pines appear at a height of 3,762 feet, birch and aspen reach 4,620 feet, spruce runs to 4,785 feet, and above 5,610 feet the fir and Siberian pine predominate. The pine forms the timber line at a height of about 6,600 feet. Higher up, they give way to vegetation of the high-mountain zone.

In the Tuva Valley there is no typical wooded-steppe district like that of the Minusinsk Valley. In the bordering strip of the forest and steppe zones, with the ascent into the mountains, taiga vegetation becomes more profuse but is confined to the north-facing slopes. Steppes descend from the high slopes into valleys and onto steep rocky slopes of southern exposure. The predominant tree is larch, grouped in open groves. Between the scarce but sturdy trees are located vast glades, overgrown with various shrubs—honeysuckle, wild rose, black currant, rhododenron, and succulent grasses—and with globeflower, forget-me-not, and gentian. Close by, on terraces of river valleys, steppe-like meadows are developed with artemisia, cinquefoil, aster, astragalus, and feather grass. On steep rocky slopes facing south, amid moist taiga, steppe plants with feather grasses may be found.

Fig. 8-24. Ulu-Khem River, with laurel-leaved poplar in the foreground; below Kyzyl.

Fig. 8-25. Pine–fir–spruce taiga of the Sayan type in northeastern Tuva.

Typical mountain taiga prevails in the mountainous districts of the eastern part of the region. From a high observation point can be seen an endless sea of dense forests throughout which rivers and lakes are scattered. In the lower forest zone many deciduous trees (birch, mountain ash, and bird cherry) are mixed with the coniferous species. In the upper forest zone the coniferous forest acquires the uniform character of the "black forests" of Siberian pine with admixture of fir, spruce, and birch. On the moss cover under the forest canopy there are a few flowering plants and higher sporophytes, small bushes—bog bilberry, whortleberry, and red bilberry—and a series of taiga ferns. Sometimes the second formation produces elder (*Sambucus racemosa*) and honeysuckle (*Lonicera coerulea*). On glades in the middle of the forest, there are tall-grass meadows with aconite and ramsons, and on moist spots there is

much water arum (*Calla palustris*). On rocky slopes the herb *Bergenia crassifolia* grows abundantly. Usually Siberian pine, spruce, and alder cover the low, swampy sections, and larch, pine, and birch grow on the steep, drier mountain slopes.

Among the vast taiga expanses, bogs and meadows are often found. Many swamps are connected with river valleys. Muddy peat bogs are overgrown with cranberry, cloudberry, wild rosemary, and small polar birch. Peat bogs at heights of 4,600 feet and above are devoid of many typical swamp plants. The abundance of peat bogs lends to some regions a tundra character. Typical for sedge bogs is a solid cover of sedges (*Carex gracilis,* and *C. vesicaria*), horsetail, and cinquefoil. Amid the forest grow meadows of two types: forest meadows and tall-grass meadows. Characteristic of the forest meadows are globeflower, and geranium. Tall-grass meadows which grow to heights of 6 feet, have sparse roots and are composed of larkspur, ramson, and cow parsnip.

The coniferous forests, which cover the mountains of the western part of the Kemchik basin, consist mainly of larch grouped in open groves and occupy approximately 65 per cent of the area. On Tannu-Ola Range also larch forests of a park-like character are plentiful. On the south-facing slopes of the range, forests are rare, and larch rather than Siberian pine forms the timber line.

The taiga zone of Tuva is rich in forest fauna, among which valuable fur-bearing and commercial animals are abundant. Dwelling in the forests are: brown bear, wolverine, sable, otter, weasel, fox, squirrel, beaver, mountain goat, elk, Siberian stag, musk deer, and reindeer. The fur industry is important in the economy of Tuva; furs are available in quantity, and are noted for their high quality. Some types of sable and squirrel are considered equal in quality to those of Trans-Baikal. Stag are plentiful in the taiga, and form the core of intensive animal husbandry. The wild reindeer lives in the Sayans. Domestic deer is the basis of the economy of the nomadic people in the northeastern part of the region. Among the birds living in the dark-coniferous taiga are: nutcracker, wood grouse, crossbill, trydactylous woodpecker, black grouse, hazel grouse, and deaf cuckoo. Mosquitoes and midges are inhabitants of the moist forest jungle and swarm in clouds above a party traveling there. In the park-like larch forests the bird species include the white-capped yellow hammer, chiff-chaff, sparrow, and flycatcher. Birds commonly seen in the zone of sparse mountain forest are the mountain double-snipe, and the drab-colored chiff-chaff.

Vegetation of a subalpine character begins 5,280 to 5,610 feet, is dominant at 6,600 to 7,260 feet, and extends as far as the high-mountain alpine belt, that is, to approximately 8,080 feet. It is developed along dry rocky slopes of ranges and on extensive high-mountain plains in the Western part of the region. The vegetation of the belt is sharply distinguished and compre-

hensive, both in terms of the floral composition and in terms of phytophenological structure. The subalpine belt in Tuva has two basic types of vegetation: a distinctive shrub growth and mountain-steppe. The subalpine shrubs are low-growing and cover a large area near the timber line. As flora, they differ sharply from one another in the various regions of Tuva. On the greater part of the Tannu-Ola Range, shrub subalpine growths are of a uniform nature: dwarf birch (*Betula humilis*) in the lower part of the belt and dwarf birch (*B. rotunifolia*) in the upper; intermixed with them are dwarfed cinquefoil (*Potentilla fruticosa*) and alpine spirea (*Spiraea alpina*). In the southeastern part of Tuva, where the subalpine belt is represented only by sparse small patches, the shrub growths have a more xerophytic nature. The basic shrubs are pea tree (*Caragana jubata*) and rhododendron (*Rhododendron parvifolium*). In the southwestern part of Tuva, shrub growths are not characteristic.

The steppes in the subalpine belt are at 6,600 to 8,080 feet. They extend in a narrow belt along the southern spurs of Eastern Tannu-Ola and have a wide development on the high-mountain watershed plateaus, in the wide valleys and canyons of southwestern Tuva, and also along the rocky-rubbly exposures of southeastern Tuva. The steppe flora is of a mixed character, with typical steppe species, mountain xerophytes, and alpine species combined. On the high-mountain steppes of Tannu-Ola, tulip (*Tulipa uniflora*), cinquefoil (*Potentilla acaulis*), and gentian (*Gentiana angulosa*) are dominant. The high-mountain steppes of southwestern Tuva are influenced by the desert. Predominant is the high-mountain cereal–artemisia steppe with low, sparse grass. The grass stand of the steppe is cereals and mixed grasses. Some 25 per cent of the grass species are alpine. Present also are types common to the southeastern Altai and northwestern Mongolia, such as crazyweed (*Oxytropis tragacanthoides*).

The high steppe plateaus, abounding in sheer cliffs, and the wide steppe valleys are a favored habitat for the mountain ram, mountain goat, the red-billed jackdaw, and the Altai gyrfalcon. The steppes offer high-mountain pastures for small-horned cattle, horses, and yaks which range the year round.

The high-mountain zone is located in separate islands above the timber line (6,270 to 6,600 feet) of the mountains surrounding the Tuva Valley. Attaining their greatest development on the treeless summits, certain alpine plants (globeflower, columbine, violet) grow far below the timber line to a height of 3,960 feet. Growing above the forest zone in the form of a transitional narrow strip are such dwarf brushwoods as: small polar birch (*Betula rotundifolia*), scrub alder (*Alnus fruticosa*), willow (*Salix myrsinites, S. herbacea*), scrub cinquefoil (*Potentilla fruticosa*), and rhododendron (*Rhododendron chrysanthum*), amid which one may often see partridge grass, dragon's head, and other alpine plants. Alpine meadows are characteristic of lower sections of the high-elevation zone, and along the valleys of mountain streams they are found at the upper timber line. They are composed of columbine, chive, anemone, snakewood, and alpine poppy; and forest plants such as ramson, sorrel, white hellebore, pinks, aconite, and geranium.

Above the alpine meadows, on level plateaus with ample precipitation and weak drainage, lies the mountain moss-lichen tundra, characterized by a thick moss-lichen cover mixed with reindeer moss (*Cladonia rangiferina*). Among mosses and lichens are beds of small polar birch and small willow, together with sparse low-growing alpine plants such as alpine sweet grass (*Hierochloe alpina*), chickweed (*Alsine arctica*), snow crowfoot (*Ranunculus frigidus*), partridge grass (*Dryas octopetala*), and gentian (*Gentiana algida*). In the upper part of the zone a stony mountain tundra is developed on rocky patches and the rubbly soil of steep mountain slopes. Vegetation is scanty: Individual specimens of the hardiest, cold-enduring species, such as whitlow grass (*Draba algida*), saxifrage (*Saxifraga oppositifolia*), and gentian (*Gentiana tenella*), are scattered amid the rocks. Near snow patches are seen alpine willows and crowfoot. Small bogs are thickly overgrown with alpine sedges, rushes, and cotton grasses. On drier sites the vegetation is even scantier; mosses and lichens are rare, and the rocky areas are almost entirely bare.

The occasional alpine mountain summits rise above the solid sea of dark-coniferous taiga; that is why the fauna on them is numerous, but it is clearly foreign to the taiga world. In the mountain district of Eastern Tuva reindeer are abundant, ascending in winter from the snow-covered taiga into the region of mountain tundra, where the flat summits of the mountains have been swept free of snow. Birds dwelling amid the brushwood thickets are the mountain pipit (*Anthus spinoletta blakistoni*) and white ptarmigan (*Lagopus lagopus*). The tundra ptarmigan (*Lagopus mutus*) and "foolish" plover (*Charadrius morinellus*) dwell on flat rocky sections devoid of brush. The Altai snow pheasant (*Tetraogallus altaicus*) is common to the craggy mountains in the western part of the region, where the mountain tundra and mountain steppes touch each other.

CHAPTER 9

Baikalia: Trans-Baikal and Pre-Baikal

The Trans-Baikal (east of Lake Baikal) and Pre-Baikal (west of Lake Baikal), known as Baikalia, and the areas adjoining them on the north and northeast form a unique, well-defined geographic region. Baikalia is comprised of ancient, highly dislocated schists and gneisses and of large granite blocks. In the west and north, it drops off in a high, steep escarpment to the Central Siberian Plateau. In the southwest, it is separated from Eastern Sayan by the deep and narrow Tunkin graben. In the south and southeast, it adjoins the national border of the Mongolian People's Republic and Manchuria. The region is not well defined in the northeast, where the border passes along a line dividing the basin of the Zeya River from that of the Aldan.

In Baikalia, the mountains are of average height and do not have a snow line; the plains are of secondary importance. The mountains do not belong to any one center. With the exception of the Stanovoi Range and a series of plateaus, the mountains are situated in parallel ridges similar to each other in outward appearance and origin, and are extended generally in an east-northeast direction. This direction is most strongly expressed in western Trans-Baikal. The Yablonoi Range is the watershed between the Pacific and Arctic drainage.

The ranges are massive, broad water divides, with occasional dome-shaped summits. They are separated from one another by broad and deep depressions. High ranges with alpine relief forms are found only along the outskirts of the region (Barguzin and Udokan). The hydrographic network is laid out in long, parallel valleys of a northeast-southwest trend. These valleys are wide with gentle slopes and contain exceptionally thick Quaternary deposits. The valleys result either from synclinal sagging or from subsidences along large fault lines, as in the valleys of the Khilok, Muya, and Chara rivers. Many valleys were formed from old lake bottoms and are now islands of steppes amid a solid forest landscape. Lateral eroded valleys are small, meandering and narrow, and have steep rocky slopes; such, for example are the lower valleys of the Khilok, Chikoy, and Ingoda rivers. In the southeast, an intricate drainage system is developed, consisting of dry broad ravines and valleys of varying direction.

The structure and relief in the southeast have been created by Caledonian and Mesozoic folding, by large tectonic breaks and shifts of separate blocks, by twofold ancient glaciation, and by modern exogenous processes.

To the sharply continental climate are added climatic features of Eastern Siberia and Mongolia, plus the strong climatic influence of Lake Baikal. The rivers, which belong to the Yenisei, Lena, and Amur systems, possess the typical regime of Eastern Siberia rivers: extremely small discharge of water in winter,

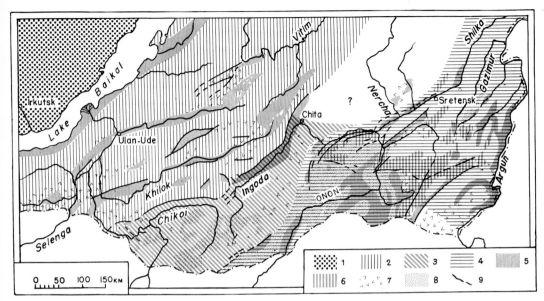

Map 9-I. Tectonic map of Trans-Baikal: 1—Siberian platform (shield); 2—Caledonian folds; 3—Hercynian folds; 4—Mesozoic folds; 5—Cenozoic depressions; 6—Mesozoic and Permian sea deposits; 7—Mesozoic volcanic deposits; 8—Middle Paleozoic sea deposits; 9—Lines of displacement and their projection.

minimal high water in spring, and heavy summer floods. Although there are many shallow, mineralized lakes, the greatest geographic interest is evoked by Baikal, the largest, oldest, and most original fresh-water lake. Baikalia lies between 49° and 60° north latitude. Its vegetation corresponds in latitude to the subzone of mixed forests and wooded-steppe between Leningrad and Kharkov, or to the Western Siberian taiga, wooded-steppe, and steppe zones, approximately from the mouth of the Irtysh to Karaganda. Therefore in one area, the Siberian taiga runs into the Mongolian steppes, in the middle of which are scattered patches of high-mountain landscape. Here we find (1) all the basic soil types, from chestnut to podzol and peat-gley soil, and (2) Siberian taiga, Mongolian steppe, and Amur-Ussuri and high mountain species of plants and animals, to which are added diverse relics of the glacial and xerothermic periods.

Administratively, the Trans-Baikal and Pre-Baikal belong to the Buryat-Mongolian ASSR, the Chita region, the Irkutsk region, and the Yakutsk ASSR.

GEOLOGIC HISTORY

The relief of the Baikal region has been formed by processes of the remote past and by modern exogenous processes. The tectonics are extremely complex. Intensive folding took place in the Caledonian (lower Paleozoic) period; only the southeastern part is affected by Mesozoic folding. Trans-Baikal has a series of broad and flat anticlines, divided by comparatively narrow and deep synclinal sags; the anticlines are sometimes overthrust on synclines, and in places breaks have occurred, accompanied by a subsidence of the synclines and even by their crumpling. Others maintain that at the end of the folding process, the region, as a result of

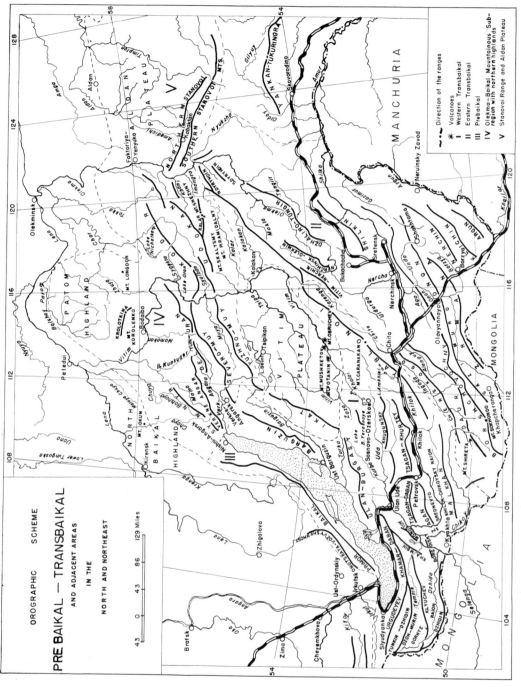

Map 9-II. Orographic scheme of Pre-Baikal and Trans-Baikal.

repeated upheavals, was brought several times to the state of a peneplain. At different times tectonic breaks dissected the region into long sections, of which some subsided, forming grabens, and others remained in place as horsts. These processes have been complicated by volcanic eruptions both of the fissure type, yielding vast mantles of basalts (for example, in Borgoy steppe), and of the central type linked with a few ancient volcanic cones. Craters and streams of lava have been preserved on the Vitim Plateau. Tectonic movements have not yet terminated, as indicated by the frequent earthquakes.

The upheaval of the ranges has created severe climatic conditions on their summits, contributing to the development of glaciation which centers in the highest ranges and on the separate bald mountains (Khamar-Daban, Barguzin, Udokan, and Sokhondo). The thawing of glacial ice has produced many turbulent mountain streams, the waters of which have accumulated in deep depressions, forming large lakes. Sand and gravel carried here by the streams form thick deposits on the bottom of the depressions.

The shifting of separate blocks, having raised or lowered the erosion level of some river systems, has caused the formation of three to four terraces, as well as the capture of some rivers by the system of a neighboring river. For example, the river Argun once emptied into Lake Dalay-Nor, but was later captured by tributaries of the Amur; its subsequent deepening led in turn to the capture of the Khaylar River, which had also emptied into Dalay-Nor. With the upheaval of the blocks there occurred (1) intensification of stream erosion, (2) creation of antecedent valleys, (3) damming of rivers, and (4) formation of large lakes on whose bottoms thick layers of sediment accumulated. During the subsidence, lakes were drained either entirely (being converted into broad sandy plains in which the rivers began to cut their channels), or were only partly drained, leaving chains of shallow lakes which have survived to the present. Energetic erosion occurs today, and the lengthwise profile of most rivers appears young. The degree of erosion in the river valleys is directly related to the composition of the rocks through which the rivers flow.

The sharply continental climatic conditions (especially the great daily amplitudes), the altitude of the ranges, and the steepness of the mountain slopes favor physical weathering; hence vast areas of rocks, rock patches, and talus are typical of the relief. The hot, short summer contributes to chemical weathering of the rocks. Salts thus produced are carried off with surface and ground water into locked-in basins, resulting in the mineralization of many lakes. The wind, under conditions of arid climate, has created a variety of deflational rock forms in many regions (the valleys of the Barguzin and Chikoy rivers). Substantial expanses of ancient lake sediments, freed from under the water and sand, have been worked over by aeolian processes, and subsequently covered by pine groves. Felling and burning of the forests, together with the plowing and trampling of the fixed sand, has resulted in the renewed drifting of sand and the formation of wind-eroded basins and sandy hillocks (Khilok Valley). Permafrost is important in the formation of the region's relief.

GEOMORPHOLOGIC SUBREGIONS

Baikalia may be divided into five large geomorphologic subregions, each distinguished by a number of characteristics in its geological history, details of geologic composition and structure, and predominance of certain relief forms: (1) Western Trans-Baikal, (2) Eastern Trans-Baikal, (3) Pre-Baikal, (4) Olekma-Baikal, and (5) the Stanovoi Range with the Aldan Plateau.

Western Trans-Baikal

Western Trans-Baikal belongs to the region of Caledonian folding (lower Paleozoic). It is formed of granites and Pre-Cambrian crystalline rocks. In the southern half of the subregion there are small patches of marine sedimentary Paleozoic rock. Marine Mesozoic sediments have not been discovered, and only comparatively small strips and patches of fresh-water Jurassic and Cretaceous sediments are present. These are absent on water divides but occur undisturbed in large valleys in which each outcrop has a separate profile. This indicates that Mesozoic rocks, just as Tertiary ones, were deposited in valleys already existing at an earlier time. These valleys filled with water and formed a system of elongated lakes. Geomorphologically, Western Trans-Baikal is comprised of the following: (1) Tunkin-Dzhidin mountain region, (2) Khamar-Daban Range, (3) Barguzin Range, (4) the intermediate-elevation Khilok-Chikoy region, (5) the Vitim Plateau, and (6) the Yablonoi Range.

The Tunkin-Dzhidin mountain region connects Khamar-Daban with Eastern Sayan. It consists of four ranges stretching from east to west: two northern ones—the Urgudeyev Mountains (9,279 feet) and Dzon-Murin Mountains (9,282 feet)—which rise above the timber line, and two southern ones—the Klyuchev Mountains and the Ainek-Dzhidin Mountains—which are lower and completely covered with forest. All ranges constitute parts of a single plateau and are divided by zones of low mountains. The main water divide is not coordinated to a single range, but passes along a broken line from one range to another. The ranges have more gentle southern slopes and very steep northern ones, along which fault traces are marked by cold and hot mineral springs. The higher, steeper, and more intensely moistened northern slopes are more strongly dissected than the southern slopes, and the river valleys are gorges with almost perpendicular sides. The broad, level, and horizontal surfaces of the ranges, despite their dissection by the dense river network, have the appearance of real plains, owing to: (1) ancient peneplanation, (2) basalt blanket deposits lying on the eroded, leveled-out surface of steeply placed rocks, (3) permafrost which has solidi-fied the surface and preserved the ranges from rapid erosion and also (4) intensive surface weathering, contributing to the leveling-out of the general area. Almost everywhere there are signs of ancient glaciation in the form of glacial troughs (sometimes enclosed in one another), and cirques. Large areas of the bald mountains are covered by rock waste.

The Khamar-Daban Range, extending along the southeastern shore of Lake Baikal, is a mountain chain without pronounced peaks but with massive rounded mountain shapes reaching more than 6,600 feet high. Closer to Baikal, the high bald mountains look like flat benches heaped one on the other—easily accessible from the southern side, but steeply cut off on the north toward Lake Baikal. Where there are many glacial cirques the mountains are dissected and craggy, with tops in the form of combs, pyramids, and peaks exceeding 7,260 feet in height. The eastern part of the range beyond the Selenga River, called Ulan-Burgasy Range, gradually widens and is converted into high plateau-shaped hills.

The Barguzin Range lies along the right bank of the Barguzin River, sloping gently toward Baikal and steeply toward the valley of the Barguzin. This range, composed mainly of granites and rising to a maximum height of 8,910 feet, has sharply expressed alpine forms—jagged narrow crests, sharp snowy peaks, and steep, almost inaccessible cliffs. Vast alluvial fans formed at the foot of the range by mountain streams are composed of large boulders, rubble, and sand. The northern sections contain abundant evidence of glaciation, and resemble the glacial landscapes of Finland: there are glacial troughs and lakes with fiord-like bays, together with islands of bedrock *rôches moutonnées*.

The Khilok-Chikoy region of an intermediate height has a series of approximately parallel ranges, such as Tsagan-Daban, Khudun, Zagan, Tsagan-Khurtey, and Malkhan, extending in a southwest-northeast direction and reaching, on the average, 3,135 to 3,630 feet, and in individual mountains 4,290 to 5,280 feet maximum. The main ridges, especially in the east-

Fig. 9-1. Vitim River in the granite region of the southern part of the Vitim Plateau.

ern part, have massive, broad, slopes, above which rise low, flat summits. Where there is more intensive dissection, the ridge is broken into large dome-shaped or elongated hills. The rivers frequently merge in the longitudinal depressions and rush through transverse valleys into the neighboring depressions. Some of these are the Selenga and Uda rivers, Arey, Bludnaya (Khilok system), Ingoda, and Chita. Longitudinal river valleys, diverging from the depressions into the mountains sometimes form peculiar types of regions. On the valley floor in a series of depressions are lakes, such as Chitiuskiye, Yeravnyye, and Gusinoye lakes. The tops of the water divides represent the base level surface of a high plateau which has been divided into parallel ridges by dislocations and erosion. In the relief of the region, depressions are insignificant. Many of the broad, straight valleys are of tectonic origin; the secondary narrow and meandering valleys are erosional.

Valleys in the west are notched more deeply; their bottoms lie at an altitude of 1,650 to 1,980 feet; valleys in the east lie at 2,970 to 3,300 feet. Therefore, the relative height of the ranges and their dissection increases toward the west.

The Vitim Plateau, geomorphologically, is a monotonous region drained by the Vitim River. It consists of low hills and boggy plains extending for dozens of miles. A solid forest cover conceals irregularities of the relief and emphasizes the soft contours of the mountains. The chief watersheds, reaching an altitude of 5,610 to 6,171 feet, rise 1,320 to 1,980 feet above the bottom of the valleys. Along its periphery the plateau is higher, more dissected, and assumes a high-mountain character. For example, Ikat Range, with altitudes of nearly 6,600 feet, drops as a precipice of tectonic origin from the plateau to the valley of the Barguzin River. Valleys of the large rivers are notched deeply between adjacent water divides; small streams flow in shallow and open valleys; only where they pass through igneous rocks have streams cut canyon-shaped channels. Most river valleys follow two prevailing directions—east-north-east and west-northwest—conditioned not only by the direction of folding and large faults but

Owing to the basalt cover, erosion of the Vitim Plateau is retarded in comparison with that of the southern sections; water-divide expanses have not yet been converted into ranges, but contain preserved features of the ancient peneplain.

Fig. 9-2. Pass in the Yablonoi Mountains at 3,500 feet, with a forest of Dahurian larch and Siberian pine.

also by the direction of the old river network. In tectonic valleys (for example, that of the Tsipa River), there are many hot springs. In the central part of the plateau, which is formed of ancient metamorphic schists and granites, basalts are exposed along the upper course of the Vitim River. These basalts are from extinct volcanoes—Obruchev, Mushketov, and Lopatin. Lava flows and craters are still preserved, such as fissure eruptions of basalts, and the Kropotkin volcano in the basin of the Dzhida River. The Mushketov volcano is a truncated cone rising 528 feet; its crater, today filled by a lake, is 2,475 feet wide. The basalt flow of the volcano covers 76 square miles and has a thickness of 50 feet. The lava from the volcanoes is very fresh, with good columnar structure.

The Yablonoi Range is the watershed of the rivers flowing to the Pacific and Arctic oceans. In the north, it is the water divide between the Vitim and its right tributary, the Karenga. The average altitude of the range varies from 3,960 to 4,950 feet, and its highest point is the bald peak, Greater Saranakan (5,200 feet). The crest of the range is steep. North of Chita it breaks off in a steep wall 1,155 feet high. The rivers flowing off the eastern slope have a steep gradient and form valley gorges with high, precipitous, craggy slopes, overgrown with pine and deciduous forest. The western slope rises imperceptibly, so that from the west the range appears to have a low elevation with a series of very flat summits. The valleys of this slope are broad and swampy, with gentle inclines covered by dwarfed larch and some spruce. Where the valleys converge they form cirque-shaped terminals containing many shallow ponds and swamps. The Karenga River intersects the Yablonoi Range at an impassable gorge, and it continues farther to the northeast as the water divide of the Vitim and Olekma rivers. Here it is a chain of smooth bald mountains with an elevation up to 4,620 feet, with tops flat and frequently swampy; farther on, it terminates as the Northern and Southern Dyryndin Ranges.

The Kyakhtir Mountains differ from the neighboring Khilok-Chikoy by having lower and shorter ridges. The landscape of the region is like that of the Gobi desert: residual and island mountains, poorly drained or undrained depressions containing saline lakes, and aeolian forms with thin alluvial deposits on their slopes.

Mineral resources of Western Trans-Baikal consist of: (1) placer gold in the Barguzin taiga, on Vitim Plateau, and in the system of the Dzhida River; (2) large contact Balbagar deposits of iron ore in the Ulan-Burgasy Range with reserves of 92 million tons and an average iron content of 37 per cent; (3) the Dzhidin wolfram deposit, of national economic importance; (4) beds of brown coal of Jurassic age at Gusinoye Lake, near Ulan-Ude and Chita (Chernov mine); (5) mineral lakes with great supplies of soda and Glauber salt (Selengin, Kiran); (6) numerous mineral springs—hot sulphuric, cold carbonate, and chalybeate springs—where there are many health resorts, such as Yamarovka or Darasun; (7) stone construction materials; particularly igneous rocks.

Eastern Trans-Baikal

Eastern Trans-Baikal, unlike Western Trans-Baikal, belongs to the region of Mesozoic folding. Besides pre-Cambrian deposits of highly dislocated (principally in a northeast direction), widespread granites and small patches of young Quaternary basalts, there are known marine deposits of the Cambrian, Devonian, Carboniferous, Permian, Triassic, and the Ju-

rassic. Jurassic and Tertiary fresh-water deposits are found. The Mesozoic folds have a northeast strike, and are tilted toward the northwest. Mesozoic and alpine folding took place as follows: (1) weak folding between the Triassic and Jurassic Periods; (2) folding at the end of the Jurassic; (3) extensive folding in the second half of the Cretaceous Period; (4) strong folding during the Tertiary (but nonetheless weaker than that of the Cretaceous). The folded area has been complicated by faulting, as indicated by thermal discharges.

In the development of the relief, ancient repeated glaciation has also participated, leaving its evidence in several regions. A lake-river period during which valleys were well established, was followed by an arid "Gobi" period, which is characterized (especially in the southeastern part of Trans-Baikal) by the formation of undrained basins, the old-age river system, and the accumulation of coarsely fragmental alluvial fans. Accumulation ended with upheaval of the subregion and the rejuvenation of the hydrographic network.

In the high-mountain district, at the sources of the Ingoda and Chikoy rivers, and the left tributaries of the upper Onon River, are peaks of Trans-Baikal—Sokhondo (8,190 feet) and Borun-Shebetuy (8,434 feet). Morphologically, the region is a highly elevated peneplain, greatly dissected by erosion. Often individual water-divide summits do not conform to the geologic structure. The region appears to be a single unbroken upland; it is without sharp ridges of the alpine type. The summit of Sokhondo, formed of dacites, is a broad, flat dome with graduated slopes. It is notched by steep cirques which contain patches of snow or small lakes. The valleys of rivers originating in the flat swampy basins are almost impassable—in some places they are extremely narrow, and in others wide but completely inundated.

The central part of Eastern Trans-Baikal east of Yablonoi Range, with Cherskogo, Daur, Borshchovochny, Gasimuro-Onon, and Ermana ranges is typical erosional country. Its highest elevation is 3,300 feet and it is deeply dissected by the numerous tributaries of the Ingoda and

Onon rivers. The water divides are typical erosional ranges, with an approximately parallel northeast direction. The northern part of Cherskogo Range is a remnant of the ancient peneplain, dissected first by fault dislocation, and later by erosion, which developed the contours of the rolling hills. The regularity of distribution of the ranges may be explained by the fact that most of the rivers of the subregion flow in a northeast direction (characteristic for Trans-Baikal) in conformity with the strike of folds, although there are a few valleys or separate parts of valleys with a northwest trend, intersecting the main ranges (the Ingoda River Valley, which cuts through Cherskogo Range; or the Onon River Valley, cutting across Borshchovochny Range). Only the valleys which have been formed by fault dislocations are wide. Erosional valleys are narrow and deep with high, steep, craggy sides and straight, rapid-filled channels. Intensive erosional activity has been sustained by repeated upheavals of the subregion, and at the present time the intensified erosion of the Amur tributaries indicate a rejuvenation of the relief.

The southeastern part of Trans-Baikal contains a group of parallel low ranges—Nerchin, Klichkin, and Argun. In contrast to other districts of the subregion, these ranges are relatively stable. This section of Trans-Baikal is characterized by the Gobi relief: (1) features of old age; (2) relative heights from 300 to 500 feet; (3) flat watersheds with dry rocky slopes, having the appearance of dome-shaped hills; (4) wide river valleys filled with sediments, or dry ravines. Weak streams meander on the broad, flat bottoms of the valleys forming braided channels (especially on the Argun River). Old dry river beds are exposed as a result of the predominating lateral erosion. In the large ravines neither channels nor terraces nor other traces of erosional activity may be found. Some striking Gobi features are the isolated crags, which often have unusual weathered shapes. These are edged by thick trains of mountains debris, and contain vast enclosed basins with many lakes (Khara-Nor, Borzin, Barun-Tarey lakes), which at the present time

are dried up and surrounded by a white border of effloresced salts.

In the mountain district of the upper Olekma basin, or at Olekmin Stanovik, comparatively short ranges of a northeast trend predominate (Dzhaliro-Tungir, and Nerchinsk-Olekmin). They lie in parallel, echelon-like positions and are separated from one another by deep and broad lengthwise valleys. Despite the heights (4,290 to 5,610 feet above sea level and 1,650 to 2,640 feet from the valley floor), the relief forms are massive, with the smooth, rounded contours of dome-shaped bald mountains and with vast alluvial deposits at their summits and taluses on their slopes.

Eastern Trans-Baikal is rich in mineral resources. Between the Onon and Argun rivers, in the large granite massifs, are deposits of wolfram, with metal content up to 73 to 76 per cent, estimated at 7,500 tons. On the contact zone of metamorphosed calcareous-clay shale and granite intrusions west of Nerchinsk, there are deposits of iron with reserves of more than one hundred million tons. In the same subregion lie polymetallic deposits: tin, silver, lead, zinc, mercury, antimony, arsenic, fluorspar, precious stones (beryls, aquamarines, topazes, and amethysts), construction materials, and many mineral lakes and springs.

Pre-Baikal

The northwestern shore of Lake Baikal, for its entire length from Kultuk to the northern tip of the lake, is bordered by flat-topped mountains and bald ranges, which lie at a distance of three to six miles from the lake. The mountains form an abrupt bench 660 to 1,485 feet high, separating the lake depression from the lower, neighboring Central Siberian Plateau, and serving as a water divide between the Baikal tributaries and the Irkut and Lena. In the Pre-Baikal area (west of Lake Baikal) there are clear traces of recent upheaval and comparatively recent subsidence.

Between Kultuk and Olkhon Island, the mountains are known as the Primor Range. In its southern section, to the Angara, the range has an intermediate-mountain landscape raised to 990 feet above Baikal. It is close to the lake, often descending to it in sheer, highly abraded walls. Farther north the range increases in height, but the width remains constant, resulting in a sharp relief with steep scarps and increased river gradient. The range is part of Olkhon Island, from the northern tip of which the underwater Akademiche Ridge (lying at depths of from 1,980 to 3,300 feet) extends to Cape Valukan on the northeastern shore of Baikal. Extending parallel to, and west of, the Primor Range in the massive Onot Range, which contains individual flat summits 4,290 to 4,620 feet high.

Baikal Range begins at the latitude of the northern end of Olkhon Island and averages from 3,960 to 4,950 feet in height from the base-level of Lake Baikal, thus rising above the timber line. From Olkhon to the source of the Lena the range is massive and rounded, with a level crest capped by low, flat bald peaks, with no evidence of glaciation. Farther north, the range becomes alpine in character, with pointed crests separated by saddles covered with talus. The range gradually broadens into uplands, rising to heights of from 6,105 to 6,930 feet, with passes at 3,300 to 4,290 feet. Alpine relief forms are concentrated in the western part. The western rim of the upland is a steep cliff 990 to 1,650 feet high, and the eastern rim drops off steeply toward Baikal. On the west-facing slope, glacial traces have been preserved almost untouched by erosion; but on the east-facing, Baikal side, the Baikal tributaries have destroyed all glacial evidence.

Olekma-Baikal

The Olekma-Baikal mountain subregion lies, as the name would suggest, between the Olekma River and Lake Baikal. It consists of a system of parallel ranges with a general northeast trend, divided by many lengthwise valleys, mostly of tectonic origin. The ranges are composed of pre-Cambrian crystalline schists and gneisses, with granite outcrops. Only in the valley separating the ranges are continental Jurassic deposits (for example, in Verkhne-Char Valley) and Quaternary deposits (in the valleys of the Muya and Upper Angara) found. The subregion was almost leveled to a peneplain, remnants of which are found in plateau-shaped water divides. Then a period of upheaval, accompanied by faulting, resulted in the formation of a pronounced cliff dropping to the adjacent Central Siberian Plateau. Modern mountain ranges and high plateaus were created, and grabens were formed parallel to one another. The erosion levels of the river systems were altered, resulting in the rejuvenation of erosion and the intensive dissection of relief. Indications of this are the entrenched river terraces and the increased depth erosion of the large rivers. There is energetic notching of the rivers into the bottoms of glacial valleys, intersection of high ranges by rivers, and stream capture. For example, the Olekma River, having a greater gradient, has captured the streams of the Kalar-Vitim system. Intensive erosion still continues.

In the subregion are abundant and varied indications of ancient glaciation: thick moraines, fluvioglacial deposits, glacial troughs, and cirque lakes. These are not evident in the adjacent sections of the Central Siberian Plateau. The landscape indicates twofold glaciation: lakes on the bottom of crumbling glacial cirques located at 3,300 feet in the Udokan Range, and erratic boulders on the tops of high bald mountains indicate early glaciation resembling continental glaciation of the Scandinavian type; broad glacial valleys containing cross moraines 100 to 300 feet high, *rôches mountonées,* and striated rocks indicate more recent glaciation. Cirques at 6,600 to 7,260 feet indicate the alpine character of the last glaciation, and there is evidence of thick glaciers in the valleys. After the retreat of the glaciers, rivers by-passing the moraine obstructions cut narrow gorges through bedrock, notched bottoms of glacial troughs, and formed the last terrace. Despite the height of the ranges and the severe climatic conditions, there is no sign of present-day glaciation; however, large snow patches last all summer on the tops of many bald peaks. The absence of modern glaciers is due to the small amount of winter precipitation, the thinness of snow cover, and the exceptionally low humidity. In several ranges (for example, Yuzhno-Muy) cirques are developed by frost weathering.

Between Lake Baikal and Vitim River there are three main parallel ranges: Delyun-Uran (bearing the name Angar in the southwest), Severo-Muy, and Yuzhno-Muy, divided by the lengthwise valleys of the Upper Angara and the Muya. Delyun-Uran Range, more than 6,600 feet high, and with mountain passes at a height of about 4,950 feet, is a chain of sharp-toothed, high bald peaks which rise sharply above the mountains adjacent on the north. Severo-Muy Range is the same height and, with its alpine relief forms, presents a distinct contrast to the more southerly Yuzhno-Muy Range. The latter has massive bald peaks more than 6,600 feet high. In the southwest it breaks into a series of isolated mountains with dome-shaped tops. In the northeast, owing to stronger tectonic processes and the changing from granites to shales and limestones of the pre-Cambrian and Lower Cambrian, the Yuzhno-Muy range acquires a high-mountain landscape, with sharp peaks, steep slopes, and a well-developed valley network. The range represents an asymmetrical horst; its gentle northern slope has very little talus and is covered solidly with forest.

A similar system of three ranges (Kodar, Udokan, and Kalar) is located between the Vitim and Olekma rivers. These ranges are a continuation of the Muy ranges. They are separated from one another by the Verkhne-Char, Verkhne-Tokko, and Verkhne-Kalar tectonic valleys. These ranges are massive and do not have an orographically expressed main range. The mountain system is symmetrical: In the middle range, Udokan, both slopes are steep; in the more northerly range, Kodar, only the south-facing slope is steep, and in the southerly Kalar Range the north-facing slope is a cliff.

Kodar Range may have been formed of a single massif raised above Verkhne-Char Valley and dissected by rivers into a series of separate bald mountains and mountain groups with heights of 6,600 feet. Alpine relief is pronounced in the highest parts. The south-facing steep slope, in contrast to the gentle north-facing one, is highly dissected by glacial troughs, steep hanging valleys, and cirques.

Udokan Range is a zone of irregularly scattered bald mountains and mountain groups 24 to 30 miles in width, more highly dissected toward the Olekma. Mount Typtur, one of its highest points, is 9,900 feet high. Udokan appears higher when viewed from the Verkhne-Char Valley side, which is 2,310 feet lower than Verkhne-Kalar Valley. Ancient glaciation has carved alpine forms in the highest peaks. Exposed, sharp-ribbed, craggy crests and summits are covered by talus and marked by large belts of perpetual snow. Part of Udokan is weakly dissected and capped by flat summits. The height of the widespread flat summits corresponds to that of the alpine forms, indicating that they are probably the preserved remnants of a post-Tertiary peneplain.

In the Kalar Range, flat, smooth bald mountains are covered with rubble and fine alluvial deposits. Often they are separated by narrow saddles with almost perpendicular walls. In the upper stretches of the Kalar River, there are bald mountains more than 8,250 feet high (Skalisty, 9,240 feet; Snezhny, 8,299 feet). The range drops off abruptly into Verkhne-Kalar Valley and descends to the south, imperceptibly changing into lower mountain districts.

The lengthwide valleys (Verkhne-Char, and Muy) dividing the ranges are typical grabens, as confirmed by the line of hot sulphur springs parallel to Kodar. Typical moraine landscapes are found in these valleys, with moraine-dam lakes and almost impassable bogs. In some swampy depressions, an intricate system of small lakes is all that remains of a larger lake basin. The rivers flowing in these lengthwise valleys, such as the Char or Kalar, diverge from the longitudinal tectonic valleys into lateral ones; where they intersect the ranges their character and morphologic features sharply change. The gradient of their channels abruptly increases, speeding up erosion, and the valleys become narrow and contain many rapids. The largest rivers of the subregion—the Olekma and Vitim—cut across the ranges. The Olekma, from the mouth of the Khana River to Yenyuka village, carves a deep gorge, narrowing, in places, to 247 feet; this section of the river contains a series of turbulent rapids.

West and northwest of the Kalar system of mountain ranges are the North-Baikal upland (from Baikal to the lower course of the Vitim), and the Patom upland (to the north of the North-Baikal upland). The uplands are distinguished by the absence of clearly expressed ranges, the approximately uniform height of all mountain summits, and a sharp escarpment dropping to 1,320 to 1,980 feet to the adjacent Central Siberian Plateau.

Deep in the North-Baikal upland there are scattered groups of bald mountains, some of which contain alpine relief forms. In these mountains is a river network containing both broad flat-bottomed valleys and narrow gorges. The right tributaries of the Kirenga and Lena, flowing from the upland onto the Central Siberian Plateau, force their way through almost impassable gorges.

Along the lower courses of the Mama and Vitim rivers, on an area 60 by 15 miles and lying in striated pegmatite veins, there are extremely rich deposits of mica (muscovite). In quantity and quality they may compete with those of India for the world market.

The broad water divides of the Patom upland are 3,960 to 4,290 feet high, with almost level surfaces, above which rise individual flat summits or dome-shaped bald mountains 3,300 to 4,950 feet high. Between the mountains lie broad valleys with gentle slopes. The highest point of the district—Mount Longdor, 6,464 feet—is distinguished for its sharp-edged peaks. The bald mountains north of Bodaibo are incorporated in short Kropotkin Range with maximum height of 5,445 feet (Mount Korolenko). The Patom upland contains the Lena gold district, which is famous for its abundant

and valuable placers. The richest deposit is in the basin of the Bodaibo River.

Stanovoi Range and Aldan Plateau

The Stanovoi Range extends in a latitudinal direction from the Olekma River to the source of the Maya River (left tributary of the Uda River) where it continues as the Dzhugdzhur Range. It consists of two or three bald mountain chains, divided by lengthwise valleys. The highest range is intersected by the sources of the Lena and Amur rivers, and the main watershed passes from one range to another. For example, the water divide between the basins of the Zeya and Lena is a high (4,290 to 4,785 feet) plateau, edged on the north and south by high mountain chains. Rivers of the Lena basin begin not on the north-facing slope of the highest northern chain (6,600 to 8,250 feet) but at the base of the south-facing slope—cutting northward through the range. West of the Timpton River, the chief mountain groups of the Stanovoi Range are the northern one, 6,600 feet high, and the southern one, 4,950 feet high. These are divided by the upper valleys of the Timpton and Aldan rivers, which flow in a northwesterly direction. The ranges are broken through by the Olekma River, west of which is the Olekma-Baikal mountain subregion. This subregion is considered the direct orographic and tectonic continuation of the Stanovoi Range because of its geologic composition, tectonics, similarity of granites, and deposits of mica.

The height of the Stanovoi Range generally exceeds 4,950 feet, and reaches its maximum (8,190 feet) at the source of the Zeya (Mt. Skalisty). The range rises above the timber line (which lies at 4,950 feet) and is covered by rocky bogs, lichenous tundra, and vast patches of stone. Despite the height of the mountains, they are predominantly massive, with rounded ridges and dome- or cone-shaped bald peaks. These are separated by broad, swampy saddles and valleys. In the highest ranges, there are pronounced features of alpine relief: sharp crests and craggy peaks, steep rocky slopes, deep and narrow gorges. The Stanovoi Range, as a result of fault dislocations, has a series of steps dropping off steeply (especially to the south) to the lower regions. Although it is likely that early glaciation took place in the range, it has not been proven. The Stanovoi Range is formed of crystalline schists and gneisses of pre-Cambrian age, with extensive intrusions of uniform gray granites. The sedimentary rock cover is eroded everywhere owing to the recent upheavals of the range. Among the mineral resources are placer gold (Upper-Timpton gold-bearing region) and mica (Chulman deposit).

North of the Stanovoi Range, between the Olekma and Uchur rivers, the Aldan Plateau falls off in an escarpment toward the Central Siberian Plateau. The almost horizontal Cambrian limestones of the Central Siberian Plateau are abruptly replaced by a highly dislocated strata of pre-Cambrian schists and gneisses, shot through by granite intrusions and, in places, by younger extrusions. The plateau, which has average heights ranging from 2,310 to 3,300 feet, is highly dissected and contains separate bald peaks and mountain groups with heights of 4,950 to 5,610 feet; but nowhere are there pronounced mountain ranges. Dome-shaped bald mountains are often solidly covered with talus. Broad, flat valleys of east-west strike contain meandering rivers, yet in several places the rivers are filled with rapids. Linked with the quartz veins of crystalline schists are the rich supplies of placer gold near the Timpton gold-bearing region.

CLIMATE

The climate of Pre-Baikal and Trans-Baikal, which are far inland and high above the sea level (1,650 to 2,640 feet), is extremely severe and continental. Here the characteristics of the Mongolian climate are combined with the pronounced climatic features of Eastern Siberia, to which is added the strong climatic influence of Lake Baikal. The climate has large daily and annual temperature amplitudes (Ulan-Ude 82.6 °F, Nerchinsk 93.4 °F, annual), and low annual precipitation. It also has extremely irregular seasonal variation of precipitation and very dry air.

In Baikal a typical Eastern Siberian anticyclonic winter prevails, with many calm days, negligible precipitation, low humidity, little cloudiness, many hours of sunshine, and an exceptionally thin snow cover, which contributes to radiation and consequent lowering of temperatures. The average temperature of January is extremely low: −16.0°F at Ulan-Ude, −17.8°F at Olovyannaya, −24°F at Nerchinsk. But the January temperatures near Lake Baikal rise sharply, as indicated by a closed pattern of isotherms. For example, the January average on Ushkanye Island reaches only −1°F. The minimum temperatures are extremely low: −56.0°F at Ulan-Ude, −63.8°F at Nerchinsk, and −66.0°F at Petrovsk which is made lower by the influence of relief.

In snowless, cloudless, and dry Trans-Baikal, the relief—more than the latitude—influences the temperature regime of a region. In winter, the inverse distribution of temperature typical of the Eastern Siberian climate is observable, but the intensity of the inversion is not the same everywhere, depending on the flow of the cold air masses. In valleys, where cold air accumulates in winter, the temperatures are lower, and the annual and daily amplitudes are greater; but in higher places (even several dozen feet higher), the temperatures modulate. Petrovsk, in an enclosed valley at 2,643 feet, has, from December to February, temperatures 5.4 degrees lower than Khilok, almost at the same altitude (2,673 feet) in a more open locality. Again in December and January it is 10.8 degrees warmer than Nerchinsk, which is only 214 feet lower; however, in summer the temperature differences are slight. Chita, at an altitude of 2,253 feet has a January average of −27°F, and a July average of 65.8°F; but

Perevalnaya Station (Turgutuy), at 3,370 feet has a January average of —9.5°F, and a July average of 61.4°F. During intense cold, despite the low humidity, thick fogs occur.

Spring is late, cold, and dry, but owing to the negligible snow cover temperatures may increase rather rapidly. The average temperature of March greatly exceeds that of January. For example, at Olovyannaya the January average is —17.7°F, and the March average is 8.8°F; at Kyakhta the January and March averages are —9°F and 14.3°F, respectively. May brings warmer weather, although night frosts are still common—thus making early sowing hazardous. Also unfavorable to agriculture are the large daily amplitudes (up to 82.8 degrees), characterized by daily insolation of the soil and nightly heat loss owing to radiation and strong drying winds.

The southern part of Baikalia lies on, and to the south of, the same latitude as Kiev and Kharkov; hence the summer is warm. The average July temperature is 66.3°F in the north and 75.2°F in the south. At Ulan-Ude it is 66.5°F, at Olovyannaya it is 68°F, and at Nerchinsk it is 68.5°F. At Ulan-Ude the highest temperature is 98°F. At Baikal there is a sharp curve of the July isotherms to the south under the cooling influence of the lake. For instance, the average July temperature on Ushkanye Island is only 68°F, and the August average is 72.5°F. July is the only month in the year in which there are but a few night frosts. In contrast to winter, summer temperatures regularly decrease with an increase in altitude. In summer the ground thaws to an average depth of ten feet. The growing period lasts about 150 days (147 at Ulan-Ude, 143 at Chita, and 150 days at Nerchinsk), and the frost-free period is about 100 days (92 at Ulan-Ude, 97 at Chita). From August 15 nightly frosts become more frequent; in September the temperature drops to half that of August; in October it drops below 32°F; and in November it drops more rapidly. For example, at Ulan-Ude the average October temperature is 30.8°F, the average November temperature is —13.0°F; during the same months at Olovyannaya the

temperatures are 31°F and 7.5°F; at Kyakhta they are —0.1°F and —10.8°F. In autumn the winds are stronger than in summer.

Baikalia is characterized by small average annual precipitation—12.7 inches at Chita, 10.6 inches at Olovyannaya, 8.0 inches at Ulan-Ude, and 6.6 inches at Selenginsk. On the windward slope of Khamar-Daban facing Baikal precipitation increases sharply (more than 28.0 inches). Periodic alternations of dry and moist years are characteristic of the region. At Petrovsk 23.4 inches of precipitation fell during one year, and 7.0 inches in the next. During certain years the maximum August precipitation has exceeded the established average by 250 per cent. In 1869 there was two and one-half times the average annual precipitation, which resulted in extensive floods; Lake Baikal rose 6.6 feet above its average level.

The seasonal distribution of precipitation is irregular—a characteristic feature of the Mongolian climate. Throughout the year, precipitation has the following distribution: in winter, 2 to 6 per cent; in spring, 7 to 18 per cent; in summer, 51 to 76 per cent; and in autumn, 13 to 16 per cent. At Chita, July has an average of 3.6 inches of rain, and February has an average of 0.08 inch; at Olovyannaya, 3.5 inches fall in July, and 0.04 inch falls in February. During the entire winter there are 2.7 gallons of water for every 2.4 square yards of land, but in summer a single downpour may yield more water than falls in an entire winter. For example, at Mysovsk on the shore of Baikal, there were 9.0 inches of precipitation during two days at the end of August. In the southern half of the region, the difference in the amount of winter and summer precipitation is especially sharp. Here, during the seven cold months the amount of precipitation is so slight as to be negligible. Summer, however, has no less than 70 per cent of the annual amount of precipitation; frequent and torrential rains result in extensive floods. Erosion of the upper horizon of loose earth and soil is extensive on treeless mountain slopes, causing the destruction of railroad embankments and damage to bridges. Baikalia has relatively few days of precipitation: In the central part of the region, there are more than 60 rainy days a year, with the most rainy rays in July and August, and the fewest in January and February. At Olovyannaya in August there are 13 rainy days, and in January, one day with precipitation.

Because of the small amount of winter precipitation, the snow cover is extremely light, is established late (the second half of November), and disappears very early (toward the beginning of April); altogether it lasts about 140 days. The snow cover decreases in thickness to the southeast: in the north of the region and on the southeastern shore of Baikal it is 24 to 36 inches deep; at Ulan-Ude it is 6.8 inches deep; at Kyakhta, 5.2 inches deep; at Chita, 3.0 inches deep; and at Olovyannaya 0.8 inch deep—in some years being entirely absent. Owing to the thin snow cover, the ground freezes, permafrost is well preserved, and the river ice attains great thickness, like that on the northern rivers. Long before the soil thaws and the average temperature rises above 32°F, the thin snow cover is blown off into depressions by the strong spring winds and partly evaporated by the extremely dry air; thus there are relatively few spring floods.

Meltwater from the slowly thawing earth is not absorbed by the long-frozen underlying soil, and runs off without benefitting grain crops. A large increase in precipitation is characteristic on the leeward side of high ranges just over the crest because of the blowover but precipitation decreases far out beyond the ranges, because the air is warmed and dried in descending from the crests. From Pereyemnaya on the shore of Baikal to Selenginsk lying on the east shore at a distance of little more than 60 miles, the annual precipitation of 27.5 inches drops to 6.4 inches, and that of winter drops from 3.0 to 0.2; that is, it decreases 15 times.

Cloudiness in Baikalia is relatively small: 53 per cent at Ulan-Ude, 47 per cent at Petrovsk, 41 per cent at Olovyannaya, 38 per cent at Nerchinsk. Corresponding to the winter anticyclone, cloudiness is at a minimum in January and February and at a maximum in July and August. During the summertime cloudiness is distributed uniformly throughout the region; in winter, however, it decreases from northwest to southeast. Average July cloudiness at Petrovsk is 59 per cent, at Nerchinsk, 54 per cent; average January cloudiness at Petrovsk is 35 per cent, and at Nerchinsk, 19 per cent. The duration of sunshine is very long, especially in winter. The number of days duration of sunshine at Akatuy, for example, comprises 72 per cent of that possible, and in March 85 per cent, and in July 59 per cent. Twenty-three days a year are recorded to have cloudiness all day. Relative humidity is greatest in December and least in May. Ulan-Ude, with an average annual relative humidity of 64 per cent, has a relative humidity of 74 per cent in December and 49 per cent in May. The air in the region is often so clear that the peaks of mountain ranges more than 36 miles away are clearly visible, and even the shadowed side of the crescent moon—completely invisible from the European part of the USSR—may be seen. The great transparency of the air is responsible for the beautiful hues of the Trans-Baikal sky.

The absence of a permanent or sufficiently thick snow cover prohibits the cultivation of winter grain crops and perennial fodder grasses such as legumes by exposing their root system to frost destruction. Because of the peculiarities of climate, black fallow is not practiced in the region. Fall tillage is unsuitable, because with the snowless winter and dry air a field under cultivation may be deprived of its last moisture and completely dry up. With abundant sunshine and good local soil, grains are harvested during those years when the seasonal precipitation is most favorable. Usually during the leafing out and blooming periods of the grains, there is very little rain, owing to the fact that the air currents ascending from the insolated soil disperse and drive off the rain clouds passing over the forested ranges. The abundant precipitation of July and August hinders the harvesting of grains and grasses. July and August rains and a prolonged sunny autumn contribute to the good growth of truck-garden plants and fodder root-plants. The rains of June and early July fall on fully thawed earth and are absorbed by the soil just at the period when moisture is most needed. Orchard fruits are not grown, owing to the cold, snowless winters and the brevity of the period with average temperatures above 50°F. The climate, with its dry and clear air, has a healthful effect on consumptives; the sharp daily fluctuation of temperature, however, is considered harmful to people who are afflicted with heart disease.

HYDROGRAPHY

Baikal is one of the largest and most interesting lakes in the world, occupying seventh place in area (12,159 square miles), and second place in volume of water (23,000 cubic kilometers). Its length is 394.3 miles, its greatest width is 49.2 miles, and its average width is 29.7 miles. If it were placed at that same latitude in the European part of the USSR, it would occupy an expanse approximately between Moscow and Kursk. The lake is the deepest continental depression in the world. Its surface lies at an altitude of 1,495 feet and it reaches 5,745 feet in depth; that is, its bottom drops 4,250 feet below sea level. Considering that the mountains at the shore of Baikal rise to an altitude of 6,600 feet, the relief in this region of the earth's crust is most remarkable. Baikal is one of the oldest lakes in the world. The continuous history of its development has been reflected in its original fauna. The lake has a tremendous influence on the sharply continental climate of the surrounding region, modifying it to the extent that a marine climate is approached. It is the source of the Angara, one of the largest rivers of Eastern Siberia. Lake Baikal, a natural water reservoir, is directly connected with the problem of the utilization of the Angara's energy resources by providing a steady flow. The lake lies in a mountainous region of exceptional beauty, and is a major tourist attraction.

The lake shore is irregular, except where it conforms to the underlying tectonic lines. The straight lake shore from Kultuk to the Angara is demarcated by parallel step-like faults, along

Fig. 9-3. Western shore of Lake Baikal near Goloust.

which basalts have issued. Also affecting the character of the shores is the active creative work of rivers in building alluvial fans. Exceptionally strong wave-cutting action tends to straighten out the shore line and destroy promontories. Many rivers like the Selenga, Upper Angara, and Barguzin form deltas. The Selenga delta is the largest. In 1861 its northern section suddenly dropped below the surface of the lake, forming Proval Bay. Olkhon Island and the four Ushkaniye islands are extensions of the submarine Akademy Range, which intersects Lake Baikal obliquely.

When shallow lagoons of a lake are cut off from the lake proper, they are called *sory*. In Baikal, one may find examples of each stage of this process, from Istok *Sor* (just beginning to be cut off) to the completely separated Posol *Sor*.

On the shores of Baikal, there are three groups of terraces at heights of from 6.6 to 26.4 feet, 66 to 82.5 feet, and 165 to 280.5 feet. These terraces were formed when the lake level subsided as the Lower Angara lowered its outlet. The northwestern shore of Baikal is a region of strong upheaval, as indicated by the rejuvenation of the hydrographic network. There are narrow canyons, and rapids on the rivers; islands are joined with the mainland by low isthmuses and cone-shaped deltas. On the northeastern shore, there are indications of subsidence: inundation of the river valleys, the absence of deltas, and the development of a new terrace 182 to 198 feet lower than the old one.

Bathometrically, the lake may be divided into three depressions: (1) a northern shallow basin, extending from Olkhon Island and submarine Akademy Range to the northern tip of the lake, morphologically homogeneous, with its greatest depth at 3,243 feet; (2) a southern depression, occupying the part of the lake south of the Selenga delta, with a trough along the northern shore where the greatest depth reaches 4,738 feet; (3) a central depression, with a vast area more than 3,300 feet deep and a maximum depth of 5,745 feet. The lake bottom sediments are extremely diverse. The central part of the

lake bottom is covered with diatomaceous silt containing a large proportion of silica and iron. In many places on the eastern shore, sand predominates, and the eastern shore of Olkhon Island is rocky.

The deep basin of Baikal could only have been formed tectonically. The modern relief of Trans-Baikal is based on vast deep grabens of an approximate northeast strike. A complex of three or four grabens forms the present depression of Lake Baikal. Beyond the limits of the modern Baikal depression there are similar depressions, situated one after the other according to the direction of ancient folding. To the southwest, extending as a continuation of the Baikal graben is the Tunkin graben, which terminates in the tectonic depression of Lake Khubsugul. To the north is the graben of the Upper Angara, the bottom of which is up to 132 feet higher than the lake level and the Verkhne-Charskaya depression, which ends before reaching the Olekma River. Beyond the above-mentioned group are the Barguzin and Tsipo-Tsipikan lakes, and other grabens. Evidence of the past connection between Baikal and old Trans-Baikal water reservoirs is the polychaetous worm, *Manajunkia baicalensis*. It is a relict of specific original Baikal fauna, but is found also in the lakes of the Vitim River basin. All the above-mentioned grabens are filled with a thick mass of loose deposits, the lower layers of which contain fauna of confirmed Tertiary age. In the grabens are evidence of dynamic processes: large, graduated faults and dislocations (a fault near Olkhon Island has a length of 57 miles), and chaotic shattering of rocks into fine particles. Smaller traces of these processes may be detected under a microscope in the form of hairline cracks and broken rock flakes.

The Baikal basin was formed no later than the middle of the Tertiary Period. This may be confirmed by the character of the present-day fauna of Baikal, which bears the impression of great antiquity. Core samples taken in the southern part of the present-day Baikal Valley reveal gray, middle Tertiary lake sediments up to 3,300 feet thick, which contain coal and remnants of fresh-water mollusks, indicating that the depression already existed in some form during the Tertiary Period. Renewed upthrust in the Quaternary Period along the old lines of fracture has led to further deepening of the grabens and to the appearance of new ones. This is indicated by the fossilized remains of Baikal fauna (for example, sponges of the family Lubomirskiidae) on old Baikal terraces, 1,650 to 1,980 feet higher than the present terrace. Some shores indicate upheaval and others subsidence. The processes of upheaval and subsidence continue at the present time; for example, the shore at Kultuk rises 0.4 inch a year, and at Mishikha subsides 0.4 inch a year; thus the difference between levels increases 0.8 inch a year. This is corroborated by the increased seismism of the entire shore of the lake and the relatively recent large subsidence of the northeastern part of the Selenga delta (Proval Bay). The outlet of the Lower Angara was formed in comparatively recent times.

Baikal has frequent storms brought about by strong winds maintaining a steady direction. Owing to the difference in temperatures above the lake and over the land, nightly winds spring up in the gorges. These are especially strong in the late autumn and are called *kholoda*. Other winds are: the southwest, or *Kultuk*, the north, or *Angara*, the northeast, or *Barguzin*, and the north-northwest, or *Kharakhaikha*—raging in the Goloustnoye Valley in winter and autumn. The "mountain" wind, or *Sarma*, descends from the Sarma River valley, which enters the lake opposite the southern tip of Olkhon Island. The *Sarma*, coming on suddenly, blows in autumn for whole days with a velocity reaching up to 90 miles per hour. During freezing weather the wind raises water spray which freezes in mid-air. The mast and rigging of a boat caught in such a wind are covered by a thick layer of ice. The *sarma* does not affect a large area: 12 to 18 miles east of the mouth of the Sarma River it is not directly noticeable, although it creates great swells on the lake.

The total area of the Lake Baikal basin,

equaling 12,159 square miles, is distributed unevenly: the largest water-collecting area lies to the south and southeast of the watershed on the western shore. Of the total number of Baikal tributaries (336), only 6 large, mature rivers are significant sources of water. These are the Selenga (83.4 per cent of the entire water-collecting area), the Turka, Barguzin, Upper Angara, Kichera, and Goloustnaya. All of the remaining tributaries are of comparatively recent origin and are mountain streams with a small discharge.

The second source of lake water is precipitation: the average annual amount is 12.5 inches. Underground springs feeding into the lake bottom also contribute to the water supply. The Lower Angara River is the chief outlet for Lake Baikal, with an average discharge of 2,330.8 cubic feet of water per second. The water enters the Angara from different depths depending on the thermic condition of the lake, the force and direction of wind at the outlet, and—in winter especially—the position of the temperature discontinuity. Evaporation comprises only about 6 per cent of the annual discharge from Baikal.

There is a characteristic seasonal fluctuation of from 0.8 to 5.7 inches in the water-level of Baikal. Local fluctuation occurs with the driving and piling up of the water by wind, and standing waves, seiches, or tides of slight amplitude (up to 0.4 inch). Characteristic dynamics of the Baikal waters are: (1) counter-clockwise currents south of the Selenga River delta and at Barguzin Bay, where they are 33 to 66 feet deep; (2) the difference in properties of the Baikal water and the amply watered Selenga River, resulting in a certain current pattern. In summer, the water of the Selenga is warmer than that of Baikal; thus it circulates along the surface of the lake to a depth of about 6 to 8 feet. In winter, however, the density of the cold and highly mineralized water of the Selenga is greater than the water of Baikal, and consequently it sinks upon entering the lake.

In thermic regime, Baikal belongs to the lakes of the temperate type. In the winter, the surface layers are colder than the deep layers;

in the summer, however, temperatures increase from the bottom up. In annual temperature variations, only the layers of water within 660 to 825 feet of the surface reflect change; the layers close to the bottom are characterized by extremely gradual and slight drops of temperature with depth. The water at the greatest depths has a temperature of 37.5°F. In March the sun's direct rays penetrate the ice and warm the surface layers. In June, influenced by the wind, water circulates in the deeper layers; increase of temperature is accomplished slowly, despite the continuous rise in the air temperature. Water interchange with the subsurface zone slows down, and thermic stratification becomes, for some time, more stable. After this the temperature of the surface water increases rapidly, and the deep water masses are slowly heated through. Autumn water circulation begins with the lowering of surface temperatures, and is accelerated by the strong autumn wind. The greatest heat exchange with the deepwater zone occurs in November, retarding the cooling of surface water in spite of the sharp lowering of air temperature. With the establishment in December of definitely expressed inverse stratification, water circulation comes to a halt. Surface water of the open part of the lake has in general the following monthly average temperatures (in degrees Fahrenheit):

January........	32.18°	July............	43.88°
February.......	32.36°	August.........	48.32°
March.........	32.36°	September......	46.58°
April..........	33.26°	October........	42.08°
May...........	34.70°	November......	38.04°
June...........	41.18°	December.......	33.08°

YEARLY 38.1°

Near the shores, especially on vast shoals, the summer water temperature is higher. For example, it is 54.6°F at Olkhon in August, and 66.5°F at the Selenga delta (Kharauz). Surface water is intensely warmed (to 68°F and more) in shallow bays, which are thermally indistinguishable from ordinary shallow lakes. Strong prevailing northwest winds, perpendicular to the lake axis, drive the upper, heated layers of water from the western to the eastern shores, causing the underlying cold water at the western shores to well up from a depth of more than 1,320 feet.

Baikal does not freeze over till the beginning of January, owing to the extremely slow cooling of the large water masses and to strong autumn gales which break open newly formed ice. In individual years, the dates of freezing fluctuate for different points. The earliest freezing has occurred at Listvyanka (November 30, 1905), and the latest at Goloustnoye (February 22, 1892). At its outlet the Angara River does not freeze over at all. The average thickness of the ice is 36 inches, with variations of from 26 to 56 inches. In winter, sharp changes of air temperatures cause cracks to form in the ice. These may vary in width from inches to a yard, and make it hazardous to travel along the ice. Certain ones are formed from year to year at the same place and bear local names, such as "Stanovaya Fissure." In places where gases discharge from the bottom of the lake, ice will not form. Such areas increase in number and size toward springtime, and may reach several dozen yards in diameter. The breakup of ice does not take place all at once. Broken ice, driven by the northwest wind, accumulates primarily along the eastern shore, where it gradually melts, chilling the water and hindering navigation. The navigational period at the western shore (Listvyanka) is 293 days, but at the eastern shore, it is only 169 days. Almost all the broken ice melts in place; only a small amount enters the Angara River outlet. Most of Baikal is free of ice for an average of 110 days.

Chemically, the water of Lake Baikal does not differ from that of other fresh-water lakes. To a depth of 4,290 feet, so much aeration takes place that there is a high per cent of oxygen— contributing to favorable conditions of life both in the mass of water and in the bottom sediments.

Like the ocean, Lake Baikal varies in transparency and color from place to place and from time to time. The average transparency is 85.5 feet, and the maximum 132.5 feet. In the

Selenga shoal region, however, transparency may drop in summer to only 6.6 feet. The water is usually most transparent in July and December. Generally, the more transparent the water, the bluer its color. With transparency to a depth of 100 feet, the water color is dark blue —little different from the color of the open sea. Near the eastern shore the water is a greenish shade; in the Selenga shoals it is gray-green; and at the mouth of the Selenga River it has a brown tint. The water has its darkest and clearest blue tint in June and on individual days when cold subsurface water is brought to the surface by the wind. In autumn the color becomes somewhat greenish; in the period of the greatest heating (August through September), it has a grayish tint.

Baikal is a classic example of the influence of a water reservoir on dry land. Almost all the climatic isolines, even those at a great distance from the lake, are affected in one way or another by this reservoir. The extraordinary crowding of isotherms near the shores of Baikal, their bending around the lake to the north in winter and to the south in summer, and

their being closed characterize the typical distribution of temperatures on dry land close to a large water basin. Places adjacent to the lake approximate the climate of places adjacent to the sea.

The thermic and water regimes at points on the shore of Baikal differ to a great extent from

Map 9-III. Bathymetric map of Lake Baikal.

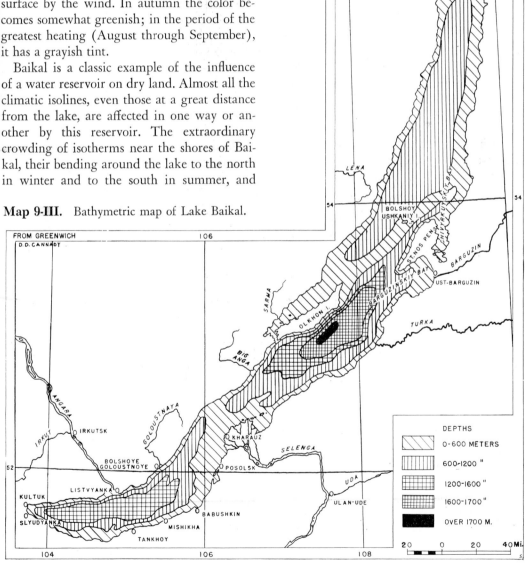

DEPTHS

	0-600 METERS
	600-1200 "
	1200-1600 "
	1600-1700 "
	OVER 1700 M.

those at points lying some distance away. The reason for this is that the large volume of water —contained within a relatively small but extremely deep area—effects a heat exchange with the air over the surrounding dry land. Water is more conservative than dry land: in winter it gives off warmth, accumulated during the summer, more gradually, and in summer it absorbs heat more slowly. The moderating influence of Baikal shows climatically in the decrease of annual and daily amplitudes and in higher winter and lower summer temperatures at its shores. Whereas Listvyanka, on the shore of Baikal, has an annual temperature range of 55.6 degrees, Ulan-Ude, about 108 miles to the east, has a range of 84.6 degrees. On Olkhon Island, the daily temperature range in July is only 4.5 degrees, and in March 8.6 degrees. At Ulan-Ude the difference between the average temperatures of March and April is 22.5 degrees (10.5°F and 33°F); at Listvyanka it is only 15.8 degrees (14.2°F and 30°F). The difference between the average temperatures of October and November at Ulan-Ude is 21.7 degrees (30.5°F and 8.5°F), and at Listvyanka, 15.1 degrees (35.1°F and 20.1°F).

In winter, the temperatures of the lake and the surrounding locality differ most in December, when the lake is not yet covered with ice. For example, at Listvyanka, the average December temperature is −11.3°F, at Ulan-Ude it is −6.2°F, and the difference between temperatures on Ushkanye Island and at Verkholensk is 28.8 degrees; that is, on the average, there is a temperature drop of 1.8 degrees for every 6 miles away from Baikal. In summer, average temperatures differ most in July, because the lake is just freed of its ice cover in May, and warms up much later than the land. For example, the average July temperature at Listvyanka is 54.8°F; at Ulan-Ude it is 66.8°F. Spring (March and April)—when the heat reserves of the lake begin to be exhausted—and autumn (August and September) are the periods of the least temperature differences: at Listyvyanka the average April temperature is 30°F, and at Ulan-Ude it is 33°F; the September average at Listvyanka is 47°F, and 47.2°F at Ulan-Ude. The climate close to Baikal becomes less continental and the highest air temperature at Listvyanka is not in July but in August, and the minimum is not in January but in February, as is generally the case in oceanic climates. The proximity of cold Lake Baikal retards the spring; for example, in the middle of June, when vegetation near Baikal has just begun to appear, at a distance from its shores things are in full bloom.

The shores of Baikal, with the exception of the southeastern section, have little precipitation. North of the 52nd parallel there is less than 12 inches of precipitation (10.4 inches at Barguzin, 9.8 inches on the Ushkanye Island, and only 6.4 inches on Olkhon Island). Therefore, the shore is covered by steppe, with scattered saline lakes and salt marshes with halophytic vegetation. The inhabitants employ irrigation. On the Khamar-Daban mountains, which project steeply from the windward shore of Baikal, ascending northwest air currents increase the vapor condensation so that there is a sharp local increase in precipitation on the northwest-facing slope, and a consequent decrease on the leeward slope facing the Selenga. For example, there are 30 inches of precipitation a year at Murins, 27 inches at Pereyemnaya, 21 inches at Mishikha, 19 inches at Mysovsk, and only 6.6 inches on the other side of the range at Selenginsk. Owing to the sharp climatic differences, the northwest-facing slopes of Khamar-Daban are covered down to the lake with a solid pine-fir taiga, and the Selenginsk southeast-facing slope is covered with chestnut steppes beginning at 990 to 1,320 feet above Lake Baikal. The snow mantle on Khamar-Daban is thicker and lasts longer than anywhere else in the region because of the cooling influence of the lake in the summer and the many days with precipitation (176 days on Khamar-Daban, and only 58 days at Selenginsk, 102 miles away). The snow cover at Mysovsk is 15 inches deep and lasts 165 days; it is only 7.6 inches at Ulan-Ude, and lasts 151 days. On the shores of Baikal there is some-

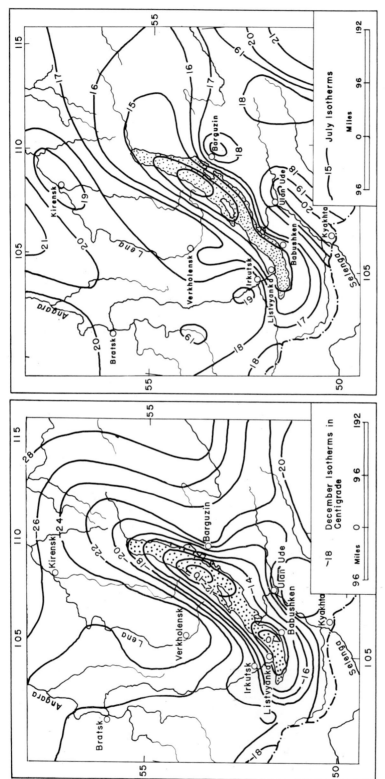

Map 9-IV. December and July isotherms in the Lake Baikal vicinity.

times local cloudiness, which is attributable to the sharp contrast between the heating of dry land and water.

The vegetation of the Baikal shores is influenced by a slow and late spring, warm summer, late and moderate autumn, and comparatively warm winter. Although the base-level of Baikal lies 1,495 feet above sea level, bald-mountain vegetation grows in many places along the shores. The forests on the middle slopes of the bald mountains are bordered by a subalpine belt of dwarf stone pine (*Pinus pumila*). Near the shores of the lake one may also find: yellow rhododendron (*Rhododendron chrysanthum*), short native birch (*Betula baicalensis*), yellow poppy (*Papaver nudicaule*), and burnet (*Sanguisorba tenuifolia*). These plants descended to the shores of Baikal from the surrounding bald peaks in response to the favorable climatic conditions; in particular, low summer temperatures.

Lake Baikal is unique both in faunal composition and in the biological peculiarities of its species. In the other Trans-Baikal reservoirs, as well as in the shallow sory of Baikal, an ordinary Siberian fauna is found. But Lake Baikal contains many endemic species, many of which have considerable geologic significance. Of the 890 species, 649 (73 per cent) are endemic to Baikal; only individuals live outside the limits of Baikal: for example, the leech (*Torix baicalensis*) has related forms in Tonkin (Indochina).

The endemic Baikal seal (*Phoca sibirica*) is similar to the Arctic ringed seal (*Phoca hispida*) and feeds on bottom seaweeds, large crustaceans, and fish. Of the 32 species of fish living in Baikal, 14 (44 per cent) are endemic. Lake Baikal has two endemic families of fish: (1) Cottocomephoridae (seven genera with twelve species). These are peculiar creatures. The Baikal goby fish lives at a depth of 3,300 to 4,950 feet, has a jelly-like body, and bears long protuberances on its head. Other goby fish are clumsy, large-headed, and resemble toads in shape and color; they are not considered edible. In addition to these, there are agile, brightly-colored fish with huge breast fins resembling the wings of tropical butterflies, such as the widespread *Cottocomephorus grewingki*. (2) Comephoridae. This includes two unusual species of deepwater fish—*Comephorus baicalensis* (up to 3.6 inches in length) and *C. dybowskii* (up to 8 inches in length)—most often found at a depth of 1,000 to 1,650 feet. These semitransparent, white fish are scaleless and bear delicate, web-like dorsal fins; their young are born alive. They do not resemble any species in other water basins, and their origin remains a mystery.

Goby fish may be found at depths of more than 3,300 feet; they can live under very great

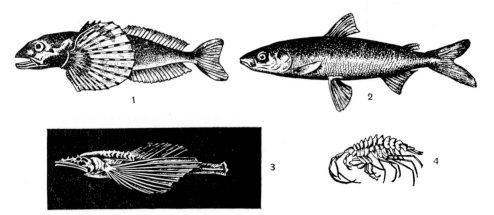

Fig. 9-4.   Some characteristic Lake Baikal fauna. 1—Goby (*Cottocomephorus grewingki*); 2—Omul (*Coregonus migratorius*); 3—Golomyanka (*Comophorus baikalensis*); 4—*Brachyuropus nassonovi*. (Scale not observed.)

pressure, but unlike most deepwater fish they do not perish upon being brought to the surface, and can even live in the upper levels of water. They seem to be recently adapted to living at such great depths—an indication of the young age of the Baikal deeps. There are only two true deepwater fish (of the family Cottocomephoridae): *Cottinella boulengeri,* dwelling at depths of 2,310 to 4,950 feet, and *Batrachocottus multiradiatus,* dwelling at a depth of 1,650 feet.

The fish of the greatest commercial importance is the Baikal whitefish (*Coregonus autumnalis migratorius*), a member of the salmon family, which lives in winter at depths of 1,320 to 2,640 feet, and in spring moves in masses to the shores and remains all summer in the shoals, feeding intensively on plankton, bottom fauna, and the roe of goby fish. At the beginning of October it enters the rivers (with the exception of the Lower Angara), where it spawns. The Baikal whitefish has an exceptional flavor and its meat is easily canned, salted, and cured. Baikal salmon are grayling, *Salmo thymallus,* and char. All the remaining fish related to the carp, pike, and perch families belong to fauna common to Siberia and bear the local name *sorovaya* fish, because they live primarily in the *sory* and near the mouths of rivers.

Baikal's mollusk fauna is abundant. Altogether there are about 85 known species, among which are two endemic fresh-water families—Benedictidae and Baicalidae. The mollusks display a certain similarity to the mollusks of the Upper Tertiary briny-water deposits of southeastern Europe and also to the mollusks lying today in Lake Ochrid on the Balkan Peninsula. The mollusk Baicalia is encountered in a fossil state in the Lower Cretaceous fresh-water deposits of Trans-Baikal. The most widespread crustaceans are crayfish of the family Gammaridae. On the entire globe outside of Baikal, there are only 150 species of Gammaridae, but in Baikal itself there exist 230 species. Most of the Gammaridae are endemic —of the 66 genera only five are found outside of Baikal. The Baikal crayfish are distinguished

for their large size (up to 3.2 inches long). Almost all of them have variegated coloring of red, brown, bluish, and green hues, and many have various growths on their bodies, in addition to spines; therefore they are more like the spiny sea crayfish, than like fresh-water ones. They are abundant from the shore to great depths, although they are not conspicuously adapted to a deepwater environment. Species that inhabit the deep zones have weak eye-color, pale bodies and well-developed feelers— organs of touch especially necessary for life in the darkness. Turbellaria (planarians) number more than 80 species, of which 60 are endemic, and they reach a large size for this group (up to four inches). Oligochaete worms, most of which are endemic, are extremely primitive, reflecting the antiquity of the order; some are similar to marine species. Lake Baikal sponges are different from sponges found elsewhere and are related to marine families. Even many of the protozoan species are endemic.

The origin of the unique Baikal fauna has long been a subject of research. The Baikal fauna may be divided into the following four categories:

(1) Relics of a fresh-water fauna with a marine resemblance, which inhabited the reservoirs of Asia, Europe, and North America in Upper Tertiary time. This fauna has been far more warmth-loving and luxuriant in the past. Relics of this fauna are concentrated at Baikal, but solitary species are scattered throughout the region in other reservoirs. Most of the Baikal species belong to this category, making Lake Baikal a living museum of Tertiary fauna.

(2) Species which developed in Baikal itself during its long geologic life and do not have direct links with modern fresh-water and marine forms, but some are encountered in a fossil state. To this category belong certain fish and mollusks, of the Cottocomephoridae and Comephoridae families. Among these endemic species some investigators distinguish another category, consisting of those species whose closest relatives are marine, or relics of a marine environment.

(3) The few species from the North Arctic Ocean which invaded Baikal along the river systems during the last marine transgression, when the cold climate forced northern species to migrate far to the south. To this group belong: Baikal seal, whitefish, salmon, and certain crustacea (for example, *Gammaracanthus loricatus*).

(4) Fresh-water fauna, widespread in Siberia, but encountered only in the bays of Baikal, where the bottom relief, heat regime, and chemism differ from those of the open lake. To this category belong fish and plankton.

The many other lakes of the region occupy large areas. Collected in large groups (Yeravnyye lakes) or scattered as solitary lakes (Onon), they are located in locked-in depressions sometimes of tectonic origin (Gusinoye Lake) or in large river valleys (Bauntov lakes in the Tsipa River valley). Most of the lakes are remnants of Quaternary lakes, evidence of which are traces of former higher levels. For example, the surfaces of the Bauntov lakes today lie at a height of 3,273 feet, but formerly they lay at 3,725 feet.

The Yeravnyye, Bauntov, and Chitin groups consist of several large and many small fresh and slightly mineralized lakes of round or ob-long form. Flat sandy shores and shallow depth (less than 18 feet) lend to the lakes the aspect of large pools. The lake dimensions are dependent on the water supply, and hence are subject to seasonal change. The water inflow ceases altogether in summer, owing to increased insolation and rapid water evaporation; in arid years the lakes dry up, being converted into salt marshes. In spring the lakes fill with water.

The largest and best known of the isolated lakes is Gusinoye (15 miles long, 92 feet deep), which lies in a vast tectonic depression. The present Gusinoye Lake is a young formation: it did not exist in the year 1720; on its site there were two small ponds. In the year 1730 the water began to rise in the lakes. Later the water of the Temnik River filled the lower part of the valley and formed the modern lake. From the year 1810 the water began to recede and islands appeared in the lake, but in 1865 a new rise took place. At the present time the lake has once again receded.

The hot, though short summer hastens the evaporation process in locked-in basins, resulting in the concentration of various salts, and in the subsequent formation of many small mineral lakes, such as Selenga Lake (0.9 mile long

Fig. 9-5. Goudzhir Lake, near Ganganyr, on the left bank of the Borzi River.

and 6 feet deep). Thick salt beds in several lakes are indications of a former period of drought, during which effluence processes were intensive. These reservoirs were never linked with the sea, and are remarkable examples of lakes with salts of continental origin. Some of them contain salts formed from chemical weathering of crystalline rocks; others are mineralized by leaching of continental sedimentary rocks impregnated with salts in the past; many lakes are simply the concentrated residue of large vanished reservoirs. Many fresh lakes which have lost their outlets have begun to grow salty.

The composition of the lakes depend on the types of rocks surrounding them. If the lake lies, for example, in the midst of igneous rocks, it usually has an alkaline character; that is, it contains soda (Lakes Doronin, Onon, and Borgoy). As these lakes freeze, crystalline soda, or *gudzhir*, forms a white coating on the surface of the ice. To extract artificial *gudzhir* the inhabitants flood the ice with lake brine, which they pump through holes in the ice; then they gather the *gudzhir,* receiving 20 to 25 tons from 2.4 acres. Strong winds blow particles of the *gudzhir* off the ice and carry them throughout the vicinity, thus contributing to the mineralization of ground and surface water. If the lake lies in Jurassic sedimentary rocks, sulphates—especially Glauber salt (mirabilite)—will pre-

dominate. Under a layer of silt in Lake Selenga there is a bed of mirabilite many feet thick, with up to a million tons of Glauber salt in reserve. Gudzhirnoye Lake, of the Algin lake group, contains very pure stores of mirabilite.

The accumulation of salt is slow. It takes a long time for each ton of salt withdrawn from the lake for commercial use to be restored; as a result, there is a conspicuous drop in the concentrations of the salt in lakes, and frequently a change in their mineral composition. Selenga Lake, which has supplied table salt for two hundred years, is now a sulphate lake; Kiran Lake, also, has lost its commercial importance. The brines of mineral lakes are as medicinal as the water of mineral springs. Many lakes (for example, Kiran) possess large supplies of excellent medicinal mud.

The rivers of the region belong to three systems: Those of one are through Baikal linked with the Yenisei system, carrying water to the west; those of the second belong to the Lena basin and flow north and northeast; those of the third deliver water eastward into the Amur. There is very little flooding in springtime, owing to the light winter snowfall. However, sudden floods and destructive overflows occur in summer, when precipitation—because of the mountainous relief and extensive permafrost cover—does not percolate into the soil and runs off almost entirely into the rivers.

LANDSCAPE ZONES

Trans-Baikal and Pre-Baikal, along with the territories adjacent to them on the north and northeast, constitute a unique region where Siberian taiga meets Mongolia steppe. Steppe and taiga landscapes are distributed according to geographic position and relief.

In the southern part of the region, steppe landscapes have continuous spread, jutting in finger-like patterns from the Mongolia steppes northward into the Selenga valley on the west and the Nerchinsk valley on the east. Steppe and wooded-steppe landscapes are found far to the north in broad valley-grabens and individual locked-in depressions, where higher summer temperatures, scanty precipitation, intense evaporation by drying winds, and sandy-clayey saline soil favor their growth. They form isolated centers of steppe soil, plants, and animals amid the wooded taiga landscape; such steppes are found at Nerchinsk, Chita, and in the Barguzin Valley. Farther north, almost to the Yakutia border, individual steppe plants and animals are found along the dry, insolated, south-facing slopes.

Similarly, in the northern half of Baikalia (north of the 53rd parallel) there is continuous taiga interspersed with steppe centers (in the valley of the Barguzin or the Upper Angara), belts of pine groves on sand, and swamps along narrow and deep river valleys.

The taiga extends southward to the sources of the Onon and Ingoda rivers. Its dense mossy forests invade the dry steppes of Mongolia along the mountains, whose lower temperatures, greater precipitation, higher relative humidity, and wide distribution of rubbly podzolic soil constitute a suitable taiga environment.

The diversity of landscapes between the western and eastern half of the region is appreciable. In the west, owing to lower summer temperatures and increased precipitation (under Lake Baikal's influence), Dahurian larch is admixed in varying amounts with dark-coniferous woody species—spruce, fir, and pine, Eastward from the eastern slope of the Yablonoi Range mountain taiga, spruce, and other dark conifers are gradually replaced by larch and pine forests. Some species are peculiar to the Amur-Primorye region, such as Mongolian oak, elm, filbert, and black birch.

South to north transitions of dry chestnut-soil steppes to meadow steppes occur in higher landscapes, corresponding to climatic changes and type of soil cover. On the low, gently sloping parts of dry rocky slopes are found the non-solonetz soil and sandy-rubbly, dark-chestnut soil poor in humus content (3 to 5 per cent). Higher up, the soil changes into thin southern chernozem having a close and continuous carbonate layer. Still higher, the vegetation becomes richer and more dense, the soil is enriched, and leached rubbly chernozem under meadow steppe predominates; these areas are widely used for agriculture. Frequently the replacement of the chestnut soil by leached chernozem is extremely rapid and sharp, with no transition through a zone of the ordinary southern fertile chernozem, which in the European USSR extends for hundreds of miles.

Owing to the high altitudes, vertical zonality has evolved. There are four vertical zones: (1) steppe—found in subdued relief at altitudes of from 1,650 to 3,300 feet; (2) wooded-steppe—

in the intricate labyrinth of broad ravines at 2,970 to 3,960 feet; (3) forest—on massive, flat waterdivides at 3,960 to 6,270 feet, sometimes divided into a lower zone of mixed aspen-birch–larch forests and an upper mossy taiga zone of larch, spruce, and pine; and (4) the high-mountain, or bald-mountain, zone—on rocky slopes and the tops of high peaks, with a subalpine belt of dwarf stone pine and areas of mountain tundra above 6,270 feet.

Because of the interlocking latitudinal and vertical zonality, the limits of vertical zones are influenced by the latitude of the area: The farther south, the higher the steppes rise and the higher the taiga zones and bald mountains are forced. In the north, the timber line lies at a height of about 3,960 feet; in the south, at a height of 5,610 feet, and on Sokhondo bald mountain the forest rises to 6,510 feet. On slopes protected from the north winds pines are found at a maximum height of 6,700 feet. Dry steppe on chestnut soil is not encountered above 2,640 feet, in neighboring Mongolia it grows at 3,300 and even 4,290 feet. On the north-facing slope of mountains near the northern tip of Baikal, the forest rises to a height of 4,785 feet; on the southern slope, which is under the cooling influence of the lake in summertime, it reaches only 3,300 feet.

In Baikalia, the distribution of soil and vegetation, and cultivated plots and settlements, conform to the basic northeast direction of orographic lines. Broad, inhabited steppe valleys alternate with uninhabited and almost inaccessible wooded ranges on rocky slopes and in swampy, narrow ravines. The cultivated lands are concentrated in the lower altitude belts. Meadows and pastures are found at a height of approximately 1,650 to 2,805 feet, and plowed fields rise on slopes to 2,970 to 3,630 feet. The character of the soil and vegetation is influenced by the direction of the mountain ranges and the exposure of the slopes. The north-facing slopes, with their moister and colder climate, are the sites of a more northern taiga landscape; the south-facing insolated slopes are predominately a steppe or wooded-steppe landscape. In the upper stretches of the ngoda, on the north-facing slopes, the taiga descends to 3,300 to 2,970 feet; at the same altitude, the south-facing slopes are covered with continuous steppe.

In the northern part of the region, on north-facing slopes with crypto-podzolic clayey soil, larch taiga is developed with a subgrowth of Middendorf birch, and a bog rosemary and solid moss cover. On south-facing, drier slopes with rubbly soils, there are pine groves with a subgrowth of Dahurian rhododendron and sparse grass cover. Valley vegetation varies, depending on the vertical location of the valley: In the zone of dry steppes there are halophytic plants, in the mountain steppe and wooded-steppe zone there are meadow valleys, and in the taiga zone there are bogs. The vegetation varies also with the character of the rock strata. Sand, especially widespread in the southern part of the region, in most often covered with pine groves. Limestone outcrops on south-facing slopes of the northern part of the region, contain karst formations and are poor in surface water. They contribute to the development (for example, on the northwestern shore of Baikal) of a humus-carbonate soil wholly uncharacteristic of the region, which is covered by a rich steppe vegetation of feather grass, koeleria, artemisia, and steppe sedge.

Frequent fires have, in a number of places, almost destroyed the dark-coniferous taiga of Siberian pine, fir, and spruce—formerly more widespread—and have contributed to the extension of pine and birch. After the fires have destroyed the larch, birch, and pine forests on steep south-facing slopes, steppe plants are first to grow. In general, Siberian taiga, Mongolia steppe, high-mountain and Amur-Ussuri species contribute to the richness and diversity of a flora which also contains many unusual Dahurian xerophytic species: astragalus, cinquefoil, and artemisia. The uneven mountain relief, the exposure, and the climatic heterogeneity, establish the complex ecological conditions favorable for a diversified vegetation.

Likewise, the soil of the region is extremely diverse in its composition, origin, and properties. It is possible to find all the main soil types: chestnut, different variants of chernozem, solonchak and solonetz, soil of a podzolic type from clearly expressed podzol to dark-colored slightly-podzolic soil, meadow and peat-gley soil.

The fauna, like the flora, contains a mixture of Mongolian steppe, Siberian taiga, high-mountain, and Amur-Ussuri species. Many of the species in this region are peculiar to it alone. In the faunal makeup are: steppe species, including Mongolian antelope and Mongolian lark; typical taiga species, such as sable and hazel grouse; high-mountain species, such as the mountain sheep and tundra ptarmigan; Amur-Ussuri species, such as raccoon-dog and dark-blue thrush; and unique local species of Trans-Baikal badger, and Dahurian hamster. Certain Amur-Ussuri fauna, such as the siskin (*Chrysomitris spinus*), ordinarily not found outside the Amur Basin, or dark-blue thrush (*Turdus hortulorum*), characteristic of the south-Ussuri district and native also to the Crimea, are found in the region of unbroken taiga at the sources of the Olekma, Aldan, and Maya rivers. Many steppe species enter other landscape zones, where they must find shelter under stringent conditions. For example, on certain small lakes of the Vitim Plateau, the red sheldrake (*Tadorna ferruginea*) nests in a larch taiga, and along riverside meadows the Eastern Siberian bustard (*Otis tarda*) nests. On the rocky precipices of northern Baikalia, the Mongolia steppe varicolored rock thrush (*Monticola saxatilis*) nests side by side with such northern taiga residents as the ordinary waxwing (*Bombycilla garrula*).

Southern steppe and Amur-Ussuri species which nest far to the north are doubtless relicts of a xerothermic period. East of Yablonoi Range many taiga species—elk, wolverines, bear, and white ptarmigan—are absent from the forest biocoenoses; on the other hand, to the east of the Nerchinsk Range, boar and raccoon-dog appear, coming out of Manchuria. In the forest zone of the eastern shore of Baikal, owing to the thick, loose snow cover, are such taiga animals as the roe deer, the elk, and the wolf.

Steppe Zone

There are three types of steppe in Baikalia: (1) artemisia–feather–fescue grass steppes on chestnut soil in the southernmost districts, where they occupy not only the valleys but spread up the slopes and summits of low ranges; (2) feather grass and mixed grasses on southern chernozem, located to the north of the region; (3) meadow steppes on leached-out chernozem, belonging to the zone of wooded-steppe.

Interspersed with these three types are white solonchak glades and patches of solonetz soil. Near brackish springs are solonchak meadows or hilly bogs with sedge, cotton grass, and scrub willow.

There are several types of dry steppes. The most arid ones are those with a soil covering of 40 to 50 per cent of the surface and a grass stand 6 to 9 inches high, developed on chestnut soil, and used as poor pasturage. The predominant plants are shallow-sod grasses, *Diplachne squarrosa,* cinquefoil (*Potentilla bifurca*), and astragalus. White artemisia-grass steppes are widespread on saline chestnut soil with soil covering up to 40 per cent of the surface and standing grass 10 to 15 inches high; the background is formed of sods of white *Artemisia frigida,* to which are added: sheep's fescue (*Festuca ovina*), meadow grass (*Poa attenuata*), feather grass (*Stipa capillata*), edelweiss (*Leontopodium sibiricum*), and veronica (*Veronica incana*). The steppes are used for pasturage in the spring and the first half of summer, before the steppe has had time to burn out and before the maidenhair feather grass has blossomed.

On sandy-gravelly, dark-chestnut soil and southern chernozem, developed on early lake sediments, are found tansy steppes with soil covering of up to 30 to 35 per cent of the surface and grass to 12 to 15 inches high. The plant cover consists mainly of Siberian tansy (*Tanacetum sibiricum*) and steppe meadow grass (*Poa botryoides*), with a dense ground cover of parmelia lichen (*Parmelia conspersa*). These steppes make good pasturage for sheep.

Sandy steppes with a soil cover of up to 30 to 40 per cent of the surface and a grass stand 7 to 9 inches high are developed on shallow soil with a chestnut-brown humus layer. They occupy wide, sandy terraces along large rivers, and are made up of feather grass (*Stipa capillata*), crested wheat grass (*Agropyron cristatum*), steppe meadow grass (*Poa botryoides*), koeleria (*Koeleria gracilis*), sand cinquefoil (*Potentilla subacaulis*), and thyme (*Thymus serpyllum*). These steppes provide poor pasturage for sheep, the grazing time being limited to 3 or 4 months. Columnar and structureless solonetz soil on the bottoms and gentle slopes of valleys are covered by small patches of steppe sedge (*Carex stenophylla*) and *Artemisia frigida,* often used as pasturage. On meadow solonchak, along the bottom of broad ravines and at dried-up lakes, thickets of chee grass (*Lasiagrostis splendens*) and *Iris ensata* are found.

The islands of steppe extend northward into the taiga zone, to the valley of the Barguzin and Muya. The soil and vegetation are the northernmost types—feather-grass and meadow steppes on chernozem, chernozem-like, and dark-colored soil covered with a mixture of steppe and meadow species. At the same time, the turfiness of soil increases to the north. In feather-grass steppes with turfiness of 50 to 60 per cent of the ground and a grass stand of 20 inches high, the predominating species are: maidenhair feather grass (*Stipa capillata*), to which are added, in different proportions, steppe meadow grass (*Poa botryoides*), *Aneurolepidium pseudoagropyrum* which is a valuable fodder plant, astragalus (*Astragalus dahuricus*), pasqueflower (*Pulsatilla patens*), and scabiosa (*Scabiosa fischeri*). The best season for pasture is from May to August. Near Yeravnyye lakes, on shallow chernozem are found mixed-grass meadow steppes with ground covering up to 60 to 70 per cent, with a grass stand 17 to 19 inches high, and a mixture of steppe and meadow forms: brome grass (*Bromus inermis*), meadow grass (*Poa pratensis*), edelweiss (*Leontopodium sibiricum*), and clover (*Trifolium lupinaster*). These steppes make

Fig. 9-6. Four-cereal steppe on chestnut soil southeast of Lake Baikal.

good hay and pasturage for all types of livestock. In the valleys of the Upper Angara and Barguzin are found meadow steppes with covering up to 80 per cent and with a grass stand to 18 inches high; *Aneurolepidum pseudoagropyrum* and steppe sedge (*Carex stenophylla*) predominate. These steppes are especially valuable in spring, when the sedge stalks are tender.

Dauriya is the center of Trans-Baikal steppe vegetation. It adjoins southern Trans-Baikal and northeastern Mongolia, where an exchange of plant species takes place. During the Tertiary Period the climate changed in the direction of greater dryness, and the environmental conditions in Trans-Baikal were correspondingly altered. On the southern slopes of the mountains, where the climate is more arid, xerophytic species developed. Some of the forests perished, and the bottoms of dried-out water basins were occupied by the xerophytes of the mountain slopes. The process of xerophytization proceeded in later xerothermal periods and goes on at present. An important part in the formation of the Dauriya steppes was played by alpine high-mountain species, which can tolerate aridity.

The wooded-steppe, lying between the true steppe and the forest zones and jutting northward along the valleys, contains large steppe areas alternating with pine groves, larch woods, birch copses, and dry brush (made up of *Betula gmelini* and *Betula fruticosa*). The wooded-steppe is developed on meadow-steppe carbonaceous soil. The steppe areas are sometimes composed chiefly of clematis (*Clematis angustifolia*), and sometimes predominantly *Nemerocallis minor*. On rocky south-facing slopes brushwood steppes prevail with dwarf elm (*Ulmus pumila*), Siberian apricot (*Armeniaca sibirica*), and reed grass (*Calamagrostis epigeios*). Along the bottoms of broad ravines, on flat, clayey, irrigated soil are found grassy meadows with *Atropis distans,* cobresia (*Kobresia schoenoides*), and gentian (*Gentiana decumbens*). The pine groves, which alternate with the steppe areas, are distinguished from the European groves by good subgrowth of Dahurian rhododendron.

The wooded-steppe with its chernozem and dark-colored, slightly podzolic soil—arable land —is densely populated, whereas the neighboring mountain taiga and dry bordering steppes are almost uninhabited. The yield of grasses depends largely on the amount of precipitation in the first half of summer. The average productivity over a period of years reaches 220 pounds for 2.47 acres. In years with little an-

Fig. 9-7.   Pine forest and steppe on the plain between the Onon River and Lake Toreysk.

nual precipitation, there is a sharp drop in the vegetative cover, with resultant migration of the population with its livestock. The arid climate necessitates the irrigation and fertilization of meadows, the practice of winter pasturage, and late harvests. Natural fodder regions suffer from the abundance of rodents and from insect blights—locust and meadow moth.

The animal world of the steppes and wooded-steppes is diverse. Rodents are most important: Eversman marmot (*Citellus eversmanni transbaicalcium*), and along with it in the southeast, suslik (*Citellus dahuricus*). The marmots (*Marmota sibirica,* and *M. kamtschatica doppelmayeri*), jerboa (*Alactaga saltator mongolica*), Dahurian hamster (*Cricetus furunculus*), and species of field rodents (*Microtus*) often spread disease. Directly or indirectly, the rodents: (1) destroy the grass; (2) directly affect the formation of the composition of steppe plants; (3) reform the soil layer, bringing out the bottom matrices and forming mounds, which are very noticeable in the steppes in thickets of artemisia and weeds; (4) destroy the root systems of plants, gather

and eat the seeds, and cut off the stems above ground.

The following carnivores are found in the steppe zone: Trans-Baikal badger (*Meles meles raddei*), Trans-Baikal steppe polecat (*Putorius eversmanni michnoi*), *Kolonocus alpinus,* wolf, and Tartar fox (*Vulpes corsak*). In the southeast the raccoon-dog is found. Ungulates inhabiting the region are: Mongolian antelope (*Gazella gutturosa*), which migrate from Mongolia at the beginning of winter and return there in the spring; the boar; and Manchurian roe deer, which occupy the steppe areas of the Barguzin Valley, where there is abundant fodder and slight snow cover.

Many Mongolian species of birds nest in the steppe zone: *Tadorna tadorna,* red duck (*Tadorna ferruginea*), crane (*Grus virgo*), Eastern Siberian bustard (*Otis tarda*), Mongolian lark (*Melanocorypha mongolica*), horned lark (*Eremophila alpestris*), and chat (*Oenanthe isabellina*). The number of steppe species rapidly decreases to the north; in the Barguzin steppes only *Otis tarda, Oenanthe isabellina,* and *Eremophila alpestris* nest. In the wooded sections of wooded-steppe, black grouse is abundant.

Taiga Zone

The taiga is varied and has uneven distribution throughout the region. The northern taiga, lying approximately in an area between the northern end of Lake Baikal and the mouth of the Gazimur River (the left tributary of the Argun), receives a large amount of precipitation and has moist soil, so that the vegetation resembles that of the Yakut taiga. The timber line lies at about 3,960 feet but individual larches are found at 4,950 feet.

The most widespread types of the predominating Dahurian larch forest are: (1) larch forest with subgrowth of Dahurian rhododendron on steep slopes; (2) larch forest with red bilberry on gentle slopes; (3) larch forest with wild rosemary on the lower parts of gentle slopes; (4) larch forest with Middendorf birch and red bilberry, growing over forest burns; (5) larch forest with continuous moss cover; (6) bottomland larch forest with wild rose, ripple-leafed spirea, and black, red, and creeping currants (*Ribes nigrum, R. pubescens, R. procumbens*); (7) larch forest with scrub birch (*Betula fruticosa*); and (8) larch forest with scrub alder (*Alnus fruticosa*).

Occasionally mixed with the larch are Siberian pine, fir, and *Ayan* spruce. Beneath larch forests is slightly podzolic or podzolic soil, and sometimes podzolic-gley and boggy soil. Some less abundant plants are: flat-leafed birch (*Betula platyphylla*) and rock birch (*Betula ermani*), aspen, balsam, bird cherry, and mountain ash, which extends to the timber line. Along the rivers lie bright bands of forests, meadows, and bogs. Scattered throughout the solid forest cover are dismal expanses of burned-over areas, and gray patches of bald peaks, covered with talus.

In the central part of the region forests of Dahurian larch predominate, with many different varieties often mixed with other woody species. Pine and fir grow in the upper mountain-forest belt and in areas influenced by Lake Baikal. Spruce and poplar line the bottoms of broad ravines and the banks of rivers; pine grows on sandy soil and is especially dense in Eastern Trans-Baikal. Birch and aspen are spread along the foothills and cover old burns. The most widespread types of pure larch forests are: those with a subgrowth of Dahurian rhododendron; those with a subgrowth of Middendorf birch, or dwarf birch; and those with bog rhododendron (*Rhododendron parvifolium*). Also there are some with a moss ground cover (hypnum or sphagnum), with a lichen cover, and with a subgrowth of dwarf stone pine. Usually, larch grows on the north-facing slopes of low ranges and the lower parts of valleys, where colder and moister clayey soil prevails. On sunny and well-drained south-facing slopes, and also on the deep sandy crypto-podzolic soil of high alluvial terraces, pine groves with a subgrowth of Dahurian

Fig. 9-8. Larch forest north of Lake Baikal with undergrowth of birch (*Betula fruticosa*).

rhododendron, and with a cover of red bilberry or lichen, are prevalent.

In the moister areas of Pre-Baikal (those directly cooled by Lake Baikal in summer), and also in the upper mountain forest zone, there is a dark-coniferous taiga of spruce, fir, and Siberian pine, to which larch is admixed. Taiga, with the predominance of spruce and a continuous moss cover, is common along the banks of the upper and middle courses of rivers and along broad, swampy ravines where frost occurs. A fir taiga is developed in Khamar-Daban on podzolic, well-moistened, and fertile soil; beneath its canopy there is a Siberian taiga grass complex of pyrola, lily, and hypnum mosses. Dense, solid spruce-pine and fir-pine forests are prevalent near the base of bald mountains on the shaded, moist, north-facing slopes, and also in narrow strips along the bottom of moist, broad ravines. Under the dark-coniferous taiga is soil of a podzolic type. Birch and aspen forests grow over sandy and clayey podzolic soil on sites that have been burned or slashed. In the eastern part of the region, they constitute a persistent independent grouping of wooded-steppe, and have a cover of pea vine (*Orobus lathyroides*), clover (*Trifolium lupinaster*), peony (*Paeonia anomala*), and reed grass (*Calamagrostis epigeios*). Poplar trees extend in narrow strips on the rocky alluvial soil of the river banks. Rising upward, pine disappears first, then fir, spruce, poplar, and birch. Remaining at the upper border of the forest are larch.

Along broad ravines and river valleys of Central Baikalia, peat-bog soil is covered by gray sedge bogs, moist meadows with prominent stands of sedges (*Carex vesicaria, C. gracilis*), moisture-loving grasses (*Agropron repens*), and mixed grass—for example, white hellebore (*Veratrum album*). These meadows have little economic value. In the valleys of large rivers, on recent alluvial-meadow soil, there are grassy bottomland meadows of good quality. Among the grasses, there is much brome and meadow grass; and among the legumes, there are clover (*Trifolium lupinas-*

ter), *Hedysarum sibiricum,* and European pea vine (*Lathyrus pratensis*).

The forest zone in southern Baikalia lies higher up than in the central part of the region: It begins at 3,300 feet, and extends to 6,600 feet; whereas, at Baikal, it extends from the level of the lake. Slightly podzolic soil prevails, owing to the dry climate and the comparatively thin crust of coarse talus on the summits and slopes of the mountains. Bog soil is negligible. In the lower ranges are mixed grassy forests—primarily birch-aspen with a small admixture of larch and pine. The south-facing slopes are noticeably drier, and contain pure pine groves and large patches of steppe vegetation. At the bottom of moist broad ravines, bogs are developed. Rising from the low secondary ranges to the primary high ones (for example, Mt. Sokhondo), the relatively light mixed forest is replaced by larch and then by pure pine forests, to which spruce and fir are added on shaded north-facing slopes and along the bottoms of narrow valleys. Trees do not attain large dimensions in the mountain taiga. Rising upward, the soil becomes more moist and cold, and is covered solidly by mosses and lichens which crowd out the grassy vegetation; thus for dozens of miles there is no fodder for horses. At an altitude of a little more than 6,270 feet, pine forests are replaced by subalpine thickets of dwarf stone pine and mountain tundra.

Found in the taiga zone of the region are: bear (*Ursus arctos baicalensis*) of large size and with luxuriant, long fur; wolf, a serious enemy to stock raisers; fox (*Vulpes vulpes jacutensis*); wolverine; polecat (*Kolonocus sibiricus*), which in summer hunts the pika (*Ochotona alpina*) and in winter hibernates underground; ermine (*Mustela erminea*); weasel (*Mustela nivalis pygmaea*); otter (*Lutra lutra*); and the valuable Barguzin sable (*Martes zibellina princeps*). Sable reserves have been severely depleted, but the sable still survives over a very broad territory. It lives chiefly in the talus zone just below the bald peaks, in impenetrable thickets of dwarf stone pine, where it finds shelter and abundant food (chipmunks, field mice, nuts, and berries). The Barguzin game preserve was established in 1916 for the protection of sables. Here, they multiply and pass across the high bald peaks into the neighboring districts. There is also a sable nursery.

The commercially important Barguzin squirrel (*Sciurus vulgaris fusconigricans*), found in all types of forest, has fur of excellent quality. In east Trans-Baikal, the permanent habitat of the squirrel is not the thick pine taiga, but the larch forests, where the larch cone is its primary food. Other rodents living here are: marmot, white hare, chipmunk, flying squirrel, rust-colored and red field mice (*Evotomys rutilus, E. rufocanus*), and birch mouse (*Sicista montana*). Among the ungulates, elk (*Alces alces*) lives in damp forests containing lakes and bogs; and Manchurian deer or Siberian stag (*Cervus canadensis sibiricus*), and sometimes boar live where forests alternate with vast meadow and steppes areas.

Birds common to the taiga are: rock grouse (*Tetrao urogalloides*), hazel grouse (*Tetrastes bonasia*), pintail duck (*Anas acuta*), teal (*Querquedula crecca*), widgeon (*Mareca penelope*), and snipe (*Capella gallinago*).

High-Mountain Zone

The high-mountain, or bald-mountain, zone occupies a small area (in the north not more than 5 per cent), but is uniform throughout the region. Unlike the high-mountain zones of other mountain regions, it has but a few subalpine, high-mountain meadows, and these form small isolated areas, disseminated on the border between the forest and high-altitude tundra. There is almost no zone of moist alpine meadows—so typical, for example, of the Altai. The subalpine belt is covered by a luxuriant development of dwarf stone pine (*Pinus pumila*) forming an almost impassable thicket. Along with it grow Middendorf birch, dwarf birch (*Betula exilis*), and characteristic Eastern

Siberian heathers, such as cassiope (*Cassiope ericoides*), alpine bearberry (*Arctostaphylos alpina*), and juniper (*Juniperus dahurica*).

The belt of dwarf pine thickets—165 to 330 feet wide in the north—contains unique ecological conditions. Dwarf stone pine forms impenetrable and high (about 7 to 10 feet) thickets, which help to hold back the snow, preventing it from being blown off. Vegetation growing under the stone pine canopy is protected from the cold north winter winds and from excessive evaporation, and the soil is guaranteed a more intensive and uniform supply of moisture. There is more energetic soil formation here than in the tundra lying higher up. The soil is enriched by a substratum of fine soil, which aids in the development of podzolic types. Lichens are replaced by a cover of shade-enduring mosses. The thickets offer shelter and give abundant food to animals of commercial importance. Pine nuts are plentiful but often large areas of the pine groves are severely damaged by the pine silkworm and by fires. Burns are grown over by Middendorf birch.

The mountain summits above the subalpine belt are covered with mountain tundra and rock deposits. The different types of mountain tundra are distributed according to the mechanical composition of the substrata, the thickness of snow cover, and type of relief and conditions of soil moistening. Slopes protected from wind contain mountain tundras with a predominance of *Cladonia alpestris,* and an abundance of bog and red bilberry; cassiope (*Cassiope ericoides*), bearberry (*Arctostaphylos alpina*), and crowberry (*Empetrum nigrum*) are absent. Growing on the flat summits of bald mountains over a fine layer of humus are "alectoria" tundras with a lichen cover of *Alectoria ochroleuca,* and a thin bush cover of cassiope and *Ledum decumbens;* lichen supplies reach eight tons per 2.5 acres. Large rocks are covered by encrusted lichens. In addition to these bald-mountain plants there are: alpine sedge, lousewort, primrose, pimpinella, diapensia (*Diapensia lapponica*), and sweet grass (*Hierochloe alpina*).

The fauna of the bald-mountain zone is typical. On many of the ranges the reindeer (*Rangifer angustirostris*) thrives; on craggy mountain slopes close to the timber line there are musk deer and roe deer (*Capreolus pygargus*); and in high parts of the Stanovoi Range there are mountain sheep (*Ovis nivicola*). Among the pikas are: *Ochotona alpina svatochi* and *O. dahurica;* and, in the southern districts, *Aschizomys lemminus*—a lemming-type field mouse. Another rodent of the south is the marmot (*Marmota kamtschatica doppelmayeri*), an important commercial animal, which lives in colonies on large, alpine grassy areas amid large rock patches. The marmot hibernates from early September to the middle of May.

Occupying the pine grove thickets is a martin-like bird *Pinicola enucleator*. Tundra ptarmigan (*Lagopus mutus*) and dotterel (*Eudromias morinellus*) nest in the bald-mountain zone.

PART **III**

FAR EAST

The geographic region known as the Far East consists of a comparatively narrow strip along the eastern coast of Soviet Asia. The Pacific Ocean is separated from the seas that border the coast by chains of volcanic islands—the Japanese, Kurile, and Aleutian. Only that part of the eastern coast of the Peninsula of Kamchatka between Cape Kronotski to Cape Lopatka, a distance of 360 miles, and the Kurile Islands are directly open to the Pacific Ocean. The natural boundary of the Far East, on the west, is formed by the continental water divide of the Stanovoi, Dzhugzhur, and Kolyma ranges. In the north, the border closely parallels the northern coast of the Sea of Okhotsk, then cuts across the narrow isthmus joining Kamchatka to the mainland, at the southern end of Parapolskiy Valley. Administratively, the region lies almost wholly within the bounds of Khabarovsk Territory, Primorski Territory (often translated Maritime Territory), and Amur oblast. Geographically, it is sharply distinguished from adjoining Eastern Siberia.

The Far East is a complex geologic region, a part of the Eastern Asiatic region affected by Mesozoic and Alpine folding. It has an unusual fossil fauna that is difficult to correlate with that of Europe. There is dislocation of all strata, except the Quaternary, by large tectonic breaks. Here there have been recent Quaternary eruptions of andesites and basalts, which are linked with the modern volcanoes of Kamchatka and the Kurile Islands.

The climate of the Far East is in many ways similar to that of the monsoon region of East Asia. Since it consists of a narrow strip between the vast mainland of Eurasia and the Pacific Ocean there are sharp seasonal changes in atmospheric pressure and in the direction and characteristics of winter and summer winds. Its complex relief affects the climate in different parts of the region, and the adjacent cold seas (especially the Sea of Okhotsk) and the coastal marine currents add their effect. The rivers have a maximum discharge in summer, during the period of monsoon rains, and a minimum in the dry winter. The region has well-developed forest landscapes; in different areas, Eastern Siberian, Okhotsk, and Manchurian flora and fauna predominate, and some landscapes penetrate deeply into others.

The Far East is divided into four geographic regions: (1) Amur-Primorski, (2) the northwestern coast of the Sea of Okhotsk, (3) Sakhalin, and (4) the Kamchatka-Kurile volcanic region.

CHAPTER 10

Amur-Primorski Region

The greater part of the Far East south of the Stanovoi Range, with the exception of the southern coast of the Sea of Okhotsk and the lower stretches of the Amgun and Amur rivers, north of Lake Kizi, belongs to the subzone of mixed forest landscapes. As in the European part of the subzone, it contains mixed coniferous broad-leaved forests with large stands of oak and its companions—maple, ash, linden, and hornbeam—but without an admixture of deciduous evergreen trees and shrubs. But the Amur-Primorski region has also many peculiarities that sharply distinguish it from the European part of the subzone and make it one of the most interesting geographic

regions of the Soviet Union. The main causes of these differences are: (1) its more southerly location—between 42° and 55° north latitude —roughly that of the European part of the USSR from Gorki to Tiflis; (2) the pronounced monsoon type of climate; (3) a different history of development of landscapes in post-Tertiary time, especially the absence of glaciation, which led to the preservation of a rich Tertiary flora and fauna and to the mixture of northern and southern species; and (4) the interweaving of the northern landscapes of Eastern Siberia and Okhotsk taiga with southern landscapes of neighboring Manchuria and Korea.

RELIEF

Geomorphologically the Amur-Primorski region is a combination of wide plains and mountain ranges of various heights, sharply differing in their trend from north-south (Sikhote-Alin, Bureya) to east-west (Yankan-Tukuringra-Dzhagdy). The entire region is formed of folded Mesozoic rocks, with which are associated valuable mineral resources.

The Sikhote-Alin Range is bounded on the east by the Sea of Japan and Tatarski Strait, and on the west by the plains near Lake Khanka, the Ussuri River, and the lower Amur River. The Sikhote-Alin system consists of

eight parallel mountain ridges of a north-northeast trend. The average heights of the ranges vary from 2,300 to 3,300 feet. In the north, individual peaks reach 4,300 feet; farther south, between the sources of the Bikin and Iman rivers, 4,900; and in the south, at the sources of the Ulukhe River, more than 6,000 feet. The highest point of the range is Mount Komarova, at the source of the Khor River, which reaches 6,360 feet. Despite the relative severity of climate, nowhere do the mountain ranges reach the snow line, and few rise even to the alpine zone. They show signs of intense disintegration, and form a solid mass of low, sloping, and smoothed-out elevations that extends in all directions and is dissected by a multitude of rivers. These elevations resemble highly eroded hills rather than real mountains. Denuded high and steep bald peaks of durable rocks or large elevated basalt plateaus with re-

markably uniform and flat surfaces exist only at the source of the Ussuri River (Daubikhe River).

Between the parallel ranges are numerous valleys, which are often connected with one another by transverse valleys. The rivers on the western slope are longer and larger, many of

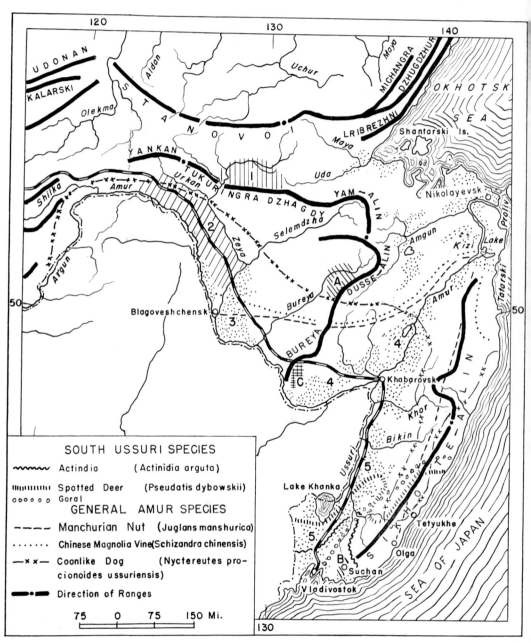

Map 10-I.   Flora and fauna of the Far East region.

hem—such as the Ussuri, Iman, Bikin, and Khor—having their sources in the eastern ranges closest to the sea. (The name of the range means "great divide of western rivers.") The streams that flow eastward into the sea, are, except for the Tumnin, Koppi, and Samarga rivers, short and small. In the south are longitudinal valleys, such as that of the Suchan River, that are open to the sea. Rivers whose upper stretches flow along these longitudinal valleys break through the ranges in transverse gorges that contain many sandbanks, rapids, and waterfalls. Because the mountain ranges are broken by faulting, there is no single uninterrupted water divide between the Sea of Japan and the lower sections of the Amur and Ussuri. In the northern two-thirds of the Sikhote-Alin the water divide shifts constantly and abruptly from one range to another; only in the southern third does it extend unbroken. The boundaries of the mountain ranges are orographically very distinct: the mountains rise sharply above the plains of the Amur and Ussuri without foothills. The base of the mountains seems sunk in the loose deposits of the neighboring lowlands, on which there are only isolated, scattered, low hills. On the eastern side, the Sikhote-Alin breaks off near the shore in sheer cliffs, making the coast inaccessible.

North of Olga Bay the coast of the Sea of Japan is parallel to the ranges of Sikhote-Alin —a longitudinal shore, unbroken, with small low sandbars at the mouths of the mountain streams that empty into the sea. The only bay in the northern section of the coast is that of Sovetskaya Gavan. In the south the mountain ranges are intersected by the coast line at a right angle; it is a typical transverse shore, highly dissected and with many bays (Amur Gulf, Ussuri Gulf) and islands (Askold, Russki).

The coast is a subsiding coast; the inundation of the river mouths has formed estuaries and deep meandering submarine channels which are direct continuations of the river, and has created a typical ria coast. But on the shores, it is possible to detect traces of periods in which the coast rose—terraces that contain shells of mollusks that still live in the Sea of Japan.

Sikhote-Alin is a folded range with highly dislocated Tertiary deposits and many faults. The range was created by the first stage of alpine folding, which took place in the earliest part of the Cretaceous Period. Its structure, in general, is very simple and consists of a system of large anticlinal folds of a north-northeast strike, complicated by a series of minor folds of the same strike.

Many tectonic breaks with a steep angle of dip run in various directions: they are a result of the most recent stages of alpine folding. In the axial section of Sikhote-Alin the most ancient rocks crop out—lower Paleozoic metamorphic schists and quartzites—and on them lies a less metamorphosed strata of phyllites and quartzite-like sandstones. Variscan granitic intrusions are also found. Rocks of the upper Paleozoic that appear on the surface in small areas, mostly in the northern part of the range, consist of a volcanic intruded limestone complex and deposits of sand and clay. In the Mesozoic there was repeated alternation of transgressions and regressions of the sea. The deposits of the Mesozoic occupy large areas of the Sikhote-Alin and are gathered in smooth steep folds. Most widespread are thick marine and fresh-water deposits of the Triassic and marine Jurassic sediments. During the Cretaceous Period, when the first stage of alpine folding occurred, there was much erosion, and thick layers of fresh-water sediments accumulated in synclinal sags with flat bottoms and steep walls. In the same depressions vegetative residue also accumulated, forming thick seams of coal. The lower layers of the deposits consist of conglomerates, shale, and ampelites, and contain seams of coal that varies in both composition and thickness but is all of high quality. In the Suchan coal district there are five main working seams of coal with a total thickness of 18 feet.

In the Tertiary Period, constant epeirogenic movements took place, and the elevation of dry land brought about intense erosion. Tertiary deposits accumulated in depressions: at present they are either completely untouched, in their original stratification, or, on the contrary, occur at very steep angles—even vertically—having been highly fractured by tectonic dislocations of dying alpine folding. In the lower sections of these deposits are seams of typical brown coal (Tavrichanka and Artem pits west of Suchan) containing entire tree trunks and branches of fossil flora, which offer an excellent record of the Tertiary vegetative cover. In contrast to the Paleozoic and Mesozoic deposits the Tertiary and Quaternary systems have more igneous rocks than sedimentary. At the beginning of the Tertiary Period and in the Late Cretaceous Period, large intrusions took place, producing valuable ore deposits. They are concentrated in the Olga-Tetyukhe district, which has some of the richest lead and zinc mines in the USSR. Lenses of polymetallic ores at the contact of porphyries with limestones contain zinc blende,

lead sulphide, copper, iron pyrite, and silver. Magnetites, molybdenum glance, manganese, and arsenic ores are found in the same district.

The beginning of the Quaternary Period was marked by thick outpourings of andesitic basalt lavas. Near Sovetskaya Gavan these rocks overlay Upper Tertiary conglomerates to a depth of 260 feet, which indicates their youth. Andesitic basalts are typically dark, close-grained, highly veined rocks with excellent prismatic basalt structures. They make fine construction material. Blanket deposits of these effusives occupy large areas along the eastern and western slopes of the northern part of the range, and in the south form individual islands among other rocks. The deposits vary in thickness from about 600 to 1,000 feet. The effusives poured out onto the uneven surface of Upper Tertiary relief, filled in the depressions and leveled the surface and then formed elevated plateaus that

Fig. 10-1. Typical rapids of a mountain river on the western slope of the Sikhote-Alin Mountains.

stretch for dozens of miles. The valleys lying amid the volcanic plateaus are canyons with vertical walls, and resemble irregular black cracks yawning in the earth. Andesitic basalts dammed up the water of moutnain springs and formed lakes such as the Shanduyski Lakes. Since the lakes have not been filled in or their dams eroded, the andesitic basalts must be quite young. No glacial deposits have been found in the Sikhote-Alin. In the last part of the Quaternary Period a series of terraces was formed along the valleys and on the seacoast.

The Bureya Range extends south-southwest from the upper reaches of the Selemdzha River to the Amur, beyond which it passes into Manchuria under the name Hsiao Khingan; on the east it borders the basin of the Bureya River. Different sections of the range have different names: the southern part is called Hsiao Khingan, the middle section Bureya, the northern part Dusse-Alin, and its continuation farther north, Yam-Alin. Bureya Range is a large mountain area that rises above the Zeya-Bureya Plain on the west and the lower Amur Plain on the east. It is cut by a network of streams into an intricate system of short ridges, separate mountain groups, and more or less dissected high plateaus. At the source of the Selemdzha River it reaches a height of 7,267 feet; in its central section more than 4,950 feet; south of the Trans-Siberian Railway seldom more than 2,300 feet; and near the Amur it descends to 660 feet. Erosion has lowered the range considerably and made the mountains smooth and bare. The upper surfaces of the watersheds in its northern part are smooth expanses arched toward the middle, like bare fields 150 to 1,300 feet wide. These descend to saddles in a series of steps or rise to dome-like bald mountain peaks with 25° to 30° slopes. Some water divides are narrow, with crests only a few yards wide. In the central part, the western slope has a steeper gradient than the eastern—a gradient that gives its rivers a very rapid fall. The role of ancient glaciation in the development of relief is negligible, although a few snow fields have developed into firns.

The geologic structure of the range is com-

Fig. 10-2. Cliff of thick effusive basalt on the east slope of the Sikhote-Alin Mountains.

plex, because folds of one direction and age were imposed on folds of a different age and direction. In the southern part of the range, three periods of folding—pre-Paleozoic, Variscan, and Mesozoic (Caledonian evidently was absent)—and three periods of magmatic intrusions are indicated. The range is considered a young fold structure of the Upper Cretaceous cycle of alpine folding: an anticlinal structure with ancient (pre-Paleozoic) rocks in the central section and a thick mass of Mesozoic deposits on the slopes. The folds and most fractures run north-northeast. The core is composed of granites, pre-Paleozoic gneisses, amphibolites, micaceous and chloritic schists, and sandy–schistous–carbonaceous deposits which, in the southern part, contain iron ores. Deposits of hematite in the Bureya iron-ore district, where there are reserves of at least five million tons, have a bedded character that establishes a certain stability of mineralization. These ores contain 37 to 43 per cent iron and much silica. Of less commercial importance are the normal rocks of the Middle and Upper Paleozoic and the large patches of young igneous rocks. Deposits of coal are found in the Mesozoic rocks that constitute a large part of the Bureya Range.

The Buryea coal basin lies between the upper course of the Bureya River north of the mouth of its left tributary, the Dulnikan, and the western slopes of Bureya Range. The basin is formed of Jurassic and Cretaceous deposits 18,000 feet thick that fill three large synclinal folds. The coal is found in the lower Cretaceous strata, which are about 2,600 feet thick, and similar to those of the Suchan coal region. The seams of coal developed throughout these strata differ in thickness and the quality of the coal they contain: there are 19 seams, 9 of which have a useful thickness, from two to six and a half feet in the north, and from two and a half to ten feet in the south. The coal reserves here are among the greatest in the USSR. These reserves indicate the possibility of the creation of a large metallurgical combine here, based on this coal and the ore deposits in the southern section of the range. Both the water divide between the Bureya River and the Selemdzha, sometimes called the Turana Range, and the region east of the Bureya Range along the upper sections of the Gorin and Kur rivers, are mountainous regions with maximum altitudes of more than 3,300 feet.

South of the Stanovoi Range and parallel to it stretches a chain of bald mountains whose various sections have been given different names. Its southern section, under the name Yankan Range, begins near the Omutnaya River, where it abuts against the ranges of eastern Trans-Baikal, and ends at the source of the Urkan River. It serves as the watershed of the Gilyuy, Urkan, and Oldoy rivers, and contains many peaks more than 3,300 feet. Its continuation is the Tukuringra Range, which runs east-southeast and serves as the water divide for the Gilyuy and Urkan rivers, tributaries of the Zeya. The Tukuringra Range continues farther east, intersects the gorge of the Zeya River, and runs to Lake Ogoron at the source of the Dep River. The average elevation of its passes is about 3,300 feet, and Mount Tukuringra rises to 5,280 feet. East of Lake Ogoron the mountains are called the Dzhagdy Range, which, at altitudes up to 4,750 feet, maintains the same east-southeast direction and serves as the water divide between the upper courses of the Selemdzha and Uda rivers. At the source of the Zeya and Uda rivers lies an isolated mountain group with a maximum altitude of more than 6,600 feet. This system of ranges, formed in part by Caledonian folding (Yankan, Tukuringra), is bounded on the south by a line of faults. Epeirogenic upheavals (Tukuringra) also contributed to the development of the mountain landscape.

Unlike the Stanovoi Range, the Yankan, Tukuringra and Dzhagdy ranges are formed chiefly of metamorphic schists, massive conglomerates, calcareous sandstones, cherts, and crystalline limestones of Paleozoic and Mesozoic age. Large masses of granite and patches of effusive rocks are found everywhere. The chain is actually a high undulating ridge dissected by erosion into a system of mountain masses with flat broad crests, which descend terrace-like toward lowlands on both north and south. The shapes of the relief are massive and have smooth outlines. The crests are flat to rolling, the slopes gentle, and there are no alpine forms. Above the general level rise the peaks of bald mountains—flat, conical, or dome-shaped, and covered with patches of rock. The relatively low altitudes, the smooth outlines, and the many passes make the water divides easily passable, and explain why the bases of the slopes and even many of the crests that rise to the height of the alpine zone are swampy.

The Amur-Zeya Plateau is situated between the Amur and Zeya rivers. It is formed of Tertiary sand and clay, under which, in the larger valleys, granites, gneisses, Jurassic sandstones, and conglomerates crop out. The plateau, whose surface undulates slightly, drops abruptly to the Amur, Zeya, and their tributaries. Its altitude ranges from 900 to 1,980 feet, the northwestern part being the highest.

Fig. 10-3. Type of relief in the northern Buryea Mountains.

The Upper Zeya Plain is situated between the southern spurs of the Stanovoi Range and the eastern part of the Tukuringra and Dzhagdy ranges and is drained by a series of left tributaries of the upper Zeya. Pressed between mountain ranges at an altitude of 900 to 1,650 feet, this region of subsidence without fault phenomena is sharply distinguished from them by the character of its rocks. It is covered by thick masses of porous Lower Quaternary deposits beneath which is the crystalline foundation of the plain. On the plain, which extends east-west, the Zeya River, which in its mountain section flows swiftly through deep gorges, has flat, low banks, a slow, quiet current, and numerous channels and meanders: that is, it has the character of a river in a late stage of development.

The Zeya-Bureya Plain is bounded on the north by the foothills of the Yankan, Tukuringra and Dzhagdy ranges, on the east by Bureya Range, and on the west and south by the lower course of the Zeya River and the middle section of the Amur. The eastern and northeastern parts of the plain have a rolling relief and the altitude ranges from 940 to 1,100 feet. In the southwest, where the plain is less than 300 feet high, a series of step-like terraces have developed along the Amur and its tributaries. The second terrace, at a height of 200 feet, constitutes almost the entire plain and is formed of horizontal Tertiary deposits—sandy-clayey shales and gray clays containing seams of coal. The varying lithological composition of the Tertiary deposits, the presence of sand and clay of differing purity, the fineness of grain, the uniformity of color, the horizontal and vertical shifting of strata, the presence of lenses and tapering seams, the diagonal and irregular stratification, the absence of marine fossils, all cause one to conclude that these deposits are sediments that were laid down in a fresh-water basin with an unstable regime. In large areas drying and inundation alternated periodically, and this created favorable conditions for the accumulation of vegetative detritus and the formation of coal. Apparently, at the beginning of the Quaternary the Bureya Range was deeply eroded, and during that period a large part of the plain was converted into bottomland of the gigantic old Amur River by an accumulation of deltaic deposits from the Zeya and Bureya rivers. The subsequent drying of the plain and the meandering of the Amur caused the development of the early Quaternary and present-day Amur terraces, as well as those of the Zeya, which are only partly coalesced with the terraces of the Bureya River. Impressions of the leaves of the gingko and elm have been found in Quaternary alluvium, which indicate the existence of a rich Quaternary flora similar to the present-day flora of Japan and China. Because of the slight gradient of the basin, erosion by water plays a small role at present, and the plain is dissected only at the banks of rivers. The network of shallow rivers is very weakly developed, and the uniform valleys have broad flat bottoms. Heavy precipitation, in conjunction with the clayey alluvial soil, causes intense swamping of low places on the terraces and of the bottoms of valleys. The terraces are covered by luxuriant meadows, and scattered on higher ground are islands of brush and trees.

The Lower Amur Plain, most of which has an altitude of about 160 feet, extends mostly along the left bank of the Amur—between it and the eastern slopes of the Bureya Range—and in the south continues into Manchuria between the Sungari and Ussuri rivers. It is a low, level, treeless expanse with numerous lakes and low ridges. Only a few isolated peaks rise as high as 2,600 feet.

The plain stretches northward to the sea from the point at which the Ussuri and the Sungari join the Amur; in some places it lies on both sides of the river. Wide basins alternate with narrow sections; the latter being found where the river cuts through the mountain ridges which obstruct its path. The width of the plain thus varies from several hundreds of yards to several dozen miles. The altitude of most of the plain is about 160 feet. Rising above it are isolated mountain ridges of resistant bedrock from 1,320 to 3,300 feet high. In its wider parts there are many well-indicated wide terraces. The Amur bottomland is 10 to 15 feet above the river, and comprises silty-dusty clay, sandy loam, sand, and gravel; it is divided by wide channels into numerous islands. Scattered on it are many

bottomland lakes of varying dimensions and outlines that are connected with the river by channels: the largest are Bolon, Udyl, Ommi, and Padali. Some of the lakes (Bolshoy Kizi, Orel, and Chlya) are in the valley of the old Amur, which had a different course, entering both Tatarski Strait, near the Gulf of Chikhacheva, and Sakhalin Gulf. Every year, during the heavy summer showers, the river may cut new channels, and form bottomland lakes and islands. The bottomland is swampy, although in some places near the river, where there are sandy deposits, the wind forms low dunes, 7 to 17 feet high. The second terrace of the Amur, 20 to 23 feet high, is made up of Quaternary powdery clay, sand, sandstone, and conglomerate. It is quite wide in many places. The narrow parts of the plain, between Komsomolsk and the Udyl-Kizi Basin and also at the point where the Amur cuts through the Chayatyn Range, have few terraces and channels; the river flows between sheer banks. Downstream the Amur valley widens, and the river changes course and forms a huge arc, terminating in a wide shallow mouth—the Amur estuary.

The Lower Amur Plain is a young plain, like the Khanka-Ussuri; a tectonic depression formed in the Quaternary Period. At that time, the advance of the sea, the formation of large lakes, and the slowing currents of rivers caused the depression gradually to fill with thick layers of friable lake and alluvial deposits. Poor drainage led to the raising of the level of ground waters and the general swamping of the bottomland.

The Pre-Khanka-Ussuri Plain is a depressed dislocated region with mountains on both west and east, and has an average altitude of 85 feet. Loose Quaternary deposits up to 316 feet thick cover the lower slopes of the adjoining mountain spurs and a few isolated hills which are composed of Paleozoic rocks, Triassic and Tertiary granites, and andesitic basalts. It is assumed that at a comparatively recent period there was a strait that ran from Vladivostok through Lake Khanka and along the present course of the Ussuri and Lower Amur rivers which separated the Sikhote-Alin Mountains from the mainland. This is confirmed by the presence of marine terraces in the Sikhote-Alin.

CLIMATE

Its proximity to the ocean, its location at the edge of the Eurasian continent, and its relief give the Amur-Primorski region a climate that differs sharply from that of neighboring Eastern Siberia. The region is under the influence of the East Asiatic monsoons—seasonal winds that blow in different directions in summer and winter. During the winter atmospheric pressure is high and north and northwesterly winds blow from the mainland to the ocean, where the pressure is low. Continental winds from the depths of the supercooled mainland, the domain of the Eastern Siberian anticyclone, carry cold and exceptionally dry air, bringing cold, clear, and dry weather. In spring the pressure over the ocean begins to rise and by April south and southeast winds are blowing from the ocean to the land. These winds bring warm humid air from the sea, producing fog, rain, and a warm summer. Monsoon rains seldom penetrate west of the Bureya Range, but the indirect influence of the monsoons extends much farther. The seasonal distribution of prevailing winds is clearly marked: during one year, at Voroshilov, 53 south winds were observed in summer and only 9 in winter; in winter there were 20 north winds, in summer only 6.

Despite the nearness of the ocean, the climate is not typically marine. A dry spring and autumn, a severe winter with little snow, as cold as that of Trans-Baikal or Yakutia, do not suggest proximity to the sea. Only the foggy, damp, rainy summer has the characteristics of a marine climate. The region in general is much cooler than others at the same latitude: much of its heat is lost to the Asiatic mainland, with its low winter temperatures, the two comparatively cold seas—the Sea of Japan and the Sea of Okhotsk—and the cold coastal current of Tatarski Strait. Vladivostok lies farther south than Sochi on the Black Sea or Nice on the French Riviera, where lemons ripen and roses bloom the year round, yet although its winter is short, its harbor is frozen over three months a year, and ice-breakers are used in order to maintain navigation. Polyarkovo, some 500 miles inland, at the same latitude as Poltava, has the same average July temperature (70.2°F) as the latter, but its January temperature of —17°F is 34.2 degrees colder, April is 9 degrees colder, and October is 10.8 degrees colder.

A monsoon climate has an extremely irregular seasonal distribution of precipitation. Summer rain predominates: here, from April to October 86 to 96 per cent of the annual total of precipitation takes place; from November to March only 4 to 14 per cent. The period from July to September has, in general, 50 to 65 per cent of the annual precipitation, and July and August are the rainiest months. The smaller the amount of precipitation, the greater the percentage arriving during summer. The winter months are practically devoid of precipitation: summer precipitation in the continental part of the region (e.g., Blagoveshchensk) is 69 times as great as that in the winter months, and in the Primorski section (Olga) it is ten times as great, while in Moscow it is only twice as great. Spring and autumn rains are mainly of local origin and hence are heavier on the plains than in the mountains. This is confirmed by comparing the monthly precipitation at an inland point (Blagoveshchensk) with one on the coast (Olga).

Precipitation varies greatly from year to year: that of winter from 0.04 to 7.2 inches, of spring from 0.24 to 15.5 inches, of summer from 2.4 to 31 inches, and of autumn from 2.1 to 18.8 inches; the difference between two years may amount to 27.5 inches. The snow cover in one year may be 3 to 4 times as thick as in the next. Winter precipitation is usually light—seldom does more than 0.04 inch fall in one day—summer averages range between 0.28 and 0.4 inches a day. At the end of summer, saturated warm marine winds may meet cold air blowing off the continent and cause cloudbursts; in one day from 4 to 9.5 inches of rain may fall—that is, more than the average rainfall for an entire summer month. Along the coast the contact between warm and moist marine monsoons and air cooled by the adjacent cold marine current causes persistent fogs. But they do not penetrate deep into the mainland, and a short distance inland their number drops sharply: for example, at Nizmenni Cape both June and July have 26 days with fog, but at Olga, separated from the cape by a small wooded mountain, only 9 and 11 days. In winter there is very little fog; summer and spring have more than 70 per cent of the annual amount. Because of the cool summer and the proximity of the ocean, the timber line in the mountains is low: on the slopes of Sikhote-Alin facing the ocean north of 44° north latitude, few trees grow above 4,000 feet. On the other hand, because of the light winter precipitation there are no glaciers in the mountains.

In accord with the shift of monsoon winds, winter is less cloudy than summer. Spring and autumn are moderately foggy. The number of overcast and clear days, and in consequence, the intensity of insolation, varies from year to year. In winter and in autumn of an average year the sun is obscured only 20 to 30 per cent of the time along the coast; inland, no more than 10 to 15 per cent: in summer it may shine for no more than 15 per cent of the daylight hours. This intense summer cloudiness decreases the supply of solar heat and thus lowers the air temperature, and the lack of cloudiness in winter contributes to the intensification of radiation, which cools the earth greatly. Winds also play a role in the temperature regime: south winds bring warm air and cloudiness from the sea and raise the air temperature although they decrease the insolation;

cold northern winds, which decrease th cloudiness and increase insolation, lower th temperature.

Relative humidity is high in winter and i summer, and low in spring and in autum Annual fluctuations of relative humidity reac 19 per cent. The monthly distribution of rela tive humidity (in percentages) at a continer tal and a coastal point are shown in the ac companying table.

MONTH	BLAGOVESHCHENSK	VLADIVOSTO
Jan.	73	68
Feb.	71	69
Mar.	67	69
Apr.	56	72
May	60	77
June	71	86
July	73	88
Aug.	78	85
Sep.	73	78
Oct.	65	68
Nov.	73	65
Dec.	74	67
Yearly	70	74

The climate of the region varies latitudinall and longitudinally as well as vertically. Th lowest temperatures have been recorded in th Upper Zeya Plain, between the Stanovoi and Tukuringra ranges, and summer is warmes and winter least severe in the Lake Khank district, the Ussuri Valley, and the middl section of the Amur. January averages de crease from south to north: Kraskino, 12.2°F Voroshilov, −2.5°F; Khabarovsk, −9°F Blagoveshchensk, −11°F; Mazanova, −20.2 F; and Dambuki, −26°F. The July aver ages of the same places vary less; from 65 (Dambuki) to 70.1° (Blagoveshchensk). Cor respondingly the length of growing season a the points mentioned decreases from south t north: 199, 186, 172, 164, 155, and 138 days The length of the continuous frost-free perioc varies from 141 days in the south to 75 day ir the north. Nowhere in the north can even th ardiest fast-growing grains ripen, but in the outh the cultivation of such warmth-demanding plants as rice and soy is carried on with omplete success. Although the annual precipitation decreases from south to north, more now falls in the north. In the south, 10 per ent (2.4 to 3.2 inches) of the annual precipitation consists of snow, e.g., at Nikolayevsk nore than 30 per cent (6.5 inches). The duration of the snow cover increases from 145 days n the south to 208 days in the north; its thickess is negligible in the south, 1.7 to 2.4 inches n the middle section, and 5.2 to 6.0 inches in ne north.

In the inland areas the temperature drops nore rapidly in winter and rises more rapidly n summer than it does along the coast, alnough temperatures may differ greatly in laces exposed to the sea: for example, the anuary average at Vladivostok is 10.4 degrees igher than at Voroshilov, which is only 48 niles away. The Sikhote-Alin Range seems o be the boundary between the coastal strip nd the continental part of the region: winter nd autumn on the coast are much milder than n the other side of the Range, but summer and pring are colder. The cooling influence of the ea in summer does not extend far from the oast, and temperatures rapidly increase inand: Olga has a January average of 12°F, and n the warmest month, August, an average of 7.5°F; Voroshilov, lying at the same latitude, ut 165 miles west, has a January average of −2.6°F and a July average of 70°F. Inland he absolute minimum decreases rapidly—)lga, −22°F; Voroshilov, −45°F; Mazanovo, −59.2°: the duration of the growing eason decreases—Olga, 185 days; Khabarovsk, 72 days; Blagoveshchensk, 164 days; and Mazanovo 155 days: the frost-tree period shortens—at Vladivostock it is 68 days longer than t Anuchino, 89 miles farther inland. Inland, precipitation decreases rapidly: along the coast he annual average is 34.4 inches, in the Ussuri basin 20 to 24 inches, and in the northwest 4 inches. The heaviest summer rains fall along he coast of the Sea of Japan; farther west the rains are lighter but more frequent. As the distance from the coast increases so do the number of days with snow, and the duration of the snow cover and its thickness.

The relief causes local variations in climate and may also affect the climate over a large area. In the mountains the climate is cooler and more humid than in the valleys. The July average at Obluchye (963 feet) is 66.5°F, the January average is −16°F; in Poyarkovo (386 feet) the July average is 69.8°F and the January average −15.3°F. The length of the growing season at Obluchye is 152 days; at Poyarkova, 163 days. The greater the altitude, the heavier the precipitation, especially on slopes facing the sea. This is particularly noticeable in the Sikhote-Alin and Bureya ranges, which run at right angles to the prevailing direction of the summer monsoon and condense moisture on their crests. At some places in the Sikhote-Alin the annual precipitation is almost 20 per cent greater than that at sea level with each 330-foot increase in altitude. In the south, the crests of low mountain ridges only 1,100 to 1,500 feet high, forested to the summit, are enveloped in clouds and fog much of the time. Air saturated with vapor that blows in from the ocean leaves most of its moisture on the eastern slopes or the crests of the mountains. The remainder of the moisture, gradually condensed by cold air from the forests on the western side falls there.

Although precipitation is heavier along the coast than farther inland, there are fewer days with precipitation there—the annual average is 70 days, whereas it is 100 days on the eastern slope of the ranges, and 130 to 140 on the western. Winter precipitation in the mountains is heavy; thus the snow cover is deeper than on the neighboring plains. In clear weather, the influence of the relief on temperature is particularly noticeable, except in the coastal strip. On clear, calm nights cold air accumulates in valleys and depressions, causing a marked decrease in temperature. The higher a place lies (to known limits of 165 to 264 feet) above the bottom of a valley, the less likely there will be early frosts. All slopes, especially in the north, are warmer than the valleys during the entire year: the average annual temperature is 3.6 degrees higher, the frost-free period is 20 to 40 days longer, and daily fluctuations during the growing season are 5.4 degrees less. These differences, however, are not so pronounced here as in neighboring Trans-Baikal.

Many plants that cannot be grown in the valleys ripen on the slopes. The seasonal distribution of moisture on the slopes is more favorable for agriculture than it is in the valleys: in the dry months (May and June) more rain falls on the slopes than in the valleys, and during the rainy months (July to September) air is somewhat drier on the slopes. Because of this, grain is not likely to suffer from spring droughts or from excessive summer dampness and the fungus diseases connected with it.

The seasons, in general, are uniform throughout the region. Winter is cold, sunny, and dry, with little snow. The city of Voroshilov, at the same latitude as Yalta, has an average January temperature of $-5°F$, that is, 45 degrees lower than that of Yalta and 23.7 degrees lower than that of Leningrad, which is more than a thousand miles farther north. Even in the south daily temperatures may fluctuate more than 36 degrees. Because of the small amount of precipitation the snow cover is thin: on the Zeya-Bureya Plain from 8 to 16 inches; on the Pre-Khanka–Ussuri Plain, during some winters, no snow at all. Only near the ocean and in the mountains is the snow cover deep. The light snow cover and the fact that snow seldom falls before the ground is already frozen foster the freezing of the soil to a great depth: on the Zeya-Bureya Plain more than 10 feet; at Grodekovo, 8 feet; at Voroshilov, 6 feet; at Vladivostok, 4 feet. Until the middle of June one can find ice on the Zeya-Bureya Plain at depths of 6 to 8 feet. Because of the deep freezing, the soil thaws slowly in spring, and since the snow cover is thin there is little meltwater. Because of this condition it is possible to cultivate winter wheat and perennial grasses such as clover and alfalfa only in the very southern part of the plain.

Throughout the entire region spring is very late, long, dry, and cold. Much of the snow has already melted off by the time the average daily temperature rises above $32°F$. The soil, damp and cold, thaws very slowly: this prevents the rapid growth of plants. During the day branches, leaves, and young shoots exist in a summer atmosphere because of the abundance of sunlight, but the roots are still deep in winter. The first spring plants bloom and the foliage opens in May, while there are still early-morning frosts. The high temperature of the air and strong dry winds evaporate the light spring precipitation and the water from melting of snow before it can penetrate the soil, and as a consequence young crops suffer from drought, and forest and grass fires are frequent.

Summer is warm and has abundant rain. In the period of the regular monsoon rains, from the second half of June to September, the rain drips, drops, drizzles, and mizzles without pause for ten or twenty days at a time. When the rain stops the sun may still remain hidden behind the clouds: suddenly, cold piercing fogs from the sea drift in. In both north and south the temperature lowers, there is little heat during the day, and the nights are cold. At this time of year it rains continuously in the mountains, and when, in the valleys, the rain stops for breath, the sun has his chance to add to the discomfort. The warm air saturated with water vapor reminds one of the atmosphere of a bath house or a warm, moist hothouse. Three or four times during the summer there are intense downpours lasting from one to four days. After these downpours, the rivers overflow their banks and cause enormous destruction, washing away buildings near the river banks, destroying young crops, and carrying away harvested hay and grain. In the mountains the downpours erode slopes that are not secured by forest, remove the soil, and wash out forest undergrowth, dead trees, and branches, which form large jams in the swollen mountain streams.

When great amounts of summer rain fall in a short period, the heavy soil of the region cannot absorb the moisture readily and its surface becomes supermoistened, which greatly hampers the work of agricultural machines. In the large areas where permafrost exists, rain water accumulates in the surface layers of the soil. In protected valleys of the south the abundance of summer precipitation and warmth create the atmosphere of a hotbed, which leads to the rapid growth of luxuriant vegetation. The small amount of sunlight that filters through the ever-present clouds is nevertheless sufficient for the majority of plants, even those that ordinarily demand much light. The summer dampness makes the trees hollow and short-lived, gives fruit a high water content and makes it sour, and prevents the development of a strong fragrance in flowers.

The constant high relative humidity (to 90 per cent) in summer creates favorable conditions for the mass growth of epiphytic ferns, such as linear fern (*Polypodium lineare*), on trees, and for the formation of overhead roots on vines of the genus *Actinidia*. Agriculture is hazardous here: during a dry spring, young plants suffer from drought, and each year the heaviest rainfall takes place during the period when cereals blossom, ripen, mature, and are harvested. The high humidity gives grain a small content of albumen (11 to 13 per cent), makes harvesting difficult, and creates favorable circumstances for the mass attack of parasitic Ustilaginaceae, rust, and mold fungi on cultivated plants. The fungus *Fusarium roseum*

make grain poisonous. Essential to its eradication are: treating seeds with fungicide, crop rotation, early sowing of grain, good cultivation of the soil. In order to guarantee moisture to the soil during a dry spring, plowing during the preceding summer is necessary (fallow cultivation of the field).

The heavy monsoon rains soften the bed of dirt roads and make summer a season of bad roads (*rasputitsa*). During the warm and moist summers all objects not protected from the humidity—e.g., leather—become covered with mildew during the night.

Autumn is a more favorable time of year for man, beast, and plant. After the rainy period, late in August or early in September, clear warm weather may set in very rapidly, with azure skies and transparent, relatively dry air that is completely calm. These conditions are favorable for the development of plants on the soil that has been soaked by the monsoon rains. Until the end of September or the beginning of October sunny weather continues; then come the first frosts, and leaves begin to fall. By the end of autumn there is still little snow, and the soil begins to dry out and freeze. Autumn is the period of forest fires. The dry remnants of grass cover, the dry deadwood, and the dying leaves of the underbrush are highly inflammable; fires in the forests are frequent and cover large areas.

HYDROGRAPHY

Hydrographically, almost the entire Amur-Primorski region is part of Amur Basin; its rivers are fed mainly by rainfall. Winter precipitation is usually light, and because of the poverty of the snow cover, its melting supplies a negligible amount of water; thus the rivers do not rise much in spring. In summer, however, the abundant rain water runs rapidly down the steep slopes into the rivers, which rapidly overflow their banks. Smaller rivers may flood after every intense downpour. The inundations are aggravated because man has

destroyed many of the forests that once covered the mountain slopes: the water, unchecked by forest litter, underbrush, or the roots of trees washes off the soil, destroys the thin vegetation, and pours into the rivers. Two regions have greater discharge than the others. The first is the Sikhote-Alin Range, where the isolines of flow parallel the axis of the range and the coast of the Sea of Japan. Inland the discharge diminishes and reaches a minimum on the Khanka-Ussuri Plain. The second region with heavy discharge is the Bureya Range,

Fig. 10-4. The Lower Amur River.

especially along the upper stretches of the Selemdzha River.

The Amur, the largest river of the region, is longer than the Volga (2,860 miles, Amur-Argun), and has a larger basin. The upper Amur, to the mouth of the Zeya, has high banks covered with trees. Where the Amur breaks through the Bureya Range it flows through a narrow gorge about 2,000 feet wide; farther along its course the banks become low, the river breaks up into many branches, and its width increases until below Nikolayevsk it is 9 miles wide. In the Lower Amur basin there are many lakes, of which Bolon and Kizi lie within its valley and are directly linked with it. Kizi is five miles from Tatarski Strait and is separated from it by a ridge 180 feet high; therefore it would be possible to construct a canal and an outlet for the Amur here. The water of the Amur is usually pure and transparent, becoming muddy only near the mouths of its large tributaries (Zeya, Ussuri), which carry much material in suspension. It is highest not in spring but in summer, when the continuous monsoon rains and frequent cloudbursts may cause intense floods. At Khabarovsk the water level is highest between May and

September, lowest in the middle of March; the average difference in levels is about 20 feet, the greatest recorded difference, 35.3 feet.

The Amur is covered with ice at Khabarovsk for 151 days, at Nikolayevsk for 189 days—that is, approximately as long as the rivers that empty into the Gulf of Finland—which indicates the severity of local winters and reduces the value of the river as an agency of transportation. The average speed of the current of the lower Amur is 1.8 to 2.1 miles per hour. Nowhere in its lower course is it less than 10 feet deep, and it would be navigable by large ocean-going vessels for a distance of 300 miles upstream were it not for a bar 10 to 13 feet beneath the surface at its mouth; this prevents the entry of large vessels and necessitates transshipment of goods.

In spite of these drawbacks the Amur is an important avenue of communication: it is easily navigable in the summer and provides the only access to most of the towns and villages in the region. Down the river from Khabarovsk and Komsolmosk move manufactured goods shipped from the west on the Trans-Siberian Railway. Up the river to the railways terminals move oil from Sakhalin, petroleum products, and fresh and canned fish. Timber is floated along the rivers of the Amur system, grain is shipped down them, and supplies for the gold mines along the northern tributaries are shipped on them.

The water power of the region's large and small rivers should be utilized—there is much of it. And the regulation of the rivers' flow that would be a prerequisite to harnessing their power would also do much to solve the problem of frequent flooding.

The Amur system is rich in fish: the rivers of the Volga Basin contain 75 species, but the Amur and its tributaries contain 99. One of the reasons for this diversity is the infiltration of northern and southern kinds of fish. In the Amur are many species widespread in Siberia, among them lamprey, *Salmo thymallus,* char, and umber; but sterlet, Siberian sturgeon, whitefish, roach, dace, perch, and ruff are absent. Also found are many Chinese varieties of carp, sheatfish, and tropical snakehead mullet (*Ophicephalus*). In the southern tributaries of the Amur there are more southern Chinese species than northern ones. Sturgeon are indigenous to the Amur: Amur sturgeon (*Acipenser schrenki*) and long-snouted sturgeon (*Hucho dauricus*).

Salmon of the genus *Oncorhynchus* are extremely important commercially: Siberian, humpback, and silver salmon spawn in the Amur, but spend the greater part of their lives in the sea. Each year great numbers of Siberian salmon from the Sea of Okhotsk and humpback salmon from the northern part of the Sea of Japan rush headlong into the rivers, moving up the Amur 300 to 600 miles to their spawning grounds at the dead ends of shallow mountain streams fed by springs. After spawning, nearly all the salmon that have ascended the river die; countless dead fish are thrown out on sandbars and covered with alluvium, thereby enriching the soil. Soon after hatching the young fish swim downstream to the sea where they quickly grow to maturity (Siberian salmon after four years, and humpback salmon after two). Catching these Pacific Ocean

salmon as they head for their spawning grounds is the basis of the Amur fish industry, and the mouth of the Amur is the most important fishing district of the region.

Lake Khanka lies in the middle of a plain in the southern part of the region; its northernmost part is in Manchuria. Despite its length (57 miles) and width (24 to 51 miles), its greatest depth is only 33 feet. The eastern, northern, and southern shores of the lake are low, bordered by plowed fields, meadows, or swamps; the western shores are higher and covered by forest. Parallel terraces which border the lake indicate that it is slowly drying up. The lake's outlet is the Sungacha River, a tributary of the Ussuri. The water is fresh and clear and sturgeon live in the lake.

The Sea of Japan is one of the marginal seas of the Pacific Ocean. Its western border is the continent of Asia; on the east it is separated from the Pacific by Sakhalin, Hokkaido, and Honshu islands; in the south it is connected with the Pacific by the Tsushima and Shimonoseki straits; in the north La Perouse and Tatarski straits connect it with the Sea of Okhotsk. The straits are shallow, but the Sea of Japan is a deep basin that slopes away from the Japanese coast more gently than from the mainland coast of Asia. About a half of the sea is more than 6,500 feet deep and about one-quarter more than 10,000 feet deep. Only near its shores is the sea shallow. The greatest measured depth, 12,959 feet, is in the eastern part.

Although the basic hydrologic regime of the Sea of Japan is determined by its character as a deep basin separated by shallow straits from the Pacific Ocean, the East China Sea, and the Sea of Okhotsk, its surface layers have all the features of those of a marginal sea. The constant counterclockwise movement of the surface water results from infiltration of a branch of the warm Kuro-Shio Current through Tsushima Strait. This current enters the Sea of Japan under the name Tsushima Current and then divides in two. The main current swerves to the northeast, flowing along the western

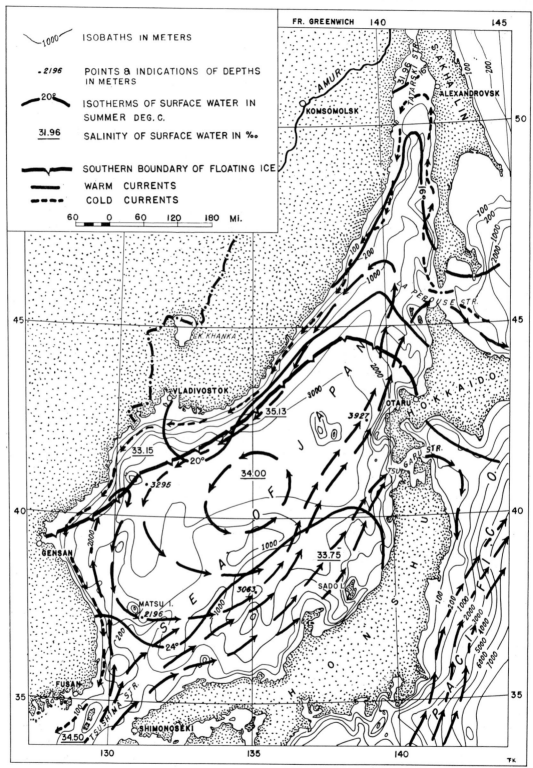

Map 10-II. Bathymetric map of the Sea of Japan.

shore of Japan. The weaker current flows along the eastern shore of Korea and, meeting a cold current from the north, joins it, turns southeast, and fuses with the main current. Northward the main current narrows: much of its water passes through Tsugaru Strait into the Pacific; most of what remains goes through La Perouse Strait into the Sea of Okhotsk. Only a small part maintains its movements to the north into Tatarski Strait and along the western shore of Sakhalin. Near Sovetskaya Gavan the current encounters large submarine ridges that rise from the bottom; these force it downward, which causes cold subsurface water to rise to the surface. This mixes with the surface layers, so that here they are colder and somewhat more saline than in adjacent areas. This cold water flows south along the coast of the mainland, carrying with it the fresh water of the many streams that flow off Sikhote-Alin. This is the current that meets the western branch of the Tsushima Current approximately off Vladivostok, blends with it, withdraws from shore, drops into the depths, and moves slowly to the coast of Japan.

The temperature regime of the Sea of Japan changes not only from south to north, but also from west to east. The average January air temperature in the northern part of Tatarski Strait is —7°F; at Tsushima Strait 25°F. The August average near the mainland at Tatarski Strait is 59°F; at Tsushima Strait 78.8°F. In winter the western coast of Primorski is under the direct influence of the continent and the climate has a continental character, although that of summer is marine. The cold current from Tatarski Strait that passes along the mainland coast lowers temperatures considerably. Along the eastern shore of the sea (the islands of Japan), the sharp temperature contrasts between winter and summer are moderated by the warm Tsushima Current, which warms the cold winter monsoon that blows from the continent before it reaches the coast. Precipitation decreases from south to north: the annual average in the south is four to five times as great as in the north. In the east it is appreciably greater than in the west. Along the mainland coast, it is much heavier in summer than in winter: near the eastern shores the seasonal distribution of precipitation is not so sharply expressed; that of summer is but slightly greater than that of winter.

The temperature of surface water follows the climatic pattern: in the south it is higher than in the north; near the Japanese coast it is higher than along the mainland. Near Tsushima Strait the temperatures of surface water vary from 78.8° to 57.3°F; near Tsugaru Strait they vary from 75.2° to 41°F; at La Perouse Strait from 71.7° to 34.5°F; and in the northern part of Tatarski Strait from 62.8° to 28.5°F. They are highest in August or September; lowest in January or February. In February the Tsushima Current warms the southeastern part of the sea; in August, the mainland coast is cooled by the current flowing south from Tatarski Strait.

The water temperatures of the Sea of Japan are like those of an inland sea. In summer the temperature drops rapidly with depth. Only the surface layer of the water is warmed; just below the surface the temperature drops sharply; deeper, it decreases slowly. In the central part of the sea temperatures have been taken in July; on the surface they were 69°F, at a depth of 165 feet 38.4°F, and at 330 feet only 33.5°F. Below 1,650 feet the temperature remains slightly above freezing the year round. Temperatures below freezing are not found even at great depths. Near the shores of Japan, in the path of the warm Tsushima Current, the temperature at a depth of 660 feet fluctuates from 59° to 41°F, and at a depth of 1,320 feet from 41° to 33.8°F. In the southern and southeastern parts of the sea, ice never forms. Along the coast north of Vladivostok floating ice appears every winter. The southern boundary of the ice, driven from the north by winds and currents, extends from northern Korea to the middle of the western coast of Hokkaido. In the north, many sheltered bays and gulfs are covered with firm solid ice during winter. The northern part of Tatarski Strait is covered by floating ice and ice land-floe forms along the shore. The Amur estuary freezes solid and horses may travel on it in winter.

Summer fogs are frequent in those sections where the temperature of the surface water is low. The southeastern winds that prevail in summer bring warm masses of air almost saturated with water vapors to the continental coast. Passing above the cold shore current, they are chilled and give off their excess moisture as fog all along the coast of the mainland. On the 40th parallel, July may have as many as 22 foggy days. Fog is especially frequent and thick near Sovetskaya Gavan. There is much fog in La Perouse Strait, but it is rare in the southeastern part of the sea.

Strong winds make navigation hazardous on the Sea of Japan. In winter, cyclones from the depths of the Asiatic mainland move across the sea. They are accompanied by clearing weather, by an abrupt rise in temperature, and by a marked increase in the intensity of the wind. In summer, cyclones of oceanic origin, or typhoons, originate in the Pacific near the tropics, and, following rapidly one after another, travel toward the continent of Asia and then swerve to the northeast. These typhoons create large waves on the sea, and lead to destructive floods along low coasts. The inflowing tides of the Pacific Ocean penetrate mainly through Tsushima, the widest of the straits. Because of the great depth of the southern part of the Sea of Japan, the incoming water spreads very rapidly and the time of the high tide occurs at regular 12-hour intervals almost everywhere. The average height of the tide is not great (2.95 feet), although in Tatarski Strait it increases to 8.9 feet.

The distribution of salinity of surface water is similar to the distribution of temperatures. The water is saltiest, as well as warmest, in the south and eastern parts of the sea, and the least salty and the coldest along the continental coast. Water of high salinity (34.56 parts per thousand) enters through Tsushima Strait; northward the salinity decreases, dropping to 31.96 parts per thousand in the northern part of Tatarski Strait. This fresher water is carried south by the cold current along the continental coast, receiving on the way the fresh water of many streams, but to the south the salinity gradually increases. In the winter the surface salinity rises and may reach more than 35 parts per thousand, a result of the great decrease in the inflow of fresh water and of the release of salt by the water that freezes along the continental shore.

The water of the Sea of Japan, to the very bottom, contains a great deal of oxygen; thus plants and animals live and grow even at great depths. This is a result of the excellent aeration of the water in winter, when, because of the increase in salinity, the cold surface water, which is both dense and rich in oxygen, descends to great depths. The transparency of the water varies from 30 to 75 feet, averaging about 50 feet. Near the Amur estuary it is very low because of the influx of muddy river water. In most of the sea the water is dark blue; in Tatarski Strait, near the mainland, it is greenish-yellow.

The fauna of the Sea of Japan comprises both northern and southern species. Physicogeographic conditions are different in the eastern and western parts of the sea. The Tsushima Current carries many warm-water species northward, and many Arctic species similar to those in the Sea of Okhotsk and the Bering Sea are carried far to the south by the cold current that flows along the continental coast. The crab (*Paralithodes kamtschatica*) is of commercial value; in spring and autumn it migrates from the depths of the bays, where it passes the winter, to the shores, being attracted by the higher temperature of the coastal zone and the rich coastal flora and fauna, which provide favorable conditions for propagation. Submarine "meadows" of seaweed are also of economic importance, especially those containing sea kale, from which iodine and gelatine are obtained.

DEVELOPMENT OF LANDSCAPES

The flora and fauna of the Amur-Primorski region not only comprises many species like the tropics, but also presents some extraordinary contrasts. Its mixture of plants and animals differ in origin, age, and bioecology—of northern Siberian taiga species with southern Chinese and Indian species—makes it truly a transitional region. The landscapes suggest those of the subtropics, but have much in common with cold Siberia. Here the south impinges upon and lives in harmony with the north: grape twists around spruce; white birch and pine grow beside cork oak trees; and subtropical Dioscoreaceae live side by side with such a typical taiga resident as wood sorrel. The same is true of animals. Sable and brown bear share the Ussuri forests the year round with tiger, goral, and spotted deer: in the rivers are such northern Siberian species as umber and *Salmo thymallus,* many Chinese species, and even tropical fish of the genus *Ophicephalus*. In summer, on the same taiga path where in spring the modestly colored Yakutsk butterfly (*Leucobrephos middendorffii*) was found, the large brilliantly colored tropical butterflies *Danais tytia* and *Papilio raddei* warm their outstretched wings in the sun. Where the northern night-butterfly (*Endromis versicolora*) was caught in early spring, the large southern blue night butterfly (*Actias artemis*) is found in summer.

The Amur-Primorski area is at the junction of four floral and faunal regions—East Siberian, Dahurian, Okhotsk, and Manchurian—and their peculiarities are strikingly interwoven in certain areas. The East Siberian element penetrates from the northwest, usually being found in mountainous country where the climate is cold and there is permafrost beneath rocky peat soil; it constitutes most of the subalpine vegetation. The Dahurian element, which is typical of the southern part of the Trans-Baikal region with its steppes and pine groves, brings in from the west such grassy plants as edelweiss. The Dahurian butterfly (*Colias aurora*) is not abundant on northern slopes of valleys of the Amur system, especially in the western part, but is even found on the shores of the Pacific. The Okhotsk element—spruce-fir forests with rock birch, such grasses as clintonia, and the fauna accompanying them—penetrates from the northeast into the northern sections of the Sikhote-Alin and Bureya ranges.

The Manchurian element covers the greatest area and dominates the landscapes of the region. It consists of mixed broad-leaved forests of southern trees—such legacies of the Tertiary Period as cork oak and aralia—and Manchurian-Indian animals such as Himalayan bear, goral, Indian oriole, and blue flycatcher. Some plants and animals are encountered throughout the entire region: these are the species most capable of bearing low temperature—for example, Mongolian oak, which extends to the coast of the Sea of Okhotsk; maple, which grows north of Nikolayevsk; and filbert in the Deptski district. Few Manchurian species are found north of Nikolayevsk, which marks the northern boundary of the occurrence of such plants and animals as Korean pine, cork oak, Manchurian walnut, grape, Chinese magnolia vine, and racoon-dog (*Nyctereutes procionoides ussuriensis*). Southern species of currant and spotted deer are not found north of the Iman River, which is the northern boundary of the south Ussuri district. Not only latitudinal zones, but vertical zones as well, are clearly marked. For example, in the southern Sikhote-Alin three types of vegetation are found: Manchurian, running along southern slopes below 3,300 feet, and, higher, Okhotsk and East Siberian. The zones are noticeably lower on northern slopes than they are on southern slopes.

In the Amur-Primorski region are a large number of relic plants, for example, in the South Ussuri district, the endemic Manchurian species of prinsepia (*Prinsepia sinensis*), which grows nowhere else in the USSR and supplies proof of the past existence of a flora of a more

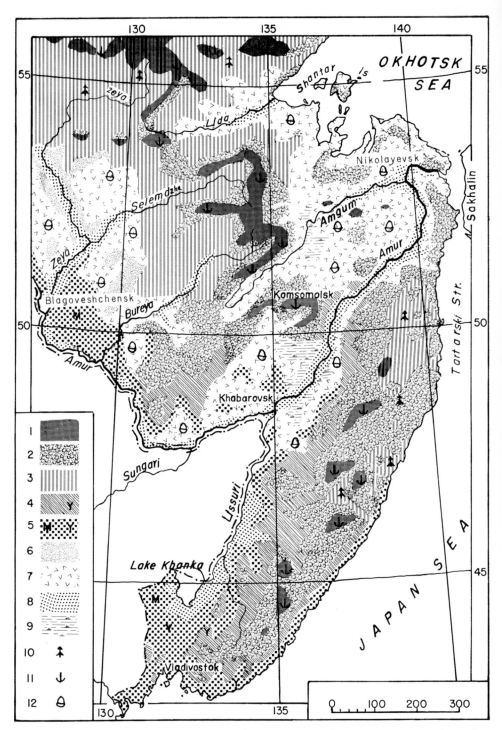

Map 10-III. Distribution of vegetation in the Amur-Primorski region: 1—Mountain tundra or mountain tundra and brush; 2—Fir–pine–larch mountain forest; 3—Deciduous mountain forest; 4—Pine–fir–broadleaf forest; U—Same as South Ussuri species; 5 —Oak forest; M—Manchurian oak; U—Manchurian oak with South Ussurian; 6

southern character. That there are old elements in the fauna is confirmed by the abundance of endemic species and subspecies of birds that have narrowly restricted habitats, are small, variegated, and brightly colored. Species not encountered anywhere else in the USSR are the water hen, the Chinese ibis, and the mandarin duck.

The similarity between the flora and fauna of the Amur-Primorski region and those of the Mediterranean region is remarkable. Many kinds of plants and animals common to both are not found in intervening regions: proximate varieties, different species of one genus, or even one and the same species. For example, no trees resembling English oak (*Quercus robur*) and its companion the filbert (*Corylus avellana*) are found east of the Ural Mountains until the Amur is reached; only there grow the closely related species, Mongolian oak (*Quercus mongolica*) and heterophyllous hazelnut (*Corylus heterophylla*). The same is true of hornbeam, elm, and several other trees and shrubs. There is a similar break in the distribution of many birds, amphibians, and fish: among them blue magpie, white stork, green frog, carp, and loach. All examples point to a discontinuity in what was once a single habitat, the cause of which must be sought in the unusual history of development of the landscapes of the Far East.

Since the beginning of the Tertiary Period, life has proceeded far more peacefully in the Amur-Primorski region, than in the European part of the USSR or in Western Siberia, where recurring glaciation changed the organic world fundamentally. In the Amur-Primorski region the flora and fauna bear clear traces of descent from Tertiary ancestors. Fossil remains in Tertiary coal deposits indicate that subtropical forests grew in the warm, moist Tertiary climate, containing such trees as sequoia, bog cypress, five-leaved pine, chestnut, beech, and elm. This flora preceded the modern impoverished and altered flora of the South Ussuri region and resembled that of modern Japan and China, which does not contain the northern elements of the modern South Ussuri flora.

A few living remnants of Tertiary flora are found in both the Amur-Primorski region and Trans-Baikal: grape, jasmine, and yams, which are represented in the Caucasus by *Dioscorea caucasia* and in the Far East by *Dioscorea polystachya*. Tertiary faunal relics are the beetle (*Callipogon relictus*), a representative of a genus whose three other species live in Central America, or the Acanthopterygian fish (*Percottus glehni*), which has close relatives in Mexico, Central America, and the West Indies. In the Tertiary mountain landscapes grew such plants as *Microbiota decussata* and Olga larch (*Larix olgensis*), which have close relatives in distant countries. Beneath the Tertiary forests was a red soil formation, as shown by fossil red soils in the Zeya-Bureya Plain. Until the beginning of the glacial period Tertiary flora and fauna developed without disturbance: the climate was warm, as indicated by fossil remains of gingko, elm, and other trees that have been found in the Quaternary alluvial deposits of the Zeya-Bureya Plain.

Although there was no Quaternary glaciation here, the weather became colder, and this caused the disappearance of the more warmth-loving species of plants and animals, the withdrawal of Tertiary flora to the south, and the appearance of a northern flora and fauna. In the South Ussuri region this cooling was less intense than elsewhere in the Far East and it was at this time that the phytocoenosis of modern forests of the Manchurian type was evolved. Many Tertiary species were able to adapt themselves gradually to new conditions of existence, and with the return of a milder climate the warmth-loving southern plants began to return. The influence of glaciation, which was

—Pine forests; 7—Deciduous, middle, central, and south taiga forest; 8—Meadows, brush, forest area (flooded in spring); 9—Marshes, mixed forests; 10—Firs; 11—Pine brush; 12—Oak.

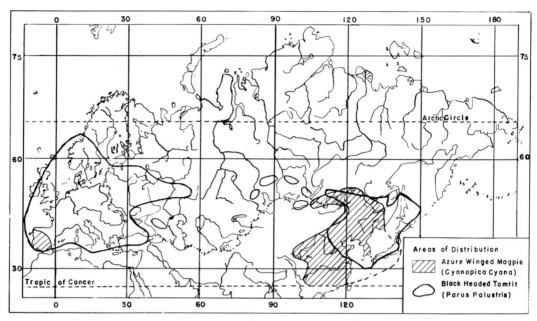

Map. 10-IV. Distribution of azure winged magpie (*Cyanopica cyana*) and black headed tomtit (*Parus palustris*).

strong in most of Siberia but weak in Southern Europe and the Amur-Primorski region, explains the discontinuity of the once unified Mediterranean and Far Eastern habitats.

Some warmth-loving Manchurian plants of the present day were living in the European part of the USSR during the interglacial period: water shield (*Brasenia purpurea*) has been discovered in a fossil state in interglacial deposits at a number of points between Minsk and Kostroma, and seeds of the *Euryale ferox* have been found in interglacial deposits in Tula. Some species of Manchurian plants and animals were able to move northward in the xerothermic period, when the climate was warmer than at present. Thus certain Amur caddis flies (*Trichoptera*) quite recently moved as far north as Yakutsk. It was evidently in this period that the drought-resistant Dahurian flora penetrated the Amur plains from Trans-Baikal. At present, the continued cooling of the climate causes the Manchurian flora to move slowly southward, while the northern, Okhotsk flora advances onto the areas it vacates. The most warmth-loving Manchurian species, as they move south, cling to well-warmed and protected southern slopes but gradually lose the ability to bear mature fruit.

Thus the modern forests of the Manchurian type contain only a few kinds of trees and shrubs, but the species that have survived have brought down to us not only the astonishing history of their life, but many valuable qualities they have acquired in the course of thousands of years of struggle with an antagonistic climate. The excellent development of the forest trees and their amazing endurance offer great hope for their acclimatization in other regions of the USSR, possibly far in the north. Such beautiful and valuable trees as Manchurian walnut or cork oak should adorn the streets, gardens, and parks of Russian cities.

Economic necessity has caused many landscapes to lose their original appearance. They have been most affected by the felling of trees and fires set to clear the land of brush that have gotten out of control. Fires have completely wiped out some species of trees and have greatly changed the original composition of the vegetation of many areas. The first to be destroyed were the conifers, which are incapable of restoration from their roots. Thus mixed coniferous-broad-leaved forests have been replaced by groves of oak, which is readily restored by suckers that grow from the stumps. Animals are driven from the forests by fires, and many species are now found only in the portions of primeval forest that have escaped destruction. In order to guard the valuable forests and hunting areas, and also because of the exceptional scientific interest in forests of

the Manchurian type as living museums of the rich legacy of the Tertiary period, the Soviet government has set aside a state reservation of about 2,500,000 acres in the Sikhote-Alin Range. Many species of Far Eastern animals of commercial value can be acclimatized to other regions of the USSR. For example, the raccoon-dog has been acclimatized to Central Asia, the Caucasus, and the forests of the Leningrad, Novgorod, and Kalinin regions, and the spotted deer has been acclimatized to the Altai, to the Teberdinsk game preserve, and to Buzuluksk forest.

SOIL, FLORA, AND FAUNA OF THE MOUNTAINS

Most of the forests in the Sikhote-Alin Range are of the Manchurian type. In the dissected mountain relief with steep slopes and rock outcrops shallow and rocky soil has developed beneath them.

Despite the thinness of the soil, the processes of soil formation are expressed quite clearly. Podzolic soil forms beneath the rich forest vegetation because of the widespread carbonate-free matrices and the abundance of summer rain, which rapidly leaches the upper layers of the soil. Although almost all stages from little-formed crypto-podzolic soil to distinctly podzolic can be found, there is no typical podzol.

In the southern part of the range the soil has the following features: (1) the invariable presence of dark-colored structural humus layers in which the high humus content of the upper parts drops sharply with depth; (2) a yellow or pale yellow podzolic layer; (3) thin layers; (4) indistinct separation of the eluvial layer from the gangue; (5) firm, dust-like, clayey mechanical composition; (6) the inclusion of a large amount of coarse rubble; (7) a high capacity for absorption despite a distinctly unsaturated absorbing complex.

These properties distinguish this soil from the podzolic soil of the northern part of the range and make it akin to the podzolic soil of

the forests of the mountains of the Crimea and part of North Caucasus. Southern podzolic soil has many good qualities: high humus content, structured upper layers, and a wealth of nitrogen and calcium obtained by the mineralization of oak-, hornbeam-, and maple-leaf humus. The introduction of clay detritus improves the drainage of the soil and excludes the possibility of over-moistening during an excess of summer rain, thus contributing to normal forest growth. A dense forest cover and a thick grass matting secure the thick humus horizons and protect the soil from erosion. Soil beneath thick coniferous forests does not erode as fast as that under the thinner groves of oak. Since the soil in the oak groves undergoes constant rejuvenation, it does not have well-developed humus layers, and is not very thick. In the northern Sikhote-Alin, podzolic soil typical of the taiga is found.

The thickest forests grow in the South-Ussuri region; Manchurian forests of broad-leaved trees, pine, and fir that cover the well-moistened slopes to a height of almost 2,000 feet. Here are intricate stands with three tiers of trees, a thick growth of underbrush, and two or three tiers of grasses. The forest is dense and shady; the crowns of the trees are intertwined, and their trunks are straight as a candle and

Fig. 10-5. Pine and fir forest in the southern Sikhote-Alin Mountains.

free of branches to a great height. Side by side are blue-green pines, elms with enormous light trunks, dark green firs, and walnut trees with dark gray trunks. Vines twist around their trunks and branches, almost to their tops. Epiphytes cling to the trees. Because of the variety and thickness of the vegetation and the presence of vines and epiphytes, the forests resemble those of the subtropics. But here, in contrast to the real subtropical forests of Trans-Baikal, there are no broad-leaved evergreens, because they cannot grow in the Far Eastern climate. The forests must endure cold dry winters with little snow and sharp daily variations in temperature, extended springs with frequent morning frosts and hot sun during the day, rainy and warm summers with cloudbursts and floods of destructive force, and dry autumns with fires and hurricanes that break and uproot the trees. In forests of the Manchurian type conditions are favorable for the preservation and development of Tertiary species: *Actinidia*

polygama and *A. arguta* bear fruit only here, and yew, ash (*Micromeles alnifolia*), and *Kalopanax ricinifolia* grow tall only in such forests.

The first tier of the forest is composed of big, widely spaced conifers: Korean pine and fir. Korean pine (*Pinus koraiensis*) is the giant of the South-Ussuri forests and over a hundred of them may grow in an acre of mixed forest: most are 250 to 300 years old. The root system of the pine is superficial in the shallow mountain soil and the trees are easily blown down. The cones are coarser than those of the Siberian pine, contain twice as many nuts (up to 150), and are productive until they are very old. Young pines require shade, and, with the regular development of a forest, pine renews itself excellently, but frequent fires hinder restoration. Pine does not grow on bottomlands. The strength and workability of its wood make it the most important tree in the timber industry. Fir (*Abies holophylla*) grows best in well-lighted places and on loamy soil. The trees are as large as the pines but their wood is not of high quality.

Somewhat below the canopy of fire and pine is a tier of deciduous trees: yellow birch (*Betula costata*), a shade-enduring tree with rose-yellow bark; elm (*Ulmus montana* var. *heterophylla*); linden (*Tilia amurensis*), which grows plentifully along the outskirts; and in depressions and on southern slopes, narrow-leaved maple (*Acer mono*). Manchurian walnut (*Juglans mandshurica*), a valuable tree with straight trunk and dark-gray wrinkled bark, grows in forests along ravines and in valleys where the soil is fertile and moist, but does not grow at altitude above 1,000 feet. The young walnut is shade-enduring, but it is very sensitive to spring frosts and protects itself from them by late development of leaves. Walnut has many practical uses: its wood is light, tough, uniform, and beautiful, and is highly valued for cabinet-making, the preparation of veneer, and the manufacture of rifle stocks. The bark yields tannic acid (10 per cent tannin) and is also used to make a brown dye. The nuts are edible and nutritious; the leaves are used as a home remedy for various ills; the tree itself is often used as an ornamental. It is possible to cultivate Manchurian walnut in more northerly parts of the USSR. In districts with a warm spring it revives earlier than in its native habitat, but since the slightest frost kills its leaves it is necessary to retard the development of sprouts artificially until the early-morning frosts are over. This is done by covering the ground under the tree with snow and ice as soon as winter ends, and in turn covering the ice with straw, dry leaves, sawdust, or other heat-insulating materials, in order to retard thawing of the soil.

The Amur cork tree (*Phellodendron amurense*), of the rue family (Rutaceae), has a well-shaped straight trunk with bark two to three inches thick that, on young trees, is smooth, light, and resilient. The root system is deep and highly branched. The leaves appear late in spring and fall early in autumn, thus protecting the tree from frost. Its seeds germinate well, it can reproduce by means of shoots, and it grows rapidly, especially between 20 and 40 years, when the yearly gain in height is one and a half feet. Young trees require shade. The Amur cork is a very valuable tree; the beautiful and durable wood resists decay and is used in the manufacture of veneer and for furniture; the bark yields cork, although it is heavier, less homogeneous, and less resilient than that of the true cork oak; from the fibrous inner bark, which contains a high percentage of tannin, a yellow dye for fabrics is extracted. Bees gather honey from its many blossoms. Since it has excellent adaptability to severe climatic conditions, is drought resistant, and grows rapidly, the Amur oak could be widely cultivated in northern USSR: many specimens survive the winter without protection in the vicinity of Moscow, Leningrad, and Gomel.

On gentle southeastern and southern slopes it is possible to find large solitary specimens of Mongolian oak (*Quercus mongolica*) and small groups of kalopanax (*Kalopanax ricinifolia*) of the family Araliaceae. These have beautifully grained golden yellow wood that is a valuable furniture and veneer material. Here and there, throughout the whole southern Sikhote-Alin, are old isolated yew trees (*Taxus cuspidata*).

The third tier of these forests comprises hornbean (*Carpinus cordata*), which is the most common, Manchurian linden (*Tilia mandshurica*); Manchurian maple (*Acer mandshuricum*); cherry (*Cerasus maximowiczi*); and Amur lilac (*Syringa amurensis*). The undergrowth consists of many kinds of shrubs: hazelnut (*Corylus mandshurica*), wild jasmine (*Philadelphus tenuifolius*), wild pepper (*Eleutherococcus senticosus*), false spirea (*Sorbaria sorbifolia*), and barberry (*Berberis amurensis*).

The many vines that wind around bushes, climb to the top of tall trees, and run from one tree to another in long garlands, increase the density of the forest. Some vines may grow 50 feet long and have a trunk 8 inches thick. Vines grow best in the lighter openings in the shady pine–broad-leaved forests, along the banks of mountain rivers, and on areas thinned by lumbering or fires. The most common are various species of grape, magnolia vine, and currant.

Amur grape (*Vitis amurensis*) has round, dark blue-black, sourish-sweet fruit that ripens at the end of September and drops in clusters in the middle of October. It is used to make wine and jelly, and in the confectionary industry. The vine grows rapidly and endures the northern climate (at Leningrad, for example) very well. When plants with the largest and sweetest fruit are selected and hybridized with cultivated varieties, the result is good.

shaded places, or on completely exposed southern slopes. The berries are used in medicine and as flavoring in tea. The liana is easily propagated from seeds or cuttings.

Actinidia arguta, of the tropical family Dilleniaceae, is the largest and the most warmth-loving vine. It is common only in the South Ussuri region, where it grows on the rocky well-drained soil of northern slopes. The young plants demand ample shade, but older plants grow most luxuriantly in lighted spots. In moist shady places this vine may develop aerial roots. Its large green juicy fruit, sweeter than the grape and with a distinctive flavor, ripens

Fig. 10-6. "Zhen-shen" plant.

Magnolia vine (*Schizandra chinensis*), which is popularly called *limonnik* because of the strong lemon-like scent given off by the bark, has solitary rose-white blossoms. Its round juicy berries are tart and ripen in the middle of September. This vine grows at altitudes of 1,600 to 2,000 feet; it is not found in the spruce-pine forests lying above, in highly

in October and produces a superb wine; the fruit is also dried for winter use as a sweet.

Actinidia kolomista, the most abundant and most northerly growing vine of the region, is found even in the spruce-fir forests of the Okhotsk type. This vine has colorful variegated leaves and produces a sweet fruit which is used for compotes and preserves. It is well adapted to artificial propagation, as it is resistant to cold, does not demand special shading, and grows rapidly.

There are many epiphytes on the trunks of the trees. For example, the fern *Polypodium lineare,* whose creeping, branching rhizomes are concealed beneath a moss cover from which the linear short-petiolate leaves project upward in rows.

In spring the arboreal canopy of the pine-broad-leaved forests is open and translucent because of the different times at which the trees put forth their leaves. This permits the growth of a rich and diverse, but not dense, grass cover. It contains many ferns, such as oak fern or wood fern (*Dryopteris crassirhizoma*), and such tall plants as peony (*Paeonia obovata*), miterwort (*Mitella nuda*), and ginseng (*Panax ginseng*) of the Araliaceae, whose roots have an unlimited market in China, where they are widely used in medicine. In the grass cover are not only many species peculiar to the Manchurian region but also others with a wide habitat. Side by side with relic plants such as sweet cicely (*Osmorrhiza amurensis*) or Chinese yam (*Dioscorea polystachya*), are the *Maianthemum bifolium* and European wood sorrel (*Oxalis acetosella*). Moss grows on the trunks of the trees but not on the ground.

The pine–broad-leaved forest presents a clear picture of seasonal change in vegetation. In early spring (April), before they have leaves, various willows, alder, hazelnut, and aspen begin to blossom, giving a light-yellow tint to the riverside forests. In mid-spring (May) maples blossom, their green-yellow flowers attracting a multitude of bees: everywhere are seen the snow-white blossoms of the cherry (*Prunus triflora*) and the big rose-colored racemes of the pear (*Pyrus ussuriensis*). Late spring (end of May, beginning of June) brings the blossoming, along the banks of rivers, of bird cherry, apple, *Spiraea chamaedryfolia,* and oak.

By the beginning of summer, the leaves of trees and shrubs have fully developed, sunlight does not penetrate into the forest, and the shade is dense. In early summer (June) the forest is embellished by the white blossoms of jasmine, and the many vines, the Korean pine, and cork trees are blooming. In midsummer (July) the pink and lavender blossoms of wild rose (*Rosa dahurica*) and spirea (*Spiraea salicifolia*) and the white flowers of false spirea (*Sorbaria sorbifolia*) stand out. Along the river banks fragrant lilacs (*Syringa amurensis*) bloom, and the blossoming linden fills the air with the odor of honey. With the blooming of bush clover (*Lespedeza bicolor*) summer ends and autumn begins. In autumn only certain ginsengs such as aralia (*Aralia manashurica*) are in flower; the fruit of other plants has ripened. The first early-morning frosts, at the end of September, color the leaves bright yellow, red, and dark brown, and in October the leaves begin to fall.

Where a recent fire has destroyed a pine–broad-leaved forest dense thickets of aralia grow. In winter the upright trunks resemble stakes 10 to 12 feet high covered with numerous firm woody spines, but in summer crowns of large trifoliate pinnately decompound leaves and large white complex umbellate racemes grow from the tops. A few years after the fire oak and black birch has replaced the aralia.

In the river valleys, the pine–broad-leaved forests contain fir, ash (*Micromeles alnifolia*), apple (*Malus mandshurica*), and bird cherry (*Prunus maackii*). After a fire, thickets of false spirea and eastern raspberry (*Rubus crataegifolius*) appear; then maple, cork oak, and apple restore themselves, later fir, and last of all, pine.

Oak–pine–broad-leaved forests are situated along narrow ridges and well-drained, dry, and warmed southern slopes. Under the forests is a rubbly, dark-colored crypto-podzolic or weakly podzolic soil. The trees of these forests —Mongolian oak, Korean pine, *Betula dahurica*—produce such dense shade that no other trees can grow beneath them. Predominant in the subgrowth is bush clover (*Lespedeza bicolor*), a shrub of the legume family that grows as much as six feet high, with paniculate rose-violet racemes. It provides nectar for honeybees and fodder for spotted deer. Like all legumes it enriches the soil with nitrogen, and breaks it up with its long branching roots.

Thus, after a fire conditions are favorable for the growth of thickets of deciduous shrubs, oak groves, and the later restoration of coniferous trees. The composition of the thickets depends on the exposure and steepness of the slope: on steep southern slopes aralia and lespedeza predominate; on gentle southern slopes, eastern raspberry; on southeastern and southwestern slopes, hazelnut. In a few years black birch and oak raise their heads above the shrubs and the thickets are converted to oak groves.

high) and with trunks about ten inches in diameter. There is a solid undergrowth of shrubs—mainly heterophyllous hazelnut and bush clover, to which are added wild rose and raspberry. Grape vines are plentiful. This type of forest yields only firewood, but much nectar for bees and great quantities of wild grape for vintners. It binds the soil of mountain slopes, but is often cleared to make plowed fields and gardens.

Scrub thickets are all of secondary origin and

Fig. 10-7.   A sparse stand of Mongolian oak with a ground cover of lespediza.

Oak groves are common in the mountains, especially in inhabited areas. They have sprung up where oak–pine–broad-leaved forests have been destroyed by fires. Under them, weakly-podzolic argillaceous soil has developed on slopes and slightly rubbly soils on the crests of hills. The groves are sparse and consist mainly of Mongolian or Manchurian oak, much of it crooked, low (about 30 to 35 feet

owe their existence largely to the activity of man. On the inhabited plains and slopes thickets of hazelnut are most common; in the thinly populated mountains bush clover takes over. The composition of the accompanying vegetation and its quantity depend on the density of the thickets. In dense thickets there are a number of spring plants that are able to pass the complete cycle of vegetation by the time the leaves of the hazelnut and bush clover open—for example, adonis (*Adonis amurensis*) and a few species of violets. The thinner the thickets, the more diverse the plant cover. Many creeping plants, such as *Clematis mandshurica,* and Chinese yam make an appearance.

Riverside forests grow on alluvial deposits of varying mechanical composition. Under these forests residual weakly podzolic soil has developed, soil which is rich in organic substance and has but slightly differentiated profiles; in a few places the soil is of a bog type (mudgley). The mechanical composition of the soil and the age of the substrata determine the type of vegetation that grows on it. On young conglomerates, cemented by sandy-clayey alluvium, is humus-rich soil that has been subjected both to erosion and deposition of new material. Along lower stream channels are thickets of willow (*Salix viminalis* and *S. thunbergiana*) under which, because of flooding, the grass cover is extremely meager and consists largely of reed grass (*Calamagrostis langsdorffii*) and sedge (*Carex vesicaria*). Along the middle and upper courses of rivers, on sandy-conglomerate deposits along the edges of the first terraces near the river, is thick mulch-podzolic soil on which grow large patches of butterbur (*Petasites palmata*) or thickets of chosenia (*Chosenia macrolepis*). Adjoining them are forests of gigantic poplars (*Populus maximowiczi*) that reach 150 feet in height and are more than 6 feet in diameter. These forests protect the river banks and the neighboring plowed lands during floods.

A pine–broad-leaved forest that contains an admixture of Okhotsk conifers is the basic type of forest in the northern Sikhote-Alin, and is rather common in the South Ussuri district, where it grows on plateaus and the middle sections of mountain slopes. Under the forests is either a rubbly variety of podzolic soil or a heavy slightly podzolic soil. The dominant tree in the first tier of these forests is the Korean pine, with which is admixed Yeddo spruce (*Picea jezoensis*), yellow birch, Amur linden, and Mono maple. The second tier is formed by other species of maple, hornbeam, and Okhotsk white-barked fir (*Abies nephrolepis*). There are many grape and magnolia vines. The undergrowth consists mainly of ferns, and the moss cover is not continuous. Burned-over sections are first overrun by growths of bush clover, aralia, and false spirea; after them appear Amur linden, maple, and yellow birch; finally the coniferous trees of the original forest re-establish themselves. Complete destruction by fire or clearcutting over a large area results in the elimination of pine from the forest. In moist valleys where cold air stagnates these forests contain a higher proportion of Yeddo spruce and white-barked fir. Some forests contain cork oak, Manchurian walnut, ash, and apple.

The life cycle of the animals of the mixed forests and their distribution in the Amur-Primorski region are affected by its geographical peculiarities: the mountainous character of the relief, the vertical zonality of vegetation, and the mosaic distribution of plants are reflected in the distribution of animals.

The cold winters also affect the lives of many animals: some birds migrate to more southerly latitudes; a number of mammals hibernate throughout the winter; reptiles, amphibians, and some insects enter a torpid state. Because the snow cover forms late and disappears early, and is frequently blown away by the wind or covered by falling leaves, few animals turn white in winter (white hare, ermine). Southern Chinese or Himalayan animals that stay for the winter may even become darker; for example, the spotted deer loses the white spots on its sides in winter.

The thinness of the snow cover on southern slopes causes intraregional winter migration of ungulates in search of food. On these slopes spotted deer, kaban, leopard, forest cat, and pheasant dwell the year round. The warm, moist, and long summer guarantees rich and diversified food for animals not only throughout the period of vegetation but also in winter: Korean and Manchurian pine nuts, the basic food of the squirrel, sable, and kaban;

Fig. 10-8. Characteristic fauna in Amur coastal region. Upper left: "Kharza" or yellow-breasted marten (*Martes flavigula*); upper right: Antelope goral (*Nemorhaedus goral*); middle right: Long-haired tiger (*Tigris longipilis*); middle center: Blue magpie (*Cyanopica cyana*); middle left: Spotted deer (*Cervus nippon*); bottom right: Amur pheasant (*Phasianus colchicus pallasi*); bottom center: "Mandarinka" (*Aix galericulata*); bottom left: Ussuri raccoon-like dog (*Nyctereutes procionoides ussuriensis*). (*Mounting by S. P. Suslov; drawing by V. V. Trofimov.*)

acorns; grapes and actinidia berries, on which the raccoon-dog and pheasant feed; the leaves of the ash, linden, maple, lilac, and jasmine, and the evergreen winter horsetail, which provide for the hooved animals. The soil is rich in earthworms, ground insects, and mollusks, and these provide food for numerous small mammals and birds. Many different plants serve as food for hordes of rodents, which, like the small insectivorous mammals and birds, provide food for the carnivores. The flooding caused by cloudbursts often kills great numbers of animals in the river valleys.

Many carnivores live in the Manchurian-type mixed forests: (1) The long-furred tiger (*Felis tigris longipilis*), a large, strong, clever, and indefatigable cat, whose coat resembles that of his subtropical relative although his silky and luxuriant yellow-ochre fur is less brilliant—more nearly the color of fallen yellow leaves. He endures cold of −20°F, but summer heat drives him high into the mountains. He roams at any time of day and night in search of boars, wild goats, and Manchurian deer; (2) The eastern panther (*Felis pardus orientalis*), who has a rich gold, pale-yellow coat with black spots; (3) The Amur forest cat (*Felis euptilura microtis*), who lives in forested ravines, where he hunts from sunset till dawn for mice, squirrels, Manchurian hares, and small birds; (4) The Manchurian bear (*Ursus mandchuricus*); (5) The black Ussuri bear (*Ursus tibetanus ussuricus*), who has shiny black fur, and feeds on succulent roots, berries, and the honey of wild bees. He is an excellent climber and willingly sits in trees for hours. In winter he does not hibernate in a lair but settles in the crotch of a tree, where he sleeps in a sitting position; (6) The Korean polecat (*Kolonocus sibiricus coreanus*), a bold carnivore with beautiful soft fur, who pursues mice and small birds.

Other predatory animals are: red wolf (*Canis alpinus*), Amur badger (*Meles leptorhynchus amurensis*), fox, otter, weasel, and lynx. The Ussuri raccoon-dog (*Nyctereutes procinonoides ussuriensis*) prefers small copses along valley meadows where there are many

shallow lakes and small streams; in winter he hibernates in his deep burrow. The raccoon-dog eats mice, frogs, eggs, and young birds, although he prefers fish, acorns and grapes. Ungulates living here include: East Asiatic boar (*Sus scrofa continentalis*); Korean musk deer (*Moschus moschiferus parvipes*); Siberian roe deer (*Capreolus pygargus blanfordi*); spotted deer (*Pseudaxis dybowskii*), which today is almost extinct and is protected in breeding reserves; Manchurian stag (*Cervus canadensis xanthopygus*); and goral (*Nemorhaedus crispus*), a beautiful antelope that lives on rocky cliffs. Characteristic local insectivora are the Ussuri mole (*Mogera robusta*) and Amur hedgehog (*Erinaceus amurensis*). Among the common rodents are: Primorski white hare (*Lepus timidus mordeni*), Manchurian hare (*Allolagus mandschuricus*), flying squirrel (*Pteromys volans arsenhevi*), Ussuri chipmunk (*Eutamias sibiricus orientalis*), Manchurian squirrel (*Sciurus vulgaris mandshuricus*), and many different species of field mice. The latter, especially *Mus agrarius,* infest grain fields in great numbers, and as every sheaf is raised from the earth dozens of them scatter in all directions.

A characteristic bird of the Manchurian forests is the Manchurian pheasant (*Phasianus mongolicus*), which is found as far north as the mouth of the Ussuri River. Its habitats are the riverside forests and the brushy thickets along broad river valleys. In spring and winter it moves near human settlements—near grain fields, threshing floors, and gardens—where it can find seeds, which, with snails and acorns, make up its food. The mandarin duck (*Aix galericulata*), the most brightly colored of the ducks, lives along slowly flowing small streams. Many southern species of birds nest in the region but winter farther south. Some winter in the Philippine and Sunda Islands and in Indochina—*Eurystomus orientalis calonyx,* blue Chinese flycatcher (*Muscicapa cyanomelana cumatilis*), and white Chinese sparrow (*Motacilla alba leucopsis*): others winter in India and Indochina—Chinese black-headed oriole (*Oriolus chinensis diffusus*) and Indian blue kingfisher (*Alcedo atthis bengalensis*). The blue Ussuri magpie (*Cyanopica cyana*) is indigenous to the region.

The warm rainy summer and the rich vegetation of the Amur-Primorski region provide favorable conditions for reptiles, amphibians, and mollusks. The East Asiatic water tortoise (*Amyda sinensis*), which lacks a horny shell, lives in Lake Khanka and the Ussuri River. There are several species of lizards and snakes, their spread being promoted by the abundance of mice: the East Siberian tiger-grass snake (*Natrix tigrina lateralis*), beautiful and harmless; the Japanese grass snake (*Natrix vibacari*); the red-backed snake (*Elaphe rufodorsata*), an excellent swimmer and diver; Amur snake (*Elaphe schrenki*)—large (as much as six feet long) and strong, living in open meadows, in thickets of shrubs, and along the borders of the forest; and a poisonous moccasin of the genus *Agkistrodon*. Amphibians include: the Ussuri triton (*Geomolge fischeri*), the East Asiatic frog (*Rana nigromaculata*), the eastern tree frog (*Hyla stepheni*), and the eastern toad (*Bombinator orientalis*).

The insects of the broad-leaved forests are many and varied and include a number of indigenous species, particularly of bright-colored butterflies. In the daytime the following species flutter about the forests and meadows: the large blue-green butterfly (*Papilio bianor maacki*), the *Danais tytia,* the *Satyrus brice, Parnassius eversmanni, Apatura nycteis,* and *Niphandra foxa.* On warm dry nights, the large *Dictyoploca japonica,* the *Schecodina caudata,* the magnificent *Iotophora admirabilis,* and the blue ribbon (*Catocala fraxini*) stream through the air, their paths illuminated by thousands of fireflies. The large Far Eastern beetle (*Callipogon relictus*) has several close relatives in South America. Many insects feed on the leaves, bark, and wood of trees valuable as timber, causing much damage: among them are the larvae of certain butterflies, capricorn beetles, and over a hundred species of bark-eaters. The forests are filled with blood-sucking Diptera: midges, mosquitoes, gadflies, and horseflies. These drive the wild animals wild and force them to seek surcease by leaping into streams and lakes or changing their habitat. Some species of ticks and mosquitoes are carriers of the dangerous disease encephalitis. Even here, the multitude of honey-bearing plants assures an exceptional collection of honey, sometimes as much as 35 pounds of honey in one beehive in a single day.

At an altitude of 1,300 feet on the slopes of the Sikhote-Alin, fir-spruce forests of the Okhote type begin to replace the Manchurian forests. White-barked fir appears first in the undergrowth and then, higher, as full-grown mature trees. Higher still, large Yeddo spruce trees are added. On well-drained slopes where the soil is well warmed and cold air does not stagnate, the spruce-fir forests contain an admixture of Manchurian species, and farther down the slopes blend into forests of the Manchurian type. In the first tier of these mixed forests the crowns of Korean pine, yellow birch, and mountain elm intermingle with those of Yeddo spruce. White-barked fir dominates the second tier, which contains also white birch (*Betula mandshurica*), bird cherry, and Amur linden. In the undergrowth are false spirea and thorny wild rose (*Rosa acicularis*). The grass cover is thin and the moss cover is thinner. The soil under these forests is transitional to the normal podzolic soil of the northern forest regions and is distinguished from it only by a greater content of humus, clayeyness, and less acidity. Near the upper stretches of rivers, at an altitude of about 2,000 feet, spruce and fir begin to drive out the other trees; in some places the young trees grow so thickly that they hamper the development of the underbrush. In the soil cover appear green moss, club moss, and grasses found in northern mountain forests. The typical spruce-fir forests that begin here rise to an altitude of 2,600 feet. Yeddo spruce forms the first tier, white-barked fir the second. Underbrush and grass cover are absent and mosses cover the entire surface of the ground, sometimes even rising upward on the trunks of the trees. Beneath the forests the soil is podzolic or slightly podzolic, rubbly, and argillaceous.

The spruce-fir forests are not important commercially but their protective role is very great. If they are destroyed by felling or fire, the thin soil cover may be entirely washed off, leaving bare mountain rocks from which rain or meltwater runs off rapidly, which greatly increases the danger of floods.

The fauna of the spruce-fir forests has a northern character: there are few species, most of them Siberian ones. Characteristic mammals are: the yellow-breasted marten (*Martes flavigula borealis*), a real forest animal found in the dense taiga of the southern Sikhote-Alin; the Sakhalin sable (*Martes zibellina sachalinensis*); the polecat (*Kolonocus sibiricus*), which destroys a vast number of rodents (not less than 700 a year); the eastern lynx; the wolverine; the Ussuri elk (*Alces alces americanus*); the northern cony; the Manchurian squirrel; and the rust-colored field mouse. There are many grouse: rock grouse (*Tetrao parvirostris*); Ussuri grouse (*Lyrurus tetrix ussuriensis*), which range rather far to the south through the mountain spruce-fir forests; and the Amur hazel grouse (*Tetrastes bonasia amurensis*), which is very abundant and prefers the sunniest spots in the forest. Where the Okhotsk taiga spreads there lives the grouse (*Falcipennis falcipennis*), a bird which never moves far from the thickest, mossiest sections, although in autumn it descends until it reaches a region rich in berries. Biologically, it is close to the American grouse found in the spruce-fir forests of Canada and Alaska.

Above the spruce-fir forests are larch forests, which occupy the belt below the bald peaks in the northern Sikhote-Alin and individual summits in the south. The larch forests here are similar to those in Trans-Baikal. The trees are scattered sparsely: in the underbrush are dwarf stone pine (*Pinus pumila*), scrub birch (*Betula middendorffii*), and *Rhododendron dahuricum;* beneath them are bilberry, *Ledum decumbens,* and black bearberry (*Mairrania alpina*). The larch forests, which are as yet completely unexploited, contain unswamped mountain peat soil.

In the subalpine zone, the belt between 2,300 and 5,100 feet altitude, impenetrable thickets of dwarf stone pine (*Pinus pumila*) and *Rhododendron crysanthum* form narrow bands along protected slopes and along saddles between bald mountains on poorly developed soil covered with a slightly rotted mulch of needles. The thickets contain many animals, including bears and tigers that hunt the other animals that seek refuge there. In this belt grows the only endemic conifer in the USSR: *Microbiota decussata,* a squat plant of the genus *Thuja,* family Pinaceae. It forms a narrow border along the edges of patches of rock on the slopes of the Sikhote-Alin that face the Sea of Japan. Forest fires spread rapidly in it because of the intense pitchiness of its branches.

The bald-mountain zone of the Sikhote-Alin comprises the high points of plateaus and many gentle slopes at high altitudes; in the south these are covered with patches of reindeer-moss tundra and in the north by solid areas of it. Against a background of reindeer moss (*Cladonia rangiferina*) are scattered small perennials, mainly heathers and bilberries: red bilberry, bog bilberry, *Cassiope ericoides,* creeping wild rosemary (*Ledum decumbens*), and *Rhododendron redowskianum.* Here too is a plant of the alpine tundra—partridge grass (*Dryas octopetala*). The strong winds on these open heights prevent the growth of trees. The rocky soil of the bald mountains has a slightly differentiated profile, usually without indication of podzolization.

The vegetation of the Bureya Range is unusually diverse because of the complexity of relief and the convergence here of the boundaries of three floral regions: the Manchurian, the Okhotsk, and the East Siberian. In the northern part of the range where there are low temperatures, cold fogs, and frequent winds, the summits and upper parts of the mountain slopes that lie between altitudes of 2,000 and 3,000 feet are covered by gloomy, shady forests of spruce and fir, where lichens hang from the branches and the trunks of the trees are covered with moss. In the first tier of these forests are Yeddo spruce and white-barked fir, and a few yellow birch and rock birch (*Betula ermani*). Where there is a second tier it consists of maple (*Acer ukurunduense*). The ground cover of shade-loving grasses is very sparse and is interspersed with moss. The valleys of the mountain streams have a vegetative cover that differs greatly from that of the slopes. In their upper sections are forests of larch, spruce, and fir; lower, extending approximately to the middle section of the rivers, are pure larch forests; still lower, the forest consists of a narrow strip along the river—beyond it are grassy meadows, which surround low hills covered with thickets of hazelnut, groves of white birch and aspen, oak groves, and remnants of the pine–broad-leaved forest. The spread of larch is favored by the fact that cold air flows from the mountains into the river valleys and stagnates there; larch infiltrates far to the south along these cold corridors. In the lowest valleys is a strip of pine–broad-leaved forests that contain some spruce. The southern part of the Bureya Range and its spurs have pine–broad-leaved forests, oak groves, and their derivatives that are similar to those of Sikhote-Alin.

The vegetation of the northwestern part of the Amur-Primorski region resembles that of Trans-Baikal and Yakutia. The cold climate, the extensive development of permafrost, and the low plains, flat uplands, and long gentle slopes contribute to the stagnation of water and the formation of countless large sphagnum-moss bogs; it is possible to cross these bogs with relative ease because permafrost lies extremely close to the surface. These bogs, in which a few larches grow, constitute the most common landscape of the region. They contain the usual sphagnum-moss bog plants—wild rosemary, casandra, and the others—but instead of polar birch they have scrub birch (*Betula midden-*

dorffii), and instead of swamp pine, larch. The northwestern forests are composed of larch and white birch; they contain no underbrush and the soil cover is made up of forest and bog grasses. The soil under the trees is rocky bog, semi-bog, or podzolic. Pine grows on sandy dry sections near rivers and is common west of the

Fig. 10-9. Pine–spruce–fir forest on the southern Buryea Mountains; to the left a large Korean pine.

Zeya River; farther east it grows sporadically although it extends as far as the southern part of the Okhotsk coast. On semi-bog and podzolic soil in the Yankan and Tukuringra ranges, forests of larch with an underbrush of dwarf stone pine (*Pinus pumila*) and scrub birch (*Betula middendorffii*) reach an altitude of 3,300 feet; higher up is a subalpine belt like those of Trans-Baikal.

SOIL, FLORA, AND FAUNA
OF THE PLAINS

The plains of the Amur-Primorski region are exceptionally level and are covered by a uniform thickness of alluvial deposits. Their semi-bog soil is rich in humus, and they have few trees but much thick, tall, and luxuriant grass. Heavy rains during the growing season, the high clay content of the soil, and the levelness slow surface drainage and create favorable conditions for periodic swamping; thus a large part of the plains is covered by half-swamped soil. There are small islands and strips of podzolic soil only on the higher places, where the mechanical makeup and drainage of the underlying strata differs from that of the level plain. The humus layer of the semi-bog soil is intensely black, thick, and, when moist, without structure. The lower layer is dirty-gray with dark humus stains; in depressions it has a dark-blue tint that indicates deoxidization. With the onset of summer rains the humus layer becomes saturated with water, breaks down easily, and forms a sticky clayey mass.

The plains resemble a chernozem steppe, but the soil has nothing in common with chernozem. Chernozem develops where there is little moisture, here there is too much moisture during summer; chernozem has a grainy or clotted structure, but this soil is structureless; chernozem has carbonate salts in the lower layer, this soil has the dark-blue color that indicates gleying. The luxuriance of the vegetation aids the accumulation of humus (up to 15 per cent). Excess moisture and weak aeration of the soil in summer slows the decomposition of the dead grass and prevents the formation of chernozem. There is some peat-bog soil on the plains.

Meadows cover most of the plains. Their type and distribution depend on the amount of moisture in the soil, which in turn depends on the dissection of the relief: bog, beach grass, mixed grass, and cereal grass. These four types and their variants give the plains a variegated appearance. The distribution of meadows is clearly marked on the Pre-Khanka Plain.

1. Bog meadows occupy the lowest and wettest places. They are swamped the year round, and their peat-bog soil is underlain by heavy clay. Their vegetation is quite uniform: the grass is tall (up to 28 inches), dense, and turfy. The most important plants are a species of reed grass (*Calamagrostis neglecta*) and one of sedge (*Carex meyeriana*). The productivity of the meadows is about one and a half tons of dry hay per acre, but the quality of the hay is rather low (legumes 1 per cent, sedge 26 per cent, cereal grasses 54 per cent, other grasses 19 per cent). It is necessary to harvest twice a summer.

2. Reed grass meadows predominate on low slopes that are rather moist but are swamped only temporarily. The bog soil of these meadows is underlaid by a layer of sticky clay. The grass grows three or four feet high but turfiness is slight. Reed grass (*Calamagrostis langsdorffii*) is good fodder, and these meadows are the best hay harvest lands (legumes 3 per cent, sedge 11 per cent, cereal grasses 69 per cent, other grasses 17 per cent).

3. Mixed-grass meadows are prevalent on gradual slopes where moistening is moderate and swamping is of short duration. The semi-bog soil is clayey or sandy, contains no peat, and has traces of slight podzolization. The composition, height, and turfiness of the meadows varies greatly. They contain lilies (*Lilium dahuricum*), day lilies (*Hemerocallis minor*), globeflowers (*Trollius ledebouri*) with large orange flowers; clover (*Trifolium lupinaster*); and many cereal grasses. The meadows comprise about 5 per cent legumes, 8 per cent sedges, 24 per cent cereal grasses, and 63 per cent of other grasses. They produce comparatively small quantities of coarse but very nutritious hay.

Fig. 10-10. Luxurious meadow on fertile soil of the Zeya-Buryea plain: purple *Hemerocallis grami-nea* in bloom and narrow-leaved *Sanguisorba tenuifolia* in bud.

4. Cereal-grass meadows occupy drained crests and slopes; in midsummer they are half dried up, and even in moist years they are not swampy. The soil often has clear traces of podzol formations. In some places the most common grass is bent grass (*Agrostis clavata*), and in others meadow grass (*Poa pratensis*), with which may be mixed *Koeleria gracilis*. Meadows of this type contain 2 per cent legumes, 1 per cent sedges, 75 per cent cereal grasses, and 22 per cent other grasses and herbs. The average height (10 to 12 inches), density, and turfiness is less than on the other types of meadows. Productivity is low—600 to 800 pounds of dry hay per acre. The vegetation dries out rapidly and only by early mowing is it possible to obtain even this much hay.

In drier parts of the plains the character of vegetative cover is somewhat different: bog meadows are replaced by reed-grass meadows, and the latter by meadows of mixed grasses, which in turn give way to cereal-grass meadows. Where it is driest, the latter are quite xerophytic, as on southern slopes in the Zeya-Bureya Plain, where the soil lies on beds of well-drained sand and gravel. This permeable soil has small capillary capacity and dries out to a depth of 20 inches despite the abundance of rain. Here, near the steppes, are such typical taiga plants as maidenhair feather grass (*Stipa capillata*) and tansy (*Tanacetum sibiricum*), which is also found on the eastern Trans-Baikal steppes.

In many districts, especially in the eastern half of the Lower Amur Lowland, are swampy sparse larch forests in which peat mosses cover gray podzolized Tertiary clay. The upper tier of these forests contains white birch (*Betula japonica*) as well as larch, and the undergrowth contains much scrub birch (*Betula middendorffii*) and many bog plants such as *Ledum palustre* and bog myrtle (*Chamaedaphne calyculata*). The quality of the timber is low, but the soil, if drained and cleared, is suitable for agriculture. Near streams these forests change their character: swampiness decreases, the growth of larch improves, and the undergrowth consists of huge osmund ferns (*Osmunda cinnamomea*) and silvery wild rosemary (*Ledum hypoleucum*).

Along the rivers that flow through the plains are narrow, slightly elevated terraces. These are well drained and do not flood; the soil on them is fine in texture, has its upper horizon strongly stained by humus, and is only slightly podzolized. On them are found forests of aspen, white and black birch, larch, pine, Okhotsk conifers such as Yeddo spruce, and such Manchurian broad-leaved trees as Mongolian oak or cork oak. In the western part of the plains there are coniferous forests of larch and pine. Farther east these forests contain ash; and on dry slopes oak—gnarled, with irregularly developed crowns and twisted trunks. There are also scattered small groves of white and Dahurican birch (*Betula dahurica*), the latter a light-loving variety with brown or chestnut-colored bark that hangs on the trunk in tatters. Under the translucent green canopy of the coniferous forests grows lespedeza, and on the margins many Manchurian shrubs and grasses.

On sandy-muddy deposits in stream channels in the South-Ussuri region are: lotus (*Nelumbium nuciferum*), with rose-colored blossoms up to 10 inches in diameter, a plant that grows also in the delta of the volga and along the lower stretches of the Aras River but nowhere between there and the Ussuri; water shield (*Brasenia purpurea*), which once grew in Europe; water nut (*Trapa incisa*). The giant water lily (*Euryale ferox*), with bright blue-violet flowers and leaves up to 50 inches in diameter, grows in a few places; more abundant is the small water lily (*Nymphaea tetragona*). The fruits, seeds, and rootstocks of most of these plants are used as food.

Among the mammals in southern plains are the raccoon-dog (*Nyctereutes procionoides ussuriensis*), the Manchurian hare (*Allolagus mandshuricus*), and a species of mouse (*Micromys minutus ussuriensis*) that is found in great numbers and is a serious pest. Common birds are hazel grouse, woodcock, pheasant, and various waterfowl. Lake Khanka is a station on the migration route of great flocks of ducks, geese, swans, snipes, and gulls: migration lasts more than two months in spring and autumn. In the central plains are the great bustard, quail (*Turnix maculatus*), and Ussuri quail (*Coturnix japonica ussuriensis*); such waterfowl as large grebe, rust-colored heron, and Chinese ibis (*Nipponia nippon*); and, in the grassy swamps, Indian water rail (*Rallus aquaticus indicus*) and small rail (*Porzana pusilla*).

The history of development of the landscapes of the Amur-Primorski plain is very complex. Evidently, after the drying up of the gigantic lake that once filled the plain, northern vegetation moved onto the cold swampy soil of the drained bottomland—larch forests and extensive bog meadows. As the climate grew warmer, the abundant summer rains, the water-tightness of the alluvial and lake soil, and its weak aeration, permitted the growth of luxuriant meadows. The rich organic residues decomposed slowly and thick layers of humus were

Fig. 10-11. Stand of black and white birch trees in the Zeya River Valley.

formed. Several ferrous streaks in the gley horizon of present-day semi-bog soil indicate that the soil was once swamped and that the level of ground water was close to the surface. The downcutting of the rivers and the conversion of bottomland into terraces caused the level of ground water to lower and the terraces to dry out, which created favorable conditions for the growth of trees and shrubs. The better-drained and dried-out crests with their warm soil became covered with Manchurian vegetation, which descended from the slopes of the adjacent ranges.

In the xerothermic period, which was not particularly dry here, steppe plants and animals infiltrated from the neighboring steppes of Mongolia and Trans-Baikal: plants such as maidenhair feather grass, birds such as the great bustard (*Otis tarda dybowskii*), and mammals such as the suslik (*Citellus eversmanni*), settled in areas with light, well-drained soil. These have survived to the present because of the southern location of the region and the light precipitation in spring, during which season steppe plants complete the cycle of their development. In the xerothermic period the soil dried so thoroughly that thickets of brush could grow on the higher ground, paving the way for the forests that followed them and that are now slowly encroaching on the meadows. As the trees take over, bog soil changes into podzolic soil. Today young forests grow on weakly-podzolic argillaceous soil where, fifty years ago, semi-bog soil was covered with thick grass. The forest consumes moisture rapidly and the humus layer of the soil gradually divides in two: its lower part lightens, acquires a foliated structure, and is converted into the leached-out layer characteristic of podzolic soil.

The advance of the forest and the podzolizing of semi-bog soil has been interrupted by human activity. Man's struggle for existence has brought about changes in the vegetative cover and created new interrelations between plants and animals and between them and their environment. The main ways in which man alters the landscape are by: (1) felling and burning forests, (2) plowing, (3) cutting hay, (4) grazing livestock, and (5) burning off unmowed grass. Great areas of the plains have been deforested by man and forests on the slopes have also undergone clearcutting, their place being taken by thickets of brush or by cultivated fields. The destruction of forests has led to the drying up of creeks, the shoaling of rivers, and the lowering of the level of lakes. Hay can be mowed from late in July until early in September; constant mowing hastens the replacement of one type of meadow by another that is able to exist with a smaller amount of moisture. Grazing of livestock converts a bog meadow into wet pasture; on a reed-grass meadow, the packing of the earth by cattle leads to the destruction of the nourishing reed grass; on a meadow of mixed grass, inedible weeds replace the edible grasses; on a cereal-grass meadow the basic plants maintain their dominance over weeds, which need more moisture for growth.

Unmowed grass and stubble remaining from the past year is usually burned off in spring. Old vegetation left on the meadows hampers mowing, retards drainage, brings about swamping, decreases the warming of the soil and its aeration, and prevents the normal growth of young grass. Spring burning affects both the warmth and moisture content of the soil: the black surface of a burned meadow absorbs much of the sun's heat, so that on burned sections the level of the seasonal frost lowers more rapidly and to a greater depth (a difference of up to 16 inches); the destruction of the moss cover contributes to the evaporation of excessive moisture; and the ashes increase the supply of nourishing substances in the soil. Burning destroys and suppresses some species of plants and stimulates the growth of others, especially reed grass. In general burning increases the yield of hay from bog, reed-grass, and mixed grass meadows by about 600 pounds per acre; the yield from dry meadows, however, is not affected by burning. It is necessary to dig trenches or to plow the ground around areas to be burned, and also to burn only in early spring, because in summer the peaty layer of soil catches fire easily and may lead to forest fires.

Dilatorily but inevitably, the meadows are being replaced by cultivated fields: with cultivation the temperature and water balance of the soil changes. The destruction of the forests, the trampling of grass by grazing cattle, the burning off of meadows and their plowing contribute to (1) better warming of the soil (its summer temperature may be raised as much as 18 degrees); (2) a rise in the night temperature of the air; (3) the reduction of daily amplitudes of temperature; (4) a decrease in the number of spring and autumn frosts; (5) the surface drying of the soil; and (6) a decrease in the amount of water discharged into streams. These conditions lead to the wide distribution of steppe plants on uncultivated sections—pasque flower (*Pulsatilla patens*), *Koeleria gracilis,* and couch grass (*Agropyron repens*)—to which are added a thick growth of reed grass (*Calamagrostis epigeios*). Where there are cultivated fields, there also is the suslik, which in its movement to the east has already crossed the Bureya.

Summer wheat, spring rye, buckwheat, and sunflower are cultivated on the plains. Many crops common in the European USSR do not succeed here, and it is necessary for new settlers to accustom themselves to plants that have been grown in neighboring Manchuria for at least a thousand years: (1) Manchurian or soybean (*Glycine hispida*) which is well adapted to Far Eastern climate and soil. The plant resists spring drought and light frosts, endures an extremely wet summer, and is not subject to fungoid diseases; it can be cultivated as far north as Blagoveshchensk. Since it is a legume and enriches the soil with nitrogen, it is useful in crop rotation. The beans contain 15 to 51 per cent oil, 38 to 41 per cent albumen, and a number of healthful mineral substances: the soybean flour, sauce, oil, etc., are prepared from them. (2) Rice, which can be cultivated as far north as Khabarovsk. (3) Foxtail millet (*Setaria italica*) and (4) sorghum (*Andropogon sorghum japonicum*), whose dried stalks provide feed for cattle and are used as fuel and to cover roofs. Corn and hemp are also cultivated, but spring frosts and the damp summers prevent the development of all but a few indigenous frost-resistant fruit trees: for example, the small-fruited Siberian apple tree (*Malus mandshurica*) and the Ussuri pear (*Pyrus ussuriensis*).

CHAPTER 11

Northwestern Coast of the Sea of Okhotsk and Sakhalin Island

The northwestern coast of the Sea of Okhotsk and Sakhalin island, which is separated from the shore by a narrow strait but extends farther south, have similar climates—climates whose characteristics are determined by the proximity of the monsoon region of East Asia and the cold Sea of Okhotsk. Both island and coast have the same flora, which not only is composed of a peculiar combination of species but also has an unusual vertical distribution. Yet each has its own geologic history and structure, its own orography, its own local climatic variations, and its own landscapes. Administratively, the northwestern coast of the Sea of Okhotsk lies entirely within Lower Amur oblast, and Sakhalin comprises Sakhalin oblast, both of which are parts of Khabarovsk Territory.

THE SEA OF OKHOTSK

The Sea of Okhotsk has a direct influence on the climate of its coasts. It is a typical marginal sea of the Pacific Ocean, separated from it only by the chain of Kurile Islands. Its southwestern part is connected with the Sea of Japan by La Perouse Strait, and to the Pacific by straits between the Kuriles. It washes the west coasts of Kamchatka and the Kurile Islands, the eastern coast of Asia from Shelekhova south to the Amur estuary, and the north and east shores of Sakhalin. The northern part of its western shoreline is dissected more than the southern part, but even in the north, between large gulfs and bays (Shelekhova Gulf, which is divided by Taygonos Peninsula into Gizhiginskaya and Penzhinskaya bays, Tauya Bay with Nagayevo Cove) large sections of the coast run almost in a straight line. The shore consists in most places of solid rocks that disintegrate slowly, and thus drop abruptly to the sea. Only in the inner sections of large bays and gulfs and along the western coast of Kamchatka are there low shores. There are few islands in the Sea of Okhotsk (the Shantar Islands, the Yamsk Islands near Pyagin Peninsula, and the small rocky St. Iony Island). On the bottom of the sea, in the extreme southeastern part, along the Kurile chain, is a deep, narrow depression: here is found the deepest spot in the sea, 11,060 feet. A steep ridge that borders this depression runs northward along the Kurile chain to Kamchatka, and westward along Hokkaido to Sakhalin. Along the northern and western shores the sea is nowhere much more than 660 feet deep, and near steep shores may be less than half of that.

The water balance of the sea is maintained largely by an exchange of water with the

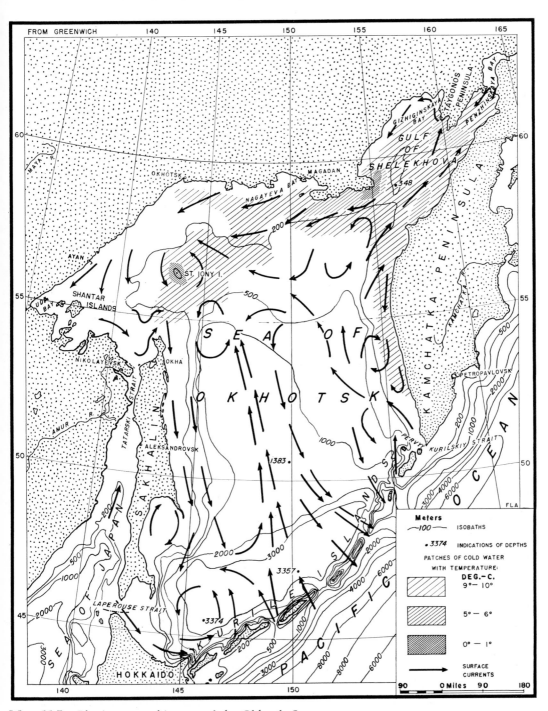

Map 11-I. Physicogeographic map of the Okhotsk Sea.

Pacific—the water received from precipitation and removed by evaporation, and the exchange with the Sea of Japan through La Perouse Strait are unimportant. Through the northern Kurile straits the surface layers of the sea are constantly replenished by Pacific Ocean water, through the southern straits Okhotsk water flows into the Pacific. The currents caused by this water exchange flow in a counterclockwise direction. The Pacific water that enters through the northern Kurile straits turns north along the west coast of Kamchatka, then passes along the north shore of the sea, is deflected to the southwest by the mainland coast and by currents flowing out of Shelekhova Gulf, washes St. Iony Island, reaches the northern shores of the Shantar Islands, where it receives a tangential impetus from water from the Amur that forces it eastward. It then flows south along the eastern coast of Sakhalin, is joined near La Perouse Strait by the current from the Sea of Japan, and, increasing its speed, pours out through the southern Kurile straits into the Pacific, thus completing the circle.

The incoming water from the Pacific Ocean causes regular tides throughout the sea. The amplitude of the tides on the open sections of the coast is about 13.2 feet; in the constricted gulfs and bays it increases sharply and conspicuously—at Gizhiginskaya Bay, for example, it reaches 43.8 feet.

The low temperature of the air throughout the year, the cold winters, and the short cool cloudy summers with their persistent fogs give the water a very low temperature. During the summer only a relatively thin layer of water, 100 to 165 feet thick, is warmed; the temperature of the underlying cold water is below freezing the year round. The frequent emergence of this layer onto the surface causes dense fogs that prevent the sun's rays from reaching the surface of the sea. The surface temperature of the water in July and August fluctuates from 48.3° to 50°F in the north, and from 42° to 44.8°F in the south. To a depth of 45 feet the temperature of the water drops gradually; below 45 feet it drops sharply, reaching approximately 32°F at 60 feet. Below this level the drop in temperature continues, although not so sharply, for a few hundred feet. Between 250 and 500 feet the temperature is 29.3°F; below 500 feet it begins to rise gradually, and on the bottom may reach 34°F in the north and 36.5°F in the south. When surface water freezes the salt it releases increases the density of the surrounding water. If the water is cold,

the added salt will cause it to sink into the lower layers.

The Sea of Okhotsk has patches of very cold surface water in the region of the Yamsk Islands, near St. Iony Island, and between the northern tip of Sakhalin and the Shantar Islands. The temperature of the surface water surrounding these patches is close to the norm, but in the cold patches—for example, at the mouth of Penzhinskaya Bay—the temperature is five to nine degrees colder. The origin of the patches is connected with the general circular movement of the water in the sea. When the current meets an obstruction it is deflected downward and forces water from the depths to the surface. Near the Yamsk Islands is a patch with a summer temperature of about 37.4° to 39.3°F; as the current carries this cold dense water toward St. Iony Island it gradually sinks. Near St. Iony Island a ridge rising from the bottom and the mass of the island itself again deflect the current downward and cause the rise of water with a temperature as low as 33°F; the current carries this to the northern tip of Sakhalin, near which it sinks beneath the warmer water flowing in through La Perouse Strait. Beneath these cold patches the drop in temperature with depth is gradual, and even at a depth of 500 feet the temperature seldom goes below 32°F.

Fog is created by the emergence of cold water onto the surface. In summer, when saturated air passes over the cooled surface of the sea its temperature is lowered, water vapor is condensed, and fog is formed. The lower the temperature of the seas' surface, the stronger and more persistent the fog. Summer fogs often last for weeks: nowhere are they as steady and continuous as in the Yamsk Islands and in the neighborhood of St. Iony Island—these are covered for almost the entire navigational period by dense shroud-like fog. Winds spread the fogs over the whole sea, but they thin and disappear in regions with warm surface water.

The Sea of Okhotsk, which juts deep into the mainland and has long, cold winters during which much ice forms on its surface, differs little from the polar seas. Most of the northern bays are solidly covered by ice throughout the winter, and in January and February all of the northern half of the open sea is covered with thick masses of floating ice—at times this ice consolidates into vast areas of immovable ice, but these break up with the first strong storm. From the middle of November to February or March the thickness of the ice increases steadily. By the middle of April, when the temperature of the air has risen above 32°F, ice stops

of its area. In favorable years navigation is possible as early as the middle of June.

The salinity of the Sea of Okhotsk is less than that of other marginal seas of the Pacific. The saltiness of the surface waters fluctuates from 32 to 32.5 parts per thousand; in coastal areas and close to the outflowing waters of the Amur it is fresher (to 31 parts per thousand). The salinity increases gradually with depth and at the bottom reaches 33.5 to 34.5 parts per

Fig. 11-1. Rocky shore of the Okhotsk Sea; in the distance are the Malmin Islands.

forming, and in May it begins to melt. The coastal rivers have opened, their water destroys the connection of the ice cover with the shores, and winds blow the ice into the open sea where the counterclockwise current carries it to the southwest—to the region of Uda Bay and the Shantar Islands. The great quantity of ice that accumulates here melts very slowly, mainly because of the cold water that rises from the depths, and it is not until the second half of June that the sea is clear of ice over most

thousand. In the eastern half of the sea, water flowing in from the Pacific Ocean raises the salinity.

In the south the water is more transparent than in the north, reaching a maximum of 58 feet. The color of the water ranges from bright blue in the south to dirty brown in the eastern part of Sakhalin Gulf.

The Sea of Okhotsk contains many Pacific salmon: great numbers of Siberian salmon and humpback salmon spawn in the streams of

Kamchatka. Such fish as herring, Japanese sardine, cod, navaga, and sea perch are also found in the sea. The fishing industry, concentrated along the western coast of Kamchatka, has been mechanized, a great fishing fleet has been created and many canneries constructed. Many crabs are also caught off the western coast of Kamchatka, and seal, white grampus, and whale are hunted there.

NORTHWESTERN COAST OF THE SEA OF OKHOTSK

The narrow coastal strip bordering the Sea of Okhotsk from the lower course of the Amur River near Lake Kizi to the city of Okhotsk, is the narrowest section of the Far East: here the water divide of the Pacific and Arctic oceans is extremely close to the Pacific shore. Its geologic history, tectonics, and climate are quite different from those of the Central Siberian Plateau on the west, and those of mountainous northeastern Siberia on the north.

The boundary between this region and the Amur-Primorski region, roughly, follows the Uda River to the point where the Maya enters it, passes along the northeastern foothills of the Yam-Alin, Dusse-Alin, and Badzhalski ranges, cuts across the northern Amur valley, and then through the northern extremity of Sikhote-Alin to the coast of Tatarski Strait just south of the town of De Kastri.

The northern part contains the complex Dzhugdzhur Range, which extends along the watershed between the Sea of Okhotsk and the basin of the Aldan and Lena rivers and forms an arc convex to the southeast. In the north the range extends to the upper source of the Maya River (a right tributary of the Aldan, not the river of the same name that enters the Uda), where it abuts against the Yudomo-Maya Plateau; in the southwest, at the source of the Maya River that is a left tributary of the Uda, it merges with the Stanovoi Range. The Dzhugdzhur is an independent orographic range that is sharply distinguished geologically and tectonically from the neighboring mountain ranges. It consists chiefly of magmatic rocks with very few sedimentary lower Paleozoic rocks, and originated as a result of extremely large fractures that trend northeast and demarcate the range on both sides. Both the composition of its rocks and its trend differ decidedly from those of the main part of the Stanovoi Range. The pre-Cambrian gneisses and crystalline schists so common in the Stanovoi Range are here encountered only in small patches, whereas Mesozoic extrusives—such as diabases and andesites—that are linked with the fractures occupy the entire northern part.

Throughout its whole extent the range has sharp alpine relief. The most prominent peaks reach an altitude of about 7,200 feet—4,000 to 6,000 feet above the bottoms of the valleys. The eastern slopes of the Dzhugdzhur are much steeper than the western ones. The westerly drainage of the water divide is distinctly marked by the more intensive intrenchment of its rivers. The slow upheaval of the range increased the erosion by the rivers, causing the formation of low saddles 300 to 500 feet above the sources of certain rivers; these have erased the boundaries between adjacent valleys and thus created almost continuous corridors.

West of the Dzhugdzhur Range and parallel to it is the Mikchangra Range, which has rather high (up to 3,300 feet) but smooth bare peaks, some composed of crystalline and some of sedimentary Lower Paleozoic rocks. Along the coast of the Sea of Okhotsk, dropping off directly to it, are the Pribrezhnaya mountains, some of whose peaks are more than 3,000 feet high: these are separated from the Dzhugdzhur by well-defined longitudinal valleys with rather large rivers—e.g., the Ulya.

Near the southern Okhotsk coast, along the lower course of the Amur, Amgun, and Uda, are broad flat basins among low hills. They contain Triassic and Jurassic deposits amid which are patches of granite, Mesozoic extrusives, and post-Tertiary basalt. Along the valleys of the Amur and Amgun, Tertiary deposits are widespread.

An alluvial plain extends from Komsomolsk to the Tugur Gulf: on it are two large lakes—Chukchagirski and Evoron. The plain, on which are low hills that rise no more than 330 feet above it, is a subsided block whose formation was accompanied by fractures and fissure eruptions of basalt. Well-expressed old lake terraces 60 to 160 feet above the edges of the plain indicate that large lake basins existed here at an earlier time. The gradual rise of the entire region caused these lakes to drain; their outlets cut through high water divides in the neighboring mountains, and captured the tributaries of other basins, thus creating the complex hydrographic network of the plain. The narrow V-shaped valleys of the upper mountain sections of the rivers have steep gradients. Where these streams leave the mountains and flow on to the plain, they widen; the gravel in their beds is replaced by fine sand and dusty loam; their currents slacken; they begin to meander and low islands and bottomland lakes appear along their courses.

The eastern half of the region along the southern coast is occupied by the northern sections of the lower Amur plain and the Sikhote-Alin range (see Chapter 10). The southern shore line is much more irregular than that of the northwestern Obhotsk coast; there are deeply penetrating gulfs, such as Ulbanski or Nikolay, and complicated peninsulas, such as Tugur.

Off the southern Okhotsk coast are the Shantar Islands. The group consists of twelve islands, of which the largest are Bolshoy Shantar (33 by 27 miles) and Feklistov. The islands are mountainous; some peaks rise to an altitude of about 2,000 feet, but have comparatively smooth outlines. The shores of the islands drop abruptly to the sea and the islands abound in rivers and springs.

Climate

The climate of the Okhotsk coast is much colder than the climate of other coastal regions at the same latitudes. For example, the average January temperature at the city of Okhotsk is −13°F, while at Leningrad, lying almost at the same latitude, it is 18.3°F. It is mainly the Sea of Okhotsk that makes the difference—its masses of ice, its cold water, its fog, and its constant winds. The influence of the wind extends as far inland as the lower course of the Bureya River, where north and northeast winds prevail in summer. The winds have a pronounced monsoon character. In winter they blow from the cold continent to the sea and in summer from the sea to the mainland: summer winds are weaker than those of winter and early spring. From October to March gusty winds, often stormy, blow from the northwest. At Okhotsk, during this period, north and northwest winds with an average velocity of about 16.5 feet per second blow 83 per cent of the time, only 5 per cent is calm; at Nikolayevsk the velocity of the wind decreases to 12.5 feet per second, and the percentage of time during which it blows to 64—the percentage of calms increases to 14 per cent. The Okhotsk region of high pressure has a strong influence in summer. From May to August southeast marine winds with a velocity of 10 to 11.5 feet per second blow 50 to 52 per cent of the time, but it is often calm.

The temperature of the air, both on the shores and above the sea itself, is affected by the wind. In the long, narrow coastal strip the annual average ranges from 26.5° to 21.2°F, the summer average from 58.8° to 57.2°F, and that of winter from −3.8° to 5.3°F. The temperatures on points of land that extend into the sea vary with the extent of protrusion, the direction of the shore line, the closeness of the mountains. For example, Point Prange, a cape that juts into the sea 25 miles from Nikolayevsk, is considerably warmer than the latter in autumn and in the first half of winter (the January average is eight degrees higher) and is colder in summer (the July average is two degrees lower). In winter, winds blowing from the super-chilled mainland bring cold air to the sea and the coast. Winters are coldest at Okhotsk (January average —13°F) and warmest at Ayan (—4°F). Even so, the weather at Okhotsk is warmer than it is on the other side of the Dzhugdzhur Range (at Ust-Maya, at the same latitude but 300 miles inland, the January average is —41.3°F). In the summer the wind blowing from the still unwarmed water of the sea lowers the temperature on the coast. The temperature of the warmest month at Okhotsk is 54.8°F (August), and at Ust-Maya it is 66°F (July).

The coast of the Sea of Okhotsk has a greater annual precipitation than any other part of northern Asia. In general, precipitation increases to the south: at Okhotsk, 11.3 inches; at Nikolayevsk, 18.8 inches. The exceptional precipitation at Ayan (35.4 inches) results from its exposure to the warm, moist sea winds that rush through Tatarski Strait and meet the high mountain range near the shore. Okhotsk lies on a coastal plain, several miles from the closest mountain range. Sharp annual variations in the amount of precipitation are typical: at Nikolayevsk, with an annual average of 17.8 inches, one year may have as much as 28 inches, another only 7.8 inches. This is characteristic of a monsoon climate.

Most of the precipitation takes place in summer and early autumn: 87 per cent at Okhotsk and 91 per cent at Ayan. August has the most precipitation; February and March the least: August, the most days with precipitation; January, the fewest. Snow accounts for 14 per cent of the annual precipitation at Ayan and 18 per cent at Okhotsk. Seasonal variation in precipitation decreases from north to south (in percentages):

SEASON	OKHOTSK	NIKOLAYEVSK
Winter	3	11
Spring	12	18
Summer	57	38
Autumn	28	33

Cloudiness has a regular annual trend: low in winter, increasing in spring and summer until the maximum is reached in July, then decreasing through autumn and winter. Seasonal distribution of cloudiness is more regular in the south (in percent possible in each season):

SEASON	OKHOTSK	NIKOLAYEVSK
Winter	37	42
Spring	58	56
Summer	76	60
Autumn	48	55

The climate of the coast is milder than that of adjacent areas farther inland—winter is warmer and summer is cooler—maximum temperatures do not exceed 86°F, but minimums may reach —52°F, and absolute amplitudes 138°F. Winter on the coast begins in the middle of October; there is little snowfall, relative humidity is extremely low (in January only 65 per cent), there is little cloudiness, and many clear days. Spring begins at the end of April, but early morning frosts continue through May.

Precipitation in spring is very light. Plants begin to grow with the disappearance of the snow cover at the end of May or the beginning of June. The accumulation of ice at Uda Bay retards the onset of spring on the Shantar Islands. In June and July, the thermic difference between the warm interior of the continent and the cold sea is great, and the negative influence of the sea is strongly manifested on the coast. Summer is cool, damp, and cloudy, and has very few clear days (in July 1 to 4); relative humidity is high (85 per cent), exceeding that in the summer months at Colchis on the Black Sea; there are many overcast days during which the dense fog settles like fine rain. Autumn on the coast is warmer and moister than spring; it is sunny and relatively long so that flowers may blossom until late in September. Early in October the weather becomes cooler. The first snow falls in the mountains in September and in the valleys in Octo-

creeping among the rocks. The thickets also contain scrub birch (*Betula middendorffii*), alder (*Alnus fruticosa*), golden rhododendron (*Rhododendron crysanthum*) and small red rhododendron (*R. redowskianum*).

Many species of high-altitude tundra plants grow on bald mountains. Here are small sedge bogs and large patches of lichens, the latter serving as pastures for deer. Higher, where it is often cloudy and misty, are sphagnum bogs. In hollows on steep slopes, where there is no swamping and fine soil can accumulate, many interesting plants appear: alpine sweet grass (*Hierochloe alpina*), snow cinquefoil (*Potentilla nivea*), *Hedysarum obscurum,* anemone (*Anemone narcissiflora*), and Siberian patrinia (*Patrinia sibirica*).

The fauna of the Okhotsk coast comprises not only such Okhotsk species as Siberian spruce grouse (*Falcipennis falcipennis*) but also southern Manchurian species such as Japanese waxwing (*Bombycilla japonica*). In the Okhotsk forests live musk deer, elk, and reindeer, but no racoon-dogs, wild sheep (*Ovis nivicola*) live in the mountains. The Shantar Islands constitute a sable reservation, and there the squirrel, the sable's chief food, cannot be hunted by man. Of the other valuable fur-bearing animals, otter, fox, and wolverine are common.

SAKHALIN

Sakhalin is a narrow island, almost 600 miles long, separated from the mainland by Tatarski Strait—which, where it narrows to 4 miles opposite Cape Lazareva is called Nevelskogo Strait and from Hokkaido by La Perouse Strait.[1] Its longitudinal coasts are parallel, but the western half of the island extends farther south than the eastern; this southern extension is called the Notoro Peninsula: the eastern half extends farther north to form Shmidt Peninsula; its southern end is Cape Terpeniya. The northern and southern coasts are more broken than the parallel eastern and western coasts; on the north coast are Baikal and Pronge bays and on the south, Aniva and Terpeniya bays. The island is situated between 54°25′ (Cape Yelizaveta) and 45°54′ north latitudes (Cape Krilon), that is, approximately between the latitudes of Tula and Odessa in the European USSR. The area of Sakhalin is 48,000 square miles.

The relief of Sakhalin is somewhat diversified. The highest mountain peaks are in the central part of the island. From them the two main ranges of Sakhalin extend north and south along both coasts. Toward the north the ranges gradually lower, break up into a series of parallel ridges, and withdraw from the shores, leaving narrow lowland strips along the coasts.

The chief water divide between the basins of the Sea of Okhotsk and Tatarski Strait is the Western Sakhalin Range, which consists of several parallel ridges separated by longitudinal valleys; the eastern ridges extend farther north than the western ones. The coastal ridge has a narrow crest with sharp peaks, steep slopes, and gorge-like river valleys; the central ridge is more massive, and has gentler slopes and broader river valleys. The highest peak in the range—Mount Sikoku-Yama—is 4,506 feet high. The Western Range is formed primarily of Cretaceous and Tertiary deposits with intrusions of gabbro-diorites and dikes and veins of basalts and andesites.

The Eastern Sakhalin Range, which is higher than the western, consists of three mountain chains that parallel the eastern coast of the island. The central chain has the highest peaks —Mount Lopatina (5,514 feet) and Mount Nevelskoy (6,604 feet), the highest point on Sakhalin. To the north, the Eastern Range drops gradually and merges with the lowland. It is composed of metamorphic and sedimentary rocks that form isoclinal folds of northwest and northeast strike; with these are

---

[1] Recently a ship captain reported that a causeway had been constructed across Nevelskogo Strait.

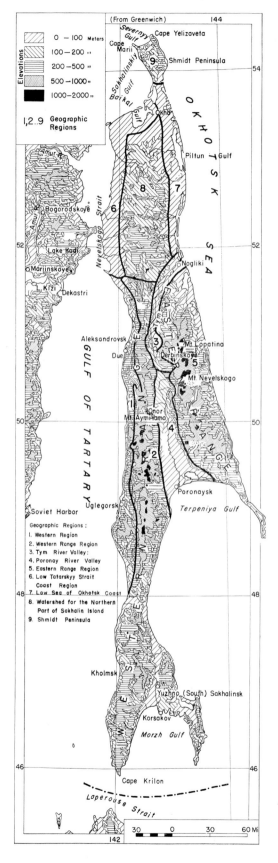

Elevations

	0 — 100 Meters
	100 — 200 "
	200 — 500 "
	500 — 1000 "
	1000 — 2000 "

1,2..9 Geographic Regions

Geographic Regions:
1. Western Region
2. Western Range Region
3. Tym River Valley
4. Poronay River Valley
5. Eastern Range Region
6. Low Tatarskyy Strait Coast Region
7. Low Sea of Okhotsk Coast
8. Watershed for the Northern Part of Sakhalin Island
9. Shmidt Peninsula

mixed much igneous rock. Metamorphic schists, the most solid and resistant to erosion, constitute the highest points of the range. In the south the mountains drop sharply to the coast and the shores of the many bays and inlets are rocky and steep.

Shmidt Peninsula, the northern tip of Sakhalin, has the same structure as the two ranges, but is not so high (2,300 feet). The coasts of the peninsula drop off abruptly into the sea. Cape Marii and Cape Yelizavety are the northernmost extremities of the island.

The general trend of the lowlands follows that of the mountain chains. In the central part of Sakhalin, between the Western and Eastern Ranges, at an altitude of not more than 500 feet, a long narrow depression from 3 to 18 miles wide that is evidently of fault origin runs from north to south. In it are the Tym River, which flows north, and the Poronay River, which flows south. Their sources are separated from one another by a low watershed; this does not destroy the continuity of the depression, which narrows at this point and has the appearance of a deep valley. Along the course of the Tym River the depression is clearly demarcated from the steeply descending foothills. Northward the depression turns toward the eastern coast and the Tym turns with it, entering the sea at Nogliki. North of the Tym's mouth the depression follows the coast, gradually widens, and becomes the predominating geomorphologic element in the north of the island. As the coastal ranges disappear, the depression takes over their function as a watershed. The floor of the depression consists of marine Tertiary sediments and aluvial Quaternary deposits. The Poronay River flows into Terpeniya Bay.

The largest of the coastal lowlands is that on the western coast. Here the beach abuts against a scarp six to sixteen feet high, beyond which a series of marine terraces rise to heights ranging from 500 to 900 feet. The lowland is composed of post-Tertiary marine gravel and sand interbedded with thin layers of clay. North of Aleksandrovsk the ranges move inland and the

Map 11-II. Relief of Sakhalin Island.

mountainous and inaccessible shores of the south are replaced by low beaches, many of them covered with dunes. The west coast has no good harbors: at the only port at which large vessels call—Aleksandrovsk—they are forced to load and discharge cargo in an exposed roadstead.

The lowland on the northern part of the east coast of Sakhalin is less extensive than that on the west. The eastern coast, as viewed from the sea, has an extremely smooth curved shore line, because of the many narrow alluvial sandy spits that parallel the shore. These spits mask the intensive irregularity of the steep inner shores of the numerous bays.

Between the spits and the shore are vast lagoons, similar to those along the Baltic Sea. These lagoons provide convenient channels of communication. Large ships can enter some of them, thus avoiding the dangers of navigation on the stormy Sea of Okhotsk. Because of the abundant inflow of river water, the water in the lagoons is fresh—only near entrances to the open sea is it salty, and then only for a short time after high tide. The lagoons are formed by two opposing movements of water—that of the inflowing river current and that of the ocean waves—which, where they meet, cause the formation of submarine bars that gradually build up into coastal embankments. This process often leads to the closing of river mouths after storms and to the locking of bays and their conversion into coastal lakes. The rectilinear outlines of the shore, the coastal lagoons, the lakes, and also the existence of marine terraces on the west coast indicate a recent upheaval of the island.

The extremely complex modeling of the relief of Sakhalin is a result of the activity of running water. The pattern of the hydrographic network and the regularity of its branching distinctly reflect the north-south trend of the chief morphologic elements. Many of the rivers—for example, the Poronay—are set in longitudinal valleys. Nonetheless, although lateral valleys are small, there are more of them. Near their sources the rivers have exceedingly gentle currents, where they break through

the coastal ridges their currents are swift; beyond the ridges they are even and gentle. The upper stretches of some rivers—the Tym, for example—flow along longitudinal valleys, but lower down the river may turn, follow a lateral valley or cut through either the eastern or western ridges and emerge on the lowland coast.

Cretaceous and Tertiary deposits play the chief role in the structure of the island, with the exception of the southern part of the Eastern Range, which is Paleozoic. The thick Cretaceous deposits consist of conglomerates, sandstones, and clay shales. They form large asymmetrical folds of a north-northeast strike, broken by a multitude of faults, and many are several hundred yards long. Tertiary deposits are found in the Western Range and the northern part of the Eastern Range, and apparently fill the bottoms of longitudinal river valleys, where they are covered by Quaternary deposits. Formed into folds, they are broken by both longitudinal and transverse faults. These dislocations occurred at the end of the Tertiary period, before the post-Tertiary marine transgression, the sediments of which are almost horizontal. The simple outlines of the western and eastern coasts of the island are a result of similar faulting that was accompanied by volcanic outpourings. During the post-Tertiary transgression, Sakhalin was joined to the mainland in the region of Nevelskogo Strait, and this greatly affected the development of the flora and fauna of the island. Almost all the geologic strata of Sakhalin, with the exception of the Paleozoic of the Eastern Range, are carboniferous. The coal in the numerous seams of working thickness, which lie beneath Cretaceous and Tertiary deposits, varies from bituminous coal to lignite and has a high heat value. The petroleum deposits on the eastern coast of the island —of which the best known are those near Okha—are found in Tertiary strata.

Climate

The climate of Sakhalin is severe. Although its northern tip lies at the latitude of Tula and its southern end at the latitude of Odessa, winter here is even colder than on the shores of the White Sea. Only the southwestern part of Sakhalin has a milder climate. Here it approximates that of northern Japan because of the warmth brought by one of the branches of the Tsushima Current. The meridional position of the island and the protected central Tym-Poronay Valley diversify still more the climate of the island. The difference between northern and southern temperatures is great in winter, although summer temperatures are rather uniform. The average for the coldest month varies from −9.3°F in the Tym River Valley (Kirovskoye) to 17.5°F on the southern tip of the island (Cape Krilon), but summer temperatures vary only from 59°F at Kirovskoye to 62.8°F at Cape Krilon: the lowest recorded temperature in the north is −54°F, in the south, −23.2°F. The length of the growing season increases toward the south; from 97 days in the north (Okha) to 146 days in the central valley (Kirovskoye) and to 167 days in the south (Korsakov).

In winter the central valley is much colder than the coastal lowlands, which are exposed to cold sea winds and constant fogs. Thus, the average January temperature on the west coast is −2°F and in the central valley −10°F. A short distance inland, under the shelter of the mountains, winter is noticeably colder than on the coast. Zhonkiyerski lighthouse has a January average of 2°F, but the average at Aleksandrovsk, just half a mile away, across a range of hills, is −2°F. In the central valley, protected by mountains from the sea winds, the climate has distinct features of continentality; July heat reaches 89.8°F and winter cold −54°F. On a March day, before dawn, the temperature was −27°F—by noon the snow had melted. The valley has less wind than the coasts, and fogs are fewer and less intense.

The west and east coasts of Sakhalin are under the influence of seas of different heat regimes. From the southwest, the warm water of one of the branches of the Tsushima Current approaches the west coast, but the eastern and northern parts of the island are washed by the cold water of the Sea of Okhotsk. The yearly precipitation on the west coast is 24 to 32 inches, half of which is snow. It rains very frequently; in July and August there is hardly a day without rain, and the skies are usually filled with dense clouds. The central valley has 22 to 30 inches of precipitation: the maximum in September and the minimum in February. Average annual relative humidity varies from 77 to 89 per cent. In north Sakhalin the mountain ranges gradually become a chain of low hills, and the entire northern part of the island is exposed to the cold winds from the sea.

Winter on Sakhalin is harsh and cold, and the prevailing north wind brings frequent snowstorms. Snow accounts for more than one-third of the annual precipitation. Winter lasts five to six months, and in the north, seven months. March is a winter month, with an average temperature of 12°F and an abundance of snowstorms. Snow covers the ground not less than 200 days out of each year. Strong winds sweep the snow into low spots and river valleys, where enormous snow drifts that could completely cover dwellings accumulate. On most of the island, spring is long and cold: snow remains on the ground and frosts are common until the first half of June. Summer lasts two to two and a half months. Only July and August are frost-free, although the temperature drops as low as 39°F during the night. There are light but comparatively frequent rains in summer. On the southwestern coast and in the central valley, however, summer is at its height by the beginning of June, and grass grows vigorously on the fertile alluvial soil. On the eastern and northern coasts, along which ice floes still float on the sea, the snow cover lasts until July and only sparse vegetation of a bog type can grow on the frozen soil. Autumn, lasting two months, is warmer and rainier than spring. Early-morning frosts begin in September.

In general, the climate is unfavorable for agriculture: the late spring retards the growth of grain, and it ripens and is ready to harvest in the period of summer and autumn rains. Agriculture is possible up to 52° north latitude in the central valley and on the southwest coast, where spring rye and wheat, oats, potatoes and cucumbers are raised. The abundance of moisture provides outstanding pastures, so that animal husbandry plays a large part in farming.

The rivers of Sakhalin are fed largely by precipitation, and usually have three periods of high water each year. From October to April, they are covered by ice, but in spring they rise quickly as the thick snow cover in the valleys melts. Somewhat later, the mountain snow begins to thaw, and the water level rises again, often much higher than the first time. Finally, at the end of July or in August, the monsoon rains bring a third period of high water. In any of these flood periods, the water may rise more than 13 feet above the average mid-summer level, and cover crops and plowed fields on first terrace (6 to 8 feet high). Water that backs up behind jams of logs or ice may rise even higher. The trees covering the slopes are important in the regime of the rivers, and denudation of mountain slopes by clearcutting of the centuries-old coniferous forests may cause catastrophic floods. The dense spruce groves on the slopes not only prevent rapid runoff but also keep snow from blowing off into valleys and slows its melting; thus on Sakhalin the forest has an especially important protective significance and should be guarded with great care.

Flora and Fauna

The latitudinal position of Sakhalin is the same as that of the wooded-steppe zone of the European USSR, but its climate and vegetation are those of a more northerly zone—that of taiga and mossy bogs. Its flora consists for the most part of Okhotsk-Kamchatka species, but comprises also many Kurile, Japanese, and Manchurian plants. In the southwest it resembles that of northern Japan, but northward the number of Japanese-Manchurian species gradually diminishes and they are replaced by northern, East Siberian, and Kamchatka plants.

Sakhalin soil is mainly of podzolic and bog types. On the mountain slopes the products of weathering become podzolic soil, although the dissected relief and the abundance of coarse rubbly material makes even clayey soil porous, and this greatly retards podzol formation. Peat-bog soil is widespread in the central and northern parts of the island, where it has developed on Quaternary deposits poor in mineral salts. In bottomlands and on the first terraces of river valleys recent alluvial soil is found.

The complex relief, which causes the climate and soil to vary from place to place, greatly complicates the distribution of vegetation. Vertical zonality here is analogous to that of the Okhotsk coast. The central valley is very swampy because of its heavy precipitation, the low rate of evaporation in its cool climate, the abundance of clay just beneath the soil, and the flatness of its bottom and its slight gradient to the sea (in 180 miles, from the highest part of the Tym Valley to the river's mouth, it drops only 410 feet). Most of the old broad valley of the Poronay consists of a mossy bog of peat-bog soil up to six feet thick, on which scattered sickly larch trees grow. Only on sandy ridges are there fairly thick larch forests with an admixture of birch and a ground cover of reindeer moss (*Cladonia rangiferina*).

In the Tym Valley alluvial soil covers the bottomland and first terrace and muddy-bog and podzolic soil has developed on the old river terraces and low slopes. Beneath the soft argillaceous alluvium lies a layer of sandy loam and coarse river sand, which in turn is underlain by gravel. These underlying layers of sand and gravel, on the one hand, provide natural drainage, and on the other, allow the circulation of water to feed the roots of plants. The fine-grained structure of this soil guarantees easy access of air to roots. The soil contains from 6 to 8 per cent humus, and along the river bank its richness has been increased by the decomposition of the bodies of salmon that enter the river to spawn and then die. Cast up on the banks, they are covered by silt, and add phosphorous and nitrogen to the soil. Alluvial soil near the river is inundated and intensely eroded in flood periods.

In the deciduous forests of the southern part of Sakhalin are many Japanese-Manchurian trees: yellow maple (*Acer ukurunduense*), Manchurian ash (*Fraxinus mandshurica*), Mongolian oak tree (*Phellodendron amurense*), Manchurian oak (*Quercus mongolica*), and elm (*Ulmus laciniata*) which grows also in the north. In the undergrowth are found *Evonymus sachalinensis,* holly (*Ilex rugosa*), and Chinese magnolia vine (*Schizandra chinensis*). In these forests, however, many typical Amur plants, such as bush clover (*Lespedeza bicolor*), are missing. On bottomland, another kind of deciduous forest covers the rich alluvial soil in places protected from the wind. Thick groves containing various species of willow border the rivers; in them the tall (up to 80 feet) well-shaped trunks of Korean willow or chosenia (*Chosenia macrolepis*) are especially prominent, and there are also many huge poplars (*Populus maximowiczi*) approximately 20 feet in circumference. Beneath the trees is a dense herbaceous undergrowth that comprises plants that attain the most extravagant growth of any on Sakhalin. Ferns (*Struthiopteris filicastrum*) the height of a man alternate with clumps of butterbur (*Petasites japonicus*) that may grow 8 feet high—the solid green crown of the enormous leaves of this plant is striking. In places are groups of huge, tall (up to 9 feet) cacalia (*Cacalia hastata*), gigantic nettles, enormous groundsel (*Senecio cannabifolius*), meadow-sweet (*Filipendula kamschatica*) and enormous umbellates: *Angelophyllium ursinum* and cow parsnip (*Heracleum barbatum*). On moist places bog beach grass and reed grass grow extremely high. Farther from the river, in unflooded places, grows a mixed forest of poplar, elm, ash, spruce, and fir, with an undergrowth of alder, willow, and bird-cherry. After felling or fire, these trees are usually replaced by birch and aspen.

Larch is widespread in the river valleys. It covers old riverside dunes with their dry ground, swamped depressions, and poor soil. Because its fine seeds are carried great distances by the wind and its very rapid early growth permits it to outstrip even the tall Sakhalin grasses, larch conquers grassy expanses and the burned-over sites of former spruce forests. In the course of time, spruce begins to grow beneath the larch and sooner or later crowds it out. However, spruce disappears very quickly if the soil becomes swampy. Almost pure single formation larch forests with a very thick grass-stand grow on the muddy-boggy soil of river terraces underlain by gravel. The thick trunks, which have few lower branches, yield long straight logs of high-quality grained wood. On well-drained argillaceous soil of river terraces, there are sparse growths of gigantic old larches, under which is a dense tier of healthy spruce admixed with Sakhalin fir.

The sea coasts of Sakhalin with their turfy expanses, numerous small shallow lakes, and permafrost at a depth of 20 inches, have a sparse bog vegetation made up of wild rosemary, cranberry, cloudberry, cotton grass, and sedge, that resembles that of high-altitude tundra; in the north, the vegetation is like that of the subarctic. Here, the luxuriant high grasses of the Tym Valley are lacking and trees and shrubs are much smaller. The soil cover consists mainly of poor podzolic and bog soil. The valleys are filled with huge, cold, peat bogs, with a cover of sphagnum mosses 6 to 9 feet thick. Above this cover grow not only the ordinary plants of peat bogs, but also many gnarled and twisted larches with wide spreading crowns from which hang thick strands of lichens. These larches, only 30 feet tall but with sound wood are as much as 400 years old and grow in narrow belts along the deep streams of rust-colored water that flow quietly through the bogs. Forests of ordinary larch trees cover many of the water divides; beneath them is a solid cover of reindeer moss (*Cladonia rangiferina*) on sand and sandy-loam podzolic soil. Many plants found here are characteristic of northern Siberia—meadow grass (*Poa arctica*), kinni-kinic (*Arctostaphylos uva-ursi*), and others—but Japanese-Manchurian plants are absent.

In contrast to the lowlands, the mountain slopes are covered with a continuous spruce-fir taiga of Yeddo spruce (*Picea jezoensis*) and the indigenous Sakhalin fir (*Abies sachalinensis*).

The soil here is rocky or rubbly, well-drained, and slightly podzolic. Its upper layer is mellow, gray, and clayey, rich in humus, and two to five inches thick; it is underlain by coarse rock. Trees grow best on the leeward slopes of the Western Range, where they are sheltered from the sea winds, and there is a comparatively large amount of heat, heavy precipitation, and soil rich in mineral salts that is well-drained and aerated. Conditions on the eastern side of the Western Range and in the Eastern Range are not so favorable for forest growth.

In the upper tier of Sakhalin forests spruce is found almost exclusively; in the lower, fir predominates. The spruce yields wood that can be used in construction although it is somewhat soft and is susceptible to decay because of its high moisture content. Fir dies before it attains full growth, and consequently there are a great number of dead trees in the taiga—standing or fallen—which serve as the dwelling place of innumerable wood-borers, such as cerambycidae or long-horned beetles, and other insects. A small fire can easily reach disastrous proportions and only a heavy rain can put it out. These forests resemble the spruce forests of northern Europe: the same tall trees with straight limbless trunks, the same dampness and shade, the same resinous odor, the same cover of glistening mosses. A younger generation of spruce and fir may spring up in places where fir is not especially dense. After a destructive fire, the first growth consists of willow herb (fireweed), whose flowers give the countryside a solid rose tone; later the burn becomes a birch grove with an admixture of aspen.

Higher in the mountains, more and more rock birch (*Betula ermani*) is added to spruce and fir, so that summits and passes are covered with spruce-birch forests. In the Western Range, Sakhalin bamboo (*Sasa kurilensis*)—a northern relative of the bamboos of Japan and tropical Asia—is found in the high-elevation rock birch forests. This bamboo forms dense thickets, may reach five feet in height, and is hard to cut because of its unusually strong, slippery, and resilient trunks. On the highest ranges or on slopes exposed to the constant cold winds from the Sea of Okhotsk, are impenetrable thickets of dwarf stone pine (*Pinus pumila*) similar to the thickets below the bald peaks of Eastern Siberia. Bear and sable, who eat pine nuts, find both shelter and abundant food here. Above the belt of dwarf stone pine, on the bald peaks, are thickets of yellow rhododendron (*Rhododendron chrysanthum*).

The fauna of Sakhalin, like the flora, consists of a mixture of Okhotsk and Siberian species: among the mammals one may encounter here bear, wolverine, wolf, fox, lynx, sable, chipmunk, squirrel, flying squirrel, rabbit, musk deer, and reindeer. The latter is represented by a special Okhotsk-Kamchatka form *Rangifer tarandus setoni* and here reaches the extreme southern limit of its distribution (46° north latitude). There is not a single animal of southern origin on Sakhalin: elk, roe deer, Manchurian deer, badger, and mountain snow sheep are absent here.

Among the birds, side by side with such typical Okhotsk species as Siberian spruce grouse are many common Siberian species of nutcrackers, tomtits, small and varicolored woodpeckers, owls, and hawks. In addition, there are at least fifteen Himalayan and Chinese species in the southern part of the island, among them Japanese fly-catcher (*Muscicapa narcissina*); Sakhalin thrush (*Turdus sibiricus*), which lives on Sakhalin and in Japan but winters in Southeastern Asia; and Japanese long-beaked bullfinch (*Uragus sibiricus sanguinolentus*), which lives on Sakhalin, in Japan, and on the Kurile Islands. Living in the tundra-like areas of northern Sakhalin are Sakhalin white ptarmigan (*Lagopus lagopus okactai*) and speckled pipit (*Anthus hodgsoni inopinatus*). On the rocky coasts of the Okhotsk Sea are countless marine birds: guillemot, noddy, and many others. On the island are the viviparious lizard (*Lacerta vivipara*), and the Amur frog (*Rana amurensis*), which lives in hilly bogs.

Many Siberian salmon and humpback salmon spawn in Sakhalin's rivers. Bering mussels and Sakhalin pearl oysters (*Margaritana sachalinensis*) are also found in the rivers of Sakhalin Island.

CHAPTER 12

Kamchatka-Kurile Volcanic Region

KAMCHATKA

Kamchatka is a large peninsula in northeastern Asia that extends approximately 720 miles from north to south. In shape it resembles the flint tip of a Stone Age spear. Its northern end lies at the same latitude as Leningrad, its southern end at that of Kiev. In the north, at about 60° north latitude, near the southern end of Parapolskiy Valley, Kamchatka is joined to the mainland by an isthmus 60 miles wide. At its southern end, 51° north latitude, it tapers off into the lowland Cape Lopatka, which is separated from Shumshu Island, the first island of the Kurile chain, by the First Kurile strait. Most of Kamchatka is mountainous. The highest mountains lie in the broad central part of the peninsula, where it is 290 miles wide; to the north and south the altitude decreases gradually. Kamchatka, together with the Kurile Islands, is the only part of the USSR where there are active volcanoes at the present time. Administratively Kamchatka Peninsula is the southern part of Kamchatka oblast, Khaborovsk Territory.

Relief and Morphologic Regions

There are few data on the tectonics of Kamchatka. The predominating trend of all its geologic formations is north-northeast or northeast. The more recent the rock strata the less it is folded or metamorphosed. Paleozoic rocks (mica schist, gneisses, metamorphosed extrusives, phyllite) usually compose the cores of the anticlinal structures, whose limbs are complicated by inclined, horizontal, or overturned folds. All Paleozoic rocks are highly dislocated. The Tertiary deposits (continental Oligocene, marine and volcanic Miocene, continental Pliocene) are dislocated even less. They are found chiefly on the coasts of the peninsula and are not a part of the structure of the folded ranges, but only lean against them, lying monoclinally, or are gathered in anticlinal and synclinal folds of a north-south strike. Quarternary formations (post-Pliocene marine, river, and glacial deposits) are not folded. The steep and abruptly rising slopes of the Kamchatka ranges indicate the existence of large faults. The largest and probably the oldest is the one that passes through the upper course of the Bystraya River, along the valleys of the Kamchatka and Yelovka rivers, and continues northward along the bottom of Litke Strait between Karaginski Island and the Kamchatka coast. Parallel to this is another fault, along which all the volcanoes of the east coast and the southern end of the peninsula are concentrated. Post-Tertiary faults are shorter and have a different strike than the older ones—they trend northwest. Along these faults are volcanoes and groups of hot springs, and they sometimes form the outlines of the sea coast—for example, the steep rocky shore west of Cape Shipunski. Thus, on Kamchatka, folds created anticlinal ranges, and faults the fault-block inner structure of the peninsula and the large scale overthrusts that displaced the mountains to the Pacific Ocean side. There is some recent folding combined with faults that intersect lava deposits.

Orographically, Kamchatka may be roughly divided into three zones: the central ranges, the west coast, and the east coast. The two parallel central ranges of Kamchatka are tectonically independent folds that begin in the south, approximately on a line from Petropavlovsk to Ust-Bolsheretsk, and extend northward to Parapolskiy Valley. The valley between these ranges contains the Kamchatka River and its left tributary the Yelovka. A third independent fold along the eastern coast of the peninsula has been strongly dissected and eroded and only remnants have survived: the eastern capes, low, hilly plateaus up to 1,320 feet high; coastal reefs; and submarine crags.

The Western Range of the central mountains extends along the axis of the peninsula in an unbroken chain consisting of separate ridges, mountain groups, and isolated peaks. In the southern part, even the passes are rather high —2,900 to 3,900 feet. The highest peak, the extinct volcano Ichinskaya, is 11,834 feet high. The Western Range is asymmetrical. Its western foothills are 6 to 12 miles wide and slope gently to a scarp that divides them from the lowland of the west coast of the peninsula; its eastern slope is 3 to 4 miles wide, dropping off steeply into the Kamchatka River valley. The range is basically an anticline whose crest forms the mountain passes. It is composed of crystalline schists and gneisses of the Paleozoic that are highly crumpled and do not erode readily; intrusions of granites are associated with them. These rocks are bordered by dark sandstones, shales, and masses of green volcanic rock that lie conformably and are evidently Mesozoic.

In the central part of the range, in the region of recent volcanism, great areas of andesites, alternate with more basic basalts. In places the range consists of a series of sharp-ribbed peaks, in others of rounded and cupola-shaped heights, and, farther north, of a chain of mesas.

In the morphology of the central part, traces of old volcanic cones (Ichinskaya), old craters, and the ruins of highly eroded volcanoes are clearly discernible. Past glaciation is indicated by dead glacial cirques and hanging glacial troughs, which have been somewhat altered by subsequent erosion. The rivers flowing from the slopes of the Western Range begin in glacial lakes and snowfilled cirques and have broad, well developed valleys with many terraces, even within one or two miles of a mountain pass. To the north, the range widens out on both sides and produces a network of spurs that extend laterally from its axis. Where the peninsula narrows it splits into many small ridges, none higher than 3,000 feet, then follows the western coast until it dies out on the tundra of Parapolskiy Valley.

The Eastern Range of the central mountains, unlike the Western Range, is broken up into three separate chains of mountains that stretch north-northeast one after another. Like the Western Range the Eastern Range is asymmetrical, and the slopes that drop off toward the Kamchatka River Valley are narrower and steeper than those facing the coast. Spurs of the Eastern Range extend close to the shores of the Pacific along a raised volcanic plateau that is an independent morphological unit.

The southern end of the Eastern Range is a dissected picturesque mountain chain, Ganalski Vostryaki, composed of a series of almost sheer crests and peaks, the highest of which is 6,800 feet. Where the western slope of the chain borders the Bystraya River Valley, it is smooth, high, and steep, devoid of dissected foothills. Every three or four miles this slope is cut by the deep narrow latitudinal valleys of the left tributaries of the Bystraya, none of them more than five miles long. There are many remarkably beautiful mammoth cirques in the chain, especially along the steep western slope: in them are accumulations of snow which do not melt during the summer, but form small firm fields and miniature glaciers. The height and narrowness of the range and the steepness of its western slopes are a result of its purely tectonic origin. The Ganalski Vostryaki chain becomes lower and dwindles to nothing south of the extinct Kamchatsk Vershina volcano (7,319 feet). North of the right source of the Kamchatka River the Valaginski chain begins; it is similar to Ganalski Vostryaki in structure, having a great number of cirques and the same steep, high western slope devoid of foothills, although its eastern slope has well-expressed foothills of Tertiary deposits. The deep valleys of the rivers are in many places dammed with enormous blocks of rock. Where the range is

formed of easily weathered Mesozoic rocks it has smoother surfaces. Indicative of its tectonic origin, are its sharp, steep, rectilinear western slope, and an uplifted lava mantle that lies farther east on a lower volcanic plateau. The most northerly chain of the Eastern Range is Kumroch, also of northeast trend, which begins with Mount Shish (7,975 feet) and farther north crosses the lower course of the Kamchatka River.

The Central Kamchatka Valley is pressed between the Central Range on the west and Valaginski and Kumroch ranges on the east. The width of the valley, which contains the Kamchatka River and its left tributary, the Yelovka, varies greatly: in the south where it is constricted by the ranges, it is from one to two

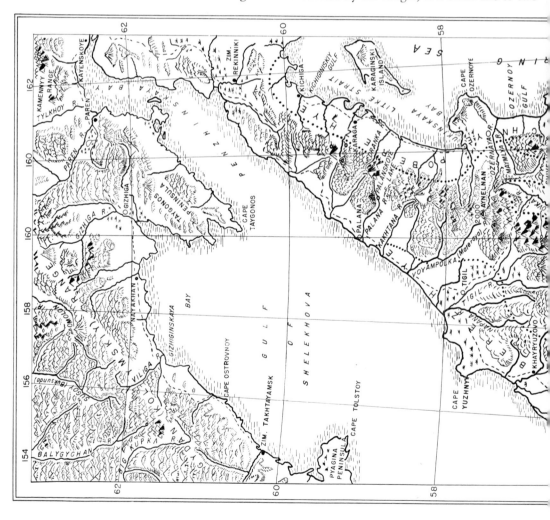

and a half miles wide, but to the north it rapidly widens to thirty miles. On both west and east, the borders of the valley are sharply demarcated by the steep slopes of the adjacent ranges. The almost level bottom of the valley, inclined toward the north, is covered with alluvium, and there are two terraces, the upper one dryer, more dissected, and rolling. The loose soil of the high river banks show profiles of bedded alluvium in which bones of the mammoth are often found. The Central Kamchatka Valley is more suitable for agriculture than any other part of the peninsula.

The Ganalski tundra, which constitutes a small independent geographic district with maximum altitudes of about 1,700 feet, is the water divide between the basins of the Kamchatka and Bystraya rivers. Moraine and glacial lakes on this plateau-like, dry, and hillocky tundra indicate past glaciation. It is traversed by the dry, rocky, meandering channels of small streams along which are old rubbly and gravelly alluvial deposits.

The west coast lowland extends in a broad (43 miles wide in the central part) strip along the eastern shore of the Sea of Okhotsk that gradually narrows and almost disappears in both the northern and southern parts of the peninsula; it rises gently from the seacoast to the foot of the Central Range. For its entire length, the shoreline is smooth and slightly wavy. A sloping beach of sand and gravel borders the sea, and this in turn is bordered by a strip of sand 300 to 650 feet wide and 10 to 15

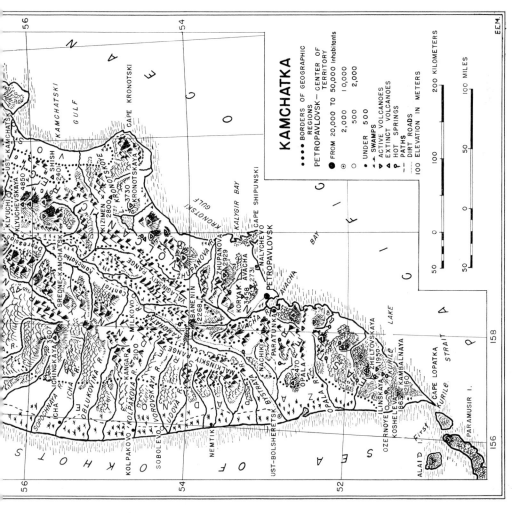

Map 12-I.   Relief of Kamchatka.

feet high, directly inside which is a chain of narrow lagoons. In some years this sandy strip grows, hampering the discharge of water from within the peninsula; in others it disintegrates or is broken through by rivers. Sand and clay deposits of the coastal strip are covered by a layer of peat thick enough to be of commercial value. Large amounts of it are destroyed by the sea during storms and high tides, and by rivers during floods. Farther inland the landscape presents a monotonous picture: vast expanses of lowland covered with mossy bogs alternate with low (65 to 100 feet), gentle, latitudinal watershed ridges on which there are groves of rock birch. Only in the north do small spurs of the Central Range extend toward the coast —on these the dry tundra serves as good pasture for deer.

The rivers of the west coast that rise in the mountains are shallow and swift, with clear water, but there are streams with dark-brown water that drain the moss bogs of the coastal zone. Near their estuaries, the rivers form labyrinths of channels, old river beds, and lakes with turfy banks. When the rivers reach the coast and encounter the high sandy strip that borders the shore they abruptly change their courses and flow inside the sand bar for several miles before they finally break through it and enter the sea. The river valleys are well developed and are 2 to 6 miles wide in their lower courses. The main banks are sharply defined and near the coast rise 100 to 130 feet above the rivers—in their upper sections they may be 330 feet high. Three or four terraces, varying in width from a quarter of a mile to 6 miles, are clearly distinguished in the valleys. These are covered with park-like groves of rock birch that alternate with luxuriant tall-grass meadows and sedge bogs.

The west coast is formed of thick strata of Tertiary (Neogene) deposits, either horizontal or compressed into folds, that consist of sandstones and sandy-clayey layers containing friable volcanic material. In the Tertiary sandstones are seams of coal of high heat capacity that are as much as 43 feet thick. Signs of oil-bearing strata have also been noted—for exam-

ple, in the Tigil region. The levelness of the west coast is a result of one or all of three processes: the retreat of the sea, which once reached the base of the range; the leveling action of erosion and the deposition of sediments by the rivers; and slight epeirogenic movements.

The northern part of the east coast is washed by the Bering Sea, the southern part by the Pacific Ocean. It is level, low, and open and slopes gently to the sea. Here, as in the west, are many sand bars, vast peat bogs, meadows that contain small bogs, lakes, old river channels and beds, and low hills with groves of rock birch.

Spurs of the Eastern Range reach the coast, where they may form capes that jut far out into the sea (Shipunski, Kronotski, Kamchatski, Ozernoye); between these are large open bays, such as Kronotski or Kamchatski. Numerous smaller bays such as Avacha, which is an excellent harbor, and small coves south of it and on Shipunski peninsula make the shores exceptionally irregular. Along the southern shore are high headlands which drop to the sea in sheer precipices 600 to 1,000 feet high; just offshore are small islands and many rocks that may be covered with water at high tide. The smooth sections of the high sea coast—that west of Cape Shipunski, for example—are linked with post-Tertiary fractures. Some of the deep coves which complicate the shoreline are a result of volcanic activity; Tarya Cove in Avacha Bay, for example, is the caldera of an old volcano which has been invaded by the sea. The shoreline changes as a result of the activity of the surf and the rivers that flow into the sea. Coves are separated from the sea by offshore bars and are thus changed into lakes; large but shallow Lake Nerpichye was once a bay, and was cut off by alluvium from the Kamchatka River, and by a sand bar raised by the surf.

Volcanoes and Hot Springs

The eastern volcanic region consists of hilly plateaus, averaging about 2,500 feet in height, with volcanic cones set upon them. They are formed of thick bedded deposits of lava, tuff, volcanic sand, ash, and other friable pyroclastic material. These volcanic materials have produced the flat relief—rocky plateaus from 1,650 to 3,300 feet high—on which most of the vol-

Of the 38 undestroyed volcanoes, 13 are considered active—periodically active, or in a stage of solfataric activity. After a rest of nearly a century some volcanoes have once again erupted violently, for example, Gorely and Zheltovskaya Peak.

Fig. 12-1. Koryak Volcano from the Avacha River: flooded forest of Maxsimovich poplar trees.

canoes of Kamchatka are concentrated. The plateaus are dissected by broad, deep river valleys (Avacha, Zhupanova, Tolbachick) into vast mesas with nearly horizontal, dry surfaces; some have gentle slopes, others sheer cliffs.

Kamchatka and the Kurile Islands together constitute the only region in the USSR where there are active volcanoes. Kamchatka lies along the Pacific volcanic rim and is a northern continuation of the Kurile volcanic chain. A second volcanic arc extends eastward from Kamchatka through the Aleutians. The intensity of the peninsula's volcanic activity is greater than that of any part of the volcanic rim of the Pacific except Java. Altogether, 127 volcanic cones have been counted; most are almost completely destroyed, some have domes and others craters, some are flooded with water.

The Kamchatka volcanic region is divided into two zones: western-extinct; eastern-active. The east has 74 volcanic cones, including all the active ones. The volcanoes of the west are all extinct and most are highly eroded; many of them were but slightly active, even at their apogee.

The beautiful, sharp-pointed, volcanic peaks, many truly conical, are scattered from the southern tip of the peninsula to 57° north latitude (Mount Shiveluch). They serve as a picturesque embellishment of Kamchatka, creating a unique landscape in the eastern region. The volcanoes on Kamchatka are arranged primarily in groups or rings on the high plateaus around centers of early eruptions, which have either collapsed, becoming lakes (Kurile and Kronotskoye lakes) or large craters, or are simply horizontal lava flows. Moreover, the disposition of volcanoes seem to be related to the orientation of two series of tectonic breaks: one that corresponds to the strike of the Kamchatka volcanic zone (northeast), and another that is almost perpendicular to the first. The volcanoes Shiveluch, Klyuchevski, and Tolbachik lie in the northeast direction. Although Shiveluch's lava differs sharply from that of Klyuchevski there is a definite interlinking of volcanic phenomena along this line. After prolonged eruption, Klyuchevski suddenly became quiet in 1854 as though to replace it, the more northerly Shiveluch, considered extinct, opened up and began to display energetic activity. Several volcanoes (Koryak, Avacha, and Kozel) are situated along a single fracture with a northwest strike. Extending in the same direction are outcrops of acid rhyolites which have associated mineral springs.

Present-day volcanic activity in Kamchatka is considerably weaker than the intense activity of the past. Volcanism probably began before the Paleozoic, was renewed several times in the Paleozoic and Mesozoic, in the late Tertiary and at the beginning of the Quaternary, and continues to the present. Indicative of its intensity in the geologically recent past are the enormous areas covered by present-day and Quaternary lavas, which occupy 40,000 square miles—more than 40 per cent of the area of Kamchatka. During the Tertiary, the lavas erupted through numerous fissures and tubular channels. Such eruptions were later replaced by central eruptions, which are the only type observed at present.

The volcanoes of Kamchatka have many different shapes—that of any one of them depends on the age of the volcano and the character of its eruptions. There are seven basic types, and these produce unusual shapes when combined.

1. Active volcanic peaks—these have a regular conical shape and long, sharp ribs that separate deep depressions. Klyuchevski Peak, one of the greatest volcanic cones in the world (15,912 feet high), is one of these. The shape of its perfect regular cone is maintained by frequent eruptions of loose volcanic material. This material, together with discharges of lava

that alternate with accumulation of snow and ice, form the volcanic cone. The sheer rocky walls of the crater enclose clouds of poisonous gases with an acrid odor. Other volcanoes with remarkably regular cones are Kronotskaya Peak (11,909 feet), on top of which the lava has congealed in an enormous mass that completely plugs the crater and the violently active Karymski Peak. The tops of some volcanoes are truncated cones; these are usually found on peaks that have undergone several small disasters and which have secondary or freshly restored craters. Koryak Peak (11,411 feet), for example, has an obliquely truncated top, a main crater, and two parasitic ones.

2. Eroded-top volcanoes—these have crumbling craters and parasitic cones. An example of this type is Avacha Peak (8,960 feet), which is a twin volcano with a Vesuvius-type crown, but is twice as high as Vesuvius. The active volcano lies inside a broad old crater-like depression—a caldera two and a half miles across. The andesite ridges of the old crown are pitted with depressions that are occupied by glaciers and present a sharp contrast to the gradually growing regular cone that has been formed inside the caldera and down which descend a series of lava streams of recent eruptions. Others of this type are: Krasheninnikova (6,094 feet), Zheltovskaya (6,406 feet), Kosheleva (6,110 feet), and Ichinskaya (11,834 feet).

3. Caldera volcanoes—their craters are not funnel shaped, but have vertical inner walls and large flat bottoms. These were formed when the central part of the volcano sank along circular faults, which may have been caused by the development of large cavities below the crater or by huge explosions during eruption. The crater may remain dry (Uzon, Mutnaya), or may be inundated by the sea (Tarya Cove—part of Avacha Bay) or filled with fresh water (Kurile Lake). Uzon (5,084 feet) has a crater about six miles in diameter. After the formation of an andesite-basalt cone, a gigantic explosion carried off the entire mountain. On its site was a vast crater, which filled with water and finally overflowed, eroding an outlet through the crater wall. Both constant and erratic

fumaroles, mud holes, and hot springs whose waters are not alike in chemical composition are found in the crater of Uzon.

4. Cupola-shaped volcanoes—these were formed by a single extrusion of viscous lava. These do not have a crater (Ivanov Peak, 3,444 feet high).

5. Ridge-shaped volcanoes—these developed when lava emerged through short tectonic fissures. These volcanoes have many small craters: for example, Tolbachik and Zhupanova (9,606 feet).

6. Slag cones—these are small volcanoes whose activity is ordinarily limited to one explosion, the ejected slag forming a small cone.

7. Completely destroyed volcanoes—these have lost their conical form and are now mountains with several low peaks. Such are Ipelka, the remains of a large volcano, highly eroded, with gently sloping outer walls and steep inner walls, and the crests of Shisel, the remnants of a colossal caldera.

The eruptions of some Kamchatka volcanoes are like those of Etna—relatively quiet outpourings of lava flows: others are like those of Vesuvius—violent explosions that eject huge quantities of pyroclastic debris and volcanic ash. In 1907, during the great eruption of Shtyubelya (2,963 feet) the bottom of the crater was demolished, volcanic sand and ash were expelled with such force that all of Kamchatka was covered: the volcano ejected more than four billion cubic yards of loose material. So much ash was suspended in the air that in Petropavlosk lights in windows could not be seen from across the street. Ash covered the snow so thickly that it stopped dog-sled travel.

Lava is the main volcanic product, and streams of it descend far down the peaks; tuffs and breccias are far less widespread. The greatest known lava flows were those from Tolbachik and Klyuchevski, which flowed for 19 miles. In different stages of volcanism, the composition of the lava has varied: older eruptions

Fig. 12-2. Volcanic funnel in a lava flow near Tolbachik Volcano.

yielded porphyries and diabases exclusively, the younger lavas are primarily andesites and dacites. Most lava flows are completely covered by loose pyroclastic debris, from beneath which emerge outcrops of lava that subsequently weathers into fantastic shapes. The surface of much of this block lava is pitted with various kinds of sinks, craters, and depressions that create insurmountable obstacles for horses, and caves in block lava provide bears with custom-built dens. Such "volcanic karsts" keep the lava fields completely dry. The water that runs off the slopes of the volcano easily erodes the loose debris, forming deep narrow channels and dropping in waterfalls from the shelves of old lava. Streams rising in volcanoes often carry a mixture of water and ash, and sometimes sulfur, as does the stream draining the crater of Mount Mutnaya. Water from rapidly melting snow on the tops and sides of active volcanoes, carries along with it volcanic ash, sand, lapilli, and small volcanic bombs, to form so-called "dry streams" as much as 27 miles long. In the volcanic regions of Kamchatka there are a billion cubic yards of pumice—a firm, light, fireproof, and low heat-conducting construction material—and many deposits of pure sulfur.

High seismic activity correlates with volcanism on Kamchatka—since 1790 there have been more than 150 known earthquakes. The epicenters of the most powerful earthquakes have been found to be in the zone of active volcanoes.

Hot spring and geysers are frequent companions of the volcanoes of Kamchatka. More than 60 groups of hot springs are located in districts with past and present volcanic activity. The dense distribution of hot springs near active volcanoes in the solfataric stage indicates that they are linked with magmatic centers lying close to the surface beneath the extinct volcanoes, and are the last manifestations of volcanic activity. Most of the hot springs are in south Kamchatka, where there are many active or recently extinct volcanoes; there are few in the Central Range; and on the west coast there are none at all. Local thermal lines are well expressed: the mineral content of the

Fig. 12-3. Kluchevsk Volcano in action.

water from all springs situated along a given line is almost identical—for example, the Paratunsk thermal line, with its three groups of springs. The majority of the springs discharge in river valleys—either on the surface, at the base of terraces, or in the river bed. Springs linked with fumaroles are found at altitudes up to 3,300 feet. Most hot springs have temperatures above 122°F (Middle Paratunsk Springs, up to 145°F), there are a few warm springs with temperatures below 122°F (Kronotski Springs, 95°F), but springs with cold water are rare. Hot springs in river valleys, where there is much underground water, have a large discharge (Paratunsk, 17 to 23 quarts per second); those linked with fumaroles discharge much less. Quietly flowing springs discharge more than those that bubble and spurt. South of Lake Kronotskoye, near Uzon and Kikhpinich peaks, in the valley of the warm Geyzernoy Creek, numerous geysers have been discovered.

Asiatic continent, that is, from the west and Here, the water escapes with a rush from holes that range in diameter from less than an inch to more than a yard, accompanied by steam and spray and strange sounds that blend with the continuous rumble of the overflowing water. The largest of these geysers, Velikan, hurls a column of boiling water and steam about 165 feet in the air; the interval between its eruptions is 2 hours and 46 minutes, and each eruption lasts 4 minutes. The temperature of its water varies from 203° to 206°F.

Some hot springs are linked with centers of acidic magma (granodiorities), others with centers of basic magma (andesites). The first are slightly mineralized soda-sulfate springs, which release nitrogen and a small amount of hydrogen sulfide, but do not precipitate lime. The Machikinski Springs west of Avachina Bay are of this type. Springs linked with basic igneous rocks have soda-chlorine water containing carbonic acid and considerable concen-

trations of salts of zinc, antimony, boron, and especially arsenic, and are accompanied by accumulations of calcium carbonate. The Nalachevski Springs east of Avacha Peak, for example, are unusually rich in boron and arsenic, and thus have medicinal importance. Hot-spring fields and the beds of hot brooks are surrounded by a border of unusual warmth-loving vegetation.

Climate

The climate of Kamchatka is far more severe than might be expected from its geographic position, largely because of its proximity to cold seas and cold ocean currents. Nevertheless, it is considerably warmer than the opposite mainland coast. Even as far north as Kamchatka the Far Eastern climate has a monsoon character. Two main currents of air affect it: in winter, one from the region of high pressure on the Asiatic continent, that is, from the west and

Fig. 12-4. Hot springs with lime deposits on the edge.

northwest; in summer, one from the region of high pressure above the Pacific Ocean, that is, from the east and southeast. The winter monsoon has much more effect than the summer one; not only is it of greater duration, but the wind is stronger and there are more stormy days. The summer monsoon is active during June and July only. At Petropavlovsk the average velocity of the winter monsoon is 26.73 feet per second, that of summer is 13.86 feet per second. In winter large areas of the Sea of Okhotsk contiguous to the Asiatic mainland freeze over, and thus the sea gives little warmth to the Kamchatka coast, although it somewhat lessens the harshness of the winter monsoon. In summer, the cold water of the sea near the west coast of the peninsula greatly cools the coast. The Bering Sea and the portion of the Pacific Ocean that adjoins the southeast coast of Kamchatka are warmer than the Sea of Okhotsk in both winter and summer, and this keeps the east coast warmer the year round.

In addition to the monsoon shifts of wind, a local isobaric relief in the air over Kamchatka affects local winds. In winter an area of high pressure forms above the center of Kamchatka —a deep, narrow tongue from the region of the East Asiatic anticyclone whose axis coincides with the Central Range and Kamchatka Valley. Therefore, the pressure decreases from the center of the peninsula to its periphery and from north to south, and air masses from the center spread to the coasts. On the east coast, the direction of this wind coincides with the direction of the winter monsoon, and on the west, it is opposite to it. In summer the distribution of pressure on the coasts and in the center of the peninsula is the reverse of that of winter, and winds blow from the cold periphery to the warmer center, but these summer winds are not strong. The prevailing monsoon winds are dry and cold: in winter because they blow from the cold centers of Eastern Siberia, in summer because the Sea of Okhotsk has a low temperature and produces little water vapor. The east coast of Kamchatka is under the influence of warm maritime winds from east and northwest—especially Pacific Ocean cyclones—with abundant moisture. In winter their influence is greater than that of the cold dry western monsoon and creates weather absolutely untypical of a monsoon region.

The great length of Kamchatka from north to south and its complex relief cause local differences in its monsoon climate. The interior of the peninsula is colder than the coasts in winter; in summer it is warmer. The lowest average monthly temperature in the Kamchatka Valley (Milkovo) is —12.5°F, in February; and on the east coast (Petropavlovsk) it is 12.3°F, in February. In April, the temperature is rather uniform throughout the peninsula. The average temperature of the warmest month is higher in the valley (Klyuchi, 58°F in July) than on either the west coast (Ust-Bolsheretsk, 53.8°F in August) or the east coast (Petropavlovsk, 53.6°F in August). In October, temperatures are again approximately the same. The highest temperature (82.3°F), the lowest (—57.8°F), and the greatest daily amplitude (more than 27°F) have all been observed in the valley.

The growing season usually lasts from the last of May or the first of June to the first of October on the southeast coast of Kamchatka; in the interior it begins earlier: in Kamchatka Valley (Klyuchi) it lasts 134 days, on the east coast (Petropavlovsk) 127 days, on the west coast (Ust-Bolsheretsk) 107 days, in the northwestern lowlands (Tigil) 96 days.

Annual precipitation gradually decreases from southeast to northwest: on the southeast coast, it is more than 32 inches, on the northwest coast, it is about 14 inches—the Kamchatka Valley protected from the seas by high mountain ranges, averages 16 inches. The number of days with precipitation varies from 120 to 200, and the number with snow from 70 to 96. Snow begins to fall in September and the snow cover lasts until the end of May; in the mountains it lasts through June. It is not unusual for snow to fall even in June. The first snow, on the other hand, falls later than at similar latitudes in the European USSR, and snowfall in September is very rare at Petropavlovsk. Relative humidity is lower in spring

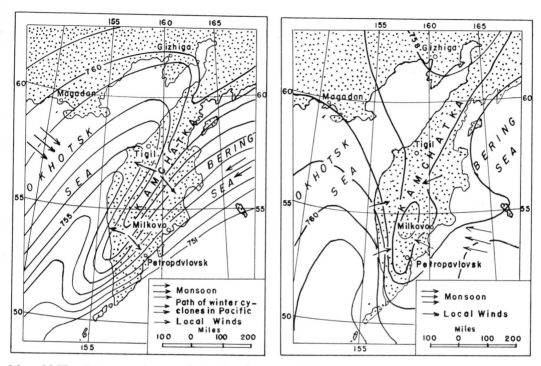

Map 12-II. Diagram of atmospheric distribution, including pressure and basic types of winds, on Kamchatka.

and autumn than in winter and summer. The humidity is adequate for the growth of vegetation, and on the coast, even excessive (up to 87 per cent in August).

Cloudiness is frequent on the coasts, especially in the west, and reaches its maximum, as is generally the case in monsoon regions, in late spring and summer, during the southeastern monsoon; it is much less cloudy in autumn, winter, and early spring, during the cold and dry northwestern monsoon. On the west coast (Ust-Bolsheretsk), July is cloudy 89 per cent of the time, December, 49 per cent. The seasonal distribution of clear and cloudy days, and also of days with fog is not the same on the coast as in the valley. In January, Ust-Bolsheretsk has 2 clear, 14 cloudy, and 1 foggy days: Milkovo, 18 clear, 6 cloudy, and 3 foggy. In July, at Ust-Bolsheretesk, no clear days, 25 cloudy and 25 foggy: at Milkovo 3 clear, 16 cloudy, and none foggy.

The climate of the eastern coast is affected by the Pacific monsoon in summer, the north-

east Pacific cyclones in winter, the cold Oyashio Current in the north, and the warm Kamchatka Current in the south. The southeast coast has a rather low annual amplitude (40.8°F), mild winters (average February temperature, 13.8°F), and cool, short summers with very little sunshine (average August temperature, 54.6°F). A cold spring and warm autumn, late arrival of autumn and winter, maximum temperatures in July, minimum in February, and insignificant winter freezing of soil (not much deeper than 4 inches)—all these are characteristics of a typical oceanic climate.

Seasonal distribution of precipitation on the east coast is unusual: there is no sharp contrast between winter and summer precipitation, although the minimum is in winter and the maximum in summer and autumn. Annual precipitation on the east coast is made greater than that of other districts by the exceptionally abundant winter precipitation that is brought by northeast winds that have passed above the warmed sea—winter precipitation here is several times as great as in the valley or on the west coast. In a single October day, 7.5 inches of rain fell at Petropavlovsk. Warm winters may have more than half of the entire annual precipitation, and as a result a snow cover of exceptional thickness forms—sometimes as much as 10 feet thick. The southeastern coast, the least sheltered from moisture-bearing ocean winds, has extraordinarily frequent snowstorms of great strength and duration; it is truly the region of snowstorms. Because of the thick snow cover and the frequent snowstorms, only dogs can be used as harness animals, and they are necessary in every village. At Petropavlovsk snowdrifts often cover all but the roofs of houses. The snow cover is established in the first half of November. By the middle of March, strong winds have so packed the snow that in many places it supports a man's weight and travel by dog sled is accomplished with exceptional speed. The snow melts by the end of May or early in June. In years when volcanic ash falls on the snow it may melt earlier. Summer has much cloudiness and fog (in July, 15 foggy days) but almost none in winter.

The west coast is subjected to the influence of the Sea of Okhotsk, the cold dry winter monsoon, and the east-northeast winds from the center of the peninsula. As a result it has a dryer and colder climate than the east coast. It has only a quarter to a third as much precipitation, summer is moist and foggy, winter is relatively snowless—the total snowfall is only 16 inches and irregularly distributed; for much of the winter the tops of the hills remain bare, although some snow may remain in the deep valleys until autumn. Snowstorms are not common on the west coast, which, unlike the east coast, has a typical monsoon distribution of precipitation—much more in summer than in winter. The west coast is extremely foggy, especially in summer; when the warm and moist air currents from the interior encounter the cold Okhotsk Sea (where in places the ice lasts until August), they produce fog and clouds that envelop the coast and hide the sun for weeks. There is little fog in winter. The high cloudiness and fog throughout the grow-

ing period hinder the development of agriculture.

The climate of the Kamchatka Valley, protected by high mountain ranges from both cold and warm sea winds, has many features of a continental climate; a severe winter, with an absolute minimum of −57.8°F; a relatively warm summer; an early warm spring. Winter temperatures are lowered by the flow of cold air onto the bottom of the valley, where it may stagnate in calm and clear weather. Because of the early warm spring, rock birch blossoms in the middle of May, whereas in the coastal regions it does not bloom until the second or third week in July. Central Kamchatka is the driest part of the peninsula. The northwest monsoon that prevails here in winter is dry, and summer winds from the east and south have lost their moisture on the mountain ranges which enclose the valley. Thus, there is far less precipitation here, winters are not snowy, relative humidity and cloudiness are low, and in summer there is little fog.

The climate of the valley is favorable for agriculture: melting snow supplies moisture to the soil during the spring; the dry and clear spring weather is favorable for plowing and sowing; the warm but moderate summer temperatures favor the growth of plants; the dry and clear autumn permits unhindered harvesting of grain. Nevertheless, it is necessary to cultivate varieties of plants which demand little warmth: garden vegetables, root plants, clover, and flax grow best here.

Glaciation

Kamchatka has a type of glaciation unlike that of other glacial regions of the USSR. Because it is washed by cold seas, has a short cool summer, much snow in the east, and high mountains, Kamchatka would seem to have conditions favorable for the extensive development of glaciers. However, little snow and ice can accumulate annually, except in the craters of extinct volcanoes, since the active volcanoes bring about the rapid melting of snow. Most existing glaciers are thus remnants of ones formed in the past, and are slowly disappearing. The largest and most interesting are concentrated around the volcanic cones, especially on the Pacific side of Kamchatka, where winter precipitation is heaviest. Permanent snow on the high volcanoes descends to a height of of only 5,280 feet (Klyuchevski, Shiveluch), which is 3,960 feet lower than in the central part of the Alps. Sometimes thawed patches appear in the snow because of the activity of erratic fumaroles. During volcanic eruptions, water from the thawing snow and ice feeds the numerous dry streams of the volcanic slopes. Volcanic debris from early eruptions, frozen in snow, preserves the slopes of the volcanic cones. Like the cones of many South American volcanoes, that of Klyuchevski Peak has alternating layers of firn and volcanic ash mixed with loose debris.

The most common glaciers are the caldera glaciers that lie in craters of both extinct and active volcanoes: for example, between the cones of Avacha Peak and its crater ring. Many star-shaped glaciers encompass the tops of volcanoes—from their firn domes sharp tongues descend to a height of about 4,000 feet (Klyuchevski). From Shiveluch, six rather large glaciers diverge radially; those on the northern slope reach a length of 3.6 miles. Glaciers of the hanging and cirque types are widespread, both on the Central and Eastern ranges and on many volcanic cones.

The largest glaciers on Kamchatka are Bogdanovich and Erman which descend from Ploski and Klyuchevski to a lower altitude than any other glaciers on Kamchatka: 2,640 feet. In deep, extensive depressions among the mountains of Cape Kronotski are more than ten large glaciers (the largest is Tyushevski, 5 miles long) and dozens of small ones.

Volcanic activity on Kamchatka has not died out, thus, it is a very special factor in the thawing of glaciers.

Every volcanic eruption on Kamchatka melts part of the glacial armor covering the volcano and brings about a change in the relief of the slopes that causes a rearrangement in the distribution of ice and creates erratic glaciers that do not have their own permanent channels. Between eruptions, ice is melted by the active fumaroles, as it is in the crater of Mutnaya Peak, where a flat glacier that ends chaotically in a broken ice chute lies beside a warm lake along whose surface the wind drives a yellow layer of sulfur—a lake fed by meltwater as the glacier is thawed by the white hot gases that escape from the fumarole with a roar. Volcanic materials—for example, mealy ash containing free sulfur, and the products of disintegration of andesites with pyrite and gypsum—are usually enclosed in the solid ice body of such a glacier, and, as it melts, color the moraine and ocher-yellow. The ash that accumulates on the surface of the ice color is black and promotes its thawing.

At the beginning of the Quaternary period glaciation was far greater than it is today, as is indicated by the widespread traces of former glaciers, many of which have been concealed by lava flows or pyroclastic debris. Trough-shaped glacial valleys and glacial cirques cut deeply into the slopes of the ranges and the sides of individual volcanoes. *Roches moutonnées,* rocky semicircular terminal moraines at the bases of volcanoes (Shiveluch), and countless moraine lakes—both on moraines and the mass of ice itself (Klyuchevski)—create, in places, glacial landscapes that are gradually being altered by volcanic activity and erosion.

Hydrography

The largest river on the peninsula is the Kamchatka. Its water is warmest in July, coldest in January: yet even in winter it is warmer than that of most streams at similar latitudes because of the numerous and copious hot springs that discharge into it. Its swift current and the high temperature of its water make the ice cover extremely unstable: unfrozen patches dot the surface of the river in the coldest winter. In summer the Kamchatka River is the chief means of communication between the interior of the peninsula and its eastern coast. It is navigable up to Milkovo for small craft with shallow draft. Runoff from the eastern volcanoes provides most of its water, although warm underground springs contribute a great deal. Seldom, however, does the drainage basin supply more water than the river can carry. Spring floods are rare, and occur only when enough volcanic ash is precipitated to cause exceptionally rapid and early thawing of the snow.

a thousand feet deep. The lake is surrounded on all sides by volcanoes, which descend to it abruptly, so that the lake's banks, both above the water and below it, are steep and rocky. Evidence that the lake once had a higher level is visible on these banks. Extrusion of andesitic lava has formed three islands in the lake. Numerous mountain streams warmed by water from hot springs feed it. Its outlet is the Ozernaya River, which freezes only superficially

Fig. 12-5. Kamchatka River.

There are few lakes on Kamchatka outside the volcanic region because of the good drainage afforded by the coarse skeletal soil and porous lavas and the low snowline and comparatively high position of the sun. There are five main kinds of lakes: (1) small crater lakes, some containing hot water; a few of these have cut outlets through the side of the volcano and their water has been drained off down the slope; (2) lakes formed from lava dams (Palanskoye Lake in the northern part of the peninsula; (3) the basins of hot springs; (4) lakes of fault origin, which have extremely simple outlines (Lake Dalneye in the Avacha district); and (5) big crater lakes (Kurile and Kronotskoye).

Kurile Lake is an old volcanic crater filled with water: it is about 7 miles in diameter and

each winter. The transparency of its water is only 21.4 feet. Despite the lake's comparatively small area, its water is intensely chilled to the very bottom—a depth of 1,004 feet—each winter, although the great depth contributes to late freezing-over.

Lake Kronotskoye in many ways similar to Kurile Lake, far exceeds it in area, but is only 422 feet deep. The surface temperature of its water is lower than that of Kurile Lake but it cools only to a depth of 66 feet. In December the lake is completely covered by ice about 3 feet thick, but its outlet—Kronotskaya River—does not freeze over. On the coasts are lagoons, some separated from the sea by sand spits (Lake Koyger), some by accumulation of sediment from a river (Lake Nerpichye).

Soil, Flora, and Fauna

Kamchatka, surrounded by seas and bordered on the north by vast expanses of tundra, should logically have a strongly endemic flora. But it does not—few of its plants are indigenous, and it comprises no more than 800 species, most of them plants of the Arctic, the Okhotsk continental coast, Sakhalin, and the Kurile Islands. This flora poverty is a result of intense volcanic catastrophes and early glaciation, which crowded out and destroyed its early vegetation, which consisted of species found both in Alaska and Japan. The coniferous forests of the central valley and a single islet of fir (*Abies gracilis*) on the east coast, close to the mouth of the Semyachik River, are surviving relics of the earlier vegetation. Most of the present species came from the Anadyr region in the north or from the coasts of the mainland. Sea currents carried seeds, shrubs, and even whole trees, which were washed into the sea by the rivers of Sakhalin and of the mainland, to the southwest coast of the peninsula, so that, despite the cold, foggy summer, such Okhotsk-Manchurian plants as *Thermopsis fabacea* and *Swertia tetrapetala* now grow there. Many seeds from the Kurile Islands were brought in by birds. Much of the vegetation seems to suffer greatly from the environment: Early frosts sometimes kills their leaves and prevents ripening of their seeds. In some winters the snow cover is so thick that vegetation is still surrounded by snow in the middle of July. Often, volcanic eruptions cover the plants with ash and dry them out or singe them with hot cinders and lapilli. Torrents of water may pour down the slopes of volcanoes, tearing out even large bushes and carrying them far below. The thick masses of loose volcanic debris that are the matrices of the soil contain few compounds that are absorbed by plants, but are extremely rich in silicic acid. Water drains so quickly from the debris, and to such a depth, that roots of plants have a difficult time finding water.

The distribution of vegetation in Kamchatka, as in every mountainous region, is governed by local climate and relief. It is as though there were three different plant worlds: (1) the Kamchatka Valley with its dry continental climate, which contains coniferous forests of a taiga type, groves of aspen and white birch, and vast meadows; (2) the mountainous eastern coast with its predominant rock-birch groves; and (3) the lowlands of the western coast with their many swamps. Vertical vegetative zones are clearly marked in the high mountains bordering the middle section of the Kamchatka River. The proximity of the sea and the abundance of precipitation cause the lowering of the snow line (especially in the south), and with it the timber line. Spruce and larch forests reach only an altitude of about 1,100 feet; higher, a zone of rock birch runs to about 2,500 feet (on Shiveluch to 1,980 feet). Alder thickets, a few subalpine meadows, and pine groves replaces the rock birch, and are replaced in turn by a belt of alpine meadows at an altitude of about 3,350 feet (on Shiveluch, 2,950 feet). Because of the local differences in climate the borders of vertical zones vary greatly: near Petropavlovsk, not far above sea level, the vegetation has a mountainous character (rock birch, alder thickets, pine groves); in central Kamchatka such vegetation appears only above 1,100 feet.

A narrow strip of coniferous forest extends along the Kamchatka Valley on alluvial deposits bordering the Kamchatka and Yelovka rivers, on terraces, on hills, and low foothills. Pure larch forests are rare and occupy a relatively small area. They contain many huge full-grown trees, 100 to 200 years old and with sound wood. Many of these have bottle-shaped trunks—at the base the trunk is 30 to 40 inches in diameter; at chest height 18 or 20 inches. In the undergrowth is wild rose (*Rosa amblyotis*), pyrola, and red bilberry. Dead needles and leaves cover the ground—in only a few places does moss appear. The dense, bright-green second growth of larch indicates how favorable conditions are for restoration, and hence for the establishment of a regular lumber industry. On argillaceous, slightly podzolic, recent alluvial soil grow forests of larch and birch with a predominance of spruce in the second tier. For-

Fig. 12-6. Layers of volcanic ash along the shore of the Studyonoy River.

ests of Yeddo spruce, with which is mixed larch, birch, aspen, mountain ash, and willow, and which have an undergrowth of honeysuckle (*Lonicera edulis*) and wild rose (*Rosa acicularis*), occupy a still smaller area, being found only on shaded, well-drained but moist soil. Some hills have their northern slope covered by spruce and the southern by larch. Forests of white birch (*Betula japonica*) grow luxuriantly in the Kamchatka Valley as well as in other districts. On alluvial soil that borders the rivers are narrow strips of forest that have poplar (*Populus suaveolens*) and Korean willow (*Chosenia macrolepis*) in the first tier, and Sakhalin willow (*Salix sachalinensis*), alder (*Alnus hirsuta*), and bird cherry in the second. In these shady forests the undergrowth consists largely of tall grass. Dug-outs made from poplar trunks are used for transportation on the rivers of Kamchatka.

The river and forest meadows of Kamchatka are one of the main resources of the region but they have not been adequately exploited. In the river valleys are extensive meadows of tall reed grass (*Calamagrostis langsdorffii*): The soft leaves and stems of this grass are rich in nutrients, and are eaten avidly by domestic animals in spring, before they become tough. The monotonous green areas of reed grass contain islands of bog vetch (*Lathyrus palustris*), the only meadow legume of Kamchatka, and burnet (*Sanguisorba tenuifolia*). Other riverside meadows have more diversified stands of grasses and herbs, well fertilized by the bodies of salmon which have died after spawning. Their alluvial soil, rich in nitrous and phosphoric compounds, is covered with dense growths of cow parsnip (*Heracleum dulce*) as much as 14 feet tall and 4 inches thick, as well as *Angelica ursina,* Kamchatka nettle (*Urtica platyphilla*), and groundsel (*Senecio palmatus*) —all amazingly large. Kamchatka meadowsweet (*Filipendula kamtschatica*) grows with fantastic speed; two weeks after the plants break through the soil they may form a wall of succulent and massive stalks 4 to 6 feet high. These same plants, on the mountain slope just above the river meadow, seem starved and are almost unrecognizable.

On the mountainous eastern coast, the slopes of the mountains, from the base to the belt of alder thickets, are occupied by pure stands of rock birch. They are light and park-like, with many glades. Some have solid brushy undergrowths of mountain ash and alder; in others the undergrowth consists of tall herbaceous plants and there is no moss cover because there is so little shade. In spring, they have a low herbaceous cover of anemone, violet, and sedge. Later, lady's-slipper (*Cypripedium*) and *Orchis* blossom, but by the middle of July they have disappeared beneath the high stand of mugwort (*Artemisia vulgaris*), *Angelica ursina,* and the grasses which are fellow travelers of birch —for example, ramose millet (*Milium effusum*). In the coastal strip, rock birch grows even on slopes open to moist and cold sea winds, but here it is deformed and weathered, with squat, distorted, highly branching trunks,

their shores: sea otters (*Enhydra lutris*) and seals. Up to the end of the eighteenth century, great numbers of sea cows (*Rhytina stelleri*) inhabited the sea near the islands but they have long been extinct. Steller's sea lions (*Eumetopias jubata*) live on the islands in winter. They form large rookeries on offshore rocks among the breakers, where they feed on cephalopod mollusks, herring, codfish, and crustaceans. The hides of these seals have little commercial value, and the natives use them to cover their canoes; they also use the seal's intestines to make waterproof clothing. The Komandorski fur seal (*Callorhinus ursinus*) has summer rookeries on the islands, but winters on the shores of Japan where it does not form rookeries. Like Steller's sea lions, they eat codfish, cephalopod mollusks, and crustaceans. Next to

man, the greatest enemy of the fur seal is the killer whale (*Orca orcinus*). For several years hunting has been regulated on the islands, and all possible measures for the preservation of the fur seal have been taken, with the result that there are now many more than there were before regulation was begun.

The blue fox, whose fur is extremely valuable, lives in the tundra of the islands. Gigantic flocks of birds inhabit the shores: puffin (*Fratercula cirrhata*) of the same family as the guillemots; petrel (*Fulmarus glacialis*) a relative of the stormy petrel; kittiwake (*Rissa tridactyla*), a kind of gull; and other sea birds which nest in colonies. Tundra partridge are abundant, and there are many migratory birds such as snipe and seagulls.

THE KURILE ISLANDS

The Kurile Island arc is the northernmost of the three volcanic island arcs, convex to the east, that constitute the so-called "outer coast of Eastern Asia." The islands link the volcanoes of Hokkaido with those of Kamchatka. There are 36 large islands, 20 small ones, and many uninhabitable rocks that just barely project above the sea. The archipelago is subdivided into a long chain of large islands that extends almost 750 miles from Shumshu Island to Kunashir Island and a short parallel chain of small islands—the Lesser Kuriles—that extends 60 miles from Nemuro Peninsula on Hokkaido to Shikotan Island. The overall area of the Kurile Islands is more than 6,000 square miles, and the four largest islands, Iturup, Paramushir, Kunashir, and Urup, make up 40 per cent of this. The northern end of the island chain—Alaid Island—lies at 50°56' north latitude, approximately the latitude of Kiev, and the southern end—Shuishio Island—at 43°26' north latitude, corresponding to the latitude of Sochi in the European USSR.

There are two special features in the structure of the Kurile arc. The first is the disposition of

the islands in an echelon at either end of the Kurile arc. This is particularly clear at the southern end, where the long axis of the islands, which run from northeast to southwest,

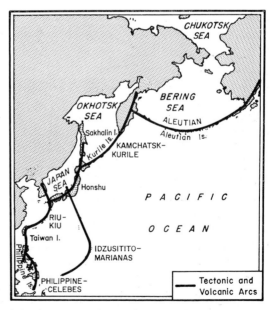

Map 12-III. Volcanic arc of the North Pacific Ocean.

recede to the northwest, i.e., toward the continent, in proportion to their distance from the central part of the arc. The second feature is the morphologic difference between the islands in the middle of the chain and the islands at the ends of the arc. The middle islands are solitary or double volcanic cones that rise directly out of the sea; their bases are thousands of feet below the surface. The islands at the ends of the arc consist of several volcanic cones joined by low dikes and all have extensive level surfaces of varying heights.

water from the Sea of Okhotsk flows into the Pacific through the southern straits.

Geologic Structure

The Kurile Chain is evidently the top of a folded zone of Paleozoic and Mesozoic rocks that was forced far below sea level during the development of the East Asiatic geosyncline. The geosyncline began to form in the Early Cretaceous, continued to sink during the Mio-

Fig. 12-9.   Makanrushi, volcanic island of the Kurile group, seen from Onekotan Strait.

The sea bottom in the region of the Kurile Islands has an extremely complex relief. To the west is the deepest part of the Sea of Okhotsk, 11,060 feet. East of the chain, in the Pacific Ocean, is the narrow Kurile depression (Tuscarora Deep) whose average depth is about 24,500 feet, and whose greatest is 27,929 feet. Near Simushir Island an isobath of 590 feet passes close to the shore. The islands are separated from one another by straits of various widths, many of them quite deep: Boussole (Kitsuruppu), more than 6,600 feet; Kruzenshtern (Mushiru), 5,940 feet; and Friz (Etorofu), 2,079 feet. These straits are the main channels through which water is exchanged by the Pacific Ocean and the Sea of Okhotsk. The surface layers of the Sea of Okhotsk are replenished primarily through Boussole Strait, and

cene, and then and later accumulated sediments thousands of yards thick. The sinking was accompanied by folding and strong magmatic activity. At the end of the Tertiary and the beginning of the Quaternary the folds were complicated by numerous longitudinal and lateral fractures. Along the lines of the longitudinal fractures there were overthrusts and faults, which, as the surrounding sea floor subsided, formed deep narrow depressions along both sides of the chain. Thick flows of lava along the fractures raised and metamorphosed the sedimentary rocks of the geosyncline and formed high volcanic cones that emerged from below the water—the central islands of the Kurile chain. Movements of the earth's crust and the formation of the islands will continue as long as there is intensive volcanic and seismic activity. Epeirogenic upheaval of the islands is further indicated by their young marine terraces.

Almost all the islands are composed of igneous rocks—andesitic lavas and their tuffs—only the extreme northern (Shumshu) and southern (Sikotan) islands consist exclusively of sedimentary rocks. On some islands, dislocated metamorphic schists of Paleozoic and Mesozoic age emerge from lava deposits in depressions covered by slightly eroded Tertiary sediments.

Volcanoes and Earthquakes

The Kurile Islands are almost all volcanic. There are nearly a hundred known volcanoes, of which 38 are active (Sarychev Peak on Matua Island, 4,900 feet high; Prevo Peak on Simushir Island, 4,488 feet high; and others). They have a stratified structure—alternating layers of congealed lava and compacted volcanic ash. Volcanic activity takes different forms. Some volcanoes, such as those on Raikoke or Simushir, manifest a "full cycle"—a subsurface rumble, short violent outbursts accompanied by the crumbling of the upper part of the volcanic cone, ejection of ash, rocks, and gases, and finally a violent outpouring of lava. From other volcanoes (e.g., those on Matua and Shirinki islands) streams of lava pour out with a soft hissing sound, without any discharge of gas, ash, or rock. Some volcanoes have not only an active main crater, but also small parasitic cones, and many fumaroles from which sulfur-dioxide gas is continuously ejected.

The northwestern Pacific Ocean volcanic rim has many earthquakes—37 per cent of all recorded epicenters are here. Many of them take place in the Kuriles: between 1797 and 1888, 16 destructive earthquakes, and from 1923 to 1937, ten extremely powerful ones; Urup averages seven a year. Most of these quakes are accompanied by tectonic movement of large

Map 12-IV. The Kurile Islands.

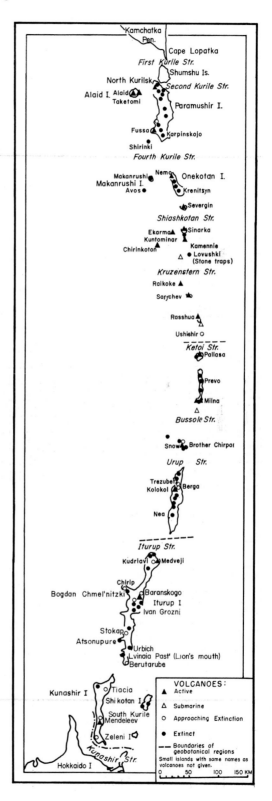

faults on the ocean's floor, and have their focuses far beneath it. Earthquakes have sometimes been accompanied by activation of volcanoes, but few earthquakes are brought about by volcanic eruptions. Often seismic waves pass from the lithosphere into the hydrosphere to become seaquakes which are felt in the open sea without visible swell and rarely reach the strength of a destructive shake. Eruption of underwater volcanoes or collapse of the sea floor often raise enormous waves, *tsunamis,* several of which may follow closely after one another and cause much destruction when they reach the coast. The highest on record—210 feet—is the one that broke on the southern tip of Kamchatka in 1737.

Mineral Resources

Because of their volcanic origin, the Kurile Islands have little mineral wealth. The most abundant resource, which is directly linked with volcanic activity and easily available, is sulfur, long exploited on Kunashir Island. On Paramushir and Shumshu, traces of silver and iron ores have been detected, on Urup galena and sphalerite have been discovered, and on others there is much pumice and other material that could be used in construction.

Relief

The mountains of the Kurile Islands are of many different sizes and shapes, as are the islands themselves. On most of the larger islands the mountains consist of a single ridge running the length of the island and occupying almost all its area. On some, however, they are divided into two, three, or four ridges, and on others are a complex system of short ranges. On some there are single majestic volcanic cones; on others the peaks form short ridges with tooth-like crests. No less than 46 peaks of the island chain are from 1,650 to 3,300 feet above sea level; 30 peaks are from 3,300 to 4,290 feet high; and 12 rise above 4,290 feet. The highest of these are

covered with permanent snow. For example, the permanent snow fields on Mount Oyakoba (7,657 feet) on Alaid Island descend to 1,650 feet above sea level. The few lowlands and hills on the islands coincide with outcrop of sedimentary rocks. They are either compressed between the mountain ridges, or extend in wide strips from one coast to another (Iturup Island). Low islands (Shumshu) are the rare exception. The volcanoes have many shapes. Many are volcanoes of ideally regular form (Ekarma) or with a truncated cone (Raikoke); others resemble Vesuvius, and have excellently expressed crowns (Severgin on Kharimkotan Island, 3,976 feet high); the depression between the crown and the young cone of these may contain a lake (Krenitsyn Peak, 4,350 feet high, on Onekotan Island). The ruins of some destroyed volcanoes have crests that look like a saw (Shirinki)—some like a saw that has lost most of its teeth (Mount Tsirip on Iturup Island). Craters of destroyed volcanoes along the coast have been inundated by the sea and have become deep sheltered bays (Brouton on Simushir Island, with a depth of 650 feet). Some groups of small islands and reefs (Lovushki) are the highest points on the edge of an old volcanic crater.

Many islands have simple shapes: a circle, an oval, a rectangle. Others are irregular and intricate—with capes that project far into the sea and deeply notched bays. The high cliffs that are prominent along the shores of most islands have been eroded into fantastic shapes; countless rocks near their coasts have been polished by breakers and high tides; and steep banks have been striated with wave-cut niches and grottos. The formation of new islands, the rebuilding of the relief of existing ones and changes in their shore lines take place rapidly, almost before one's eyes. In 1934, 12 miles from the coast of Alaid Island a small volcanic island rose from a depth of 2,600 feet; named Taketomi, it is a parasite cone on the underwater slope of Mount Oyakoba, from which, at the same time, a thick stream of lava descended to sea level and formed the long flat Cape Lava. Sea-abraded terraces, found at heights of 900 to 1,300 feet, indicate that slow vertical movements have taken place at different times.

In the mountains is a dense network of deeply notched narrow valleys that diverge radially from the high mountain masses. Many emerge onto the lowland coasts in estuaries or bays; some are gorges that cut through coastal precipices; the mouths of others hang at varying heights above the sea. The slopes of these river valleys are terraced.

The mountain slopes generally consist of bedrock, and the bases of the mountains and cliffs are covered by disordered heaps of stone, since the products of weathering cannot adhere to the steep slopes, and roll downwards, leaving the surface of the bedrock exposed. The bare windward slopes of the mountains, almost devoid of snow cover, are thus subject to energetic frost weathering.

Climate

The position of the Kurile Islands in the temperate latitudes and in the midst of vast expanses of water should give them a mild marine climate. However, they have long cold winters and cool, wet, and humid summers, much cloudiness and fog, and sharp changes in weather. In winter the islands are under the influence of the large Asiatic anticyclone on the west, and the Aleutian cyclone on the east. The winter monsoon brings masses of cold continental air with low humidity. Winds are very frequent, with northwest winds with an average monthly velocity up to 46 feet per second prevailing 70 per cent of the time. In summer, warm masses of sea air from the south and southeast sometimes reach the islands, but only as weak winds. The occasional summer storms are linked with typhoons from the south, which bring winds with a velocity of as much as 45 miles an hour. The cold water of the Sea of Okhotsk and the warmer Pacific water on the east both have their effect on the weather: an effect complicated by the influence of ocean currents. On the east the cold Oyashio Current flows southward from the Bering Sea;

farther east the warm Kamchatka Current flows northeast, carrying water about 11° to 14°F warmer than that of the Oyashio Current. The depth of these currents changes with the season. In winter, the Oyashio Current becomes even colder but is much narrower than in summer. A minor branch of the warm Tsushima Current approaches the southern islands through La Perouse Strait, but it does not have any great climatic significance. The constant oceanic currents near the islands are somewhat concealed by tidal currents, which are tremendously strong in many of the straits.

The temperature of the surface layer of water on both sides of the islands is, on an average, less than 46°F even in August. Constant northwest winds push floating ice across the Sea of Okhotsk toward the Kurile Islands; there it chokes the straits and much of it is carried out into the Pacific, where it gradually drifts south. In winter, ice forms in some coves of the Kuriles, but it is unstable.

The rather even temperature that prevails on the islands—no abrupt changes: small annual amplitude—with the lowest monthly average in February and the highest in August is a characteristic feature of a marine climate. (At the village of Syana on Iturup Island the February average is 20°F, the August average 60.8°F, and the annual amplitude 40.8°F.) Because of the great north-south length of the chain the climate of the northern islands differs greatly from that of the southern. Moreover, on the northern islands winter begins earlier and it is colder the year round. The frost-free period is 120 days long in the north, 180 days long in the south.

Because of the monsoon and relatively frequent typhoons in the summer, precipitation on the islands is heavy. Annual precipitation varies from 30 to 40 inches—it is heaviest in August and September (in September 3.6 to 6.0 inches), lightest in January and February (in February 0.8 to 2 inches). The number of days with precipitation varies from 129 to 225 per year. Rain falls in both summer and winter—very often as a fine drizzle—but there are about twice as many days with snow as with rain. The only months in which no snow falls are July, August, and September. The snow cover forms at the end of October and stays until the middle of May: its thickness may reach 40 inches. Strong winds and cyclones from the Pacific Ocean bring intense snow storms.

The water that surrounds the islands, the nearness of both warm and cold marine currents, and the frequent winds contribute to the excessive humidity. The relative humidity in winter never drops below 60 per cent, and the summer average exceeds 90 per cent—that is, the air is close to the saturation point. It is usually cloudy near the islands: there are 229 overcast days, and only 15 completely clear ones each year. Winter and summer are the cloudiest seasons: at Syana there are 26 overcast days in January; in June, 20; in March, 16; in September, 15. The islands receive only 11 per cent of the possible sunshine; in winter, about one hour a day, in summer six hours.

Fog is very frequent, and covers the islands in a thick shroud almost continuously throughout the navigational period. Southern winds cross the warm Kamchatka Current, whose average summer temperature is 77°F, and then pass above the cold Oyashio Current, whose temperature varies from 43° to 44.8°F. Because most summer winds are weak—13 to 16 feet per second—the air is thoroughly cooled by the cold water, and the moisture it contains condensed into fog. The foggiest period is from June to August; there is little in winter. At times the fog hugs the surface of the water, at others it may form banks 60 to 80 feet thick, at others it may turn into a light mizzle. Strong northern or western winds disperse it, carrying it away to the ocean.

In winter cold northwest winds prevail, lowering the average monthly temperature to 17.6°F. Precipitation in the winter averages 10 inches in the south and 7 inches in the north. The number of days with precipitation—chiefly snow—is 20 to 27 a month in the south, and about half that in the north. Winter is cloudier in the south than in the north. Throughout the islands spring is cold and stormy, and there

are only 3 to 7 foggy days a month; northwest winds still prevail, but they are gradually replaced by the summer monsoon, rains become frequent and snowfall rare. In April and May there are many strong storms. Summer is short and cool: the average monthly temperature ranges from 53.6° to 57.2°F, although there may be some days as hot as 88°F, and some when it is below freezing (in June, as low as 25°F). Ten inches of rain may fall in the course of the summer: there are 12 to 16 rainy days a month in the south and 10 to 14 in the north. Summer is cloudy, having no more than 5 completely clear days, and 10 to 12 foggy days each month. Autumn, despite the heavy precipitation (14 inches) and the passing typhoons, is the best time of year. The weather is generally clear and calm, and there is almost no fog, but as the wind shifts to the northwest at the end of the season, the period of storms and snowfall begins.

Hydrography

On almost all the Kurile Islands there are hot and highly mineralized springs with temperatures ranging from 95° to 126°F. They emerge almost anywhere—at the base of cliffs, in cracks in solidified lava, in the craters of volcanoes—and they vary in output. The water of many is colorless and transparent, even though it contains sulphur, which is deposited along the edges of the springs in yellow grains. The natives use this water for medicinal purposes. Cold springs with palatable fresh water, are uncommon, and some islands (e.g., Raikoke) have no fresh springs.

Because of the heavy precipitation and its regularity the islands have a great deal of water, which their mountainous surfaces divert into numerous small streams. The patterns of many river networks is unusual, but, in general, they form a system of radial streams that extend outward from the main elevations. The gradients of the rivers are steep, and the rapidity of their currents are swift, and they have many rapids and waterfalls. Few rivers meander calmly along plains, if for no other reason than that there are few plains. Most rivers begin in the mountains as small creeks, but some flow out of bogs and a few out of lakes. Some rivers empty into the sea over high cliffs, as waterfalls (e.g., Raknibedu Falls on Iturup Island, 460 feet high), others emerge onto a sandy or swampy lowland coast. The mouths of many of these rivers contain sandbars, gravel spits, or fills, which do not allow small boats to enter the rivers even at high tide. Because the rivers are fed mainly by precipitation, and, to a lesser degree, by meltwater from patches of old snow in the mountains, and only a few receive much ground water, there are floods after the intense rains of spring and summer. Only the few slowly flowing lowland rivers are covered with ice every year (in the north for 4 or 5 months); mountain streams seldom freeze over, and waterfalls freeze only in exceptionally cold winters. The water of many rivers is not fit to drink because of its high sulphur content, or, where rivers flow through bogs, the abundance of organic material in it.

There are a few dozen lakes on the islands. Some are linked with volcanic activity: small, deep mountain lakes in the craters of extinct volcanoes (for example, a lake in the crater of Mount Golovino on Kunashir Island) or in the depression between the crown and the young volcanic cone (Yusen-Ko Lake on Krenitsyn Peak, with a depth of 660 feet). Some are volcanic dam lakes (Lake Yeda on Paramushir Island), whose water derives from sulphur springs and is acid and yellowish: such lakes may be either hot or cold. Far from the coast, in locked-in basins on valley floors or old marine terraces, are a few lakes up to 6 miles long and 43 feet deep, some containing fresh water. The majority of coastal lakes are much like lagoons. They are the expanded mouths of rivers, separated from the sea by dunes: some are connected with the sea by small channels, or by filtration of the water through a fill (Lake Tokhutsu on Kunashir Island). The more elevated of these lakes contain fresh water; the water in the lower ones is brackish. There are a few cirque lakes on the islands, and a few suffusional lakes that were formed by the washing out of fine pyroclastic debris.

Soil, Flora, and Fauna

Much of the surface of the Kurile Islands is covered with a loose mantle of weathered rock, whose formation is fostered by the moist climate, the penetration of water into cracks, and the frost weathering that results from the frequent shifts of temperature from above freezing to below and back again. Resisting these forces are the massiveness and great sturdiness of the volcanic rocks. Intense erosion and the steepness of the mountain slopes make the mantle unstable and prevent the accumulation of fine soil and its normal development. Only on comparatively level surfaces—terraces, bottoms of river valleys—can alluvium accumulate and develop into fertile soil, but here, too, the fine soil is easily washed away and blown off by winds. The soil that develops is podzolic—some of it only slightly so—friable, porous, and easily leached out. It contains little organic matter and has a limited agricultural potential. On some islands there is much gleyed bog soil and shallow peat soil (Shumushu Island).

The flora of the Kurile Islands comprises 992 species of plants, which belong to 417 genera and 100 families: 43 species of trees (including 5 conifers), 84 shrubs, 9 semishrubs, 9 vines, 5 bamboos, 75 annuals, 23 biennials, and 744 herbaceous perennials. Nearly two-thirds of these are found very rarely on the islands. By far the greatest number of plants belong to only 20 species, of which the Kurile bamboo and scrub pine are most common. There are five species of evergreen plants (not counting conifers, heaths, and bilberries): three plants holly (*Ilex rugosa*), skimmia (*Skimmia repens*), and gaultheria (*Gaultheria miquelliana*). The flora contains 26 young endemics, among which are six types of dandelion.

The history of the Kurile flora is complex. The intense cold of the glacial period destroyed nearly all the vegetation—dark conifers, for example—in the northern and some of the central islands, leaving only a few subalpine and arctic species. Consequently, the Kurile flora is not uniform and is made up of species of various origins: 78 per cent of the species are also found in Japan, 67 per cent on Sakhalin, 54 per cent in the Amur-Primorski region, 44 per cent on Kamchatka. The broad-leaved forests, coniferous forests, and forests of elm-leaved rock birch on the islands are but impoverished variants of the forests of Hokkaido. Nearly half of the plants found on the southern islands that are not present on the northern ones either appear again on Kamchatka or have close relatives there. North of Urup Island Japanese species are less common than Kamchatka species. The Kuriles and the northwestern coast of North America have some species in common.

Climate is the major factor affecting the present-day distribution of the vegetation of the Kurile chain. The cold current of Oyashio, which cools the eastern shores of the islands intensely, establishes unfavorable conditions for the northern spread of warmth-loving southern plants. The climate of the western shores is warmer and drier in summer. The majority of southern species are concentrated on the Okhotsk shore of the two southern islands, where they bloom 8 to 12 days earlier than elsewhere. Tomatoes, cucumbers, corn, and pumpkins ripen here, but cannot be grown on the Pacific Ocean coast. In places protected from cold, moist, strong sea winds by mountains, forests are thicker and their trees taller. Volcanoes, either directly or by their heating of ground water, have a strong effect on the vegetation. Eruptions may burn entire forests or smother them with ash, thus preventing extension of their habitat. Various complexes of warmth-loving southern plants are concentrated around fumarole centers or hot springs: cultivation of southern crops should be possible in valleys containing many fumaroles. Many species of plants do not grow in the northern and some of the central islands, not because of the climate, but because their steep mountain

slopes, rocky deposits, and lava flows, do not permit the development of fertile soil.

Obviously, the great extent of the Kurile chain from south to north prevents the development of a uniform vegetative cover. The southern islands have the richest vegetation, that of the northern islands is somewhat poorer, and that of the central ones is highly impoverished. From the forests of Hokkaido, which contain many different species, through Kunashir, Iturup, and Urup islands, the vegetation gradually becomes thinner and many species disappear. Most island forests have only one tier, but that one contains many different kinds of trees: the undergrowth is sparse but there are many vines. The northern boundary of the dark-conifer forests—Yeddo spruce (*Picea jezoënsis*) and Sakhalin fir—passes through the southern half of Iturup. Kurile bamboo is widespread on the islands as far north as Ketoi, where thickets of it serve as a haven for a number of southern plants such as sumac and tissa. On Urup and Iturup it grows more than six feet high and forms dense, almost impassible undergrowth in the forests. The density of the bamboo and its height depend directly on the thickness of the snow cover: where the snow blows off there is no bamboo; where much snow has piled up bamboo develops. It exerts a strong and many-sided influence on the whole development of the forest. Taking up all the open space, the bamboo forms a dense cover, which stifles the undergrowth and prevents the growth of young trees. North of Ketoi there are no forests or bamboo thickets and the only woody plant is scrub pine, which is found on all the islands except those of the Lesser Kuriles. As the forest area decreases the area of heath increases. To the north, the lower zones of vegetation gradually disappear: first the belt of broad-leaved trees, then that of dark conifers, which seldom rise above an altitude of 1,650 feet. At the same time, the upper zones descend and take the place of the disappearing ones; north of Iturup, forests of rock birch grow on the coastal lowlands, farther north these are replaced by groves of stone pine and alder, and finally heaths appear on the coast.

Two kinds of vegetation extend almost unchanged throughout the Kurile chain: the offshore marine vegetation, and the vegetation of the coastal sands and shoreline rocks. Near the coasts of the islands, at depths of 60 to 100 feet, underwater "meadows" of gigantic brown here. The thick growths of seaweed act as breakwaters and hamper the approach to the shores. On sandy beaches, just above the high-water line, are growths of briar rose (*Rosa rugosa*) and juniper (*Juniperus conferta*); farther from the shore, but still on the sand are *Elymus mollis* and creeping *Lactuca repens*.

Fig. 12-10. Mixed forest on Iturup Island (Kurile Islands).

seaweed spread out in a belt around each island, especially near Sikhotan, Urup, Brouton, Simushir, the Lovushki, and Makanrushi. The most noticeable seaweed is the giant seaweed (*Nereocystis lutseanus*), which grows rapidly: its development begins in April, and by July it has reached a length of more than 150 feet and rises to the surface of the sea; toward the end of August the plant dies, is broken up by the current, and is tossed up in great heaps on the shore, in places forming a soft bed for marine animals which have their rookeries

The Kurile Islands are subdivided into four geobotanical regions: the North Kurile, the Central Kurile, the South Kurile, and the Lesser Kurile. The North Kurile region extends from Shumushu to Ushishir. This is a region with a greatly impoverished Kamchatka flora: almost no forests, many thickets of scrub pine and Kamchatka alder, and well-developed heaths. The highest parts of the mountain slopes have a rock mantle covered with lichens and mosses and a few scattered flowering plants such as low-growing crazyweed (*Oxytropis pumila*) and saxifrage (*Saxifraga merkii*). On Alaid Island are alpine meadows with many anemones (*Anemone narcissiflora*). Below the bald-mountain zone the dry slopes of the mountains are covered with heaths of crowberry (*Empetrum nigrum*), bog *Ledum palustre*, Alpine ptarmigan-berry (*Arctous alpina*), and Arctic willow (*Salix arctica*). At altitudes of 1,650 to 2,300 feet are Kamchatka alder (*Alnus kamtschatica*) and dwarf stone pine (*Pinus pumila*). In the valleys are meadows of Alpine timothy (*Phleum alpinum*) and sheep's fescue (*Festuca eriantha*), and also meadows of tall Kamchatka grasses and herbs—bear-root, nettle, cacalia, and meadowsweet. The lowest sections are swampy and covered with sedges and grasses. In the valleys and small hollows, protected from cold wind and fog, there are groves of stunted Sakhalin willow (*Salix sachalinensis*), Maksimovich alder (*Alnus maximoviczii*), and elm-leaved rock birch (*Betula ulmifolia*) with twisted, contorted trunks.

The Central Kurile geobotanical region includes the islands from Ketoi to Urup, inclusive. It differs from the northern region in having southern species and, on Urup, forests of elm-leaved rock birch with an undergrowth of Kurile bamboo. Urup is the northern boundary of such southern species as Chinese club moss (*Lycopodium chinense*), skimmia (*Skimmia repens*), and maple (*Acer ukurunduense*). Throughout the region are thick growths of dwarf stone pine, groves of elm-leaved rock birch, and, along the banks of rivers, thickets of Sakhalin willow and Maksimovich alder. Dwarf stone pine is the basic landscape plant of the region; it is usually admixed with Siberian mountain ash (*Sorbus sambucifolia*), grows above a sparse cover of grass and club mosses, and covers a greater area than any other plan in the region. Next in area are groves of elm-leaved rock birch with an undergrowth of Kurile bamboo; growing with the birch are Maksimovich alder, ash (*Sorbus commixta*), Kurile cherry (*Prunus kurilensis*) on Urup, and a large number of shrubs and grasses; horensia is the only vine. The trunks

of birch, which grows 40 feet high, provide good lumber for all kinds of construction. On the tops of hills and on terraces, just as on the northern islands, are heaths of crowberry, golden and Kamchatka rhododendrons (*Rhododendron chrysanthum* and *Rh. kamtschaticum*), and cassiope (*Cassiope ericoïdes*). On the slopes of hills and marine terraces are meadows of Langsdorf beach grass, and on alluvial deposits in depressions and along rivers, meadows of tall grasses and herbs such as meadowsweet and cacalia. Grass bogs contain mostly Lyngby sedge (*Carex lyngbyei*)—on the coastal plains Middendorf sedge—and sphagnum bogs occupy large areas. The small islands, such as Brouton or Chirpoi, have the least vegetation; most of their surface is covered by a rock mantle on which are scattered a few flowering plants, mosses, and lichens.

The South Kurile geobotanical region consists of the two large southern islands, Iturup and Kunashir, and has dark-coniferous and mixed forests and a large number of southern plants. Passing through Iturup are the northern boundaries of many Manchurian species, such as dimorphant, lespedesa, and actinidia; on Kunashir is the northern boundary of magnolia (*Magnolia obovata*), Glehn spruce (*Picea glehni*), Japanese alder (*Alnus japonica*), and oak (*Quercus dentata*). The tops of mountains and the upper sections of slopes are covered with impassible thickets of dwarf stone pine that alternate with heaths, and a sparse grass cover on the talus slopes. Lower on the slopes is a narrow belt of elm-leaved rock birch with an admixture of mountain ash and Jamisso honeysuckle and an undergrowth of dwarf stone pine; still farther down the dwarf pine gives way to Kurile bamboo, which squeezes out all other vegetation under the trees. The lower parts of the mountain slopes and the foothills of the islands are covered with forests of Hokkaido spruce and Sakhalin fir; in damp places in the eastern part of Kunashir Island Glehn spruce predominates in the coniferous forests. Where spruce-fir forests have been logged off or destroyed by fire they have been replaced by groves of white Japanese birch

(*Betula japonica*). At the center of Iturup are forests of Kurile larch, oak (*Quercus crispula*), birch (*Betula tauschii*), and maple, and in the southern part of Kunashir are groves of broad-leaved trees—Amur linden, cork-bark oak, Manchurian ash, Mongolian oak, and maple. In the river valleys groves of chosen poplar, willow, and Maksimovich alder are common, as are tall-grass meadows of the Kamchatka type. On poorly drained spots are grass and sphagnum bogs.

The geobotanical region of the Lesser Kurile chain has no dwarf stone pine, little Kurile bamboo, and a great deal of Sargent's juniper (*Juniperus sargentii*). Below the narrow belt of elm-leaved rock birch are forests of Hokkaido spruce and Sakhalin fir, with an admixture of tissa, cork-bark oak, maple, ash, and bird-cherry.

The forests of the Kurile Islands have an exceptional soil-conserving and water-holding significance. The dense forests of the mountain slopes with their undergrowths of Kurile bamboo and tall grass pack the soil about their roots and turf the slopes, forestalling soil washout and aiding the accumulation of fine soil and its development. The forests of the southern islands provide building material for local needs and export, but the quality of the lumber is not high: the high humidity of the air makes the wood porous and spongy, so that it rots easily. Experimental planting of rye, wheat, barley and the cultivation of kitchen gardens on the large islands have been successful.

The chief occupations of the inhabitants of the Kuriles are hunting and fishing. In the past fur seal and sea beaver were commercially the most important, but they have been almost exterminated: at present Steller's sea lion is the most widely hunted. The whaling industry is of considerable importance, because the migrational route of whales, which feed in summer in the Bering Sea and in autumn move southward to their winter residence near the shores of Korea, passes along the Kuriles. After the decimation of seal and beaver the fishing industry acquired greater importance. Cod, navaga, halibut, and herring, which live near the shores, and Japanese sardine and anchovy, which come from the south with the warm Kamchatka Current, are caught throughout the year. In summer enormous shoals of salmon rush into the rivers to spawn—Siberian salmon, humpback salmon, red salmon, and silver salmon—and are caught there. Near Kunashir oyster pearls and crabs are obtained.

The fauna of the Kurile Islands is not rich. Almost all the mammals are linked with the forest: brown bears, wolves, foxes, and on the southern islands, otter, a few sable, squirrels, rabbits, and countless small rodents. On many of the islands, foxes introduced from the Komandorski Islands have acclimatized themselves, and are now found in great number (Ushisihr is called "island of foxes"). There are few domestic animals—a small number of cows, sheep, and dogs. On the northern and central islands the breeding of reindeer is possible. Altogether more than 170 species of birds have been counted on the Kurile Islands, the majority of them in the south. Multitudes of coastal marine birds nest on the islands, forming great rookeries on inaccessible cliffs: guillemot, puffin, noddy, and kittiwake-gull. On the fresh-water lakes are ducks (mallard, merganser, teal, pintail, turpan), and many snipe. During the period of migration, the islands are visited by swans and geese from the far north. Many northern taiga birds are found on the northern islands—nutcracker, black woodpecker, bullfinch, and tomtit. The tundra grouse (*Lagopus mutus kurilensis*) nests on the treeless tops of the mountains in the northern and central islands. Japanese and Chinese species live on the southern islands—blue flycatcher, Japanese long-tailed tomtit, and Japanese quail.

There are very few reptiles on the Kuriles, and they live only in the south (lizards, and occasionally snakes, on Kunashir Island). There are many insects on the southern islands, few on the northern ones, and almost none on the central islands. The great swarms of mosquitoes and gnats in the southern forests compel one to work outdoors in mosquito-nets and gloves.

PART IV

CENTRAL ASIA

Central Asia extends from 50° north latitude southward to the national boundary between the USSR and Iran and Afghanistan—its southernmost point, near the city of Kushka, is at about 35° north latitude; its western boundary is the Caspian Sea, its eastern is Sinkiang Province of China. It comprises the union Republics of Turkmen, Uzbek, Tadzhik, and Kirghiz, and the central and southern part of the Kazakh SSR. Its climate is sharply continental, with cold winters and hot summers. Both annual and daily temperature amplitudes are great; most of the region has many hours of sunshine and very little precipitation; even the mountains are arid. Central Asia is part of the vast undrained interior Eurasian basin whose low arid plains surrounded by high mountain ranges, control the regime of the many large rivers within it. The unusual climate of Central Asia gives the process of soil formation a pronounced seasonal character, and has resulted in the broad development of arid soil. In its flora and fauna—which comprise, for the most part, species from the neighboring Iran-Mediterranean and Central Asiatic phytogeographic and zoogeographic regions—are many remarkable examples of adaptation to geographic conditions. The greater part of the region consists of semideserts and deserts; forests occupy a negligible area. In Central Asia crops have been irrigated for many centuries, and the construction of irrigation systems is still going on. Cotton and fruit are perhaps the most important agricultural products.

Central Asia is subdivided into three geographic regions: semidesert, desert, and mountain.

CHAPTER 13

Semidesert Region of Central Asia

The semideserts of Central Asia extend in a relatively narrow strip from the sources of the Emba River in the west to Lake Zaysan in the east. They are part of the undrained Eurasian basin, and constitute the transitional geographic zone between the steppes of Siberia and the northern deserts of Central Asia. Summer temperatures are higher and precipitation is lighter than on the neighboring steppes, and because of this ground and surface water is saltier, there are many salt lakes, and the soil is but slightly leached. The greater part of the soil is light-chestnut in the northern part and brown in the southern, but there are many large patches of solonetz (which disappear to the south) and solonchak scattered throughout the region. The thin plant cover consists of a complex combination of shallow-turf steppe grasses, arid halophytes, and, especially, many different species of the genus *Artemisia*. The association of soil and vegetative cover is extremely clear. The boundary between the flora of the Western Siberian steppes and that of the Central Asiatic semideserts and deserts coincides with the northern boundary of semidesert. The southern steppes, although they lie outside the Western Siberian Lowland, are closely related to the other Western Siberian steppes, whereas the semideserts are not part of Siberia, but the northernmost section of Central Asia.

RELIEF AND HYDROGRAPHY

The region of semideserts, together with the adjacent steppes on the north that extend to the southern border of the Western Siberian Lowland, is divided into three clearly defined districts, sharply distinguished from one another by their geologic composition and structure, their relief, and the nature of their surface and ground water: the Mugodzhar Mountains, the Turgai Plateau, and the Kazakh folded country.

The Mugodzhar Mountains

The Mugodzhar Mountains, the natural continuation of the Urals, consist of a long narrow ridge that extends from north to south through the monotonous steppe and semidesert for 120 miles, then begins to rise, splits into two parallel ridges 9 to 12 miles apart and continues for another 120 miles. Neither of the two ridges is continuous—both are broken by narrow valleys or basins into a series of low hills and isolated masses. The range is asymmetrical, but, unlike the Urals, has a steep western slope and a gentle eastern one. In the south the Mugodzhar Mountains break off with a steep porphyritic scarp to an Upper Cretaceous and Tertiary plain. The chief, or Western, Range of the Mugodzhar Mountains has a more pronounced relief in the south, where the highest peaks are —Ber-Chogur, 2,145 feet, and double-peaked Ayryuk, 2,075 feet—but since relative heights

are only 690 to 850 feet the range does not rise very high above the adjacent plain. In the north it breaks up into a series of hilly ridges and disappears before reaching 50° north latitude. The main range is formed primarily of diabase and porphyry, among which lie metamorphic and sedimentary rocks of the Paleozoic, and shales, jaspers, and quartzites of the Devonian. Carboniferous and Permian sandstones and limestones have survived in islands. The Eastern Range, on the other hand, has

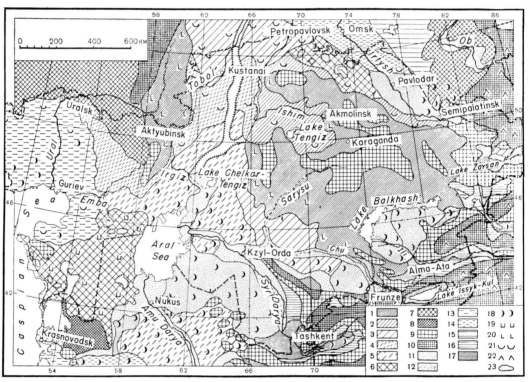

Map 13-I. Geomorphologic divisions of Kazakhstan: 1—Gently sloping low foothills; 2—Stratified isolated plains; 3—Stratified undulating plains; 4—Stratified graded slopes (on plains); 5—Stratified table plains and degraded uplands (plains of denudation); 6—Tableland uplands (undulating); 7—Sloping uplands; 8—Ridge escarpments (cuestas) with tectonic faults or faulted scarps; 9—Low and medium uplands; 10—Medium and high uplands (monadnocks) on plains of depositional lowlands; 11—Old alluvium or diluvium; 12—Recent alluvium–submerged marine lowlands or plains of emergence; 13—Marine and alluvial lowlands or lake and sea alluvium; 14—Old marine lowlands of ancient lake alluvium; 15—Recent lake alluvial lowlands; 16—Ancient piedmont plains; 17—Recent piedmont plains with additional relief-forming processes; 18—Degrading surfaces (weathering and formation of sand massifs); 19—Karst; 20—Old abraded or eroded surfaces; 21—Eluvial processes (ancient and recent); 22—Old and contemporary glacial formations; 23—Large depressions.

Fig. 13-1. The Mugodzhar Hills.

sharper relief in its northern section; in the south it is lower, with very smooth hills buried under masses of greenstone rubble. The range is formed, in the west, of diorite, changing in the east into gabbro and gabbrodiorite, among which are islands of jasper and quartzite.

The area between the ranges in the south is called the Alabassk Valley. The northern part of the depression is occupied by a slightly hilly plain, complicated by small narrow ridges linking the two ranges. The depression has a structure as complex as that of the ranges themselves. It is formed of intensely and intricately dislocated metamorphic slates of the Devonian with a northeast strike, and of conglomerates and limestones of the Carboniferous and Permian that are more gently folded. Radial dislocations took place here. Both the borders of the range and the surrounding plain are shaped by a system of faults that run north-south. East of the mountains is a granitic-gneiss zone—an abraded platform that slopes toward the horizontally bedded Tertiary sediments of the plains west of the mountains. Gneisses crumpled into folds, primarily of a north-south strike, are cut through by stocks and stratified

seams of granites and quartzitic porphyries. Exceptional development of gneisses is marked in the relief by a monotonous plain, but where there are many intrusions the landscape is hilly, with scattered crests and mounds strewn with rubble, among which are outcrops of igneous rocks.

A traveler on the semidesert is attracted to these blue mountains from afar as though by a magnet. Reaching them, he finds only a series of hills running along the plain, covered by monotonous steppe and semidesert vegetation. This landscape developed because of the diversified composition of the rocks forming the ranges, the mechanical weathering that results from the sharp daily fluctuations in temperature, especially in the south, and the rapid removal of the mantle rock. The peaks of the Western Range are outcrops of bedrock with sharp rocky crests strewn with rubble and almost devoid of fine soil. The slopes of the range are steep and rocky, and many are covered by streams of large angular rubble moving downwards. Thus fresh surfaces are continually being subjected to weathering and erosion. This explains the development here of a very coarse rubbly soil that contains only a small amount of fine particles. In the Eastern Range the relief is gentler; individual elevations have flat, smooth tops and are roughly the same height; the hollows between them contain clay.

In the axial part of the range, many narrow ravines are pressed between outcrops of bedrock. When these emerge onto the plain they widen and become broad flat-bottomed valleys with faintly marked channels. The external indications of water that are found in their upper sections all but disappear here. The southern part of the Western Range serves as the water divide between the Caspian and Aral seas. Farther north the watershed is a hilly plain between the ranges; the rivers of its western slope cut through the Western Range, and those of its eastern slope cut through the Eastern Range. In the highest parts of Mugodzhar, which are formed of crumbling massive crystalline rocks, an abundance of fresh water, often of good quality, flows out along fissures. There are many springs at the bases of slopes in both longitudinal and lateral valleys, especially in the western foothills, and some of these erode small channels six to eight inches wide and deep. On the banks of these channels, the scanty semidesert vegetation gives way to bright green ribbons of succulent grasses; and along deep mountain ravines into which springs flow there are strips of small trees and shrubs. The northern part of the Mugodzhar Mountains, which has more water, is rather picturesque. Deep ravines contain thickets of birch, bird cherry, aspen, buckthorn, honeysuckle, hawthorn, and willow, and on nearby slopes are buckbean, pea tree, and wild cherry intertwined with wild berry bushes. The farther a spring is from the axis of the ranges, the more highly its water is mineralized, because of the concentration of the salts by evaporation and the decelerated discharge. Here, in Tertiary (some gypsiferous) and Quaternary deposits, the water is consistently hard, although its mineral content may vary.

Despite the relative low elevation of the Mugodzhar Mountains above the neighboring plains, they have a marked influence on the distribution of geographic landscapes. Within their limits soil and vegetative zones show a clear southward extension.

The Turgai Plateau

Turgai Plateau lies between the Mugodzhar Mountains on the west and the Ulu-Tau Mountains on the east. It has a general drop southward toward the Aral Sea, which is the direction of discharge for surface water of the Turgai and Irgiz River basins. In its center is a long depression that runs north-south and is from 260 to 330 feet in altitude. Along this depression numerous lakes stretch in the same direction, beginning with Lake Kushmurun in the north and ending with Lake Chelkar-Tengiz in the south. This depressed strip coincides with the ancient Turgai Strait, which existed in the Tertiary Period and united the Lower Tertiary Siberian basin with a similar basin on the Turan Lowland, and is considered to be of tectonic origin. North of Lake Kushmurun it gradually widens and emerges onto the broad, slightly hilly plain that constitutes the southern part of the Western Siberian Lowland; in the south it gradually merges with the lowland near the Aral Sea. Both west and east of the central part of the depression the region rises; the relief becomes somewhat more diverse and is enriched by hills. In the south the greatest height of the Turgai Plateau is 660 feet, in the central part it is 742 feet, and on the water divide of the basin of the Turgai and Ishim it is 940 to 990 feet.

The entire elevated part of the region and most of the central depressions are formed of horizontally lying Tertiary, marine Oligocene, and continental Miocene deposits. Since the Oligocene Period, this country has not been occupied by a sea; the water of the Aral Sea did not reach here, and only Lake Chelkar-Tengiz, lying at the same level as the Aral Sea (171 feet), constituted a bay of somewhat fresher water. One of the general features of the deposits is that everywhere fine-layered clays with streaks of clayey and siliceous marls, often very rich in gypsum and salt, occupy the lower part, and sand with pebbles and conglomerates form the upper part. Clay and sand are variegated, being stained in bright red, white, yellow, blue-gray, and dark green tones. Leaching and weathering of these deposits conditioned the formation of salt lakes and solonchak, on which specialized fleshy halophytes make the best of the highly salty soil. At different heights in the central part of the main depression salifer-ous and gypsiferous sand and clay of post-Ter-tiary river and lake origin are found, and among the surface deposits white quartzitic sand and loess-like clayey soil are noted.

That the unusual conditions of the Tertiary Period have their distinct mark on the develop-ment is clearly indicated by the complete de-pendence of the forms of relief on the geologic composition and structure. The susceptibility to erosion of the loose, weakly cemented Ter-tiary deposits, their great salinity, and the height of the ancient unbroken Tertiary pla-teau have contributed to the intensity of ero-sion. In one of the more humid post-Tertiary periods, broad flat-bottomed ravines were formed; these were the first streams to carry the products of erosion out of the region. Later, a system of secondary deep ravines developed, dissecting the earlier single plateau into many separate isolated elevations or mesas. After fur-ther erosional activity, the isolated elevations were lowered and converted into flat-topped buttes. The destroyed upper layers of Tertiary strata freed the lower-lying saliferous clays, which were more easily weathered, and this contributed to further erosion and leaching of the soil. The subsequent disappearance of sur-face water resulted in the drying of the entire region and contributed in great measure to arid weathering. In the districts of greatest ero-sion, partly drained, aeolian-formed basins de-veloped which comprised a system of lakes. Thus, owing to the absence of forests, the work of the water was strong enough to dissect the region into a series of mesas, but the work of the wind was not energetic enough to destroy these elevations.

At the present time the Turgai Plateau has a clearly expressed landscape of mesas which distinguishes it sharply from the adjacent geo-morphologic districts. The tops of the mesas are almost perfectly flat, and even though little water runs off, the steep sides are gullied. The valleys of the plateau are extremely broad and in some places are dozens of miles in width. They are situated rather low and have slight gradients to the south; thus long narrow chains of small lakes are found in them. Small rivers flow along the central part of the valleys but do not approach the original banks and do not produce lateral erosion.

Closely linked with general geologic and physicogeographic conditions are the occur-rence and character of ground water. The arid climate is unfavorable for the formation of large supplies of ground water since 95 per cent of the precipitation evaporates; only 5 per cent goes into runoff or soaks into the soil. Most of the ground water accumulates in spring from the melting of snow. It occurs regularly in the Tertiary saliferous deposits, but it is not abundant and is strongly saline. The hardness of ground water is less in the loess-like clay soil cover. Rich water-bearing layers are developed in alluvial sandy deposits along the course of the main rivers. Springs of these water-bearing layers guarantee excellent drinking water for pasturing herds.

Lakes are common, and are an original for-mation amid broad depressions of deflation. The valleys are shaped only according to the degree of discontinuation of the life of the lakes and the eroding of the beds in the lake deposits. All of the valleys have both flowing and undrained lakes which, intercepting the surface flow, partly regulate it and partly stop it completely. Over-all features of the lakes are: a shallow depth (6 to 9 feet) even over a great area, a sudden rise (as much as 10 to 13 feet) in spring with a rather rapid drop, and the drying up of the majority toward the middle of summer. The amount of water in the lakes depends on the precipitation of a given year and the precipitation of foregoing years, on the supply of water in the snow cover, and on the size of the water-collecting area and the slope of the banks. In this region are fresh and salt lakes, permanent lakes, and temporary lakes that are filled only in the spring, becoming dried beds (*sory*) or solonchak in the summer. As a rule, all the fresh lakes have outlets and are associated with valleys. Undrained salt lakes are in the most depressed portions of relief, such as the end points of an outlet from the elevated parts of the region. They have a watertight bottom of saliferous clays and are fed by mineralized ground water. In the spring high-water period, these lakes are freshened; in low-water periods, they become salty. All the main rivers of the area are merely tributaries of Lake Chelkar-Tengiz, a typical terminal, dam lake lying in the lowest depression, which is dammed on the south by the sand of the Kara-Kum Desert, north of the Aral Sea. This large lake occupies a shallow depression with a flat, muddy, sticky bottom, and has gentle sandy banks and acrid water.

The rivers of the Turgai mesa country have little water. The river network is denser at the borders of the neighboring elevations. In the southern part the rivers flow only in spring; in summer the river channels become separated stretches of water. The difference between the discharges of water during the period of spring high-water and during the period of average water level is great, especially in the big rivers. The rivers are fed by melting snow. Snow accumulates in the depressions of the neighboring mountains, having been blown off the higher places. Spring flooding is rapid and violent, and during this time almost 100 per cent of the annual flow passes through the rivers. Summer precipitation is insignificant and has no effect on the river regime because of the high evaporation. Erosion and deposition are limited to the short period of spring high-water. The channel of the Turgai, the largest river, is enclosed between the two parallel natural levees formed by the deposit of spring flood alluvium; consequently, the water level is often higher than the lowest levels of the valley.

Along the banks of the larger rivers are woody and brushwood thickets and also diversified bottomland meadows. Along slopes of Tertiary saliferous rocks grows halophytic vegetation, especially saltworts, which extend quite far to the north on such substrata.

The Kazakh Folded Country

The Kazakh folded country extends from the Western Siberian Lowland approximately to the latitude of the northern shore of Lake Balkhash. In the west it ends in the Ulu-Tau Mountains and in the east abuts against the Altai and the boundary of China. The relief of the region is intermediate between mountainous and hilly or simply occupied by gently sloped hills, not connected with one another and formed of Paleozoic rocks. Among these hillocks are scattered individual, comparatively high, ancient, folded massifs formed of the same rocks. In the central part the highest massifs extend in an east-west chain: the Ulu-Tau Range (3,730 feet), the Karkaralinskiye Mountains (the highest point is Mount Kyzyl-Ray, 4,800 feet), and Chingiz-Tau (4,100 feet). In the east the country rises even more. The Saur and Tarbagatay ranges rise sharply above Zaysan Basin to the snow line and possess glaciers. The Mus-Tau group of the Saur Range reaches 9,711 feet.

From this high central zone the land slopes gradually to the north, west, and south. The slopes are broken by the irregular development of isolated elevations or their extensions, such as the Kokchetavskiye Mountains. This central zone is the water divide between the drainless basin of Lake Balkhash and the Aral Sea, on one side, and the Irtysh and the central undrained basin of Lake Tengiz on the other. From the slopes of the Kokchetavskiye Mountains the main rivers of the country flow in all directions; the Sary-Su to the southwest, the northern tributaries of the Balkhash to the south, the rivers running to the Irtysh to the north and northeast; only the Nura River carries water from the interior part of the region to the central undrained basin.

The Kazakh folded country has a complex

geologic structure. The geologic period of its origin may be considered along with that of the northern Tien Shan ranges and the Altai Mountains. All of these ranges are formed of Paleozoic rocks and possess a similar geologic history, the most intensive folding processes being in the lower Paleozoic (Caledonian folding) and the less important ones in the upper Paleozoic (Variscan folding). In individual localities, pre-Cambrian highly dislocated gneisses and crystalline schists are found in folds which approximate a meridional strike and have somewhat predetermined the direction of subsequent dislocations. Strata of the lower Paleozoic occupy large areas, lying in unconformity on pre-Cambrian strata, and contain various metamorphosed schists, quartzites, sandstones, and limestones. The two tectonic phases of Caledonian folding are rather distinctly marked, with a predominating northwest direction of folds. The last phase was more vigorous, as a consequence of which mountain forming took place more intensely and vast intrusions occurred which elevated the country. Only at the end of the Lower Devonian Period did the deposition of marine sediments begin again. The two strong subsequent phases of Variscan folding in the Carboniferous and Permian, with a predominantly northwest direction, were accompanied by an intensification and complication of folds, as well as intrusions of granites and grandiorites. Discontinuous faults were widespread, and overthrust folding of northeast and northwest trend took place. These brought about the formation of a system of fissures and breaks in the strata along tectonic joints, which is of great significance in the hydrogeology of the region. Both Caledonian and Varsican intrusions were of tremendous importance in the formation (on their peripheries) of copper, silver, lead, cobalt, asbestos, and other deposits.

The mountain ranges were built by strong repeated folding, and the entire region emerged irregularly from beneath sea level, creating shallow seas in depressions. Along the banks of the rivers and lakes, near the receding sea, a luxuriant vegetation grew, and these littoral forests and bogs accumulated plant materials which subsequently produced coal (Karaganda). In depressions amid Paleozoic deposits are Jurassic delta, bog, and lake formations containing brown coal. At the end of the Jurassic Period there occurred a strong Mesozoic (New-Kimeridgian) tectonic phase, indicated by the folding and faults with which the region is bordered. In depressions there are horizontal marine Tertiary deposits. Dislocations of the Tertiary were faults, upthrusts, and overthrusts, often with very great dislocations along former faults. At this time, many fault blocks were formed, with interlaying depressions. At the end of the Tertiary Period the relief in general corresponded to that of the present, except that it was more sharply defined. Subsequently, the ranges were intensely eroded, and the products of erosion were deposited in depressions, which led to modification of the relief. Quaternary deposits, developed everywhere, are sandy loam and a clayey soil, sometimes of a loess-like character. On the slopes, eluvial and diluvial sand, clay, and gravel are found.

The Kazakh folded country has long been famous for its mineral resources, but only recently have large deposits of metallic ores been discovered. Supplies of copper are established at millions of tons (57.4 per cent of the USSR reserves), of which 80 per cent is concentrated in three large deposits: Kounrad, Dzhezkazgan, and Boshchekul.

The Kounrad deposit, located in the arid lowland plain approximately 11 miles from the north coast of Balkhash, is a high cone-shaped mountain formed by quartzite, granite, and syenite. The large supplies of copper ore are concentrated in a very small area, the distribution of ore is irregular, and the copper content fluctuates considerably. Oxidized ores are chrysocolla and azurite. The Kounrad deposits forms about a quarter of the total supplies of Kazakhstan copper and contains a little gold and silver.

Dzhezkazgan, the largest deposit of copper ore, is in a semiarid locality in the southern part of the Ulu-Tau Range. Its favorable aspects are: undisturbed and shallow occurrence of the ore, sturdy ore-containing rocks that require little bracing, and a negligible inflow of ground water.

Besides the big Boshchekul deposit (between Pavlodar and Akmolinsk), there are many smaller ones scattered in the eastern part of the region. In addition to copper, polymetallic deposits (of the Altai type) of tin, nickel, wolfram, and manganese are found. Of the nonmetallic minerals, coal is of the greatest importance—the largest supplies are concentrated in the Karaganda coal basin in the center of Kazakhstan. Its reserves (up to fifty billion tons) put it in fourth place in the USSR, after the Kuznetsk, Donets, and Bureya coal basins. The productive series is formed of sandy-clayey Carboniferous deposits, containing many pure seams of coal. Above them lies a mass of Jurassic deposits with lenses of brown coal and brown iron ore. The Karaganda coking coal has a sulphur content of up to 1 per cent and ash from 9 to 19 per cent. The great problem is the lack of water, although abundant artesian water has been found.

The stages of development of the region's relief are: extremely complex tectonic activity, which created a series of mountains and large undrained basins; a prolonged continental period from the end of the Palezoic to the beginning of the Tertiary, which led to the gradual destruction of folded mountains and their conversion into a peneplain; modern erosional and aeolian weathering processes, which have created forms such as ellipsoids of granites and fantastic crags, as are found in the Bayan-Aul Range. The complex lithological composition is important from the standpoint of its contribution to the folding of the more resistant rocks. The highest points are formed by the closest-grained rocks—quartzites; igneous rocks produced the smaller elevations; and sandstones of the Devonian and Carboniferous periods are revealed more often in depressions. Thus the modern forms of relief must be considered as residuals from the former folded mountains. At the present time there are three types of relief:

1) Rocky massifs with relative heights of 1,650 feet and heights of 4,950 feet possess the features of a real mountain landscape—narrow gorges; sheer, highly abraded cliffs; deep, often fresh, lakes in depressions; and pine forests amid steppes (Ulu-Tau Range, Karkaralinskiye Mountains, Chingiz-Tau Mountains, Kokchetavskiye Mountains, and Bayan-Aul massif).

2) Less prominent ridges composed of high hills with elevations of 2,310 feet are also dissected by valleys, but lakes are absent in the drier depressions (the heights near Karkaralinsk).

3) The mound country proper (maximum elevation 660 to 1,000 feet) is a series of scattered hills with gentle slopes and smooth rounded profiles, often with bedrock outcrops at the top—granite, syenite, porphyry, diabase, and sedimentary Palezoic rock. The heights of the hills relative to the neighboring depressions vary from only a few yards to several dozen yards, and the hills are so monotonous it is very easy to lose one's bearings in them. The shape of the mounds depends on their lithological composition: quartzite forms sharp-pointed summits, granite makes smooth tops, porphyry develops still more rounded profiles. Among the hillocks are numerous locked-in basins, many of which are occupied by salt lakes. The diameter of these random depressions varies from dozens of yards to many miles, and their depth reaches from 65 to 130 feet. The slightly rolling central basin of the Lake Tengiz country is one of these depressions. The basins are apparently the result of aeolian processes which were active in the preceding, drier period. The valleys are extremely wide and are not at all consistent with the small flow of water.

A typical feature of the mounded country is the lowness of the upper reaches of rivers and the low watersheds lying between them. Nowhere on the slopes of the depressions are terraces or residual river deposits visible. The mounded country owes its origin and development to erosion and denudation processes of long duration. The long denudation processes are evidenced by the development of compact Paleozoic rocks not covered by later sedimentary deposits to any appreciable degree—they were removed by the continuing denudation processes, which even deeply affected the basic rocks—and by the lack of tectonic breaks (at least they are not clearly shown in the relief).

The age of the denudation origin of the mounded country is demonstrated by geomorphologic evidence: (1) distribution of a single type of relief on rocks of varying composition; (2) comparatively small fluctuation of relief; (3) coincidence of quartzites and acid igneous rocks on hills and ridges with rock outcrops, these being the least liable to destruction.

The moister climate of the Cretaceous and lower Tertiary periods caused erosion-denudation processes to be more intense than they are today. This is exemplified by the extreme concealment of the old erosion process in the mounded country. However, the old buried valleys, discovered in the mounded country's depressions beneath a thick layer of local alluvium, are evidence of a different erosion cycle. The formation of the mounded country is linked almost exclusively with the denudation process under conditions of a dry, sharply continental climate, which replaced the earlier moister climate. Connected with it are the intensive development of mechanical weathering and the accumulation of rubbly products of weathering on the lower sections of slopes. Obstructed drainage is characteristic of the mounded relief, and there is a weak carrying power and limited washout of friable products by flowing water. This alluvium is moved slowly down the slopes and fills the lowlands, contributing to gentle slopes and soft relief forms. Weak washout in the more desert-like region aids in the preservation of locked-in valleys.

Near its outer edges the mounded country turns into a rolling hilly plain with scattered islands of hills. The old tectonic depression of Lake Tengiz belongs to this type of relief. These areas differ not only in having a special evenness and few mounds, but also in having lower relative elevation. The abrasion of the Tertiary basins occurred here, and the accumulation of marine sediments took part in the

development of relief. The thickness of the accumulation varies, but in some places it is 3,000 feet (near Akmolinsk). The surface of the mounded country was covered with marine deposits, above which only rarely did the tops of the mounds emerge and become islands during the marine transgression. In later times, the erosion of the marine Tertiary-Cretaceous surface deposits exposed the buried massifs of the old mounded country. Along the valleys of large rivers this zone is affected by secondary dissection of the leveled plain created earlier.

The problem of supplying industrial and drinking water to the growing industrial centers in waterless, semiarid localities demands special attention. Because of rock jointing, the top of the water table of the interstitial water usually is within 10 yards of the surface. There is a steady discharge of this water, with only slight fluctuations, throughout the year. In general, the water is fresh or has low mineralization. The local population avails itself of this water by digging shallow wells or by collecting spring water. Water is also prevalent in the rocks of the Devonian and Carboniferous folds, and often forms artesian water. The chemical composition of this water depends on the lithological character of the rocks along which it moves; thus it is sometimes fresh, sometimes saline. The discharge of these springs is not large, but is constant and is independent of the season. Woody vegetation appears wherever fresh springs discharge.

The hydrographic network is widely developed in this region but, in the main, it belongs only to the locked-in basins. The largest rivers, such as the Ishim, Sary-Su, Nura, Chiderty, and Selety, retain water all summer, but the shallower rivers have a steady flow only in their upper sections. The central sections of the shallow streams give the appearance of separate isolated stretches of water. The lower sections are but shallow channels which fill only in the spring. The greatest annual discharge (90 per cent) of the rivers takes place in spring. The rapid onset of spring melts the snow that has accumulated in valleys and basins and brings about turbulent flooding. At this time the speed of the current is so great that even in the central section the river beds are filled with gravel and large rocks. Additional floods caused by heavy summer and autumn rains are characteristic of the upper channels of rivers. In winter, the shallow streams often freeze solid. The water of the rivers is usually fresh; however, if they are joined by salt lakes or pass along saliferous Tertiary and Quaternary deposits the water becomes highly saline and acrid, and unfit for drinking or industrial uses.

In this region there are many small basins in solid rocks, which lead to the development of countless temporary and permanent lakes. The lakes are fresh, brackish, salt-bearing, or sometimes salt-depositing, depending on the degree to which the basin is locked in, the character of the rocks of the lake-bed, and the chemistry of the water brought by the rivers. The largest lakes—Tengiz and Kurgaldzhin—comprise a single lake-river system which is situated at an elevation of 1,000 feet at the bottom of the vast central valley and which is typical of the level of erosion of the rivers of this district. Lake Tengiz lies in a saucer-shaped basin with gentle banks, formed of compact clays, abounding in inclusions of gypsum; thus the water of the lake is acrid. Both lakes are shallow, with a maximum depth of 20 to 25 feet at the northern shore. The bottoms are clayey and in places covered with algae and black ooze. A large part of Lake Kurgaldzhin is thickly overgrown with reeds. The Nura River, entering Lake Tengiz, freshens the northern part of the lake, but the many springs issuing from the gypsum-bearing clays at the other end make its whole southern part salty. Surviving traces of a former, higher level of the lakes indicate that they previously constituted single salt-water basin and that only in a period of prolonged drought did their division take place. As a result of the division, Lake Kurgaldzhin has an outlet and became fresh, and Lake Tengiz remained terminal and became increasingly salty. In 1931 most of the water of the Nura River began to pass into the Ishim River, and the flow into Lake Tengiz was decreased.

The biggest lake is Zaysan, the fourth largest in the Asiatic part of the USSR. It lies at an altitude of 1,280 feet on the bottom of an enormous graben between the Saur and Tarbagatay ranges on the south and Southern Altai on the north. The shores of this flowing lake, which extends in a northwest direction, are for the most part low and sandy, except for Chakilmes Mountain, formed of clay shales, which rises in the northeast. The low shores are occupied by dry halophytic meadows covered with chee grass (*Lasiagrostis*), by impassable brackish marshes, and by reed bogs. The Black Irtysh River enters Lake Zaysan on the east side through several distributaries which form a broad, overgrown, swampy delta. The current caused by the entry of the Black Irtysh stops 1.8 miles from the mouth. The underwater channel of the Black Irtysh continues along the lake bed 1.2 miles wide and is 33 feet deep. This channel is the basis for considering Lake Zaysan as a flooded valley of the Black Irtysh River. The main Irtysh River flows out of the northern end of the lake. With the exception of the deep channel, lake depths vary from 13 to 19 feet. The water is fresh, brownish-green, and its greatest transparency is 9 feet. Because of its shallowness, the water of Lake Zaysan warms throughout. On summer days the surface temperature rises to 85°F, and even at the lake bottom the water does not drop below 67°F. In winter the temperature of the bottom water remains above 39.3°F. These high winter temperatures are the cause of sudden breaks in the ice in the central part of the lake and an unfrozen area at the source of the Irtysh. The numerous streams flowing off the mountains toward Zaysan lose their water to evaporation or irrigation before reaching it. Therefore the level of Lake Zaysan depends exclusively on the Black Irtysh. In spring, at the time of the melting of the ice cover, the lake is at its lowest level. In summer, when the Black Irtysh begins to rise with the meltwater of the mountains, the maximum rise of the lake occurs.

The fauna of Lake Zaysan consists of common representatives of the fish of the Black Irtysh and Ob, such as sturgeon, and salmon

(*Salmo thymallus*), but not the fish of the basins of the Aral, Chu, and Balkhash, with which Zaysan has never been linked. In the hydroelectric development of the Irtysh the lake will serve as a gigantic water reservoir, as a regulator of the flow of the Irtysh, and as a source of irrigation water for the surrounding semiarid territories.

CLIMATE

As in all of Central Asia, the climate of the semidesert regions is distinctly continental: sharp annual and daily temperature fluctuations, hot summers and cold winters, a short spring, aridity, and little precipitation. There is regular change of climate both from north to south and from west to east. The semideserts lie between the January isotherms—3.1°F in the north and 12.1°F in the south, and running in a strictly east-west direction. The July isotherms—71.5°F in the northern part and 78.8° in the southern part—run up to the Ulu-Tau Range in an east-west direction, but then drop sharply to the south, rounding the elevations of the Kazakh folded country. Owing to the increase in continentality from west to east, winters are severer in Kazakhstan than they are in European semideserts, the amount of precipitation is less, and the absolute temperature amplitude reaches 154.8 degrees (at Kokpekty), and the transition from frosts and snowstorms to thaws and calms often takes place in a single day.

The annual precipitation of the semideserts is less than 12 inches. Annual precipitation may—as, for example, at Kokpekty—fluctuate from 15.5 to 7.5 inches (average of 11.8 inches). Seasonal precipitation is irregular: in general, the greatest precipitation occurs in summer, the least in winter. For example, precipitation records for Karkaralinsk show: summer, 5.2 inches (44 per cent); autumn, 3 inches (26 per cent). From 20 to 40 per cent of the annual precipitation is snow. To the south, maximum precipitation shifts from June to May, and minimum precipitation shifts from winter to summer. Winds greatly influence the water balance of the region, since they blow frequently and with great force. At Irgiz 81 per cent of the observations showed some wind.

Wind velocities at Turgai vary from 15.8 feet per second in August to 20.4 feet per second in February. The greatest relative humidity is observed in winter (January, 83 per cent), and the least in summer (July, 35 per cent at Irgiz). Owing to strong and prolonged winds and low summer humidity, evaporation from open water amounts to 80 inches a year. The greatest cloudiness is in December, the least in August. Cloudiness decreases notably to the south.

Winter temperatures may reach figures extremely low for these latitudes: —43.3°F in the west (Irgiz) and —56.5°F in the east (Kokpekty). In winter strong northeast winds blow from the periphery of the Central Asiatic area of high pressure, bringing severe snowstorms but only a negligible amount of precipitation and depressing the already low temperature. The snow cover is thin (28 inches in the north, 8 inches in the south), owing to the minimum precipitation during the winter. Because the thin snow mantle covers the soil for only a comparatively short period (up to 120 days) and is easily blown off by the strong winter winds, the soil freezes to considerable depths. The low-growing semiarid vegetation is poorly protected from the cold, which comes on before the snowfall. The thin snow cover permits the maintenance of livestock on fodder in winter; however, since intense freezes often set in after thawing, causing the formation of an ice crust, livestock frequently cannot obtain food and perish en masse. Thus, reserve fodder stocks are necessary.

Spring is characterized by sudden shift from winter cold to summer heat—April is 23.4 degrees warmer than March; May is 20 degrees warmer than April—and often the change occurs within a few days. This is attributable to the thin snow cover, which requires little heat for thawing. Spring is extremely short, often lasting no more than 10 to 13 days. Because of this, the duration of the growing period is increased, and is about 164 to 190 days. In spring, the frozen ground cannot absorb all of the water from the rapidly melted snow and the spring rains. Part of the water quickly evaporates, some runs off into the rivers, and only a little soaks into the soil. The remnants of snowdrifts packed by the winds into a firn-like mass melt slowly. This delayed melting and the spring rains, along with the relatively low temperatures and slight evaporation, guarantee moisture to spring vegetation, which has adapted its activity to this moist period.

Summer temperatures in the semideserts may reach 104°F, but frost is possible in June. Although precipitation is highest during the summer months, it is not excessive, amounting in three summer months to from 6 to 10 inches. The summer winds (north and north-north-east) do not reach velocities as high as do the winter winds, but they too are dry. Summer downpours wash along the gulleys, unretarded by vegetation, and not soaking into the soil. Evaporation is high, owing to the high temperatures and the frequent winds. The summer dryness is unfavorable for vegetation; thus growth takes place principally in the moist spring, and autumn.

The influence of unfavorable climatic factors on vegetation is, to a great degree, increased by the plants themselves. The low, sparse, semi-desert vegetation does not protect the soil from intense heating in summer or from deep chilling in winter. Furthermore, it does not prevent the snow cover from being blown off nor does it hinder the rapid runoff of surface water.

SOIL

The soil-forming process in the semideserts is unique. In comparison with the more northerly steppes, the soil of the semidesert is far less leached, owing to the drier climate and the higher summer temperature. In addition, the poor, scattered vegetation yields a small amount of organic matter to the soil. These basic factors bring about (1) a gradual decrease of humus layer, in comparison with steppe soil; (2) a lesser intensity of chemical processes in the soil; (3) a weaker decomposition of the minerals; (4) an approach of the layer of effervescence to the surface; and (5) a discharge of calcium carbonate and a formation of a layer containing soluble salts. Because of the decreased role of water in soil formation, the parent stratum's physical and chemical properties take on importance. The high salinity of the parent stratum and ground water is a legacy of the preceding xerothermic period. The clayey and generaly compact, impervious layers are more subjected to salting than are sandy and loess-like strata. Each parent stratum has its own soil diversities; thus, the profiles of soil patches are sinuous and irregular. As the climate becomes dryer, solonetz appears at first in the soil of the semidesert (that is, heightened concentration of alkali from the abundance of alkaline carbonates); and then solonchak follows, conditioned by water-soluble salts in the upper soil layer. The soil-forming process reaches its greatest energy in the moister spring and autumn periods, when there is more water in the soil and plant activity revives. In summer the soil-forming process slows down; because of the lack of moisture, the soil solutions become concentrated, and the development of vegetation is retarded.

Complex soils cover the semidesert; changes of soil are frequent even over a small section of diverse combinations of soil types—steppe, semidesert, and desert. The small intake of moisture and the excessive evaporation result in little redistribution of precipitation. The influence of the micro-relief controls abrupt changes in the different soil elements, both in moisture and in salt content. The complexity is best expressed on clayey lowlands of semidesert, where the differentiated influence of the micro-relief is exhibited strongly. On the steeper slopes the complexity lessens and disappears.

The basic soils in the northern part of the region are light-chestnut; brown soils are widespread in the warmer and more arid south. These soils are found everywhere in an intricate complex with solonetz, solonchak, and the dark-colored solodizing soil of small depressions. The humus layer of the soil is from 12 to 16 inches thick, contains a small amount of humus (1.3 per cent), is light-chestnut in color, and is clearly packed in the lower part. Below this is a soil layer containing abundant lime spots washed out of the humus layer; these lime spots cause soil from a given depth to effervesce. The shallow-lying humus layer is important to the life of vegetation, since moisture percolates through from above, in spring when the snow melts or in autumn and summer in the event of heavy rains, and remains a long time. Transitions from intense drought to considerable moisture in the humus layer may therefore be accomplished rapidly. The soil ends in a layer of water-soluble salts (in particular, gypsum). Agriculturally, the soil is of low quality: under the plow the compact and sticky lower part of the humus layer is turned up; in summer the plowed soil dries out and makes the fields cloddy, and during the rains it becomes watertight and floods easily. In arid years crops suffer not only from the lack of moisture but also from an increase in the concentration of soil solutions and their alkaline reactions; therefore, harvest on this soil is possible only in the most favorable years.

Brown soil is similar in its morphologic and chemical properties to the sierozem of the deserts. It is extremely deficient in humus; usually it is carbonaceous from the upper layer down. Thus it effervesces at the surface, has a weakly dissected profile with a humus horizon of a yellow-gray color, a brown, packed, slightly platy horizon of accumulation, and is sharply enriched downwards in carbonates.

Light-chestnut and brown soil on bedrock at higher elevations is poorly developed because of the close occurrence of bedrock, rubbliness, lack of fine soil, sandy mechanical composition,

and the decrease or absence of effervescence. This rubbly soil is good only for growth of pasturage.

The character of soil formation in the valleys is completely different. Here, there is more moisture, vegetation is richer, and therefore dark-colored solonetz, solonchak, and solodized meadow alluvial and bog soil have developed. In locked-in undrained basins an extremely intricate complex of soils is found, with the predominance of solonchak and solonetz soils.

Solonchak forms a characteristic element of the landscape of the semidesert, especially in its southern part. It is difficult to visualize the semiarid country without the white patches of solonchak. It is formed in places of excessive, though periodical, moistening by ground water. Ground water, rising upward by capillary action, evaporates rapidly, leaving salts in the upper layers of the soil. Morphologically, solonchak does not have an independent soil profile and is structureless. During more intensive rising of salts, surface solonchak forms, containing a great amount of salts on the surface as efflorescences and incrustations. Sometimes a swollen, friable layer forms, oversaturated with salt crystals, chiefly sodium sulphate (swollen or puffy solonchak), in the solonchak under an incrustation of ocherous matter cemented by salts. Solonchak is of little value for agricultural purposes.

Solonetz soil is developed out of solonchak (1) in those places where the ground water lies deep and salt-bearing solutions cannot rise by capillary action, and (2) under conditions of downward percolating of precipitation, but with periodic interchange of ascending and descending streams of soil solutions. With an increase of descending water the upper layer of the original solonchak soil is gradually freed of chlorides and sulphates, which had retained the colloidal part of the soil in a coagulated state. The sodium which is in a saturated state begins to be displaced in the soil solution, producing a highly alkaline reaction. Because of the interaction of the ion of sodium with the ion of carbon in the soil solution, soda develops. The soda formation is accompanied by the de-

Fig. 13-2. Profile of columnar solonetz soil showing silaceous loess on top of columnar lower horizon.

struction of the organic and mineral portion of the soil and the movement into the depths of the colloidal particles. The latter coagulate and form a compact illuvial layer, brown in color, becoming clayey and enriched in humus, ferric oxides, aluminum, and loose silica. In a moist state this layer swells easily and becomes watertight and viscous; when it finally dries (which takes a long time) the colloidal particles adhere closely.

Under the influence of alternate spring moistening, accompanied by the swelling of the soil, and summer drying, accompanied by a sharp reduction in volume, the horizon is split into compact prismatic fragments 1.2 to 3.2 inches thick. Soil solutions stand over this horizon

a long time; they have a sharp alkaline reaction and thus highly corrode the soil. Therefore, during subsequent solonizing the prismatic structures are made columnar and their tops are corroded, which gives them the shape of caps sprinkled with siliceous powder. This powder also descends onto the lateral faces of the columnar structures. The process may continue until there is intense destruction of the illuvial horizon. Subsequently, the soil is more sharply differentiated into an eluvial above-solonetz layer and an illuvial solonetz layer. Moreover, the former is already acquiring a neutral reaction (phase of the columnar solonetz). Later, with continuing leaching, the podzol-like, whitish, above-columnar horizon is noticeably isolated, but the illuvial horizon loses much of its alkalinity (phase of the solodizing solonetz). Conditions of diversified local drainage vary the stages of solonizing, solonetzing, and solodizing of the soil.

Solonetz soil is of little value for cultivated crops because of its unfavorable physical properties and chemistry. In a moist condition it rapidly swells, becoming watertight and sticky, and on drying out, it is cemented together and becomes compact; also the soda content is harmful for cultivated plants. To improve the solonetz soil agriculturally, the sodium must be eliminated and replaced with calcium; this may be achieved by the adding of gypsum to the soil.

VEGETATION

The features of vegetative cover are uniform for the whole semidesert area, from the Emba River to Lake Zaysan. The semidesert type of vegetation is a gradual transition from steppe to desert type. In the steppes the chief plants are sod grasses, and in the northern deserts they are semiscrub desert *Artemisia*. The semidesert has a complex combination of real steppe turf grasses and semiscrub desert *Artemisia* and halophytes. On a large geographic scale such a vegetation transition is due to the general change in climatic conditions and in the soilforming process. In the northern lowlands grasses are the predominant vegetation; farther south the number of grasses decreases, and *Artemisia* begin to prevail; and in the southern semidesert halophytes are predominant. Vegetation changes are much more rapid in the semidesert than they are in the taiga zone because the moisture-deficient semidesert vegetation reacts more quickly to climatic and soil changes. Whereas forest phytocoenosis itself strongly influences the surrounding natural habitat, semidesert vegetation is almost wholly subordinated to physicogeographic changes. Semidesert vegetation has little capacity for evening out surrounding conditions, and reflects their slightest variations; it reacts readily to a minor redistribution of precipitation and salts, depending on the micro-relief. As a consequence, extraordinary diversification is observed in the scanty vegetative cover (which is analogous to the soil complexity) which results in a mosaic quality and a mottled composition over small areas. Finally, large forms of relief play a leading role in the distribution of the vegetative cover.

In the semidesert region, three different geomorphologic districts intersect in a line that is roughly perpendicular to the east-west zonality. This introduces a series of variations into the general picture of vegetation. In the highest parts of the Kazakh mounded country, where the dissection is greater and where there is an abundance of rubbly soil, vegetation of a more northern zone is found—feather grass and mixed grass (rocky steppe), and pine groves of the typical northern species (granite areas). Low forms of relief allow two principal deviations from the zonal type of vegetation. Depressions without drainage or with weak discharge, and with impermeable clay, are favorable for the solonizing of soil; in them, solonchak meadows and bogs are found. In other depressions increased moisture from precipitation or from ground water washes through the soil; here is found vegetation characteristic of the more northern moist zone. Along the latter depressions steppe grass and steppe brushwood may penetrate deep into the semidesert. The degree of solonizing of the bedrock plays a certain role in the distribution of vegetation. Along the mountain slopes of the Turgai table country, characterized by their outcrops of saliferous and gypsiferous clay, brushwood halophytes of the southern type penetrate rather far to the north.

In general, the vegetation of the semidesert is somewhat sparse, low-growing, and of a monotonous light gray color. The leaves are concentrated in a 2 to 4 inch layer, which contributes to less evaporation from their surface. The plants occupy little more than half the surface of the ground, and thus pale patches of soil appear everywhere amid the vegetation. In the distribution of aboveground parts, the semidesert phytocoenosis is not dense but open; however, root systems are highly developed in order to utilize soil moisture to the fullest extent. The root systems have many branches in the different layers of the soil—from the surface layers, where the moisture from rain and melted snow is concentrated, to the deeper layers where moisture penetrates in lesser amount but is preserved longer.

Certain ecological conditions cause poverty in the semidesert vegetative cover, which contains several species from the neighboring steppes and deserts. There is so much fescue grass (*Festuca sulcata*) that the semidesert vegetation might be called fescue–*Artemisia*. There is also an abundance of koeleria (*Koeleria gracilis*) and feather grasses, both of the maidenhair and pinnate types. But these grasses are sparse and form comparatively fine turfs. In the north a rather rich mixed grass is observed, but to the south it grows very poorly.

Several drought-resistant small shrubs with relatively little annual growth have a conspicuous position in the plant makeup of the semidesert. These have grayish or whitish leaves, because of the aerated fibers which cover them abundantly, and they discharge volatile oils which protect the plants from increased evaporation. These plants undergo abrupt changes in life activity during the different seasons of the year. Most typical of them are the Artemisias, which may be considered the emblem of the semidesert. Slightly saliferous clayey soil is covered by white *Artemisia maritima ssp. incana,* which is a small low shrub with branches and leaves growing directly from the roots. The top roots are up to a yard in length and produce lateral roots by which more soil is reached. The cycle of growth of *Artemisia* is extremely clear. In a moist spring it grows a cluster of leaves rapidly, but with the onset of summer heat its life activity decreases. With the advance of autumn rains it blooms, opening out blossoms that are from 8 to 10 inches high. The ripening of the seeds continues even during frost. With the coming of winter the aboveground part

dies. Clay and more saliferous soils are covered by black *Artemisia pauciflora.* After a rain the leaves of the *Artemisia* straighten out, but in dry weather its black stalk, rising 2 to 4 inches above the ground, is almost leafless. In very dry periods it loses its leaves completely. *Artemisia* contains a great amount of volatile oil; therefore a specific *Artemisia* scent is very typical of the semidesert. Other semidesert plants are *Kochia prostrata* and the squat saltbush (*Atriplex canum*) of the halophytes.

The ephemeral and perennial plants are abundant in the semidesert and grow only in spring. Water from melted snow and spring rains soaks into the soil and is retained on the packed waterproof layer, thus saturating the surface layer of the soil which is utilized by the ephemerals. In spring the surface of the soil becomes slightly green from the very fine coating of confervoids of blue-green algae and mosses awakening to life activity. Later there appear rapidly-blooming flowering plants: tulip (*Tulipa biebersteiniana, T. schrenkii*), crowfoot (*Ranunculus polyrhizus*), rhubarb (*Rheum tataricum*), and *Rindera tetraspis.* With the coming of summer heat and the disappearance of moisture in the upper layer of the soil, the annuals and perennials conclude their vegetative cycle.

Woody vegetation occupies an insignificant area in the semiarid region. In deep mountain valleys having a good supply of fresh water are groves of birch, aspen, maple, poplar, and pine; willow beds grow near rivers.

Herds pasturing the year round deplete the vegetative cover of the semidesert. In areas of intensive grazing perennial steppe turf grasses gradually disappear, *Artemisia* grow, and the number of annuals increases. Complete uncovering of the soil follows.

On solonetz soil is found a vegetation with special species and with a unique ecology that is not native to the neighboring light-chestnut and brown soil. This singularity enables one to discern even small patches of solonetz soil lost amid the other soils. In summer several types of xerophytic and soda-bearing plants grow in the dry solonetz soil. Besides black *Artemisia,*

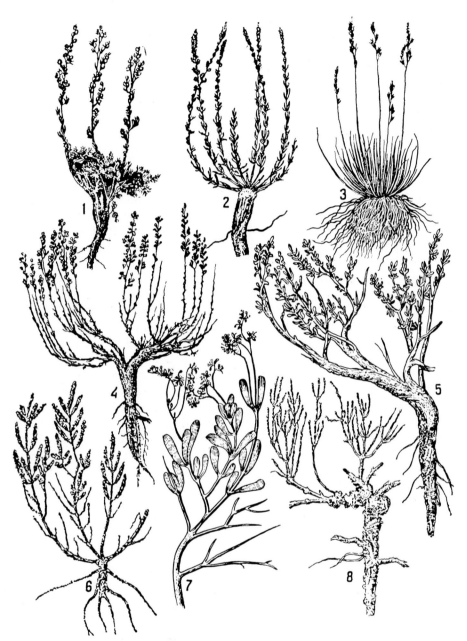

Fig. 13-3. Characteristic semishrubbery and cereals of semidesert zone of Kazakhstan. First row: plants of clayey, slightly salty regions: 1—*Artemisia incana;* 2—*Kochia prostrata;* 3—Tipchak (*Festuca sulcata*). Second row: plants of saliferous (solonetz) regions: 4—Black *Artemisia pauciflora;* 5—Kokpek (*Atriplex cana*). Third row: solonchak plants: 6—glasswort (*Salicornia herbacea*); 7—"Zamanikha" (*Nitraria schoeberi*); 8—"Sarsazan" (*Halochemum strobilaceum*). (*Mounting by S. P. Suslov.*)

there grow small shrubs of the goosefoot family Chenopodiaceae: *Camphorosma monspeliacum,* saltbush (*Atriplex cana*), kochia (*Kochia prostrata*), and sand ceratocarpus (*Ceratocarpus arenarius*). They bear clear features of xeromorphism: the bases of the stalks are highly branched; the leaves of some are awl-shaped or needle-like and thickly covered with gray-white hairs or scales, lending a grayish color to the vegetation; and many contain volatile oil. The vegetation is very sparse, covering about one-third of the soil surface. Any one species may predominate and may occupy vast areas. Some of these plants are important as fodder (ceratocarpus); others are used as fuel (saltbush and kochia).

As is true of solonetz soil, the high content of easily-soluble chlorous acids and sulphates on solonchak soil causes a paucity of flora and pronounced plant variation. Solonchak is very moist, even in the dry period, because it is constantly fed ground water moisture by capillary action. As a result, the root system of a halophytic plant is small, and descends to a depth of only 2 to 3 inches. Of the halophytic plants, the most widespread are the saltworts of the goosefoot family (Chenopodiaceae): *Halocnemum strobilaceum;* glasswort (*Salicornia herbacea*); *Nitraria schoberi;* and sea lavender (*Statice suffruticosa*).

Because of the strong development of a water-bearing tissue, the assimilating organs of these plants are very succulent. In some they are well-separated fleshy leaves; in others, such as glasswort, the leaves grow together with the stems into fleshy shoots. The pulpy organs and their succulent tissues constitute a reservoir which fills with water in the spring and autumn when the water in solonchak soil is slightly salty. When the concentration of saline solution in the soil increases later in the summer, the plant can absorb only an extremely limited amount of water, and that under conditions of great osmotic pressure of the cell fluid. The halophytes are able to accumulate in their assimilating organs, without damage to the plant, a large amount of easily soluble

mineral salts because the development of the watery tissues and the relatively large size of their vegetative parts do not allow an inordinate increase of the concentration of salts in the cell fluid. This gives them the opportunity to acquire moisture from the hard soil solutions, since under these conditions the suction power of the roots exceeds the osmotic power of the soil saline solutions. Evaporation in halophytic plants is very slight, and they have definite xerophytic characteristics. If the evaporation were greater, the tissues would be filled with salts and the plant would die. Nevertheless, the constant intake of solutions is necessary for sustaining the plant water balance; the water stores protect the plant from excessive heating and from an inordinate accumulation of salts in its cells. The leaves of these plants have the appearance of beaded scales, or are cylindrical, pulpy, small stems growing together with the stalk (glasswort), or are cylindrical or thread-like. Their runners are covered by a thick membrane. Owing to the large volume of the assimilating organs, their outer evaporating surface is small. Because of the absence of furriness, which is typical of the leaves of xerophytes, pulpy halophytes have a green color even during the hot summer, which lends a beautiful contrast to the white crust of salt efflorescences. In autumn the color of saltworts turns to reddish-purple.

Other types of solonchak plants (such as tamarisk) constantly exude easily soluble salts onto the surface of the leaves during their growing period. Early in the morning these plants are coated with acrid droplets, which crystallize when the temperature rises. The crystals are broken by the wind or are washed off by rains. Since these plants are free of a harmful excess of salts, they do not experience a water deficiency and thus they have a well-developed leaf blade. During the entire year halophytes serve as green fodder for sheep, and are also readily eaten by camels.

In distribution of vegetation the semidesert region may be divided into two parts: (1) the subzone of northern *Artemisia*-fescue grass semideserts on light-chestnut soil, and (2) the subzone of southern fescue-*Artemisia* semideserts on brown soil. The uniqueness of physicogeographic conditions of the three basic geomorphologic districts mentioned earlier introduces a series of essential modifications into the general distribution of vegetation.

Along the axis of the Mugodzhar Mountain range, feather-fescue rocky steppes on dark-chestnut, rubbly soil predominate, with an abundance of feather grasses (*Stipa kirghisorum, S. lessingiana*), fescue grass (*Festuca sulcata*), and *Artemisia austriaca*. Steppe brushwoods grow along the slopes, and small birch groves grow in the moist ravines. In the foothills *Artemisia*-fescue rocky steppes are plentiful on light-chestnut, carbonaceous and saliferous, rubbly soil with an abundance of other species of *Artemisia lessingiana* and *A. maritima* ssp. *incana*. In the south are fescue-black *Artemisia* rocky semideserts with black *Artemisia pauciflora*, and on solonized soil are saltbush and other halophytes.

In the lower and widespread Tertiary salt-bearing clay of the flat Turgai table country, complexes of salty soil with halophytic vegetation acquire much importance. In the northern subzone, semideserts of feather grass, white *Artemisia*, and fescue grass develop on light-chestnut carbonaceous and saliferous soil with several species of feather grasses (*Stipa lessingiana, S. sareptana*), arid grass (*Agropyron desertorum*), and poor xerophytic mixed grass. Scattered among them are shallow depressions with slightly clayey and sandy, dark-colored, solodizing soil, on which is found a rich meadow-steppe vegetation. In the locked-in solonetz and solonchak basins a diversified complex of black and white *Artemisia* and saltbush has developed. Along the valleys of rivers are saline meadow soils of river bottomlands and lakeside terraces, and an *Artemisia*-grass halophytic complex with *Anabasis salsa, Halocnemum strobilaceum,* and chee grass (*Lasiagrostis splendens*). Prevalent in the southern subzone are fescue-*Artemisia* halophyte semideserts with gray, black, and white

Artemisia terrae albae and fescue grass on brown saliferous and alkaline rubbly or gravelly-clayey soil. Scattered among the solonetz soil, and occupying up to 40 per cent of the surface, grow the halophytes.

In the higher, strongly dissected Kazakh mounded country, the signs of vertical zonality are clearly expressed in the more northern types of soils and their accompanying phytocoenoses and patches of pine groves. The background vegetation in the northern part comprises a feather-fescue-grass, rocky semidesert. Under this intricate complex of vegetation are light-chestnut, carbonaceous and saliferous, alkaline, rubbly, and sandy soils, with patches of solonetz soil occupying about 40 per cent of the area. Along the axis of the greater elevations appear feather-grass-*Artemisia*, fescue-grass, rocky steppes with thickets of steppe pea tree (*Caragana frutex*) and birch groves. Developed under them are mountain chernozem. In the foothills this is replaced by *Artemisia*-fescue rocky steppes on mountain dark-chestnut soil. In the deeper ravines provided with the water of fresh springs, dense thickets of birch, aspen, willow, bird cherry, buckthorn, and hawthorn are found. On higher places there are pine groves with elements of northern forest and swamp species, pyrola, and cotton grass. On the mountain heights of the eastern part of the region appear feather–fescue grass and feather grass, mixed grass steppes on mountain-chestnut soil and mountain chernozem. In the Lake Zaysan depression there is a complex of black-*Artemisia*–halophyte–fescue grass semideserts, partly on sierozem. In the southern part of the region, fescue–halophyte–*Artemisia* semideserts are developed with white, black, and gray *Artemisia* and with such halophytes as saltbush and its more southern species, such as *Nanophyton erinaceum*. This complex is developed on brown saliferous and solonchak, partly rubbly, soil, with large patches of solonetz soil.

The northern border of the region of semideserts is the southern frontier of continuous agricultural crops, beyond which begins oasis agriculture with irrigation. The chief wealth is the abundant pasturage of good fodder plants—*Artemisia* and halophytes. Through the entire region grows the rubber-yielding chondrilla, a perennial plant, about 3 feet high, of the family of thistles. At the present time it is cultivated.

FAUNA

The severe continental climate of the semidesert makes a sharp impression on the composition, geographic distribution, and seasonal and daily conditions of life of the animals.

In the summer months, when cloudiness is slight, the ground is heated by the sun, and southern warmth-loving animals, such as scorpions, desert lizards, and certain birds (the Indian rail, for example), penetrate into the semidesert far to the north. The animals, being nocturnal and crepuscular, either flee from the direct, strong heat of the sun, or in the hottest hours of the day hide in burrows. Color camouflage—the color of the soil—is characteristic of the semidesert animals during the summer months. Most of them are grayish or reddish-brown with small brownish stripes and spots, which corresponds with extraordinary accuracy to the tone of the dry, cracked, clayey soil. Among the larks the actual adaptation in coloring of plumage is sometimes so successful that they gain the color of the soil.

During the severe winter there is paucity in semidesert life; only hibernating animals (the jerboa) or those which gather supplies of grain or hay remain. Many species of birds, such as larks and snipes, migrate. The snow bunting, the white ptarmigan, and the polar owl, come here from the north, which points up the polar nature of the winter. Because the winds blow the light snow cover off the hills, it is possible for the large hoofed animals (the antelope) and some upland birds (the gray ptarmigan) to obtain feed from the ground. The vegetation in winter is principally roots, which have excellent fodder qualities for the herbivores. Owing to the duration of the snow cover, birds (white ptarmigan) and mammals (white hare, ermine, and Dzungarian hamster) often wear a camouflaging white coat for almost 6 months.

Since semidesert has water only in reservoirs of poor quality, animals become accustomed to the distinctive water conditions in different ways. The antelope makes long, rapid migrations from grazing lands to places where drinking water is obtainable; in winter, snow serves as drinking water. Grouse make migratory flights to water reservoirs dozens of miles from their feeding places. Carnivores (wolf, fox) ordinarily inhabit places near reservoirs. Rodents (the suslik, marmot, jerboa, and hamster) use water very seldom or not at all, and are satisfied with the moisture which they obtain from their food. When the vegetation dries out during the driest periods of the summer, the yellow marmot enters a summer sleep. Some underground rodents feed on succulent bulbs and roots. Since the food supply is scattered, as are the rare watering places, animals must be capable of rapid migration. The following animals are characteristic of the open landscape of the semideserts: jumping rodents (jerboas), and jumping straight-winged birds (plover). The predominance of insects which do not fly but creep, and of heavy insects such as beetles, is attributable to the frequency and velocity of high winds.

The conditions of existence on the open plains having a broken grass cover are especially favorable for some groups of burrowers. Particularly widespread in these areas are the sluggish burrowing rodents, the suslik marmots: the yellow suslik (*Citellus fulvus*) and the small suslik (*C. pygmaeus*). The semidesert is rich in various species of jerboas, including the Severtsov jerboa (*Alactaga severtzovi*), the small jerboa (*A. elater*), and the large jerboa (*A. jaculus*). Jerboas feed on bulbs, seeds, worms, grubs, and beetles, and some species of jerboa raid melon fields. Widespread among the other rodents are the steppe vole (*Lagurus lagurus*), the hamster (*Cricetus eversmanni*), the mouse (*Microtus gregalis*), the meadow mouse (*M. socialis*), and the mole (*Ellobius talpinus*), which lives underground. The antelope (*Saiga tatarica*) is the chief ungulate of the semidesert; in the past there has been a relative of the wild ass and tarpans (related to the Przhevalsky horse). The following carnivores live in the semidesert: the *Vulpes corsak*, a fox with slender legs and relatively long ears; the wolf; the steppe ermine.

The most noticeable landscape birds of the sermidesert are the larks—the white-winged *Melanocorypha leucoptera*, the black *M. yeltoniensis*, and the horned *Eremophyla alpestris* —and the buntings—the Caspian (*Eupoda asiatica*) and the thick-billed *Cirrepedesmus leschenaulti*. Among the other birds are the *Burhinus oedicnemus,* a large, nocturnal, fast-running bird; the grouse—the white-bellied *Pterocles alchata*, the black-bellied *P. arenarius,* and the *Syrrhaptes paradoxus*—the rails; the *Chlamidotis masqueenii;* and the bustard (*Otis tarda*). The abundance of rodents attracts many carnivorous birds, such as the desert *Athene noctua*, the steppe falcon (*Falco naumanni*), and the *Falco columbarius.*

Of the semidesert reptiles there are the steppe tortoise (*Testudo horsfieldi*); the vari-colored lizard (*Eremias arguta*); the round-headed lizard (*Phrynocephalus reticulatus*); the western snake (*Ancistrodon halys*); the steppe snake (*Vipera renardi*); and the patterned *Elaphe dione.*

CHAPTER 14

Desert Region of Central Asia

The deserts of Central Asia make up a well-defined, arid, geographic region with sharply continental temperatures. This region is south of the semideserts of Central Kazakhstan—roughly south of a line running from the northern scarp of the Ust-Urt Plateau eastward to the Aral Sea and Lake Balkhash and on toward the southern slope of the Tarbagatay Range. The region extends southward to the base of the mountains on the international border. Mesozoic, Tertiary, and Quaternary rocks are widespread. Desert landforms, considerably weathered, are characteristic of the region. The region is a locked-in, undrained basin having several large transit rivers that bring abundant water from the mountains. The zonal soils are sierozems and solonchaks that are poor in humus. The plant world has unique ecological features; it comes to life in the moist spring and dies off in the hot summer. Oasis agriculture, under artificial irrigation, is predominant.

CLIMATE

The climate of the deserts of Central Asia is unusual. Since the region is thousands of miles from the oceans, it has a sharply expressed continental climate: very hot summers, cold winters (for these latitudes), sharp annual and daily fluctuations of temperatures, little and irregular seasonal precipitation, dry air, little cloudiness, and many hours of sunlight. Owing to its southern location, the region is insolated, even in wintertime. The desert region is encircled on the south and on the east by systems of high mountains, but it is completely exposed on the north, from which direction waves of cold air penetrate without resistance and spill through the plains areas, lowering the winter temperatures. The extreme climate is modified somewhat by the entrance of warm and moist air masses from the western side.

The prevailing winds, and their qualitative and quantitative characteristics, are controlled by the distribution of barometric pressure in the surrounding regions. The deserts of Central Asia lie southwest of the East Siberian anticyclone with its zone of high pressure. Thus during the entire year the pressure decreases from north to south, the isobars trending in an almost east-west direction and winds from the north prevailing. This transfer of air, primarily from one part of the mainland to another, from the higher latitudes into the lower ones, from the colder to the warmer localities, tends to change the air masses from a state of saturation to one of low humidity. This not only prevents precipitation, but even heightens evaporation on the plains and causes cloudless skies, especially in spring and summer. In winter, when the air pressure in the deserts decrease in a southwest direction from the region of the East Siberian anticyclone, very cold northeastern winds prevail which are the cause of the low winter temperatures. In summer the East Siberian anticyclone disappears, and above the warmed interior parts of Asia forms a region of low atmospheric pressure. At the same time the Azores maximum of high pressure of the Atlantic Ocean increases, sending a branch eastward across southern Europe; consequently, the air currents emerging from it are, in Central Asia, northwest winds. Thus, on the plains of Central Asia, winds of a northern bearing prevail the year round; in winter they are more often northeastern, and in summer northwestern.

Variations from this general distribution of the winds are caused by local geographic conditions, such as the influence of water basins (on the coasts of the Caspian and Aral seas), the proximity of mountains (the eastern portion of Kazakhstan), and geomorphologic peculiarities (Fergana). The climatic influence of water basins is not great. Neither the Caspian nor the Aral Sea, because of their relatively small size, appreciably influences the climate of the interior of Central Asia. Their influence is limited to only a narrow coastal strip. In comparison with the thermic conditions of the inner portions of the desert region, the climate of the littoral belt of the Caspian Sea has a number of peculiarities: winter is more gentle, but summer is cooler; autumn is warmer than spring; the annual temperature maximum is somewhat retarded; the frost-free period is lengthened to about 275 days a year. The influence of the Aral Sea on its coast is negligible in winter, while in summer it increases considerably. Finally, a diversity in climatic conditions of the river valleys and the deserts adjacent to them is characteristic. In winter the difference is slight; at the height of summer, however, the temperature is higher in the desert than in the river valleys.

Winds in the desert zone are of low velocity; weak winds or calms predominate. In some districts 62 per cent of the daily observations record calms. On clear days the calms occur in the evening and at night, and during the day a comparatively strong wind blows, reaching a maximum in the afternoon hours. The intense warming of the soil creates favorable conditions for the increase in wind velocity, whereas very often at night after a strong daytime wind a complete calm sets in.

Because the relief of the region is monotonous through 10 degrees of latitude, latitudinal thermic zonality is observed in the desert of Central Asia. Isotherms trend in an east-west direction; that is, the average temperatures for July and January are increased from north to south; however, this increase does not have a constant pattern. Every 60 miles southward the average yearly temperature increases 1.6 degrees, July 0.5 degrees to 0.6 degrees, and January 2.3 degrees to 2.7 degrees. Summer temperatures are more uniform than winter temperatures, and the influence of the latitude of a place is three to four times greater in winter than it is in summer—an effect of the long duration of snow cover in the northern deserts. Owing to the southern geographic position of the deserts (and the high position of the sun), insolation is increased, and this together with the clearness of the skies and dryness of the air contributes to the exceedingly intense heating of the ground of Central Asia in summer. From the standpoint of average temperature of the warmest month (July) and of summer in general, the southern half of the desert region is the hottest part of the USSR. It may be compared with such hot localities in the world as North Africa, the northeastern outskirts of Iran, or the northern part of Mesopotamia.

In the northern part of the region (Kazalinsk) the July average temperature reaches 78.8°F, in the middle (Turtkul) 82.5°F, and in the southern part (Bayram-Ali) 85.8°F. Under favorable geographic conditions (for example, at Termez), it increases to 90.5°F. On individual days in summer in the southern part of the desert region, the air temperature may reach almost 122°F in the shade. January is the coldest month. On the northern shores of the Aral Sea the average January temperature (8.8°F) is barely above that of

Arkhangel, and only in the southern part of the desert region is it above 32°F (Kazalinsk 17°F, Turtkul 23°F, Bayram-Ali 32.5°F, Termez 35°F). The temperature rises rapidly in spring and drops almost as rapidly in autumn: in the north it changes approximately 21 degrees per month (Kazalinsk: March, 28.8°F; April, 49°F; September, 62°F; November, 36°F). To the south this difference is somewhat modified.

Annual and daily amplitudes of the desert temperatures are great. Because of the cloudless skies and the thin vegetation cover there is intense radiation at night, which contributes to sharp fluctuations in the air temperature. The absolute maximum temperatures are generally very high, and increase to the south (Kazalinsk, 108.5°F; Bayram-Ali, 113.3°F). On the other hand, the absolute minimums are extremely low and are rather modified to the south (Kazalinsk, −27°F; Bayram-Ali, −14°F). Absolute amplitudes are high (Kazalinsk, 135.7°F; Bayram-Ali, 127.4°F). Daily fluctuations are greatest in August and September, when the small amount of cloudiness contributes to intense heating during the day and considerable chilling at night. In Turkmenia daily fluctuations as much as 45° have been observed (6 A.M., 37.5°F; 9 A.M., 68°F; 1 P.M., 82.5°F), and fluctuations as great as 93° have been noted. The duration of the frost-free period increases considerably from north to south (Kazalinsk, 172 days; Bayram-Ali, 215 days), as does the length of the growing season (Kazalinsk, 204 days; Bayram-Ali, 288 days).

In summer the ground is heated much more intensely than is the air. For example, on May 16 at an elevation of 6.6 feet in the Kara-Kum Desert an air temperature of 92.4°F was observed, but the temperature of the soil was 147.3°F. Even in January the temperature at the surface of the ground may reach 116.6°F, and in summer it may be as much as 158°F. At Repetek, on June 20, 1915, a temperature of 174.8°F at the surface of the ground was recorded. Daily amplitudes at the surface are as great as 108°, and annual amplitudes are as great as 180°. Warming of the soil does not extend far downward—the heat is not felt at a depth of 3 feet. On May 15, at 3 P.M. a temperature of 120.2°F at the surface of the ground was observed, and at a depth of 36 inches the temperature was only 71.8°F. This coolness with depth is of great importance to the organic world, since high surface temperatures often are destructive to animals and plant roots. Animals attempt to survive by burying themselves as deeply as possible in the ground.

Extraordinary dryness of the air is a characteristic of the desert. The average annual relative humidity is a comparatively small figure: 67 per cent in the north (Kazalinsk) and 49 per cent in the south (Bayram-Ali). Relative humidity reaches its minimum in summer: In July, 50 per cent in the north (Kazalinsk), and 30 per cent in the south (Bayram-Ali). There have been times when the humidity has dropped to 5 per cent in the desert. In the dry, sandy hillocks the summer relative humidity drops to such small values that it cannot be determined exactly by standard methods of meteorology. This dryness of the air is reflected strongly in the intensity of the evaporation of water from plants and from the surface of the soil. Maximum relative humidity is measured in the winter, especially in January: 84 per cent in the north (Kazalinsk), and 74 per cent in the south (Bayram-Ali). The influence of relief is clear in the distribution of moisture: the most exposed points, situated in the middle of the desert, are driest in comparison with points more sheltered and closer to the mountains (such as Tashkent). Everywhere in the region, low areas have less humidity than elevated ones. And on the coast of the Caspian Sea the influence of the adjacent desert is more pronounced than that of the sea. Only in the oases, with their high temperatures and vast irrigated lands, occupied by wild and cultivated vegetation, is the relative humidity greater than that of the neighboring deserts.

Cloudiness in the deserts of Central Asia is slight. The average annual cloudiness in different districts varies from 27 to 41 per cent. In winter, cloudiness is relatively frequent: January, 48 to 58 per cent average annual. Summer is almost completely clear: August, in the north, 17 per cent; August, in the south, only 4 per cent. In the second half of summer there are no overcast days; at the beginning of summer and in autumn they are comparatively rare; and only in the middle of winter do they exceed the number of clear days in a month. Early summer clouds for the most part are cirrus and high stratus and shade the sun's rays relatively little. Much uniformly distributed annual cloudiness is observed along the shores of the Caspian (average annual, 41 per cent; January, 43 per cent; August, 21 per cent).

In wealth of sunlight the deserts of Central Asia may be compared with such regions as Egypt and California. In summer and autumn there are more hours of sunshine here than in Egypt. At Bayram-Ali, in August, solar radiance comprises 94 per cent of the possible. At Termez (Surkhan-Darya Oasis) there are 202 clear days and 37 cloudy days annually. Such clear skies are found nowhere else in the USSR (for example, in the Moscow region there are 50 clear, 150 cloudy, and 165 partly cloudy days in a year).

Because of the slight cloudiness, the low humidity, the summer heat, the dry winds, and the low precipitation, evaporation can reach unusual intensity. It may exceed by many times the annual precipitation: Tashkent, 3 times; Fergana, 7 times; Nukus, 27 times; Turtkul, 36 times. In certain years evaporation exceeds precipitation by as much as 85 times (Nukus) and even 270 times (Turtkul). Evaporation reaches a maximum in July and a minimum in December. The actual amount of moisture evaporated in the deserts cannot be great because of the lack of water, but wherever rivers and lakes exist their water is evaporated in large quantities. The annual evaporation from the surface of rivers is considerable: Syr-Darya (Kazalinsk), 57.6 inches; Amu-Darya (near Kerki), 86.1 inches. Seventy per cent of the annual evaporation takes place from April to September.

The entire plains region of Central Asia receives less than 10 inches of precipitation annually. The number of days with precipitation also is small—often less than 40 days a year—and precipitation is distributed irregularly. Increases do not follow the latitudinal zonality but are determined by the relief. The lower stretches of the Amu-Darya River lack precipitation (Turtkul, 3.8 inches; Nukus, 3.1 inches annually), but closer to the mountains the amount of precipitation increases (Kerki, 6.4 inches; Ashkhabad 9.2 inches). Despite the diversity in the amount of precipitation, there is an over-all pattern of distinct seasonal distribution: most precipitation is in spring and winter; summer and autumn are dry. In the north the spring maximum is in May, in the central part of the region in April, and in the south in March. The least precipitation is in August, September, and July. The relative abundance of spring and winter precipitation is caused by cyclones bearing moisture from the west across the southern part of Central Asia. In summer, although there is an upward current, the air is so dry that the vapors do not condense. This sharp seasonal distribution is clearly expressed in the growth of vegetation and the life of animals. There are essential differences between the seasonal distribution of precipitation in the north and the south of the region. Precipitation is distributed more regularly in the north than in the south. In the north, under conditions of Central Kazakhstan climate, there are two periods of maximum precipitation: spring and winter; the December maximum is a little less than that of spring (Kazalinsk: May, 0.6 inch; December, 0.58 inch). In the south, the maximum precipitation is in March, when for a short time vegetation in the deserts revives. Thus, to the south the amount of spring precipitation increases and that of summer decreases.

STATION	INCHES OF PRECIPITATION				
	SPRING	SUM-MER	AU-TUMN	WIN-TER	AN-NUAL
Aralskoye More	1.04	1.0	1.24	.92	4.2
Kzyl-Orda	1.5	.6	.9	1.24	4.3
Bayram-Ali	2.36	.08	.56	1.9	4.9
Kerki	2.78	.04	.68	3.0	6.5

Summer in the southern part of the country is completely rainless. Throughout a 10-year period of observations at Bayram-Ali, not a drop of rain fell during July, August, September. At Tashkent it has happened repeatedly that from the beginning of July through August, to the end of September no rain has fallen at all. Normally, in each of these three months, on the average, one rain has occurred yielding 0.8 to 0.9 inch of precipitation. Sharp fluctuation in annual amounts of precipitation is characteristic. In individual years the amount of precipitation may decrease in comparison with the average annual amount. In Merv it fluctuated from 5.8 to 1.8 inches a year, and at Chardzhou, from 4.4 to 1.2 inches a year. In such dry years even desert vegetation and animals are in a state of extreme impoverishment. In a broad sense, these fluctuations from year to year greatly increase the selection of species and intensify the struggle for existence. In Bet-Pak-Dala as little as one or two drops may fall on a square yard of surface; at other times great downpours occur, but these are very rare. At Golodnaya Steppe Station, in November 1902, 4 inches of precipitation (of the annual 11 inches) fell in one day. At Bayram-Ali, in March of one year, 1.7 inches (of the annual 5.1 inches) fell in one day. Water from cloudbursts rapidly runs into the rivers without benefiting vegetation.

The amount of snow cover and its duration decrease sharply from north to south: at Kazalinsk it is 2.4 inches; at Nukus 1 inch, at Bayram-Ali less than 0.04 inch. The number of days with snow cover are: in the north (Kazalinsk), 70 days; in the central part (Tashkent), 37 days, and in the south (Bayram-Ali), in exceptional years, 4 days. Despite the small amount of precipitation and the high temperatures, there is no foundation for asserting that the desert region is in an uninterrupted state of drying.

The seasonal climatic character and the seasonal distribution of precipitation differ sharply in the northern and southern halves of the desert region, between which runs the boundary roughly along a line from Kara-Bogaz-Gol to Nukus to the northern tip of the Kara-Tau Range. Because of this difference, each of these types of deserts is characterized by a different composition, ecology, seasonal change, and origin of plant and animal world.

Winter in the northern deserts is relatively severe, and average monthly temperatures from November to March are below freezing. In the middle of October or at the beginning of November the first frost begins; by the end of November winter has already set in. The Aral Sea freezes over for four or five months; the lower course of the Syr-Darya River also freezes over, and, in individual years, all of Lake Balkhash. Sometimes the ground is covered with deep snow, and cold, sharp, northeast winds blow. Raging storms, which often blow off the snow cover, and sleet are the usual companions of a severe winter. On calm days the sun warms intensely and the absolute maximum temperature, in the winter months, reaches a considerable magnitude (January, up to 41.3°F); even so, winter is certain here. In the southern deserts, winter is far more mild and is shorter. In the most southern districts, only January and part of February may be considered winter months. Even the coldest month—January—has above-freezing temperatures (Bayram-Ali, 32.5°F). Often in the middle of winter, summery days are observed: In Repetek there are days in January when the temperature rises to 68°F; there have been years when the January average was 7°F. But even the areas farthest south are not free from sudden drops in temperature. Occasionally during strong northerly winds, the temperature may drop sharply to −13°, but cold spells last a very short time. The snow cover is slight and not stable—the snow alternates with rain and quickly melts. Because of the absence of snow cover, the soil and vegetation are not well protected from intense freezing and thawing, winds, and solar heating.

Spring is of importance in the life of the plant and animal world because at this time of year there are rather frequent rains. But although spring brings the greatest amount of precipitation, the absolute amount is small. In the northern deserts the last frost occurs at the end of April. Spring arrives early and sets in quickly; a few warm days are sufficient to erase all signs of winter. Hot days soon come, but the nights are still cool. The soil is saturated to the limit from the abundant precipitation, which creates extremely favorable conditions for the development of vegetation. Spring does not last long; at the beginning of May a sharp transition takes place from a short spring to a long summer. Summer days arrive, the rains stop, the skies become clear, and the sun begins to heat the desert unbearably. The air becomes drier and drier, clouds of dust rise, the soil rapidly loses its moisture, becoming air-dry and hard, and grasses commence to burn out. Spring in the southern deserts starts in the beginning of March. At this time the snow vanishes everywhere, rains fall, the days become warm, and almond and apricot trees blossom. In May the heat sets in.

Summer in the desert region is extraordinarily hot and dry. Combined with the intense heat is the complete absence or only a negligible amount of precipitation, little cloudiness, and low relative humidity. The heat of the ground causes an unstable condition in the lower layers of air which creates an increased turbulence of the atmosphere, resulting in a multitude of whirlwinds. As a consequence, dust raised by the wind is carried into the highest layers of the atmosphere and reduces its transparency. Dry haze is observed often in summer. In the southern deserts the period of summer

rest is very sharply noted in plants. Terrestrial turtles are deep in slumber, and termites conceal themselves deeper in the moist layers of the soil.

Autumn brings the second period of the revival of vegetation, owing to the rains. In the south, at the end of August and not before September the heat decreases somewhat during the day, and the nights become colder. In the north, in September it becomes cool during the day also. Early autumn is warm, dry, clear, and sunny. Then the rains begin to fall, and vegetation is revived. The first frost in the north is at the beginning of October, and in the south at the end of October. In the oases the leaves begin to turn yellow in October, and drop from the trees at the start of November. Autumn, with its gentle, warm days and quiet, transparent atmosphere is the most propitious time for travel over the plains of Central Asia.

The essential difference between northern and southern deserts is in the effect of seasonal distribution of precipitation on the seasonal growth of the vegetative cover. In the southern deserts a distinct periodicity is observed in precipitation. The irregular distribution of precipitation, wherein during three summer months only 6 per cent of the annual amount falls, causes the pronounced cyclic quality in the development of the grassy vegetation and the predominance of spring annuals, among which Mediterranean species predominate. Because of the adequate early spring moisture, the landscape in these months is brilliant with a diversity of colors and has a luxurious stand of grass. But by the second half of spring the vegetation withers to the roots, owing to the lack of moisture. Only sand and rocky, rubbly substrata have a high water table. Because of this they are more favorable in regard to their water regime and at this time of year are able to support growing vegetation comprising shrubs, semi-shrubs, and large grassy perennials with deep root systems. In the northern deserts, where there is a small amount of precipitation, the amount of summer precipitation is greatly increased over that of spring. The slight moistening of the soil in the spring is the cause of the poor development of spring vegetation. The shorter period of summer dryness and partial summer rains create conditions under which the entire soil is covered by semi-shrubs and shrubs of a Central Asiatic variety which grow all summer and up to late autumn. In the Chu River basin, owing to an adequate amount of spring precipitation, spring vegetation grows abundantly, but toward the middle of summer it gradually withers to the roots. At this time it is replaced by more drought-resistant species, which grow during the entire summer.

The plentiful sunlight and warmth and the fertile, unleached soil make the plains of Central Asia extremely auspicious for agriculture under conditions of irrigation. The long and hot growing season gives such warmth-demanding plants as cotton and rice a chance to ripen. The three summer months are warmer in the deserts of Central Asia than they are in the cotton-growing regions of the United States and Egypt. The almost complete absence of summer rains and the negligible amount of autumn rains make possible the cultivation of the best varieties of cotton. The abundance of sunlight and warmth contributes to the ripening of the seeds and fruits and to the increase of the albumen and sugar content in them and the gluten content in cereal grains. Grapes, apricots, and melons are famous for their sweetness. These same conditions contribute to the formation of fragrant volatile oil in plants; thus, wild flora of the deserts abounds in highly redolent ester-bearing plants. The cultivation of many aromatic plants is possible, such as lavender (*Lavandula vera*) and muscatel sage (*Salvia sclarea*).

The annual distribution of precipitation is exceedingly favorable for various crops. Spring rains are beneficial for grain, and the dryness of September is no less auspicious for the harvesting of cotton and fruit. In the dry climate, with the aid of artificial irrigation, man is the master of water and can give plants exactly what they need; a surplus of water increases the danger of frost in the spring and retards ripening. The determination of this optimum of moisture for each variety of cultivated plant is the work of experimental stations. Hence, neither drought nor excessive moisture is feared; thus together with rice, which demands plenty of moisture, crops requiring little water can be grown. In irrigated districts one may observe the luxuriant and rapid growth of vegetation. If poplar trees are planted along a reservoir, in six years they grow to a size suitable for use in construction, and after 12 to 15 years the trees have become very large. In three or four years one may raise an orchard and enjoy its fruit.

Climatic characteristics definitely affect transportation. The slight and broken snow cover is not favorable for sleighs, whereas rail transportation is little affected by the infrequent snowstorms. The usual alternation of warm and cold periods during winter and part of spring, along with the relatively abundant precipitation which forms sticky, clayey soil, greatly hampers movement along dirt roads.

The high summer temperatures are easily endured not only by the local inhabitants but also by travelers. The dryness of the air promotes rapid evaporation from the surface of the body and cooling of the skin. Hence there is not that burdensome stuffiness which makes even lower temperatures hardly endurable in a moist climate. When the humidity increases, cool nights are a great relief for man in the desert. The hot, dry climate is favorable for the treatment of lung diseases, but regions with dust storms must be avoided. The dust circulated by dust storms is responsible for numerous eye disorders.

RELIEF

The Caspian Lowland extends from the eastern shore of the Caspian Sea along the northern outskirts of the Ust-Urt Plateau in a southeasterly direction to the national boundary with

Iran. It is sharply demarcated on the east by the high, steep cliffs of the Ust-Urt Plateau and the Mangyshlak Mountains. The lowland is formed of the post-Tertiary deposits of clay and sand laid down by the Caspian transgressions. In places one may observe as many as seven terraces and shore embankments—traces of former levels of the Caspian Sea. The highest of these terraces (containing Caspian mollusks) lies at an elevation of approximately 247 feet above the Caspian, which is the same elevation as the Aral Sea. In the period of this transgression the lowlands of western Turkmenia were inundated by the water of the Caspian to Kyzyl-Arvat. Between the Bolshoy (Big) Balkhan and Malyy (Little) Balkhan mountains there was a strait joining the Caspian Sea with the Uzboy Basin. The Sarmatian Tertiary transgression, which was on the site of the Caspian, extended farthest east, along the base of Kopet-Dag almost to the meridian of Geok-Tepe (near Ashkhabad). The surface of the Caspian Sea lies at —92 feet, but the pre-Caspian lowland in places drops considerably below this level. In southern Mangyshlak Peninsula there are many depressions below sea level, such as Koshkar-Ata at —148 feet or Kaundy at —65 feet. Batyr or Karagiye is the deepest depression (with a large salt marsh on the bottom), at —427 feet. The shores of this basin, whose dimensions are 24 by 12 miles, rise 759 feet above its bottom. Batyr is the deepest dry depression in the entire USSR. In depth it can be compared to the well-known Lyukchunskaya Basin near Turfan in Chinese Turkestan, which has an absolute bench mark of —429 feet, and the arid Qattara Depression in the Libyan Desert, which has an absolute bench mark of —332 feet. Because of its depth, Batyr Depression may be the site of a hydroelectric station with a tunnel for the passage of sea water into the depression, and may be used also as a reservoir in which Caspian water can be evaporated for the extraction of salts. It is fortunate that the water divide between the Batyr Depression and the Caspian Sea lies only 16 feet above the level of the Caspian.

The Caspian oil field is the most interesting district of the lowland. It is the area lying in the southern portion of the lowland, and includes Cheleken Peninsula and the group of hills of the Nebit-Dag district.

Cheleken Peninsula is 20 miles long and extends across the entry into Krasnovodskiy Gulf. In the middle of the peninsula stretches elongated Chokhrak Hill with a height of 343 feet above the level of the Caspian. Cheleken is formed of dislocated Tertiary deposits, which are underlain by Mesozoic rocks. The tectonics of Cheleken are extremely complex. Faults play an essential role. The Tertiary deposits are oil-bearing; the productive horizon lies at a depth of 660 to 742 feet. On the peninsula are active low mud-volcanoes with craters up to 6 feet in diameter, filled with oil, through which gases are actively given off. The oil of the old eruptions has saturated the rocks surrounding them. The sand cemented by oil, is called solidified petroleum, and even under energetic desert weathering it has been well preserved as mesa-shaped, blanket deposits with sheer edges. On drying out, these deposits break into prisms, similar to basalt structures. Besides oil, the richest deposits of ozocerite or mineral wax in the USSR are found here. These are connected with the faults in the oil-bearing rocks. In these same faults are numerous springs precipitating sodium chloride or brown hematite and giving off gaseous hydrocarbons. In the salt springs there is so much salt that with the intense evaporation in summer the streams are dammed by terraces of sodium chloride. On the peninsula is the original Lake Porsu-Gel, which is the crater of an old mud-volcano flooded with water. The extraction of gas and oil from the lake is being carried on at the present time.

In the very southern portion of the Caspian Lowland are found solitary small mounds which are a variety of brachy-synclines and appear to be independent centers of upheaval. They are formed of dislocated Upper Tertiary (Apsheronsk and Bakinsk) deposits, often highly broken by numerous faults. Belonging to these elevations are: plateau-shaped Nebit-Dag Hill, or Neftyanaya, 148 feet high, rising above the Baba-Khodzha Salt Marsh; Boya-Dag Hill, lying farther east, 386 feet high; Monzhukly Mountain, 386 feet; and the mud-volcanoes at Chikishlyar, among which Zelenyy Bugor has an elevation of 224 feet. In these salt domes are countless outcrops of oil and ozocerite, large cone-shaped, oil-sand deposits, such as on Cheleken, and abundant salt springs (sometimes warm ones). The mud mounds emit mud, oil, and gas. Geologic prospects of the oil-bearing potentialities of Nebit-Dag are favorable, and the deposit is being made use of today.

The Caspian Mountain system—a group of isolated desert ridges—extends between the eastern Caspian coast and the Ust-Urt to the northern tip of Kopet-Dag. Belonging to this are the Mangyshlak Mountains, Dzhanak Plateau, Krasnovodsk Plateau, and the Big Balkhan, to which we may add with certain reser-

zonality and bear the same character as the adjacent plains.

The Mangyshlak Mountains extend for 120 miles between the gulf of Kochak on the west and Kaydak salt marsh on the east. In the central part, the Kara-Tau Ridge stretches in a west-northwest direction. Two ridges parallel Kara-Tau, one north of it and one south of it, bearing the names North and South Ak-Tau, respectively. They are separated from Kara-Tau by longitudinal depressions. Mangyshlak-Kara-Tau is an undulating plateau with elevations of 1,000 to 1,122 feet in the western part and 1,122 to 1,551 feet in the remaining portions; the highest point is 1,752 feet. The surface of the plateau is rather level. In some places it is a plain broken only by deeply notched gorges, and in other places it becomes slightly rolling. Often residual buttes of hard sandstones rise on it as rectilinear

Fig. 14-1. Geological cross section of the Mangyshlak Mountains.

T—Triassic strata of the Kara-Tau Range which are greatly dislocated (folding greatly generalized); Cr_1Cr_2—Lower Cretaceous strata forming the longitudinal basins; Cr_3—Upper Cretaceous marl, chalk, and limestone of the northern and southern Ak-Tau Ranges; J_1, J_2, and J_3— Jurassic strata.

vations the Little Balkhan Range, which is similar to them in nature. These landforms are plateaus with precipitous slopes dissected by deep gullies. Geologically, with the exception of Malyy Balkhan, the elevations are anticlines, formed by dislocated Mesozoic deposits on which, in many places, lie horizontal upper Tertiary deposits. The most intensive folding took place in the Mesozoic. The major forms of meso-relief are created by water and wind under conditions of desert climate. These comparatively low mountains in the neighborhood of the vast deserts are devoid of signs of vertical

crests, while the surface of the plateau cuts off the folds and steeply elevated beds of the rocks composing the ridge. The sides of the longitudinal depressions are extraordinarily steep. The southern sides are rectilinear, and the northern sides diversified by deep depressions, as a consequence of which the width of the surface of the plateau ranges from two to five miles. The slopes for the most part are dissected by deep sheer-walled ravines several miles long. Geologically, Kara-Tau is a large anticline, formed of highly dislocated marine Triassic rocks, of sandstone, metamorphosed clay shale, and black limestone. It also contains Jurassic and Cretaceous rocks, which are less dislocated. The folding must be related to the early-Kimeridgian phase (between the Triassic and Jurassic). The North Ak-Tau Ridge, with heights up to 1,056 feet, is formed of Upper Cretaceous deposits. It extends from Ust-Urt along the entire Kara-Tau, marked by a snow-white escarpment, and on the west is completely buried under Upper Tertiary limestone. South Ak-Tau, on the other hand, begins in the west with a sharply defined cliff, extends south of Kara-Tau, and in the east disappears, becoming a gentle turfed-over slope. There is a longitudinal depression between the Kara-Tau and Ak-Tau Ranges, formed of Jurassic and Cretaceous rocks. It possesses a complex relief, both as a result of the undulation along the line of strike of the sides of the fold and the diversity of lithological makeup. Characteristic features of the relief are the long isoclinal ridges and isolated residual table mountains of sandstone. Deep and broad gateways cut through North Ak-Tau in places, provide an outlet for the valley.

The present-day agents of erosion of the Mangyshlak Mountains are water and wind under the conditions of a desert regime. Exfoliation, forming protective crusts on soft rocks, is common, as are niches, overhangs, and small holes resulting from wind erosion. Yet water is important in the formation of not only the small but also the large forms of relief. It cuts deep gorges, narrow winding gaps, and numerous small gulleys, all having the appearance of gigantic furrows. Water from torrential rain works episodically here, converting sinuous, dry valleys into turbulent, impassable streams which carry out a large amount of erosional material from the gorges. Kara-Tau Range is the source of water for the region surrounding it. It serves as a depository for summer rain and winter snow. The water runs deep along the cracks in the rocks and appears at the source and on the bottom of deep gulleys as excellent fresh springs. No small part is played by the capacity of rock waste to condense the water vapors from the atmosphere,

under conditions of their heating during the day and cooling at night. Therefore the water is not mineralized at all, and only at a distance from the ridge does it become brackish. The springs usually dry up toward the end of summer; hence the water is used carefully by the population for irrigation.

In the Kara-Tau Range no indication of vertical zonality in the distribution of soil and vegetation is observed. Here we find coarse, skeletal, shallow soil, devoid of any differentiation into layers. Developed on this soil is a vegetation of the northern desert variety, composed of Artemisia, halophytes, and feather grasses. The nature of the vegetation allows large herds of horses to pasture on the Kara-Tau Plateau. People do not settle on the plateau permanently because of the lack of water.

Dzhanak is the district between the southeastern ridge of Kara-Bogaz-Gol and the western scarp of Ust-Urt. The relief is made up of the monoclinal Mesozoic ridges Irsary-Baba, with a height of about 1,254 feet (of Upper Cretaceous rocks), and Tua-Kyr (of Jurassic rocks), which extend in a northwestern direction. Dislocations of the Mesozoic are gentle folds of a northwest trend. Intense dislocations are related to the same early Kimeridgian phase as in the Mangyshlak Mountains.

The Krasnovodsk Plateau is between Krasnovod Gulf in the south and Kara-Bogaz-Gol in the north. In the west it does not quite reach the shores of the Caspian Sea; in the east it extends to the Chil-Mamet-Kum sand. Average elevation of the plateau is about 660 feet, but some parts are above 1,000 feet. The plateau is definitely bounded by scarps having different elevations: in the north 858 to 924 feet, in the south about 1,023 feet, in the west 280 feet. Krasnovodsk Plateau is formed of Tertiary rocks, the youngest of which are the horizontally occurring Akchagylskiye beds (Pliocene). At the southern and northeastern borders of the plateau, Tertiary deposits overlie an eroded fold, consisting mainly of highly dislocated Mesozoic rocks (Jurassic and Cretaceous). The fold is an anticline strongly inclined to the north with crumbling southern walls running along a fault trace and marked by outcrops of igneous rocks (the summit of Kuba-Dag). Near Krasnovodsk is the mountain Sha-Kadam (absolute height 544 feet), formed of porphyrite and diorite. A peculiarity of the relief of the plateau is the numerous undrained basins with relative depths from 165 to 396 feet. The Krasnovodsk district is known for its seismism, which was evidenced in 1895 by a destructive earthquake with an epicenter along the coast of the Caspian Sea, between Krasnovodsk and Uzun-Ada. At its eastern end, the plateau abuts the Bolshoy Balkhan Range.

With certain reservations, the Big Balkhan may be considered morphologically as a plateau sloping from north to south. Its elevation reaches 6,154 feet (Mount Dyuvnesh-Kals). In the north and west, Bolshoy Balkhan is bordered by steep, inaccessible, rocky cliffs 2,640 feet high. On the south and partly on the west, it is bounded by the bed of the Uzboy. The northern sheer slope is dissected by extremely deep ravines with a drop of more than 1,650 feet, but only 1.5 to 2.5 miles long. Alluvial fans from these gulleys have merged into a solid belt 3 miles wide and rising to a height of 660 feet. The Bolshoy Balkhan system consists of several anticlinal folds. In the structure of the mountains, thick masses of light-gray, close-grained highly fractured limestone, belonging to the Upper Jurassic and Lower Cretaceous, are most important. At the eastern end are the remains of horizontal (Akchagylsk) deposits, similar to those of the Krasnovodsk Plateau. On all sides except the north, Bolshoy Balkhan is edged by Caspian deposits containing shells of mollusks (*Cardium trigonoides*).

The Little Balkhan is south of the Big Balkhan and the Trans-Caspian railroad. It is a desert range rising at one point to 2,646 feet and extending from northeast to southwest. On the north along a longitudinal fault it descends to the Kara-Kum Desert in steep bluffs. It is a very long and precipitous anticline, the northern side of which dips sharply to the north. On the northern slope, Lower Cretaceous rocks are developed—limestone, sandstone, clay, and marl. Upper Cretaceous and Tertiary rocks are found only in the southern foothills. Upper Tertiary deposits here, in contrast to other elevations of the Caspian Mountain System, are dislocated Akchagylsk deposits, surrounding the range on all sides as foothills. Processes of folding took place in the Mesozoic and Tertiary. The northern slope, formed of solid Lower Cretaceous limestones, is dissected by short but very deep (about 660 feet) gorges with sheer walls.

The southern slope, formed of marl and gypsiferous clay of the Upper Cretaceous and Tertiary rocks, is characterized by karst and other purely erosional processes. Intense fracturing, friability, and high solubility of the rocks explain the formation of a unique karst, despite the desert climate. Along with the remarkably regular ravines, diverse forms of desert clayey karst are found. Everywhere are deep holes, sometimes turning into underground pits of a sinkhole character. "Hanging" gullies are evident, on the floor of which are deep craters and pits joined to one another by underground channels. With the destruction of the outer gully, the underground one emerges to the surface and the hanging gully is converted into a normal valley. Sometimes completely enclosed, dry, deep basins are formed. Very deep canyons are abundant, with openings for underground cavities. This extreme dissection of relief by erosion and the processes of the desert clay karst create a pronounced "badlands" landscape.

The morphologically simple forms of the northern Tertiary plateaus have very extensive spread. They existed in the Pliocene as large, original Tertiary-Cretaceous plateaus occupying a large area in the northern part of Central Asia which was subsequently dissected into individual isolated mesa-butte elevations. Characteristic geographic features common to all of these elevations indicate their unity of origin: wide occurrence of horizontally lying Tertiary rocks, plateau-like tops, pronounced similarity in character of bluffs or escarpments, absence of an external hydrographic network, deep occurrence of saline ground water, and, finally, continuous development of a rocky desert landscape with a predominance of *Artemisia*-halophytic vegetation on structural sierozem. Some of the plateaus belonging to the area are Ust-Urt, Zaunguz, and the western Bet-Pak-Dala Desert.

the Sarmatian are thin limestones, sometimes white, sometimes with a green, yellow, or rose tint, alternating with light saliferous marl and clay. At the base of the steep scarps can be seen the older rocks of the Paleozoic, Cretaceous, and Jurassic directly underlying the Sarmatian. In the southwestern part, under the Sarmatian,

Fig. 14-2. Northern cliff of the Ust-Urt Hills showing strata of limestone and sandstone.

Ust-Urt is the plateau between the Caspian and Aral seas. Its central elevation does not exceed 660 to 693 feet, but in the southwest corner it reaches 1,089 feet. On all sides the plateau ends in steep cliffs or escarpments, which are its only borders. The western cliff in its southern portion is the eastern shore of Kara-Bogaz-Gol. The eastern bluff is an abrupt wall 627 feet high, above the western shore of the Aral Sea; farther south it borders the Sarykamysh Basin. The northern escarpment rises 214 feet. The entire surface of Ust-Urt is formed of horizontally lying rocks of Sarmatian age, especially its lower series (upper Miocene). Their general character remains rather constant over this vast area. Strata of

there is a strip of folds extending from northwest to southeast composed of Mesozoic and Paleozoic rocks, which are a continuation of the Mangyshlak folds. This suggests that the Ust-Urt is a region of Kimeridgian orogeny— not very intensive, it is true, but more pronounced on the boundary of the Jurassic and Lower Cretaceous.

During the post-Pliocene, Ust-Urt began to be separated from the adjacent areas. In the formation of its escarpments, many faults took place on the eastern Pri-Aral cliff. Abrasion of the early Caspian and Aral seas and stream erosion (of the Uzboy, for example) separated Ust-Urt from the solid continental block and made it an isolated plateau. Subsequently, it underwent the influence of karst processes and desert weathering. The surface of Ust-Urt is a monotonous plain, sometimes nearly level (the northeast part). In some places there are small hills together with flat broad gullies, and enclosed basins with sand, salt marshes, and salt lakes. The origin of these basins is explained by erosion, by karst processes in gypsiferous clay, and by aeolian action on the Sarmatian limestone. Within the limits of Ust-Urt, there are several sandy areas, two of which are the Sam Sand at an elevation of 231 feet, situated near the lake of the same name, and the Matay Sand, near Lake Asmantay-Matay.

There is no running water on the surface of the Ust-Urt plateau. Only in spring are the depressions filled with water. Underground water is diverse; sandy areas are the water-bearers, and they quickly absorb precipitation. Also, water is supplied by means of condensation. Water may always be found in the sand at varying depths, but its quality differs. In the Sam Sand at a depth of 6.5 to 10 feet, there is fresh ground water. Within the Sarmatian series ground water lies very deep (65 to 165 feet and even 230 feet), and it is usually brackish or salty. In this series there are a number of watertight seams which cause several layers to contain water with diversified chemical composition. The most constant and dependable water horizon is at the base of the Sarmatian. It is detected quite definitely in many places, and belonging to this horizon are the numerous but weak springs emerging along the Aral escarpment in its southern part. They yield acrid, salty, and, more rarely, fresh water. Southeast of the plateau are found dissected elevations, formed by the same Sarmatian deposits. On one of these—the Ishek-Ankren-Kyr Plateau—there is a large dry basin, the bottom of which lies 303.6 feet below sea level and lower than the near-by Sarykamysh Basin.

The Zaunguz Plateau lies southeast of Ust-Urt and is separated from it by the Uzboy Valley. On the east, it reaches to within 49.6 miles of the Amu-Darya and, on the south, it is sharply demarcated by the Unguz Depression. Elevations of the plateau usually range from 200 to 330 feet above the surrounding locality. The plateau slopes gradually northward; on the south abruptly breaks off in an escarpment similar to that of Ust-Urt. The line of escarpment is tortuous because of its multitude of spurs and valleys, and the upper third of it is covered by sandy hillocks from the weathering of friable sandstone. The plateau is formed of horizontal strata of Upper Tertiary age: at the base is Lower Sarmatian, above are clay and sandstone, corresponding possibly to middle and upper Sarmatian. As a result of heightened activity of running water on the precipitous southern edge of the plateau, a unique badland landscape, lying to the south, was formed. It consists of narrow and long plateau-like parts which are separated from the southern edge of the plateau, having steep slopes and stretching almost in a meridional direction. These small elevations, with an area of a few square miles and a height of several dozen yards, are sometimes completely detached from the plateau, are sometimes joined to it by bridges, or else project in the form of promontories. Between the badlands are found elongated, flat-bottomed valleys, the bottoms of which form a level surface covered with a clayey alluvium.

More denuded, low, circular and conical hill-elevations, rising only 65 to 100 feet above the surrounding locality, are found. Similar mounds situated in groups over a large expanse in the Shiikh pit district are well known for their deposits of sulphur. The best known is Chemberli mound, formed of horizontal seams of gypsiferous sandstone, marl, and solid quartzite, above which lies a cap of light-gray, friable, Middle Sarmatian sandstone, with which the sulphur is linked. The amount of sulphur in the rock reaches 40 to 50 per cent, and the ratio of rock-containing sulphur to barren rock is rather favorable (1:4). Supplies of sulphur are estimated at approximately one million tons; that is, the deposit may be considered of primary industrial importance. The origin of the sulphur is not clear. Evidently it accumulated as a result of chemical processes taking place in the rich sulphates of sedimentary rocks under conditions of desert climate.

At the base of the southern scarp of the Zaunguz Plateau stretches the so-called Unguz —a chain of dry ravines and locked-in basins occupied by salt marshes, the bottoms of which lie at elevations of 313 to 379 feet. The abundance of salt marshes is explained by the fact that rain water running off the nearest portions of the plateau brings into these depressions those salts which it has dissolved on its way along saliferous clay and sandstone, together with suspended particles of clay and sand. Water evaporating on the watertight clay of the depressions leaves the salts on the surface of the soil. Some explain the origin of the Unguz as original karst denudation; others consider Unguz one of the old channels of the Amu-Darya. It is the underground channel for drainage of the water from the Kara-Kum Desert.

Bet-Pak-Dala extends from the Sary-Su River almost to the western shore of Lake Balkhash. Its southern border over a considerable extent is determined by the middle and lower course of the Chu River. The northern boundary is less regular, following approximately 46°30′ north latitude, and is distinct only in the western portion, where it corresponds to an escarpment. Farther east it merges gradually with the adjacent districts. In terms of surface structure, Bet-Pak-Dala is a large plateau or rolling upland, with average elevations of 990 to 1,155 feet. Its surface, in general, dips in a southwest direction: elevations in the northern part reach 1,108 feet, in the west, 825 feet, and on the southern border near the Chu River, 594 feet. In the mountainous eastern part, maximum elevations increase sharply, reaching 2,145 feet in the Baygara Mountains and 3,220 feet in the Dzhambul group. In relation to the adjacent regions, Bet-Pak-Dala is uplifted and separated from them in some places by escarpments. In the northwest, the plateau breaks off toward the Sary-Su River in a steep cliff 132 to 200 feet high, while the transition to the valley of the Chu River is a more gentle slope.

Because of the small amount of precipitation, and the high summer temperatures and strong winds, the water supply of the plain is limited. It does not have a surface hydrographic network, and running water is lacking. The Chu River, passing along its southern border, receives no surface water from the plain. Hydrographically, Bet-Pak-Dala is a region of internal drainage, inasmuch as it dips on all sides toward the center. The many shallow rivers flowing off the mountains of the eastern and southern parts of the plain very rapidly lose their channels in the locked-in depressions. Only in spring do the rivers contain temporary meltwater, and in summer only small salt-water pools remain. Small lakes of a temporary nature are observed. Nevertheless, the plain is useful for the grazing of thousands of herds of livestock because of adequate underground water. The hydrographic locked-in quality of the plain and the permeability to surface water of the almost unbroken mantle of coarse-rubbly soil promote rapid absorption of precipitation, and therefore considerable ground water is accumulated despite the desert regime. The abundant ground water, tapped by wells and springs, often has a high quality.

The distribution of underground water depends mainly on the geologic structure of the plain. It consists of two different parts, according to relief and geology—the western and the eastern, each of which has its own hydrographic peculiarities. The western part is a typical uplifted plain with extremely monotonous landscape. This uniformity is conditioned by the absence of any noticeable influence of the activity of running water—here, there are no deep gullies and in general no sharp traces of erosional activity. This part of the plain is formed of horizontally lying Tertiary deposits. Continental and marine Paleozoic strata of sandstone, clay, and gravel are found. Farther east lies a narrow strip of Upper Cretaceous, consisting of conglomerate, gravel, and sand. A characteristic of the relief of the western part of Bet-Pak-Dala is the combination of two elements: flat waterdivides and undrained locked-in depressions covered with salt marshes and saline lakes. Aeolian weathering has been suggested as the origin of the basins. The constant strong winds carry the dust-like material beyond the borders of the region, not giving it a chance to accumulate here. This explains the large clastic or coase character of debris and its shallow depth. Rain water, flowing into the basins, carries an abundant quantity of salts and fine mineral particles, which are material for the formation of solonchak soil that readily yields to surface weathering.

Over the entire western part of the plain, formed exclusively of horizontal strata, ground water has a very slow inflow. Water is found in wells at varying depth (from 15 to 66 feet), depending on the position of the watertight rocks. On the water divides of the plains the water is of comparatively good quality and only slightly mineralized. On the other hand, the water from the different depressions is highly saline. On the southern outskirts of the desert (Chu River valley) fresh artesian water with good pressure offers the opportunity of irrigating large areas of land and guarantees water for future population.

The eastern part of Bet-Pak-Dala possesses completely different features, being a hilly country—a continuation of the Kazakh hill country. On the level or slightly undulating surface, scattered at a distance from one another or gathered in groups, are numerous dome-shaped hills, with relative heights of not more than 16 to 33 feet. The soft horizontal lines from time to time are broken by low ridges. In places the relief takes on the features of a mountain region. The most prominent elevations of the more resistant rocks are in the northeastern and southeastern parts (Dzhambul and Baygara groups). The eastern part of Bet-Pak-Dala is formed of Paleozoic sedimentary rocks—shale and sandstone—and also various igneous rocks, among which gray and red granite crops out frequently. On low hills formed of granite are heaps of granite blocks rounded off by the wind and embellished by weathering. In places where schists have developed, the surface of the hills is eroded lower.

The depressions have the appearance of locked-in basins devoid of surface drainage. The basins possess very gentle slopes and flat bottoms, lying 33 to 50 feet below the level of the plateau. Their size differs, varying from 3 to 4 miles in diameter. The basins are the only places on the whole plain for the accumulation of loose alluvium. Wind and rain water carry salts and the fine soil from the water divides and slopes of hills, into the depressions. As a result of this process, the soil of elevated portions is coarse and becomes rocky, and the loose fine soil of the basins increases in thickness. Some basins possess artesian water of constant pressure and springs with a large output. Their soil is well leached and is low in salts. Many other basins have brackish, highly saline ground water lying close to the surface.

In the eastern part of Bet-Pak-Dala, in contrast to the western, the Paleozoic rocks are watertight, as a consequence of which a considerable number of mineralized springs of an exclusively interstitial character are developed with feeding from great depths. The water of the springs is adapted to tectonic fissures; thus the distribution of local water is irregular and bears a spotty character. The number of wells and springs is considerable.

Sandy Deserts

The sandy deserts are interesting because of their unusual history of development, special landforms, hydrologic regime, and uniqueness and complexity of structure, and because they differ from other landscapes of the plains region of Central Asia. The sandy deserts begin at the coasts of the Caspian and Aral seas and prevail without break for many hundred of miles to the foothills of the Tien Shan. The large areas are Kara-Kum Trans-Caspian, Kyzyl-Kum, Kara-Kum Pre-Aral, Big and Little Barsuki, Muyun-Kum and the sand of the southern Balkhash area.

The origin of the sands has not been definitely determined. The idea is prevalent that they are the product of weathering of bedrock of a sandy composition under conditions of desert climate. While the importance of the wind as one of the chief relief-forming forces in the deserts is exceptionally great, its role in the creation of blanket deposits of sediments is far less certain. One may consider that the sand was formed as the result of the weathering of bedrock by continental climatic elements. This is clearly indicated by the petrographic similarity of the sand with the bedrock underlying it. Usually, however, such sand has only a relatively limited local spread. The accumulation of most of the sand has stopped, and new sand is being formed only on the outskirts of the present Amu-Darya Valley and in certain places of the northern Kara-Kum. The sand has not been formed in the present era; the deserts of Central Asia are old. The majority of the Turan lowland has not been covered by the sea since the Eocene; only along the outskirts are remnants of Oligocene, Miocene, and Pliocene marine deposits found. In the western portion of Kara-Kum, transgressions of the Sarmatian and Akchagylsk seas took place, which could have left sandy sediments. In the Quaternary period the plain was not covered by water of the Aral-Caspian Sea. The Aral Sea was never joined to the Balkhash, and at its highest state, in the period of union with the Caspian, it covered eastern and southeastern shores for only a few dozen miles from the present shore line. The level of Balkhash stood much higher. Balkhash was raised 100 feet above its present level, covering a considerable part of its southern shore, and was connected with Ala-Kul and Ebi-Nur lakes.

Most of the sand is of continental origin. The largest desert sand areas are the product of aeolian reprocessing on the site of loose sand and sandy, clayey alluvial deposits. In the glacial period when the rivers contained much water and carried sandy, clayey material in suspension, the Turan lowland plain was the main center of flooding with deposition of large amounts of alluvium. Everywhere, beneath the wind-blown sand of Kara-Kum lie gray micaceous sand. Its pronounced stratifi-

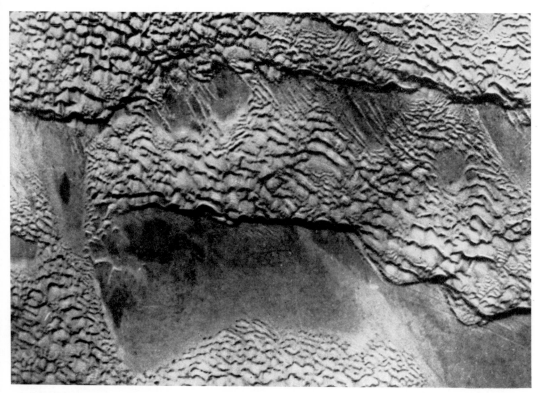

Fig. 14-3. Barchan sands on the Kara-Kum Desert.

Fig. 14-4. Growth on barchan sands in the Kara-Kum Desert; scattered bushes are sand acacia.

cation and streaks of clay indicate its alluvial origin, and it is analogous to modern alluvium of the Amu-Darya.

Signs of past flooding of the sandy deserts are shown in the relief by well-preserved old channels and large dry deltas. Perhaps the large Kara-Kum depression was a region of an intricate Quaternary delta of the Amu-Darya, Tedzhen, and Murgab, which drained into it and filled it with the products of erosion and weathering from the Pamir-Alay, Hindu Kush, and Paropamiz mountains. The dry deltas of the Tedzhen and Murgab are watered at present only in the central and southern parts. Old channels of rivers are numerous in Central Asia. Some areas dotted with dry, old channels, from weakly to deeply notched, are: the northern part of Kyzyl-Kum, the Kunya-Darya district, and the Kashka-Darya system —the old tributary of the Zeravshan entering into the Amu-Darya. The Pre-Aral sandy areas may have come from the alluvium of lakes and rivers formerly bringing their water into the Aral Sea. The sandy belt of Big Barsuki is an alluvial lake terrace formation of an old

basin, in the middle of which, at occasional points, rise residual mesas formed by the erosion of Tertiary bedrock now undergoing little weathering. The newest sandy, clayey alluviums of the modern rivers may serve as material for aeolian sand. The present shifting sand is the product of weathering of the river shoals of the Amu-Darya and Syr-Darya. Finally, a possible source of the sand in the shoreline deserts is sand deposited by waves on the level shores of the seas and large lakes, such as the areas along the Caspian, Aral, and Balkhash shores. Sand of different origin was later subjected to energetic weathering.

The continental period in the Kara-Kum has lasted since the post-Sarmatian, or, in any case, from the post-Akchagylsk period. In these eras the climate was even drier than it is now, as indicated by the unusual Turkestan xerophytic flora and fauna. The modern epoch is characterized by a climate that is moister than the foregoing one; thus, the sand has become secured in recent times. Historical evidence denotes a former immobility of many expanses of sand which are now covered by barchans formed as a result of man's agricultural activity.

The Trans-Caspian Kara-Kum is a sandy desert bordered on the south by the rather sharp but low bluff of the inclined foothill plain of Kopet-Dag and Paropamiz. In the north it extends to the bluff of the Zaunguz Plateau, on the west it runs to the depression of the Uzboy, and on the east it is bordered by the Amu-Darya. The roughly defined area is a rectangle extended in a northwest direction. Maximum heights do not vary much over the entire desert. Kara-Kum is on the site of a young Turkmenian graben, with an over-all area of 15,000 square miles, nine-tenths of which is occupied by sand. The shapes of relief of this sandy desert are extremely diverse —from active, moving barchans to sandy plains.

Barchan sand, a type of unsecured shifting sand, is found along the left bank of the Amu-Darya in a belt 24 to 30 miles wide. A barchan is a crescentic, sloped hill of bare shifting sand devoid of vegetation, that yields easily to the influence of the wind. Its profile is asymmetric, and its convex (windward) slope has a gentle rise with an angle of 5 to 12°. On the windward slope are branched sandy ripples perpendicular to the direction of the wind. The sharp crest of the barchan is curved in an arc, and the leeward slope is steep. Particles of sand crossing the crest roll down the leeward slope,

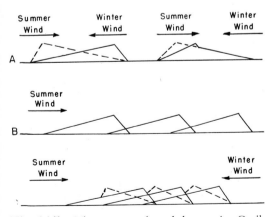

Fig. 14-5. Three types of sand dunes: A—Oscillatory; B—Progressive; C—Progressive-oscillatory.

and therefore the angle of incline is the angle of falling of the sand particles of a given diameter and varies from 28° to 36°. The profile of the leeward slope is almost a straight line, from the crest to the base.

During a strong wind, large particles which have begun the movement down the leeward slope fall to its base, but the finer particles of dust and sand are carried beyond. The crest cannot remain stable. With increased pressure of the wind, it dwindles as though melting, but during light wind it is re-established. The steep leeward slope moves only in a direction parallel to the trend of the crest, both during a wind perpendicular to the crest and during a wind blowing at an angle.

Individual barchans of perfect crescent shape are rarely found in the deserts of Central Asia and seldom are any barchans more than 16 to 26 feet high. This is because many conditions control their formation. A level, almost horizontal surface is essential, with a solid rocky or clayey bottom incapable of undergoing weathering. (In these deserts are unusual clayey strata where the sand dunes may actually reach a very great height—perhaps 115 feet above the level of the clay.) Also, the amount of sand should not be very great. Moreover, the wind, at least during a definite time of year, should have a single prevailing direction. Barchans are rarely encountered in the valley of the Amu-Darya.

Barchan chains are not formed by the consolidation of the sides of two or more dunes but are a special form of sandy accumulation. They are distinguished from individual barchans by their shape, large dimensions, little mobility, and by an abundance of loose sandy material under conditions of uneven relief. They have parallel asymmetrical embankments with a length of from 100 to 1,320 feet, extending perpendicularly to the direction of prevailing winds. Barchan chains also have a gentle windward slope with an angle of 12 to 15° and a steep leeward slope with a gradient of 32 to 36°. The line of the permanently sharp crest reveals a smooth undulation both in a vertical direction (in profile) and in a hori-

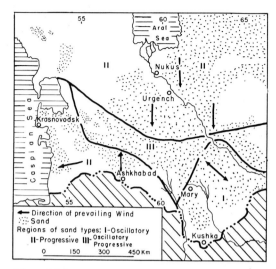

Map 14-I. Distribution of types of sand dune movement in Turkmenia and Kara-Kalpak.

zontal direction (in plan) because in depressions, where the depth of the sand is less, it advances more rapidly than on elevated areas. Dune ridges are relatively inert, slightly movable formations. Despite the definite predominance of north winds in the Kara-Kum, the sand has not buried the narrow cultivated zone of oases stretching along the base of Kopet-Dag. This relatively stationary quality of the sand is explained by the fixing, in part, by vegetation and by local characteristics of the wind regime.

At first the depressions are overgrown with vegetation. This suspends the feeding of the barchan ridges, which become lower, and their mobility is lessened, which gives vegetation a chance to settle on and secure the barchans themselves. Even if the direction of the prevailing wind shifts, the ridges are not able to shift the position of their base, and no movement of the sand forward in a single direction is observed. With the prevalence of north winds in summer, the summits of barchan ridges are moved roughly 65 feet south; in winter, however, when southeast winds are more frequent, a compensating movement in the reverse direction takes place, but the base of the barchan ridges remains in place. Some shifts in the direction of the wind do not play a role in the

movement of the ridges, because the direction of the ridge, with its shift, does not become perpendicular to the new direction of the wind but is deflected to the side.

The cultivated areas, situated on the outskirts of the desert, experience all the negative consequences of dynamic processes in the sandy desert. Formerly cultivated lands in the lower sections of the Murgab and Zeravshan were covered by sand. Even today, sand in the flourishing valley of the Amu-Darya attacks the fields and dwellings. In the zone of contact of barchan ridges and oases, the wind carries sand freely into the oases, but with a shift in the wind the sand deposited on the plain cannot return to the ridge because vegetation, fences, and dwellings, etc., prevent this.

The process of secondary weathering of already secured sand is widespread and is due to many natural causes and the activities of man. A strong factor is the ground burrowers —the long-pawed marmot, settling in great colonies, breaks up the surface, destroys the continuity of the plant cover, and thus contributes to the scattering of the sand. Tortoises dig burrows under the overhang of sandy cornices, which are subsequently destroyed by the action of the wind. Moving sand most often develops near populated places or regular stopovers of nomadic livestock herders. The excessive grazing of a great number of livestock at one time, eating and stamping the already sparse vegetation of the sand, the felling of *saxaul* forests and the brushwoods which secure the sand, and the disruption of the plant cover along roads and near wells where livestock drink are all factors leading to the energetic movement of sand and to its conversion into bare shifting barchans. With the curtailment of wasteful methods of pasturage of sheep in the southeastern Kara-Kum from 1918 to 1928, local sand recovered its vegetation at a rapid rate.

Ridge sand is widespread in the northwestern part of Kara-Kum, where long parallel sandy ridges extend in a general meridional direction. In contrast to barchan ridges, the ridge sand extends in the direction of the prevailing wind. The size of ridges varies greatly;

relative heights, on the average, are 50 to 65 feet, with individual tops at 80 to 100 feet. The distance between the ridges usually is about 200 to 250 feet. The ridges are joined to one another by sandy bridges, as a consequence of which the interridge depressions are divided into locked-in basins stretching lengthwise. This gives to areas of ridge sand an extremely intricate honeycombed structure. The basins have clayey areas or solonchak.

A transverse profile of a sand ridge is more or less symmetrical, and in the shape of a gen-

flatly oval, have a steeper upper edge, and are completely devoid of vegetation.

The origin of the ridge sand is not clear. Its formation is linked with the shrinkage of large lakes which existed in Quaternary time, as indicated by Quaternary lake deposits. The ridge sand south of Zaunguz Plateau is explained by the relief of the plateau. The continuation of every large gully, furrowing the edge of a plateau, into the plain adjacent on the south intensified deflation, and the formation of the interridge gullies took place. In the shelter

Fig. 14-6. Cross-bedded sands in the northern Kara-Kum Desert.

tle, low arch which is sometimes depressed. The length of a ridge exceeds the width by many times. The longitudinal profile is an elongated trapezoid with a gentle, undulating crest. Sometimes a ridge has a steeper western slope (in western Kara-Kum) or eastern slope (southeastern Kara-Kum). Ridge sand does not move and is secured by vegetation. In some places its form is complicated by secondary aeolian effects. As a result of secondary scattering under the influence of excessive pasturage of livestock, small barchan accumulations are found on top as well as on the slopes and in deflation depressions. These depressions are

from the wind, at the southern tip of each projection of the plateau, sand became deposited as a ridge, continuing the projection in a southern direction. The trend of the sandy ridges in a meridional or nearly meridional direction facilitates the movement of caravans from the foothill oasis zone near the base of Kopet-Dag to Khivinskiy Oasis. Caravan routes run along the depressions between ridges, most often along the clay base, and only occasionally cut across transverse bridges between ridges.

Sand hills are fixed bodies of sand on mound sand secured by vegetation. They are low sandy hills, irregularly shaped and in no observable order. The original landscape of the sand hills is widespread in all the sandy deserts of Central Asia. The mounds, 20 to 25 feet high, have rounded tops and gentle slopes, with no morphologic differentiation on windward and leeward sides. The hills overlap one another and either merge into short ridges with a few rounded tops or form irregular groups. The sand hills, as can be seen from an airplane, extend into ridges. Locked-in basins are formed between the hills and are also irregular in shape. Sand hills are quite immovable and produce the best impression because of the rich vegetation. Here are gathered all the diverse plants of the sand of Central Asia. In places, under the influence of intensive grazing of livestock, sand hills are subjected to secondary weathering and are converted into shifting sand. The formation of typical sand hills is the result of partial fixation of the movable barchan sand by the rather dense vegetation.

Securing the sand, the plant pioneers divide the barchan ridge into a series of fixed sections. The sand between the sections may move, but the secured portions are converted into hills. What is left of the barchan ridges expands to the sides, becomes lower, begins to move more slowly, and becomes still more accessible for the growth of vegetation. As a result, the barchan ridge is converted into a series of fixed mounds.

Similar in origin to the sand hills are the bush mounds—accumulations of sand with considerable admixture of clayey particles—in the shelter of individual bushes or thickets. The bush mound forms where vegetation is distributed in separate groups amid bare areas of thin sand. If the sand is thick, the plants may be entirely covered by it. When the sand is brought in in small quantities it slowly fills in between the branches and stalks of the bushes, which, having time to grow in height, remain living and secure the accumulated sand.

Fig. 14-7. Fixed sand dunes along the Kunya-Darya dry river bed.

The accumulation is limited, and is different for different plants (it varies from 6 feet to 20 feet). With the further covering of the sand mound, the upper limit of the moist layer is somewhat raised, but always to a lesser elevation than the surface of the mound. The plant must obtain water from a greater and greater depth and begins to suffer from lack of moisture, not being able to reach it with its roots. Then begins the withering of the shrub and the destruction of the sand mass by the wind.

Sandy or sandy, clayey plains—flat or slightly hilly sandy expanses—are developed in the eastern part of the Kara-Kum and in patches in other parts of it. A feature of the sandy plain is its thinness of sandy cover (loess-like sands). The layer of sand is underlain by a slightly layered, sandy, clayey mass which prevents further weathering. Plains having only a fine layer of sand on their surface rapidly become covered with vegetation. Sandy, clayey plains are concentrated exclusively in dry river deltas and are without doubt the result of deposits of sandy, clayey alluviums by these rivers.

Many flat-bottomed, clearly demarcated depressions are covered with a fine clayey alluvium and are inundated for a prolonged time during spring rains and occasional downpours. The size and shape of these basins may vary from small spots of a few yards width to large areas of the most fantastic shape, having a width and length of several miles. They occur on fine-particled alluvial and proluvial depositions. A zone of these basins, 20 to 24 miles wide, extends north of Kopet-Dag and parallel to it. Here, they occupy 50 per cent of the surface. These basins are widespread not only on the upper terraces of the Amu-Darya and Syr-Darya valleys and the Murgab and Tedzhen valleys, but also in old locked-in basins such as in the Sarykamysh Basin, on saline alluvial and lake clayey deposits very often underlain by gray river sand. Similar forms may be located on plateaus, occupying the flat depressions. Examples are the countless depressions of the Ust-Urt and Krasnovodsk plateaus. In spring they are flooded. The streams, carrying a mass of turbid water, quickly overflow the basins, which are dammed by the sandy mounds.

In spring, the basins are continuous lakes with a width of 1.5 to 3 miles, but with a length of tens of miles. These lakes are about a foot and a half deep, have yellowish water colored with suspended mud, and give rise to broad but low terraces. During the stand of spring water the lake bottoms are not deeply penetrated by the water. These ephemeral lakes disappear very quickly under desert heat. Whereas one traveler may be gladdened by the blue surface of a broad basin of water, another may find, a week later, a salty clay puddle or an impassible sticky swamp. When the water disappears, a barren, muddy, and completely level plain forms, hardening in the sun's rays and cracking in all directions from the shrinking of the surface.

In summer, with further drying, the surface of the basins changes into a flat, smooth, glistening surface so hard that it clanks under horses' hooves. With the intense and rapid drying out of the moist, sandy, clayey alluvium, the surface is broken by deep cracks into polygonal structures. Flakes of the soil surface have a thickness of about 1 inch and are usually weakly connected, both between themselves and with the next layer down. By thrusting the end of a knife between the cakes and easily lifting them out, one finds that they are somewhat convex, owing to salts. In cross section the crust is seen to be highly porous, but on the surface the pores are usually imperceptible. Owing to the rapid hardening of the surface by the sun's warmth, water entering such basins quickly evaporates. The deposition of dissolved chemicals forms a hard, thin, and very strong crust of a rosy, pale-yellow, or sometimes bright orange color. This crust gives the surface a hardness and a reddish tint. The basins of the northern part of Kara-Kum, lying at a higher level, have a white crust.

Even a weak wind carries great quantities of sand across these basins, but their surface is so smooth and level that not a single sand particle will remain on it, and therefore barchans

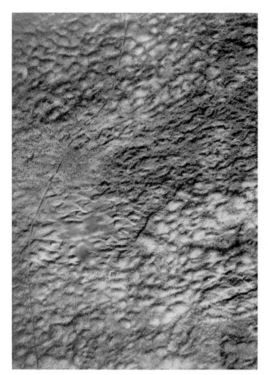

Fig. 14-8. Air view of sand dunes in Central Asia.

do not form. However, the smallest obstacle on a basin will cause an accumulation of sand, especially at the edges. These desolate tracts, as smooth as though they had been polished, are absolute wastes without a single bush or blade of grass. The sand slowly advancing at the edges is soon populated with spring ephemerals, which fasten little heaps of sand with their roots. Along the periphery of basin areas, closer to the sand, grow solitary artemisia and halophytes.

The main characteristic of the soil-forming process of these basins is the long-standing surface water which creates conditions for the hydromorphous soil process, by which the soil is distinguished from sierozem. Particularly characteristic of this soil is an excellent thin-leaf stratification, corresponding to the annual spring inundation. The upper layers are sandier than are the deeper ones. The clayey layer, lying at a depth of 8 inches, is a water-resistant stratum, which does not let the flood water

percolate downward. The water-resistant strata in northeast Kara-Kum are milk-chocolate colored clays, which evidently are the deposits of glacial meltwater in lake basins. The soil has various layers. On top lies the very porous crust of brownish shades, with negligible humus content 1 to 2 inches thick. Its upper part is a strong fine crust, more often reddish in color. Under the crust lies a flaky, foliated, friable layer with a thickness of 2 to 4 inches. Below this layer is clay, underlain by sand.

The chemism of the basin soil is unique. Carbonates are distributed more or less uniformly through the soil, or their quantity increases toward the bottom, which denotes the washing through of the soil. An increase in the content of alkaline carbonates close to the surface indicates a solonetz quality of the crust, leading to dispersion, condensation, and little water permeability. At a certain depth in the basin, salting by gypsum and sodium chloride appears. Thus the chemism of the soil is complex. In general, it is a deep-seated solonchak, but the condensed surface crust, containing absorbed sodium, includes within it the rudiments of the solonetz process. Often the soil becomes saline at the surface, turning into wet or inflated solonchak; sometimes it is salted with the formation of solonetz soil in which a columnar layer is seen under the surface crust.

Water is the chief agent of destruction of the basin, effecting its work by means of chemical solution and mechanical erosion. By carrying away dissolved substances, chiefly gypsum, the water creates basins on the smooth surface of the soil, which finally develops pockets. These pockets serve as the erosion base for precipitation flowing off the surrounding sand. The deeper the pocket the more running water dissects the surface of the soil, uncovering and destroying the water-resistant layer of the base. With the destruction of this base the basin as such is destroyed also. The wind, plants, animals, and man are only continuers of the destructive work begun by the water.

These clay basins are of extraordinary importance in the life of the sandy deserts because they serve as watertight storage places in the middle of the desert. Caravan routes often converge at them. Water from precipitation falling on them, or running off the surrounding higher areas of relief, is retained and runs off either along a natural slope or along specially constructed ditches to a single place. A pit serving as a collector of rain water may be formed by natural means on the bottom of a basin. Sometimes rain water from the basin runs off into depressions in the sand outside, enters the ground, and is diffused in lenses above the more dense and salty ground water. These pockets serve to feed wells, which may be constructed here, yielding excellent fresh water. An artificial pit on the surface may be used by Turkmenian livestock breeders to draw off rain water. The amount of water and the length of time it lasts depend on the amount of winter and spring precipitation and the dryness of spring. Livestock graze the year round on the desert. This is possible only because of the rain water collected in wells. In spring (two to two and a half months) if it is possible to construct a temporary well on every basin and gather rain water, herds can be grazed several miles away from the main well. With the onset of summer the water of all these temporary reservoirs dries up and cattle breeders are forced to return to the main wells where they pass the remainder of the year. In addition to the utilization of rain water for drinking, it is also used in the cultivation of watermelons and muskmelons.

The bottoms of some depressions that lie at a lower level than the clay basins are covered by solonchaks. In the moist period of the year, the bottom of the depression is swampy and covered with saline mud or water, but in the dry period it has a surface of small knobs formed by the dried-up saline mud with white efflorescences of salts. Beneath this crust, which for the most part sinks underfoot, lies an inflated mealy layer, and below that a green, strongly gleying, sandy layer, sometimes with clayey layers. Near the surface lies a gypsiferous layer. In the southern Kara-Kum these depressions occupy a strip 18 to 24 miles wide,

extending from northwest to southeast along the southern outskirts of the ridge sands. They are located in the larger depressions between ridges, being independent elongated depressions, following one after another in a chain and separated by low sandy bridges. The sides of these depressions, on which one can sometimes observe terraces, are rather high, reaching 50 to 65 feet. The zones of depressions, which extend parallel to the trend of Kopet-Dag and which some geologists consider brachysynclines, are characteristic for the structure of this mountain region. Many such depressions have been formed in the greater depressions amid barchan sands into which surplus irrigation waters are discharged, resulting in solonchak flats and lakes. The origin of some is attributed to karst processes. The Baba-Khodzha salt marsh, a large depression, was the former bottom of the Caspian Sea.

The Kyzyl-Kum Desert is the large plain lying between the middle and lower courses of the Amu-Darya, Syr-Darya, and Zeravshan rivers. The forms of relief of the desert are diversified both in outer appearance and elevation as well as in their origin. There are three basic types of relief: (1) mountain (Paleozoic) elevations; (2) foothill (Mesozoic) plateaus; and (3) plains with a series of Quaternary deposits. The name Kyzyl-Kum, meaning red sand, could be applied only to the third type. In the southeastern corner of the plain the folded spurs of the Turkestan Range are broken to form the Nura-Tau Mountains. Spurs of this range, like small folded residual mountain ranges, are spread to the northwest and cover the central part of the desert and the zone lying to the southwest of it. The largest mountain groups are the Tamdy-Tau and Bukan-Tau, with maximum elevations of 3,399 feet and 2,313 feet, respectively. On the boundary of the Amu-Darya delta lies a small, isolated ridge called Sultan-Uiz-Dag.

All of these mountains have a uniform geological composition. They are formed of Paleozoic crystalline schists, limestones, granites, and other igneous rocks. Many mineral resources are associated with these rocks, such as copper, asbestos, mica, and such rare elements as wolfram, lithium, and others. The Paleozoic rocks are highly dislocated in shallow folds, which are complicated by faults and intrusions of igneous rocks. A Tertiary sea covered the surface of the old Paleozoic rocks, by then highly eroded and destroyed by denudation processes. The water level did not reach the highest points, so individual mountain groups rose out of the water as islands; these have survived to the present day as separate, crumbling, residual mountains. Paleozoic folds are usually asymmetrical, which causes the steepness of the northern slope and the smoothness of the southern (with the exception of the Sultan-Uiz-Dag Range). The mountains to the south of the Kyzyl-Kum Desert plains have the highest elevations, and those to the north are somewhat lower. However, because the southern slopes of both mountain groups are usually gentle and hilly and the northern ones steep, the greatest mountains appear to be those in the north and not the south. The mountains have been leveled off by erosion; sometimes the summits are flat, as on Bukan-Tau. Peaks rising abruptly are the more highly dissected and are formed of solid, resistant, crystalline rocks. Strong dissection is characteristic of slopes with large, deep, and twisting ravines. Most of the products of disintegration remain on the site, gradually burying the bedrock and creating a landscape of stony deserts. The northern slopes are covered with soil and some vegetation; the southern ones, which are usually being actively disintegrated, have no vegetation. There is no fresh surface water in the mountains. The main type of ground water is interstitial water. It often emerges onto the surface as rather abundant, fresh, cold spring water—the best water in the Kyzyl-Kum.

At the base of the mountains are flat, almost horizontal Tertiary-Cretaceous plateaus. They are formed of sandstone, conglomerate, sand, clay, and marl, often well cemented. The Tertiary-Cretaceous series is broken by processes of folding and fault phenomena, but to a far lesser degree than are the Paleozoic rocks of the mountains. Tertiary-Cretaceous rocks are gathered in long anticlinal folds or in small dome- and ridge-like folds. Like those folds of the Paleozoic, these have a trend close to meridional, and possibly northwest, directions. The development of broad and low folds very often interrupts the apparent horizontal occurrence of the beds. The surfaces of the plateaus are covered by rubbly proluvial and gravel-sand-clay alluvial deposits, and sometimes by sand. The edges of the escarpment of the plateaus are dissected by many short and deep (130 to 160 feet) ravines. On the plateau are small locked-in depressions of karst origin created by the dissolving of gypsum lying not far from the surface. The supply of ground water of the plateau is extremely poor and variable; the maximum flow of mountain springs occurs in spring and autumn, the minimum in summer.

The Kyzyl-Kum lowlands occupy a large area. The widespread sandy plains are formed of old alluvial and subaerial sand. Most extensive is the highly bedded, steel-colored alluvial sand, with a thickness of 33 to 40 feet, linked with the somewhat higher position of the old Amu-Darya channel. Ridge sand is often found, which distinguishes the Kyzyl-Kum from other deserts. The meridionally extended ridges vary widely in width. The sand is covered by a dense vegetation, and has a few wind-blown depressions. In the central part of the desert are sand mounds; barchans are very rare in Kyzyl-Kum and are usually found only in the farming areas. The sand is incomparably richer in ground water than that of the Tertiary-Cretaceous foothill plateaus. The shallow occurrence of watertight rocks contributes to the accumulation of ground water, which is saline and not good for drinking. In certain places artesian water occurs. Clayey plains are widespread along the dry channels of the Kuvan-Darya and Jany-Darya rivers. Large enclosed basins are highly developed here and abound in ground water discharges. There are also saucer-shaped, salt-lake marsh depressions with low and gently sloping shores. The extreme over-all dryness and the lack of water circulation contribute to the accumulation of salts in the soil, which often collect into a crust.

The Pre-Aral Kara-Kum, bordering the northeastern shore of the Aral Sea, is covered by fixed sand hills. Barchans are developed only where the vegetation has been destroyed by man. In places, individual table mountains are encountered of the same type as those in the Turgai table country. The northern part of Kara-Kum belongs to the semi-arid zone.

The Big and Little Barsuki sand approaches the Aral Sea west of the Pre-Aral Kara-Kum. It is secured by vegetation over a great part of its area.

The Muyun-Kum Desert lying between the Kara-Tau and Kirgiz ranges and the Chu River and extending almost 300 miles from west to east from the lowlands of the Sary-Su River to the Kuragaty River, is wide in the eastern part and narrow in the western part (24 miles). The desert is bounded by well-marked escarpments from the foothill plain and the bottom lands of the Chu and Talas river valleys. The greatest elevations—about 2,310 feet—are found in the southeastern part of Muyun-Kum, and toward the lower stretches of the Chu and Sary-Su rivers the elevations gradually drop to 900 feet and at As-Kazanyn-Sor salt marsh are only 363 feet. The desert has a widely developed early aeolian relief, in the form of ridge-mound, hill, and low-ridge sand. In the northern part, sections of rolling sandy-loam, a clayey soil, are equally distributed. In those places where the sand is broken down it is complicated by barchan accumulations, which in general occupy not more than 7 to 10 per cent of the area of the sand. Besides the aeolian forms, there are various depressions having the appearance at times of old river-beds (with bottoms below the level of the Chu River) and at times of bead-like depressions with lakes separated by sandy bridges.

The geological structure of Muyun-Kum ap-

Fig. 14-9. Typical *takir* in the Kara-Kum Desert: rear, large sand ridges; in front, polygonal cracks in the soil.

Fig. 14-10. Large partly dry *shor* in the Kara-Kum Desert.

pears as a gentle syncline. At the base lie Paleozoic rocks, which crop out in the surrounding mountain ranges. An isolated bed of carboniferous limestone crops out in the Chu Valley where the river forms rapids. Resting on these old rocks is a thick series of Cretaceous and Lower Tertiary clays, sands, and sandstones. These rocks are covered by thick sand with streaks of clayey soil. Sand of a yellowish-rose color, fine-grained and well-sorted, is more or less enriched in the upper soil layer by dust-like and clayey particles, which are most numerous in the interridge depressions. The main bulk of the sand appears to be early alluvial deposits.

The rich hydrographic network in the period of the great Quaternary flooding of Central Asia, in connection with the discharge of glacial meltwater, led to the accumulation, within the limits of the present desert, of the products of erosion of basement rock and fluvioglacial sediments. Apparently the Chu River, at its emergence from the mountains, directed its water to the west along the mountain ranges, merged with the water of the Talas and Sary-Su, and finally reached the Syr-Darya. Broad meandering of the river among the mass of alluvium is indicated by the terrace-like slope of the Muyun-Kum in the north and the abundant channel-shaped depressions of latitudinal

trend. Also, clay streaks in the sand and the clearly expressed maturity of the Chu River valley, meandering and accompanied by four to five terraces, bear this out. It seems that already in historic time the Talas stopped delivering its water to the Chu River, and the latter, severed from the Syr-Darya, accumulated several intra-valley deltas, which were indicative of the stages of a receding river. The water-deposited sand did not become fixed and, in the dry postglacial period, underwent aeolian reprocessing, which resulted in the formation of an intricate network of mounds and ridges and depressions between them. In the formation of relief, no slight role was played by small streams, rich in sediment, flowing off the slopes of the fans at the base of the mountains and contributing to the strong silting up of the depressions.

Supplies of ground water in the desert region are almost inexhaustible. The occurrence, on a practically watertight Paleozoic foundation, of Cretaceous and Tertiary rocks, gently dipping north from the base of the southern ranges and containing a series of water-bearing layers, favors the formation of abundant artesian water whose level drops from south to north 6.6 feet for each 0.6 of a mile. Meeting the resistance of the Paleozoic rocks near the southern edge of Bet-Pak-Dala, the ground water swerves to the west toward the lowlands of the Sary-Su and Syr-Darya. Indicative of artesian water are the abundant self-discharging springs and the recently formed lakes in the sands on the sites of shallow excavated pits. The sources of the artesian water are the heavy precipitation, snow, and glaciers of the southern mountain ranges, and, partially, the filtering into the sand of the water of the Talas and Chu rivers. Precipitation, especially in winter, penetrates deep through the mass of loose bare sand or accumulates in the depressions; only a portion of it is expended through evaporation from the soil and by vegetation, because escape through surface discharge in the sand is almost eliminated. Important in the accumulation of ground water is the condensation, by the sand, of water vapors from the air.

The ground water nearest the surface (3.3 to 5 feet) is that of the central part of the desert, where it often emerges onto the surface to form lakes surrounded by reed thickets and grasses. The deepest ground water (66 to 132 feet) is that in the western part of the desert, which is drained on the north and south by river valleys. The ground water is rather fresh, soft, and good for drinking and irrigation. However, when the surface gradient decreases and the ground water approaches the base of accumulation of salts, as in the lowlands of the Chu and Sary-Su rivers, mineralization increases noticeably.

The sandy desert of south Pre-Balkhash lies within the Balkhash-Ala-Kul depression, between Lake Balkhash and the foothills of the Chu-Ili Mountains, Zaili, and Dzungarian Alatau. In contrast to the elevated northern coast, formed of bedrock, the southern coast of Balkhash is low and formed of loose alluvium. The large sandy areas are: the Tau-Kum Sand between the Chu-Ili Mountains and the Ili River, the Sary-Ishik-Otrau Sand between the old delta of the Ili River (Bakanasskaya Plain) and the Kara-Tal River, and the Lyuk-Kum Sand between the Kara-Tal River and the Lepsa River.

The basic forms of relief are sandy plain; sand hills; mound-ridge; ridge sand with over-blown material of great thickness; low elevations covered with a fine layer of sand; secondary forms of sandy relief transformed by deflation; barchans; mound-dunes; and dune-ridge sand. The Bakanasskaya Plain is formed of delta-lake sandy, clayey sediments. Half of the area here is occupied by sand ridges. The plain is intersected by many old channels of the Ili River, from several dozen to several hundred yards in width, the bottoms of which are covered by coarse, reddish sand and gravel. South Pre-Balkhash is cut by the broad valleys of the main rivers—the Ili, Kara-Tal, Ak-Su, and Lepsa—which, on reaching the lake, form deltas with a swarm of channels, lakes, and large thickets of reeds, alternating with sand and salt marshes.

The origin of the sand of south Pre-Balkhash, like that of the sand of Muyun-Kum, is linked with the colder and moister climate of the glacial period. At that time the neighboring mountain regions underwent heavy glaciation, and abundant streams flowing off the mountains deposited a thick, sand-gravel, fluvioglacial mass. At that time the Balkhash lake basin reached its maximum size, forming a single unit with the modern lakes Ala-Kul, Sasyk-Kul, and Ebi-Nur. In the postglacial, dry period, there occurred the great shrinking and lowering of the level of the old Balkhash water basin and its division into Balkhash and the lakes of the Ala-Kul group. The meandering of the streams continued, which rewashed and redeposited the loose fluvioglacial deposits and, owing to the lowering of the erosion base, gradually cut into the plain which was leveled by depositions. The majority of secondary streams, decreasing their water volume, broke off their connection with the water reservoir. In this same dry period occurred the most intensive process of scattering of the sandy rewashed deposits covering the plain. Under present climatic conditions the sand of Pre-Balkhash is well secured by vegetation and in the majority of cases is undergoing the processes of soil forming. The existence today of shifting sand is the result of secondary deflation, coinciding with the outskirts of the modern river valleys.

roads, wells, and places of the grazing of numerous livestock—that is, it is linked with the activity of man.

In regard to a guarantee of water, the sand of Pre-Balkhash is in close connection with the rivers of the region and with Lake Balkhash. Upon emerging from the mountains, the rivers, slowing their currents, enter the region of loose alluvium. Filtration of much water in this alluvium, the formation of countless lakes, old high beds, and channels in the river valleys, and the utilization of water for irrigation in the zone at the base of the mountains contributes to the complete dying out of the surface discharge in secondary rivers. But this loss is compensated for by the rather strong underground flow, directed toward the level of erosion at Lake Balkhash. Many quicksand areas, forming near the rivers, produce near-surface (3.3 to 10 feet), fresh ground water, which deepens considerably (to more than 45 feet) at a distance from the rivers. In the Balkhash coastal strip this underground flow encounters ground water from the lake and flows out on the surface in places, but the water is somewhat salty. The water regime of the sand is supplemented by the night-cooling condensation and precipitation of water vapor from the air.

Loess Foothill Plains

The discontinuous and irregular zone of loess foothill plains at the base of the mountains, with local relief of not more than 100 feet, extends from Kopet-Dag in the west to Zaili Alatau in the east. The large intermountain valleys should be included in this zone. The loess plain includes the Fergana Valley, Golodnaya Steppe, the foothills of the Kirghiz Range, Zaili Alatau, and part of the valley of the river Chu. They are absent at the base of the Dzungarian Alatau. This sloping, foothill plain appears to be the first level of vertical zonality, providing a transition zone from the landscapes of the lowlands to the mountainous zones of Central Asia. It is covered, as its name indicates, by an almost solid mantle of loess.

Loess lies in a rather thick mass on the different heights of the foothills, giving to it softly rounded forms of relief.

The origin of Central-Asiatic loess is not clear. It lies on bedrock of the most diversified origin. Loesses are developed on masses of glacial sediment carried onto the plain by glacial water, on thick proluvial depositions of the postglacial period, and on old and modern alluvial deposits. The process of loess development occurred under conditions of a dry climate; it is an easily pulverized material. The plowing of loess soil, the destruction of the loess mantle at the surface by pasturing livestock, and the movement along roads contribute to the raising and movement of loess dust which is a common feature of all the plains. In summer, cities of Central Asia may be recognized, even from far off, by the thick shrouds of loess dust. Carried along by wind and convection currents, the extremely fine dust rises to considerable heights. A misty, whitish color of the air is characteristic for this country. Typical productive sierozem soil is developed on the loess. Therefore, these foothill plains were the centers of the earliest cultures, and at the present time the majority of the valuable workable lands of the Central-Asiatic union republics occupy this region.

Golodnaya or "Hungry" Steppe is situated between Dzhizak and the Syr-Darya River. It is a vast and sparsely populated plain, lying at elevations of 825 to 1,000 feet. The plain is gently inclined to the north and northwest, and imperceptibly merges with the sandy expanses of Kyzyl-Kum. On the south it is bordered by the sloping, sandy, clayey plain of the foothills of the Nura-Tau Mountains and the Turkestan Range, and drops off to the Syr-Darya in a pronounced shelf 20 to 60 feet high. The flatness of the Golodnaya Steppe is broken only in places adjacent to the Syr-Darya, where there are many locked-in, elongated depressions, which are the remnants of old river channels. The plain is covered by a thick mantle of uniform saline and nonsaline, clayey alluviums. Only in the very lowest spots does solonchak and salt marshes occur. Running

Fig. 14-11. Loess cliff in the Arys River Valley.

water is absent on this plain. Rivers flowing off the Turkestan Range, adjacent to it on the south, are exhausted almost immediately upon emergence from the mountains. Ground water is found at depths of 15 to 30 feet, but in wells it is usually brackish or salty.

On the plain, typical sierozem soil predominates, which is uniform in mechanical and chemical composition and devoid of harmful salts. Almost everywhere, ephemeral vegetation grows on this soil that is occasionally broken by solonchak. Large irrigation works are being built on the plain because there are many favorable conditions for irrigation by the Syr-Darya River; in places, it lies above the surrounding portions of the plain. There are a number of settlements in the steppe (for example, the small village of Ilich). The main canal, Kirov Canal, is near Begovat, and it feeds a number of smaller ones. Kirov Canal is in a good cotton-farming region where there are more than a hundred collective farms (Pakhta-Aral, Malik).

Fergana is a large clearly defined valley enclosed on almost all sides by the Kuraminskiy, Chatkalskiy, Fergana, Alayskiy, and Turkestan ranges. Its length is about 180 miles and its width 100 miles. At the entrance into the valley near Leninabad, it is only five miles wide and is joined with the Golodnaya Steppe plain. The bottom of the Fergana Valley is a plain, gradually rising toward the east from 1,056 feet at Leninabad to 1,659 feet at Andizhan and 3,369 feet at Osh, which is in the foothills. Flatlands project eastward along the valleys of the large rivers. The Syr-Darya cuts through the northern rim of the valley floor for its entire length. In its upper section, called the Naryn River, it breaks through the Fergana Range, bordering the valley on the east, and on the west breaks through a spur of the Mogol-Tau Mountains, where it forms the Begovat Rapids. Not one of the tributaries of the Syr-Darya reaches the central part of the valley or the main river because their water is entirely used in irrigation.

The central part of the Fergana valley is desert. Here are vast, salty expanses, for the most part dry, yet in some years flooded by high river water, and sometimes salty lake-swamps in the process of drying out (such as Dam-Kul). Intensive processes of weathering of Tertiary conglomerate and sandstone, and also of Recent sandy alluvial deposits of the Syr-Darya, lead to the creation of considerable areas of shifting sand. Only along the margin of the valley is this sand somewhat secured by vegetation. The partially mobile sand of the center accumulates in recent barchans, with heights up to 50 feet, which move to the east, covering fields and settlements. The remaining area of central Fergana is cultivated. Broad fans of proluvial and deluvial gravel deposits occur at the bases of the mountain ranges as steep slopes having the appearance of stony deserts. Gradual erosional disintegration of these formations creates, at first, individual table mountains and, later, a highly broken relief. The rivers have large dry deltas, as for example, the huge alluvial fan of the Sokh River, which irrigates Kokand Oasis, and the

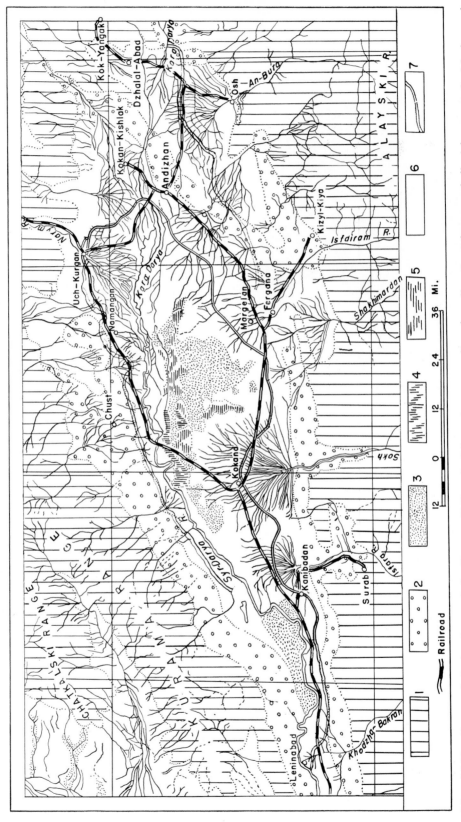

Map 14-II. Geomorphologic scheme of the Fergana Valley: 1—Mountains surrounding the valley; 2—Adyr area of alluvial terraces; 3—Moving and fixed sand; 4—Solonchak; 5—Marsh; 6—Cultivated oases; 7—Fergana Canal.

delta of the Isfayram River. Important in the formation of the relief of the valley are the erosional features which are caused by cloudburst torrents.

Nearer the mountains the plain of central Fergana gradually changes into an extremely dissected hilly zone. These hills, from 330 to 1,320 feet relative elevation, are formed of Upper Tertiary and Quaternary deposits. On top they are covered with loess and loess-like loamy soil, a mantle of which is prevalent in the foothills and on mountain slopes up to 9,900 feet elevation. These hills are formed of friable sedimentary rocks which erode easily and are subjected to intense dissection, mainly by intermittent streams. The mantle of soft alluvium—loess and loess-like loam soil—explains the rather softly rounded forms of the hills. They rise to 3,300 feet maximum elevation and are covered by halophytic semi-deserts; higher up a rich cereal and vari-grass steppe predominates. Beyond the hill zone the higher zone of foothills rises abruptly, often with a smooth, relatively soft relief. Still farther on is located the zone of mountainous, craggy, highly dissected, often inaccessible relief.

Fergana is an old region of irrigated crops, converted by modern irrigation into a continuous oasis. At present its southern portion is irrigated by the water of the Great Fergana Canal. It is one of the most populated districts of the Central Asiatic republics, having more than 2 million people. The foothill ring is the most thickly populated, where under conditions of relatively mild climate on the most fertile soil there is located a continuous belt of cultivated, irrigated land which receives water from the numerous mountain streams and creeks. In places, the density of population is 750 per square mile, while the central part of the valley is almost unpopulated. Fergana is the greatest cotton-growing center in the USSR, yielding about two-thirds of the cotton production of the Central Asiatic republics. Moreover, it is one of the main orchard-grape districts of Central Asia. A great amount of mineral wealth is concentrated here—about 70 per cent of all the Central Asiatic coal, the main deposits of oil in Central Asia, considerable stores of iron ore, mercury, antimony, natural sulphur, wolfram, fluorspar, bauxite, and an abundance of construction materials.

HYDROGRAPHY

On the plains of Central Asia the role of water in the economy is very important, and in places life depends on it. Here are combined simultaneously dryness and abundant water, i.e., waterless desert expanses with large rivers cutting through them. This contradiction is explained by the orographic heterogeneity of Central Asia: arid, lowly situated plains and low plateaus exposed on the north and west; high, mighty mountain structures on the south and east, the hydrological conditions of which are extremely diversified. The water regime of the plain is determined primarily by the climatic features: small amount of precipitation, high temperatures with sharp and extreme fluctuations, slight cloudiness, low relative humidity, greatly increased evaporability. In addition to these climatic conditions, which are

unfavorable for moisture, the water regime is further controlled by the level lowland relief and comparatively uniform geomorphological landscapes ranging from barchans to low-rolling foothill plains and low plateaus. Owing to the combined effects of conditions, there is no moisture from evaporation from the plains, as is the case in the foothills near the mountains. The underground flow on the plains lies rather deep and to a great degree has no connection with precipitation and the evaporation of moisture.

The systems of high ranges lying south of the plains are distinguished by other physicogeographic features. The windward slopes of the ranges are accumulators of precipitation brought by west winds. Because of the predominance, in the high-elevation regions, of almost polar winter temperatures, much precipitation forms great fields of snow and large glaciers and also accumulates in the deep depressions of mountain lakes. High summer temperatures and intense sunshine melt the snow and glaciers rapidly. The highly dissected mountain relief with its steep slopes, the relatively negligible water absorption by the rocks composing the ranges, and weak evaporation because of the low temperatures cause a rapid runoff onto the adjacent desert plains, creating a good water supply where little is precipitated.

The incoming water balance of the arid plains is supplied by: (1) surface waters entering from the neighboring mountain regions; (2) filtration from the large river arteries; (3) the emergence, onto the surface, of river water flowing underground within alluvial fans in the foothills; and (4) the condensation of water vapor in sand. The plains receiving this water do not increase it but actually decrease it because their evaporation capacity is high. The moisture accumulated by the mountains disperses rapidly and passes back into the atmosphere. Open water surfaces (the Aral Sea, Lake Balkhash) contribute even more to the conversion of the discharge into atmospheric moisture. The territorial junction of the deserts and the large streams brings with it man's intensive utilization of the river water in irrigating land devoid of water. Because of this, the territory with actual predominance of evaporation over precipitation actually increases. From 2.4 acres of irrigated area, 1,307 to 10,456 cubic yards of the water supplied to the fields evaporates per year. Thus, the activity of man becomes one of the main factors in water discharge. Only the underground flow, having different depths of occurrence, does not essentially vary its amount. Therefore, the process of constant accumulation of atmospheric moisture in the mountains, and the subsequent dispersal of it back into the atmosphere on the plains, is a characteristic hydrological feature of Central Asia.

Central Asia has a closed hydrologic cycle. It is a locked-in, drainless basin cut off from the oceans; inasmuch as it receives little or no discharge from outside, it exhausts its own interior supply. The character and regime of the rivers are unusual. Owing to the slight gradient and the strong evaporation, the shallow streams emerging onto the plain run along the surface forming swamped expanses, or are broken up into distributaries for irrigation and end in an intricate fan of irrigation canals (Sokh River). The larger rivers flow into the main arteries, or, not reaching them, end in a system of lakes (Chu River), or in the dead ends of dry deltas (Murgab River). The largest rivers (Amu-Darya, Syr-Darya, and Ili) flow into large, rapidly evaporating lakes (Aral Sea, Lake Balkhash). These lakes are the base level of erosion for the rivers entering them. A lowering of the base level of erosion—the level of the Aral Sea—before the beginning of the present period, conditioned the increased erosional activity of the rivers, which still has not been completed. In the lower stretches of the Amu-Darya and Syr-Darya a sharp intrenching of the channels is observed. The deepening of the main river channel, where the main bulk of the water passes through naturally, leads to the gradually dying out of the less important subsidiary channels and their conversion into old river-beds on a higher level. After the historic period, the old bottomlands were finally formed into the recent terraces, which are now the second terrace. Because of the deepening of the rivers water was not able to enter into the head portion of the main reservoirs, even in high water, and the old irrigation system could not be used. Early cities lying on the banks of rivers (Termez and others) thus gradually moved downward to the deepening river.

To a great degree, the character and regime of the rivers depend on the geographic conditions of their source regions. Rivers of mixed glacial-snow feeding (Amu-Darya, Syr-Darya, Zeravshan), having their source above the snow line (not lower than 11,500 feet), have a continuous heavy flow during almost the whole year. They have two high-water periods: in spring (April-May), from the melting of snow in the mountains, and in summer (June-July) in the period of energetic thawing of ice. These rivers are the chief source of irrigation. Rivers of snow feeding (Angren, Malyy, or Little Kebin), beginning at an altiude of 6,600 to 11,500 feet, have a more variable discharge. There is a great difference between average discharges and flooding during the maximum discharges in May-June. In April these rivers manifest violent activity, and in July, because of the depletion of supplies of seasonal snow, an abrupt reduction of the discharge is observed. Rivers of ground feeding, to which belong comparatively small streams located in the lower belt (not higher than 6,600 feet) of the mountains, are fed by ground water and showers and have a small but steady discharge. They may have flash floods during cloudbursts, which discharge large quantities of water suddenly.

All rivers flowing through the desert lose an enormous amount of water by evaporation and much is taken by many for irrigation. Rivers in regions with an annual amount of precipitation less than 12 inches do not receive water from their tributaries. In the majority of rivers the amount of solids in suspension during flooding is so great that the water has the appearance of a thick brownish mass, and to become clear it must settle for many hours. This large amount of alluvium is derived from the disintegration of the undercut banks, which are composed of loose alluvium. In periods of flood, cultivated lands are torn off by the raging torrents: in particular, farms on the right banks of the Amu-Darya and Syr-Darya suffer. Part of the sediments settle in the channel, forming shoals and islands and raising the bed itself, which in time may prove to be higher than the surrounding plain. In the lower section of the Syr-Darya, or on the Murgab, the channels rise rapidly, even in the canals fed by the rivers.

The rivers of the desert plains have tremendous national economic significance for the republics of Central Asia. "Water is dearer than gold," runs one of the widespread Central Asiatic sayings. In those places where there is water, flourishing oases exist, and in those places where there is none, there stretches a desert seared by the sun. With the exceptional fertility of the desert soil, only water from an irrigation canal is needed for the rapid growth of luxuriant vegetation and to cause fields and gardens to appear. Water in the desert is the very source of life; it contributes to an increase of the area of cultivated land and to the prosperity of agriculture. In the recent past, irrigation in the deserts of Central Asia was developed only in those areas where, with favorable geomorphological and soil conditions, water could be conveyed to the fields comparatively easily by gravity or with the aid of primitive methods. Most of the available water was not utilized, owing to the primitive techniques and because the water was private property. Modern techniques permit the widespread utilization, for irrigation, of the water resources of the large rivers of the desert. Their winter and flood discharge is regulated by means of mountain reservoirs and by the improvement of unfavorable sandy soil (brought about by enriching with silt from the rivers). And today water in the desert is public property.

The Fergana Canal

One of the examples of a change in the geographical landscape, in the interests of the national economy, by means of a reorganization of the hydrographic network is the construction of the Fergana Canal, named after Stalin. Because of an insufficient amount of rainfall, the welfare of the Fergana Valley is promoted by artificial irrigation. Throughout the centuries, the people have altered the nature of this district, converting great expanses of desert into oases. The valley owes its prosperity to the existence of irrigation systems based on rivers of the northern slope of the Alayskiy and Turkestan ranges (Isfara, Sokh, Shakhimardan, and others), but the amount of water is still not adequate. The excessive length of the water table passing through the alluvial fans contributes to the loss of much water by infiltration and evaporation. Water along faults, together with the underground discharge from the mountains, raises the level of the ground water and leads to the salinizing and swamping of lowlands. Therefore, orchards and kitchen gardens, cotton and rice fields, melon fields and vineyards stop immediately at the end of the water table. Here the green ring of oases constantly runs short of water, and in the center, and occupying about half the area, of the valley lies a sandy or gravelly desert.

For centuries the interesting idea had been entertained of constructing a great canal which would utilize the water of the mighty Naryn, upper course of the Syr-Darya, and which would saturate all the land of the valley. The Syr-Darya, flowing in the very low, central part of the valley, could not, because of relief conditions, be utilized, and uselessly it carried its abundant water through the valley to deliver about 20 billion cubic yards of water annually into the Aral Sea. Enormous quantities of precious moisture were lost to evaporation while the cotton fields of Fergana were experiencing a severe need of water. The aim of the construction of the Fergana Canal is to supplement the existing irrigation systems with the water of the Naryn and Kara-Darya; therefore, the course of the canal intersects all the irrigated fans of the rivers of the southern part of the valley.

The Fergana Canal begins from the Naryn, supported by the Uch-Kurgansk installation. The water of the Naryn is tranferred along the canal to the Kara-Darya, dammed by Kuygan-Yarskaya Dam, which raises its level 13 feet and allows the water to move, by gravity, farther westward along the canal. As the canal continues along the southern part of the valley it receives additional water from the rivers flowing off the mountains. The canal is one of the greatest hydraulic structures of the world. Its over-all length to the Khodzha-Bakhirgan River is 210 miles; the depth of the channel is 40 feet in the head section and 6 to 26 feet in the central part; its width varies from 20 to 82 feet. The bed of the canal is partially in earthen levees. It breaks through gravel and conglomerate in the east, and through sandy loam, argillaceous soil, and gravel farther west.

The canal unites rivers of different regimes, that is, rivers of glacial feeding (Sokh, Isfara), with their main high-water in summer, rivers of snow feeding (Kara-Darya), with spring high-water and rivers of mixed feeding (Naryn), with two high-water periods. It forms, so to speak, a new ideal river with an almost completely adjusted regime, sufficiently full of water in both spring and summer. The artificially created river, with a water discharge up to 130 cubic yards per second at the head section, is four times as large as the Tedzhen River and twice as large as the Murgab River.

The canal is intended to completely resolve the problem of the irrigation of the southern half of the Fergana Valley. Its water will irrigate 2,090 square miles of both developed lands and those suitable for development and awaiting only water. Lack of water in cotton-raising is just as much of a disaster as drought in growing grain: it limits the development of cotton-growing, lowers the productivity, and renders impossible the introduction of regular cotton-lucerne crop rotation. The cotton plant demands much water: a hectare (2.47 acres) of cotton requires, for the winter and spring irrigation, an average of 7,800 cubic yards of water. (The sowing of lucerne, besides creating a good fodder base for livestock-raising, is the most effective means of combating "wilt," that most dangerous disease of the cotton plant, the losses from which amount to 60 thousand tons of cotton a year. Within three years after the introduction of lucerne to crop rotation, the infection of cotton with wilt had decreased 80 to 90 per cent.) Crop rotation is entirely carried on in newly irrigated areas, without the curtailment of planting of cotton. The canal guarantees adequate water to the orchards and vineyards and will bring about their optimum expansion. In the arid and barren Yaz-Yavanskaya Steppe (north of Margelan), which formerly was in danger of salinizing, the washing of the soil with the water of the canal has permitted the planting of mulberry trees and the creation of the largest center of silkworm breeding in the USSR. The canal has freed labor for the development of new territories and provides water for actual needs. The construction of the canal has been a source of pride to the inhabitants, and it is pointed out that it took 180,000 collective farm workers only one and one-half months to complete the digging work in 1939.

The Amu-Darya River

The Amu-Darya is the largest river of Central Asia (1,401 miles in length). It begins on the northern slope of the Hindu-Kush Mountains at an elevation of 16,170 feet. Its source is considered to be the Vakhdzhir River, lower down called the Vakhan-Darya, which upon uniting with the Pamir River receives the name Pyandzh. The latter, on the right, takes on the tributaries Gunt, Bartang, Yasgulem, and Vanch, and after the entry of the Vakhsh bears the name Amu-Darya from the name of the city Amulya, which existed on the site of present-day Chardzhou. Its people call it simply Darya, meaning river. After receiving the rivers Kafirnigan, Surkhan-Darya, and Shirabad from the right, the Amu-Darya does not receive any more tributaries all the way to its mouth, but instead discharges much water to evaporation and irrigation. On the plain the river has a channel, during high water, of 1,650 to 6,500 feet in width (on the average, 4,950 feet), but during two months it narrows to 1,155 feet. Approximately 240 miles from the Aral Sea the river channel begins to braid, and only near Nukus, 90 miles from the Aral, does the real delta begin. At first in the delta the channel is 2 to 3 miles wide; farther down it narrows and breaks up into several channels whose water overflows, during floods, along the lowlands and are lost amid dense thickets of reeds. In the lowest part of the delta the water is once again collected in definite channels and pours into the Aral Sea.

Within the plain the Amu-Darya flows in a valley having a width at first of about 5 miles, and later gradually widening. The surface, on which the central part of this valley was formed is composed of Tertiary and Cretaceous rocks. It is broken by a slight folding, resulting in small, ridgelike elevations. Strictly speaking, the valley of the Amu-Darya is its channel and is of very recent origin. The fine, easily eroded, alluvial soil comprising its valley is only about 20 feet thick. Valley sections of considerable width, successively touching first one shore then the other, are formed of alternating thin seams of clay and sand. The first terrace rises above the average level 6 to 16 feet and is formed of frequently alternating, compact clayey soil and sandy loam. It is covered by thick woody-brushwood and cane thickets. Only below Chardzhou does the sand approach almost to the river on both sides. The second terrace rises above the average level 26 to 33 feet, and the third 52 to 66 feet. Both terraces are formed of loose, micaceous sand and clay. In regard to outer appearance and vegetative cover they are a sharp contrast to the lower, richly overgrown terraces, and are little distinguished from the deserts adjacent to the river.

Amu-Darya is fed by the thawing of snow and glaciers in the mountains; thus it has two floods. The spring flood (April-May) comes from the thawing of snow and consists of rapidly rising and quickly abating discharges; the summer flood (June-July) comes from the rapid melting of glaciers with the onset of hot weather. The average discharge (at Nukus) is 1,944 cubic yards, the maximum 8,333 cubic yards, and the minimum 691 cubic yards per second. The range between the highest and lowest levels of water is 6.6 to 9.9 feet. The smallest discharge of water is observed in January and February, the greatest in July. High water abates at the end of September; toward the beginning of November the water enters the norm and remains at approximately the same level until March of the following year. The following tabulation shows (in cubic yards per second) the monthly average discharge at Kerki.

January.........	598	July.............	3,376
February........	596	August..........	2,932
March..........	698	September.......	2,299
April...........	1,237	October.........	954
May............	2,002	November.......	726
June............	2,906	December........	650

Between Kerki and Nukus the Amu-Darya loses an average of 25 per cent of its water (in May 38 per cent and in February 8 per cent) to evaporation and irrigation.

The lack of maturity of the present lengthwise profile, characteristic for the central and lower part of the Amu-Darya, checks the comparatively high speed of the current. The gradient of the river at the emergence from the mountains is relatively steep—ten times as great as that of the Volga. Local declivities are still greater, and the rate of flow during high water may be as much as 13 feet per second. Owing to the speed of the current, the strong fluctuation of the level of the water, and the easy washing of the banks, the Amu-Darya is both destructive and creative. The depth of the river varies constantly: at low-water it can, in places, be forded. In general the depth varies from 20 inches on sandbars up to 28 feet in deep places. The channel may change entirely in a single summer. Sometimes in one day deep places are filled in by shoals, and where sandbars were, great depths form. The banks are sometimes destroyed with amazing rapidity, and at times almost 6 feet of bank is washed away in a minute. Destroying the bank, the river washes out fields, orchards, and buildings, and almost every year necessitates a change in the direction of irrigation canals. Because the valley is formed of very light soil, the mobility of the channels (that is, the change of their shape and profile) also is very great.

The Amu-Darya meanders widely within the limits of its valley and even on its first terrace moves its channel, during short intervals of time, hundreds of yards and even miles. Because of these characteristics of the channel, the entire central and lower courses of the river are intensely braided and separated by shoals and sandy islands. There is no definite chan-

nel; frequently it changes in a week or even in a day, shifting sometimes hundreds of yards to one side. In the individual channels the river flows with varying speed, having different lengthwise gradients, and the difference in levels at opposite shores may reach almost 2 feet.

There is no other river in the world that carries as much suspension material as does the Amu-Darya. Even at average level the water is a muddy, dirty yellow; in high water it becomes still more turbid and takes on a dark yellow-brown color. The Amu-Darya carries twice as much suspended alluvium as does the Nile. At Kerki, from October 1911 to September 1912 it carried 390 million cubic yards of suspended alluvium; 92 per cent of this was carried in the summer. During the passing of the first, very high water the maximum amount of debris is observed; the minimum is seen in November-December. In those places where loose sand comes up to the edge of a steep bank, the slightest movement of the air brings sand rolling down, thus increasing the amount of suspension debris in the water. The depositional activity of the river, owing to the abundance of suspension material, is very great. After high water a layer of sand and silt 10 inches and more remains. New shoals and even whole islands may grow in a week, and in the week following they sometimes disappear. At such a rate of sedimentation the first terrace may form on the site of valleyland in the course of 15 to 20 years. New lowland areas deposited by the river, gradually rising and drying, are covered by reeds and woody thickets and with the passing of time they become useful for agriculture.

The exceptional productivity of the Amu-Darya bottomland soil is a result of the favorable mechanical and chemical composition of the alluvium; its soil does not require artificial fertilizing and therefore is of great agricultural value. The alluvium is made up of such small particles that even after repeated filtering the water remains muddy. There is an especially large percentage (64.3 per cent) of particles from 0.01 to 0.05 millimeters in diameter. The alluvium contains a great amount of lime (7.3 per cent), potassium (2.1 per cent), and phosphates—the most important elements for soil productivity. The amounts of these mineral substances entering into the makeup of the suspension debris in the soil are considerable. In the irrigation of 1 hectare (2.47 acres) over 1 year they may be as much as: lime, 3,784 pounds (in the Nile Valley, only 756 pounds; potassium, 1,080 pounds (in the Nile Valley, 122 pounds); phosphoric acid, 97 pounds (in the Nile Valley, 61 pounds). Moreover, in the Amu-Darya water itself is a considerable amount of soluble salts, greater than in the water of the Nile. On the average the Amu-Darya carries (at Kerki) about 22.5 million tons of soluble salts a year. The smallest amount of salt in the water is observed in summer, owing to the increase of meltwater in the river discharge, which lowers the concentration of solutions. After the subsidence of high water, the percentage of salt in the water increases, reaching a maximum in February (0.601 grams of salt per liter), although the absolute discharge of salt at this time decreases. The average daily discharge of dissolved salts during the summer of 1912 was 81 thousand tons, and during the winter of the same year it was 42 thousand tons. Thus the water of the Amu-Darya is extremely valuable for agriculture, because in addition to its irrigation function it brings in fertilizer. Despite the muddiness of the water, its great amount of soluble salts, and its extreme hardness, it is perfectly good for drinking and has a pleasant taste.

The Amu-Darya rarely freezes in its middle section, but its lower stretches are covered with ice every year for 2 to 2½ months (December to February). The river freezes only in the canals and at the shores. The ice is not thick and not stable, and only in cold winters does it freeze to a depth of as much as 12 inches. The ice flow passes almost imperceptibly in the middle of March.

The regime of the Amu-Darya is extremely favorable for irrigation. Toward the beginning of the growing season (March), supplies of water in the river begin to increase, and they reach a maximum just at the time of the greatest need for irrigation, that is, in June-July. There is sufficient water in the Amu-Darya for the irrigation of an area upwards of 12 million acres, and at the present time there are only about 1,720,000 acres of irrigated land. The techniques of irrigation are extremely intricate because of the difficulty of connecting irrigation canals with this powerful and freakish river and because of the small area of the land good for cultivation in proximity to it. Today only a narrow strip of bottomland is cultivated, and here farming is made difficult. Because of the restless nature of the river, the riverside inhabitants are forced, from year to year, to alter the network of irrigation canals. Often the river tears away the head sections of the canals and destroys existing cultivated lands. It is true that the river deposits new fertile plots in other places, but a great outlay of labor is required to bring them to a cultivated condition. Millions of tons of silt carried by the river are deposited on the bottom of irrigation canals, and the inhabitants using the canals must spend up to 60 per cent of their working time in clearing out the silt. Settling basins are sometimes constructed at the head section of canals, and dredges and excavators transfer part of the silt to the shore, which enables water somewhat cleared of alluvium to enter the irrigation canals. The nearest irrigated, sandy areas of the Kara-Kum are improved by enriching them with the fertile Amu-Darya silt, but this is feasible only with large-scale engineering installations. Erection of such installations is hindered by the loose foundation soil and the destructive activity of the river.

Transportation on the Amu-Darya is very slight because the basin of the Aral Sea is locked in and because the great rapidity of current, the changeability of the channel, and the abundance of sandbars make the river unfavorable for navigation. Steamboat service has been established along the entire lowland portion of the Amu-Darya, but it encounters many hardships. The usual methods of utilization of a river for transportation are rendered impracticable. The channel cannot be marked by shore markers; often it must be determined by the color of the water. Thus navigation takes place only during the day. The main volume of shipments goes on large ferryboats with a maximum draft of 28 inches, which is, in general, equal to the shallowest depth of the sandbars. These boats float downstream and are towed up.

The commercial fishing industry on the Amu-Darya begins below Turtkul. Such European species as carp, barbel, bream, and sheatfish are caught. The shovel-nose (*Pseudoscaphirhynchus*) is an unusual fish of the sturgeon family, similar to the species living in the Mississippi River in North America. The fishing near the mouths of the Amu-Darya on the Aral Sea is of importance.

Dry Channels

The plains of Central Asia are intersected by several dry channels of which the best known is the Uzboy. The Uzboy system comprises a combination of channels and the val-

leys linked with them, along which water formerly flowed from the Aral basin into the Caspian Sea. Subsequently this depression was converted into a channel for the discharge of part of the water of the Amu-Darya into the Caspian Sea. The Uzboy system consists of the dry bed of the Kunya-Darya, Sarykamysh Valley, and the dry channel of the Uzboy itself.

The Kunya-Darya is the old, dry bed of the Amu-Darya, which had extended its lower course westward to the Sarykamysh depression. When the water of the Amu-Darya is high, a small quantity enters the Kunya-Darya, but it usually does not run far. In 1878 water from the Amu-Darya broke through into the Kunya-Darya and reached the two Sarykamysh lakes, which lie in the center of the depression, raising their level approximately 26 feet. At present the channel of the Kunya-Darya is partitioned by two large dikes. The channel to the Sarykamysh lakes is 438 feet wide. Close to Sarykamysh the width of the river bed decreases, but the depth increases, and the banks become almost sheer, displaying reddish and gray lami-

Fig. 14-12. Ostatochnoye salt lake in the lower Uzboy Valley; deposits of salt on the shore and saxaul trees in the distance.

Fig. 14-13. Iolatan dam on the Murgab River.

nated clay (about 132 feet thick) sediments of old Lake Sarykamysh.

Sarykamysh Valley is southwest of the Amu-Darya delta. Its border on the north and west is the Ust-Urt escarpment; on the south it extends to the Charyshly pits where once many lakes were situated, from which the Uzboy began. The lowest spot in the depression is occupied by the two Sarykamysh lakes, which in dry years evaporate and are converted into salt marshes. Within the valley are well-expressed systems of early shore terraces and blanket deposits of early lake sediments. They indicate the recent existence of a lake basin which was filled to approximately 178 feet, that is, to the height of the surface of the old Aral Sea and the outlet of the Uzboy from the valley. The slightly brackish water of Lake Sarykamysh was connected with the Aral Sea on the site of the recently dried-up Aybugir Gulf and joined with the Caspian Sea by means of the Uzboy.

The Uzboy itself extends from the southern tip of the Sarykamysh Valley to the southwest, a distance of 330 miles, with an over-all gradi-

ent of 247 feet. The channel of the Uzboy is excellently defined for a long distance. Only in places has it lost its valley shape as a result of the most recent denudation and covering of individual sections with sand. Traces of the recent passage of water along the Uzboy are clearly expressed in the relief: it possesses a well-developed channel, blanket deposits of alluvium, and systems of terraces. At first the Uzboy passes near the base of Ust-Urt Plateau, following the curves of its southeastern margins. In places it intersects Sarmatian limestone, forming cliffs up to 26 feet high. In the middle section of the Uzboy there are some fresh and brackish lakes, and many sumps. The lakes receive water from a multitude of salty or fresh water springs and from the retention of snow and rain water on clayey soil. Some of them, e.g., fresh Topiatan Lake, are typical dried-up river channels. The shores of these lakes are overgrown by reeds, tamarisks (*Tamarix*), and individual poplars. A little south of the railroad, the bed of the Uzboy disappears. Here the Uzboy formerly entered a gulf of the Caspian Sea, on the site of which today the vast Baba-Khodzha salt marsh is located. It is at the same level as the surface of the Caspian Sea and is separated from it by sand and brackish marshes. The Aktam channel runs from the Baba-Khodzha salt marsh, entering the Caspian Sea by way of Balkhan Gulf. In the spring strong winds from the west drive sea water from the Caspian into Aktam, tens of miles along the channel, and during the hot summer months locked-in lakes form along the channel, in which salt of high quality is deposited. Near Molla-Kara, a salt-deposit lake, there are medicinal muds and a sulphur spring, around which a health resort has been established. There are indications that in historic time part of the water of the Amu-Darya flowed into the Caspian Sea; for example, from the middle of the thirteenth century to 1573 water flowed along the Uzboy and the river was navigable.

West of the Amu-Darya there are other dry channels. The Kelif Uzboy is a dried-up branch of the Amu-Darya and at the same time the channel of the North Afghanistan rivers. The Kelif Uzboy does not have a continuous channel, and in places it is divided by land bridges into individual depressions, situated in a line. Brackish water, and occasionally fresh water, is found near the surface. In 1907 water from Afghanistan rivers penetrated into the Kelif Uzboy and flowed almost 60 miles from the national border into the Kara-Kum, but in the spring of 1911 the Kelif Uzboy was dry.

The Syr-Darya River

In their general nature and regime the other large rivers of Central Asia are analogous to the Amu-Darya, but each of them has its own peculiar characteristics.

The Syr-Darya, called the Naryn in its upper section, originates in the region of permanent snow and glaciers on the ranges Ak-Shiyryak and Terskey-Ala-Tau of Central Tien-Shan south of Lake Issyk-Kul. Breaking through Fergana Range the river merges with the other large tributary, the Kara-Darya which collects

waters from Fergana Range, and, under the name Syr-Darya, flows through the central portion of the Fergana Valley to the southwest. Here it receives short channels only from a lake in the Kuraminskiy and Chatkalskiy ranges, and not a single tributary from the south because the southern rivers (Sokh and Isfara) while still at the Alayskiy Range foothills, are entirely broken up for irrigation and do not reach the main river. Farther on, the Syr-Darya bends around the spur of the Chatkalskiy Range—the Mogol-Tau Mountains—and beyond the Begovat rapids emerges on the plain, swerving northwest toward the Aral Sea. Above Kyzl-Orda the Yany-Darya, the old channel of the Syr-Darya, cuts off, heading across the Kyzyl-Kum sand to the Aral Sea. During low water it is completely dry; in high water it flows for more than 180 miles. Approaching the mouth, the Syr-Darya is braided and forms its own modern delta which juts out prominently into the Aral. Everywhere in its lower course the Syr-Darya flows on a gentle rise formed by natural levees; thus there is a down gradient from the river inland. For example, sections situated 9 miles from the river lie 13 feet below its level. Because of this, even with a slight rise in the level of the river the water overflows across the banks and floods vast expanses. This is observed in the summer flood or at the time of ice jams in the breakup of the river. The depth of the river (16 to 32 feet) is fully adequate for navigation of small vessels. In comparison with the Amu-Darya, the Syr-Darya has less water discharge, and, owing to the composite feeding, the maximum water discharge shifts from July to June. The annual discharge at Zaporozhskaya is 765 cubic yards per second, the minimum in January is 436 cubic yards per second, and the maximum in June is 1,640 cubic yards per second. The Syr-Darya has less suspended solid substances than does the Amu-Darya. Its water contains a large quantity of mud particles; as a consequence, the shoals and the bed of the river in general are more stable than on the Amu-Darya. The river is covered with ice below Kzyl-Orda at the beginning of December,

Fig. 14-14. Large canal in the Khorezmsk Oasis.

breakup is around the first of April, and the river is free of ice for 242 days.

The Ili and Other Rivers

The Ili River begins at the junction of the Tekes and Kunges rivers. The Tekes collects the water of the Terskey-Ala-Tau ranges and the mountain massif Khan-Tengri. After the entry of the tributary Chilik, the Ili River becomes a purely transit river, inasmuch as its would-be tributaries lower downgrade are wholly taken up for irrigation. In its lower stretches the river meanders amid a vast sea of sand, where we find its numerous, old dry channels. The modern Ili River enters Lake Balkhash in three large, open distributaries, forming a narrow and long delta solidly overgrown with reeds. The Ili River is compositely fed. In April the spring flood from the melting of winter precipitation in its entire basin passes slowly and is not high. In the first half of May a rapid and high flood from the downpours rushes through. In the first half of July the river reaches its maximum level when the glaciers and snow fields rapidly melt and a great amount of precipitation falls in the mountains. The discharge in November is 391 cubic yards per second, in June 1,211 cubic yards per second. The summer high water continues for some time because the tributaries of the Ili are fed variously and therefore have diversified maximums. In addition, the Ili has significant underground feeding from channels of numerous tributaries whose water partially escapes through gravelly alluvial fans upon their exit from the mountains.

Whereas the Amu-Darya, Syr-Darya, and Ili enter large lakes, the other rivers of Central Asia end in small, shallow lakes (Chu River), form large dry deltas (Tedzhen, Murgab), or dry up amid the sand (Zeravshan). Nevertheless, their irrigational importance is great.

The Chu River rises from several springs in the heart of Tien Shan between lakes Issyk-Kul and Son-Kul. It then passes several miles to the west of Lake Issyk-Kul, being joined with it only by the short, narrow, boggy Kutemaldy Channel. The main bulk of its water

Fig. 14-15. *Chigir,* primitive water-well construction for irrigation.

breaks through Kirghiz Range in deep Buam-skoye Gorge. It receives, in the mountainous portion from the right (Kungey-Ala-Tau and Zaili Ala-Tau ranges and the Chu-Ili Mountains), a series of partially glacial tributaries (Bolshoy Kebin). On the left enter many shallow streams from Kirghiz Range. On the plain the Chu does not receive a single tributary, but flows slowly along the desert to the west near the base of the Bet-Pak-Dala Plateau, loses a large amount of water to evaporation, gradually shallows out, and finally is lost in the small Lake Saymal-Kul 66 miles from the channel of the Syr-Darya. In the glacial, moist period, uniting with the Sary-Su River on the right it enters the Syr-Darya below Kzyl-Orda near the beginning of its old delta.

A large part of the watershed of the Tedzhen and Murgab rivers lies outside the borders of the USSR in the Paropamiz Range where a great part of their water is expended in the irrigation of Afghanistanian oases. The regime of these rivers is similar: they receive the max-

imum water in spring from the thawing of snow in the mountains and from abundant rains, but in summer they lose much water to evaporation, filtration, and irrigation. In summer the water of the Tedzhen vanishes in the gravel, yet in some places, because of topographic peculiarities, water does appear in the channel evidently from springs and by filtration from irrigation canals. The Murgab is partitioned by dams, which form large reservoirs for the retention of flood water. The alluvium of both rivers is less valuable in its chemical composition than that of the Amu-Darya. The fine mud of the alluvium precipitated from the irrigation water gives a compactness to the soft, sandy soil, increases its moisture capacity, and decreases water permeability. Along the banks of both rivers the lack of water is felt in large areas of land fit for irrigation; thus, careful utilization of this water is essential. The rivers flow in clearly defined valleys, but in the very lowest sections they combine with the lowland to form large, dry deltas—sandy-clayey plains with cultivated fields, with thickets of reeds, with bare surfaces, and with an abundance of old, dry river-beds of varying age.

The Zeravshan, rising out of the large Zeravshan Glacier, is completely taken up in irrigation.

The Kashka-Darya, which was the left tributary of the Zeravshan in the moist glacial period, begins with several branches in the Gissar Range, but does not reach to the Zeravshan at present, being lost in the Karshinskaya Steppe.

The large lake basins of lowland Central Asia—the Aral Sea and Lake Balkhash—are virtually the large terminal overflows of the rivers entering them—the Amu-Darya, Syr-Darya, and the Ili—which have considerable influence on the regime of these water basins.

The Aral Sea

The Aral Sea is a large brackish lake; in all Eurasia it is second only to the Caspian in size (greatest length 230 miles, width at the 45th parallel 170 miles). It is a locked-in basin with no outlet, receiving only two rivers, though large ones—the Amu-Darya and the Syr-Darya. The Aral Sea belongs to the lakes of the desert regions, where little precipitation falls, where the activity of running water is slight, and where, consequently, the lake basin has the greatest chance of all of surviving since it is not being filled with the products of denudation.

The shores of the Aral Sea are varied in nature. The northern shores, very often rather high, are broken by large, open, little dissected, comparatively deep bays. The western shore, with an almost meridional trend, is rectilinear and steep (relative heights of about 627 feet), with small, wide, open bays scarcely penetrating into the mainland. Here extends the high eastern escarpment of Ust-Urt, which neither forms a single bay nor detaches a single island. The activity of running water is negligible; over the entire Aral area there is not one constant stream, and the shores are arid and water-

less. The small amount of rainfall is quickly absorbed by the permeable Sarmatian limestone and produces springs emerging on the line of contact of the limestone with clay. The eastern shore is low and sandy, and is highly dissected by small branching bays penetrating deep into the mainland. The eastern coastal strip is studded with many low sandy islands. Such dissection is the result of the rising of the level of the Aral Sea and the inundation of its sandy shore. Flooded coastal valleys were converted into bays, and the higher portions became islands and peninsulas. Dunes, secured by vegetation, are encountered along the entire extent of the eastern shore. The southern coast is formed by the northern edge of the Amu-Darya delta. The Syr-Darya on the eastern shore also forms a great delta.

The depth of this large water basin is not great. In the middle of the Aral Sea depths of 66 to 82 feet predominate, and along the western shore extends a narrow zone of depths greater than 99 feet. On this shore is the greatest depth—224 feet. With a 13-foot lowering of the level of the lake all the islands except those lying far from the shores (such as Barsa-Kelmes and others) would be joined with the mainland. A great part of the surface of the sea bottom at depths of 33 to 99 feet is a gray thick silt. In the deep western part this is replaced by a slimy black mud which contains colloidal hydrate of ferrous sulphide. Nearer the shores the silt is replaced by sand, and, toward the mouths of the rivers, by light-brown silt like that of the rivers.

The level of the Aral Sea fluctuates considerably. Over 15 years (1900 to 1915) the level rose more than 6 feet, and by 1920 it had lowered 45 inches. There are annual fluctuations, depending on the entry of water from the rivers, evaporation from the surface, and the amount of precipitation. About 4 inches of precipitation falls, but the evaporation from the surface of the water is about 40 inches; the difference is made up by the inflow of river water. The sea reaches its highest level from May to September, its lowest level in winter. Daily variations in level are the result of long-

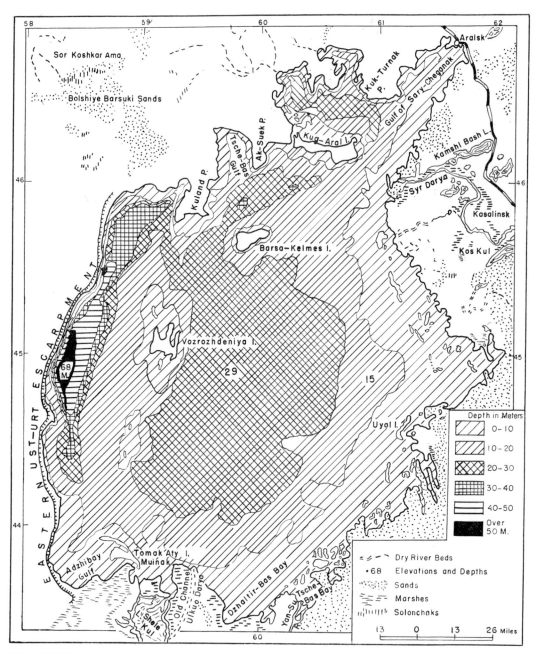

Map 14-III. Bathymetric map of the Aral Sea.

period (22-3/4 hours) seiches averaging 9.6 inches in height. The seiches owe their origin to rapid changes in atmospheric pressure and to strong winds. Because of the shoals at the southern and eastern shores, during winds there is a considerable driving and piling up of the water (up to 6.6 feet). In the Aral Sea there is a clockwise rotation of water. Along the western shore the current passes north with a maximum rate of 0.78 mile per hour, carrying water partially freshened by the Amu-Darya. This current is caused by the driving of the water in the southwestern corner of the sea by strong northeast winds and the mass of fresh water brought here by the Amu-Darya. Another current runs from the mouths of the Syr-Darya southward along the eastern shore. Near the mouths of the rivers compensating currents are observed. The salt water brought from the sea to the mouths rapidly settles mud and sediments brought by the river, which leads to the formation of bars.

In summer the water at the surface of the Aral Sea, even far from the shores, may warm up to 79° to 80°F, and near shore it may warm to 86°F. Daily amplitudes may be as great as 13°F. As far as the distribution of temperatures in depth is concerned, the Aral Sea fits perfectly the fresh lake type: low temperatures (34° to 37°F) persist at extreme depth even in summer. Every year the northeastern and often the northern parts of the sea freeze over. The ice cover lasts 140 to 160 days, and is 28 to 40 inches thick. The salinity of the Aral Sea is not relatively high—1 kilogram of water contains 10 to 11 grams of salt—it is only a little less saline than the Caspian Sea, and is only a third as salty as ocean water. If the Aral Sea were to dry up, a bed of salt only 3 inches thick would be deposited on the bottom. For such a locked-in basin lying in the center of a region poor in precipitation, the salinity is extremely slight. This is all the more surprising in that enormous amounts of salt are brought into the Aral by the Amu-Darya and Syr-Darya. It would require approximately 300 years for those two rivers to bring to the sea as much salt by weight as it contains today. The salinity of the water increases rapidly with depth, and the surface layers are fresh even in the central part of the basin. Everywhere water lies in thin layers. Because of the rapid increase of salinity (specific weight) with depth, vertical circulation of the water is hampered: in spring the sea does not warm rapidly, and in autumn it cools slowly; thus deep water remains cold a relatively long time in spring and even in summer.

In comparison with ocean water, the chemical composition of the water of the Aral Sea shows a greater amount of sulphates and a smaller quantity of chlorines. In composition, it is closer to the water of the Caspian Sea but differs from it by having a larger amount of calcium. The sulphates and calcium are brought by the Amu-Darya and Syr-Darya, both of which are rich in these minerals. The water of the Aral is very transparent. In its central part, at a depth of 72 to 79 feet, the bottom is often visible during summer. The greatest transparency (79 feet) is noted not far from the western shore, and the least in the southwestern part, where the Amu-Darya pours in muddy water. In the middle of the sea the water is as blue as that of the Aegean Sea. Fresh water and salt water near the mouths of the rivers differ sharply in color.

The fauna of the Aral Sea, in comparison with that of the Caspian, is poor: here, for example, there are no sponges, hydroideans, or bryozoans. There are a number of species common to both seas, such as barbel and carp and some mollusks and crustaceans. Seal, herring and goby are found in the Aral, but not in the Caspian. The number of endemic species is small, that is, the fauna of the Aral Sea is of recent geological origin; about 20 species of fish are found. The chief fishing districts are located close to the mouths of the Amu-Darya. The fish caught are carp (45 per cent of the catch), bream (40 per cent of the catch), roach, small sturgeon, barbel, and sheatfish.

Navigation of the Aral Sea is insignificant, owing to the locked-in character of the basin and the dryness of the shores. Regular steamboat communication exists between the mouth of the Amu-Darya and Aralskoye More station.

The history of the evolution of the Aral Sea is not clear. Traces of an old level of the sea are shown by terraces only 13 feet above its present level and developed comparatively close to its shores. During its greatest spread the sea covered the eastern and southeastern shores for no more than a few dozen miles from the modern shore line. To the northeast, its fresh-water inundations extended to Lake Chelkar-Tengiz, whose level lies at the same elevation as the Aral. Comparing the slight occurrence of Aral sediments, the poverty and unusual composi-

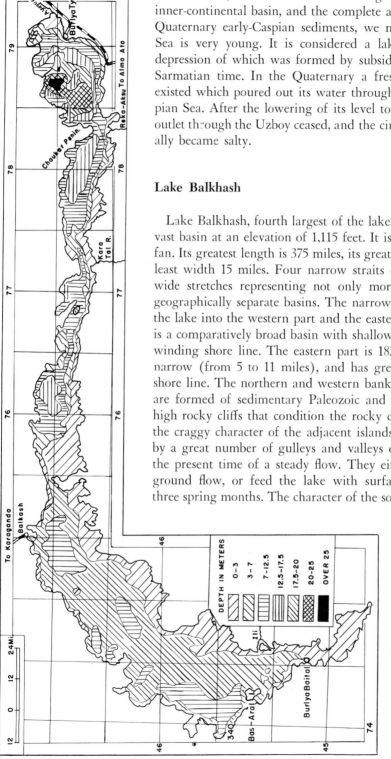

Map 14-IV. Bathymetric map of Lake Balkhash.

tion of fauna, the small amount and original makeup of salts of this inner-continental basin, and the complete absence of connection with Quaternary early-Caspian sediments, we may deduce that the Aral Sea is very young. It is considered a lake of tectonic origin, the depression of which was formed by subsidence along faults in post-Sarmatian time. In the Quaternary a fresh-water circulating basin existed which poured out its water through the Uzboy into the Caspian Sea. After the lowering of its level to the present-day level, the outlet through the Uzboy ceased, and the circulating fresh lake gradually became salty.

Lake Balkhash

Lake Balkhash, fourth largest of the lakes of Central Asia, lies in a vast basin at an elevation of 1,115 feet. It is shaped like an elongated fan. Its greatest length is 375 miles, its greatest width 55 miles, and its least width 15 miles. Four narrow straits divide Balkhash into five wide stretches representing not only morphologically but physico-geographically separate basins. The narrow Uzun-Aral Strait divides the lake into the western part and the eastern part. The western part is a comparatively broad basin with shallow depths and an extremely winding shore line. The eastern part is 182 miles long and is quite narrow (from 5 to 11 miles), and has greater depths and a simple shore line. The northern and western banks are high and steep, and are formed of sedimentary Paleozoic and various igneous rocks in high rocky cliffs that condition the rocky character of the coast and the craggy character of the adjacent islands. The shores are notched by a great number of gulleys and valleys of dry streams, devoid at the present time of a steady flow. They either have a slight underground flow, or feed the lake with surface water during two or three spring months. The character of the southern and eastern shores is completely different. They are bordered by a large sandy plain, which is either the product of lake deposits of a gradually receding lake or is completely made up of the modern alluvium of the Ili River. Great areas are covered with barchan and mound sand—the result of the working over of coastal dunes. The shores and also the offshore islands have level lowland beaches dozens of miles in length. Many sandy sections are covered by cane thickets. The southern coast has a great number of shallow lakes, occurring as continuations of its bays. The lakes are relics and are of very recent age. With the lowering of the level of Lake Balkhash, which is occurring at the present time, the lakes are cut off; this increases mineralization, and the most remote lakes dry up and become salt marshes. The southern Pre-Balkhash sandy plain is intersected by many rivers delivering their water to the lake. Balkhash receives its main rivers in the southwestern part.

The average depth of Lake Balkhash is only 20 feet and its bottom is very level. The western part of the lake is shallower than the eastern part. The distribution of isobaths in the western part reflects the constant deposition of much alluvium by the Ili River near the southeastern shore and the leveling action of the waves and currents, which uniformly distribute these deposits along the bottom and create broad submarine shoals. The 9-foot isobath is pushed toward the northwestern shore and, in places, is 10 miles from the southern shore; therefore this shore is little accessible for vessels with a draft of over 3 feet. From a depth of 36 feet near the northwestern shore the depths gradually decrease toward the mouth of the Ili River. The depths of the narrow eastern part of the lake vary from 20 feet to 39 feet. Depth increases toward the northeast shores, where the greatest depth of 87 feet is found. Bottom deposits of Lake Balkhash are extremely diversified. With the increase in depth to the east the bottom is more heavily covered with light-gray muds, which are typical of the deeper sections. From east to west the zone of darker silt and sand, characteristic of the shallow-water sections of the lake, enlarges. The silt is poor in

Fig. 14-16. Rocky northwestern shore of Lake Balkhash.

organic substances, and in the majority of cases it is highly mineralized.

The water balance of Lake Balkhash, which is a drainless water basin, is regulated by two factors: the intake of river water, and intense evaporation, brought about by high summer temperatures, low salinity of the water, large areas of shallow water, and the long and narrow shape of the lake which contributes to intensive warming. River discharge, especially that of the Ili River, decisively influences the lake level. During the winter the level rises somewhat, and during the summer it falls. The river discharge has a reverse trend: in winter it is minimum, in summer it is maximum. The fluctuations in the level of the lake depend without question on the discharge of the Ili River. Nevertheless, the annual amount of precipitation, however small, has a certain importance in the level. Underground feeding is not great.

Variations in level are also caused by currents

of two types. Water currents flow over large areas and have high speeds, depending on the force and duration of the wind. These currents are most pronounced during violent but brief western and northwestern winds in narrow parts of the lake, and flow at 1.6 to 4.3 feet per second. The other type of current, originating from the inflow of the water of the Ili River in the western part of the lake, has a steady circular motion in a clockwise direction. Fluctuation of the lake level over several years is common, with a maximum lowering of 8 feet; hence, in planning permanent installations in the immediate vicinity possible rises of the lake must be considered. The periodicity of the full range of rise and fall of the lake is approximately 36 years. In connection with the fluctuations of the level over a period of years, there is a steady shift in the salt content of its water.

The surface temperature of Lake Balkhash begins to rise in March, reaches its maximum in July (approximately 84°F) and toward December lowers to 32°F. The annual thermic curve for the water of the western part of Balkhash, during the entire navigational period, conspicuously exceeds the same curve for the eastern part, with its more severe Siberian type of climate. In winter the water of the shallow half of the lake (western part) is more intensely chilled than that of the deeper (eastern) part. The greatest warming is displayed in the upper layer (not below 10 inches) of water only on hot days and during prolonged calms. Under ordinary conditions great areas of shallow water maintain an approximately uniform temperature, owing to the constant disturbance of thermic stratification by prolonged wind. The lake usually begins to freeze in November. The average thickness of ice is 24 to 28 inches, and the freeze lasts from 124 to 139 days. The ice breaks up in the first half of April, though in the eastern part of the lake the breakup is delayed for 10 to 15 days.

In regard to the salt regime of the water, Balkhash is an unusual geographic subject: its water is partially fresh, partially slightly brackish, despite the fact that it has no outlet, that it is in a desert climate, and that the rivers bring many salts into it, as a consequence of which gradual salting of the lake should take place. The unusual coastal outlines of the lake, its bathimetric data, and also the distribution of the hydrographic network create a special chemical regime of the water of individual parts of Balkhash. The narrow neck of the Uzun-Aral Strait isolates eastern Balkhash from western. The small number of rivers in the eastern part and the large tributary, the Ili River, in the western part bring about the gradual and regular increase in the over-all mineralization of the water from west to east, with an abrupt change at the Uzun-Aral Strait and with the maximum amount of salinity occurring in the extreme eastern end of the lake. An especially abrupt freshening is displayed along the western shores opposite the mouth of the Ili River, which in the degree of mineralization of its water is one of the freshest large rivers of Central Asia. The western part of Lake Balkhash, with its slight mineralization, belongs to the fresh water reservoirs. The eastern part, with its chlorides and sulphates and with its over-all salt content, must, without doubt, be linked with brackish lakes. The concentration of individual mineral salts in the eastern portion is several times greater than in the western part. In the bays of the lake an increased mineralization is observed, as, for example, in the southern bay of Ala-Kul (despite its position in the freshened western part of the lake), which is separated from Balkhash by a narrow strait overgrown with vegetation.

The transparency of the water increases from the western tip of the lake toward the east. The slight depths, the rather vigorous regime, and the great amount of soil particles in suspension brought by the Ili River make its water rather turbid. In the western part the water is transparent to no more than 3 feet, and in the extreme eastern part a maximum transparency of 18 feet (summer) has been observed. The color of the water changes from a muddy yellowish-gray in the western part to a greenish and bluish in the center, and to emerald-blue in the extreme eastern part.

The fauna of Lake Balkhash is very poor, owing to its unusual hydrological regime, its chemism, and apparently its youth. The comparatively poor zooplankton of the exposed part of the lake bears a pronounced lake character, but in the sections which are under the influence of the rivers it bears a pond character. The benthos of the lake is abundant and varied, and includes great quantities of small mollusks, vermes, and crustaceans. There are only four species of fish: native Balkhash perch (*Perca schrenki*), one species of loach (*Nemachilus*), and two species of minnow (*Schizothorax*)—a valuable fish with tender meat but with a poisonous peritoneum.

In the past Balkhash was considerably larger. There are indications of old lake terraces at heights of 99 to 352 feet on the area adjacent to it. Terraces extend in many of the northern shore points, having a regular graduated shape and reaching heights of 10 to 13 feet. Nowhere along the shores are there traces of Aral-Caspian deposits; Balkhash was never joined to the Aral Sea. The slight salinity of the water of this desert lake and the relative poverty of its fauna indicate that in its present form Balkhash inundated a dry basin and is a comparatively young lake. That is why it has not yet succeeded in becoming a salt lake and being colonized.

Lake Ala-Kul

In the eastern part of the large Balkhash-Ala-Kul depression, which is a single drainage basin, lies large Ala-Kul Lake, at the present time drainless, but once linked with Lake Balkhash. Lake Ala-Kul lies between Tarbagatay and Dzungar-Alatau at an altitude of 1,155 feet. The islands and the rapid increase in depths close to them (the greatest measured is 59.4 feet) indicate the unevenness of the bottom. The morphology of the shores varies. Along the northern and northwestern shores are many sand bars and coves—low accumulative shores. The southwestern and eastern shores, breaking off toward the lake in terraces

formed of lake deposits, have a typical erosional character. The lake has six well-expressed terraces (from 6 to 221 feet high). The high terraces and plains, having a lake origin, indicate a former, very large lake of which the present lake is a residual part, having survived in the deepest part of the Balkhash-Ala-Kul depression. The chemism of the water of Ala-Kul is distinguished from that of the usual sea water by large quantities of sulphates and by small amounts of carbonates, which is usually characteristic of relic lakes. The modern water balance is maintained by underground water flowing from the surrounding mountain ranges.

The Kara-Bogaz-Gol

The Kara-Bogaz-Gol is the eastern gulf of the Caspian Sea; it is somewhat isolated from the Caspian and juts deep into the mainland. It is a water basin whose regime reflects distinctly the climatic influence of the surrounding desert. The gulf is joined to the sea by a narrow (660 feet to 2 miles), short (8 miles), shallow (6 to 18 feet) strait, enclosed between two sand bars of meridional direction. The Kara-Bogaz-Gol, occupying the lower part of an Upper Tertiary syncline, formerly was an open gulf freely circulating with the Caspian Sea, but later was separated from the sea because of the growth of alluvial sand bars. The northern and eastern shores of the gulf are formed by high banks (495 to 990 feet) of the Mangyshlak and the Ust-Urt, leaving a lower narrow terrace rising 3 to 6 feet above the level of the gulf. In the south a lowland shore with spits, lagoons, and salt lakes separates the shelf of the Krasnovodsk Plateau from the water line. The low western shore is covered with hill sand amid which there are numerous salt lakes.

Owing to the difference of levels between the gulf and sea (ranging from 17 to 42 inches), a constant flow of water into the gulf takes place. The regime of the Kara-Bogaz-Gol is due partly to this constant inflow of sea water and the absence of a reverse exchange of water between the gulf and the sea. Also, influencing the regime are the large area of the gulf (6,973 square miles), its shallowness, and its climate. The relief of the bottom of the gulf is monotonous. The prevailing and average depth is 33 feet, and the greatest depth is 42 feet. Close to the shores the depth does not exceed 5 feet.

The Kara-Bogaz-Gol experiences a desert climate with an extremely hot summer (maximum temperatures 104 to 114°F), a moderately cold winter (minimums from −5.3°F to −9°F), a slight amount of precipitation (less than 4 inches), a small relative humidity (59 to 66 per cent), and with the prevailing (55 per cent) winds from the east, the direction of the desert, having an average velocity of about 20 feet per second. These climatic features condition the extreme evaporation from the vast surface of the gulf. During the year a 51.2-inch layer of water evaporates. The amount of water evaporated is replenished by a steady flow from the Caspian Sea into the gulf. In the mouth of the strait, where the rapidly flowing water of the strait encounters weakly circulating dense water of the gulf, the rate of the current drops sharply, and alluvium is deposited and bars are found. Owing to the cumulative activity in the mouth of the strait, its length increases at an average rate of 108 feet a year. The strait itself becomes shallow and it is necessary to clear it out.

The water temperature of the Kara-Bogaz-Gol has a considerable yearly amplitude. Intensive warming occurs in summer when the temperature rises to 92°F, but in winter it may drop to as low as 12.2°F. Even at such a low temperature the water does not freeze, owing to its great salinity. The water level of the Kara-Bogaz-Gol has a yearly seiche, different from that of the Caspian. The water is lowest in October (February, in the Caspian), highest in April-May (July, in the Caspian). The annual amplitude of the fluctuations in the water level of the gulf is 9.2 inches. Transparency of the water is not great (6 inches), and the color is lead-gray or bluish-yellow, depending on the season.

Water from the Caspian, on entering the gulf, is subjected to evaporation exceeding the evaporation in the sea; thus, the concentration of salts in the gulf is considerably greater than that in the sea. The salinity of the gulf, on the average, is 16.39 per cent; the salinity of the Caspian is 12.6 per cent. In comparison with the Caspian, the saline composition of the gulf shows an increase of the percentage content of chlorous salts and a decrease of the percentage of sulphates. Such a change in composition is explained by the reactions taking place in the gulf water under the influence of meteorological conditions of the mutual interchange of the pairs of salts—$2NcCl + MgSO_4 \rightleftarrows Na_2SO_4 + MgCl_2$—and by the precipitation taking place during this reaction of Glauber salt. With the lowering of the temperature in autumn and winter the water of Kara-Bogaz-Gol becomes saturated in regard to Glauber salt and unsaturated in regard to sodium chloride and magenesium chloride; thus the Glauber salt crystallizes out perfectly pure. The period of thickening of mirabilite (decahydrate Glauber salt $Na_2SO_4 \cdot 1OH_2O$) begins usually in November, when the temperature of the water is 41 to 43°F, and continues up to the first half of March, when the temperature rises. At this time the mirabilite begins to dissolve and the reaction runs in reverse order. The Glauber salt settles out pure without the admixture of sodium chloride, because in comparison with the sodium chloride the brine remains unsaturated. The total amount of Glauber salt which may be deposited in Kara-Bogaz-Gol equals 6 million tons. Supplies of mirabilite increase annually because the inflow of water into the gulf is constant. Mirabilite is not only deposited on the bottom of the gulf but is also thrown onto the shores by waves. At the present time three methods of extracting mirabilite are employed:

1) In the method of utilizing natural storm discharges of mirabilite the mirabilite thrown onto the shore is raked up by hand and is carried inland where it is accumulated in stockpiles. Under the influence of high temperatures, dry air, and constant winds, the mirabilite loses its crystallized water and changes to anhydrous salt-sulphate (Na_2SO_4). Mirabilite is not thrown out along the entire shore strip, but

only on the northeastern and southwestern shores, where the configuration of the shores and the bottom, as well as the direction of the prevailing winds, are contributing factors.

2) The method of excavation consists in sucking in the mirabilite from the bottom of the gulf by means of salt pumps. It requires platforms for dehydration, a calm station for the barge near the shores, and thick bottom deposits of mirabilite.

3) The method of basining provides for pumping the brine which contains mirabilite at the time of its greatest concentration (September-November) into artificial or natural shallow-water basins with a watertight bottom. After the temperature drops to 41 to 43°F (December-February) the brine is pumped out, and on the bottom of the basin a layer of mirabilite remains, which is subsequently subjected to dehydration.

Products of the processing of mirabilite are: soda, sodium sulphide, and sulphuric acid. By means of successive utilization of brines, conducting the process with the aid of evaporation in the basins, it is possible to precipitate a great amount of sodium chloride, magnesium chloride, and bromine chloride.

Fish penetrating across the strait from the Caspian Sea into the strong salt solution of Kara-Bogaz-Gol lose their ability to swim, become blind, and throw themselves onto the shore where they become plunder for the birds. Many fish naturally salted and dried in the sun are preserved for a year.

SOUTHERN AND NORTHERN DESERTS

From the standpoint of a uniform desert climate, with its aridity and high temperatures, all desert landscapes of Central Asia have certain features in common. But within the extent of the desert region, from north to south, there are rather distinct variations in climate, in the rate of the soil-forming process, and in the ecological peculiarities of the plant and animal world, which, in turn, results in a heterogeneity in the landscapes. From north to south evaporation increases, because of the gradual rise in temperature; in addition, summer rain decreases and spring rain increases, which heightens the seasonal contrast of precipitation. In the southern deserts the seasonal nature of the soil-forming process is strengthened, the complexity of the soil cover decreases, and structural sierozem of the north is replaced by typical sierozem of the south. In turn, the influence of these factors on plant and animal life in the southern deserts is intensified. The mosaic quality of the plant cover and the number of long-vegetating perennials decrease, the life cycle is more pronounced in both plants and animals, spring pasture grounds take on greater importance, and the lack of summer fodder for domestic animals is more strongly felt.

These characteristics, imposed in the remote past, have conditioned the predominance in the northern deserts of Central Asiatic species of plants and animals, and the predominance in the southern deserts of Mediterranean (Iranian) species. Thus there are two distinct types of desert in Central Asia: the northern, and the southern. The ground itself is responsible for significant changes in the geographic landscapes. Its inherent properties and chemism strongly influence geomorphological and soil processes and thus the ecology of the plant and animal life.

Southern Deserts

From the standpoint of climate, composition, and development of the plant and animal world, the southern deserts of Central Asia are a continuation of the deserts of Asia Minor and North Africa—they are the Mediterranean subtropical type. However, in spite of similarities, there are genetic differences in the southern, Central Asiatic deserts and the African deserts: the former are conditioned by their position within the mainland; the latter are conditioned by trade winds. The southern deserts of Central Asia have a very hot summer and a rather warm winter—the January temperature is usually above 32°F. Even though the precipitation for the entire desert region is negligible the distribution of precipitation is seasonal and sharply periodic in southern deserts. More rain falls in the short spring than in the remaining portion of the vegetative period. The soil is saturated during winter and spring, but its upper layer dries out in summer. These sharp contrasts have pronounced rhythmic and seasonal effects on the development of soil, vegetative cover, and animal life. The abrupt change from abundant rain to intense dryness causes a uniform soil condition of some leaching in spring and the rise of solutions in summer. Thus, soils are not complex, and solonchak processes are broadly developed. Against the background of these general attributes of the southern deserts, the ground acquires much importance. By its physical and chemical properties, it acts strongly on the character of soil-forming and on the development of the plant and animal life, that is, on the landscape as a whole. According to this criterion the southern deserts are divided into (1) loess foothill plains, (2) sandy deserts, and (3) salt deserts.

Loess Foothill Plains

Loess foothill plains belong to the loess or ephemeral deserts. They are characterized by the almost unbroken occurrence of loess, on which typical sierozem is developed that is strongly influenced by the chemism and physical properties of the loess. Here, more than in the sandy deserts where the more favorable water regime of the sand somewhat modifies the seasonal contrast, is expressed the rhythm of the development of soil, plant cover, and animal world. This explains the important role of ephemerals in the composition and development of vegetation. The amazing fertility of irrigated soil makes the loess desert a region of very valuable crops.

An essential feature of soil formation in the loess deserts is the complexity and seasonal character of the soil processes. There are three distinct periods in the climatic regime: (1) the hot summer—wide ranges of day and night temperatures, extremely slight precipitation, a great amount of vaporization, low humidity during the day; (2) the cold winter—little snow; (3) the spring and part of fall—warm and more humid. Such annual climatic differentiation strongly influences the soil-forming process, which varies with each season. In summer the intense heating apparently causes a reverse capillary flow of the salted soil solutions to the surface and complex reactions of mutual interchange among the soil salts. During the winter soil formation probably ceases. In spring and fall, along with the disintegration of the mineral and organic mass of soil and the arrival of salts from outside, a diversified shift of salt solutions take place. Most often this is an accumulating of salts from the surface layers to a certain depth. Because of the slight washing and removal of salts in the hot, dry climate, the role of primary salting of the parent rock is considerably heightened.

On the foothill loess plains typical sierozem is developed. This normal zonal soil occurs usually on loess, and in mechanical and chemical composition is similar to it; because of this, sierozem was formerly taken for loess. The significance of loess as a parent material is important in the soil-forming process, which is characterized by weak disintegration of minerals, under conditions of low moisture, the influence of salts, and the small role of vegetation. This results in the formation of soil with little humus (less than 0.8 to 0.9 per cent) and with almost no differentiation into horizons. Abundant carbonates in the soil and in the loess are partly washed down into the lower-lying layers; thus the maximum of carbonates in typical sierozem is not in the surface layer (10 to 15 per cent) but at a lower depth (up to 25 per cent). This increased carbonation contributes to the great fertility of the soil. Vegetation on irrigated sierozem grows rapidly and luxuriantly. In contrast to the wealth of carbonates, the salting of typical sierozem is slight. It is linked entirely with the rather favorable hydromechanical properties of the loess: the loess is permeable to water and permits rapid leaching out of water-soluble salts.

Ground water usually lies deep, and the soil is outside the influence of ground moistening; consequently, the soil is not saline. Water extractions do not reveal soluble salts in noticeable quantity to depths of 3.3 feet or even 6.6 feet, but deeper layers may be salted, especially by gypsum. If the ground water has easy access to the surface the sierozem quickly becomes saline and is converted into brackish sierozem, and sometimes even into solonchak. This may occur if the soil is incorrectly irrigated during cultivation. A wealth of soil fauna is characteristic of the typical sierozem, and it forms a layer which is perforated by countless borings. A typical sierozem has the following structure: (1) an upper layer 4 to 4.8 inches thick, light gray-brown in color, and slightly-humus with a flaky-foliated structure; (2) a more compact, lumpy, and carbonaceous layer with calcium carbonate precipitated in the form of webs and concretions; (3) a layer highly bored by worms and grubs, which is saturated in the moist period of the year; (4) a layer containing plentiful precipitations of carbonates. From 32 to 40 inches (and lower) down, there is usually unchanged loess. In regions of typical sierozem development there are brackish meadows and vast solonchak areas, occasionally wet and overgrown with grass.

The loess foothill plains belong to the landscape of ephemeral desert. The characteristic peculiarity is the contrast in the development of vegetation. This is caused by the contrast in climate—the sharp difference between moist spring and dry summer. The correspondence between the character of moistening and the rhythm of the growth of vegetation here is exceptionally distinct and indicative. In the loess foothill plains the summer climate is favorable for the development of ephemerals and just as unfavorable for the development of perennial xerophytes. Inasmuch as the deep ground water is inaccessible to the short root system of desert ephemerals (which are fully

represented on loess) they are completely dependent on precipitation. Ephemerals emerged in the desert as a result of a long selection directed to shortening the growth time of plants in order that they might escape the effects of summer drought. During the brief moist regime of spring, the desert is settled first by ephemerals capable of vegetating in 1½ to 2½ months. They grow rapidly during this short period of moisture and warmth when the sierozem is fertile on the loess. The first sprouts appear early in March; the plants bloom in April; by the middle of May they have scattered their seeds.

Another biological feature of ephemerals is their curtailed growth under the influence of insufficient moistening. When moisture and warmth is sufficient, many of the ephemerals, such as trigonella and veronica attain heights of 4 to 8 inches, but in dry years these plants grow to no more than ½ to ¾ inch during their full cycle of development. The rate of development of certain ephemerals is partially related to the fact that they are winter crops, sprouting in late autumn when precipitation begins and the weather is warm. In the life of ephemerals no small role is played by the favorable properties of typical sierozem on loess. Such soil is porous and capable of taking in a large quantity of water. Being fine-grained it lets little water through to the lower layers. Instead, it retains moisture in the upper layers where it is available for the roots of the ephemerals. Although there is very little humus in the soil, all of the substances necessary for the development of plants are found in it.

Vegetation in the ephemeral deserts does not develop much under conditions of the ordinary desert regime. The short period of rains could not be better utilized by the ephemerals. In a particularly moist spring the density of the vegeative cover reaches the maximum which may be attained by grassy vegetation. There may be several hundred plants per square yard, and soil is completely covered by vegetation. The appearance is that of a continuous sod, and the cover is so cohesive that it is hard to penetrate the soil with a shovel. Ephemerals do not reflect the influences of summer dryness; they bear distinct features of typical mesophytes—traits of meadow vegetation indicative of surplus moisture however temporary.

Ephemeral-annuals are single-stem dwarf plants with a herbaceous stalk and soft bright-green leaves which fade quickly and which have well-developed, thin blades, like those of plants of moist localities. They do not require special devices for the reduction of evaporation. Their roots are spread out in a thick network in the surface layer of soil, which is well moistened by spring rains. The root mass exceeds the aboveground herbaceous mass by fifteen times, and the particles of the soil are covered with root hairs. The numerous roots contribute to the porosity of the soil and thus facilitate the entry of air and water. With the help of ephemerals, areas little suited for plants are converted into productive areas; humus appears, and structure is developed.

Inconstancy of the weather is characteristic of loess deserts. A dry spring arrests seed reproduction, often causing the plants to dry up without having opened their buds. In such cases the failure of seed reproduction is compensated for by vegetative reproduction. Ephemeral-perennials, or ephemeroids, survive summer drought as underground organs—roots, rootstocks, tubers, and bulbs—in which moisture and nourishing substances are accumulated in spring. The aboveground organs are short-lived; the stems die yearly, and renewal comes from the tubers, bulbs, or rootstocks.

The vegetation of the ephemeral desert is uniform in its makeup and in the character of grassy cover. It could be called sedge-meadow grass desert, since the spring cover is made up of two ephemeroid plants—desert narrow-leafed sedge and viviparous meadow grass—whose role is similar to the role of grasses in the steppes.

Narrow-leafed sedge (*Carex pachystylis*) is a plain, low herb with short linear leaves. It reproduces by means of rapid growth of rootstocks (¾ to 3 inches annually). The rootstocks, looking like long braided whips (up to 20 feet in length), are buried in the earth

to a depth of 2 inches, and they bear rosettes at short intervals along the fascicle of stalks. The roots, branching out abundantly from the base of the rosettes, are concentrated at a depth of 2 to 6 inches, forming a compact turf layer. The life of the shoot seemingly is completed in two years, but in unfavorable years it is prolonged. In the first year barren rosettes of leaves appear from the top of the rootstock. In the second year the shoot is restored and sends out a flower. Sedge is distributed evenly in the cover; its stems, standing ½ to 2 inches from one another, cover 75 to 80 per cent of the surface of the ground.

Viviparous meadow grass (*Poa bulbosa* var. *vivipara*) is a low grass, with narrow, soft leaves, growing in shallow sods on the surface of the soil and not buried in it like steppe grasses. Meadow grass reproduces vegetatively in two ways. In the spikes, in the axillae of the flowering leaves, instead of blossoms there form small bulbs which substitute for seeds, and which fall and start a new plant. Thus meadow grass is proliferous. In addition, its sprouts have thickenings at the base in the form of bulbs, which, owing to destruction of the root connection between them, break up and start a new plant. The bulbs of meadow grass do not lose their capacity to germinate even after several years of exposure to the air, as for example, in an herbarium; therefore, it has extreme resistance to drought. Meadow grass is a good fodder plant.

A few more ephemeroids capable for the most part of vegetative reproduction enter the main center of the sedge-meadow grass deserts of Central Asia. One of them, ixiolirion (*Ixiolirion tataricum*), sends out three to five horizontal shoots from a short rootstock, which swell at the ends into small pitcher-shaped tubers and very soon separate from the mature plant. On crowfoot (*Ranunculus sewerzowii*) the terminal node of the rootstock expands without losing its connection with the mother plant. On the node appear the first additional roots, and before long a young rosette is released from the mature plant.

The diversity of plant species and their varie-

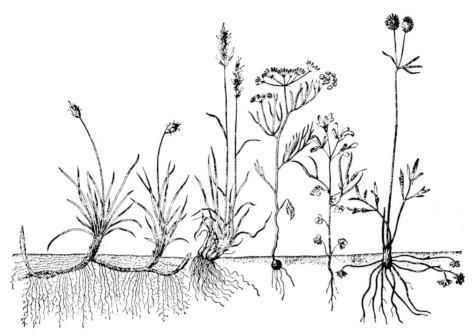

Fig. 14-17. The characteristic ephemoroids of loess deserts of Central Asia. From left to right: narrow-leaf sedge (*Carex pachystylis*); meadow grass (*Poa bulbosa vivipara*); *Bunium capus;* Trigonella (*Trigonella grandiflora*); crowfoot (*Ranunculus severtzovi*) with young rosettes.

gation depend on the abundant ephemeral-annuals. During the short period of vegetation their stalks and leaves are soft, but even when they are dry they are eaten by livestock. In the over-all fodder balance of the desert, this vegetation occupies a conspicuous position since it is of very good quality and is highly edible. The annual vegetation of monocarpic plants, whose life cycle ends with the bearing of fruit, is of short duration. In the first two years only a rosette appears; the stalk develops in the third to sixth year, after which the plant blooms, bears fruit, and dies. In some instances these herbaceous plants, which have an unusual rate of growth, attain sizes that are exceptional for grasses. Their short roots do not penetrate to the zone of ground water; therefore they must utilize the spring moisture in the surface layers. Two examples of monocarpic plants are the giant umbellates, asafetida (*Ferula foetida*), which has an unpleasant odor and a thick stalk with globular raceme and a large rosette at the root, and *Dorema aitchisonii,* which is wide-spread on the Karabil Hills in southeastern Turkmenia, and which has a 6-foot stalk thickened in nodes, with a raceme in the form of a panicle. The roots and stalks of monocarpic plants contain gum-resin, which has medicinal importance. Santonica (*Artemisia cina*), or wormwood, grows in the loess desert of the Chimkent, Dzhizak, and Dzhambul regions, in an area of about 10,000 acres. This plant is valuable because its unexpanded flower heads contain santonica, from which is derived santonin, a remedy for intestinal worms. The USSR is the only world source of santonica-wormwood.

The rate of growth in the ephemeral desert differs highly from that of other types of desert. In early March rain falls every four or five days, and the plain begins to revive. After each rain the soil is so saturated that one's feet leave deep tracks on its surface. Moisture conditions are established which resemble those of meadow soil. Early spring is the time of the greatest activity in the growth of vegetation: the seeds of monocotyledonous ephemeroids—sedge and meadow grass—germinate, the shoots of underground rootstocks sprout, the roots of many grasses begin to accumulate moisture and food substances for the summer and following spring. Toward the middle of April, vegetation attains its full growth. The sedge blossoms, and bulbs appear on the meadow-grass panicles. Poppies bloom, covering areas with a red carpet, and other plants tint the desert a violet color. Later in the month dicotyledonous ephemeral-perennials such as crowfoot blossom. Near the end of April the seeds of most plants mature.

Early in May the rains decrease, the temperature rises, and evaporation is intensified. Part of the moisture is absorbed by the soil itself and part by the abundant plant cover. The soil dries out, retaining some moisture at a depth of about $1\frac{1}{2}$ feet, but becoming rock-hard at the surface. The summer sun scorches the vegetation, and the desert turns yellow. Annuals quickly wither into standing hay, and perennials become dormant.

In autumn the rains come again, and the plain revives. Ephemerals begin to germinate, and some animals emerge from their burrows. With the approach of spring, the vegetation once more begins its life cycle.

The ephemeral deserts provide fodder for two to three months, and so serve as spring pasturages. The productivity of the vegetation is extremely variable—from 225 to 1,100 pounds per acre. In dry years there is little vegetation, but in especially moist years the grasses form excellent meadows. Unless livestock is driven into the mountains after the disappearance of spring fodders, it faces a semi-starvation diet in the desert.

The meadows yield the greatest harvest when meadow grass predominates. Any circumstance bringing about the development of meadow grass, such as pasturage of livestock, which scatter the bulbs, or cultivation of the soil, increases the harvest. With the help of agricultural engineering, the ephemeral plants may rise to the caliber of excellent meadow grasses. The ephemeral deserts are potential cotton regions, and if the relief and soil are favorable, they are highly capable of cultivation.

Animal life in the ephemeral desert also is influenced by the seasonal variations. The dense spring vegetative cover offers abundant food to a great number of animals. Early in March, tortoises (*Testudo horsfieldi*) and yellow marmots (*Citellus fulvus oxianus*) emerge from their burrows and begin to seek food. The Eversmann gerbil (*Meriones erythrurus eversmanni*) stores great quantities of grain in his burrow for the winter and causes serious damage to the fields. The large jerboa (*Alactaga severtzovi*), and the fox (*Vulpes vulpes caragana*), which is now becoming extinct, make their appearance. The bustard (*Otis macqueni*), crested lark, and other small birds feed on insects, grubs, and grain. Everywhere there are flocks of large griffon vultures. Lizards and snakes appear, as well as arachnids, insects and termites. With the almost complete extinction of vegetation in early summer, the life of animals in the ephemeral desert changes suddenly. Deprived of food and water, the yellow marmot hibernates, for 8 to 9 months, right up to the following spring. Tortoises bury themselves in the ground. The gerbil emerges from its burrow only at night; lizards leave their refuge early in the morning or before evening. Birds finish nesting and fly away, close to the banks of rivers. In winter many birds leave the deserts and fly south, but some fly in from the north.

Sandy Deserts

In the sandy deserts organic life exists within the narrow limits delineated by moisture. Sandy deserts have much less moisture than do the other types of deserts. The amount of annual precipitation fluctuates greatly from year to year. It may be as little as 1 inch or as much as 6.8 inches. There is no running water, and ground water, mostly salty, is at great depth. Between the Amu-Darya and the Murgab there is an area where wells yield salty water to a depth of 100 feet; from 100 feet to 460 feet the water is fresh.

Although the sandy deserts receive much less precipitation than do the loess deserts, they utilize moisture much more efficiently. Sand left to itself becomes covered with vegetation, owing to the ability of the substratum and the soil to store water. Old desert sand of river and lake origin is always well washed and consists almost exclusively of quartz grains with few admixtures of dust particles. Only rarely is sand of continental origin found in the deserts of Central Asia; it is formed by weathering of local bedrock which contains quantities of clay particles, lime, and iron oxide.

The sand of the southern deserts is dirty-yellow or red-yellow, and only on the shores of the Amu-Darya is it a steel-gray. The tops of barchans are pure sand, owing to the excellent sorting action of the wind; the depressions contain admixtures of dust. The mechanical composition of barchans is rather uniform: the chief mass is fine sand, the amount of dust in it not exceeding 1 to 1½ per cent.

The small amount of dust in barchan sand makes it highly water-permeable, and permits infiltration of the meager precipitation. A high percentage of moisture is absorbed, and very little evaporates from the surface, owing to the weak capillary lift of pure sand. In moist years much water accumulates at the boundary of the barchans and the underlying watertight rock. Thus, sand at the tops of barchans is coarser than sand in basins, where there is an admixture of dust particles.

A certain amount of water is formed by underground condensation of water vapor. The amount of water vapor saturating an area increases with a rise in temperature, since in moist sand varied vapor tensions in temperature layers cause water vapor to flow from higher-temperature layers to lower-temperature layers. The surplus received above saturation condenses to water, which under its own weight drops into the adjacent layers of sand. The greater the difference in temperature between soil layers, the more favorable are the conditions for accumulation of condensed moisture. Many circumstances contribute to this process. Continental deserts experience wide daily tem-

perature fluctuations, both in the air and in the soil, and sand, because of its intensive radiation, cools more than does clayey soil. In the sandy deserts the night absorption, by the parched surface sand, of water vapor from the lower layers of air is great. Because pure sand is very porous and its upper layers are dry, the saturated air circulates freely.

As a result of such condensation, a "hanging horizon of moisture," underlain by dry, shifting sand, forms below the surface sand of the barchans. In this horizon, the temperatures of the upper and lower borders alternately rise and fall, condensation takes place, and water is accumulated. This water is fully available for utilization by the shallow root system of sand vegetation. The depth of the hanging horizon of moisture varies with the season. In spring it is near the surface; at the beginning of summer it is more than 8 inches below the surface. A second horizon of moisture is formed at a depth of 40 to 56 inches, and it remains year round.

Little study has been made of the relationship between different kinds of sand from the standpoint of soil formation. A common characteristic of all sandy-desert soil formations is their primitiveness. This primitiveness is a result of the excellent water- and air-permeability and the low content of active (colloidal) particles. Soil forming is expressed in the formation of different salt regenerations: water-soluble salts are leached out of sand, and carbonates of cal-

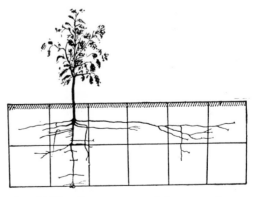

Fig. 14-18. Root system of desert sand vegetation.

cium in sand possess greater mobility than they do in loess. At a certain depth, dendritic calcareous concretions are abundant. They are formed during the evaporation of soil solutions, and their development is closely linked with plant root systems, which often are enveloped in lime. Near Repetek station there are accumulations of gypsum in the sand in the form of large (6 inches long), well-developed crystals. These crystals contain 40 to 60 per cent gypsum, and the remainder is sand. They are formed from fluctuations in the level of strongly mineralized ground water.

Since continued soil forming can take place only in fixed sand, areas of barchan, ridge, and mound sand do not have a clearly formed soil cover. Under some shading and lower temperatures, and influenced by growing woody vegetation, the surface layer of sand undergoes changes in mechanical composition and chemical properties. The dying vegetative mass enriches the soil with salts and humus. Beneath bushes is formed porous, sandy crust up to 4 inches thick, and with a clay content of more than 2 per cent. In ordinary sand the same type of crust is only 0.5 to 0.6 per cent clay. On sandy plains, arid sandy sierozem is developed having a certain graying of the upper layer due to a small amount of fine soil and a slight accumulation of humus (about 0.5 per cent). Beneath this are a uniform sandy mass and, in the lower layers, formations of carbonates of calcium and accumulations of gypsum. In many districts sandy-desert sierozem is entirely suitable for crops.

The low precipitation, aggravated by high summer temperatures and by the desiccating action of wind, causes an extraordinarily intense transpiration by plants. At Repetek station, during the hot season, over a 24-hour period a plant changes its supply of water several times. Under such conditions a plant subsists on precipitation which has infiltrated into the sand and, especially, on a steady condensation of moisture. Because the upper-hanging horizon of moisture disappears in summer, it can be utilized only for spring grassy vegetation. The lower one serves as the water-supplying horizon for shrubs, whose horizontally directed roots lie at the level of the lower layer of condensed moisture. Intense transpiration from the aboveground parts of plants and the slight, though constant, presence of moisture at the roots compel the plants to preserve their water balance by a decreased absorption. Plants vegetating during the dry period are xerophytic. Shrubs have no leaves, and other plants have spines rather than leaves.

The first plants to settle on barchan sand are subjected to mobility, owing to the dryness of the air, the looseness of the sand, and the strong wind. Plant pioneers are so closely linked with the sand that their very existence is determined by the looseness of the sand. Here we find many clear facts testifying to the role of selection in the development and formation of vegetation. The scattering of sand and its piling up are conditions between which the life of plants revolve. They are liable to be either completely buried or completely exposed (the root system included). In a strong wind lasting only two days, grassy plants and even bushes up to 10 feet tall may be covered.

A few endemic, sand-preferring plants are biologically and morphologically adjusted to life on a movable substratum. They can endure continual covering and deflation, and their fruits and seeds remain on the surface of the moving sand. The winter leaf buds of these plants are often buried, which means that the shoot must pass through a layer of sand sometimes 6 to 8 inches thick to reach the surface. Because of the looseness of the sand and its excellent aeration, the shoot is able to germinate without damage to the plant. Sand-preferring plants have a rapid growth, which to a certain degree protects them from being entirely covered. (One of the astragals, *Astragalus confirmans,* grows 36 inches in 6 weeks.) On shrubs, accessory roots may appear at various points on buried stalks, and they often eventually replace the main roots. The latter grow into a deeper layer of soil and die out, and feeding shifts to the accessory roots.

The scattering of the sand by the wind, and the consequent exposure of the shorter roots

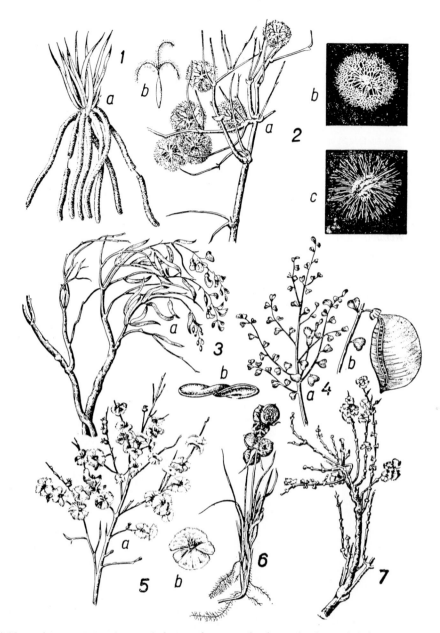

Fig. 14-19. Characteristic plants of the southern sandy desert in Central Asia.

1—Selin grass: a—root system with sandy hoods; b—seed with anchor-flying apparatus; 2—"Dzhuzgun": a—Leafless branch with fruit; b—flying seed, "Dzhuzgun" ball (*Calligonum caput medusae*); c—another species of fruit *C. arborescens;* 3—Sand acacia; a—branch with leaves and flowers; b—fruit-pod-propeller; 4—Smirnovia (*Smirnovia lurcestana*); a—branch with leaves and flowers; b—fruit, inflated bean; 5—Saltwort (*Salsola richteri*); a—branch with fruit; b—individual seed with flying apparatus; 6—Sand sedge; 7—White saxaul, branches with fruit. (*Mounting by S. P. Suslov.*)

of grassy plants as well as the long roots of large bushes, is deleterious to plant life. Even though the long surface roots can stand considerable exposure, they eventually dry out and the plant dies. The roots of pioneer psammophytes have a corklike texture which collects sand and thus enables them to adapt against deflation.

The fruits and seeds of sandy-desert plants do not sink into the loose sand, but are dispersed by the wind. The fruit has adapted itself by an increase of surface and a decrease in weight, attained by a reduction in the number of seeds and the formation of a thin, webbed tissue. The fruit is caught up and carried along by the wind, skipping on the surface. When the wind ceases, the seeds stop moving and, remaining near the surface, may germinate and produce shoots.

Despite the unfavorable environment for plant life, the conquest of the barchan sands by vegetation proceeds inexorably and at an exceptional rate.

A pioneer plant of barchan sand is the endemic psammophytic grass, three-awn (*Aristida pennata var. karelini*). It grows in bunches about a yard high, which sometimes unite to form small groups of vegetation occupying less than 10 per cent of the surface. Its extremely thin leaves with pin-shaped filaments indicate its xerophytic character. In the shade of neighboring bushes three-awn dies out. Accessory roots often run horizontally for 30 feet or more in the subsurface layer of moisture. When the grass is covered by sand, rootstocks with long internodes and sharp tips develop from buds in the hearts of the leaves and quickly shoot through the sand to develop a new cluster of leaves and then a stalk at the surface. With strong deflation of sand the large bushes of three-awn are exposed. Dead

Fig. 14-20. Selina (*Aristida pennata* var. *karelini*) bushes on sand.

leaves, which do not decay for a long time, protect the plant from desiccation. When roots are covered with a solid blanket of sand, they are at first connected with the root filaments, and later firmly cemented by salts. The pericarps of three-awn have, at one end, a downy beard divided into three branches, each bending outward in an arc, giving the seed pod the shape of a three-pronged anchor. Because of the elasticity and fluffiness of its beards, it rolls along the surface of the sand.

The settling of three-awn introduces subtle changes in the regime of the sand. A certain decrease in its mobility prepares the soil for the appearance of other plants—plants less equipped for the struggle with the shifting sand but able to propagate under the indirect aid of three-awn. To such plants belong root-sprouting forms such as heliotrope (*Heliotropium arguzioides*), tournefortia (*Tournefortia sogdiana*), and plants with a capacity to send out accessory root shoots; for example, Jurinea, Acanthophyllum, and semi-brush woods of the shoot variety. Calligonums and sandy acacias are prevalent. The acacias are different from real brushwoods in that, parts of their branches do not become woody and perform assimilation functions.

Calligonum (*Calligonum*), a semi-brushwood of the buckwheat family *Polygonaceae,* is widespread in the sandy deserts of Central Asia, and is represented by many species. The plant is circular in profile, stands about six feet, and pierces the dunes with countless, highly branching stalks and intertwining branches. Calligonum is a typical plant of the leafless xerophytes. In place of leaves the bush is covered with fine, green, resilient fibers. Some of them continue the growth of the shrub, maturing in the same year, and are covered with a thick glittering husk. Other fibers are flower bearers and assimilators, and fall off at the end of summer, after the fruit ripens. The majority of species of calligonum are light-loving. Its auxiliary roots extend as far as 100 feet horizontally in the lower subsoil horizon seeking moisture. The more the sand covers calligonum, the more rapidly its branches grow,

thus the plant always succeeds in narrowly out-distancing the sand. Its brush retards neither the wind nor the wind-blown sand. Because calligonum sends out auxiliary roots from the covered portions of the stalk, each root contributes to the over-all root feeding of the plant. With the dying out of deeply buried stalks, an auxiliary root may become a separate plant, taking root near the surface. The surface roots of calligonum have a corklike texture which protects them from drying out. Its seedlets are covered with small, finely branched bristles, which converts them into springy little balls that roll and bounce along in the slightest breeze, outdistancing particles of sand moved by the wind and thus escaping being covered.

Another pioneer psammophyte is the saxaul (*Ammodendron conollyi*) a member of the legume family, and a plant endemic to the sandy deserts of Central Asia. It is a well-shaped, semi-brushwood with small silver leaves, drooping branches, and racemes of dark-violet, fragrant flowers. Sometimes it has a treelike shape. When covered by sand it sends out lateral auxiliary roots as far as 10 feet from the base of the trunk. These roots are amply covered with root shoots, which contribute to the nourishment of the main plant. With the deflation of sand from under the roots to a depth of 4 to 6 feet, saxaul remains alive and standing upright owing to the support of the auxiliary roots. The fruits of the saxaul are light, spirally coiled, propeller-shaped beans. They remain air-borne a long time and so become widely scattered throughout the desert.

The seed of the semi-brushwood-psammophyte, smirnovia (*Smirnovia turkestana*), also a member of the legume family, is a thin-walled bean with a dry pod. The pod is almost the size of a hen's egg and contains only two or three seedlets, smaller than peas; thus, the wind rolls it easily along the sand.

The physicomechanical and water properties of the soil is changed by such pioneer psammophytes. The plants which do not form a dense surface cover send roots through the sand easily and abundantly and are buried almost to their tops, thus decreasing the mobility of the sand.

Fig. 14-21. White saxaul in the Kara-Kum Desert.

With substantial development of vegetation the transpiration of the plants causes an excess of moisture discharge of the sand over its intake. Part of the precipitation does not reach the sand but is retained and evaporated by the vegetation. In addition, dust is retained on the branches of shrubs, and where the leaves decompose under the bushes they enrich the sand with fine particles which are washed into the ground by rains. The amount of such particles in the soil is only 0.15 per cent in barchan sand, but under the pioneer psammophytes it is 0.5 per cent, and ultimately increases to 8.8 per cent. Because these particles fill in the spaces between sand grains, the water permeability of the upper soil layers drops; water is held longer at the surface and consequently quickly evaporates. Also, the fine soil increases the capillary rise of moisture from the soil and its subsequent drying out. Under these conditions the formation of condensation moisture decreases, and the desiccation of the soil eventu-

ally results in destruction of the pioneer plants. Also, because the thick plant cover tends to shield the light-loving psammophytes, they die out, old bushes become deadwood, and natural restoration ceases.

Freed expanses are occupied by new semi-brushwoods and grasses which are not as well-adapted to life on shifting sand. Other species of calligonum—*Calligonum eriopodum,* and *C. setosum*—together with large bush halophytes —*Salsola subaphylla* and *S. richteri*—and white saxaul first take possession of the basins and the lower part of gentle slopes, rising later to the tops of ridges and mounds. The mature white or sandy saxaul (*Haloxylon persicum*) is a tree 13 to 15 feet tall with a diameter at the base of 8 to 12 inches; it is a semi-brush-wood, or a small tree. It has a light gray bark, and instead of leaves it has fine, spiney scales. The yearly shoots of saxaul retain their chlorophyll from April to late autumn. Most of the seeds, which are winged, drop off during ripening. Saxaul puts out small auxiliary roots, which help it to tolerate the slow covering up with sand. Saxaul requires a somewhat loose soil for seed reproduction; therefore, it can endure some shifting of the sand, but it avoids saline soil. It is very abundant, but grows in individual bushes, never interlocking, and the projection of its crown covers less than half the soil surface.

With the complete deterioration of soil water properties, the only surviving plants are the grassy vegetation, which utilizes precipitation. Perennial ephemerals are abundant and diverse, and among them are a few bulbous and tuberous plants. Under grassy vegetation the content of dust particles in the sand increases, and the sand changes to light sandy loam.

A typical plant of overgrown fixed sand is desert sedge (*Carex physodes*). In March sprouts of this ephemeroid appear; in April it attains full growth; and in the middle of May it withers under the hot sun, but remains standing until autumn or even until winter. Sedge has long-branching rootstocks, which lie at a depth of 2 inches, from which numerous roots branch out almost vertically to a depth of 6 inches. Like smirnovia, its large, inflated, globular fruit is easily blown about by the wind. However, the seeds within sedge fruit are imperfect and do not germinate, and sedge reproduces exclusively by development of the rootstocks, preserving its life activity despite drying. Sand sedge is the chief fodder of sheep. Being a perennial, it is less subject to the influence of weather than the rest of the spring

Fig. 14-22. Sandy sedge (*Carex physodes*), a typical ephemeral of the compact sands of the Kara-
Kum Desert.

flora, which lends a stability to desert sedge pasturages. The appearance of a grassy ephemeral vegetation on the sand is the final stage of development of the sandy desert landscape.

The process of the overgrowth of sand may be disrupted by the haphazard pasturing of livestock or by the broken paths of nomad camps. These and other causes of the scattering of fixed sand result in distinct changes in the vegetation. The evolution begins with the dying out of sand saxaul, and in place of it appear plants that are periodically covered and uncovered by sand (calligonum and sand acacia).

The vegetation of fixed, compact ridge sand is called sedge-herbaceous vegetation. It repeats the peculiarities of the loess desert both in character of cover and in rhythm of development. The main role is played by various ephemeroids, especially sand sedge and viviparous meadow grass, which are admixed with fine quack grasses (*Agropyron*) and gray brome grasses (*Bromus tectorum, B. oxyodon*). Of the dicotyledons there are many bulbous and tuberous species, but those with rootstocks and those capable of developing additional roots are absent. Early in April the vegetation of ridge sand begins to revive, and within 20 days a uniform grassy cover colors the sand a uniform light-green. The ephemerals begin to die out in the first days of May, but the perennials live until the end of May. On small, uncovered areas of sand there are many of the semi-brushwoods.

The sandy clayey plain is formed of stratified sandy loam and clayey seams and at the top is covered by a layer of wind-borne sand up to 9 or 12 feet thick. The composition of vegetation, to a considerable degree, is determined by the thickness of this sandy layer. In places not covered by sand the plain is bare clay or clay sparsely covered with ephemerals. If the sand layer is less than 3 feet thick, soil with Turansk *Artemisia terrae albae* and *A. turanica* predominates. If the sand layer is more than 3 feet thick, the usual fixed-sand semi-brushwoods appear, such as white saxaul and sand sedge. The diverse composition of vegetation makes

the sandy clayey plain rather good grazing land. Some sections of the plain are suitable for the development of irrigation agriculture.

The zonal vegetation of the Kyzyl-Kum desert is *Artemisia terrae albae,* which associates it with the vegetation of the northern deserts such as Ust-Urt and the northern Aral deserts. The vegetation of the Kyzyl-Kum sand is similar in nature to that of Kara-Kum sand; that is, the composition of vegetation and the general character and formation of plants are very similar. A peculiarity of the Kyzyl-Kum desert relief are low scattered hills. Owing to the slight elevation of the mountains, there are no new types of vegetation different from those of the adjacent lowlands. Vertical zonality is not present. However, a different substratum of Paleozoic rocks results in the growth of certain unusual types of vegetation. On the rubbly soils of these hills is sierozem soil with ephedra (*Ephedra intermedia*), cousinia (*Cousinia pseudaffinis*), and meadow grass. On sand, old world winter fat (*Eurotia ceratoides*) grows. The vegetation of the rubbly slopes is extremely sparse, with artemisia and ephemerals predominating.

Sandy deserts are regions of livestock pasturing. In comparison with the grazing lands of other types of deserts, they offer the following advantages: high productivity, good fodder quality of the grasses and bushes, little dependence on the weather, and a guarantee of fodder in winter—the critical period for animal husbandry. The most important fodder plants are sand sedge and three-awn; annual grasses and the pea family, especially various astragals, are second in importance. In the sandy deserts are found the best conditions for the karakul sheep, which yield valuable hides.

The animal world of the sandy deserts is unique. Only those animals exist that can adapt to the high temperatures of air and soil and the lack of water. In the midday heat many animals retreat into burrows located at the suspended horizons of moisture, emerging only at night for feeding. Some animals that retreat underground during the day stopper the burrow entry with an earthen plug, which tends to stabilize underground temperature and moisture and make them independent of the temperature and moisture at the hot, dry surface. Other animals shelter themselves in pits and caves or simply lie down in the shade.

The long-toed sand suslik (*Spermophilopsis leptodactylus*) is a typical sandy desert mammal and is widespread from Turkmenia to Semirechya. It has long, thin toes with long claws, and its feet are covered with stiff hairs which aid it in running in the loose sand. The suslik avoids compact ground. Singly, or in colonies, it digs large burrows in the slopes of barchans. It does not hibernate during the winter, but its wool becomes long and thick. Viviparous meadow grass is the suslik's basic food.

In mound sand the large jerboa (*Rhombomys opimus*) is encountered in great numbers, forming numerous colonies in the depressions between mounds. The ground is so broken up by burrows (averaging more than 500 an acre) that sometimes it gives way under a horse. In bad weather and in winter the jerboa rarely emerges from its burrow. It gathers and stacks dried green hay at the entrance to the burrow, and secures the windward side of the stacks with wooden pins. As much as 5 pounds of hay is accumulated at each burrow. The burrows cause the soil to dry out and, consequently, to break up and scatter; this results in the dying out of brushwood and saxaul and, thereby, the rodent's own eventual destruction.

In addition to the large jerboa, there are the three-toed jerboa (*Dipus sagitta*) and the brush-toed jerboa (*Paradipus ctenodactylus*). All are nocturnal and feed on seeds, roots, tubers, and insects. They obtain the water by eating the bulbs of tulips.

The large ungulates in the sandy deserts are goitered-gazelle (*Gazella subgutturosa*), wild ass (*Equus hemionus*), and saiga antelope (*Saiga tatarica*). The last two animals are very rare and are disappearing; they have been declared inviolable. The most important desert animal is the camel, which even in summer does not require water more often than every 2 or 3 days. Also, it will drink very salty water. Because the camel travels rapidly, it can be moved far from watering places.

Birds are not uncommon in the sandy desert. During the midday hours they are silent and hide from the sun in the shade of bushes. Larks settle in the shade of telegraph poles and move around with the shade. Predatory birds and sparrows build their nests in saxaul groves, not within the bushes but on the peripheral branches, and although they are in the full sun, they are nevertheless above the scorching ground surface. To protect their eggs from the high temperature, some birds (grouse) sit on the eggs as soon as the first one is laid, and the male and female sit alternately so the eggs are never subjected to the direct rays of the sun. The most unusual bird of the sandy desert is the chough thrush (*Podoces panderi*) of the crow family. It does not leave the mound sand even during the winter. In spring and summer it feeds on grass seeds and on the grubs of beetles, and in spring and winter on the seeds of saxaul, colligonum, and other brushwoods. The most abundant birds are saxaul sparrow (*Passer amodendri*), desert wheatear (*Oenanthe deserti*), desert raven (*Corvus corax*), desert warbler (*Sylvia nana*), the best songbird of the desert, and desert speckled shrike (*Lanius excubitor*).

The sandy desert is an empire of reptiles, and the sand is streaked with the tracks of lizards and snakes. Most of the lizards have a thin, elongated body and long legs, and can move with amazing speed. Owing to their widely set legs, their body weight is distributed over a large area and thus they can move about on the surface of the sand. Some lizards can bury themselves by rapid, lateral body movements; they literally sink into the sand. Lizards appear on the surface, but they hide at certain temperatures. Only with sufficient heating of the air and soil do lizards become active. During the midday heat they conceal themselves in the shade by retreating into burrows or climbing onto plants.

The long-eared toadhead (*Phrynocephalus mystaceus*) is a typical resident of the sand,

Fig. 14-23. Animals of Kara-Kum Desert: large "peschanka" (*Rhombomys opimus*); steppe agama (*Agama sanguinolenta*); big-eared "roundhead" (*Phrynocephalus mystaeus*).

and a true day animal. In the hotter part of the day this lizard creeps onto the crest of a swelling sand dune, where the temperature is lower than in the basins and any breeze can be felt, and stands raised high on all four feet. It feeds on insects and smaller lizards. The Turkestanian agama (*Agama sanguinolenta*) is common. During the hotter time of the day these large lizards with a bulging sack on the neck rest motionless on bushes, since the temperature at a height of 6 feet is 18° lower than the temperature of the soil in the shade, and 50° lower than the temperature of the soil in the sun. At other times of day the agama remains in thickets of saxaul and tamarisk. This lizard is able to change color: when it is annoyed its neck, normally a sandy color, becomes tinted a deep blue, and the blue spreads to its belly and the legs.

The gray monitor (*Varanus griseus*), giant of the lizards, is over 4 feet long. Most monitors are native to Africa or Southern Asia, since it prefers compact sand. This predatory reptile roams a great deal, its movements having the side-to-side motion characteristic of snakes. It eats smaller lizards, snakes, small birds, eggs, and small mammals; it does not grind its food but swallows it. The monitor has a strong bite, and delivers blows with its long, powerful tail. Only at high temperatures does it warm up and become active. At 59°F it is very sluggish and at 50° it is entirely motionless. The hide of the monitor is beautiful and durable. Since it withstands stretching and nailing, it is used for women's shoes.

Of the other lizards there are the tiny sand toadhead (*Phrynocephalus interscapularis*), the veined and striped lizard (*Scapteira grammica* and *S. scripta*), the lobe-footed gecko (*Crossobamon pipiens*), and the fringe-toed gecko (*Teratoscincus scincus*).

Desert snakes, like most of the lizards, can also bury themselves rapidly in sand. Little flaps on the front of their mouth form a forward-projecting comb, and their lower jaw is smaller than the upper and rests inside it, so when the snake is in sand its mouth is protected. A typical sandy desert snake is the 30-inch sand boa (*Eryx miliaris*), a day animal. The boa is not poisonous and it buries itself in the sand with amazing speed. Insects, lizards, fledglings, and small animals are its food. The beautiful long and slender arrow snake (*Taphrometopon lineolatum*) is exceptionally fast, and climbs in saxaul bushes. It eats lizards and spiders, and is poisonous only to small animals.

One of the most common insects of the sandy desert is the big darkling beetle (*Sternodes caspia*). Spiders and scorpions are common arachnids. Among the Coleoptera there are the sand eel (*Thinorycter*), whose legs have the highest degree of development of digging of any of the insects; the wingless ground beetle (*Discoptera*), which resembles a cockroach; the Rhizotrogus, which looks as though it had been dusted with flour, and whose grubs feed on the roots of calligonum. Many of the insects are nocturnal. During the hottest part of the day they rest in the shade in the middle of bushes or cling to the shady side of stalks and leaves.

With the approach of summer, animals are scarcely seen in the sandy desert. Many birds have already hatched out their fledglings and have migrated beyond their places of nesting. Lizards are hidden in the middle of the day. A number of invertebrates, such as scorpions, spiders, and myriapods, are seen during the day in spring, running along on the sand, but in summer they dig deep into the ground. In autumn, with the lowering of the temperature, with rain beginning to fall, and with the growth of vegetation, animal life begins to revive. Large insects appear, snakes crawl out of their holes, and rodents run around on the sand, and migratory birds begin their flights south. In winter many birds that nest in the desert fly away, reptiles and insects fall into a torpor, and certain mammals hibernate.

Salt Deserts

The vegetation of the salt deserts does not occupy vast continuous areas, but grows in comparatively small regions, disseminated in the desert landscapes. The chief areas of development of the halophytic landscape are river terraces where brackish water lies close to the surface. Salt marshes are one of the final stages of development of these terraces. Outside the river valleys, salt marshes occupy locked-in, undrained basins having ground water near the surface. Precipitation constantly flowing into the basins supplies the soil with salts. The development of halophytic vegetation depends on the degree of saltiness of the substratum and the moistening of the soil by ground water. The amount of precipitation and its distribution in the vegetative period are only slightly reflected in the plant life.

Halophytic vegetation is interesting because of its original composition and its form of adaptation to life on salty soil. The goosefoot family (*Chenopodiaceae*) has the ability to grow on highly saline soil, a characteristic exhibited by very few genera. Thus, halophytic vegetation is poor in species, and its form and structure do not have much diversity. There are either fleshy saltworts—succulents—or rigid plants which exude salts, such as the grasses *Aeluropus littoralis* and *Frankenia,* and the bushes of *Tamarix.* The biological properties of both types of plants are analogous to those of the halophytic plants of the semi-arid zone. Halophytic vegetation is favorable for fodder:

it contains salts in its tissues, is resistant to drought, and has a long period of vegetation. Saltworts are readily eaten year-round by camels and sheep, and after the first frost they are almost the only green fodder for sheep.

One of the most unusual plants of the halophytic desert is black or halophytic saxaul (*Haloxylon asphyllum*); it is widespread in the Kara-Kum and Kyzyl-Kum deserts, in the Pre-Syr-Darya Plain, in the Muyun-Kum Desert, and between the Ili and Kara-Tal rivers. Great thickets grow in slightly salty, sandy loam and clayey soil, but it cannot endure either strong salting of the ground or flooding. Saxaul is especially abundant in dried river valleys where there is a temporary inflow of ground water. Halophytic saxaul is a tree 13 to

Fig. 14-24. Large black or solonchak saxaul tree (*Haloxylon aphyllum*) in the southeastern Kara-Kum Desert.

26 feet tall, with a crooked, often very thick, highly branching trunk having dark gray bark and dark, extremely heavy (specific weight 1.2) wood. The wood is so hard, felling saxaul with an axe is quite difficult. After many cuttings it frequently resembles a brushwood scrub 3 to 6 feet high. Saxaul, like calligonum, is a plant without leaves. Part of the branches do not become woody and perform the assimilative functions, which is why it is classed as a semi-tree. Saxaul utilizes the ground water in depressions, which is at a depth of only a few yards.

Saxaul grows rapidly. On abandoned plowland may be found 4-year-old specimens up to 5 feet in height. Restoration of saxaul normally takes place only under conditions of some salting and sufficient depth of the surface soil layer. On very compact soil, seed restoration is rare, but close to abandoned animal burrows saxaul seeds itself abundantly. Saxaul also reproduces by shoots. Black saxaul often forms stands or groves, called saxaul forests, which are cared for by a government forestry service.

Saxaul does not have a thick stand; it averages about 300 mature trees to 1 hectare (2.47 acres). In the Kara-Kum 1 hectare of saxaul forest yields about 40 tons of wood. A saxaul grove is not dark, since there are few branches to produce shade. In hot weather the groves are even hotter than the open desert, since, being in valleys and depressions they are sheltered from the wind and little protected from the sun. Grassy cover is poor, and sand sedge is often predominant. The soil is fairly compact. There is little sound in saxaul groves, since there are few birds. The transition between black and white saxaul groves is gradual. Mixed stands of black and white saxaul grow on the slopes of sand hillocks where ground water is relatively close to the surface.

Virgin groves of black saxaul are filled with much deadwood, the total mass of which sometimes exceeds the amount of living wood. Black saxaul deadwood, in contrast to sand saxaul, may lie for 10 years without deteriorating.

Saxaul could be of importance in reforesta-

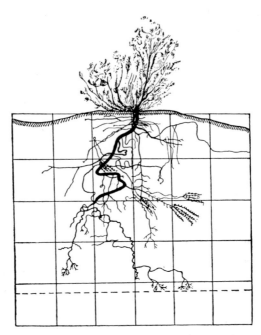

Fig. 14-25. The root system of the saxaul.

tion. Its heavy, close-grained wood (specific weight of green saxaul is 3.15), which sinks in water, is broken comparatively easily but does not split. It is an excellent fuel, with a high heat value (equal to that of coal), and is the principal fuel in the desert. In the markets of Central Asia where wood is scarce, saxaul is sold by weight. The population requires about 150,000 tons and the railroads about 17,000 tons annually. Saxaul is used for activated charcoal, which is an indispensable item in industry. Saxaul wood has little value as lumber because it is brittle and gnarled. In winter the tree is important as fodder for camels and sheep; and potash is extracted from green saxaul. Saxaul is also an excellent sand-fixing woody plant. The total area occupied by white and black saxaul is approximately 250,000,000 acres. Saxaul has disappeared in many places, as a result of wasteful cutting. But the excellent germination of its seeds, its capacity for shoot restoration, and its rapid growth create excellent prospects for a reasonable saxaul economy.

The typical salt marsh is almost devoid of vegetation. Monotonous, flat expanses stretch for many miles, the white, salt-covered surface dazzling in the sun. Halophytes are usually distributed around the periphery of salt marshes, depending on the relief and the degree of soil salinity. In the Golodnaya Steppe the lower portions of the salt marshes are covered with glasswort (*Salicornia herbacea*), halophytes (*Halocnemum strobilaceum*), and *Halostachys caspica*. In the next zone are *Suaeda arcuata* and fleshy glasswort (*Salsola crassa*). In the peripheral belt are *Anabasis salsa* and gray *Artemisia terrae albae*. Sand heaped on the surface of the marsh changes the plant life: new species appear which are absent on typical salt marshes.

Typical salt basins are also almost devoid of vegetation. It occurs only along the outskirts and where sand lies on the surface. The semi-shrub glassworts (*Salsola gemmascens* and *S. rigida*) are pioneer plants. Later, halophytic vegetation grows, and the last to appear is ephemeral desert vegetation.

Recent and old alluvial plains are widespread and are the main centers of modern agriculture. In these areas, united by a single process of development of the modern river and its valley, three basic landscapes are characteristic: valley meadows, valley forests, and oases. Each has its own structure and own course of development, and each plays a different role in the economy of the areas.

Valley meadows are most typical along the lower courses of the Syr-Darya, Ili, Chu, and Sary-Su rivers, and in the delta of the Amu-Darya. Soil of the river valleys is developed under conditions of a high level of ground water and the proximity of the river. This leads to widespread capillary rising of soil solutions —the solonchak process. The periodic surface watering of bottomlands in the flood periods establishes the opposite, short-lived process of the downward movement of the salts. The parent material is young alluvial deposits, mechanically and chemically diversified, somewhat sandy, often well-sorted, and with a small content of organic matter. Owing to the youth of the land and of the soil-forming process itself, the morphological profile is weakly developed. On bottomlands, alkaline, meadow, flaky,

alluvial soil is developed, with a sufficient amount of humus and salting from the surface; in places of prolonged flooding there is undeveloped, slightly saline soil. In higher places, primitive desert sierozem soil is widespread with an upper, dark-gray layer bedded with a uniform distribution of humus from the top down, the amount of which fluctuates from 1 to $2\frac{1}{2}$ per cent. Below the humus is a compact carbonaceous layer, wherein carbonates are scattered and deposits of calcium carbonate are absent. A certain amount of easily-soluble salts moves downward.

Sierozem is extremely diversified, depending on the chemical and mechanical differentiation of the alluvial deposits. When a terrace emerges from the zone inundated by river water during floods, soaking and washing through, which was previously periodic, ceases. The level of ground water lowers, according to the age of the terrace, and the influence of the river water is no longer felt. The dry air causes intense evaporation from the surface of the soil, which increases the capillary rise of solutions and the accumulation of salts in the upper layers. That is why solonchak is widespread on elevated terraces. In inflated solonchak the amount of sulphates and chlorine salts in the upper layer may be as much as 36 per cent. Strong winds lift powdered salt from solonchak and carry it great distances. Also, sand hillocks are found on river terraces.

Meadows of the river valleys owe their existence to the proximity of the river water, to periodic deposits of alluvium by high water, and to the high level of summer ground water, which is supplemented by the river. The elevation of river valley meadows, and the fluctuations in the level and chemism of the ground water, determine the character of the meadows, their ecology, and the diversity of their vegetation. Owing to the salinity of the soil, the abundance of salts in the river water, and the intense evaporation, valley meadow vegetation is composed chiefly of halophytic plants.

A vigorous rhizome guarantees the existence of halophyte (*Aeluropus littoralis*) even with comparatively deep ground water. Special glandules enable this plant to exude excess salts onto the surface of its leaves. It is readily eaten by livestock in autumn and in winter. Its constant and typical companions are the rootstock Bermuda grass (*Cynodon dactylon*) and the sod grass *Atropis distans*. In the lowest, highly moistened areas of bottomland, reed marshes often occupy vast regions, as in the delta of the Amu-Darya. The reed *Phragmites communis* is woven into mats for nomads' tents, and is

the large rivers in a broken, narrow belt. They stand out as a dark-green ribbon amid the pale-yellow sandy hills which often border the valleys on both sides. *Tugai* are situated on the lower young terraces or on islands corresponding to such terraces. *Tugai* exists under unique conditions—good soil moistening and dry desert air. Near-surface ground water is constantly fed and freshened by river water, and inundations are periodic. Therefore, *tugai* vegetation

Fig. 14-26. Tugai vegetation consisting of "dzhida" and reeds on the six-foot terrace of the right bank of the Amu-Darya.

used as a covering under the ceilings of houses; it is also used in house foundations as an inexpensive insulator from the capillary rising of ground water and salts. Herds of cows and horses pasture in reed thickets, knee-deep in water. If reeds are cut before blooming they yield excellent hay; however, water transportation and special hay-harvesting machines are essential.

In Central Asia the forests of the river valleys are called *tugai*. *Tugai* are spread along

grows under conditions of optimum soil moistening. Prolonged dryness is not noticeably reflected in the *tugai* vegetation, which remains green until the first frost. During floods, the *tugai* terraces are inundated, and the water leaves a layer of silt.

Tugai is typically a forest landscape. It has a dense, woody canopy that deeply shades the ground and inhibits the movement of air. When the temperature is high *tugai* has a high humidity, which is caused by evaporation from the river and the bottomland. The summer heat of *tugai* is tropical, which fosters the rapid growth of vegetation and at the same time makes the forests oppressive and unhealthy for humans.

In *tugai* there is a small variety of plant species, a characteristic undoubtedly due to the unusual environment. The chief woody species of the first stage is heterophyllous or Euphrates poplar (*Populus pruinosa*). Following it are the lower brushwoods, wild olive (*Elaeagnus angustifolia*) and different species of willow (*Salix wilhelmsiana*), and numerous species of tamarisk (*Tamarix*). When the tamarisk is in flower, the bottomlands are vivid with white, rose, and violet. Still lower grow the smaller shrubs: two species of boxthorn (*Lycium*) with thorny branches, the salt tree (*Halimodendron argenteum*), and the semi-bush glasswort (*Halostachys caspica*) Undergrowth in the *tugai* is not developed, and grassy vegetation is absent. An unusual appearance is given *tugai* by the woody, half-grassy, and grassy lianas, eastern clematis (*Clematis orientalis*) and pointed milkweed (*Cynanchum acutum*). Characteristic plants of the Amu-Darya *tugai* are in the south, the bamboo, and in the river deltas, *Apocynum scabrum,* a perennial fibrous plant of the family Apocynaceae.

The constantly changing river channel and shoreline condition the extreme mobility and activity of vegetation, and the formation and development of *tugai*. On newly appearing flats, the seeds of moisture-loving plants—reed, cattail flag, rush, and horsetail—germinate rapidly. The abundance of seeds brought by water and wind, in addition to the moist, fertile earth, favor rapid overgrowth of the alluvium. In the second or third year, dense and tall thickets of reed secure the young alluvium with their roots and preserve the new shoreline from washout. The littoral strip on which reeds grow increases in width, but thickets of reed situated at a distance from the river die out and are replaced by different *tugai* brushwoods such as tamarisk. Poplars, which replace the brushwoods, grow considerably more slowly and only after about 20 years do they form a completely mature

tugai. As the river cuts below the terrace, the *tugai* to a great extent emerges from the influence of the river water, and the upper soil layers become dry. The thick, woody vegetation itself aggravates these conditions by drying out the soil.

As a result the *tugai* begins to die out. Because the growth of poplar is so slow, the ability for self-renewal is lost, and it is replaced by grassy vegetation. Licorice can exist where ground water lies deep and is considerably mineralized. With further relative rises of the terrace, soil salts increase, and the soil takes on a desert-regime character and becomes populated by salt-enduring plants (primarily halophytes or black saxaul). The life of the *tugai* could still be extended if the former river channels were re-established.

Man's agricultural activities play an important role in the life of the *tugai*. He uproots the *tugai* vegetation, clears off the soil for young crops, and installs irrigation lines that change the distribution of moisture. The vegetative composition is altered by fires, by the unsystematic felling of trees, and by the grazing of goats, which strip the bark from the trees. The economic importance of the woody varieties of *tugai* vegetation is slight. Most of it is used for firewood, and because the wood is of such poor quality only an extreme need for construction material will compel its use in building. The *tugai* is important principally as a means for preserving water. The unfavorable quality of the woody plants necessitates improving their composition by the introduction of other plants, such as white acacias, mulberry trees, and plane trees.

The valley forests of the Chu, Ili, Lepsa, and Ayaguz rivers are composed of other woody plants and brushwoods, but Heterophyllous poplar is absent. A number of trees foreign to the southern *tugai* give an unusual character to them. In these *tugai* are birch, willow, wild rose, and barberry. Characteristic of the higher, dry sections of the valleys are thickets of tall chee grass (*Lasiagrostis splendens*), the sods of which are not joined to one another.

The *tugai* is a meeting of forest and water;

thus the animal population is mixed. In these inaccesible jungle thickets are wild boar, Bukhara deer, tiger, and the reed wildcat, none of which lives outside the bottomland. When the *tugai* is inundated the animals move to drier areas or wander from one island to another. The predatory animals prefer to move along the trails made by wild boar and deer, which are often tunnels through the dense jungle. During the hot part of the day, when even mosquitoes are still, the animals rest. Only at nightfall, when the enervating heat abates, does the animal life awaken and seek food. The Central Asiatic wild boar (*Sus crofa*) feeds on Gastropoda and frogs, roots, grass, and the shoots of reeds. Toward autumn it goes into cultivated fields at night, trampling and eating the young rice, cotton, and melon crops. The Bukhara deer (*Cervus elaphus bactrianus*), inhabits the more southerly districts. Most of the predatory animals are a brownish yellow color, which effectively camouflage them in the dense reed thickets. They are also able to pass through the reeds noiselessly, without breaking grass stalks. The Turan tiger (*Felis tigris virgatus*) still dwells in the *tugai* of the Amu-Darya and the Ili. It prefers the outskirts of impassable reed thickets near bottomland forests, where it can prey on grazing wild boar and deer. It avoids any encounter with man and never attacks him. The reed wildcat or swamp lynx (*Felis chaus chaus*) lives in bush thickets near the water where day and night it hunts for ducks, geese, pheasants, and rabbits. Near Semirechya is found the steppe wildcat (*Felis caudata schnitnikovi*). In the *tugai* are many rabbits, water rats, and field mice.

The pheasant (*Phasianus colchicus turcestanicus*) lives in the dense, impassable thickets of the low forest, feeding in the morning and evening on berries. At Demirechya is a Mongolian species of pheasant. In the *tugai* are also kingfishers, sparrows, chiff-chaffs, and speckled magpies. Some birds such as the *Plegadis falcinellus* fly to Africa, south and east Asia, and Australia for the winter. The shore and reed jungles are a special habitat for birds,

inasmuch as fish are their main food. Ducks, geese, snipes, sandpipers, gulls, pelicans, noddies, and flamingos dwell here.

The *tugai* areas are rich in amphibian life, not in species makeup but rather in the number of individual specimens. The lake frog (*Rana ridibunda*) is common, and at Semirechya is found the grass frog (*R. temporaria*). In the reeds, migratory locust (*Locusta migratoria*) propagates, and mosquitoes thrive.

Oases stand out as rich, green patches against the desert background. They are separated from the desert by a wall of tall poplars and dense elms. The oases are man made—lands reclaimed from the desert by irrigation. The irrigated areas of Central Asia total about 8½ million acres, on which about 32 billion cubic yards of water are expended each year. With the absence of irrigation the Aral Sea would receive an inflow of water of not less than that which the Syr-Darya yields. The water of many tributary streams, immediately on its exit from the mountains, is taken almost entirely into the irrigation system and does not reach the main river. Especially characteristic are the alluvial fans of the Fergana Valley (Sokh, Isfayram, and Isfara). Man has created a new hydrographic network of numerous irrigation canals, and under his influence the rivers are joined. The old Iskilyuy-Tartar Canal takes part of the discharge of the Zeravshan River for supplementary feeding of the shallow Sanzar River of the Syr-Darya basin, mixing the water of two of the arteries of Central Asia. Many irrigation canals have been converted into natural streams and have all their characteristics: meandering, formation of bottomland, and establishment of terraces. Along the periphery of irrigated lands swamps have been created by irrigation. The socialist economy has not only changed the techniques of irrigation but has also simplified the legal problems of a water supply for farmers by regulating, reconstructing, and expanding the overall irrigation system.

In the irrigated oases, where canals flow from reservoirs, where rich orchards and brushwood plants create shade, a unique agro-climate exists. It is a more moist and moderate climate than that of the surrounding, still un-irrigated, desert, where it is difficult to bring water because of the elevated, highly dissected relief. The summer air temperature in the oases is 10 to 18° lower than that of the surrounding desert, temperature fluctuations are less sharp, winds are not so strong, and the humidity is above 30 to 40 per cent. Nevertheless, high summer temperatures and increased humidity in the oases make them areas ill-suited for human habitation. Cooling evaporation from the surface of the skin is low, and the swamplands are hotbeds of malaria and gastric diseases.

The conversion of primitive valley sierozem soil into irrigated agricultural land results in a profound change in its natural characteristics and forms a new oasis-irrigation soil. The mechanical composition and salt-water regime are radically changed, and the additional moisture causes an increase in the microbiological activity of the soil. The oasis-irrigation soil has an increased humus layer, formed from deposition of material suspended in irrigation water, which replaces manure fertilizers. This is re-plowed every year, and, as a result, 2 milli-meters of new soil on the average is accumulated each year. In the oldest oases the oasis-irrigation layer is 3 to 12 feet deep. The amount of humus is usually not great (1 to 1½ per cent), since the systematic re-plowing distributes it uniformly through the entire depth of the soil. High carbonation may reach 20 to 25 per cent of the total volume. The absorbing complex is saturated with calcium, but because of the small amount of organic matter in the irrigated soil and the free movement and renewal of soil water, it creates only an easily broken structure.

Incorrectly supplied irrigation water, without provision for adequate drainage, causes rise of ground water, deterioration of the structure of the soil, development of the solonchak process, and swamping of the irrigated fields. Often the soil cover of an oasis is a mosaic of differently salted soils, from weakly solonchak to acrid solonchak. The accumulation of calcium in the humus layer and increased biological activity are desirable, but the considerable clayeyness, the absence of a stable structure, the lack of organic matter, and salting are undesirable. Poor irrigation may be corrected by rearranging imperfect irrigation systems and exploiting them efficiently. Agro-technical measures are valuable such as careful cultivation of the soil and the introduction of legumes (for example, lucerne) into the rotation of crops.

Oases are the centers of old irrigated agriculture, traces of which can be seen wherever there are lands which long ago emerged from inundations of the rivers. The abundant warmth and light and adequate irrigation create favorable conditions in the oases for the development of warmth-loving crops. Profitable plants are either selected from wild Central Asiatic flora or introduced from other countries. The natural flora is deliberately replaced by more productive foreign flora, and cultivation of a plant under oasis conditions may basically alter the plant itself. Arboreal plantings are self-sowing.

The oases are the main cotton growing areas of the USSR and one of the largest fruit-vineyard districts of the Central Asiatic Union Republics. Cotton is the most important cultivated plant of the oases. Not only is it widespread in all the oases, but it is also successfully cultivated in unirrigated sections of the semi-desert zone of the mountain region of Central Asia. *Gossypium,* the variety of cotton of the mallow family, is represented by several dozen species which grow wild in the tropical countries of the Old and New World. Local Asiatic cotton (*G. herbaceum*) is a grassy species, but the American cotton (*G. hirsutum*), in its Mexican homeland, is a perennial woody plant attaining a height of 9.9 to 11.5 feet and reaching 80 years in age. In the cotton area of Mexico the average temperature of the coldest month does not drop below 65°F, and the perennial cotton plant yields its first fruits in the seventh or eighth month after planting. In Central Asia, American cotton is cultivated as an annual plant; it tolerates somewhat lower temperatures than in its native land and yields a

Fig. 14-27. Picking cotton in Central Asia.

crop in the fourth or fifth month. The climate of Central Asia, with high temperatures during the main growing months, a prolonged frost-free period, and the absence of superfluous humidity, especially during the danger period of the maturing of the bolls, is extremely favorable. But below 32°F the buds, blossoms, and bolls perish. Also widespread in Central Asia is the cotton of the African and Asiatic types—having a fiber ¾ to inch in length. At present, Egyptian cotton is being developed, a cotton which belongs to a South American group and which has a long (up to 2 inches) twisting, silky fiber used in the manufacture of the finest fabrics.

Fruit orchards are important in the oases. From the standpoint of diversity of varieties, Central Asia is one of the prominent orchard regions of the world. There are numerous varieties of apple, apricot (with its hundreds of local species), plum, peach, quince, pomegranate, and fig, all of which possess a high sugar content. There are many varieties of grape; some are large and sweet, others have easy recovery of juice and can be hauled long distances without damage. With proper handling, the grape yields quite exceptional harvests. Cultivated grapes will grow unusually well without care, although the fruit is rather small.

The grain crops of sorghum (an African grass), rice, wheat, and barley are widespread. Numerous varieties of very sweet muskmelon are grown.

Black and white tapered poplars (*Populus nigra* and *P. bolleana*) and elm, lend a singular appearance to the oases of Central Asia. The lumber of tall, pyramidal poplars is used in house construction, and from their twisted branches are made rims for the wheels of bullock-carts. There are numerous decorative trees and shrubs, with species from America, eastern Asia, and Europe finding a second home here: plane tree, magnolia, tulip tree, Judas tree, and silk acacia.

The oases are a special habitat for animals that will live near man and for whom orchards and buildings offer shelter. Landscape birds commonly seen in the cities, in the villages, and along the road are the Senegal turtledove (*Streptopelia senegalensis*) and the hoopoe (*Upupa epops*), both of which build their nests under the eaves of houses. Another cohabiter with man is the village swallow (*Hirundo rustica*), which migrates to India or Africa for the winter. The earliest herald of spring is the white Turkestan wagtail (*Motacilla alba personata*). The beautiful tropical Indian paradise flycatcher (*Terpsiphone paradisi turcestanica*) arrives from India and Ceylon somewhat later, and after it comes the Indian oriole (*Oriolus oriolus kundoo*). The white Asiatic stork (*Ciconia ciconia asiatica*) roams the rice fields.

Fig. 14-28. Grapes in Central Asia.

Falco subbuteo is a predatory bird of the oases. Sparrows cause great damage to young crops and multiply in great numbers. The percentage of damage in the fields by sparrows may amount to 75 per cent of the harvest.

Of mammals there are the Baktriyskiy bat and Turkmenian red-brown bat, hedgehogs, several species of shrew, Turkestanian rats, and domestic Turkestanian mice. South of Samarkand is the lamellar-toothed rat (*Nesokia huttoni*). It does much harm to fields and stores, settling in the ground in colonies.

The Northern Deserts

The northern deserts of Central Asia differ from the southern deserts in their origin and ecological makeup. They are linked very closely with the deserts of Mongolia and possess many species of plants and animals indigenous to them. The hydrothermic regime of the northern deserts differs from that of the southern deserts. Owing to their northern location, they have a sharply expressed desert climate with high temperatures in summer and very severe winters. The amount of precipitation is small, but it is evenly distributed throughout the year, which results in a constantly low relative humidity. The northern deserts lack the spring maximum of precipitation that is characteristic of the southern deserts. The plant cover and soil-forming process are not of a pronounced seasonal character. The abundance of skeletal soil strongly influences plant life and lends uniformity to the soil-forming process. Thus the northern deserts are typical rocky deserts.

Owing to the uniform annual precipitation and to the comparatively slight evaporation, some moisture is retained in the soil during most of the growing season. Moreover, the minor precipitation contributes little to soil leaching and to elimination of mineral salts, processes that are detrimental to plant life. But the steady washing, slight as it is, balances the solonetz and solonchak processes and brings the character of the soil closer to that of the neighboring semi-desert zone. It distinguishes the soil from the soil of the southern deserts, which is devoid of this solonetz quality. Two notable features of the northern deserts are the pronounced complexity of the soil and plant cover and the effect this complexity has on the rate of development of vegetation (predominantly drought-resistant perennials). Growth is rather uniform, and ephemerals, so abundant in the southern loess deserts, are nearly absent.

The soil-forming process in the northern deserts develops under continental climatic conditions of hot summers and severe winters and of light, uniform precipitation. The slight but steady moistening (increased somewhat by the condensation of water vapor), the minor amount of leaching and downward movement of salts, and the absence of a seasonal character in the soil-forming process, results in a monotonous, level plain, with extremely weak runoff and uniformly loose alluvium.

The chemism and physical properties of the crust of young Tertiary and Cretaceous saliferous rocks are important to soil formation. The lime in the residual rock is practically inexhaustible, and there are considerable sulphates (gypsum). The surface of the soil is usually strewn with rubble and this contributes to the high absorption of precipitation. The easy downward washing of salts to bedrock prevents their removal by deflation and leaching of the upper layer. The steady carbonation and gypsiferousness of the surface and the pronounced arid hydrothermic regime cause rapid and diverse movement and redistribution of the salt within the soil. Seasonal changes in the movement of soil solutions are fundamentally a downward flow in the cold and somewhat moist winter and spring, and an upward flow in the hot summer and warm autumn.

The character of the relief and the insolation control the movement of soil solutions and the development of one or another type of soil formation. In warm areas the solonchak process predominates, whereas in shaded areas the solonetz process is more common. Salt-water accumulates in depressions, and they have a predominance of the solonchak process, but in raised areas salting of soil is inconspicuous. These factors give to the soil a mosaic quality— a rapid alternation of saline and nonsaline soil —which draws together the northern deserts and the semi-arid zone. Thus, the complexes of soil of the plains are uniform in relation to their morphology but extremely diverse in relation to their chemistry. Vegetation constantly suffers from a lack of moisture, the result of which is premature loss of leaves, curtailment of vegetation, and, consequently, a small humus content of the soil.

The basic landscape soil is a structural sierozem. Its mechanical composition is characterized by the abundance of soil skeleton and by a small amount of clayey and sandy-loam, fine soil which increases somewhat with depth. In

Fig. 14-29. Desert pavement called *khayma* on the flat surface of the Zaunguz Plateau: "ferul" trees in the foreground.

this soil the humus content in the upper horizons does not exceed 1 per cent, and it is distributed uniformly according to profile. An important characteristic of structural sierozem is the high content of calcium carbonate. The maximum of carbonates is contained in the upper layer (the result of plant activity), and the soil usually effervesces at the surface. The amount of carbonates gradually diminishes downward, which sharply distinguishes this soil from typical desert sierozem and from the light-chestnut soil of the semi-desert. In addition, a large amount of gypsum is found in the lower layers. The high content of calcium carbonate and the strong salinizing by sulphates are indications of old soil-forming processes under climatic conditions.

The structure of clayey or sandy loam sierozem is fairly uniform. At the top is a light-gray, porous, stratified, clayey crust. Beneath is a brown, slightly lumpy, packed layer showing abundant efflorescences of calcium carbonate. Next is a layer rich in gypsum deposits in the form of tufts and crusts on the rubble and even layers of gypsum. On Ust-Urt the gypsum layer is 6 to 10 feet thick. Sometimes the structural sierozem at the surface contains soda, which causes it to be saliferous; or it may contain a little soluble salt and have a tendency toward brackishness. The widespread solonetz soil of the northern deserts distinguishes the soil regime from the more solonchak soil of the southern deserts. Because of its mechanical and chemical composition, structural sierozem retards the normal development of vegetation.

The northern rocky deserts, with their severe climate, are even less favorable for the development of organic life than are the southern deserts. The following conditions are typical: extreme dryness of air and soil, due to the slight precipitation (sometimes less than in the Kara-Kum); severe winter cold; summer heat up to 117°F; and large yearly and daily amplitudes of air and soil temperatures. The absolute annual amplitude of the air temperature reaches 126 to 135°F. In Bet-Pak-Dala, in September, the soil warms to 107°F during the day and cools to 52°F in the evening. The severe climate is the cause of the uniformity of vegetation, its exceptional species poverty, and the distinct xerophytic character of squat semi-bushes that branch densely near the ground.

In the northern deserts there is almost no spring. The cold winter changes to hot summer in a very short time. The high summer temperatures, constantly cloudless skies, and prolonged dry winds contribute to the rapid loss of soil moisture. Vegetation experiences a shortage of moisture during the entire vegetative period, and the lack of seasonal precipitation leads to a uniform slow growth throughout the year. It gradually grows and gradually dies out toward winter under the influence of low temperatures, whereas in the southern loess deserts the growth of vegetation takes place in spring at a vigorous rate. In connection with this, ephemerals are not characteristic of the northern deserts; they are few in number and do not play a part in the composition of phytocoenoses and in the pasturing economy of the livestock breeder.

The vegetation comprises mainly drought-resistant, perennial semi-brushwoods and semi-bushes with a distinct xerophytic appearance. During the vegetative period the northern deserts retain uniform gray coloring and the few ephemerals are lost against this gray background. Plants whose roots penetrate into the strongly salted medium must have the capacity to endure the salinity. Certain species of the goosefoot family and some artemisias are typical plants.

The cheerless appearance of the desert is due not only to the gray tones of the vegetation but also to the thinness of the plant cover and its over-all impoverishment. The vegetation is so sparse that often there is more bare soil than soil covered by vegetation. The plant cover is thin throughout the year and does not change during its growth. In spite of the unfavorable climate and salty soil, the development of vegetation is maintained at the stage of open phytocoenoses. Large areas are bare of plant life and the process of growing-over takes place very slowly. In lowland areas the complexity of plant cover is clearly expressed: rapid and frequent alternation, even in small areas, of the different phytocoenoses influenced by slight variations of relief and soil. The vegetation is a polynomial complex. The structure of the several phytocoenoses is sometimes so simple that only one species takes part in them.

The northern deserts, like the southern ones, comprise clayey-rocky and sandy deserts. The northern clayey-rocky deserts are brushwood-halophytic, because of the predominance of the goosefoot family and artemisias. Three species of halophytes make up the vegetation of the northern deserts.

Despite the sparsity and rarity of the vegetative cover, these basic plants form different plant associations which have well-defined patterns that change from one to another, and have unusual structure. In basins, where solonchak and solonetz develops, the *Anabasis salsa* association is prevalent; on elevated sections, with slightly saliferous soil, artemisias predominate; the intermediate positions are characterized by the *Salsola arbuscula* association.

The *Anabasis salsa* is quite primitive and almost always is found alone, but sometimes with another halophyte—*Nanophyton.* Under different conditions *Anabasis salsa* varies from compact, flattened pillows to small, multi-branched bushes 4 to 5 inches high. It grows slowly, but is capable of settling on all soils and producing seeds. The annual shoots bear short, thick leaflets and single blossoms that thicken and store water (stem-succulent). The shoots remain green the entire growing season and die out completely to the base with the onset of the first autumn frost.

Nanophyton erinaceum is an unusual halophyte with fine, narrow leaflets. On Ust-Urt a similar halophyte, *Salsola gemmascens,* has underdeveloped leaves in the form of scales. There are few steady companions in this association. It occupies primarily the lowest sections of the relief, where clayey solonetz soil often is located. In spring the open soil areas are saturated by melting snow and become sticky; in summer they are compact and rock-hard. Plants are widespread, occurring mostly in small, irregularly shaped patches. The extent of surface

soil coverage does not exceed 10 to 20 per cent. Individual plants are scattered 2 feet or more from one another. These small, insignificant halophytes contrast with the taller bushes of *Salsola arbuscula* and artemisia surrounding them, and outwardly they appear to be a vegetation impoverished, struggling, and disappearing.

The artemisia association is as primitive and constant in composition as is *Anabasis salsa.* The gray *Artemisia terrae albae* is the most profuse plant. There are also the red-brown Turan artemisia (*A. turanica*), and *A. maikara,* an artemisia native to Bet-Pak-Dala, which is similar to black artemisia and is characteristic of the semi-desert zone. The growth of artemisias is very impoverished. They endure the most unfavorable time of year in a state of anabiosis, often losing their leaves in the hot summer; in fall they develop flowers. They are the main fodder of the northern desert pastures, playing the same role as sedge in the southern deserts. Artemisias are eaten by sheep, especially during the winter. They occupy elevated areas with fine, loose, and light soil. The covering of the soil with artemisia does not exceed 30 to 40 per cent. A few plants, of *koehia* are encountered among the *polyns* and bring a little variety to their thickets. Sometimes rare specimens of ephemerals are found.

Salsola arbuscula is a full-grown semi-brush-wood, 1 to 2 feet tall. Its bushes are situated 2 to 6 feet apart, but the extent of coverage of the soil is as high as 50 per cent. A few other plants, such as rhubarb, are admixed. Pure groups of *Salsola arbuscula* are also encountered. In the eastern part of Bet-Pak-Dala its usual species is replaced by the Mongolian-Siberian species, larchleafed saltwort (*Salsola laricifolia*) which grows on saliferous soil that is, to some degree, rocky. The yearly growth of *Salsola arbuscula* is small, and restoration takes place at a depressed rate. Its landscape is monotonous in its sameness, meagerness of colors, and seeming lifelessness.

The impoverished makeup and scantiness of ephemerals are a result of the slight moistening

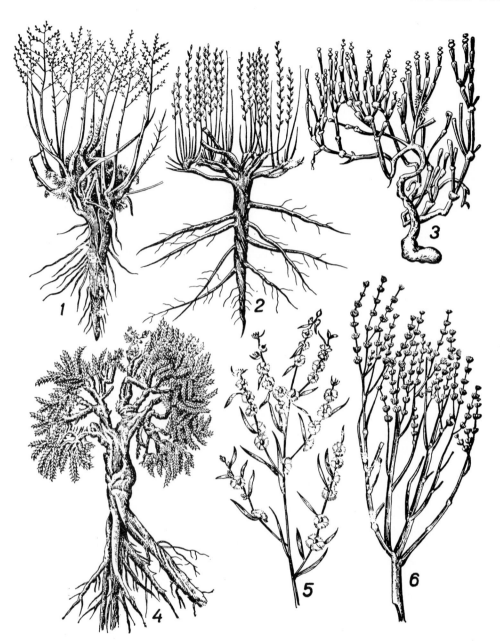

Fig. 14-30. Characteristic artemisia vegetation of clay deserts of the northern type in Central Asia. 1—*Artemisia terrae albae;* 2—*A. maikara;* 3—"Biyurgun" (*Anabasis salsa*); 4—Nanofiton (*Nanophyton erinaceum*); 5—Saltwort (*Salsola arbuscula*); 6—"Ittzegek" (*Anabasis aphylla*). (*Mounting by S. P. Suslov.*)

in summer, the comparatively low temperatures in spring, and the rockiness and solonetz nature of the soil, which is unfavorable for development of the hairlike rootlets of these plants.

In certain areas some variety is lent by tulips, onions, and spring grasses. Of the monocarpic plants a species of ferula, *Ferula paniculata,* is characteristic. Some depressions in Bet-Pak-

Dala are noted for their greenness and height of vegetation, which grows under comparatively favorable soil moistening. Spring water brings a certain amount of fine soil, and the soil is thicker and less rubbly. This creates an opportunity for the existence of vegetation which is richer in species composition and also more dense. Desert pea shrub (*Caragana grandiflora*) grows to a height of 30 inches. It forms dense thickets whose cover is almost continuous, and under the canopy of the scrub penetrate sod steppe grasses, such as feather grass and fescue. The Caragana grouping introduces a certain liveliness into the dismal desert plain. Solonetz soil is widespread everywhere but occupies comparatively small areas in the central parts of the depression. Here are the usual halophytic bushes, glasswort and saltwort. Solonetz soil bears a unique vegetation made up of chee grass.

The severe desert climate is also responsible for the impoverished makeup of fauna, the slight density of the animal population, and the characteristic daily cycle of their lives. The zoocoenosis is simple as illustrated by the realm of the animal world of the Bet-Pak-Dala Plain. The rocky plain is the kingdom of jerboas. There are many species of the genera *Alactaga, Alactagulus,* and *Scirtopoda* populating the entire desert. Since they are nocturnal animals they escape the high daytime temperatures. They travel rapidly, and, being good burrowers who have an excellent sense of smell, they can swiftly and easily cover much ground. They live primarily on the bulbs of tulips, which give them both food and water. Another burrower is the mole rat (*Ellobius*). Being an underground creature it avoids the unfavorable surface conditions of the desert. Its tunnels lie right at the depth of tulip bulbs.

In Bet-Pak-Dala grain-eating birds are entirely absent. The principal landscape bird is the desert warbler. Closer to the outskirts of the desert, sparrow and small lark are found. There are very few insects in the plain. Neither butterflies nor *Hymenoptera* are seen, and *Coleoptera* are very rare. Darkling beetles are abundant. Life in the oases of the Chu River valley is far richer: here are many waterfowl, insect-eating and predatory birds, and a number of mammals.

The migratory livestock economy necessarily conflicts with the lack of spring fodder, owing to the absence of ephemerals. Two things are essential: (1) the improvement of pasturing lands to increase their productivity, and (2) the introduction of new fodder plants from similar deserts of the world. Climatic conditions are oppressive for man: high temperatures during the day, with a sharp drop at night; the desiccating action of the air, with low relative humidity and strong winds; and the small amount of water, most of which contains laxative salts.

The northern sandy deserts are sharply distinguished from the adjacent clayey-rocky deserts and are rather widespread. Among the sandy deserts are the Big and Little Barsuki, the Pre-Aral Kara-Kum, the Muyun-Kum, and the Pre-Balkhash sand. Scattered over vast expanses, the sandy deserts are united by the unique physical properties of sand, which makes the development of its vegetation independent of local climatic differences. Therefore, conditions of life of the vegetation and its uniform composition for all the sandy deserts of Central Asia are understandable. The rather sharp climatic diversities and the different derivation of the vegetation of the northern and southern deserts are seen in the composition of the vegetation and in the change of plant associations during the fixing of the sand. Outwardly, the sand of the northern desert resembles that of the southern deserts. Semibrush vegetation consists of the same genera, but of different species. Kara-Kum saxaul (*Ammodendron conollyi*) is replaced in the Pre-Aral desert by a like species, *Ammodendron karelini,* and in the Pre-Balkhash sand by *Ammodendron sieversii.* Instead of the southern *Eremosparton flaccidum, E. aphyllum* is found. The same is true of many grassy plants. In the northern deserts some species of southern desert plants are absent (for example, those of the genus *Calligonum*), but many plants foreign to the southern desert are present, such as the rubberbearing Chondrilla, certain species of artemisia, chee grass, and ephedra (*Ephedra lomatolepis*), an excellent fixer of the sand of the Pre-Balkhash.

In the northern deserts sod grasses are instrumental in securing the sand. The first stage of this process duplicates that of the southern sandy deserts, but in the final phase, sod grasses —couch grass (*Agropyron sibiricum*), and feather grass (*Stipa hohenackeriana*)—play a large role. Being situated fairly close to one another, they form a compact sod and cover at least 50 per cent of the soil surface. Among them are scattered annuals and sand sedge. The more compact the sand the more prevalent are desert semi-brushwoods in the vegetation composition. Fixed sand enriched by clay particles is not suitable for typical sand-loving plants, but is covered with artemisia.

In the Muyun-Kum village of Alekseyevka precipitation is as follows: winter, 1.3 inches; spring, 1.7 inches; summer, 0.8 inch; autumn, 1.6 inches, and annual, 5.4 inches. Whereas in the Kara-Kum there is a thick layer of dry sand beneath the soil, and the grassy vegetation of the mound sand is burned out by the sun in May, in the Muyun-Kum green moist sand lies just below the surface, and feather grass and other plants bloom in June.

The soil-forming material is feldspar, quartz sand, highly washed and scattered and almost completely leached of easily soluble chlorous salts and sulphates but rather rich in elements of ash. The fine, rich humus layer of the soil on sand is a pale brownish color; below this is a yellowish, straw-colored carbonate layer, with concretions of lime. This fertile soil is closer to brown soil than to gray soil, though the solonetz quality is very weakly expressed because of the light mechanical composition and the leaching of the parent rock. There is also a bog-meadow type of soil in depressions, and a series of salinized solonchak-meadow, solonchak and desalinized solonetz, and clay soils.

The distribution of the vegetation of Muyun-Kum demonstrates (1) the change from south to north from grassy and semi-brushwood veg-

etation to brushwood and woody vegetation (saxaul), and (2) the distribution of the main vegetative groupings in narrow latitudinal belts.

In the southern part of the northern deserts, on the ridge-mound sand having silt-covered depressions and ground water at depths of not less than 50 to 60 feet, varigrass-artemisia growths are widespread on brown soil. The complex character of the relief and the rapid change in the mechanical composition of the soil control the diversified distribution of plant associations. In the silt-covered depressions are many grassy and semi-brushwood species peculiar to the loess deserts, such as sand sedge (*Carex pachystylis*) and iris (*Iris songorica*), forming a solid, squat cover. Along the slopes, on brown soil less enriched by fine soil, sandy-steppe species predominate: red *Artemisia scoparia,* wheat grass (*Agropyron sibiricum*), feather grass (*Stipa hohenackeriana*), and higher up camphoric *Artemisia leucodes* and wild rye (*Secale fragile*). On the loose sand of the ridge- and mound-tops there are semi-brush-woods of the sandy desert—*Calligonum caput medusae,* or *Stellera stachyoides.*

Farther north, amid hillocky relief with a gentle profile of mounds and basins, lies a zone of calligonum groves, with unequal vertical distribution of ground water. Under sandy mounds the water lies at a depth of 100 to 130 feet, under lengthwise depressions 2 to 10 feet, and where the depression widens, the ground water often emerges onto the surface and forms ponds. Scattered along the sand hills, at times uniformly and at times in groups, are sturdy bushes of calligonum amid a uniform background of ephedra (*Ephedra lomatolepis*) and wild rye. In the depressions, where the ground water is close to the surface and is almost fresh in spring and summer, are meadow grass-vari-grass associations with reed, ephedra, astragal (*Astragalus lanuginosus*), and heliotrope (*Heliotropium dasycarpum*). The depressions are valuable economic land additions. They have large stands of grass that is good for mowing. They permit the sowing of young crops of lucerne and other fodder plants and the planting of willow and black alder. The level relief and compactness of the soil invite completely mechanized plowing, sowing, and hay cutting.

In the central part of Muyun-Kum, on the old terrace of the river Chu, with ground water not higher than 15 to 30 feet, the vegetation is uniform but very limited in variety. The basic background is made up of Old World winter fat (*Eurotia ceratoides*) and astragal (*Astragalus brachypus*), in addition to wheat and feather grass. These winter fat areas are valuable grazing lands and provide watering places for sheep and camels. In the northern part of Muyun-Kum, where ground water is at a depth of 23 to 33 feet, is a belt of dense, virgin thickets of white saxaul (*Haloxylon persicum*). On the more-silted brown soil of the undulating plain, where there is fresh or slightly salty water at a depth of 30 to 50 feet, is a zone of black saxaul forests (*Haloxylon aphyllum*). An essential measure in restoring the highly exploited saxaul groves is the sowing of seeds in the loosened soil on the sites that have been cleared of stumps.

Muyun-Kum is spotted with lakes and grassy meadows. It has an inexhaustible supply of fresh ground water, and large areas of fertile soil offering the opportunity for development of dry-farming and irrigation agriculture (cotton, wheat). Within the desert are vast fodder resources and large supplies of firewood in the saxaul groves.

On the sandy areas of Tau-Kum, Sary-Ishik-Otrau, and Lyuk-Kum, where mound-ridge relief predominates, and also on ridge sand of the Bakanas Plain, the adaptation of plant associations to definite elements of relief is well expressed. The most important plants on the ridge tops are white or sand saxaul (*Haloxylon persicum*) and *Calligonum,* with a sparse cover of the usual grassy psammophytes. On the ridge slopes the vegetation is denser. Here are green *Artemisia songorica,* wheat grass (*Agropyron sibiricum*), and winter fat (*Eurotia ceratoides*). The maximum turfing-over is observed on well-consolidated sandy soil of the interridge depressions, where the predominating grouping is gray *Artemisia terrae albae,* ephe-

dra (*Ephedra lomatolepis*), sand sedge (*Carex physodes*), and *Kochia prostrata*. On clay areas grow such bushes as *Anabasis salsa* and Turkmenian saltwort.

The southern coastal belt of Lake Balkhash, with a width of several miles, has a singular water regime because of periodic inundation by the water of the lake. The shore line is notched by numerous bays, jutting far into the land and alternating with sandy ridges, sand bars, and mounds. On the ridges of looser sand grow winter fat, three-awn (*Aristida pennata*), and artemisia. Along the slopes grow *Alhagi kirghisorum,* and salt tree (*Halimodendron argenteum*), and at the base of the ridges runs a narrow belt of reeds. Interridge depressions covered with swollen solonchak or continuous efflorescences of salts are for the most part devoid of vegetation; only along the outskirts does one encounter Turkmenian saltwort, glasswort (*Salicornia herbacea*), and *Suaeda crassifolia*.

The broad valley of the lower Ili River has three well-expressed terraces. Along the first is a narrow strip of *tugai* with dense thickets of wild olive (*Elaeagnus angustifolia*) and willow (*Salix songorica, S. gmelini*), intertwined by thick networks of clematis (*Clematis orientalis*). Under the forest canopy is a formation of brushwoods made up of barberry (*Berberis integerrima*), honeysuckle (*Lonicera coerulea*), salt tree, and grasses equal in height to the brushwoods—meadow grass (*Poa pratensis*) and licorice (*Glycyrrhiza uralensis*). Beyond the belt of *tugai* begin the flooded vari-grass—beach-grass meadows with an average height of grass-stand of 3 to 5 feet. The second terrace, with a width of several miles and with ground water at a depth of 9 to 13 feet, is occupied by dry vari-grass—beach-grass, artemisia, sedge, and licorice meadows. In the low spots are swamped meadows with reed, and on elevated sections are solonchak meadows with *Aeluropus littoralis*. The third terrace, rising beyond the limits of the floods, is covered with artemisias and halophytes: *Nitraria schoeberi, Halocnemum strobilaceum,* and tamarisk (*Tamarix hispida*). The enormous delta of the Ili River has numerous meandering channels and a varying discharge of water. In the delta, the channels alternate with lakes, salt marshes, sections of ridge sand with winter fat and sand saxaul, and bog expanses with dense thickets of reeds.

The main occupation in the desert of southern Pre-Balkhash is livestock raising. The grassy vegetation of the valleys is the most important source of fodder. Four essentials for an increase of the fodder base are: (1) storing ensilage of coarse fodders, (2) mowing reeds before ripening, (3) gathering foliage fodder, and (4) sowing grass, especially lucerne. Exploitation of the saxaul groves and the cultivation of the rubber plant chondrilla (*Chondrilla ambigua* var. *crassifolia*) are also of some importance. In the delta of the Ili there are large thickets of Indian hemp (*Apocynum lancifolium*), and dry-farming and irrigation agriculture are developed. The high summer temperatures and the long frost-free period ensure the growth of valuable agricultural crops—rice, lucerne, and early ripening varieties of cotton.

CHAPTER 15

Mountain Region of Central Asia

The mountainous region of Central Asia, lying in the belt of mountains and plateaus stretching from the Atlantic to the Pacific Ocean, is the highest in the USSR. It is marked by sharp contrasts in elevation and an extremely complicated geologic structure, and is a part of one of the most seismic areas of the world. The climate is strongly influenced by the adjacent lowland deserts and the high elevations, which have produced vast areas of permanent snow, large glaciers, and deep mountain lakes. The turbulent mountain rivers, which have great water-power potentialities, provide the water for irrigation of productive foothill plains and large valley terraces. A unique floral and zoogeographic region, it is also characterized by exceptional variety of geographic landscapes and by features of vertical zonality, repeated nowhere else in the USSR.

The peculiarities of the orographic layout reflect on the structure and distribution of geographic landscapes. The systems of independent ranges extend in an approximately east-west direction for thousands of miles, and are divided by narrow longitudinal depressions, often of tectonic origin. There are also transverse ranges, such as Fergana, Ak-Shiyrak, and Akademiya Nauk, connecting the longitudinal ones. Between the main systems of ranges lie large intermountain depressions, such as the Fergana, Naryn, Issyk-Kul, and Ili depressions, which are covered by a series of old and recent alluviums. The systems of ranges are in long arcs, grouped in a concentric series. During repeated folding, the most intensive tectonic pressure was in the central convex parts of the arcs, where folds were steeply and highly elevated. To the sides, where the lateral pressure was weaker, there was less dislocation. Therefore, the mountain chains along the periphery are wider and lower, and gradually branch out and merge with the surrounding plains. The plunging of the axis of the main folds to the west at different distances causes the echelon-like grouping of the ranges.

Many mountain ranges diverge, with decreasing elevation, eastward and westward from the highest mountain centers. Examples are Stalin Peak in the Akademiya Nauk Range (24,590 feet) and the mountain center of Matcha at the source of the Zeravshan. Two mountain systems form arcs convex to the south: Tien Shan in the north and Alayskiy Mountains in the south. In the east, both systems are high and narrow ranges of Kungei Ala-Tau and Terskey Ala-Tau with maximum elevations up to 13,200 feet and Alayskiy Range 19,800 feet. In the west, the ranges fan out so that the northern branches (Kara-Tau and Nura-Tau) change from a latitudinal to a northwest direction, and the southern branches bend in a southwestern (Chatkal) or a southern (Karategin) direction. The central ranges maintain their latitudinal direction.

In the extreme south, beginning at the Trans-Alai Range (with its highest point, Lenin Peak at 23,382 feet), lies the great Pamir-Ali system which has a series of mountain arcs, convex to the north. The dividing of the mountain systems is clearly shown not only on orographic maps, but also on geological maps, by the cur- vature of petrographic formations. As a result of these characteristics of orography, the moun- tain system remains exposed only on the west- ern side. Detached from the main system are two mountain districts: Dzungarian Ala-Tau and Kopet Dagh.

GEOLOGIC HISTORY

From the beginning of the Paleozoic through the middle of the Tertiary Period, there was a warm inland basin, the so-called Tethis Sea, on the site of the present-day mountain region. In this sea, a large geosyncline, with great masses of marine sediments, accumulated. The lateral pressures of the adjacent rigid massifs raised this plastic geosyncline from beneath the surface of the sea to form the large-scale mountain chains. Tectonic movements oc-

curred repeatedly. As a result, parts of the geosyncline were gathered into folds and were not raised simultaneously to form mountainous dry land. As the sea fell back more and more, dry-land development took place from north to south.

Caledonian (lower Paleozoic) folding in- creased the amount of dry land in the north, forming the northern ranges of Tien Shan. During the Lower Devonian Period, the shore line of the sea was more or less stationary; but beginning with the Upper Devonian Period, the sea moved farther and farther to the north. Subsequently, intense Variscan (upper Paleo- zoic) folding once more forced the rapid and over-all withdrawal of the sea from the south. At this time the central ranges were formed and the northern ranges were somewhat recon- structed. In this mountainous region, a conti- nental regime began to prevail. Kimeridagian (Mesozoic) folding was weakly manifested. As a result of epeirogenic subsidences during the Mesozoic Era, the sea penetrated into the peripheral parts of the already formed moun- tain region. Countless shallow lagoons, lakes, and swamps formed in the depressions of the mountain relief, and sometimes the sea also entered. The climate in the Triassic and Juras- sic periods was moist and warm, contributing to the development of Jurassic seas and, in the coastal zone, of luxuriant vegetation composed of woody horsetails and ferns, various palms, conifers, and gingkos, the remains of which served as material for the formation of brown coal. Triassic deposits have a continental and lagoon varicolored schistous-sandstone series, often gypsiferous. Carboniferous deposits of

Fig. 15-1. Stalin Peak, elevation 24,590 feet, the tallest summit in the USSR.

the Lower Jurassic are encountered only in individual, isolated strips and patches. The continental land and fresh-water Mesozoic strata, lying unconformably on the Paleozoic strata, are distinguished from the latter by their porousness, by the variegated reddish tints, and by the absence of metamorphism.

In the Upper Jurassic Period, the transgression of the sea reached its maximum. This is indicated by the Upper Jurassic massive limestones which were the typical great barrier reefs, although continental red sandstones and conglomerates are also encountered. The red color of the continental Lower Cretaceous series, with deposition of clays, marls, and limestones, and without vegetative remnants, indicate that the moist subtropical climate of the Jurassic Period was replaced by a dry desert regime. During this dry regime the fresh-water basins dried up and the rich Jurassic flora perished. Deserts were baked by the sun and covered with a mantle of rubble and sand as a result of intense physical weathering. In the Upper Cretaceous and in the Paleocene and Eocence periods, the sea once again burst into the outskirts of the dry land, as manifested by the presence of marine sediments. Towards the Neocene the mountains were greatly lowered, modified, and converted into a near-plain (a peneplain) of the Kazakh folded country type.

With the beginning of the Neocene Period, a new stage in the geologic history began— alpine folding, which created the southern mountain chains from Mesozoic and Tertiary marine sediments. Alpine folding began in the northern ranges with powerful, tangential fractures and great block upheavals, together with which the peneplained sections of the older relief were uplifted.

Flat-topped denuded ranges, even at present, are well preserved south of Lake Issyk-Kul, in the Chatkal Range and in the Dzungarian Ala-Tau. Because of the different scale of the uplift, the old denuded surfaces are found in various parts of the country at different elevations. Along with the upheavals, there were also subsidences of various-sized depressions enclosed between the ranges. The products of disintegration were carried by the mountain rivers and deposited on the plain, near the base of the mountains as gigantic alluvial fans. These fans, which are as thick as 6,600 feet, consist of conglomerate, sandstone, and, more rarely, clay and marl. The alluvial fans merge with one another, forming a solid zone of deposits extending along the base of ranges for hundreds of miles. The bending of young deposits of gravels and the occurrence of strong earthquakes are evidence that mountain-forming processes are continuing today.

The mountain region of Central Asia consists of many various parts which can be distinguished both by age and genesis and by external appearance. A comparison of these parts with each other reveals three broad zones of mountain ranges: the northern arcs, or Tien Shan; the central arcs, or Alai; and the southern arcs, or Pamir. Since these zones gradually merge into each other, sharp boundaries between them are usually absent.

Northern Arcs

The northern arcs were formed mainly by strong Caledonian and relatively weak Variscan folding. There was no later folding. The arcs thus formed are convex to the south, because the pressure came from the north. The northern arcs were formed by highly dislocated and metamorphosed marine deposits of the Lower and Middle Paleozoic. They consist of thick strata of limestone, shale, and sandstone and continental deposits of sandstone-shale and extrusive-tuff of the Upper Paleozoic. Among these strata are small strips and patches of continental Mesozoic and Tertiary deposits. Thus, the continental sediments begin from the Upper Paleozoic. Great masses of Lower Paleozoic granites are widespread, but young intrusions are unknown. Alpine folding appeared, manifested exclusively by tectonic breaks and block movements. The folded arcs were broken into a series of blocks by many large tectonic cracks of lengthwise and transverse direction, and were moved almost vertically. The Paleozoic blocks carried with them the Upper Cretaceous and Paleocene deposits to a height of more than 6,600 feet. Sometimes the upheavals of the blocks were accompanied by lateral movement and overthrust onto adjacent, less-uplifted blocks, which led to the crumpling of Mesozoic and Paleocene deposits in the zone of their contact. These young raised blocks created the modern high-elevation relief of the northern arc which exist now as highly uplifted plateaus and the remnants of inclined peneplained surfaces. Thus the high-elevation relief may be considered only as rejuvenated, in contrast to the young relief of the southern arcs. The southern border of the northern arcs runs approximately from the base of the Nura-Tau Mountains, north of Leninabad, along the northern edge of the Fergana depression, continuing along the valley of the Naryn River, and to the mountain massif Khan-Tengri (22,-949 feet).

Central Arcs

The central arcs were formed as a result of intense Variscan folding, while Caledonian folding was only weakly developed. Since the lateral pressure, warping Paleozoic seams and folds, came from the north, the displacement of mountain masses was southward. The displacement was greatest in the central part of the folded zone, then decreased toward the periphery. There is a pronounced arc-shaped curve, with the bulge toward the south, along most mountainous ranges of Tien Shan and also along the trend of zones of the separate petrographic formations. Paleozoic beds were highly crumpled and formed diversified intricate folds, often isoclinal and inverted. The sedimentary rocks composing these folds were also subjected to strong metamorphism: clay shales were converted to crystalline slates, and limestones were changed to marbles. Folding was accompanied by numerous intrusions of granites, in the contact zones of which, in some districts, intensive mineralization oc-

curred. Mesozoic and alpine folding were comparatively weak. Under the influence of alpine folding, the structure of the central arcs became more complex. As the Mesozoic and Paleocene were intensively dislocated, the complexity of distortion to the south increased. This folding found expression also in the formation of faults. Here, the entire Paleozoic is represented by highly dislocated marine sediments; weakly dislocated rocks of the Mesozoic and Paleocene are represented by both marine and continental deposits; and only the Miocene and Pliocene are purely continental. Quaternary deposits are horizontal with the exception of small flexure curves in the foothills of the ranges and along the edges of the great valleys (Fergana). All intrusions, as relatively small islands, are Variscan. The southern boundary of the central arc passes approximately along the Zeravshan River to its upper sources, farther on along the Alayskiy Valley to Kashgar, and along the outskirts of the Tarim depression.

Southern Arcs

The southern arcs acquired their modern appearance as a result of intense alpine folding, which has destroyed most of the older folding. Variscan and Kimeridgian foldings show distinctly, but are comparatively weak. Alpine folding was strong, both in duration and in complexity of tectonic movements and forms. Many stages are noted, the most marked of which is the stage at the boundary of the Upper and Lower Tertiary. Mesozoic and Tertiary marine sediments are gathered here over the whole expanse into gigantic steep folds, in which even the Paleozoic participates. The folds, which embrace the Paleozoic and Mesozoic, are often isoclinal and even overturned, broken into separate parts, and overthrust on one another, forming real shearings and overlaps. The intensity and scope of folding increase in a southerly direction, reaching greatest development in the Pamir. All the rocks, as a result of folding, are highly metamorphosed, so that Upper Cretaceous limestone is sometimes indistinguishable from Paleozoic in outer appearance. Alpine folding was accompanied by many recent volcanic eruptions and intrusions. As a result of alpine folding, marine chalk of the Paleocene (for example, in the Trans-Alai Range) was raised to a height of more than 16,500 feet, into the region of permanent snows. Even Miocene and Pliocene conglomerates in the Darvaza Range, in places, are found above the snow line. At the time of the alpine folding, the pressure, in contrast with that in the more northern arcs, issued from the south, and thus the mountain masses were displaced to the north. The distinct arc-shaped curve, convex to the north, of petrographic formations and mountain ranges is visible. Weaker upheavals took place even after the Miocene Period, which is why Quaternary deposits are dislocated in places. In the southern arcs all deposits, with the exception of the Upper Tertiary, are marine; in the western section masses of marine Mesozoic and Lower Tertiary are widespread; in the Pamir the rocks are diversified, from ancient metamorphic strata to the Upper Tertiary, and there are great areas of granites.

MINERAL RESOURCES

The mountain region of Central Asia is a rich source of ore and nonmetallic minerals. The ample and diversified mineralization and the regularity of distribution are linked with four noncontemporary geochemical processes: (1) alpine tectonic movements with their recent intrusions of granite were accompanied by an accumulation of molybdenum, iron, gold, polymetals, antimony, mercury, and arsenic; (2) resources linked with the accumulation of sediments in the Jurassic, Cretaceous, and Tertiary seas and with their subsequent redevelopment include all the commercially important coal, all the oil, the main bulk of table salt and potash, native sulphur, gypsum, and phosphate rock; (3) the large-scale processes of Variscan folding produced such elements as iron, copper, zinc, and silver; and (4) the older formations were accompanied by zones of pyritic deposits.

The copper ores of the Amalyk formation are linked with porphyries and are similar to the ores of Kounrad in Kazakh. These reserves are second largest in the USSR. Ores of the Kara-Mazar district contain not only silver-lead-zinc but combinations of arsenic and bismuth. Reserves of lead and zinc amount to several hundred thousand tons. The Amalyk reserves are connected with contacts of Paleozoic limestone with granite and tectonic fissures in intrusive rocks. There are many unstudied and unexplored iron-ore deposits of various types—for example, the contact deposits of magnetite in the Mogol-Tau Range (western Fergana). There are also minor but important deposits of rare metals such as antimony, mercury, arsenic, bismuth, cadmium, wolfram, and molybdenum. Along the northern foothills of the Alayskiy Range is concentrated a group of mercury-antimony deposits (Khaidarkan). Of some importance is the gold of conglomerates and greenstone metamorphic schists of western Pamir.

The sedimentary complex of rocks with which coal, oil, rock salt, potassium salts, sulphur, and phosphorites are associated is especially interesting. In Fergana the deposits of coal and oil encompass the valley in a semicircle open to the west. Along the periphery are patches of Jurassic carboniferous deposits, and closer to the center of the valley are comparatively modest oil deposits associated with shell limestone of the Eocene. Known coal reserves amount to 3 billion tons, the bulk of which is the noncoking type of brown coal. The lignite of the Shurab coal district in Fergana has high heat value, small ash content, slight sulphur content, and is a fuel of high quality. In the lower part of the deposit there is a seam of pure coal 33 to 50 feet thick. The Zeravshan coal region, and particularly the Kahtut-Zaurak formation, is of great economic importance.

In the district east of Kerki Mountain on the Amu-Darya are the large Gaurdak deposits of native sulphur (with reserves of several million tons which have large salt stocks) and the Okuz-Bulak deposit of potassium salts. In the Stalinabad district the reserves of phosphorites amount to several million tons. Along a zone of deep tectonic breaks is a series of hot mineral springs: the radioactive springs of Khodzha-Obi-Garm, the sulphur springs of Vakhsh-Obi-Garm (east of Stalinabad), and the alkaline springs of Ak-Su near Mount Przhevalsk. With the nearness of great supplies of water power to mineral resources, the mining industry in a number of districts of Central Asia will continue to grow.

GLACIATION

Early Glaciation

In the Ice Age the mountain ranges of Central Asia were subjected to glaciation, traces of which are widespread, especially in Pamir, because of the severe climate and small amount of precipitation. Although, in contrast to the Alps or the Altai, the older glaciation is on a smaller scale than the modern, in individual districts glaciation was heavy. In the Pamir, in the Murgab Valley, a glacier 144 miles long received more than 55 tributary glaciers, some of which were 48 miles long. The depression of Lake Kara-Kul contained a large glacial mantle of the Scandinavian type. At this time the snow line was at the level of the lake. The drop in the snow line (in comparison with the modern snow line) of approximately 1,980 to 2,640 feet, and within the region even to 1,320 to 1,650 feet, is indicated by the spread of relic glacial forms. The lower limit of the old glaciers was along the northern slope of Turkestan Range at 6,930 to 7,260 feet, whereas present-day glaciers end at 7,975 to 11,484 feet. Although two basic glacial ages have been established for the mountains of Central Asia, three to four phases of glaciation are clearly noted in the Pamir.

Typical glacial forms of relief have been well preserved in many places. Broad U-shaped glacial valleys, with flat-concave bottoms, with comparatively small gradients, and in some places with the shoulders of the glacial trough, are observed in the upper reaches of many rivers where energetic erosion has not yet occurred. Some of the valley sides have one or more notches, often very high (to 990 feet), on which the rivers form waterfalls. But such glacial forms as hanging-side valleys, rocks polished by ice, and sheepbacks are relatively seldom encountered. At the bottom of glacial troughs old terminal moraines have survived, sometimes in several rows. Closer to the ends of the modern glaciers, the moraines are more recent, having preserved their typical morphologic features. The older moraines are deeply eroded and converted into an irregular accumulation of small hills. With further erosion by water and wind, the fine soil of these hills is carried away, and only an accumulation of rubble and large boulders remains of the moraine. In the middle of the moraine landscape are dammed high-altitude lakes, such as Issyk-Kul or Iskander-Kul. The upper parts of the mountain slopes contain gouged-out cirques, creating sharp-toothed crests typical of the high-elevation relief. There are modern active cirques which contain firn fields and small glaciers. At the lower levels are inactive old cirques, devoid of firn and revealing signs of extinction. They are losing the steepness of their sides and are being filled with rubble. The islands of relic permafrost, found on the water divides south of Issyk-Kul and in the Pamir, are linked with the older glaciation. Associated with Quaternary glaciation is the development in all the larger valleys of several rows of river terraces which indicate the alternation of periods of increased accumulation and energetic river erosion. The formation in the foothills of masses of Central Asiatic loess has been connected with the glacial and post-glacial period.

Modern Glaciation

The climate and the orography of the mountain region of Central Asia contribute to the accumulation of permanent snow and large glaciers. The glaciers, the water reserves of the Central Asian republics, are the basic source of rivers and thus determine their water regimes. They play a tremendous role in the irrigation of the deserts and mountain valleys and in the development of water power.

The snow line is much higher than in the Caucasus or in the Alps. A great difference may also be noted in the height of the snow line on slopes of opposite exposure. In the eastern part of the highland (for example, in the Terskey Ala-Tau), the snow line varies 990 to 1,650 feet between the northern and southern slopes; in the western ranges (Alayskiy), it varies 2,310 to 2,640 feet. From the zone of peripheral mountain ranges (with a relatively low snow line, 9,900 to 11,880 feet) to the mountain region to the southeast, the height of the snow line rapidly rises, reaching a maximum (18,150 feet) in the Pamir. In the latter, the height of the snow line exceeds that of the peripheral ranges by as much as 6,600 feet. The relationship of the height of snow line and the massiveness of the mountain system is nowhere as prominent as in Central Asia. Owing to the high elevation of the snow line in the central Tien Shan, mountain passes even above 13,200 feet are free of snow in summer.

The number of glaciers in Central Asia (not counting cirque and hanging glaciers) totals approximately 1,700, with valley glaciers predominating. Glaciers cover approximately 418

Fig. 15-2. Valley glacier of the Constitution Mountains in the Zaili Ala-Tau.

square miles; that is, glaciation here exceeds the area of glaciation of the Caucasus five times. Glaciation bears a diffused character. However, individual accumulations of glaciers and firn fields, corresponding to the predominant orographic centers stand out: Stalin Peak area, Khan Tengri, Trans-Alai, Matcha, Ak-Shiyrak, and the Chilik-Kebinskiy mountain pass.

The glaciation of the complex Stalin Peak mountain center is surrounded on all sides by arid regions. The role of relief in glacial development—as judged by not only the great height and the transverse orientation (in regard to the moist air currents), but also the surface features—is clearly delineated. In the flat main basin of Fedchenko Glacier, the accumulation of snow is tremendous because the transverse range, Akademiya Nauk, intercepts almost all

precipitation-bearing air currents coming from the west. The Fedchenko Glacier is the largest in the USSR. Extending north from Yazgulem-skiy Pass, it has a length of 46 miles, width of 3 miles, and thickness of 1,815 feet. The glacier, with its tributaries, contains more than 2,600,-000,000 cubic yards of ice. Fedchenko Glacier does not have a definite cirque from which the entire mass of ice discharges, but in the upper parts of the waterdivides is a solid firn cover that produces individual glacial flows. The maximum elevation at the glacier head is 17,-589 feet, and its terminal elevation is 9,583 feet. Fedchenko Glacier receives 37 tributaries, 6 of which are more than six miles long (for example, the glaciers Nalivkin, Vitkovski, Akademiya Nauk). In the upper part of the glacier, the zones of lateral and middle moraines are narrow and thin; there is more pure ice than

Fig. 15-3. Evidence of glacial "karst" on the edge of the Lower Zeravshan glacier, which is covered by a large moraine.

Fig. 15-4. The Petrov Valley glacier. The surface is dissected with deep funnel-like crevasses, usually filled with water.

moraine. Below, the ridges draw together more and more, and the strips of ice between them narrow and taper out along the downward course. For the last four miles, the glacier is covered with a solid moraine mantle. The complex interweaving of valleys, gorges, and mountain ridges has led to the formation of large and branching glaciers, such as Fortambek (15 miles), Finstervaldera (9.6 miles), and Garmo (17.4 miles). Precipitation in the firn area of Fedchenko Glacier reaches 40 inches, but to the east only 8 to 10 inches. And in the eastern Pamir, where glaciation is very slight, there is only a few inches of precipitation. The modern glaciers of eastern Pamir are confined to the greatest heights or are hidden in deep gorges. Predominating sharply in number are the semi-hanging (up to 1 mile long), hanging, and cirque glaciers.

Descending west, east, and southeast from the Khan Tengri peaks are long tongues of ice flows, occupying, with their firns, hundreds of square miles. At the source of the Inylchek River is the largest glacier in this locality,

Inylchek Glacier, 39 miles long and 1,320 feet thick. It receives more than 30 tributaries, some as much as nine miles in length. Owing to the thick fan of moraine material (up to 330 feet), which prevents thawing, the glacier descends rather low (9,513 feet). Trans-Alai has many glaciers. There are large accumulations of ice and firn fields in the massif Korundy (21,829 feet), Zarya Vostoka Peak (20,945 feet), and Lenin Peak (23,519 feet). The Matcha center, with Obryv Mountain (18,668 feet), where the Alayskiy, Turkestan, and Zeravshan ranges converge, is the focus of glaciation in this part of the region. Zeravshan Glacier, 15 miles long and about 660 feet thick, occupies the upper part of the long valley between the Turkestan and Zeravshan ranges. The transverse range Ak-Shiyrak also has heavy glaciation: both its inner parts and its slopes are covered by an unbroken sheet of ice and firn. Firns of the central part of the mountain massif are the source of a number of glaciers. The largest of these, Petrov Glacier, is 78 miles long. In the Chilik-Kebinskiy cen-

Fig. 15-5. A hanging glacier.

ter, partly connecting the Zaili Ala-Tau with the Kungei Ala-Tau, are many glaciers with an over-all area of 64.6 square miles, of which the greatest is the glacier Korzhenevski with a length of 8.4 miles, lying in the basin of the left sources of the Chilik River.

Glaciation in Central Asia is dying out at faster rates than have ever been observed in the Caucasus or the Alps. The clearly expressed features of degradation have resulted in an exceptional diversity of glacier types. The widespread valley glaciers are so different from the glaciers of other mountain districts that they are singled out as a special Turkestan variety. These glaciers may be considered as valley glaciers which are in a stage of expiration. The firns feeding glaciers of this type are disproportionately small in comparison with the long glacial tongues, the areas of

which exceed the firn areas several times (for example, by eight times at Zeravshan Glacier). The chief glacier is maintained, in the absence of a normal firn basin, by the ice of many tributaries, and the feeding of the latter is accomplished almost exclusively by avalanches. Some glaciers are fed by only the snow-covered (northern) slope, the opposite slope being free of snow. Glaciers are predominantely of the dendritic type, with a multitude of intricate side tributaries which meet in the main valley and contribute to the elongation of the tongue.

A variety of indications of glacier degradation are evident. The upper parts of some glaciers lie below the snow line; many descend as much as 1,980 feet lower than would be expected, issuing from the modern firn line. Many lateral tributaries do not reach the main glacier, and sometimes the separate flows of a glacier and its tributaries are observed in their common channel. Glaciers frequently do not touch the sides of the valley but lie as though without banks. Some glaciers are receding sideways, leaving along their sides a wide expanse of bottom. Characteristically the glacial tongues terminate in an extensive development of dead ice and an almost solid covering of thick moraine. The lower quarter or third of many glaciers is so covered by rock fragments that the surface of the ice is not visible. This abundance of rock material is at least partly the result of intense weathering of the mountain slopes surrounding the glaciers, associated with sharp fluctuations in temperature, amounting to as much as 90 degrees. The solid moraine mantle may extend as far as 12 miles (on Inylchek Glacier) and may reach a thickness of 330 feet. Moraine accumulations create a "confusion" of hills, depressions, and ridges.

Characteristic of the ends of glacial tongues, with their masses of dead, immovable ice, are the *glacial karst*—breaks, pockets, and sinkholes, brought about by the extensive development of subglacial streams, caverns, and lakes in the ice. There are also many lakes on the surface of the glacier. The water accumulated in summer under the moraines or in lakes on the glaciers often breaks through and, carrying blocks of ice along, bursts into the valleys. The thick mantle of moraine has up to now favored the preservation of glacial tongues beneath its mass as outliers, severed from their firns.

Valley glaciers are comparatively widespread with an enormous firn cirque, but with a short, seemingly severed tongue; the ratio between cirque and tongue may amount to 15 to 1. A typical representative is the Petrov Glacier. Because of the absence of lateral tributaries, it has a clean surface free of moraine accumulations. Since the thicker tongue of the glacier was not protected at the surface by moraine accumulations, the glacier rapidly began to die out. The degradation of glaciers of this type leaves the old cirque containing several small glaciers situated radially (for example, on the southern slope of the Peter the First Range). Hanging glaciers, because of their shortness and their undeveloped tongues, hang with their entire masses on the slopes and do not reach the valley bottoms.

The dynamics of the glaciers of Central Asia are extremely peculiar. The extraordinary summer dryness and warmth bring about energetic melting of the ice. For example, the

Fig. 15-6. Alpine forms of relief of the Peter First Ridge; in front, a large ice field.

surface of Zeravshan Glacier melts 1.8 inches per 24 hours and that of a glacier of the Muk-Su River system melts from 2.4 inches per day in July to approximately 0.5 inch per day in October, that is, about 16.5 feet a year. The rates of movement of the glaciers are different: Fedchenko Glacier about 11 inches per 24-hour

period (or about 330 feet a year), Semënov Glacier about 3.3 feet (or about 1,204 feet per year). The left part of Zeravshan Glacier retreated 3,960 feet from 1881 to 1932, and Fedchenko Glacier retreated 930 feet from 1924 to 1935. Although most glaciers are retreating, there is evidence that some are advancing.

EARTHQUAKES

Central Asia is a region of intense seismic phenomena. More than one thousand local earthquakes are recorded each year, and the region has been the scene of some of the greatest seismic catastrophes in world history. They rank with such well-known earthquakes as those in San Francisco (1906), Reggio-Messina, Italy (1911), and Tokyo (1923). Although the earthquakes are usually severe, there are relatively few human casualties because the population is sparse and the cities are planned with broad streets and single-story buildings. Large industrial, residential, and highway structures,

and particularly villages are subject to destruction by the quakes. In the villages, crowded adobe buildings with heavy ceilings and weak walls, even with a small shock, may be converted into heaps of debris, burying the inhabitants beneath them.

The epicenters of many of the earthquakes (Vernen in 1911) have corresponded exactly with the great lengthwise fractures. A village destroyed by an earthquake in 1930 in the Faizabad district was not more than 1.8 miles from a line of overthrust foldings. The sharp tectonic folds of the ranges and the places of

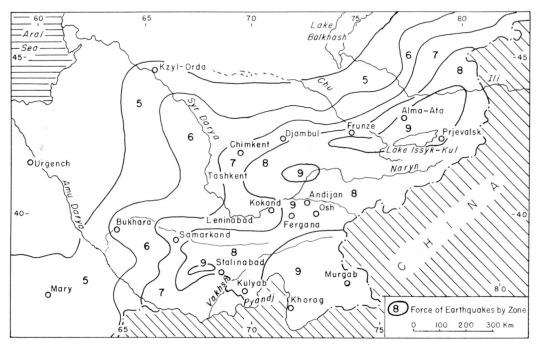

Map 15-I. Seismic divisions of Central Asia.

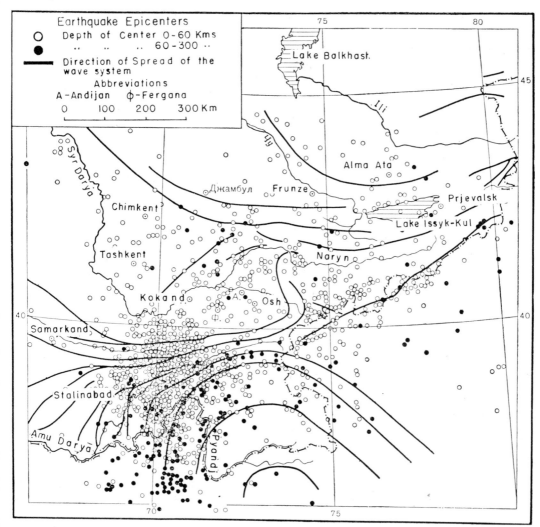

Map 15-II. Earthquake epicenters in the Tien Shan and Pamirs.

branching of tectonic elements play an important role in the activation of seismic phenomena. A series of earthquakes may occur near high elevations and deep depressions—for example, the Kara-Tag earthquake on the boundary of Gissar Range and Surkhan Basin. The seismic activity of individual districts varies with the differences in geological structure. Along with such districts as Boom Gorge, which is world famous for seismic activity, are quiet areas such as southwestern Tadzhikistan. Although in the latter district Mesozoic and Tertiary deposits are characterized by com-

plex folding and faulting, the Paleozoic foundation is untouched by tectonic processes.

The localities of strong earthquakes do not remain fixed, since consecutive earthquakes may cause a relocation of centers. In the eastern part of this region, beginning with the year 1868, the epicenters of all earthquakes seemed to move from the periphery of the Tien Shan Ranges to their central part. The Belovodskoye (Stalinskoye) earthquake seemed to prepare and determine the Vernen quake on a continuation of the same tectonic line. The latter probably influenced the Chilik catastrophe of

1889, which, in its turn, prepared the more intense Kabin (Besiri) earthquake of 1911. Some areas, after having undergone earthquakes, grow more stable, as the seismic activity moves to the south, toward Terskei Ala-Tau. This may make it possible to predict roughly the place of the next earthquake in a single seismic district.

Central Asian earthquakes produce considerable changes in the surface of the earth's crust. During great earthquakes, surface dislocations in fractures may extend for several miles. These lines are often adapted to the contacts of granitic masses with metamorphosed schists and a series of sedimentary rocks. Subsidences are rather common during strong earthquakes. At Alma-Ata in 1911, a regular graben was formed with vertical dislocation of approximately 10 feet. On the northern shore of Lake Issyk-Kul, a crack which had formed, with a depth of about 28 feet, was filled with clumps of earth, and numerous fissures appeared as overthrusts. On the bottomlands, ridges formed which dammed rivers (the valley of the Bolshoy Ak-Su). Earthquakes have been accompanied by landslides of gigantic proportions. An example is the landslide (1911) which destroyed Usoy village, blocked the Murgab River, and formed Sarez Lake. Large slides which dam up streams with thick friable rocks may cause the formation of small lakes (in the Trans-Ili Ala-Tau). Many new springs emerge along the line of fractures during earthquakes. Loose debris may become saturated with water and creep to the foot of slopes as thick mud streams. This debris, which may be as long as two or three miles, has been known to dam valleys and cause the flooding of settlements and crops and the formation of series of temporary lakes.

CLIMATE

The mountain region of Central Asia because of its position in the rather low latitudes (44° to 36° north latitude), the same as Spain, central and southern Italy, and Greece, has intense solar radiation. In the summer months the sun rises 70° to 72° above the horizon. Even during its lowest, in the second half of December, the sun at midday does not drop below 25°.

Lying a little west of the central part of the Eurasian continent and removed thousands of miles from the oceans, the region has a sharply expressed continental mountain climate. Some climatic features are: wide daily and seasonal fluctuations of temperature, dryness of the air, and little cloudiness. Leninabad, at approximately the same latitude as Lisbon, has a January average temperature of 33°F, whereas corresponding temperatures at Lisbon are: 50.5°, 71° and 29.5°F. Continentality, characteristic for the entire region, imparts some features of climatic unity, in spite of complex local climatic variations. Eastward the climate becomes more and more continental, and southward it becomes warmer. Consequently, dry climatic conditions are often found close to the line of permanent snow.

The region lies in a zone of increased air pressure, with such typical attributes as overall dryness and little cloudiness. During the summer months, as a result of the heating of the lower layers of air above the deserts and foothills, undisturbed by the inflow of outside air masses, there is pre-eminently clear, dry weather, with large daily amplitudes—considerable warming during the day and severe cooling at night. At this time the Azores High begins to play an important role, sending in western air currents which pass through at a great height (5,000 to 6,600 feet) above the hot deserts and foothills. These air currents bring moisture, most of which is precipitated in only the very highest parts as snow and almost none of which reaches the low-lying plains and foothills. In winter the region is within the limits of the large Central Asia anticyclone, the northern boundary of which is comparatively close to the mountains. It may move northward or southward and, as a result of this shift, outside air masses have an·opportunity to penetrate into the mountains.

Rather frequent winter cyclones from the shores of the Mediterranean Sea and Atlantic Ocean pass along the northern margins of the anticyclone, occasionally bursting into it and upsetting the stable state of the atmosphere. These cyclones bring with them varying winds, sharp fluctuations in temperature, cloudiness, and moisture, the latter being precipitated along the northern margins of the mountains as deep snow. Moreover, instability is created by the intrusion of cold air masses from the north, which spread along the desert plains near the mountains, contributing to the chilling and dryness of the air. Repeated intrusions, sometimes of warm masses of the cyclones from the west, sometimes of cold winds from the north, condition the strong variability of the weather during the winter months in the northern, outlying areas. Persistent snow cover in winter is found only in the high mountains. The circulation of the cold winter air is determined by the relief in the foothills and mountains, which creates an inverse distribution of temperature. Since these waves of cold air usually do not reach as high as 1,500 to 1,900 feet, the higher foothills have milder winters than the lowlands. For example, the January average for Tashkent, at an altitude of 1,580 feet, is 30°F, but for Turtkul, which lies at the same latitude but 1,320 feet lower, is 22.8°F.

The vastness and complex orography of the region could not help but affect the vertical and horizontal climatic variations. These variations not only determine the routes and characteristics of entering air masses, but redistribute the main climatic elements throughout the region. The region contains no sharply isolated climatic sections, and it is only possible to speak of climatic varieties within a known continental limit. Strong influences on the variation of the temperature regime are the complex orography, the height and character of the relief, the exposures of the slopes, the locked-in basins· and the fact that the mountains shelter

the valleys, basins, and high uplands. Although the rarified atmosphere of the high mountains allows heavy solar radiation to enter, there is also an intensive loss of heat through radiation. From an elevation of 3,300 feet and above, the frost-free period sharply decreases; frost begins earlier and ends later. The long period with below-freezing temperatures in the mountains contributes to the accumulation of moisture and its prolonged preservation as permanent snow and glaciers. The frost-free period at Leninabad (1,085 feet), Tashkent (1,580 feet), Alma-Ata (2,722 feet), Naryn (6,602 feet), Irkeshtam (9,405 feet), and Murgab (12,054 feet) is 218, 206, 173, 143, 135 and 56 days, respectively.

The east-west mountain ranges shield the more southerly localities from the penetration of cold air masses from the north in winter. In the Fergana Valley, winter temperatures are not as extreme as in the more exposed places west of the exit from the valley. The January average at Leninabad is 33°F, and at Turtkul, lying in the lowland exposed to the north, it is 22.8°F. Especially well protected from northern cold winds (and open to the south) are the lower parts of the valleys of the Pyandzh, Vakh, Kafirnigan, and Surkhan Darya rivers, lying in the area of above-freezing January temperature and possessing a July average (highest in the USSR) approximating that of Egypt. Dzhilikul in the lower section of the Vakh River has a July average of 88°F, and Termez on the Amu Darya, an average of 89.8°F. The character of the relief plays an important role in the distribution of temperatures at the same elevation: the temperature is higher on broad solid masses than on isolated summits, and slopes exposed to the south are warmer than north-facing slopes of the same locality. The temperature regime may change abruptly in locked-in mountain basins. Surrounded by mountains, these basins are warmed more intensely than unprotected plateau-like elevations or convex surfaces. In Fergana Valley, on Gissar Plain or in the valley of the Pyandzh, absolute maximums reach 81°F. In winter, on the other hand, cold and dense air masses accumulate there, dropping from the surrounding elevations which are cooled by radiation. Thus, there is a clear manifestation of an inversion of temperatures. In winter and in summer, the temperatures are higher at night on the slopes of mountains (but not of plateaus) than in the valleys. At Irkeshtam, which lies 2,755 feet above Naryn, it is colder in summer and warmer in winter than at Naryn. The July average at Irkeshtam is 55.7°F, at Naryn 63°F; and the January average in the former is 13°F, and in the latter 2°F. In the lower, locked-in basins in winter frost periods are variable; the frost lasts for only part of the 24-hour period because the temperature during the day rises above 32°F. Snow melts within a day or two. Owing to the thin snow cover, spring temperatures rise sharply, and the difference between the average temperatures of the spring months often reaches 13 degrees. On the other hand, in the locked-in valleys of the high mountains, the temperature may drop to −52°F (Murgab).

The moderating action which the large water reservoirs have on the temperature of adjacent areas must be noted. The exceptional mildness of the climate of the Issyk-Kul Lake basin is a result of this deep nonfreezing lake. Przhevalsk lies 3,300 feet above Alma Ata, but is on the shore of an ice free lake. The January average at Przhevalsk is 23°F, and at Alma Ata 16.3°F; but the July averages are 62° and 72°F, respectively. Grapes do not ripen on the shores of the lake because of the moderating influence of the lake on summer temperatures. Near deep Kara-Kul Lake in the Pamir temperatures are higher during the winter and lower during the summer, and annual amplitudes are smaller than at Murgab (about one thousand feet lower and with sharp features of continentality).

Clouds of very fine loess dust also influence the temperature regime. The dust is lifted during the hot summer by ascending air currents, and is not deposited because of the sparse precipitation at this time. A very fine bluish cloud hangs in the summer air, clouding the distances and obscuring the contours of the surrounding mountains.

Although the high mountains of Central Asia receive moisture brought by the air masses from the Atlantic Ocean, they prevent the infiltration of these masses farther east into Central Asia. The gradual increase in height of the mountain system to the east—that is, its general gradient to the west—creates conditions favorable for the condensation of the moisture brought by the prevailing western air currents. The encounter of the nearly saturated air masses with the cold mountains causes precipitation on the great heights, but not on the adjacent plains and foothills. The predominating east-west direction of the ranges and their fan-shaped divergence to the west promote the deep penetration into the longitudinal valleys, exposed on this side (Zeravshan River valley, for example), of the moisture brought by the western winds but hinder the approach of northern and southern air currents. The moist air masses entering these valleys, as along enormous troughs, is funneled into a rather confined but very high region, where strong condensation of moisture and intensive accumulation of snow take place, as, for example, in the mountain center of Matcha at the source of the Zeravshan River. Since the ranges of the western part of the region first meet the moist air currents, they receive more precipitation than those farther east; for example, the southern slope of Gissar Range receives more than 58 inches. The outside slopes of the outer ranges receive much precipitation (Talas Ala-Tau, 3,960 feet, receives as much as 60.4 inches), whereas the inside slopes of these same ranges, and the interior valleys and slopes of all the inner ranges, intercept air currents containing much less moisture.

North-south ranges, sharply distinguished from east-west ones (Akademiya Nauk and Ak-Shiyrak ranges), are barriers to air currents from the west and create conditions especially propitious for the depositing of snow on their slopes and summits. When mountain centers coincide with north-south ranges, as in the Akademiya Nauk Range, the amount of precipitation is strongly increased, and these are localities of permanent snow and large glaciers. Sometimes almost completely intercepting the moisture brought from the west, they contribute to the dryness of the basins and valleys beyond them. High uplands bordered by ranges, despite their great height, are usually very dry. (For example, Murgab in the Pamir, at 12,012 feet, has 2.4 inches of precipitation yearly.) The northern and, especially, western slopes are wetter than the southern and eastern slopes, which face dry winds blowing from the deserts. Besides, since the slopes of southern exposure are warmed more intensely than slopes of northern exposure, condensation of moisture is greater on the latter than on the former.

Increase in precipitation with increase in elevation is characteristic. Localities at different levels get from 4 to 40 inches and more precipitation a year, whereas the adjacent plains receive a more or less uniform, though small, amount of precipitation, about 4 inches. For example, Karshi (1,263 feet) receives 8.4 inches, Guzar (1,758 feet) 11.2 inches, Kitab (2,376 feet) 17.1 inches, Stalinabad (2,673 feet) 21.5 inches, and Khodzha-Obi-Garm (5,610 feet) 62 inches. In the foothills, at 1,650 to 2,310 feet, the annual amount of precipitation is only 12 to 15 inches, but beginning at 3,300 feet it may amount to more than 40 inches; that is, it may approach the degree of dampening of coastal districts. On the western slopes, for each 330-foot rise, the annual amount of precipitation may increase approximately 2.4 to 2.8 inches. Since this increase in precipitation depends on the cooling of the air currents by the mountain slope, it is limited. With the rise upward, the ascending masses of air become colder, the water-vapor content in them decreases, and consequently at a certain height there is a decrease in the intensity of precipitation.

The zone of maximum precipitation extends from approximately 5,000 to 10,000 feet. Localities within this zone which have free access of air from the west may have 40 inches or more of precipitation. The height of this moist zone depends on the relative humidity of the air masses near the base of the mountains: the closer the air is to a state of saturation at the base of the mountains, the less ascent is necessary for condensation to begin. Thus the moist zone may vary in altitude throughout the year. Condensation begins at a lower altitude in winter. One may roughly consider a height of 4,950 feet for the zone of winter precipitation and 9,900 feet for the summer. The transverse ranges may intercept all of the moisture brought from the west in winter, owing to the lowness of the zone of precipitation in winter, but in summer part of the water vapor is carried across these ranges, which explains the maximum of summer precipitation in the enclosed interior valleys (Pamir).

Broad locked-in, interior valleys (such as the Issyk-Kul, Naryn, and Alayskiy valleys) and high plateaus (Upper Pamir, the source of the Naryn) receive little precipitation. The low-moving winter clouds cannot penetrate into valleys cut off by mountains, and high summer clouds pass over the ranges. Descending air currents of a foehn form do not bring precipitation. The farther east a valley or locked-in upland, and the greater the number of ranges preventing them from receiving outside moist air currents, the drier their climate will be. In the depression of Lake Iskander-Kul in the Gissar Range at 7,484 feet, annual precipitation is about 12 inches, and in the eastern Pamir it is only 2.4 inches. In the Lake Issyk-Kul basin (5,359 feet) prevailing western air currents which descend to the lake are dry and warm; passing over its large water surface, they receive much moisture. Then, when they pass beyond the eastern end of the lake, into the mountains, they lose their moisture. This explains the increase in precipitation from west to east, from 4 to 8 inches to 20 inches, which is so unusual for this region.

The irregularity of precipitation is evident in the local landscape. Instead of a rise of the snow line to the east, so characteristic of Central Asia, in the Issyk-Kul district the reverse is observed. The snow line in the western part of the Terskei Ala-Tau Range is at 12,705 to

13,035 feet and in the eastern part at 11,550 feet. The western end of the Issyk-Kul basin, with a snowless winter, and total precipitation amounting to about 4 inches, has an arid appearance with well-developed sierozem soil and sparse vegetation; but during winter in the eastern part, deep snow falls, soil of a chernozem type develops, and on the slopes of Terskei Ala-Tau grow forests of Tien Shan spruce.

The seasonal distribution of precipitation is more marked in the mountains. The period of maximum precipitation is during warm weather, and the higher the elevation the later the period: the maximum moves at first to the middle of spring, then to its end, and finally to July, the warmest and rainiest month. In the foothills, the maximum precipitation comes in March, as in the adjacent deserts (Tashkent, 1,580 feet; Leninabad, 1,056 feet; Andizhan, 1,673 feet). In the mountains, this maximum shifts for the most part to April (Osh, 3,349 feet); higher in the mountains, the rains often fall in May (Naryn, 6,602 feet); and farther east, the maximum shifts to June (Murgab, 12,540 feet) and even to July (upper stretches of the Naryn, 11,880 feet); but summer is, nevertheless, dry. The minimum of precipitation in the mountains is not at the end of summer, as on the neighboring plains, but in winter—in January and February. During spring and summer, the amount of rain falling during a single brief downpour often equals the total monthly precipitation. On mountain slopes with loose soil and sparse vegetation, these heavy showers often form destructive mud flows. Much of the precipitation in the mountains is snow.

Not only the time of the winter precipitation but also the depth and duration of the snow cover vary with elevation. The number of days with snow cover increases regularly with elevation: Karshi (1,263 feet) 24 days, Guzar (1,758 feet) 32 days, Kitab (2,376 feet) 52 days, Khodza-Obi-Garm (5,610 feet) 127 days. Some high valleys are so filled with snow that transportation, and sometimes communication, becomes impossible. In Alayskiy Valley, the snow mantle reaches 3.3 feet in depth. In the foothills, because of the relatively mild winter and fluctuating winter weather, the snow cover does not reach a great depth and is not very constant. The number of days with a snow cover in the south is 20, and in the north 40 to 50. Its average depth varies from one to two inches, increasing in the higher foothills. In the foothills and lower mountain valleys, the annual distribution of precipitation, with maximum in spring, is generally favorable for dry farming. Although total precipitation is small, the concentration of precipitation in the short spring period provides an opportunity for good harvests.

In summer the relative humidity is higher in the mountains than it is in the neighboring plains, and is subject to sharper fluctuations. The maximum relative humidity is in winter (in December-January up to 70 and 80 per cent), the minimum in summer (in August-September to 30 per cent and lower). Relative humidity is higher in the irrigated oases (in summer, instead of the usual 30 per cent, it reaches 50 per cent). Annual cloudiness varies almost on a par with relative humidity. The winter months, January and February, are the cloudiest. From March, cloudiness gradually decreases until August or September, after which it rapidly increases to the winter maximum. Clearness of the skies, especially in the southern part of the region, is very marked; the number of clear days at Leninabad is 148, Stalinabad 146, Tashkent 148, and Khorog 169.

The wind regime is markedly affected by the local relief. Wind velocities range from 4.9 to 9.9 feet per second, and often there is a complete calm. During more than 40 per cent of the year, the weather is still. In the foothills and along mountain valleys, especially in the summer, mountain breezes or mountain-valley winds are typical, blowing upward along the slope during the day and downward at night. The day breeze is a light warm wind of variable but low velocity, the night breeze is a more steady cold wind. In the upper parts of mountain valleys which contain large snow fields and glaciers, masses of air chilled by these bodies pass downward through the valley both day and night. The thermal contrast between the cold snowy ranges and the warmed valleys leads, sometimes, to the origin of whirlwinds, duststorms, and tornadoes. In winter, cyclones passing through from the northwest along the northern margin of the Central Asia anti-cyclone seem to draw in the air of the foothills, forcing masses of mountain air to descend as foehns. Typical foehns, which are common in the foothills in winter, and especially from November to April, may be found in the Fergana Valley, near Tashkent, and in other districts. In December, during the foehns, the temperature may rise above 72°. Foehns are detrimental to agriculture because they warm and dry out the soil, bringing the premature ripening of crops.

In localities adjacent to the deserts, a very hot, dry wind, the *garmsil* (meaning "hot stream"), blows during the summer. This destructive wind, decreasing the relative humidity to 4 or 5 per cent during high temperatures (to 104°F), dries out and bakes cultivated plants: leaves roll up and dry out, bolls fall off the cotton plant, rice turns yellow and then red. Swarms of insects hatch because the dry air and heat hasten the maturation of the cocoons. To combat the destructive effect of the *garmsil* on young crops, increased irrigation and field-protecting plantings of mulberry tree and willow are practiced. In south Tadzhikistan, the hot and desiccating *afganets* (Afghan wind), blows from Afghanistan with a velocity of up to 50 feet per second. In winter it is accompanied by abundant snowfall and disastrous snowstorms.

The unique features of vertical zonality and the limits of agriculture are an index of the climate. Coniferous forests begin at the same altitude at which they end in the Alps, and chernozem steppes lie at the level at which permanent snows occur in the Alps. In the valley of the Zeravshan River, rice culture reaches to 3,828 feet, corn to 4,224, peach trees to 4,521, grape vines to 6,039, millet to 6,435, apricot trees to 7,045, and barley to 8,250 feet. On the shores of Issyk-Kul, at 5,359 feet, wheat,

apricots, and prunes are grown. In the Alay-skaya Valley, wheat is sown at a height of 8,910 feet and barley at 9,900 feet. Grapes are cultivated as high as 6,237 feet in the valley of the Pyandzh, and even up to 6,600 feet on the Obi-Khingou River at Darvaza. In the Pamir, in the Gunt River valley, white mulberry and apricots grow at 7,920 feet, wheat at 10,725 feet, and barley and pea at 11,055 feet. In the valley of the Shakh-Darya, apples and pears grow at 8,910 feet, apricots at 9,900 feet, wheat at 10,560 feet, barley and oats at 11,220 feet. In comparison, one may point out that in the Alps the limit of cultivated plants is 6,270 feet, and then only on the southern slopes.

The reason that plants can be cultivated at such great heights to the southeast is the increased continentality of climate, together with the warmer summers in this direction. Besides this, agriculture and horticulture in the mountains are adapted only to the terraces and alluvial fans in the larger river valleys, which in summer are quite warm, allowing southern trees such as walnut, peach, and apricot to bear at very great heights. The dryness of the air inhibits the growth of many of the fungi which usually attack cultivated plants, and the abundance of sunshine give excellently colored and sweetened fruit. Nevertheless, the continentality of the climate imposes definite obstacles to the cultivation of most subtropical fruit plants. In the lower and middle zones of the mountains, dry farming of grain crops is possible; all other crops—grape, fruit trees, and truck-garden vegetables—require irrigation. With great cleverness and patience, the farmers transport water to their fields and orchards along steep, even precipitous slopes, conveying it along wooden aqueducts across deep gorges. The mountain rivers permit them easy control of water on the cultivated fields.

The maximum elevations of agriculture have not yet been reached. The valleys of the highlands are endowed with an abundance of sunshine and solar radiation, exceptional dryness of the air, and favorable physical, chemical, and biological properties of soil. Frost-resistant and fast-ripening plants, such as the barleys of the Pamir, giant spring rye with a very large spike and grain, and fodder pea, have been developed. The accumulation of sugar in the tissues of high-mountain plants permits them to withstand nightly drops in temperature and to mature in the short frost-free period. Because of the rich sugar content in plants, cattle fatten rapidly after the winter starvation and horses have a high work capacity. Besides the local plants, other species from similar mountain regions of the world, as experiments have shown, can be cultivated: barley from Abyssinia and Eritrea with a growing season of 80 to 83 days, barley of Tibet, and Himalayan cereals.

The southern position of the region and the lack of water vapor and dust in the mountain air create an unusually clear and sunny atmosphere—a condition particularly favorable for the utilization of solar radiation. Direct and diffuse solar radiation is used for solar kitchens,

bathhouses, hot-water heaters, drying chambers, and hothouses. The growing season can be maintained in an artificial climate easily created and regulated in solar-operated greenhouses. In these greenhouses it is possible to grow vegetables the year round, raise more southern plants, and set up the mass production of cotton shoots. They may serve for the drying of unripe bolls of cotton and the rapid, inexpensive, and clean drying of fruits. Solar powerhouses may produce the energy for mechanical irrigation, particularly since the period when the fields need water corresponds to the period of intensive solar radiation.

Despite the great temperature contrasts, the climate is healthful and stimulating. The summers in the mountains, especially at 3,000 to 4,950 feet, are cooler than the summer temperature on the plains, the air is considerably purer, and mountain breezes set up a salubrious circulation of the air.

RELIEF-FORMING PROCESSES

Destruction of the basic tectonic forms by atmospheric and other exogenous factors leads to unusual diversity in the secondary forms of relief and alluvial formations in Central Asia. Rocks are often heated to 158°F during the day and cooled to 50°F during the night, which contributes to intense mechanical weathering. Many slopes and passes are covered by a thick mantle of coarse rubble and, in places, with huge rock fragments almost completely devoid of plant cover.

Talus slopes descend in long gray strips down to the bottoms of the gorges, where enormous alluvial fans pile up. These fans supply the rivers with alluvial materials and, in some rock-filled gorges, even conceal surface water. Meltwater soon vanishes under the mass of rubbly material and does not form surface streams. The character of the products of physical weathering differs according to the lithological composition of the rocks. The finest gravel is produced by easily weathered, coarse-grained granites. Shales and micaceous schists

form coarse, platy rubble. Because of the smooth and slippery surfaces of the slabs of rubble, it is especially mobile. Limestone and sandstone yield more stable taluses of angular rubble.

There is a contrast in elevation and a steepening of the mountain slopes because of lowering of the erosion level of the rivers. This is because of the continued subsidence of large depressions such as the Fergana Valley. The irregular upheaval of the mountain region itself conditions the youthful character of the relief, the energetic erosional work of water, the extensive development of terraces, and the formation of thick alluvial fans in the foothills. The properties of the rock in an area usually determine the general character of the erosion and relief. Compact massive Paleozoic limestone creates a sharp, angular, craggy, and little-dissected relief with sheer cliffs, some of enormous height, and valleys having steep-walled canyons: for example, the valley of the Yagnob between the Zeravshan and Gissar

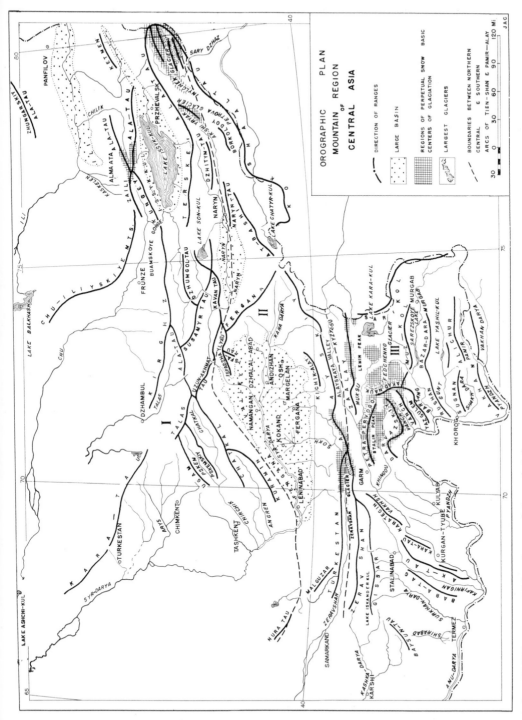

Map 15-III. Orographic scheme of Central Asia.

ranges. Continuous shales and micaceous schists create predominantly gentle, smooth forms of relief and comparatively gentle slopes, without sharp rocky ridges, and **V**-shaped valleys. Conglomerate and sandstone of the Mesozoic, with their intensive dissection by many branching gulches and ravines, resemble badlands. Gypsiferous Upper Tertiary rocks, with the development of desert karst and craters and hanging gullies, also have a badland landscape (for example, on the slopes of Kopet Dagh on hills with loess mantle in the Fergana Valley). Mountains composed of massive crystalline rocks—granites, gabbros, syenites—differ in character depending on the altitude to which they rise: if the mountains are low, they have typical rounded forms; if they are high enough to encounter high-elevation climate, they have needle-shaped or finger-shaped peaks with exceedingly steep slopes.

The products of physical weathering which accumulate at the bottoms of small side gorges are sooner or later taken up by running water and subjected to further transportation and processing. The mountain cloudbursts and the abundant fragmental material on steep and vegetation-free slopes result in landslides, particularly frequent on the slopes of the Zaili Ala-Tau, Chatkal Range, and Kopet Dagh. Because the water becomes overloaded with the mass of fragmental material, it destroys everything it encounters. An avalanche of rocks, rubble, and mud can destroy homes, roads, orchards, and crops, damming river valleys with enormous alluvial fans, clogging irrigation canals, leaving large cultivated areas and settlements without water. Efforts to control these slides involve terracing, planting of soil-holding vegetation on slopes, regulating channels by lateral dikes, and laying out artificial, constant channels at the terminal alluvial fans.

The steepness of the sides of the valleys and the disintegration of the rocks by the frequent earthquakes also cause landslides. Lakes formed because of obstructions in river valleys are encountered in many places (e.g., in the Pamir, Lake Sarez, and Lake Yashil-Kul). Some of these lakes lose their water rather soon because the energetic rivers succeed in cutting through the barriers created by slides. In place of the vanished lakes there remain level expanses formed by lake deposits (e.g., on the Magian-Darya River of the Zeravshan system).

The complex tectonics, the widespread Quaternary glaciation, and the further processing of the basic forms of relief by exogenous actions have created the great geomorphologic diversity. The ranges of Central Asia are massifs arranged in mountain chains. They may be divided into two groups: tectonic and orographic ranges, of which the former predominate in number and extent.

The tectonic ranges (Trans-Alai, Darvaza, and others) have an east-west trend, conforming with the basic strike of the strata composing them, and are distinguished by uniform, flat, slightly undulating tops and steep slopes. Their passes are few in number, lie at great heights, and are barely accessible. For example, the Kyzyl-Art pass in the Trans-Alai Range is at 14,190 feet. Orographic ranges have emerged on the boundary between river systems, often perpendicular to the direction of tectonic ranges. They have steep, fantastically jagged, pointed, and narrow crests with difficult, snowy passes (Gissar, Peter the First, Akademiya Nauk and other ranges). Sections of the tectonic ranges, after having undergone intensive glaciation, acquire a distinct alpine character. On the highest summits of the orographic ranges, not yet having undergone intensive erosion, are massive truncated tops, such as the trapezoidal Stalin and Garmo peaks in the Akademiya Nauk Range.

In the northern and central arcs of Tien Shan, typical geomorphologic elements of the landscape are the plateaus, especially developed in the mountains south of Lake Issyk-Kul, in the Dzungarian Ala-Tau, and in the Chatkal Range. They are high and broad, with relatively low and short ranges scattered along them, in which mountain streams have cut gorges. Between the tectonic ranges, parallel to this same east-west trend, are lengthwise tectonic valleys and spacious basins (Fergana, Issyk-Kul). In these basins are many of the rivers (Zeravshan, Chirchik, upper Pyandzh, and others) and lakes (Issyk-Kul) of the region. The mountain slopes are dissected by numerous transverse valleys, mostly of a meridional trend, which open into the lengthwise tectonic valleys and discharge into the main rivers.

antecedent valleys, such as the valley of the Sary-Dzhaz River, cutting through the great Kokshaal-Tau Range, or the valley of the Chu River, cutting through the Kirghiz Range via the deep Boom Gorge. These valleys are older than the ranges. The ranges were cut through by the already existing rivers, and the intrench-

Fig. 15-7. The deep canyon of the Fan-Darya River, a tributary of the Zeravshan.

The river valleys are immature; they have considerable stream gradient and steep sides covered with a mantle of rock waste, with alternation of wide sections and impassable gorges. The valley network is more fully developed on the gentle, long, and snowy northern slopes of the ranges. The southern slopes are usually shorter, with a great mantle of rock waste and an undeveloped short zone of foothills. Therefore, the river valleys are shorter and contain streams with little water. In the mountains are classical examples of typical

ment continued with the rise of the mountains.

Terraces are developed in all the larger valleys, particularly in association with early glaciation; they are indicative of the alternation of periods of increased accumulation and energetic erosion. The terraces are mostly formed of fluvioglacial alluviums and gravel (products of erosion and redeposition of glacial moraines) with sandy-clayey cement, sometimes consolidated into a conglomerate. The terraces run along the sides of the valleys, often in several stages, one above the other, and the upper ones rise several hundred yards above the present level of the river. The presence of from two to four terraces is common, and in some valleys (Zeravshan) there are as many as seven. The youth of the ranges and the recent shiftings condition the intensified erosional process, contributing to the further cutting of the rivers into the glacial material of the terraces.

The steep slopes of the narrow river valleys or gorges, the abundant talus slopes, and the sheer cliffs are obstacles to transportation. Through experience, however, special types of roads, known as balconies, have been developed. This balcony is one of the curiosities of the mountains of Central Asia. A path running along a steep slope or cornice of a deep abyss may be obstructed by a sheer cliff. In order to pass around such places, stakes are driven in recesses made in the cliff, and on the

stakes a bridging of poles and brushwoods, about a yard wide, is laid. Leaning toward the cliff, shaking under the feet of a traveler, and hanging above the churning river, the balcony path passes around the sheer cliff and comes out on the steep slope of the valley. The Zeravshan tributary district, the upper Pyandzh and other districts are famed for their many balcony paths.

The valley gorges of steep gradient present conditions favorable for the erection of high-pressure water-power installations. Solid Paleozoic and igneous rocks in many valleys offer a firm base for dam structures, and the wide valleys above them form large water reservoirs. An example is the valley of the Fan-Darya of the Zeravshan system. Upper Cretaceous and Tertiary deposits are unsuitable as a base for the erection of hydraulic structures.

Fig. 15-8. Terraces at the junction of the Big Naryn and Small Naryn rivers.

Fig. 15-9. Balconies constructed around a steep cliff on the Fan-Darya River.

HYDROGRAPHY

In the high-mountain districts, the moisture from western air currents accumulates as snow, firn fields, and glaciers. The slow and gradual melting of these maintains the ground water and mountain rivers. There is a quick runoff because of the steepness of the slopes, the compact basement rocks, and good permeability of the mantle. Because of the rock waste, with its small content of fine soil and lack of solid plant cover, and the high elevation relief, there is a very small loss of water from the time when the precipitation becomes liquid to the time the river current forms.

High-mountain regions are the origin and constant feeding source of ground water, because precipitation and snow water descends along deep cracks. The character of the water depends on the lithology of the rocks along which it moves. Ground water, circulating along the cracks in close-grained, watertight, and massive crystalline rocks, is fresh, soft and of nearly constant discharge. Where Mesozoic and Tertiary sedimentary rocks are found with frequent alternation of friable watertight and water-resistant clayey strata, interstitial water predominates, which is less constant, of slight discharge, and of very diverse chemistry and degree of mineralization. In gravel alluvial deposits in the lower courses of the rivers, in alluvial fans and trains, there is ground water of little or no pressure. The use of ground water for drinking, irrigation, and industry is of real importance in certain districts.

The rivers are typical young mountain

streams: undeveloped lengthwise profile, energetic depth erosion, rapid or even turbulent current, the presence of rapids, and waterfalls. They transport not only suspended silt and sand but also pebbles and large boulders. The rivers have a single channel restricted by the steep banks or by the sheer bluffs of gravel terraces.

At the base of the mountains, the rivers form thick alluvial fans, acquire a calmer current in a broad gravel bed, and break up into a series of distributaries. Owing to the increase in the surface area of the river, evaporation is increased. Much water filtrates into the loose alluvial ground, and much is also drawn off by the numerous irrigation canals. Thus many rivers run low before reaching the main river, entering it apparently by underground streams.

Rivers are divided into the following types according to the sources of their feeding and the character of their water regime: (1) rivers of mixed glacial-snow feeding, (2) those of snow feeding, and (3) those of pre-eminent ground feeding. A cloudburst-water regime is typical of most small mountain rivers and intermittent creeks: they rise suddenly after each heavy rain. The rate of discharge depends on the exposure of the slope and the speed of the river's flow. North-facing and west-facing slopes possess greater water-bearing capacities than south-facing and east-facing slopes. On north-facing slopes, because of their more extensive glaciation and lower snow lines, the rivers have a heavier and more stable, as well as a later maximum, discharge.

The rivers are important to the national economy not only as sources for irrigation but also as power resources. The regime of the rivers is favorable for irrigation: high water occurs in summer when cultivated crops of the fertile plains, owing to the small amount of rainfall, need water the most. In Central Asia, irrigation is many centuries old. Near Tashkent, there are irrigation canals (Boz-Su, Zakh) which were used five hundred years ago. Reconstruction, widening, and technical improvement of the irrigation system are taking place. Present-day irrigation measures are

designed to accumulate water during the nongrowing season for irrigation during the growing season and to regulate the flow of the rivers. These goals can be met by the construction of water reservoirs or by using mountain lakes (for example, Iskander-Kul) which accumulate and conserve water from cloudbursts and flooding streams. Much of the cloudburst and flood water is wasted and even does damage.

The problem of securing good drinking water for the cities and villages and of securing water for industrial use is acute. The steep gradient of the mountain rivers and their abundance of water in the lower sections create enormous reserves of water power, and geologic conditions are favorable for dams. However, the demands of irrigation and of power utilization are almost contrary: For irrigation it is necessary to concentrate the entire discharge of water for use during the growing season; for power engineering it is necessary to obtain uniform distribution of water during the whole year, which means compensating for the small winter output of the rivers. Dual regulation is necessary for the most effective utilization of the river discharge: the upper mountain water reservoirs may work primarily for power engineering, and those lying below for irrigation.

There are several different kinds of lakes in this region. The largest lakes of the region—Issyk-Kul and Kara-Kul—are of tectonic origin. Smaller lakes—Sarez and Yashil-Kul—were formed as a result of the damming of rivers by rock slides. The smaller lakes are associated with glaciers: moraine-dam lakes like Issyk and cirque lakes or tarns. In the area where variegated rocks of the Cretaceous and Lower Tertiary occur, karst lakes form as a result of leaching out of seams of gypsum. The mountain lakes have fresh or brackish water, and in districts where there are saliferous rocks they are salty or acrid.

Issyk-Kul (hot lake), a large, undrained, brackish lake, lies at 5,193 feet in a clearly-defined young basin of tectonic origin among the high ranges of the Tien Shan. It is 105 miles long and 35 miles wide. Although the

Fig. 15-10. Oases on terraces of the Zeravshan River.

shore line in general has slight dissection, in the eastern part there are two deep bays. The simplicity of the shore line is a result of the washing action of the waves and the lowering of the level of the lake in the recent past. From the northern shore the bottom descends very gradually, but from the southern shore it forms a steep descent. In its central part the lake depths reach 2,145 feet, but the greatest depth, 2,303 feet, is closer to the southern shore. On the bottom there is gray, strongly calcareous silt. The level of the lake is subject to some fluctuations. Formerly the lake was much higher, as indicated by the many terraces ranging from 8 to 165 feet above the present level. These variations of the level are linked with the history of development of the Chu River, which does not enter the lake but swerves, sharply, several miles north of it and cuts through the Kirghiz Range in the narrow and long Boom Gorge. Formerly the upper Chu River entered the lake. The lower part of the

Chu River, having cut through Kirghiz Range, as a result of later erosion approached the lake with its upper sections and partly drained it, but later captured the upper part of the river. The dried-up lower part of the upper Chu River survives today as Kutemaldy Channel, 3.6 miles long, through which part of the water of the Chu River flows into the lake every year at time of high water. Seasonal fluctuations of the level of Lake Issyk-Kul are not large; the maximum level is associated with the melting of snow and ice in the mountains.

Because of the strong, suddenly changing winds and the large water area, Lake Issyk-Kul is not very calm. The water temperature is rather high: in July the surface layers average about 66°F, and in winter do not drop below approximately 39°F. Thus the lake, with the exception of some of its bays, is free of ice in winter. The temperature drops rapidly with depth, and at 660 feet a uniform summer temperature of 40°F is recorded. The lake water does not freeze because of the relative mildness of the local winter, the large volume of water, and the salinity. The color of the lake water is blue; only near the shores does it become greenish. Transparency of the water in the area of greatest depths averages less than 50 feet in summer; the muddying activity of the tributaries is evident only along the shores. Owing to the lack of drainage, the water is somewhat brackish. Salinity is as high as 5.8 per cent in the open part. The fact that the salinity is higher than in drained lakes but lower than in other undrained ones indicates the short interval of time that the lake has had no outlet. Fluctuations in saltiness in the open part of the lake are negligible, which indicates the good intermixing of the water from the surface to the bottom. This also explains the large amount of oxygen found in the entire depth of water.

Despite its depth and size, Issyk-Kul contains very few original flora and fauna. Among the fish observed are: carp (*Cyprinus carpio*), Old World minnow (*Schizothorax pseudaksaiensis issykkuli*), and *Dyptychus dybowskii* —representatives of upland Asiatic fauna. Endemic species are: Issyk-Kul gudgeon (*Gobio gobio latus*), Issyk-Kul fish *Leuciscus schmidti, Leuciscus bergi,* and Issyk-Kul minnow (*Phoxinus issykkulensis*).

Lake Kara-Kul, in the northern part of the Pamir, is one of the highest (12,980 feet) lakes in the world. It is approximately 20 miles long, and is divided into a deeper western basin (775 feet) and a shallow eastern basin (not more than 66 feet). The tectonic basin of the lake has been highly altered by glacial and postglacial deposits, which filled the eastern section and predetermined its shallowness, but the western basin preserved its old bottom topography. Thus the western shores are precipitous and rocky, and the easten shores are low, formed of lake and glacial deposits with large masses of ground ice.

The thermal regime of the lake is as follows: in winter the temperature of the water increases with depth, and in summer decreases. During the morning hours in summer the temperature,

because of the cooling effect of meltwater from shore ice, increases with distance from the shore. In the eastern basin, because of intense insolation and because of mixing when the water is rough, the water is warmed to the bottom. Thus there is slight variability of temperatures with depth: on the surface and on the bottom (at a depth of 61 feet) temperatures differ by only 2 degrees or less. Owing to the extremely low winter temperatures, the lake is covered with three feet of ice every year. Transparency of the water is only about 29 feet because the rivers feeding the lake carry much sediment.

There are seasonal and long-range fluctuations in the level of the lake. The shores indicate that the water level was at one time 198 feet higher. Moreover, the 1934 level was 9.2 inches higher than the 1928 level, which shows the character of fluctuation. The highest annual level of the lake corresponds to the period of thawing of the surface snow and ice, of revived activity of spring water, and of rapid thawing of ground ice. The water of the lake is slightly brackish and not good for drinking.

Lake Sarez in the Pamir was formed in 1911 by a landslide which destroyed Usoy village and blocked the Murgab River. Approximately 2,600,000 cubic yards of earth formed an obstruction 2,475 feet high. The lake is now 45 miles long and 1,650 feet deep. Water from the Murgab filters through the obstruction 495 feet below the lake surface. A balance has been established between the discharge of water and its entry into the lake. Sarez Lake is the source of regulated water power.

Lake Iskander-Kul, with an area of only 1.3 square miles and a maximum depth of 237 feet, lies at 7,441 feet on the northern slope of Gissar Range. The lake had a higher level in the past, as indicated by the clearly defined terraces at heights of from 56 to 386 feet. The lake is blocked by a filter-proof dam—the terminal moraine of an old glacier, covered by the rocky material of a landslide. The dam is cut through by the lake outlet, the Iskander-Darya River, which has a yearly discharge of about nine hundred million cubic yards of water. The

Fig. 15-11. Moraine of Big Issyk Lake on the northern slope of the Zaili Ala-Tau Range; Tien Shan spruce on the slopes.

large discharge and the lack of silting of the lake permit it to be utilized as a water reservoir for the regulation of many rivers of the Zeravshan system. It guarantees a supply of water for irrigation and projected hydroelectric stations.

Bolshoye Issyk Lake, at 5,900 feet on the northern slope of the Zaili Ala-Tau Range, is a moraine-dam lake, with depths to 198 feet. The steep shores of massive crystalline rocks are covered with Tien Shan spruce.

VEGETATION ZONES

The climatic diversity and complex history of the plant and animal world of the mountain region of Central Asia explain the originality and variety in the geographic landscapes. These landscapes range from low foothill deserts to alpine meadows to permanent snows of the high altitudes, from snow fields to wild barley meadows to thickets of almond and pistachio. The mountains of Central Asia constitute a special flora and zoogeographic region. In this region coexist species of old Indo-Himalayan, Mediterranean-African, Mongolian steppe-desert, Central Asian upland, and Eurasian flora and fauna, having penetrated at different times and by various routes. The plant and animal world is distinguished by composition and ecological peculiarities not duplicated on the plains of Central Asia. These highlands are centers of origin of many cultivated plants, such as rye and pea, and the world center of the original domestication of many fruits, such as apple, apricot, cherry, plum, pistachio, almond, and grape.

The economic activity of man, begun in ancient times, has led to the modification of landscapes: to the creation of areas with a very rich collection of valuable, cultivated plants, and also to the salting and swamping of other areas. With the destruction of mountain forests, the mesophytic grassy plants which found refuge in their shade disappeared and were gradually replaced by xerophytes, which ascended from the lower zones. The intensive grazing of livestock has hastened the disappearance of valuable fodder plants, allowed woody plants to increase, and led to a sharp decrease in the density of plant cover. The mountain slopes, no longer protected by forest and meadow cover, lost their topsoil by intense erosion, which has led to the development of downpour washouts and gullies.

Complex orography and intense relief have promoted the development of clearly expressed vertical landscape-geographic zones. Each zone is distinguished by: (1) originality of climate and of plant and animal life, and (2) character of cultivated landscapes. There is a regular vertical sequence of landscapes: from deserts of the foothills with their gray soil through semideserts, dry steppes with chestnut soil, woodedsteppe landscapes with chernozem meadow steppes, and islands of broad-leafed forests to subalpine and alpine landscapes of the high mountains. The dryness of air and soil cause chernozem steppes here, with feather grass at the same heights where permanent snow exists in the Alps; but on the other hand, the vertical forest zone with its soil of a podzolic type is very weakly expressed. Forests in their typical form are widespread only in those places where conditions of relief, such as northern exposure and steepness of slopes, or great depth of valleys, compensate for the lack of precipitation. This explains the diversity and the island-like character of the forest landscape. Here oak and pine are absent and the spread of spruce and

fir is limited, but on the other hand, wild fruit trees are abundant.

The climate varies not only from north to south and from west to east, but also vertically. These climatic variations together with variations in the height of the snow line are the main factors governing the distribution and height of vertical geographic zones. Acting on these variations is the uniform regime of moisture, which in places of widely different altitude results in similar landscapes: for example, mountain semideserts with sierozems can be found at 660, 3,960, 7,260, and 10,560 feet; dry grass steppes with chestnut soil can be found at 2,310, 5,610, and 8,910 feet. The temperature regime also makes itself felt: whereas cotton or orchard-vineyard cultivation is developed in the semidesert at 660 feet, on the other hand, wheat grows in the semiarid zone at 3,960 feet; but at 7,260 feet barley alone is raised, and at 10,560 feet, in many places, agriculture is impossible. At the same altitude, permanent snow is found in one place, alpine meadows in another place, and steppes and deserts in still others. The succession of vertical geographic zones remains the same everywhere, but to the south and east their limits rise higher and higher.

The orography and geomorphology of individual districts also affect the distribution of vertical zones. In locked-in valleys, which are sheltered by the ranges and thus receive little precipitation, semidesert and steppe landscapes develop, regardless of the elevation: sierozem is found in the valley of the Chu River at 2,310 feet, in the valley of the Naryn River at 6,600 feet, and in the Pamir at 12,210 feet. Because of the great differences in latitudes between places in the region (such as there are between Kopet-Dagh, 38° north latitude, and the Dzungarian Ala-Tau, about 46° north latitude), corresponding vertical zones could not help but differ in altitude. Thus, together with the general features of the mountain belts, it is necessary to consider individual peculiarities in the individual districts, and along with this the different altitudes of lower and upper boundaries.

Desert Zone

The desert zone, at approximately 1,500 feet elevation, is the lowest of the region. It consists of low hills with gentle slopes and almost level tops, separated from one another by shallow river valleys and broad terraces, and of alluvial deposits from the mountains. Here a desert climate predominates with a hot, cloudless summer and sharply irregular rainfall. Rainfall is similar to that of the foothill plains, except that the amount is somewhat greater, reaching 10 inches a year. On fine earth, nonsaliferous, clayey sierozem is developed, and on the parent rocks, saliferous structural sierozem. Alkaline soil is encountered everywhere, and epecially in places with artificial irrigation. Mountain sierozem contains more humus and is darker than sierozem of the lowland deserts. In spring, during the rains, it is saturated with moisture.

According to the character of its vegetation, the zone is a moister version of the ephemeral desert of the loess foothill plains. In the middle of March the shoots of spring plants revive, having survived the winter as bulbs and rhizomes. First to germinate are desert sedge (*Carex pachystylis*) and meadow grass (*Poa bulbosa*), and toward the beginning of April *Crocus korolkowi*, hyacinth (*Hyacinthus ciliatus*), different species of *Gagea*, Turkestanian *Ixiolirion tataricum*, irises, and tulips begin to blossom. In late April crowfoot (*Ranunculus sewerzowii*) and countless annuals finish flowering: trigonella (*Trigonella grandiflora*), different milk-vetches, and poppies; the last to bloom is the ephemeroid blue gentian (*Gentiana olivieri*). With this ends the spring phase of vegetation. Ephemerals have delicate, soft leaves which lose their moisture and wither immediately on extraction from the soil.

The density of the plant cover is surprising. Although the number of species is not great, the number of plants reaches several thousand per square yard (for example, desert sedge up to 2,340 specimens). This abundance is due to optimum soil conditions in the mountain desert during the spring rains.

There are not many plants in the summer phase of vegetation, either in number of species or in number of specimens. The first to bloom are unusual umbrella-shaped scaligeria (*Scaligeria allioides*) and larkspur (*Delphinium semibarbatum*). The period of vegetation extends until August. The leaves, during a hot and dry summer, either fall or remain for a long time in a state of withering. Thus, during the midday hours, when the soil heats up to 158°F, scaligeria (*Scaligeria transcaspica*) seems withered; the shafts of its umbrella bend downward and the leaves droop.

Throughout the spring and summer there are two levels, or layers, of plants. In the lower layer are the spring grasses (not higher than 6 inches); in the summer period the upper layer predominates (not above 18 inches). These depend on one another only slightly because the sparse summer plant cover, growing slowly, has little influence on the lower layer. The root systems thin out at a depth of 4 to 6 inches. The lower formation belongs to the ephemerals, and the upper to the plants of summer vegetation.

Annual ephemerals and ephemeroids (such as desert sedge) are encountered everywhere. The occurrence of perennials is often limited to small areas: for example, between Tedzhen and Murgab grows the gigantic umbellate dorema (*Dorema badrakema*), along the Zeravshan River, scurf pea (*Psoralea drupacea*), and in the Nura-Tau Mountains, *Artemisia bucharica*. In the Dzungarian Ala-Tau, sedge (*Carex stenophylla*) is represented by a species taller than the desert sedge. Along the channels of the rivers in the desert zone there are many ungovernable thickets of bamboo-like, giant reeds (*Arundo donax*), or there are *tugai* sections of tamarisks, oleasters, and heterophyllous poplar. Along the Pyandzh such overgrowths serve as habitats for tiger, wild boar, and Bukhara deer.

The vertical desert zone has a higher productivity than the ephemeral desert of the foothill plains. Since the fertile soil contains more humus and has a porous structure, it is better leached of harmful salts and is favorable for dry farming. The comparatively long growing season and frost-free periods, high temperatures, and adequate water for irrigation in the main growing months open broad possibilities for the cultivation of warm-climate plants, such as cotton and rice. The desert zones are spring-summer grazing lands that produce much fodder. With further improvement of the methods of irrigation, a brilliant future is in store for these deserts, but it will be necessary to: (1) raise the productivity of high-grade varieties of cotton; (2) intensify the struggle against weeds; (3) utilize a method of seed treatment for late-ripening varieties; and (4) introduce extensive cultivation of lucerne in the struggle against weeds as well as for an increase in the fodder supply.

Semiarid Zone

The semiarid vertical zone occupies high foothill areas from approximately 1,650 to 4,950 feet, forming a highly dissected landscape. This zone has a dry and hot summer, more precipitation (up to 20 inches in the Dzungarian Ala-Tau), and a milder winter (as a result of temperature inversions). Sierozem soil is widespread and partly saline. Light chestnut soil exists on loess-like clayey soil or gravelly-rubbly-clayey alluvium. Because there is more precipitation here than in the lower-lying desert, the vegetation acquires a semidesert character. In many places the vegetation is mixed couch grass, with the absence of a solid turf and with ephemerals playing an important role, in contrast to the lowland semideserts. Artemisia is absent. In its place, there is couch grass (*Agropyron pulcherrimum*), a gray stiff grass about 16 to 20 inches high, having a horizontal rootstock and thick roots, running about 20 inches into the soil. The leaves of couch grass are not numerous and wither rapidly. Individual couch-grass plants are spaced 2 to 4 inches from one another. Bulbous barley (*Hordeum bulbosum*) is rather common. Its sods are formed by the long rootstocks that occupy the upper surface layer of the soil. The plant has a mass of stalks, up to a yard

high, and shortened leaves of a mesophytic character which wither early.

Plant makeup in the mountain semideserts is rather constant, even though some of the species are peculiar only to individual districts. The semidesert not only contains many endemic species and even genera, but there is a bond between its flora and the flora of the southern adjoining countries. For example, the genera *Bunium, Scaligeria,* and *Muretia* are also peculiar to Iran, Asia Minor, Greece, and even Italy and Spain.

The vegetation develops under moist conditions in the beginning stage of growth and under extremely dry conditions in the period of blossoming. During the first part of April, the semidesert is covered with the green of ephemerals and ephemeroids, mostly by viviparous meadow grass (*Poa bulbosa* var. *vivipara*); in places one can already note the leaves and shoots of the perennial grasses. Near Tashkent the semidesert, in April, is colored by beautiful tulips (*Tulipa greigii*), yellow or violet irises, and other richly blossoming plants. The spring phase passes without a break into that of summer. In the middle of June, couch grass blossoms, then *Inula grandis,* a tall composite with big leaves gathered into a rosette, several species of gigantic umbellate ferule (*Ferula*), and sometimes rose scabiosa (*Scabiosa songorica*). By the middle of July the semidesert is converted into scorched, dry expanses. Here there is not the solid turfing as in the steppes. Aboveground vegetation interlocks at a height of 16 to 28 inches, but one need only separate the leaves to reveal bare soil. The growing period of the summer cycle is only three to three and a half months. Because of this, the ecology of some of the plants of the semidesert is unique: there are many monocarps (*Ferula, Scaligeria*), the full cycle of development of which, from germinating to ripening of seeds, extends over three to four years. The leaves of even some long-vegetating drought-resistant plants (cousinia, perennial grasses) fall or wither in the summer heat. Plants growing before autumn (*Eryngium, Libanotis, Inula*) have leathery or fleshy leaves.

In the southeastern part of the region in the semidesert, feather grass predominates.

Fauna of the vertical semiarid zone differs little from the fauna of the adjacent deserts. Here the same burrowing rodents (jerboas, yellow suslik) and fox are found. Among the large ungulates are wild sheep (*Ovis vignei*) and antelope (*Gazella subgutturosa*). Predominant birds are the residents of open treeless expanses, building their nests either on the ground (larks) or in holes (a martin-like bird). There are many species of lizards (for example, agama). In the second half of summer, the semidesert of the Zeravshan Valley swarms with locustidae.

The mountain semidesert is the region of conditional nonirrigated crops which often suffer from drought. They are dependable only in places with more than 14 inches of rain, as on the moistened western slopes. Sowings of nonirrigated wheat are widespread; and with artificial irrigation, cotton, lucerne, grape, and fruit trees are grown. To increase the amount of arable land would require irrigation of saline soil. In order to do this, more effective watering and agricultural measures are needed, such as crop rotation, by which secondary salting of the soil could be eliminated. There are great opportunities for the development of volatile oil crops—geranium, tuberose, lemon sorghum, rose, lemon verbena, jasmine, iris, and muscat sage.

Mountainous Dry-Steppe Zone

The mountainous dry-steppe zone, at approximately 5,610 to 5,940 feet, is well expressed everywhere from Kopet Dagh in the west to the Dzungarian Ala-Tau on the east. Owing to greater moistening, together with the dark, partly saline sierozem on loess, there is a highly rubbly mountain-chestnut soil, which often does not effervesce at the surface. Solonchak and solonetz soils are absent. In some areas (for example, in the Andizhan district), sierozem is converted to soil analogous to chernozem, with considerable (about 12 per cent) humus content, carbonation, and a high horizon of effervescence. Widespread in the zone are dry feather-chaco grass steppes, very similar to the lowland chestnut steppes of Kazakhstan in development of steppe sod grasses, degree of soil covering, and participation of ephemerals. But these are distinguished from those of Kazakhstan by the homogeneity of the soil and plant cover and by the absence of solonchak and solonetz soils.

In spring there is a thick green ephemeroid cover: meadow grass, gagea, and tulips. Toward summer this mantle disappears and is replaced by the basic vegetation of the feather-chaco grass steppe, consisting of turf grasses, maidenhair feather grass (*Stipa capillata*), and chaco grass (*Festuca sulcata*) which, as in the lowland steppe, almost entirely cover the soil with their sods. Among them are found individual sods of koeleria (*Koeleria gracilis*) and pinnate feather grass (*Stipa kirghisorum*). To the grasses are added: a few species of perennial mixed grass (*Phlomis, Cousinia,* prickly almond bushes, and wild rose). On more stony areas, artemisia and its companions are developed: winter fat (*Ceratocarpus*) and *Kochia*. In certain districts there are new species of grasses and shrubs, such as feather grasses in Kopet Dagh or thickets of spirea (*Spiraea hypericifolia*) on the Kara-Tau Range.

Within the steppe and semidesert mountain zones in the southern part of the region, four valuable wild plants are abundant: pistachio, pomegranate, almond, and a shrub of the buckthorn family that bears edible fruit. Pistachio (*Pistacia vera*) has a shortened trunk (about five feet) and a broad crown. It is one of the most drought-resistant fruit trees, with an exceptionally deep root system that reaches to water-bearing horizons for moisture in the driest period. Pistachio grows on steep waterless slopes where there are saliferous or gypsiferous Cretaceous and Tertiary deposits. Pistachio may grow on dry southern slopes where other cultivated plants burn out. Thickets of pistachio have a park-like character; thus within the pistachio groves shade is lacking and the ground is devoid of a grass cover. The pistachio nuts are a valuable food product, con-

Fig. 15-12. Pistachio trees on the dry steppes of the mountains of Central Asia.

taining as much as 60 per cent oil and 22 per cent albumin. In Central Asia there are almost 480,000 acres of wild pistachio thickets of a great variety of species. Here, and especially in the Kashka district, together with the neighboring districts of Afghanistan and Iran, is the original home of this valuable fruit tree. In this zone, wild species of drought-resistant almond (*Amygdalus spinosissima* and *A. bucharica*) are also encountered, well acclimatized to the mountainous rocky slopes.

The dry mountain steppes is a zone of dependable unirrigated crops of wheat, lucerne, and cotton; and only grape and fruit trees (peaches, apricots, and apples) require irrigation. In order to provide for seasons poor in fodder, it is necessary to create meadows, both irrigated and nonirrigated, as well as to improve the fodder quality by additional sowings of lucerne, vetch, vetchling, red clover, and miscellaneous orchard grasses. Many typical desert animals, such as jerboa and suslik, have already disappeared from this zone.

Forest-Meadow Steppe Zone

The forest-meadow steppe, at approximately 3,960 to 9,900 feet, occupies large areas in the western and peripheral part of the region. Because of its height and location within the belt of maximum precipitation, this zone has a colder and moister climate (annual precipitation to 40 inches, with more or less uniform distribution for all seasons). Temperature and moisture of different places vary with altitude, exposure, slope steepness, and depth and degree of enclosure or openness. This causes interrupted distribution of various plants, lending a wooded-steppe landscape character to certain areas. On northern slopes, a complex combination of meadow mesophytes is found. Steppe xerophytes take over on the dry, better-warmed, south-facing slopes and flat water divides. Scrub thickets and deciduous forests of various types grow on the wetter, steep, shaded slopes and in deep valleys.

Because of the vigor and height (30 to 40 inches) of the meadow plants, the varied composition resulting from the many dicotyledonous plants (which grow in the absence of turf species), and the compact, multiple-stage cover, the meadows have an appearance not duplicated in other mountain zones of Central Asia. Meadow vegetation shows much diversity, depending on changes in climatic conditions. There are meadows of a northern type in the

Tien Shan and meadows of a southern type in the Pamir-Alayskiy, differing not only in plant composition but also in ecology, rhythm of development, and plant configuration. Northern-type meadows are found in the northern ranges from the Dzungarian Ala-Tau to the Talas Ala-Tau, Fergana, and Alayskiy; the southern-type meadows are found in the more western and southern mountains. Generally, there are no meadows in the Kopet-Dagh.

Variation in precipitation is the basic reason for the differences in meadow types. Where northern-type meadows occur, precipitation is uniformly distributed during the summer growing season. Where there are southern-type meadows, the precipitation is mainly in winter and spring. The northern meadows remain green a long time, not suffering a deficiency in moisture, and only the low temperatures terminate growth.

The southern meadows are subject to conditions of alternating moistness and dryness, a more acute alternation than occurs in the lower zones. Southern meadow vegetation dies with the ever-increasing summer drought. Most plants have already ended their growth by late July.

The origin of these two types of meadows also differs. The northern meadows are closely linked with the vegetation of the meadow-steppe plains of Kazakhstan. Most plants of the southern meadows belong to more southern species, whose center of development is in the Mediterranean area.

A landscape plant of the northern meadows is the *Ligularia altaica,* about a yard high, with leaves in a thick rosette pointing upward and with yellow blossoming calathi. At the height of flowering in July are: blue larkspur (*Delphinium confusum*), violet geranium, scabiosa (*Scabiosa alpestris*), various species of the pulse family, and many grasses such as Hungarian brome grass (*Bromus inermis*), orchard grass (*Dactylis glomerata*), beach grass, and meadow grass. The southern meadows have the large umbellate *Prangos pabularia.* Its leaves, broken up into thread-like globules, are gathered in a rosette close to the ground, and the root system is a thick and deep (about a yard) taproot. Amid the thickets are found: decorative lily eremurus (*Eremurus robustus*), the umbellate muretia (*Muretia transitoria*), and labiate phlomis (*Phlomis brachystegia*). In the lower stage there is a thick grassy cover of cousinia, astragals, and other plants, completely concealing the earth. Among these plants are many tubers and monocarps such as *Ferula* with seasonal falling of leaves, which indicates the sharply irregular moistening. Under the meadows on fine alluvium, unique mountain chernozem and chernozem-like meadow soil is developed, with much humus and a pronounced carbonate layer. Along steep slopes is a coarsely rubbled conglomerate, frequently with desert tarnish. Mountain meadows on drier sections tend to change to steppe vegetation. Added to the cover are various grasses rising from the zone of dry steppes, such as maidenhair feather grass, koeleria, and other grasses, which lead to the formation of meadow steppes, and on the south-facing slopes these change into dry steppes.

In the meadow-steppe belt, widespread brushwood thickets cover the more shaded slopes. These thickets, more than a yard high, are very dense. The thicker the mountain chernozem, on the slopes, the more compact and dense are the stands. Most persistent are the thickets of wild rose, added to which are bushes of spirea (*Spiraea hypericifolia*), honeysuckle (*Lonicera microphylla*), hawthorn (*Crataegus monogyna*), and barberry (*Berberis heteropoda*).

The meadows are high-grade summer grazing lands. Productive soil and good moistening permit dependable dry farming of wheat, barley, flax, and peas, which explains why the meadows are completely tilled. Irrigated orchards of apricot, mulberry, and other fruit trees are found on valley terraces and the alluvial fans of lateral tributaries.

As a result of the good and uniformly distributed precipitation in this zone, deciduous forests are adapted to the western and peripheral parts of the region. These forests are widespread in isolated groves in the midst of meadows and steppes. In the forests are more than one hundred species of trees and bushes. Fruit trees are especially abundant. The absence of oak is characteristic. Most of the woody plants are widespread, and only certain species, such as walnut, are typical of only the southern ranges. Beneath the forest, a strong humus soil is developed, of a mountain chestnut soil type, with a nutlike structure. The biocoenotic composition varies strongly according to the times of the year. Under the forest canopy, countless animals, including many kinds of insects, find good shelter and ample food. There are many insect-eating birds here in summer. With winter, the world of birds changes, too, and the summer biocoenoses disappear: warmth-loving Mediterranean or Indian visitors fly away to the south, other insectivorous birds drop to the foothills, still others flock to the *tugai,* where they begin to feed on barberries. In their place arrive some birds from farther north, such as the long-tailed bullfinch (*Uragus sibericus*), and other birds from the higher coniferous forest zone, such as the black tomtit, or from the alpine belt, such as the horned alpine lark. There are few reptiles in the deciduous forests.

The most characteristic forests are walnut (*Juglans fallax*), whose northern limit of spread is the Talas Ala-Tau and whose eastern limit is the Fergana Range. Islands of walnut forests grow in places which are protected from the north and exposed to the southwest. In these places, the temperature regime and rainfall is generally favorable. Up to the first days of July, the soil of the walnut forest is usually saturated with moisture from the rains, which permits the growth of tall and delicate grasses. After the rainy period, the period of dryness and high summer temperature sets in, and the green forest changes into a dry forest.

These forests are relics of the Tertiary Period, and included within them are an interesting combination of plant and animal species. Walnut, which plays a part in the first stage, establishes the entire tenor of life of the forest. The rays of the sun scarcely break through the thick, broad crown of the walnut, scattering only diffused light in the deep shade. The trees, with a diameter of 12 to 16 inches, are spaced far from one another; thus the forests rather resemble neglected gardens. In these forests there are also relic maple (*Acer turkestanicum*), which never becomes taller than the walnut. In the undergrowth are trees and brushwoods of moderate density and limited composition, inasmuch as there are few shade-loving species capable of enduring the darkness created by the walnut canopy. Here are plum (*Prunus divaricata*), honeysuckle (*Lonicera hispida*), rose (*Rosa beggeriana*), barberry (*Berberis heteropoda*), currant, buckthorn, spindle tree, and apple. The trees are often entwined by grapevines. The vegetation is characteristic of the growth in a shady forest, although mosses are absent. Alongside of such northern species as bishop's gout weed (*Aegopodium podagraria*) or angelica (*Archangelica decurrens*) are encountered emigrants from lower zones, such as cousinia or scaligeria, which in the shade of the forest preserve some of the ephemeral characteristics of their relatives.

Walnut, requiring a certain amount of moisture, puts up with varied soil types. Under walnut forests on slopes of northern exposure, is found a soil with a dark, almost black humus layer, deeply leached, and with a nut-like structure; in some places a podzolic layer is noted. On more gentle and better lighted slopes, soil with the same nut-like structure is developed, but with a dark-brown humus layer, weaker leaching, and a pronounced carbonate layer.

The animal life in the walnut forest is rich and diversified. Wild boar (*Sus scrofa*) enters the forest toward evening for feeding; badger (*Meles meles tianschanensis*) emerges from its refuge at night; and porcupine (*Hystrix hirsutirostris*) comes out of caves and fissures; wood mice and rats (*Rattus turkestanicus*) gather a great quantity of nuts in hollow trees and conceal themselves amid the roots or in cavities. Landscape birds of the walnut forests include the gray-crested, Old-World goldfinch

(*Acanthis caniceps*) and stockdove (*Columba oenas tianschanica*). Several southern India species, such as Indian oriole (*Oriolus oriolus kundoo*) and paradise flycatcher (*Terpsiphone paradisi turkestanica*), and Mediterranean species, such as black thrush (*Turdus merula intermedia*), arrive in summer and leave in winter. Many northern birds also enter the walnut forests.

The walnut forests are restored by seed, but restoration is very slow. The quantity and quality of the growth depend on: (1) the grazing of livestock, which destroys the young growths and the subgrowth, eating around and breaking them; (2) the devouring of fruit by wild boars and rats; and (3) the annual gathering of walnuts. In the course of hundreds of years, the walnut forests have changed their primary composition as a result of the direct and indirect interference of man. The walnut forests are of great value because of the high quality of the wood, the burls on the trunks (which are exported), and the fruit.

In some places above the walnut forests grow maple forests (*Acer turkestanicum*) with an undergrowth of shade-enduring grasses. Sites not occupied by walnut are covered with sparse deciduous forests containing apple, apricot, elm, mountain ash, poplar, and maple. There are many varieties of wild apples (*Pyrus malus, P. korshinskyi*), producing fruits which vary in time of ripening, sweetness, nature of pulp, and color. For example, in the Chimganki River valley (Chirchik River system), 25 varieties of apples have been discovered. On the western slope of Fergana Range grows an apple with red blossoms and pulp and a dark-red skin. Owing to the abundance of apples, the capital of the Kazakh S.S.R. was renamed Alma-Ata ("native land of apples," from *alma* = apple, *ata* = father). The apricot is another abundant tree. In Tadzhikistan alone there grows about 100 local varieties which are noted for their sweetness, being twice as sweet as European apricots. The trees are long lived (up to 200 years), bear early (in six or seven years), and have a high yield. The mulberry (*Morus*) is another fruit of extensive growth and many varieties. The sweet berries of the mulberry serve as food and, when carefully dried and ground, as cake flour.

Within the sparse deciduous forests, there is a large animal population. Bears and wild boars come in autumn to feed on apples. Birds found in the apple forest include the gray warbler (*Sylvia communis*), gray-crested Old World goldfinch (*Acanthis caniceps*), and eastern nightingale (*Luscinia megarhynchos*). In thickets along the Zeravshan, pheasant (*Phasianus colchicus zerafshanicus*) is encountered.

In valleys where there is running water that cools the soil, valley forests are found composed of two species of birch (*Betula altaica* and *B. tianschanica*) and wild apricot. Aspen groves are widespread in the northern part.

The deciduous mountain forests are of great significance in the development of zonal landscapes. These forests regulate the melting of snow and restrain surface runoff during downpours. As the water is absorbed by the dead plant litter, live vegetation, and soil, the erosion of slopes by cloudburst floods is averted. The forests feed ground water, regulate the flow of mountain streams, and furnish the irrigation networks with water. Mountain forests yield lumber for construction and firewood. The forests are now being protected, and many operations in natural and artificial reforestation of sparse areas are being carried out. It would be possible to develop park-like plantings of fruit trees which would yield a new source of commercial wealth.

Subalpine Zone

The subalpine zone is a complex of subalpine meadows, spruce-fir forests, juniper groves, steppes, and rocky outcrops. The variations in zone limits are considerable: in the Zaili Ala-Tau it begins at 4,950 feet to 5,280 feet, in the drier Fergana Range at 3,300 feet higher, and in Alayskiy Valley still higher (10,230 to 10,560 feet). The characteristic features of the climate of the zone are: cool summer, short growing season, and sufficient and regular moistening, which contribute to the development of meadow vegetation. Meadows of the lower forest-meadow steppe zone gradually and imperceptibly change to subapline meadows; the former are linked with the deciduous forests, the latter with spruce-fir for-

short, but thick, grass stand and complete turfing over. They have many species, rich and succulent foliage, brilliant and large flowers which blossom simultaneously. Many northern grasses grow in subalpine meadows, such as meadow grass, foxtail grass, and cold-enduring flowers: geraniums (*Geranium albiflorum*), white anemones (*Anemone narcissiflora*), or-

Fig. 15-13. Forest of Tien Shan spruce along the Aksu River near Przhevalsk.

ests. In some places the subalpine meadows extend in an almost unbroken ribbon along the mountain chains, in others they are broken up and even disappear for long distances because of the dryness of individual high ranges. The typical subalpine meadows are in the peripheral parts of the region. A chernozem-like soil is developed under the meadows, but is frequently devoid of carbonates and has a brown sod layer. Subalpine meadows differ from lower meadows in having a comparatively

ange globeflowers (*Trollius asiaticus*), and rose asters (*Aster alpinus*). Together with them, there are many representatives of the low-mountain meadows, such as phlomis, the thistle, compositae (*Ligularia altaica*), and in the southern part of the region *Prangos pabularia*. In the central part patches of high-elevation steppe are encountered with chaco grass (*Festuca sulcata*), cousinia (*Cousinia stephanophora*) and *Artemisia lehmanniana*. With their high fodder production, vast areas of subalpine meadows provide excellent summer pasturages.

Linked with the subalpine meadows are spruce-fir forests, going rather high in the dry climate of Tien Shan: in the Dzungarian Ala-Tau up to 4,950 to 7,590 feet, in the Zaili Ala-Tau 5,940 to 9,240 feet, in the Terskei Ala-Tau 6,930 to 9,240 feet, and in the Chatkal Range 5,940 to 9,405 feet. Spruce-fir forests are widespread only in the eastern part of Tien Shan to a line between the Chatkal Range and Fergana Range, where they come in contact with the eastern boundary of the walnut. They are adapted to shady, north-facing slopes and to narrow steep-walled valleys, which explains the insular character of their occurrence. On the north-facing slope of the Dzungarian Ala-Tau and Terskei Ala-Tau they play an important part in the landscape forest zone, but toward the south they are scattered in small patches along the slopes of the mountains and in deep valleys. The spruce-fir forests have a park-like character. Here one sees the regular alternation of dense woods on the steep north-facing slopes and open expanses of subalpine meadows on the other slopes. Despite the park-like character, these are cold-enduring mesophytic forests of a taiga type that completely shade the soil.

The builder of phytocoenoses is the Tien Shan spruce (*Picea schrenkiana*). It has a narrow crown, and since the short, exceedingly dense branches nowhere protrude from the general mass, the tree looks as if it has been trimmed. It reaches a height of 165 feet, and is distinguished from Siberian spruce by its sharp bluish-green color and longer needle. The natural restoration of spruce in dense plantings is completely satisfactory. The second conifer is fir. In the Chatkal Range and the Talas Ala-Tau, Turkestan fir (*Abies semenowi*) predominates, and in the Dzungarian Ala-Tau, Siberian fir (*Abies sibirica*). In the subgrowth, shade-loving trees and bushes are common: Tien Shan mountain ash (*Sorbus tianschanica*), honeysuckle (*Lonicera hispida*), and spindle tree (*Evonymus semenowi*). The lower vegetation is impoverished by decreased light and low temperatures. On the shaded loose moss cover of the Dicranum and Thuidium families are scattered solitary Siberian taiga species such as pyrola (*Pyrola secunda*) or the orchidaceous creeping plantain (*Goodyera repens*). The soil beneath the spruce forests is slightly podzolic.

The spruce forests are barren and silent: there are few insects and few birds. Some members of the animal world are attached to the spruce grove, although life on its borders is considerably more abundant. In the very thickest places live the lynx and large *manul* cat (*Otocolobus manul*). The Siberian roe deer is commonly found in the spruce groves. The stag goes off to feed in the alpine meadows above, where it pastures in the morning and evening, returning to the forest during the day to rest and masticate its food in peace. The most characteristic birds of the spruce groves are: ordinary chiff-chaff, tomtit, tridactylous woodpecker (*Picoides tridactylus tianschanicus*), black grouse, and nutcracker (*Nucifraga caryocatactes*), which live here permanently. In winter, pine grosbeak, a martin-like bird *Pinicola enucleator,* and bullfinch (*Pyrrhula pyrrhula*) fly into the spruce forests. These forests, despite wood of good grade, are little exploited owing to the difficulty both of felling on the steep slopes and of floating timber on the violent streams.

The southern part of the subalpine zone has thickets of juniper (*Juniperus globosa*), a tree of Central Asian origin. There are several species of juniper, of which the large, woody, long-lived *Juniperus semiglobosa* is abundant. Because the root system of this juniper is highly developed, it is drought resistant and defends itself against winds, erosion, and soil creep. The first of these junipers appear at 2,640 feet and rise as high as 9,900 feet in the Peter the First Range. At a height of 8,580 feet it begins to become bush-like, and at about 9,240 feet takes on a creeping form. The juniper grows on steep and very rocky slopes and usually forms sparse park-like stands. Under favorable conditions, however, it produces dense shady thickets, under the cover of which forest grasses and mosses find shelter.

Fig. 15-14. Stunted growth of "archa" on the slopes of Gissar Ridge.

The sparse, bright, and dry juniper forest on rocky slopes with vast talus trains creates an animal habitat different from that of the deciduous or spruce forests. In the depressions of rock wastes, wood mice and mountain field mice find shelter, and under the overhang of large rocks, the cony makes its home. The abundance of rodents attracts small predatory animals of the marten family, whose narrow and flexible bodies allow them to reach rodent nests among the loose rocks. Examples of such animals are: Fergana ermine (*Mustela erminea ferganae*), Turkestanian weasel (*Mustela nivalis pallida*), and rock marten (*Mustela foina*). Birds found in the juniper groves include the white-winged haw finch (*Mycerobas carnipes*), mountain yellowhammer, and bluebird (*Myophonus coeruleus*). Rock partridge (*Alectoris kakelik*) ascends from the gorges. In the groves of juniper there are no worms, myriapods, or reptiles.

The juniper forests secure the slopes, check-ing the weathering and erosion of the fine soil, and regulate the surface discharge of water, moderating floods and promoting the uniform flow of water into irrigation networks. These forests are the sole source of valuable wood for entire areas. The wood is industrially important because of its exceptionally fine grain, lightness, ability to dry without cracking, and beautiful rose-red color. As a fuel, the juniper has a limited use. It will be necessary to restore forests that have been cleared and to plant them on slopes no good for pasturage.

Alpine Zones

The alpine zone begins at the upper timber and brushwood line (9,900 to 11,550 feet), and extends to the very tops of the mountains, sometimes crossing the snow line. A short cold summer, a cold snowy winter, sharp contrasts of temperature of the soil and of the air between day and night, and strong winds are the typical features of the high-elevation climate. These features are clearly reflected in the character of the plant and animal life. Precipitation and degree of soil moistening are far from uniform in this zone. In places where sufficient rain falls and the relief promotes its retention, alpine meadows develop. In those places where there is less precipitation and the upper parts of thick taluses are without water, the meadows give way to the xerophytic vegetation of high-elevation steppes, or steppe grasses are introduced into the composition of the meadows. The fauna of the zone is poor both in number and in species. Warmth-loving species are almost absent, although species of the high uplands of Central Asia and certain northern species play a large role. Some animals live in the zone only in summer, and in winter migrate to the zones where it is easier to find shelter and food. Permanent fauna are protected from the cold and hungry winters by thick and downy fur, by the ability to hibernate, by feeding on food stored in autumn (cony), or by getting food from under the snow (field mice).

A typical alpine vegetation, in the most humid places, is formed by cobresia meadows, composed of several species of the genus *Cobresia* of the family of sedges. The meadows occupy shaded slopes and the upper stretches of river valleys in the zone of moraine deposits where there is sufficient moisture. Cobresia meadows are distinguished by uniformity, impoverished composition, limited thickness of cover, and turfing over of the soil. They contain a few of the most persistent alpine species, such as sedge (*Carex sempervirens*) or edelweiss (*Leontopodium alpinum*).

Alpine meadows differ in composition from the uniform cobresia meadows. In comparison with the subalpine meadows, they contain lower-growing (4 to 6 inches) vegetation, a thick grassy cover, bright color, and large flowers. The absence of annuals, the abundance of rosette species, the ability to reproduce vegetatively, and the exceptional frost resistance of the plants indicate the short growing season.

Only in July do the alpine plants begin to open their buds rapidly. The meadows are studded with a mass of white and varicolored starworts, yellow crowfoot, blue gentians, rose asters, and pale yellow alpine poppies. On rocky slopes are a few pillow-like semishrubs: acantholimon (*Acantholimon marmoreum*) and sibbaldia (*Sibbaldia tetrandra*). In the midst of alpine meadows are patches of chaco-grass steppes and narrow strips of damp meadows along streams. Under the alpine meadows, humus and peaty, leached-out mountain-meadow soil is developed.

Alpine meadows are excellent summer grazing lands. In the winter livestock return to the valleys. The wasteful, careless nomadic

Fig. 15-15. Some characteristic hoofed animals in the mountain regions of Central Asia. Upper left—Central Asian mountain goat (*Capra sibirica*); upper right—mountain sheep (*Ovis vignei*); bottom—sheep (*Ovis ammon*). (*Mounting by S. P. Suslov; drawing by V. V. Trofimov.*)

economy practiced in the past has greatly reduced the quality of these meadows. In the
highest parts of the alpine zone, in the region
of snow, ice, and rocks, there are many perennials which conceal themselves among the
rocks, sheltered from the strong cold winds,
and send out only their long peduncles onto
the surface. Among the plants able to cope
with the severe conditions are crepis (*Crepis
tenuifolia*), astragal (*Astragalus nivalis*), and
crazyweed (*Oxytropis pagobia*). The upper
boundary of flowering plants in the Zeravshan
Range reaches about 12,550 feet, and in the
western Pamir about 14,850 feet.

A number of unique mountain animals are
encountered in the alpine landscape. Rocky
gorges with creeks are the favorite habitat of
the Siberian ibex (*Capra sibirica*), which
climbs up to the perpetual snows. In the lower
valleys of the southern part of the region there
are flocks of goat (*Capra falconeri*). The red
or long-tailed marmot (*Marmota caudata*),

which spends a great part of its life in sleep,
is found in colonies throughout the entire zone.
Other rodents include the cony or mouse hare
(*Ochotona rutila*) and mountain field mouse.
Predatory animals include the snow panther
or ounce (*Uncia uncia*), which hunts wild
goats and marmots, and Tien Shan bear (*Ursus
pruinosus leuconyx*), which feeds primarily on
marmots and grasses and descends to the valleys when the fruit ripens. Most common birds
are: mountain pipit (*Anthus spinoletta blackistoni*), alpine accentor (*Prunella collaris rufi-
lata*), mountain finch (*Leucosticte brandti*),
and yellow-billed alpine jackdaw (*Pyrrhocorax
graculus*). Dwelling in the midst of the snowy
summits and bare crags are Himalayan black
turkey-hen (*Tetraogallus himalayensis*), red-
billed chough (*Pyrrhocorax*), and that powerful bird of prey the griffon-vulture (*Gypaetus
barbatus grandis*). The acclimatizing of the
South American llama and the valuable fur-
bearing chinchilla is being considered.

MOUNTAIN LANDSCAPES

Pamir

The Pamir is the rectangle-shaped mountainous district that extends to the south of the
Tien Shan system. On the north and south it
is bordered by mountain barriers—the Zaila
Range and the Hindu Kush Mountains—and
on the west and east by the Western Tadzhik
and the Tarim depressions. Within the USSR
the western boundary corresponds to the valley
of the Pyandzh River, and the eastern to the
crest of Sarikol Range. Administratively, this
territory belongs to the Gorno-Badakhshan
Autonomous Oblast, which is a part of the
Tadzhik SSR.

The Pamir is related to the typical southern
arcs of the Central Asian mountain region.
Geologically, it is four complex zones of deposits of different composition and age, having
the form of arcs extending in an east-west
direction with the convex side facing north:

(1) a gneiss-marble formation of Pre-Cambrian age; (2) a zone of sedimentary Upper
Paleozoic and Mesozoic deposits; (3) metamorphosed schists; and (4) Mesozoic and
Cenozoic deposits in the northernmost part
of the Pamir.

Geomorphologically, the Pamir consists of
two contrasting subdistricts—Western Pamir
and Eastern Pamir. The conventional boundary
between them passes through the Zulum-Art
mountain group, Usoyskiy Zaval, Lake Yashil-
Kul, and the junction of the Pamir and
Vakhan Darya rivers.

In Eastern Pamir, there are the most unusual
combinations of land forms: sand barchans
situated on old moraines, desert varnish on
broken stone, arctic stony polygons, peculiar
honeycombed erosion forms, dry deltas, and
solonchak in the zone of solid permafrost. The
relief bears a pronounced intermediate-mountain character, despite the high altitudes, up to

18,150 feet. Above the broad valleys the mountains rise to *relative* heights of only about 3,300 to 5,000 feet.

The small relative height of the mountains is combined with the small angle of gradient and the weak dissection of the slopes, the roundness and closeness of the summits, and the general smoothness of contours. The reason for this is the intense processes of physical weathering, the products of which cover the slopes with a rubbly stony mantle. Since the negligible amount of water prevents the fine soil from washing off, there is little movement of the material along the slopes.

The valleys of Eastern Pamir are wide with comparatively short steep slopes and flat bottoms composed of thick loose deposits. These forms are created by the intensive lateral erosion of the rivers and by the filling of the valley bottoms with the products of weathering, which compensate for the slight vertical erosion (which is limited by the permafrost) of the rivers. The finer and more uniform material accumulates in the valley bottoms. Salt appears as a white efflorescence of calcium carbonate or as yellowish concretions of gypsum. The wind also plays a certain role in the shaping of the valleys. Loose alluvium is blown off the valley bottoms (almost devoid of plant cover) into aeolian accumulations. The general trend of the relief is a gradual leveling: weathering is reducing the height of the mountains and the products of weathering are raising the level of the valley floors. The rather slightly dissected relief does not contribute to the intensity of the erosional processes.

The main relief forms of Eastern Pamir are typically glacial, linked with the great glacial cover which lay for a long period and preserved the relief from intensive erosion. Traces of glacial accumulations are widespread as moraine hilly relief and glacial moraine belts at the foot of the mountains.

The general character of the evolution of relief in the Western Pamir is completely different from that in Eastern Pamir. Westward from Eastern Pamir, the vertical dissection becomes more complicated. The rivers cut deep gorges in the broad bottoms of the Western Pamir valleys, the gentle slopes of the valleys become steeper in their lower sections, and the depths of the valleys increase. A highly dissected, high-elevation relief—sharp crests and peaks, steep slopes, and great variations in relative heights—is characteristic of Western Pamir. The northern end of Akademiya Nauk, approximately 4 miles from the bottom and of the Muk-Su River, is some 2 miles above the latter, so that the average gradient of the slope is roughly a half mile down for every mile. The relief forms of the Western Pamir are typically erosional. Running water, which is almost absent in the Eastern Pamir, is a powerful agent that breaks down the rock and moves loose masses along the slopes. Contributing to this are strong dissection, the large exposed slopes, and their sharp angles of gradient. Glaciation of the mountain crests results in saturation of the loose rock by the meltwater and the washing out of fine particles; this leads to the sliding of coarse rubble and, sometimes, to the formation of destructive slides by cloudburst torrents. Although enormous masses of rubble descend from the slopes, the level of valley bottoms is generally not raised because the rivers not only transport this rubble but carry on additional erosional work, cutting into the bedrock. Consequently, erosion does not diminish but actually increases contrast in local relief.

The high elevations, steepness and bareness of valley sides, and strong earthquakes are conditions which favor landslides, some of which are large enough to block river valleys with dams resembling terminal moraines. In the valleys, fluvioglacial and highly eroded alluvium predominates, often appearing rather high (650 to 1,000 feet) above the valley bottom. Lake sediments are also found, formed as a result of the filling up of lakes created by landslide. The petrographic character of the rocks also affects the general course of the geomorphologic process. For example, in the gneiss-marble series, there are narrow, precipitous gorges that leave only small patches for farming, but in the belt of the easily eroded schistous series, the smoothness of relief has provided considerable areas for fields. In the deep valleys lie large valley glaciers of the dendritic type.

The climate of Eastern Pamir differs sharply from that of Western Pamir. An extremely continental high-elevation-desert climate of the Central Asian type is characteristic of the Eastern Pamir. The basic factors determining this climate are: position (36° to 40° north latitude), broad valleys, and enclosure by high ranges. The thinness and dryness of the atmosphere, the clarity and transparency of the air, and the brightness of the skies, contribute to the intense cooling and heating of the air and soil. Under these conditions, solar radiation is of high intensity. This explains the low temperatures in winter and at night, and the high temperatures in summer and during the day— that is, the extremely sharp fluctuations in annual and daily temperatures, the intensive mechanical erosion, and the widespread occurrence of permafrost at a depth of 2.5 to 6 inches.

Relief forms are a strong influence on climatic conditions. In the Eastern Pamir winter temperatures are unusually low in the broad valleys because cold and heavy air masses flowing off the neighboring mountains settle there. Eastern Pamir is enclosed by ranges which intercept the western air currents and deposit their moisture on the outer slopes. Consequently, there is less precipitation in Eastern Pamir than anywhere in Central Asia: at Murgab 2.4 inches annually, and in the basin of Lake Kara-Kul 1 inch. In winter the zone of maximum condensation of the moisture brought by western winds is below the crests of the bordering mountains, which is why the air masses that drop into Eastern Pamir are already dry and why very little snow falls. In summer, when the zone of maximum precipitation is higher, some of the moisture is carried beyond the mountains to condense in the east. During the summer months, half of the annual amount falls (January 0.012 inch, June 0.56 inch).

The air is exceptionally dry. Relative humidity at 1 P.M. in the summer months averages from 21 to 28 per cent, but sometimes drops to 9 per cent. Annual cloudiness is very slight —39 per cent, and there are only about 45 overcast days during the year. The greatest cloudiness is in spring and the least in autumn (in September there are 23 clear days). There are strong (to 49 feet per second) and frequent winds, normally blowing in the afternoon and evening. The wind is often so strong that it lifts small pebbles into the air, scratching and cutting one's face and hands. Ascending air currents, brought about by intense insolation in summer, cause sandstorms, and cold air masses rolling off the mountains in winter cause severe cold winds. The dryness of the air and soil and also the frequent winds have resulted in high-elevation desert landscapes, the absence of woody plants, the development of a sparse xerophytic vegetation, and the need for artificial irrigation of crops.

Winter in the Eastern Pamir is severe and prolonged. The January temperature at Murgab averages 1°F, but may drop as low as —50°F. The daily amplitudes at these altitudes are extreme. In winter, the temperature may be —8.6°F in the morning, and after noon rise to several degrees above freezing. The difference in temperatures in the sun and shade is especially sharp. On calm sunny days it often becomes so hot that it is necessary to shed warm clothing, but it requires only a cloud or shadow obstructing the rays of the sun for the intense cold to pierce right through one. The side of the face exposed to the sun is highly warmed, but the side in the shade almost freezes. In the course of a single day the temperature of the soil may vary greatly: on a day in February, for example, a maximum temperature of 10°F and a minimum of —30.5°F were recorded. The shallow depth and short duration of the snow cover, owing to the negligible amount of winter precipitation, cause the soil to freeze deeply and maintain the permafrost; on the other hand, the lack of snow allows the nomadic livestock raiser, in the valleys, to keep his livestock on fodder all year. Summer is short and cool. The warmest month, July, has an average temperature of 56.5°F, but it may rise to 69°F (Kara-Kul). Even during the peak of flowering, however, frost is a common phenomenon, and snowstorms occur even in the middle of summer. The soil in summer may warm to 124°F, but such temperatures do not penetrate deeply. Climatic conditions are not very favorable for agriculture; only in the lowest part of the neighboring Alayskiy Valley can wheat and barley be grown.

Western Pamir, exposed to the moist air currents on the west and protected by the Akademiya Nauk Range from the cold masses that reach Eastern Pamir, has a milder, warmer, and wetter climate; the valleys tend toward deserts of the Mediterranean type. The average winter and summer temperatures are higher (to 18.5° and 71.8°F, respectively), there is more precipitation (to 9 inches, with the maximum in the winter-spring period), and summer is dry (January 1.1 inches of precipitation, August 0.04 inches).

The soil-forming process in the Pamir is unique. Under cold and dry climatic conditions, rocky, rubbly, and weakly developed soil predominates on diversified bedrock and loose strata. Local moistening and the vegetation linked with it create great extremes in the soil-forming process. The highest parts of the ranges with rocky outcrops and taluses have only small isolated patches of meadow soil. On dry sites where the vegetation cover is slight and where the ground water is far below the surface, the rocky and rubbly soil that contains only a small amount of fine particles and almost no humus belongs to the desert type, but represents unique Pamir sierozem and solonchak soils. Soil forming is more active in places with near-surface ground water and with the dense grass stand of moist meadows. Bog and solonchak soil-forming processes develop peat-bog, bog-meadow, and solonchak-meadow soils.

Against the general soil background, climatic and geomorphologic peculiarities of Western and Eastern Pamir produce unusual soils. On dry, elevated places in Eastern Pamir, a high-mountain, light-gray, generally rubbly and sandy soil is developed. On the floor of the valleys, and on gently sloping alluvial fans, there is a dust-like-clayey and dusty-sandy loam that is suitable for irrigated agriculture. In places where there is enough fine soil at the top, a grayish, friable, porous crust, as much as 1.2 inches thick and with polygonal fracturing, is formed. Below lies a darker, flaky, carbonate layer which does not contain easily soluble salts. Besides the gray soil, solonchak soil is also encountered. In places where the ground water is close to the surface, as beneath hummocky meadows, different variants of alkaline-meadow soil develop. Permafrost also plays a role in soil formation. Its buckling processes, indicated by cracks in the turf-humus layer and mottling of the soil cover, are caused by the freezing and thawing.

The soil of Western Pamir, because of the increase in the amount of precipitation, is characterized by much humus and by the absence of carbonates to a depth of 1.6 to 2.4 inches. In the midst of outcrops, rocky-rubbly taluses, and rocky patches, a soil cover is found only in small areas and strips most favored by relief—on river terraces and alluvial fans. Rocky and rubbly, light-chestnut, and chestnut-brown soils, and also high-mountain sierozem, are widespread. The irrigated soil of the river valleys is the oasis-crop type. Because of its easy permeability, it requires great quantities of water for irrigation. This soil was formed by prolonged and hard work: removing rocks and planning the tiny irrigated areas amid rocks and taluses.

The vegetation of the high Eastern Pamir should bear an alpine character but, because of the continental climate, alpine vegetation occurs only as individual scattered plants. There are small alpine meadows on amply moistened, wind-protected areas along the upper stretches of streams and at the ends of glaciers.

The entire remaining area, with the exception of amply watered riverside sections, is a cold high-elevation Central Asian desert. Vegetation grows under conditions less favorable than those in the other regions of Central Asia. The small amount of precipitation (90 per cent of which is snow), the exceptional dryness of air and soil, strong winds, sharp daily temperature amplitudes, frequent night frost in the growing season, the absence of a snow cover to protect plants from the winter cold, and the vast rocky expanses all hinder the growth of vegetation. A characteristic feature of the dry rocky places is the extreme thinness of the plant cover. The widely scattered squat plants form grazing lands of low fodder capacity.

Vegetation of the rocky deserts predominates on mountain slopes and on upper river terraces. It is primarily (about 75 per cent of the composition) small bushes or perennial grasses. The landscape plant is the squat desert semibrushwood halophyte, winter fat (*Eurotia ceratoides*). Although exceptionally sparse, it is the only source of fuel. With it grows crazyweed (*Oxytropis chiliophylla*) and certain

Fig. 15-16. Flattened ring-like form of acanthus lemon (*Acantholimon diapensioides*) with dead central part.

mustards (*Christolea pamirica*). On more cohesive and fine soil, *Artemisia scorniakowi* and also eastern feather-grass (*Stipa orientalis*) are added. On rockier and steeper slopes, the composition of vegetation is variable, but well developed is prickly thrift (*Acantholimon diapensioidese,* of the family Plumbaginacene), a cushion-shaped, squat (one to two inches) bush with fine pulpy leaves. Such plants as meadow grass (*Poa attenuata*) and fescue grasses (*Festuca violacea, F. rubra*) are of some significance in the rocky deserts.

The vegetation of the high-elevation rocky desert is unique. It is not the composition (numbering 500 species) but the form of the predominating bushes and perennial grasses, their adaptation to wasteland conditions, and their distribution that clearly show the ecological peculiarities of these deserts. Every year most plants lose their annual shoots on the soil surface, and their main woody shaft is in the soil layer itself, where the branching of the shoots also takes place. It is the layer of air, with a temperature which is still within the sphere of influence of the warmer soil, that sets the limit to vertical growth. The annual shoots, not reaching very high, cease to grow at the center of the plant and develop vigorously along the periphery, which leads to the expansion of the plant in a horizontal direction. This explains the squatness of the plants and the abundance of pillow-shaped and flattened forms, creating within themselves a special regime of moisture and temperature. The central, older parts of the plant die as a result of freezing, but the side branches are protected by the fine soil blown onto the edges of the plant, as a consequence of which the plant appears in a circular form. In the dying process of the central part of the bush and its main root, the peripheral branches form auxiliary roots, and are converted into independent plants.

The characteristics described above are possessed by many small bushes of the rocky desert: winter fat, prickly thrift, crazyweed, astragal. The intergrowth, or entwining, of one plant with another is common. For example, the large cushions of crazyweed retain the seeds of other plants on their surface, and these seeds grow there; thus it is possible to find on their cushion an entire phytocoenosis consisting of ten different species, difficult to separate from one another. Very interesting ecologically is the stalk of macrotomia (*Macrotomia euchroma,* of the borage family) with a height of 12 inches, thickly enveloped with high rosette-like leaves which protect it from sharp, daily fluctuations in temperature. Vegetation on alkaline soils with efflorescences of salts is very sparse. The rare flowering plants such as Pamir knotweed (*Polygonum pamiricum*) grow along crevices in which their roots are buried. There are also scale-like lichens and mosses distributed in patches and strips along crevices.

Meadows and bogs stand out conspicuously as emerald "ribbons" along streams in the middle of the desert. These ribbons vary from simple meadows composed of one or two species to ones with a dense cover of complex relations, from bogs with large hummocks and standing water to strongly salted, dry ones. On soil continuously moistened by ground water grow cobresia meadows containing cobresia (*Kobresia schoenoides*) and sedge (*Carex microglochin*). An integral part of the Pamir landscape is the hummocky-sedge solonchak-bog meadow, extending along the low banks of rivers and moist flat terraces. The local livestock-raising economy is based on these meadows, along which nomadic camps are scattered. In enclosed and remote valleys, since the herds will not leave the abundant fodder, they often graze unsupervised. In spring the herds graze on alpine meadows close to watersheds, and in autumn and winter descend into the valleys. To improve the fodder base, it will be necessary to create new pastures by means of irrigation, using both local grasses and legumes, and also by introducing plants from the Karakorum Tibet, and from the Peruvian Andes.

The vegetation of Western Pamir is less original, and bears a mountain-desert and partly a mountain-steppe character. The desert vegetation consists primarily of halophytic plants. Because of the rockiness of the slopes, there are not many steppes. A few small ones exist, made up of fescue grass and different species of meadow and feather grasses. Brushwoods, such as wild rose, honeysuckle, and the like, are scattered in individual groups everywhere. Meadow vegetation is good in places, for example, in the mountains above Khorog. *Ferula* plays a conspicuous role in it and is supplemented by a thick growth of diverse herbage.

The fauna of the Pamir contains a number of Central Asian species. Native to the high-elevation desert are: mammoth mountain sheep (*Ovis ammon*), which graze the year round on alpine meadows next to the permanent snows; Pamir hare (*Lepus europaeus tibetanus*); tailed marmot (*Marmota caudata*); and red cony (*Ochotona rutila*). An irreplaceable domestic animal of this area is the Tibetan yak (*Poephagus grunniens*), which yields excellent wool, delicious meat, and splendid thick milk, and is also a good pack animal. Among the birds nesting here are: Tibetan snow pheasant (*Tetraogallus tibetanus*), Tibetan sand grouse (*Syrrhaptes tibetanus*), Tibetan raven (*Corvus corax tibetanus*), *Ibidorhyncha struthersii,* and snow griffon-vulture (*Gyps fulvus himalayensis*). Indian goose (*Anser indicus*) and Tibetan short-billed plover (*Cirrepedesmus mongolus atrifrons*) spend the winter in India.

Alay Valley

The Alay Valley, between the Alay and Trans-Alay ranges, belongs to the high-mountain steppe zone. The characteristic geomorphologic elements of the valley are: (1) the smooth-undulating enclosed valley relief of moraine accumulations; (2) the gentle fans of the mountain slopes, dissected by numerous transverse gravel beds; and (3) the two terraces of the Kyzyl-Su River, which flows along the axis of the valley. The climate here is so severe that there is no frost-free period in the eastern part of the valley. The upper foothills are occupied by cobresia meadows on leached-out, high-mountain, meadow soil, and on the lower foothills subalpine meadows are developed on rich chernozem-like soil. On the diluvial-proluvial deposits of the sloping plains, fescue-grass steppes are found on high-elevation chestnut soil. Solonchak is also developed

Pamir. The level surfaces of the basins which are enclosed by mountain ranges are arid even though they are not at high elevation. There is much more precipitation here (10.6 inches at Marynskoye) than in the Pamir, and the temperature regime is more favorable. Because of the local levelness, the usual vertical zonality is absent. In these basins high-elevation

Fig. 15-17. Alay Valley with the many-braided channels of the Kyzyl River; in the rear, the wall of the Zaalaysk Ridge with Lenin Peak in the center.

here, strongly treated with gypsum. The vast reserves of fodder plus conditions favorable for their utilization seasonally, cool summers, and the absence of animal-disturbing insects have made the valley an ideal place for raising livestock. Irrigation farming in the western part is very old: barley, wheat, lucerne, oats, and even frost-resistant northern grains, such as spring rye from Yakutia, are successively cultivated.

Central Tien Shan Basins

The basins of central Tien Shan are similar in landscape to the cold desert of Eastern

steppes predominate, sometimes changing to high-elevation deserts; and only on the wetter places are there cobresia meadows—which are alpine-zone elements. Steppes in the wetter sections are meadow-steppes with chaco-cobresia base, to which are added legumes and edelweiss; the drier steppes consist of pinnate feather-grass (*Stipa kirghisorum*), koeleria, desert oats, timothy, and couch grass (*Agropyron ferganense*). The soil is carbonaceous, contains a certain amount of easily soluble salts, and resembles light-chestnut soil in appearance. The high-elevation deserts have a dismal character during the entire growing season. The soil surface, with frequent efflorescences of salts, is covered with 10 to 15 per cent vegetation, consisting of solitary bushes and isolated patches of prickly thrift, crazyweed, and Mongolian feather grass, found also in the Pamir. But white artemisia is replaced here by another species—*Artemisia rhodantha,* a small, gray, woody bush, one to two inches high.

Kopet Dagh

Kopet Dagh begins close to Kazandzhik Station, extends southeast to the Tedzhen River, and farther on withdraws into the borders of Afghanistan. That part of Kopet Dagh lying within the Soviet Union, the northern part, reaches its greatest heights at the top of Riza Mountain south of Ashkhabad, 9,695 feet. Farther south, in Iran, Kopet Dagh rises to more than 10,890 feet. The range does not reach the line of permanent snow; snow survives here to the end of summer only in patches within ravines. Three mountain chains formed of Cretaceous sediments are formed in Kopet Dagh: (1) the front range with average heights of about 3,300 feet, whose foothills are composed of Tertiary deposits; (2) the second one with heights of about 6,930 feet; and (3) the boundary range which rises to 9,900 feet. The strike of the ranges corresponds in general to that of the rocks composing them. The anticlinal part of the folds are highly eroded, and the solid strata exposed beneath form the highest points of the relief. Folds in the front range are tilted to the north, and as a result of the strong pitch there occurred a faulting of the beds in conformity with the strike of the folds. A number of springs are associated with this faulting. There are also transverse breaks which are utilized by many rivers. Mountain-forming processes occurred repeatedly during the Tertiary Period; earthquakes remind one of their continuing activity. Between the mountain ranges are synclinal valleys. Entering them are many lateral valleys (as deep, vertical-walled gorges) that have cut through Lower Cretaceous limestones. The slopes of the ranges are strikingly dissected, containing a multitude of dry lateral valleys down which, periodically, great floods flow and merge in the long valleys. Deposits of these mountain streams are common in the foothills. Karst phenomena also play a certain role in the development of relief.

The Kopet Dagh has unusually dry air during the entire growing season, which is associated with the intense desiccating action of the neighboring Central Asian and Iranian deserts. In comparison with the adjacent plains, Kopet Dagh (for example, at Gaudan, south of Ashkhabad, at 4,900 feet) has a cool summer and constant amount of precipitation (8.6 inches). However, maximum precipitation is not in March but in May (May 1.8 inches, July 0.0 inches). Kopet Dagh is very poor in water, containing only small trickling streams. The Lower Cretaceous series of limestone supplies most of the abundant springs with rather warm water. The springs are associated with the lengthwise fault line on the northern slope of the foremost range. This line of abundant springs along Kopet Dagh supplies the intricate system of underground irrigation canals which are of great importance in the adjacent deserts.

Devoid of permanent snow, Kopet Dagh is a steppe range, changing at lower elevations into a semidesert and merging in the foothills with the neighboring loess plain. The predominating vegetation differs greatly from that of the other steppes of Central Asia in its origin, composition, and ecology. The steppe vegetation bears a pronounced Iranian character. The Kopet Dagh has little precipitation, small streams, and very steep, craggy, rocky, and highly dissected slopes. These, together with the sparse accumulations of fine soil over small areas, have led to the development of upland xerophytes that are original in form and ecology. Nevertheless, vertical zonality in dry Kopet Dagh is clearly expressed, though the zones are considerably lower than those of Tien Shan. The arid mountain zone extends to 1,150 feet and is analogous in its landscape to the adjacent foothill loess plain. The mountain semidesert, to 1,650 feet, has a very sparse

Fig. 15-18. Strong dissection of the Kopet Dagh Range by torrential rains.

grassy cover on a desert-steppe sierozem which is close to light-chestnut soil. The seasonal change of vegetation is still sharply expressed here. In spring the semidesert has a continuous green, low, sedge-grass cover composed of meadow grass (*Poa bulbosa vivipara*) and sedge (*Carex stenophylla*), to which are added tulip and bindweed. In the middle of June this vegetation dies out, and the predominating plants are *Artemisia*. On rocky places there is a more xerophytic vegetation, such as cousinia and thorny upland xerophytes.

The mountain steppe zone, 1,650 to 3,800 feet, begins with couch-grass—diverse-grass steppes on light-chestnut soil. The seasonal change in vegetation is expressed differently from that in the lower semidesert. Only a few plants grow in the spring, and the predominating species, such as feather grass (*Stipa pulcherrima*), couch grass (*Agropyron trichophorum*), and astragal (*Astragalus onobrychis*), do not appear until the middle of July. The steppes are used as hay meadows and grazing lands. Wheat and barley are grown here: in rainy years they yield an excellent harvest, in dry years they are completely lost. Steppes with feather and fescue grasses on dark-chestnut

soil lie at 3,630 to 7,260 feet. The basic plants are: fescue grass, plumose feather-grasses (*Stipa joannis, S. lessingiana*), and herbs such as *Echinops ritro* and *Phlomis pungens,* which are characteristic of the Ukrainian steppes and absent in other parts of Central Asia.

Together with typical steppe phytocoenoses, upland xerophytes are abundant on rocky soil devoid of fine particles. These upland xerophytes reach greater development in Kopet Dagh, taking on real landscape significance. These are plants adapted to life on rocky terrain which is almost devoid of fine soil and rich in lime, and which warms easily but cools rapidly. The plants do not undergo a shortage of soil moisture but transpire much water because of the exceptional dryness of the air. Upland xerophytes are the most clearly expressed drought-resistant plants. Almost at the surface of the soil, the plant's small stem branches out into many short, densely leafed twigs, the upper ends of which are tightly pressed to one another, and at the top or at the side emerge elongated blossom bearers. Thus the upland xerophytes are low-growing (10 to 20 inches), compact or loose semishrub cushions; they have a semicircular shape which minimizes evaporation, restricts the interchange of the air within the cushion, and protects the plant from the wind. The leaves of many of the xerophytes are spines and are sometimes covered with excretions of lime. Many of the plants are ester-bearing. A xerophytic characteristic found in many of the plants is a deep taproot. Plants such as prickly thrift (*Acanthophyllum*) of the pink family and gypsophila (*Gypsophila aretoides*) have a pad consisting of a multitude of closely joined pedicules. Gypsophila is so compact that rain does not penetrate through it and a horse can pass through patches of it without leaving a hoofprint. The cushions of other plants (for example, *Dionysia tapetoides*) may settle on top of it. Since gypsophila burns well, it is used for fuel. Other xerophytes here include bush tragacanth astragal, yielding gum dragon, and crazyweed (*Onobrychis cornuta*) of the legumes. Upland xerophytes do not grow in close

formation but are widely separated from one another.

Woody vegetation is rather weakly represented in Kopet Dagh. Juniper (*Juniperus polycarpos turcomanica*), reaching a height of 52 to 66 feet, is found in the mountains from 3,300 to 8,250 feet. Along waterless gorges grow scrub thickets of hawthorn, wild rose, honeysuckle, and plum. In moister gorges, to 3,960 feet, there is a rather rich woody vegetation: walnut (*Juglans regia*), maple (*Acer monspessulanum*), elm (*Ulmus densa*), ash, poplar, and many wild fruit trees (including prune and white mulberry), beneath which grow shade-loving plants such as arum (*Arum elongatum*). In the southwestern part of Kopet Dagh, under approximately these same conditions, grows the woody and bush vegetation of the Mediterranean Iranian region: European plane tree (*Platanus orientalis*), pomegranate (*Punica granatum*), yellow jasmine (*Jasmi-*

Fig. 15-19. Wide longitudinal valley in the Kopet Dagh Mountains: overthrusted strata with outcrops of extrusives.

num fruticans), thickets of spiny Christ's thorn (*Paliurus aculeatus*).

Whereas the Pamir has species of Central Asian (Tibetan) fauna, Kopet Dagh contains many species from Asia Minor, Iran, and Afghanistan. The ungulates encountered include mountain goat (*Capra aegagrus*) and mountain sheep (*Ovis orientalis cycloceras*). Among the predatory animals living here are: panther (*Leopardus pardus*), cheetah (*Acinonyx jubatus*), manul cat (*Octocolobus manul*), bear (*Ursus arctos lasistanicus*), and relic Indian honey badger (*Mellivora indica*). Rodents include the rust-colored cony (*Ochotona rufescens*), mouse (*Calomyscus bailwardi hotsoni*), and, close to snow patches, snow mouse (*Microtus nivalis*), which is also found in the Caucasus. Among the birds are found: Caspian snow pheasant (*Tetroagallus caspius*) and

many pigeons (*Columba palumbus*), and, in the foothills, the beautiful mountain hen (*Ammoperdix griseogularis*). In dark gorges and caves in the foothills dwell the venomous cobra (*Naja naja*) and, in the semideserts, the large viper (*Vipera libertina*), feeding primarily on rodents. During intense heat, it retreats into the ground.

Dzungarian Ala-Tau

The Dzungarian Ala-Tau is a special region in the USSR. It is separated from the Tien Shan by the 60-mile-wide Ili depression, which varies little in elevation (1,500 to 2,000 feet). Adjoining the Dzungarian Ala-Tau from the north is the extensive Balkhash Ala-Kul plain, which has a maximum width of 60 miles and

Fig. 15-20. Pillows of xerophytes in central Kopet Dagh Ridge.

Fig. 15-21. Landforms of desert "karst" in the limestone strata of the small Balkhan Mountains showing funnels and hanging ravines.

average height of 1,150 to 1,300 feet. Eastward, it turns into a 9-mile-wide channel known as Dzungarian Gates.

The Dzungarian Ala-Tau consists of two main, almost latitudinal, ranges divided from one another by the longitudinal valley of the Kok-Su River, which descends and widens out to the west. The northern range forms an arc, convex to the south. On the gentle northern slope of the range, despite its deep dissection by transverse river valleys, one may discern five mountain ridges, which descend gradually to the west and between which are longitudinal depressions. The southern slope of the range (in China) is steep and short. The southern range, in its eastern section, is the highest of the whole mountain system, 15,701 feet, and drops to the south toward the Ili depression in steep cliffs dissected by deep erosional valleys. Toward the south, beyond the Kugaly

depression, extends the isolated range Altyn-Emel (9,497 feet).

The Dzungarian Ala-Tau has a fan-shaped structure because in the western part the folds on the northern slope are deflected to the north and those on the southern slope to the south. The main ranges represent large anticlines, the axes of which dip to the west. The valleys which separate the ranges coincide with broad synclinal dips. The cores of the anticlines consist of gneisses and crystalline schists, referred conventionally to the Pre-Cambrian. The main structure of the ranges is a complex series of Paleozoic rocks with the Silurian and Devonian strongly dislocated and metamorphosed, and the Carboniferous is less intensively folded. In lithological composition the Silurian-Devonian formations are divided into sandstone-schist and schistose-limestone. The former have a wide distribution in the northern part of the

Dzungarian Ala-Tau, the latter in the southern part. An effusive-tuff layer belongs to the Lower Carboniferous. Tertiary deposits have their greatest development in the foothills of the southern slope; in the western foothills and on the northern slope, they coincide with the intermountain valleys. The Tertiary deposits lie horizontally or form gently sloping folds. They are red clays and sands, above which lies a gypsiferous layer. The Tertiary deposits are considered to be lake deposits.

Igneous rocks have a very wide development. There are three clearly expressed volcanic cycles, of which the Variscan is the most widely and fully established. Igneous rocks of both basic and flow types are found. Among the first group, granites, granodiorites, and quartz diorites prevail. The second group of rocks is more diverse in composition and consists of quartzite porphyries, albitophyres, and porphyrites with effusive breccias, volcanic tuffs, and lavas.

The Dzungarian Ala-Tau is an anticline. Evident along the borders of the mountain massifs are overthrusts of Paleozoic over Tertiary rock. Young upheavals of the Tertiary and Quaternary periods were accompanied by numerous faults which cut through both Paleozoic massifs and Tertiary deposits. Movements along these faults caused the formation of many cliffs, and well-marked escarpments exist on the north side of each succeeding mountain ridge. The clearest traces of young upheavals are the well-preserved peneplains, flat plateaus on the ranges, at 10,000 to 13,000 feet.

Present-day glaciation is rather limited. The snow line on the northern slope is at 10,000 to 11,500 feet, and on the southern at 11,500 to 13,000 feet. There are hundreds of small hanging and cirque glaciers. Only on the northern slope of the range are there glaciers which reach lengths of 2 to 3 miles. The glaciers terminate at 9,500 to 10,000 feet.

In comparison with the Tien Shan proper, the Dzungarian Ala-Tau has a quantitative predominance of Altai-Siberian flora, although on the southern slope are many species linked with the typical desert vegetation of Central Asia. For many of these species, the Dzungarian Ala-Tau forms a northern and eastern boundary of their distribution. The limits of all the vegetation zones are somewhat lowered. From a comparison of vegetation on northern and southern slopes, it is apparent on the southern slope that there is a sharp raising of the limits of the desert and steppe zones and that there is direct contact between the steppe and alpine zones. This contact is the result of the lower limits of the forest zone.

The shrub-steppe zone on the northern slope is at 2,650 to 4,950 feet. The following soils replace one another: sierozem and solonchak up to 2,000 feet, chestnut soil from 2,000 to 2,600 feet, and chernozem higher up. The lower sections of the zone have a purely steppe cover with feather grasses dominant, and smaller stands of steppe timothy, couch grass, and mixed grasses. There are also clumps of *Artemisia dracunculus* and sage; of the shrubs, the most common are meadowsweet and briar. Higher up, the vegetation acquires a more meadow-like character, and northern European plants, such as yarrow, appear. In the upper part of the shrub-steppe zone, apple forests are rather abundant. They are made up of *Malus sierversii,* which grows in depressions on the slopes having a northern exposure. Mixed with the apple in these forests are aspen, wild cherry, and various shrubs, including briar, honeysuckle, and hawthorn. The apple, the upper boundary of which is at 5,600 feet, easily encroaches the coniferous-forest zone, but is separated from the coniferous forests by subalpine meadows.

The coniferous-forest-subalpine zone on the northern slope, from 4,900 to 7,600 feet, is composed of coniferous forests and meadows. The Siberian fir is the common forest-forming tree, as distinguished from the forests of the Tien Shan proper, where the Tien-Shan spruce prevails. The Siberian fir is most often mixed with spruce or forms fir forests. The forest occupies the slopes having a northern exposure or the shaded sides of ravines. In the lower part of the belt are many shrubs, and in the upper section alpine grasses are found.

The coniferous forests alternate with subalpine high-grass meadows of the Altai type. Developed beneath them is mountain-meadow chernozem soil.

The alpine zone on the northern slope extends from 7,600 to 9,900 feet. Developed on it is a mountain-meadow and weakly turfed soil. The zone consists of two strips: mixed grass below and sedge alpine meadows above. The vegetation of the lower strip is xerophytic grass made up of steppe timothy and chaco grass, with dictotyledons of alpine species such as violet and alpine poppy. Above the mixed grass meadows, grass-sedge meadows of a tall grass stand (4 to 6 inches) are predominant, with grasses on the elevated places and sedge swamps in the depressions. Above 10,000 feet lie snow and glaciers.

On the southern slope of the Dzungarian Ala-Tau, there are three zones: the desert zone has its upper limit at 3,950 to 4,300 feet. In the lower part of the belt is the halophyte desert with the predominance of sierozem artemisia and the admixture of anabasis, and many ephemerals. In the upper part of the desert zone artemisia, kochia, and nanophyton plants predominate. The zone occupying the greatest area on the southern slope is the steppe zone, from 3,950 to 7,900 feet. The following make up its vegetation: maidenhair feather grass, chaco grass, mixed grass, and shrubs of honeysuckle and spirea. Spruce forests are either absent or grow only on the slopes of gorges and wide valleys in sparse stands with a rich shrub and grassy cover; these sections are widely separated from one another by extensive expanses of steppe and hence they do not form a special belt.

The alpine zone on the southern slope begins with growths of scrub juniper (*Juniperus tur-cestanica*) alternating with sections of chaco grass and fescue steppes or mixed-grass meadows with the predominance of geranium and foxtail. Higher up, the alpine belt is similar to that found on the northern slope.

Although the Dzungarian Ala-Tau has a fauna basically similar to that of the Tien Shan proper, it contains species typical of Central Asia, but no Afghano-Indian species. Animals from the north come to the coniferous forests from the Siberian taiga. At various elevations live such widely distributed animals as the badger and fox.

In the steppe belt of the mountains are the long-tailed marmot, the hamster, and rabbit. Bear, lynx, maral deer, and white hare live in the coniferous forests and also move to the higher mountains. There are the typical Siberian taiga birds: three-toed woodpecker, spruce crossbill, birch owl, and also species from mountainous Central Asia such as Tien-Shan kinglet. Among the alpine meadows (from 8,200 to 14,800 feet), in direct proximity to the permanent snows, exists a biocoenosis of the following: the Central Asian mountain goat, an inhabitant of the rocky heights, and its enemy, the snow panther; mountain sheep and also the Altai, or gray, marmot, a commercial fur animal; and the Central Asian alpine jackdaw.

Seasonally, there is a vertical migration of many animals. As the snow melts, the wild boar ascends gradually from the river valleys to the belt of juniper, spruce, and alpine meadows. In winter the mountain goat descends to the less snowy southern slopes of the mountains, crossing to the northern slopes only after the snow has melted. The red-breasted redstart and the horned lark, which nest in the alpine zone, winter in the foothills.

GENERAL BIBLIOGRAPHY

1. Б е р г Л. С., Географические зоны Советского Союза, изд. 3, т. I—II, 1947—1952. — 2. Т а н ф и л ь е в Г. И., География России, Украины и примыкающих к ним с запада территорий, ч. II, в. 1. Рельеф Азиатской России, ч. II, в. — 3. Климат. Реки. Озёра, 1923—1924.— 4. Большая советская энциклопедия. Том «Союз Советских Социалистических Республик», М., 1947.— 5. Естественно-историческое районирование СССР. Труды Комиссии по ест.-ист. районированию СССР, т. I, изд. АН СССР, М.—Л., 1947.— 6. Заповедники СССР, т. I и II, Географгиз, М., 1951.— 7. А р х а н г е л ь с к и й А. Д., Геологическое строение и геологическая история СССР, М.—Л., 1941. — 8. М а з а р о в и ч А. Н., Основы геологии СССР, М.—Л., 1938. — 9. Н а л и в к и н Д. В., Геологические районы СССР. Проблемы сов. геол., т. I, № 1, 1933.— 10. А р х а н г е л ь с к и й А. Д. и Ш а т с к и й Н. С., Схема тектоники СССР. БМОИП, отд. геол., т. XI, № 4, 1933.— 11. Г о р ш к о в Г. П., Землетрясения на территории Советского Союза, Географгиз, М., 1949.— 12. Щ у к и н И. С., Общая морфология суши, т. I и II, 1938—1939.— 13. Г е р а с и м о в И. П. и М а р к о в К. К., Ледниковый период на территории СССР (физико-географические условия ледникового периода). ТИГ, в. 33, 1939.—14. М а к е е в П. С., Физическая география СССР, ч. I. Рельеф СССР, Геодезиздат, М., 1944.— 15. Гипсометрическая карта СССР масштаба 1 : 2 500 000, М., 1949. —16. Геоморфологическое районирование СССР, изд. АН СССР, М.—Л., 1947.— 17. А л и с о в Б. П., Д р о з д о в О. А. и Р у б и н ш т е й н Е. С., Курс климатологии, ч. 1 и 2, Гидрометиздат, Л.— М., 1952.— 18. Б е р г Л. С., Основы климатологии, изд. 2, 1938.— 19. К а л и т и н Н. Н., Суммы тепла солнечной радиации на территории СССР. Природа, 1945, № 2.— 20. В о з н е с е н с к и й А. В., Карта климатов СССР. Труды по с.-х. метеорологии, в. 21, № 1, 193).— 21. З е н к е в и ч Л. А., Моря СССР, их фауна и флора, Учпедгиз, М., 1951.— 22. Л ь в о в и ч М. И., Опыт классификации рек СССР. Труды Гос. гидр. ин-та, в. 6, 1938.— 23. Д а в ы д о в Л. К., Водоносность рек СССР, её колебания и влияние на неё физико-географических факторов, Гидрометиздат, 1947. —24. З а й к о в Б. Д. и Б е л и н к о в С. Ю., Средний многолетний сток рек СССР. Труды Гос. гидр. ин-та, в. 2, 1937.— 25. С о к о л о в А. А., Гидрография СССР, Гидрометиздат, Л., 1952.— 26. К а л е с н и к С. В., Горные ледниковые районы СССР, 1937. —27. В и л е н с к и й Д. Г., Почвоведение, М., 1950.— 28. В и л ь я м с В. А., Почвоведение, изд. 6, М., 1949.— 29. Ф и л а т о в М. М., География почв СССР, Учпедгиз, М., 1945.— 30. Почвенная карта СССР, 1938.— 31. А л ё х и н В. В., География растений, изд. 2, М., 1944.— 32. А л ё х и н В. В., Растительность СССР в основных зонах, изд. 2, М., 1951.— 33. Растительность СССР, т. I и II, изд. АН СССР, 1938—1940.— 34. П а в л о в Н. В., Ботаническая география СССР, изд. АН Казахск. ССР, Алма-Ата, 1948. —35. С у к а ч ё в В. Н., Ш е н н и к о в А. П. и др., Дендрология с основами лесной геоботаники, изд. 2, 1938.— 36. Р е в е р д а т т о В. В., Растительность Сибири, Новосибирск, 1931.— 37. К а ц Н. Я., Типы болот СССР и Западной Европы и их географическое распространение, Географгиз, М., 1948.— 38. Флора СССР, т. I—XIX, 1934—1953. —39. Геоботаническое районирование СССР, изд. АН СССР, М.—Л., 1947.— 40 К р и ш т о ф о в и ч А. Н., Развитие ботанико-географических провинций северного полушария с конца мелового периода, Сов. бот., 1936, № 3.— 41 Б а р а н о в В. И., Развитие растительных ландшафтов в третичное время, Природа, 1942, № 1—2.— 42. Карта растительности СССР масштаба 1 : 5 000 000, 1939.— 43. Б о б р и н с к и й Н. А., География животных (курс зоогеографии), Учпедгиз, М., 1951.— 44. Г е п т н е р В. Г., Общая зоогеография, 1936.— 45. П у з а н о в И. И., Зоогеография, 1938.— 46. Б о б р и н с к и й Н. А., К у з н е ц о в Б. А. и К у з я к и н А. П., Определитель млекопитающих СССР, М., 1944.— 47. О г н ё в С. И., Звери СССР и прилежащих стран (звери Восточной Европы и Северной Азии), т. I—VI, 1928—1948.— 48. Д е м е н т ь е в Г. П., Г л а д к о в Н. А., П т у ш е н к о Е. С., С п а н г е н б е р г Е. П., С у д и л о в с к а я А. М., Птицы Советского Союза, т. I—IV, 1951—1952.— 49. Б у т у р л и н С. А. и Д е м е н т ь е в Г. П., Полный определитель птиц СССР, т. I—V, 1934—1941.— 50. Б е р г Л. С., Рыбы пресных вод СССР, т. I—III, 1948—1949.— 51. Животный мир СССР, т. I. Историч. и геогр. введение и общий систематический обзор фауны по группам, 1936; т. II. Зона пустынь, 1948; т. III. Зона степей, 1950, изд. Зоол. ин-та АН СССР.— 52. Б о б р и н с к и й Н. А., Животный мир и природа СССР, изд. Моск. о-ва исп. прир., М., 1949.— 53. К у з н е ц о в Б. А., Очерк зоогеографического районирования СССР, изд. Моск. о-ва исп. прир., М., 1950.— 54. Ш т е г м а н Б. К., Основы орнито-географического деления Палеарктики. Фауна СССР. Птицы, т. I, в. 2, 1938. 55. Большой Советский атлас мира, т. 1, 1937.

Note: For a discussion of the general bibliography and the chapter bibliographies in the original Russian book, see page vii.

INDEX TO PLANTS

INDEX TO ANIMALS

GENERAL INDEX